NCHMCT-JEE

National Council for Hotel Management & Catering Technology

Hotel Management

15 Years' Solved Papers

(2021-2007)

With Detailed & Authentic Explanations

NCHMCT-JEE
National Council for Hotel Management & Catering Technology

Hotel Management

15 Years' Solved Papers
(2021-2007)

**With Detailed &
Authentic Explanations**

Compiled & Edited by
Arihant 'Expert Team'

arihant
ARIHANT PUBLICATIONS (INDIA) LTD

ARIHANT PUBLICATIONS (INDIA) LIMITED

ꢪ Administrative & Production Offices

Regd. Office
'Ramchhaya' 4577/15, Agarwal Road, Darya Ganj, New Delhi -110002
Tele: 011- 47630600, 43518550

ꢪ Head Office

Kalindi, TP Nagar, Meerut (UP) - 250002
Tel: 0121-7156203, 7156204

ꢪ Sales & Support Offices

Agra, Ahmedabad, Bengaluru, Bareilly, Chennai, Delhi, Guwahati, Hyderabad, Jaipur, Jhansi, Kolkata, Lucknow, Nagpur & Pune.

ꢪ **ISBN** 978-93-25796-45-4

ꢪ **PRICE** ₹275.00

PO No : TXT-XX-XXXXXXX-X-XX

Published by Arihant Publications (India) Ltd.

For further information about the books published by Arihant, log on to
www.arihantbooks.com or e-mail at info@arihantbooks.com

Follow us on   

CONTENTS

About the Exam

The National Testing Agency (NTA) has been entrusted by the National Council for Hotel Management and Catering Technology (NCHMCT), an Autonomous Body of the Ministry of Tourism, Government of India, with the task of conducting the National Council for Hotel Management Joint Entrance Examination (NCHM JEE) w.e.f 2019.

DETAILS OF EXAMINATION

MODE OF EXAMINATION

Exam will be held in Computer Based Test (CBT) mode.

PATTERN OF EXAMINATION

The paper comprises Multiple Choice Questions (MCQs) in the following areas:

Types of questions (MCQ)	No. of Questions
Numerical Ability and Analytical Aptitude	30
Reasoning and Logical Deduction	30
General Knowledge & Current Affairs	30
English Language	60
Aptitude for Service Sector	50
Total	**200**

Each question carries four (04) marks. One (01) mark will be deducted for a wrong answer.

MEDIUM OF QUESTION PAPER

- The medium of Question Paper shall be in English & Hindi only.
- Option of medium of Question Paper should be carefully chosen by the Candidate, while filling the Application Form online. The option once exercised cannot be changed.
- In case of any ambiguity in translation/construction of a question in the exam, its English version shall be treated as final and the decision of NTA shall be final in this regard.

DURATION OF EXAMINATION

Three hours (180 minutes).

ELIGIBILITY CRITERIA FOR NCHM JEE-2022

Eligibility Eequirements

- A candidate should have passed 10+2 system of Senior Secondary Examination or its equivalent with English as one of the subjects, from a recognised Educational Board. Candidate must have passed English as a subject of study (core/elective/functional) in the qualifying examination.

- Those appearing in 10+2 or equivalent examination can also appear in NCHM JEE 2022 on provisional basis. Provisional admission will stand cancelled if proof of having passed the qualifying examination (10+2 or its equivalent) is not submitted at the time of counselling or at the time of admission or latest by 30.09.2022

- The offer of admission is subject to verification of original certificates / documents, including category certificate and PwD certificate (wherever applicable) at the time of admission. If any candidate is found ineligible at a later date even after admission to an Institute, due to the inability to produce geniune certificate in original in support of passing 10+2 or equivalent examination and fulfillment of age criteria and category certificate or PwD certificate (wherever applicable), his/her admission will stand cancelled.

List of Examinations Equivalent to 10+2

- Plus two level examination in the 10+2 pattern of Senior Secondary education of any recognised Central/State Board, such as Central Board of Secondary Education and Council for Indian School Certificate Examination or State Boards of Secondary Education.

- Intermediate or two-year Pre-University Examination conducted by a recognised Board/ University.

- General Certificate Education (GCE) Examination (London/Cambridge/Sri Lanka) at the Advanced (A) level.

- High School Certificate Examination of the Cambridge University.

- Any Public School / Board / University Examination in India or in a foreign country recognized by the Council of Boards of School Education (COBSE) / Association of Indian Universities (AIU) as equivalent to 10+2 pattern of Senior Secondary Education.

- Senior Secondary School Examination conducted by National Institute of Open Schooling (NIOS) as well as State Board of Open Schooling with a minimum of five subjects including English as one of the Subjects

- H.S.C. Vocational Examination approved by NCVT and SCVT of concerned State/UT.

AGE LIMIT

- For candidates from General, General (EWS) and OBC categories, upper age limit is 25 years as on 01.07.2022. Candidates born on or after July 01, 1997 are eligible.

- In the case of Scheduled Caste and Scheduled Tribe candidates and Physically challenged candidates, upper age limit is 28 years as on 01.07.2022. That is SC/ST and Physicallly challenged candidates born on or after July 01, 1994 are eligible.

- Date of birth as recorded in the Secondary Education Board/Pre-University Certificate shall be the authentic proof that will be accepted. At the time of counseling, this certificate must be produced in original as a proof of age, failing which the candidate will not be considered for Counselling/admission.

PHYSICAL FITNESS

- All qualified candidates will have to submit a physical fitness certificate of carrying out practical claims as required in course at the time of admission from a Registered Medical Practitioner in the prescribed format.

Hotel Management Colleges

- Institute of Hotel Management, Delhi, Pusa
- Institute of Hotel Management, Mumbai
- Institute of Hotel Management, Bengaluru
- Institute of Hotel Management, Bhopal
- Institute of Hotel Management, Bhubaneswar
- Institute of Hotel Management, Chennai
- Dr. Ambedkar Institute of Hotel Management, Chandigarh
- Institute of Hotel Management, Gandhinagar
- Institute of Hotel Management, Panipat
- Institute of Hotel Management, Goa
- Institute of Hotel Management, Gurdaspur
- Institute of Hotel Management, Guwahati
- Institute of Hotel Management, Kurukshetra
- Institute of Hotel Management, Silvasa
- Institute of Hotel Management, Gwalior
- Institute of Hotel Management, Bihar
- Institute of Hotel Management, Hyderabad
- Institute of Hotel Management, Jaipur
- Institute of Hotel Management, Kolkata
- Institute of Hotel Management, Lucknow
- Institute of Hotel Management, Meerut
- Institute of Hotel Management, Shillong
- Institute of Hotel Management, Shimla
- Institute of Hotel Management, Srinagar
- Institute of Hotel Management, Thiruvananthapuram
- Institute of Hotel Management, Bathinda
- Institute of Hotel Management, Dehradun
- Institute of Hotel Management, Faridabad
- Institute of Hotel Management, Gangtok
- Institute of Hotel Management, Hamirpur
- State Institute of Hotel Management, Jodhpur
- State Institute of Hotel Management, Kozhikode
- Delhi Institute of Hotel Management, New Delhi
- Chandigarh Institute of Hotel Management, Chandigarh
- State Institute of Hotel Management, Tiruchirapalli
- State Institute of Hotel Management, Rohta
- Pondicherry Institute of Hotel Management, Puducherry
- Dr. YSR National Institute of Tourism & Hospitality Management, Hyderabad
- State Institute of Hotel Management, Balangir
- State Institute of Hotel Management, Andhra Pradesh
- State Institute of Hotel Management, Tirupati
- State Institute of Hotel Management, Indore
- State Institute of Hotel Management, Gaya
- Ranjita Institute of Hotel Management, Bhubaneswar
- K C College of Hotel Management, Punjab
- Munnar Catering College, Ernakulam
- SRM Institute of Hotel Management, Chennai
- Chandigarh College of Hotel Management Landran, Mohali, Punjab
- Shri Shakti College of Hotel Management, Hyderabad
- Oriental School of Hotel Management, Wayanad, Kerala
- Gurunanak Institute of Hotel Management, Kolkata
- Chitkara School of Hospitality Chandigarh, Patiala
- VELS College of Hotel Management, Chennai
- Desh Bhagat Institute of Hotel Management, Punjab
- Rayat & Bahra Institute of Hotel Management Mohali, Punjab
- C T Institute of Hotel Management, Jalandhar
- St. Soldier Institute of Hotel Management, Jalandhar

NCHMCT-JEE

National Council for Hotel Management & Catering Technology

Hotel Management

Hotel Management

National Council for Hotel Management and Catering Technology

Solved Paper 2021*

Instructions

- There are Five (A-E) Sections in this Solved Paper.
- For every correct attempt, the student will be awarded **1 mark**.
- All the questions are in MCQs form and each have four options.

Marks : 200
Time : 3 hrs

Section A : English Language

Directions (Q. Nos. 1-5) *Each of these questions consists of a sentence which is divided into four parts a, b, c and d. Identify the part which contains an error.*

1. (a) the Indian radio which was
   (b) previously controlled by the British
   (c) rulers is free now from the
   (d) narrow vested interests.

2. (a) A lot of travel delay is caused
   (b) due to the inefficiency and
   (c) lack of good management
   (d) on behalf of the railways.

3. (a) After having failed to revive a flagging Nano,
   (b) Tata Motors has demanded afresh last week
   (c) that the enviable sops be extended to other car models
   (d) it plans to manufacture from Sanand

4. (a) The rock paintings in Karikiyoor contains
   (b) analogous-Indus script, meaning they resemble
   (c) the script found in Indus
   (d) Civilisation sites of northern India

5. (a) As the government does not seem to want to protect the site,
   (b) we plan to put up with warning boards prohibiting tourists
   (c) from entering without our permission, and
   (d) only with a guide under exceptional circumstances

Directions (Q. Nos. 6-10) *Choose the word opposite in meaning to the bold word given in the sentence.*

6. He returned home much **inspired**, no wonder the plan had worked.
   (a) Overwhelmed
   (b) Dispirited
   (c) Disillusioned
   (d) Sceptical

7. The government is taking measures to **augment** the country's supply of food.
   (a) Prohibit
   (b) Decrease
   (c) Surpass
   (d) Compensate

8. People who hold very unorthodox views are sometimes **ostracised**.
   (a) Hated
   (b) Criticised
   (c) Befriend
   (d) Shun

9. They know by his **sophomoric** remarks that he was still naive in the field.
(a) Juvenile   (b) Immature
(c) Unacceptable   (d) Experienced

10. While the reaction to major disasters is **dismal**, the response to emergencies like accidents is equally sad.
(a) Smiling   (b) Depressing
(c) Upset   (d) Competent

Directions (Q. Nos. 11-15) *Choose the word most similar in meaning to the bold word given in the sentence.*

11. Public policy in regard to food in main economies around the world has not provided adequate **incentive**, the response to emergencies like accidents is equally sad.
(a) Acceleration
(b) Surplus
(c) Baiting
(d) Encouragement

12. The National Disaster Management agency, set up a short time ago, being a Central Government agency, has limitations relating to **infringing** the jurisdiction of the states.
(a) Obeying   (b) Violating
(c) Provoking   (d) Preserving

13. The secretary had a **derisive** attitude towards some of the members of the committee.
(a) Mocking   (b) Deprecatory
(c) Strident   (d) Respectful

14. Mohini was often teased as **corpulent** by her friends.
(a) Belligerent   (b) Gaunt
(c) Fat   (d) Garrulous

15. His **unscrupulous** pursuit of wealth finally landed him in prison.
(a) Unethical   (b) Superfluous
(c) Ethical   (d) Dedicated

Directions (Q. Nos. 16-20) *Choose the correct meaning of the idiom/phrase given below.*

16. In full swing
(a) Cheerful   (b) Appreciate
(c) Somewhat deaf (d) Very active

17. To give currency to
(a) To give a present
(b) To make popular
(c) To make a heavy load
(d) To offer a bribe

18. Play a joke on someone
(a) To trick someone
(b) To lie to someone
(c) To play game with someone
(d) To make someone smile

19. Chicken-hearted
(a) Brave   (b) Coward
(c) Intelligent   (d) Stupid

20. Sit on the fence
(a) Doubtful
(b) Having the best time
(c) Avoid doing work
(d) Avoid making a choice or decision

Directions (Q. Nos. 21-25) *Choose the correct one word for the given phrases.*

21. A nation or person engaged in war or conflict, as recognised by international law
(a) Belligerent   (b) Intelligent
(c) Sacrilege   (d) Theology

22. An examination of tissue removed from a living body to discover the presence, cause or extent of a disease
(a) Autopsy   (b) Biopsy
(c) Allegory   (d) Axiom

23. The action or offence of speaking sacrilegiously about God or sacred things; profane talk
(a) Exonerate   (b) Pantheism
(c) Blasphemy   (d) Pedantic

24. A vigorous campaign for political, social or religious change
(a) Camping   (b) Revolution
(c) Revolt   (d) Crusade

25. Lasting for a very short time
(a) Extempore   (b) Ephemeral
(c) Everlasting   (d) Eternal

Directions (Q. Nos. 26-30) *Fill in the blanks with suitable options.*

26. A stock limit of 100 quintals for retail traders and 500 quintals for wholesale traders has been ………… .
(a) Mandatory   (b) Imposed
(c) Inflictive   (d) Subrogation

27. The challenge of industrial decarbonisation looks ……… at first glance.
(a) Discourage
(b) Encourage
(c) Daunting
(d) Sympathy

28. The man was .... in financial disputes with several people.
(a) occluded   (b) recuperated
(c) mired   (d) swashbuckling

29. When the caring man saw the .... had no footwear, he offered the man the pair of shoes he wore.
(a) pauper   (b) jabber   (c) dapper   (d) hamper

30. Although my plans rarely come to fruition, ... has been good to me.
(a) ally   (b) anguish
(c) apology   (d) serendipity

Directions (Q. Nos. 31-34) *Identify the best way of writing a sentence in the context of the correct usage of standard English.*

31. (a) He is been writing a novel since October, and he is about to finish it.
(b) He was written a novel since October, and he is about to finish it.
(c) He has been writing a novel since October, and he is about to finish it.
(d) He had been written a novel since October, and he is about to finish it.

32. (a) She can count to thirty quicker than I expected and can write seven of the square-hand letters and the words which can be made with them.
(b) She can count till thirty more quicker than I expected and can write seven of the square-hand letters and the words which can be made with them.
(c) She can count to thirty quicker than I expected and can write seven of the square-hand letters and the words which could be made with them.
(d) She can count to thirty more quickly than I expected and can write seven of the square-hand letters and the words which can be made with them.

33. (a) As the number of touchpoints with other countries rise, so must our shared understanding of acceptable conduct.
(b) As the number of touchpoints with other countries rises, so must our shared understanding of acceptable conduct.
(c) As the number of touchpoints with other countries rising, so must our shared understanding of acceptable conduct.
(d) As the number of touchpoints with other countries had rise, so must our shared understanding of acceptable conduct.

34. (a) The mother bird lays her eggs in a nest and keeps them warm unless the birdlings are hatched.
(b) The mother bird lays her eggs in a nest and keeps them warm until the birdlings is hatched.
(c) The mother bird lays her eggs in a nest and keeps them warm unless the birdling is hatched.
(d) The mother bird lays her eggs in a nest and keeps them warm until the birdlings are hatched.

Directions (Q. Nos. 35-39) *Choose the misspelt word from the following.*

35. (a) Skulking
(b) Commander
(c) Legionaries
(d) Ballede

36. (a) Amid   (b) Decathalon
(c) Ancient   (d) Analysis

37. (a) Questionning   (b) Sound
(c) Nuisance   (d) Imagine

38. (a) Citation   (b) Referred   (c) Pavillion   (d) Piece

39. (a) Acquaintance
(b) Aquire
(c) Acreage
(d) Acquit

Directions (Q. Nos. 40-44) *Choose the correct spellings of the given words.*

40. (a) Quadruped   (b) Quadrupped
(c) Quadraped   (d) Quadrapped

41. (a) Allaviate   (b) Alleviate
(c) Alliveate   (d) Allaevate

42. (a) Arogance   (b) Arroganse
(c) Aroganse   (d) Arrogance

43. (a) Megnificient   (b) Magnifecent
(c) Magnificent   (d) Magnifiscient

44. (a) Suparfluous   (b) Superfluous
(c) Superflous   (d) Superfluos

Directions (Q. Nos. 45-60) *Read the passages given below and answer the questions that follow.*

PASSAGE 1

It is strange that, according to his position in life, an extravagant man is admired or despised. A successful businessman does nothing to increase his popularity by being careful with his money. He is expected to display his success, to have smart car, an expensive life, and to be lavish with his hospitality. If he is not so, he is considered mean and his reputation in business may even suffer in consequence. The paradox remains that if he had not been careful with his money in the first place, he would never have achieved his present wealth. Among the two income groups, a different set of values exists. The young clerk who makes his wife a present of a new dress when he hadn't paid his house rent, is condemned as extravagant. Carefulness with money to the point of meanness is applauded as a virtue. Nothing in his life is considered more worthy than paying his bills. The ideal wife for such a man separates her housekeeping money into joyless little piles - so much for rent, for food, for the children's shoes; she is able to face the milkman with equanimity and never knows the guilt of buying something she can't really afford. As for myself, I fall into neither of these categories. If I have money to spare, I can be extravagant, but when, as is usually the case, I am hard up, then I am the meanest man imaginable.

45. Which of the following would be the most suitable title for the passage?
(a) Extravagance leads to poverty
(b) Miserly habits of the poor
(c) Extravagance in the life of the rich and the poor
(d) Extravagance is always condemnable

46. As far as money is concerned, we get the impression that the writer:
(a) is incapable of saving anything
(b) is never inclined to be extravagant
(c) would like to be considered extravagant
(d) doesn't often have any money to save

47. What does the statement 'she is able to face the milkman with equanimity' imply?
(a) She is not upset as she has been paying the milkman his dues regularly
(b) She loses her nerve at the sight of the milkman who always demands his dues
(c) She manages to keep cool as she has to pay the milkman who always demands his dues
(d) She remains composed and confident as she knows that she can handle the milkman tactfully.

48. How does the housewife, described by the writer, feel when she saves money?
(a) Is content to be so thrifty
(b) Wishes life were less burdensome
(c) Is still troubled by a sense of guilt
(d) Wishes she could sometimes be extravagant

PASSAGE 2

Our awareness of time has reached such a pitch of intensity that we suffer acutely whenever our travels take us into some corner of the world where people are not interested in minutes and seconds. The unpunctuality of the Orient, for example is appalling to those who come freshly from a land of fixed meal-times and regular train services. For a modern American or Englishman, waiting is a psychological torture. An Indian accepts the blank hours with resignation, even with satisfaction. He has not lost the fine art of doing nothing. Our notion of time as a collection of minutes, each of which must be filled with some business or amusement, is wholly alien to the Greek. For the man who lives in a pre-industrial world, time moves at a slow and easy pace: for the good reason that he has not been made conscious of the existence of minutes.

49. According to the author,
(a) Indians are orients
(b) Greeks are very punctual
(c) Americas are orients
(d) The Englishmen live in a pre-industrial world

50. According to the author
(a) the orientals are very punctual
(b) the Americans or the Englishmen are punctual
(c) the Greek and the Orientals are very punctual
(d) the Indians are very punctual

51. A person who belongs to pre-industrial world
(a) knows the utility of time
(b) knows how to derive happiness by making use of time carefully
(c) does not care about each minute
(d) cares much for every minute

52. According to the passage, which idea is alien to the Greeks?
(a) To live in a slower pace of life in comparison to the Americans.
(b) To spend every minute of the day doing something, business or entertainment related.
(c) To be fine with spending a day idly.
(d) To live in a pre-industrial world.

53. What is the main theme of the passage?
(a) Concept of time in pre-industrial world
(b) The Greek concept of time
(c) Awareness of time in the modern industrial world
(d) The Orientals and their awareness of time.

PASSAGE 3

In an effort to produce the largest, fastest and most luxurious ship afloat, the British built the S.S. Titanic. It was so superior to anything else on the seas that it was dubbed 'unsinkable'. So sure of this were the owners that they provided only twenty life boats and rafts, less than one-half the number needed for the 2,227 passengers on board. Many passengers were aboard the night it rammed an iceberg only two days at sea and more than halfway between England and its New-York destination. Because the luxury liner was travelling so fast. It was impossible to avoid the ghostly looking ice-berg. An unextinguished fire also contributed to the ship's submersion. Panic increased the number of casualties as people jumped into the icy water or fought to be among the few to board the life boats. Four hours after the mishap, another ship the 'Carpathia' rescued 705 survivors. The infamous S. S. Titanic had enjoyed only two days of sailing glory on its maiden voyage in 1912 before plunging into 12,000 feet of water near the coast of Newfoundland where it lies today.

54. What does this passage convey?
    (a) The S.S Titanic proved itself the most seaworthy vessel in 1912
    (b) Attempts to rescue the S.S.Titanic survivors were not successful
    (c) Overconfidence by builders and owners was greatly responsible for the sinking of the vessel
    (d) The fire and panic were the only causes for the sinking of the ship

55. "Maiden voyage" is closest in meaning to ....
    (a) Inaugural   (b) Most elegant
    (c) Longest   (d) Final

56. Choose the statement which is NOT true in context to the passage.
    (a) The Carpathia rescued the survivors.
    (b) The S.S Titanic sank near Newfoundland.
    (c) The S.S Titanic was the fastest ship afloat in 1912.
    (d) Only a third of those aboard perished.

PASSAGE 4

The Printing Press has made knowledge available to the vast multitude of people - But what kind of knowledge is it? Is it of any permanent character ? Books have become common and, when we say that books like the Sexton Blake series sell like hot cakes, we have an index of the nature of knowledge which a typical person in a vast multitude seeks. Let me tell you of an incident that took place in America a few years ago. An American publisher printed a million copies of the works of Charles Dickens in the hope that he could easily sell them on the name of the author. But to his disappointment, not even the widest publicity and advertisement could enable him to sell the books. Being sorely tired, he hit on a plan, He tore off the cover pages. substituted covers containing sensational love headings for the titles and again advertised the new books, in a week, all the books were sold out. We are not concerned here with the moral of the bookseller's action. What we have to note is that only books of a sensational type are really sought for by the ordinary folk who have a great aversion to serious study. So, you will see that the grand argument that the Printing Press has made knowledge available even to the masses is certainly fallacious and quite it misleading. To put it correctly, it has created a taste for a low order of books.

57. What does the author's contention makes us feel?
    (a) He is unilateral in his argument
    (b) He is balanced
    (c) He argues convincingly
    (d) He is a typical critic

58. What is the main contention of the passage?
    (a) To stress the popularity of the printing press
    (b) To bring out the evil impacts of the printing press
    (c) To point out the disappointment of serious readers
    (d) To shed light on the morale of the publishers

59. The American publisher had chosen the works of Charles Dickens to ....
    (a) give wide publicity to Dickens' works
    (b) offer the readers what best he could
    (c) counter the trash
    (d) make money easily

60. Why are Sexton Blake series are big sellers?
    (a) They are sensational
    (b) They disseminate knowledge
    (c) They are informative
    (d) They satisfy a typically serious reader

Section B : Numerical Ability and Analytical Aptitude

61. Two persons ride towards each other from two places 55 km apart, one riding at 12 km/h and the other at 10 km/h.
When will they be 11 km apart?
(a) 2 h and 30 min
(b) 1 h and 30 min
(c) 2 h
(d) 2 h and 45 min

62. A well of diameter 3 m is dug 14 m deep. The Earth taken out of it has been spread evenly all around it in the shape of a circular ring of width 4 m to form an embankment.
Find the height of the embankment.
(a) 4.25 m
(b) 2.250 m
(c) 1.125 m
(d) 1.750 m

63. Find the amount which Shyam will get on ₹ 4096, if he gave it for 18 months at $12\frac{1}{2}\%$ per annum, interest being compounded half yearly.
(a) ₹ 5813   (b) ₹ 4515   (c) ₹ 4913   (d) ₹ 5713

Directions (Q. Nos. 64 and 65) *Study the graph carefully to answer these question.*

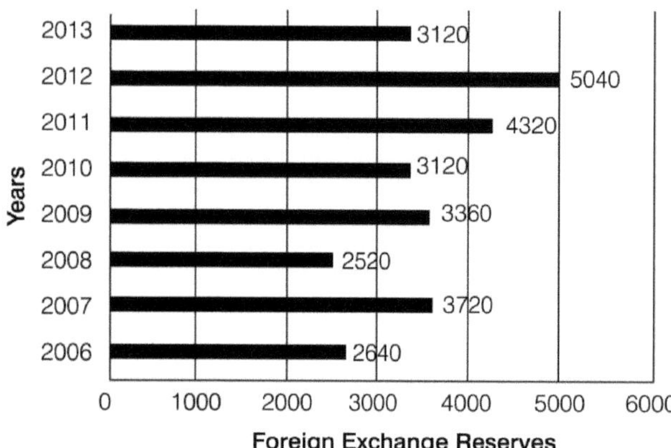

64. The foreign exchange reserve in 2012 was how many times that in 2009?
(a) 0.7
(b) 1.2
(c) 1.4
(d) 1.5

65. What was the percentage increase in the foreign reserves in 2012 over 2008?
(a) 100%   (b) 150%   (c) 200%   (d) 620%

66. A works twice as fast as B. If B can complete a piece of work independently in 12 days, then what will be the number of days taken by A and B together to finish the work?
(a) 4
(b) 6
(c) 8
(d) 18

67. In one hour, a boat goes 12 km along the stream and 8 km against the stream. The speed of the boat in still water.
(a) 12 km/h
(b) 11 km/h
(c) 10 km/h
(d) 8 km/h

68. A student was asked to find the arithmetic mean of the following 12 numbers 3, 11, 7, 9, 15, 13, 8, 19, 17, 21, 14 and x.
He found the mean to be 12. The value of x will be
(a) 3
(b) 7
(c) 17
(d) 31

69. The ratio of the number of boys and girls in a college is 7 : 8. If the percentage increase in the number of boys and girls be 20% and 10% respectively, what will be the new ratio?
(a) 8 : 9
(b) 17 : 18
(c) 21 : 22
(d) Cannot be determined

70. A committee of 12 persons is to be formed from 9 women and 8 men. In how many ways this can be done if atleast 5 women have to be included in a committee?
(a) 6000
(b) 6010
(c) 6062
(d) 6005

71. The LCM and the HCF of the numbers 28 and 42 are in the ratio.
(a) 6 : 1
(b) 2 : 3
(c) 3 : 2
(d) 7 : 2

72. A, B and C started a business with their investment in the ratio 1 : 3 : 5. After 4 months, A invested the same amount as before and B as well as C withdraw half of their investments. The ratio of their profits at the end of the year was
(a) 5 : 6 : 10
(b) 6 : 5 : 10
(c) 10 : 5 : 6
(d) 4 : 3 : 5

73. A student goes to school at the rate of $2\frac{1}{2}$ km/h and reaches 6 min late. If he travels at the speed of 3 km/h, he is 10 min early. The distance (in km) between the school and his house is
(a) 5   (b) 4   (c) 3   (d) 1

74. The length of a rectangle is 20% more than its breadth. What will be the ratio of the area of this rectangle to the area of a square whose side is equal to the breadth of the rectangle?
(a) 5 : 6
(b) 6 : 5
(c) 2 : 1
(d) Data inadequate

75. A student was asked to divide a number by 6 and add 12 to the quotient. He, however, first added 12 to the number and then divided it by 6, getting 112 as the answer. The correct answer should have been

(a) 124   (b) 122   (c) 118   (d) 114

76. A shopkeeper bought 30 kg of wheat at the rate of ₹ 45 per kg. He sold 40% of the total quantity at the rate of ₹ 50 per kg. Approximately, at what price per kg should he sell the remaining quantity to make 25% overall profit?

(a) ₹ 54   (b) ₹ 52   (c) ₹ 50   (d) ₹ 60

77. A container contains 40 L of milk from this container 4 L of milk was taken out and replaced by water. This process was repeated further two times. How much milk is now contained in the container?

(a) 26.34 L   (b) 27.36 L
(c) 28 L   (d) 29.16 L

78. At an election, a candidate secures 40% of the votes, but is defeated by the other candidate by a majority of 298 votes. Find the total number of votes recorded.

(a) 1580   (b) 1490   (c) 1470   (d) 1530

79. If $x - \dfrac{1}{x} = 2$, then what is the value of $x^2 + \dfrac{1}{x^2}$?

(a) 4   (b) 5   (c) 3   (d) 6

80. The ratio between the height of tower and the point at some distance is $5\sqrt{3} : 5$. What will be the angle of elevation?

(a) 30°   (b) 60°
(c) 90°   (d) 45°

81. The average of runs scored by a player in 11 innings is 63 and the average of his first six innings is 60 and the average of last six innings is 65. Find the runs scored in sixth inning.

(a) 60   (b) 54   (c) 67   (d) 57

82. There are 50 students in a class. One of them weighing 50 kg goes away and a new student joins. By this the average weight of the class increases by $\dfrac{1}{2}$ kg. The weight of the new student is

(a) 70 kg   (b) 72 kg   (c) 75 kg   (d) 76 kg

83. The length of side AB and side BC of a scalene triangle ABC are 12 cm and 8 cm respectively. The measure of angle C is 59°. Find the length of side AC.

(a) 12   (b) 10   (c) 14   (d) 16

84. Successive discount of 20% and 10% is given on an item of ₹ 700, find the selling price.

(a) 504   (b) 196
(c) 582   (d) 601

85. The population of a state is 20000. It increases by 20% during the first year and 30% during the second year. The population after two years will be

(a) 32000   (b) 40000
(c) 31200   (d) 30000

86. A reduction of 20% in the price of rice enable a buyer to buy 5 kg more for ₹ 1200. The reduced price per kg of rice will be

(a) 36   (b) 45
(c) 48   (d) 60

87. A man spends 60% of his income on different expenditures. His income is increased by 20% and his expenditure also increased by 10%. Find the percentage decrease in his saving.

(a) 10%   (b) 15%   (c) 20%   (d) 25%

88. A train 150 m long passes a telegraphic post in 12 sec. Find the speed of the train.

(a) 50 km/h   (b) 12.5 km/h
(c) 25 km/h   (d) 45 km/h

89. A number when divided by 6 leaves remainder 3. When the square of the same number is divided by 6, the remainder is

(a) 0   (b) 2
(c) 1   (d) 3

90. In a parade of school students, the number of boys and girls are in the ratio of 9 : 7 respectively and the total number of boys and girls are 256. Find the number of girls.

(a) 102
(b) 112
(c) 118
(d) 128

Section C : Reasoning and Logical Deduction

Directions (Q. Nos. 91 and 92) *Find the missing number letter from the given alternatives.*

91. AEN, MQZ, CGP, ?
(a) OSB
(b) PUE
(c) MPX
(d) OTC

92. 0, 4, 18, 48, ? , 180
(a) 58
(b) 68
(c) 84
(d) 100

Directions (Q. Nos. 93-95) *Select the related word/le number from the given alternative series.*

93. Apes : Gibber :: Camels: ?
(a) Grunt
(b) Cheep
(c) Bleat
(d) Whine

94. TSR : FED :: WVU : ?
(a) CAB
(b) MLK
(c) PQS
(d) GFH

95. 7 : 32 : : 28 : ?
(a) 126
(b) 136
(c) 116
(d) 128

96. Which of the following has the given figure embedded in it?

Question Figure

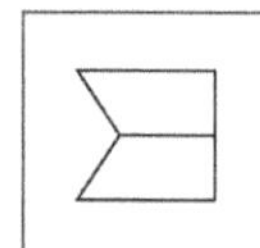

Answer Figures

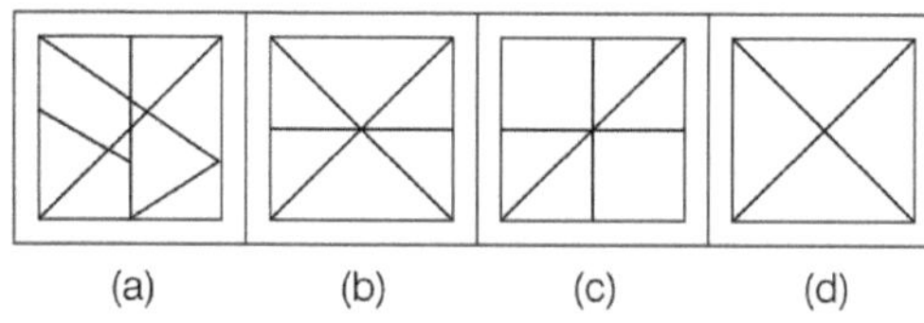

(a)   (b)   (c)   (d)

97. Which of the following diagram best depicts the relationship among English, Latin and Greek?

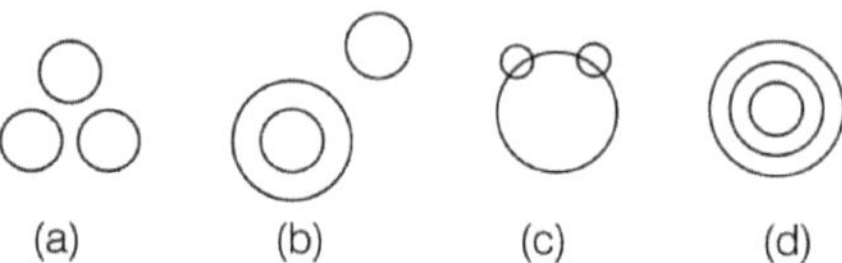

(a)   (b)   (c)   (d)

98. If 4 * 2 @ 3 = 6, 18 * 6 @ 4 =12, then what will be the value of 24 * 3 @ 7?
(a) 21   (b) 27   (c) 72   (d) 56

99. If ÷ means +, − means ÷, × means − and + means ×, then $32 ÷ 8 − 4 × 12 + 4$ is equal to
(a) 12
(b) 1/12
(c) 40
(d) −14

100. If CARPET is coded as TCEAPR, then the code for NATIONAL would be
(a) NLATNOIA
(b) LANOITAN
(c) LNAANTOI
(d) LNOINTAA

101. Arrange the following words as per in a dictionary by choosing the correct alternative.
1. Grind   2. Growth   3. Great
4. Grease   5. Greet
(a) 4, 3, 5, 1, 2
(b) 2, 1, 4, 5, 3
(c) 5, 3, 2, 4, 1
(d) 5, 4, 1, 2, 3

102. Which one of the given figure completes the given figure?

Question Figure

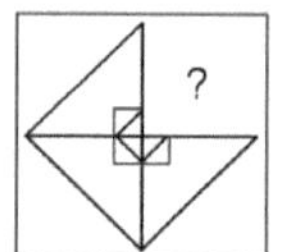

Answer Figures

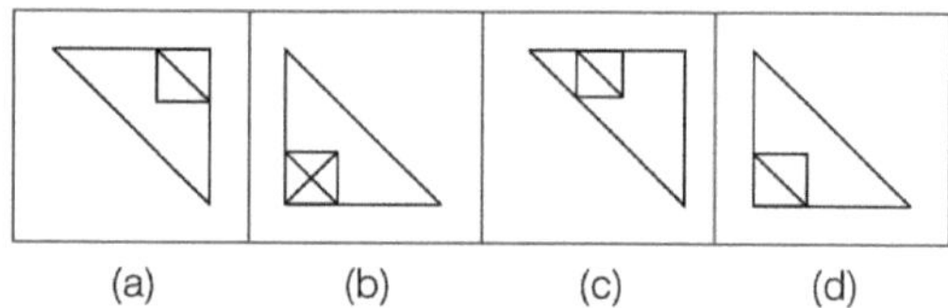

(a)   (b)   (c)   (d)

Directions (Q. Nos. 103 and 104) *Find the missing number from the given alternatives.*

103. 1, 4, 2, 3, 2, ?
(a) 2   (b) 5   (c) 3   (d) 4

104.

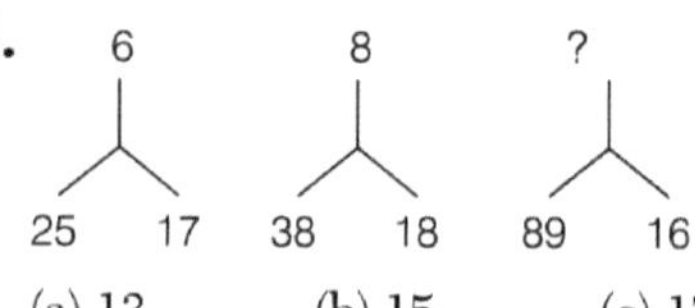

(a) 13   (b) 15   (c) 17   (d) 19

105. In this question, a statement is followed by assumptions I and II. You have to consider the statements to be true even if they seem to be at variance from the commonly known facts. You have to decide, which of the following assumptions logically follows from the given statement.
Statement Only good singers are invited in the conference. No one without sweet voice is a good singer.

Assumption I All invited singers in the conference have sweet voice.
Assumption II Those singers who do not have sweet voice are not invited in the conference.
(a) Only I follows   (b) Neither I nor II follows
(c) Both I and II follow (d) Only II follows

106. John, in the morning, started walking towards North and then turn towards opposite side of the Sun. He then turn left again and stops. Which direction is he facing now?
(a) North   (b) West
(c) South   (d) East

107. If $64 + 7 = 460$ and $25 + 8 = 212$, then $43 + 8 = ?$
(a) 360   (b) 376
(c) 332   (d) 356

108. In a certain code language, APPROACH is coded CHOAPRAP. How will RESTRICT be coded?
(a) CTRISTER   (b) ERTSIRTC
(c) CTRISTRE   (d) TCIRSTUM

Directions (Q. Nos. 109-111) *Find the odd words/letters/numbers from the given alternatives.*

109. (a) AEFJ   (b) KOPT
(c) UYZD   (d) EHIL

110. (a) 81 : 243   (b) 16 : 64
(c) 64 : 192   (d) 25 : 75

111. (a) Distinguish   (b) Scatter
(c) Differentiate   (d) Classification

112. Select the correct combination of mathematical signs to replace * signs and to balance the following equation $8 * 8 * 1 * 7 = 8$
(a) × ÷ +   (b) + ÷ ×
(c) ÷ × +   (d) + × ÷

113. Ritu is going Northwards. She turns right, moves some distance and again turns to her right. After moving some distance she turns to her left. In which direction now is the going?
(a) East   (b) West
(c) South   (d) North

114. In a row of students, Anil is 7th from left, while Sunil is 18th from right. Both of them interchanged their positions such that Anil becomes 21st from left. What will be the total number of students in the class?
(a) 38   (b) 33   (c) 31   (d) 30

115. Pointing to a photograph, man said, "I have no other or sister but that man's father is my father's son" chose photograph was it?

(a) His own   (b) His son
(c) His father   (d) His nephew

Directions (Q. Nos. 116 and 117) *In the following questions a statement is followed by two conclusions I and II. Taking the statement to be true decide which of the given conclusions difinitely follows from the given statement.*

116. **Statement** In a one day cricket match, the total runs made by a team were 200. Out of these, 160 runs were made by spinners.
Conclusions
I. 80% of the team consists of spinners.
II. The opening batsmen were spinners.
(a) Only conclusion I follows
(b) Only conclusion II follows
(c) Neither I nor II follows
(d) Both I and II follow

117. **Statement** The old order changed yielding place to new
Conclusions
I. Change is the law of nature.
II. Discard old ideas because they are old.
(a) Only conclusion I follows
(b) Only conclusion II follows
(c) Either I or II follows
(d) Both I and II follow

118. Five friends P, Q, R, S and T are sitting in a row facing North. Here, S is between T and Q and Q is to the immediate left of R. P is to the immediate left of T. Who is in the middle.
(a) S   (b) T   (c) Q   (d) R

119. A series is given with one term missing. Choose the correct alternative from the given ones that will complete the series.
XIIIII, IXIIII, IIXIII, IIIXII, IIIIXI, ?
(a) IIIIXII   (b) IIIIXI   (c) IIIIIX   (d) XIIIIX

120. Which of the following figure is the correct mirror of the given figure?
Question Figure

Answer Figures

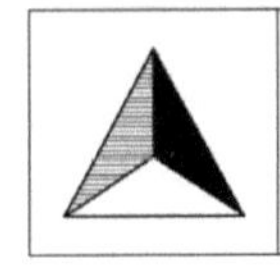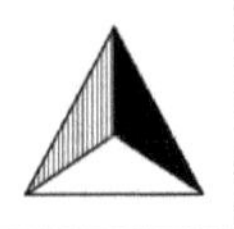

(a)   (b)   (c)   (d)

Section D : General Knowledge and Current Affairs

121. Who presides over the Joint Session of both the Houses of the Parliament in India?
(a) The President of India
(b) The Prime Minister of India
(c) The Speaker of the Lok Sabha
(d) The Vice-President of India

122. Ocean current are primarily caused by
(a) Difference in temperature
(b) Wind blowing over the sea surface
(c) Irregular shape of the continents
(d) Difference in salinity

123. Fundamental Duties of Indian citizens are provided by
(a) 41st Amendment
(b) 42nd Amendment
(c) 43rd Amendment
(d) 44th Amendment

124. Which of the following is the basis for determining National Income?
(a) Total revenue of the state
(b) Production of goods and services
(c) Net profits earned and expenditure incurred by the states
(d) None of the above

125. MK Gandhi took the leadership of the National Movement in
(a) 1919-20
(b) 1920-21
(c) 1930-31
(d) 1910-11

126. The Moti Masjid was built by Shah Jahan at
(a) Fatehpur Sikri
(b) Delhi
(c) Lahore
(d) Agra

127. Hardwood trees like sal, teak, neem and shisham are found in
(a) Tropical Evergreen Forest
(b) Montane Forest
(c) Tropical Semi-evergreen Forest
(d) Tropical Deciduous Forests

128. The Reserve Bank of India was established in which year?
(a) 1930
(b) 1935
(c) 1940
(d) 1956

129. Which among the following is the unit of measurement of the "Ecological Footprint"?
(a) Global Hectare
(b) Gallon Per Capita
(c) Cubic Meter
(d) Man Hour

130. Administration of Union Territories is dealt in
(a) Part VIII of the Constitution
(b) Part IX of the Constitution
(c) Part X of the Constitution
(d) Part XI of the Constitution

131. Shivaji was crowned as an independent king at
(a) Rajgarh
(b) Surat
(c) Ahmedabad
(d) Poona

132. One hundred years before the War of Independence (1857), a battle fought where destiny of India changed drastically. Identify
(a) Second Battle of Panipat
(b) First Battle of Haldighati
(c) Battle of Jhansi
(d) Battle of Plassey

133. Which among the following is the dangerous Green House Gas, created by the waste water?
(a) Nitrogen
(b) Sulfur Dioxide
(c) Methane
(d) Carbon Dioxide

134. In humans, the sound is produced by the which of the following?
(a) Epiglottis
(b) Oesophagus
(c) Larynx
(d) Medulla

135. What is study of fungus known as?
(a) Phrenology
(b) Physiology
(c) Biology
(d) Mycology

136. Which of the following rivers is not South-flowing?
(a) Damodar
(b) Chambal
(c) Kosi
(d) Gadadhar

137. Which of the following is an air to ground missile?
(a) Prithvi
(b) Bofors
(c) Agni
(d) Akash

138. Where is the headquarters of INTERPOL?
(a) Paris
(b) London
(c) Geneva
(d) Lyon

139. Petroleum can be categorised under which one of the following terms?
(a) Elements
(b) Hydrocarbons
(c) Polymers
(d) Salts

140. Which of the following is also used as a dry lubricant?
(a) Graphite
(b) Diamond
(c) Alpha sulphur
(d) Beta sulphur

141. What is the effect on apparent frequency when the distance between the source of the sound and listener is decreased?
(a) It increases
(b) It decreases
(c) It remains same
(d) None of these

142. Which of the following is the first state to have been formed on linguistic basis?
(a) Gujarat
(b) Andhra Pradesh
(c) Punjab
(d) Karnataka

143. Equality before law and equal protection of law is dealt with/in Article
(a) 13 of the Constitution
(b) 14 of the Constitution
(c) 15 of the Constitution
(d) 16 of the Constitution

144. The Mahadeo hills is located in which part of India?
(a) Central India
(b) Eastern India
(c) Eastern Ghats
(d) Western Ghats

145. Asia's longest high-speed track for automobiles has been inaugurated in which Indian city?
(a) Delhi
(b) Ahmedabad
(c) Telangana
(d) Indore

146. Who has become the first woman of colour to win the Oscar for Best Director?
(a) Thomas Vinterberg
(b) Lee Isaac Chung
(c) Chloe Zhao
(d) Emerald Fennell

147. Which country has become the first country to complete the official ratification process of RCEP agreement?
(a) Thailand
(b) Vietnam
(c) Singapore
(d) Philippines

148. The largest fish-exporting region of the world is
(a) North-East Pacific Region
(b) North-East Atlantic Region
(c) North-West Pacific Region
(d) South-East Asian Region

149. Which of the following is the use of Aspirin drug?
(a) Reduces fever
(b) Helps in skeletal pain
(c) Helps in preventing heart attacks
(d) All of the above

150. Which of the following electromagnetic waves in the EM spectrum has the highest wavelength?
(a) X-rays
(b) Visible
(c) Infrared
(d) UV-rays

Section E : Aptitude for Service Sector

151. If you want to start with something new and you have little saving and few employees, what will be your first priority?
(a) Generate cash flow
(b) Figure out what business to be in
(c) Launch products
(d) Develop customers

152. A football match is going on and you like one team but your group favours the other one, then
(a) you will become neutral
(b) you will try to persuade other members to like your team better
(c) you will cheer for the team the group favours
(d) you will stick to your own favourite

153. While returning home from a far away place you find that your pocket has been picked. You would
(a) try to hitch-hike till home
(b) hire a taxi and pay on reaching home
(c) go to the nearest police station and lodge an FIR
(d) call home and ask someone to pick you from the place you make the phone call

154. The newspaper hawker comes late in the morning and therefore, you go to work without reading the newspaper. You would
(a) give him a piece of your mind and tell him to deliver the newspaper early in the morning
(b) stop taking newspaper from the very next day
(c) not pay him in time
(d) apprise him about your problem

155. You want respect and reputation in the society. Then, what would you consider the right action to be?
(a) Develop friendly relationships with all the persons
(b) Keep on interacting with all the respected persons
(c) Develop strong relationships with anti-social people so that all the people give you respect and treat you as a reputed person
(d) For sake your personal selfish interests and work for the benefit of the masses

156. You get up late in the morning and your neighbour utilises this opportunity to read your newspaper. You would
(a) try to get up early in the morning so that you yourself read the newspaper
(b) tell him that he should foot half of the bill of newspapers
(c) tell him to quickly read the newspaper and return it to you
(d) tell him that he himself should buy the newspaper and read it

157. If one of your close friends does not look after his old parents who stay with him, you would
(a) feel that old people have got to live on their own

(b) feel that it may not be possible for your friend to do the needful for his parents due to certain problem

(c) tell your friend strongly that what he is doing is not quite correct

(d) like to tell your friend casually about this issue

158. When a new person joins your department in the office, you fell

(a) your boss should call you and introduce him to you

(b) you should go and meet him and help him, if he needs any help

(c) you must ignore him totally

(d) he must come and introduce himself to you

159. When you are having a walk along the sea-shore, you notice a man drowning and shouting for help. You will

(a) draw the attention of others and keep on walking

(b) not like to get involved and continue your walk

(c) go into the water to help him, as you know swimming

(d) raise an alarm and request some other swimmer to help him

160. While walking on the road, you find an envelope which contains an Aadhar Card. You will

(a) leave the envelope there only and move on

(b) post the Aadhar Card to the address of its owner

(c) give the envelope to your friend and ask him to deal with it

(d) curse the owner of the card and call him extremely careless

161. For efficient guest relations executive must have

(a) a pleasant personality and skills of courteous behaviour

(b) good controlling ability

(c) good planning skills

(d) None of the above

162. If someone involves you in an argument. Then what is your (expected) behaviour towards him?

(a) You will not hesitate in arguing with him

(b) You will try to get rid of him

(c) You will try to learn a lesson or two from the person who is arguing

(d) You will not take interest in the person who is arguing

163. While expressing your views on an important subject, you

(a) want to avoid expressing in a diplomatic way

(b) convey a truthful answer, but in a diplomatic way

(c) express what comes to your mind at the spur of the moment

(d) look for opinions expressed by other people and then speak

164. When you are not capable of taking a decision, then whose suggestion or advice you would like to take?

(a) Of your close relatives

(b) Of your parents

(c) Of your friends

(d) Of all those mentioned above

165. You are a member of the sports- team of your college. One day due to misunderstanding other members stop talking to you. You would

(a) wait till they come and start talking again

(b) go forward, sort out the misunderstanding

(c) keep to yourself and let things take their time for improving

(d) ask someone to mediate

166. You got less marks than expected in the examination, which has jeopardised your chances for further studies. You would

(a) doubt the evaluation of the papers

(b) forget about further studies and take up a job

(c) try to take up a job and go for further studies through correspondence course

(d) change your discipline and go for some easier courses

167. A friend of yours, who stays along with you, has the habit of remaining awake late in the night. Due to this habit of your friend, your sleep is disturbed. You will

(a) motivate him to sleep early

(b) tell him that he should take care of his health and sleep on time

(c) apprise him of the diseases that can arise by being awake late in the night

(d) give him information about the rules that lead to good to health

168. The responsibility of hospitality of the guest or looking after their smooth and enjoyable stay in a hotel lies on the shoulders of

(a) General Manager

(b) Guest Relations Executive

(c) Floor Supervisor　　(d) None of these

169. In an interview you are asked to describe yourself. You

(a) use monosyllables to do so

(b) go ahead full steam

(c) fumble as it is embarrassing to talk about yourself

(d) paint an unrealistic positive picture

170. Whenever I join a new group. Then

(a) I am not able to understand them

(b) I take some time to understand people

(c) I feel pretty soon that I have known all of them

(d) I take some time to identify and understand them

171. What would you as a manager do to improve employees' communication skills?
(a) Training workshop by an outside consultant
(b) Writing organisational documents at a reading level that matches the reading level of most employees
(c) Engage in 2-way communication with stress on feedback
(d) All of the above

172. You are away from your home and studying in another city. Due to an urgent piece of work, your father is not able to send you money in time. Then, you
(a) fly into a rage
(b) try to understand his handicaps
(c) enquire from him by making phone calls
(d) arrange money from another source and carry on you work

173. If someone tries to obstruct your work time and again. You will
(a) take these events seriously
(b) take these events in your stride
(c) try to stop him from obstructing in your affairs
(d) ask him the reason for obstructing/interfering and give him a suitable reply

174. If your favourite player is found to be guilty of match fixing, you would
(a) like a ban to be imposed on this player
(b) meet highly placed officials in order to save his neck
(c) like strict punitive measure to be incorporated with respect to such blunders in the rules of the game
(d) like him to be banned from playing for a period of 5 years

175. In the examination hall, you find that your question paper is too tough to be answered satisfactorily by you. The best thing you can do is
(a) try cheating from your neighbouring candidate
(b) leave the paper and walk out.
(c) try attempting those questions first of which you know something
(d) force everyone in the hall to boycott the paper

176. In case of breaking out of a fire in your neighbourhood, you would
(a) remain apathetic and unconcerned
(b) immediately call the fire brigade
(c) try to find out the causes of the fire
(d) reach the site and do your best to help the victims

177. An infectious or contagious disease has been break out spreading in your city you would
(a) inform the health centres to take necessary action
(b) help the suffering people
(c) leave that place and go somewhere else for sometime
(d) do nothing

178. While working as a primary school teacher you find a poor student is not able to pay his tuition fee. You will
(a) take him to the Principal for strict action
(b) speak to his parents and ask them to pay fee
(c) find reason for non-payment of fee and then personally help the boy, if needed
(d) punish him severely in front of the whole class

179. You see some smoke coming out of the building of your office and come to know that there is fire somewhere. First of all you would
(a) go out of the building without considering the consequences thereof
(b) make a noise and inform all
(c) inform fire brigade in no time
(d) first use the fire-fighting equipment or do something else to extinguish the fire

180. You are getting late for a meeting and while driving, you witness an accident. You would
(a) ignore the meeting and help the injured
(b) ignore it and rush for the meeting
(c) try and ask someone else to help him
(d) curse others for not helping and rush for the meeting

181. You have been sent on a visit to a rural area on a project to educate the local children. You
(a) whole heartedly take part in the project and try to put in your maximum effort
(b) start complaining about the mismanagement
(c) show no enthusiasm but anyhow complete your project
(d) bail out of the project

182. Towards your adolescent son, your attitude is correctly reflected in which of the following statements?
(a) I shall allow him to do whatever he wants providing him with full liberty and not interfere in his affairs at all
(b) I shall take all decisions about him myself
(c) I shall conduct an open discussion with him and let him make his own decisions
(d) I shall expect him to take his decisions himself after a considerable carefulness thinking

183. In case, your colleagues tell you that you are often short tempered, you would
(a) listen to it but tell them that almost everybody loses his temper, so there is nothing serious about it
(b) tell them to mind their own business and need not comment about others

(c) take sportingly and look for some ways to control temper

(d) argue with them and assert that they are wrong

184. While receiving your salary, you discover that your employer has paid extra money. You would

(a) not give the money even after employer feels he has paid extra money to you

(b) think that you are lucky and keep the money

(c) return the money immediately to the employer

(d) keep the money, but plan to return the money at a later date

185. While working as a manager in a hotel, you are informed that one of your guest has suddenly become very unwell. You would

(a) ask the guest to go to some doctor

(b) call a doctor and send him to the guest

(c) meet the guest and then urgently call the doctor and help the patient as required

(d) ask your subordinate to deal with it and need not bother you

186. You are travelling in a train and one of your co-passengers is left on a platform while the train starts moving. You would

(a) not bother

(b) look around waiting for someone to react

(c) ask others to do something

(d) get up and pull the chain

187. A guy slipped and fell in front of you while walking through the college corridor and your friends started laughing. You would

(a) join your friends in the laughter

(b) add some comment to increase the fun

(c) help him and ask your friends not to laugh

(d) just sit and watch

188. If you happen to be in a bus which meets with an accident, you would

(a) ask and motivate others to help out people who are hurt

(b) try and get away from the scene at the earliest

(c) extend physical help to people who need such help

(d) inform district authorities and police

189. A foreign tourist approaches you for some help but you don't share any common language. You

(a) would waive him off telling that you don't understand his language

(b) would try and arrange a translator in order to help him

(c) try and help him as much as you could using sign language

(d) try making fun of him

190. While watching a movie in a theatre, a small child starts crying, you

(a) yell at his/her parents for disturbing you in between the movie

(b) try to ignore but instead pass comments on the child

(c) ask their parents humbly to take their child out of the theatre

(d) ask child's parents if everything is ok with the child and if there is any help, you can give to them

191. To work efficiently in the service sector, you should be

(a) decisive or quick in decision-making

(b) extremely courteous

(c) firm in your ideas

(d) punctual

192. Your company asks you to work in another department of company, which you do not like. You would

(a) perform most inefficiently to show your disgust

(b) try to go back to your old department

(c) start avoiding your work and ask for leave requently

(d) try to get used to the new work environment and adjust

193. You have a power point presentation to make today and the hard disk, of your computer has crashed and you don't have a power back up and your presentation is after four hours

(a) you cancel the presentation

(b) you utilise the four hours and make a fresh power point presentation

(c) you change mode of the presentation

(d) you start panicking and don't know what to do

194. A stranger comes to you asking about an address while you are waiting for someone. You will

(a) ask him to ask someone else

(b) direct him casually, without being too precise about the address

(c) explain him properly and repeatedly until he understands the direction properly

(d) tell him that you are not standing there to direct people

195. After your graduation you are offered a well paid government job. However, your friend says that you have to bribe to get the appointment order. You would

(a) flatly refuse the offer

(b) accept the job by paying the bribe but firmly resolve that this is the last time you will pay bribe

(c) accept the job by-paying the bribe, consoling yourself that this is the present social set-up

(d) go to some influential politician who can help

196. One of your relatives invites you to visit them. Reaching there, you find that he is not well and is unable to give a proper welcome. You would
(a) get angry and return
(b) stay but feel disappointed
(c) stay and help him
(d) not react at all

197. When you reach your home after your office in the evening, you find your immediate neighbour has parked his car in the slot earmarked for you. You will
(a) call him and shout at him to make him realise his mistake
(b) call him and politely tell him that perhaps by mistake he has parked his car in your slot
(c) park your car in such a way that he cannot take out his car
(d) tell your other neighbours that how stupid is your neighbour and that he has no manners

198. In a park, you see two boys fighting and beating each other. You
(a) go and start beating both them
(b) ignore and walk away
(c) tell other people in the park that the fight should be stopped
(d) go to them and ask them politely to stop fighting and resolve the issue by talking and discussing

199. You finished your chocolate and now you can't find dustbin around to dispose of the wrapper. You
(a) will throw it anywhere
(b) keep it with you until you find a dustbin
(c) find a heap of trash where other people are throwing their garbage and you do the same
(d) try and stuff it in someone else's luggage

200. To make the environment of your work-place more and more congenial and worth working you would
(a) establish cordial relations among the workers
(b) use positive motivation
(c) take care of the convenience and need of the working staff
(d) All of the above

Answers

1. (c)	2. (d)	3. (a)	4. (a)	5. (b)	6. (b)	7. (b)	8. (c)	9. (d)	10. (a)
11. (d)	12. (b)	13. (a)	14. (c)	15. (a)	16. (d)	17. (b)	18. (a)	19. (b)	20. (d)
21. (a)	22. (b)	23. (c)	24. (d)	25. (b)	26. (b)	27. (c)	28. (c)	29. (a)	30. (d)
31. (c)	32. (d)	33. (b)	34. (d)	35. (d)	36. (b)	37. (a)	38. (c)	39. (b)	40. (a)
41. (b)	42. (d)	43. (c)	44. (b)	45. (c)	46. (d)	47. (a)	48. (a)	49. (a)	50. (b)
51. (c)	52. (b)	53. (c)	54. (c)	55. (a)	56. (d)	57. (c)	58. (b)	59. (d)	60. (a)
61. (c)	62. (d)	63. (c)	64. (d)	65. (a)	66. (a)	67. (c)	68. (b)	69. (c)	70. (c)
71. (a)	72. (a)	73. (b)	74. (b)	75. (b)	76. (d)	77. (d)	78. (b)	79. (d)	80. (b)
81. (d)	82. (c)	83. (c)	84. (a)	85. (c)	86. (c)	87. (a)	88. (d)	89. (d)	90. (b)
91. (a)	92. (d)	93. (a)	94. (b)	95. (c)	96. (b)	97. (a)	98. (d)	99. (d)	100. (c)
101. (a)	102. (d)	103. (d)	104. (b)	105. (c)	106. (c)	107. (d)	108. (c)	109. (d)	110. (b)
111. (a)	112. (c)	113. (a)	114. (a)	115. (b)	116. (c)	117. (a)	118. (a)	119. (c)	120. (a)
121. (c)	122. (b)	123. (b)	124. (b)	125.. (a)	126. (d)	127. (a)	128. (b)	129. (a)	130. (a)
131. (a)	132. (d)	133. (c)	134. (c)	135. (d)	136. (b)	137. (d)	138. (d)	139. (b)	140. (a)
141. (a)	142. (b)	143. (b)	144. (a)	145. (d)	146. (c)	147. (c)	148. (c)	149. (a)	150. (c)
151. (b)	152. (d)	153. (b)	154. (d)	155. (a)	156. (c)	157. (c)	158. (b)	159. (c)	160. (b)
161. (a)	162. (c)	163. (d)	164. (d)	165. (b)	166. (c)	167. (a)	168. (b)	169. (b)	170. (b)
171. (c)	172. (d)	173. (d)	174. (a)	175. (c)	176. (d)	177. (a)	178. (c)	179. (c)	180. (c)
181. (a)	182. (c)	183. (c)	184. (c)	185. (c)	186. (d)	187. (c)	188. (a)	189. (c)	190. (d)
191. (a)	192. (d)	193. (c)	194. (c)	195. (a)	196. (c)	197. (b)	198. (d)	199. (b)	200. (d)

Hints & Solutions

1. *(c)* In 'rulers is free now from the', the placing of 'now' and 'free' should be interchanged, i.e., 'rulers is now free from the' to correct the sentence.

2. *(d)* 'On behalf of the railways' should be changed to 'on part of the railways' to correct the sentence.

3. *(a)* In part (a), remove 'after' because its use is redundant with perfect participle 'having failed'. Hence, remove 'after' to make the sentence error free.

4. *(a)* The subject 'rock paintings' is a plural subject and it will take a plural verb according to subject-verb agreement rule. Hence, replace 'contains' with 'contain' to make the sentence error free.

5. *(b)* In part (b), the phrase 'put up with' means to tolerate which is incorrect in the context of the sentence. Here, 'put up' should be used which means to display.

6. *(b)* 'Inspired' means motivated and encourage. Hence, 'dispirited' meaning having lost hope is opposite to 'inspired'.

7. *(b)* 'Augment' means to increase the amount, value or size and 'decrease' means to reduce the amount, value or size. Hence, option (b) is the correct answer.

8. *(c)* 'Ostracise' means to exclude someone from the group. 'Befriend' means become a friend to. Hence, option (c) is the correct answer.

9. *(d)* 'Sophomoric' means conceited and overconfident of knowledge but poorly informed and immature. Hence, 'experienced' is opposite in meaning to 'sophomoric.

10. *(a)* 'Dismal' means causing a mood of gloom or depression. 'Smiling' means happy. Hence, option (a) is the correct answer.

11. *(d)* 'Incentive' is a thing that motivates or encourages someone to do something. Hence, option (d) 'encouragement' is the correct synonym of 'incentive'.

12. *(b)* 'Infringing' means actively breaking the terms of a law, agreement, etc. which is the same as 'violating'. Hence, option (b) is the correct answer.

13. *(a)* 'Derisive' means expressing contempt or ridicule. 'Mocking' means making fun of someone or something in a cruel way. Hence, option (a) is the correct answer.

14. *(c)* 'Corpulent' means fat. Hence, option (c) is the correct answer.

15. *(a)* 'Unscrupulous' means having or showing no moral principles. Hence, option (a) 'unethical' is its correct synonym.

27. *(c)* 'Daunting' is suitable to fill the blank as it means frightening in a way that makes you feel less confident.

28. *(c)* 'Mired' is the correct answer as it means a complicated or an unpleasant situation that is difficult to escape or make progress.

29. *(a)* 'Pauper' is appropriate to fill the blank as it refers to someone who is very poor.

30. *(d)* 'Serendipity' is the correct answer which means the occurrence and development of events by chance in a happy or beneficial way.

61. *(c)* Relative speed of both persons
$$= 12 + 10 \ = 22 \text{ km/h}$$
Now, distance between both of them
$$= 55 - 11 = 44 \text{ km}$$
∴ Time, when distance is 11 km between both of them $= \dfrac{\text{Total distance}}{\text{Relative speed}} = \dfrac{44}{22} = 2 \text{ h}$

Hence, they will be apart 11 km after 2 h.

62. *(d)* Let, height of embankment $= h$ m

Given, radius of well $= \dfrac{3}{2} = 1.5$ m

According to the question,

Volume of the embankment = Volume of the well
$$\dfrac{4}{3} \times \dfrac{22}{7} \times [(4)^2 - (1.5)^2] \times h = \dfrac{22}{7} \times (1.5)^2 \times 14$$
$$\Rightarrow \quad \dfrac{4}{3} \times (16 - 2.25) \times h = 2.25 \times 14$$
$$\Rightarrow \quad \dfrac{4}{3} \times 13.75 \times h = 2.25 \times 14$$
$$\Rightarrow \ h = \dfrac{2.25 \times 14 \times 3}{4 \times 13.75} \Rightarrow h = \dfrac{225 \times 7 \times 3}{2 \times 1375}$$
$$\Rightarrow \quad h = \dfrac{189}{110} = 1.718 \approx 1.75$$
$$\therefore \quad h = 1.75 \text{ m}$$

63. *(c)* Here, $P = ₹ \, 4096$, $R = 12\dfrac{1}{2}\% = \dfrac{25}{2}\%$

$n = 18$ months $= \dfrac{18}{12} = \dfrac{3}{2}$ yr

∴ According to the formula,

Amount $= P\left(1 + \dfrac{R}{100}\right)^n$
$$= 4096\left(1 + \dfrac{25}{2 \times 100} \times \dfrac{1}{2}\right)^{\frac{3}{2} \times 2}$$
$$= 4096\left(1 + \dfrac{1}{16}\right)^3 = 4096\left(\dfrac{17}{16}\right)^3$$
$$= 4096 \times \dfrac{17}{16} \times \dfrac{17}{16} \times \dfrac{17}{16}$$
$$= 17 \times 17 \times 17 = ₹ \, 4913$$

64. *(d)* Required answer

$$= \frac{\text{Foreign exchange reserves in 2012}}{\text{Foreign exchange reserves in 2009}}$$

$$= \frac{5040}{3360} = \frac{3}{2} = 1.5$$

Hence, in the year 2012, foreign exchange reserves was 1.5 times in comparison to the year 2009.

65. *(a)* Required percentage increase

$$= \left(\frac{5040 - 2520}{2520}\right) \times 100$$

$$= \frac{2520}{2520} \times 100 = 100\%$$

66. *(a)* Time taken to complete the work by $B = 12$ days

$\because A$ work twice as fast as B

$\therefore$ Time taken to complete the work by $A = 6$ days

Now, one day work of $B = \dfrac{1}{12}$

and one day work of $A = \dfrac{1}{6}$

$\therefore$ One day work of $(A + B) = \dfrac{1}{6} + \dfrac{1}{12} = \dfrac{2+1}{12} = \dfrac{3}{12} = \dfrac{1}{4}$

Hence, time taken by A and B together to finish the work in $= 4$ days.

67. *(c)* Downstream speed $= \dfrac{12}{1} = 12\,\text{km}$

Upstream speed $= \dfrac{8}{1} = 8\,\text{km}$

According to the question,

Speed of boat

$$= \frac{1}{2}\,(\text{Downstream speed} + \text{Upstream speed})$$

$$= \frac{1}{2}\left(\frac{12}{1} + \frac{8}{1}\right)$$

$$= \frac{1}{2}(12 + 8) = \frac{1}{2} \times 20 = 10\,\text{km/h}$$

68. *(b)* Arithmetic mean $= \dfrac{\text{Sum of total numbers}}{\text{Total number of terms}}$

$$12 = \frac{\begin{array}{c}3 + 11 + 7 + 9 + 15 + 13 + 8 + 19 \\ + 17 + 21 + 14 + x\end{array}}{12}$$

$$144 = 137 + x$$

$\Rightarrow \qquad x = 144 - 137$

$\therefore \qquad x = 7$

69. *(c)* Originally, let the number of boys and girls in the college be $7x$ and $8x$, respectively.

$\therefore$ Increased number of boys $= \dfrac{100 + 20}{100} + 7x = \dfrac{42x}{5}$

and increased number of girls $= \dfrac{100 + 10}{100} \times 8x = \dfrac{44x}{5}$

$\therefore$ Required ratio $= \dfrac{42x}{5} : \dfrac{44x}{5} = 21 : 22$

70. *(c)* Since, there are 9 women and 8 men. So, a committee of 12 consisting of atleast 5 women, can be formed by choosing.

  (i) 5 women and 7 men

 (ii) 6 women and 6 men

(iii) 7 women and 5 men

(iv) 8 women and 4 men

 (v) 9 women and 3 men

$\therefore$ Total number of ways of forming the committee

$$= {}^{9}C_5 \times {}^{8}C_7 + {}^{9}C_6 \times {}^{8}C_6 + {}^{9}C_7 \times {}^{8}C_5$$
$$+ {}^{9}C_8 \times {}^{8}C_4 + {}^{9}C_9 \times {}^{8}C_3$$

$$= 1008 + 2352 + 2016 + 630 + 56 = 6062$$

71. *(a)* $\because \quad 28 = 2 \times 2 \times 7$

$\qquad 42 = 2 \times 3 \times 7$

$\therefore$ LCM of 28 and 42 $= 2 \times 2 \times 3 \times 7 = 84$

and HCF of 28 and 42 $= 2 \times 7 = 14$

$\therefore$ Required ratio $= 84 : 14 = 6 : 1$

72. *(a)* Let their initial investments be ₹x, ₹$3x$ and ₹$5x$, respectively.

Ratio of their profits = Ratio of their investments

$$= (x \times 4 + 2x \times 8) : \left(3x \times 4 + \frac{3x}{2} \times 8\right)$$

$$: \left(5x \times 4 + \frac{5x}{2} \times 8\right)$$

$$= (4x + 16x) : (12x + 12x) : (20x + 20x)$$

$$= 20x : 24x : 40x = 5 : 6 : 10$$

73. *(b)* Let the distance between the school and the house of the student be D km and the time taken $= t$ h

Case 1. When he goes at a rate of $2\dfrac{1}{2}$ km/h, he reaches 6 min late.

$$\therefore \quad \frac{D}{\frac{5}{2}} = t + \frac{6}{60} \Rightarrow \frac{2D}{5} = t + \frac{1}{10}$$

$$\Rightarrow \quad t = \frac{2D}{5} - \frac{1}{10} \qquad \qquad \text{...(i)}$$

Case II. When he goes at a rate of 3km/h he reaches 10 min earlier.

$$\therefore \quad \frac{D}{3} = t - \frac{10}{60}$$

$$\Rightarrow \quad \frac{D}{3} = t - \frac{1}{6} \qquad \qquad \text{...(ii)}$$

On putting the value of t from Eq. (i) in Eq. (ii), we get

$$\frac{D}{3} = \frac{2D}{5} - \frac{1}{10} - \frac{1}{6} \Rightarrow \frac{2D}{5} - \frac{D}{3} = \frac{1}{10} + \frac{1}{6}$$

$$\Rightarrow \quad \frac{6D - 5D}{15} = \frac{3 + 5}{30}$$

$$\Rightarrow \quad D = \frac{8 \times 15}{30} = 4\,\text{km}$$

$\therefore$ Required distance $= 4$ km

74. (b) Let the breadth of the rectangle be x.

Then, length $= \left(\dfrac{100 + 20}{100}\right) \times x = 1.20x$

and side of square $= x$

$\therefore$ Area of rectangle $=$ length $\times$ breadth

$= 1.20x \times x = 1.20x^2$

Area of square $=$ (side)$^2 = x \times x = x^2$

$\therefore$ Required ratio $= \dfrac{1.20x^2}{x^2} = \dfrac{12}{10} = \dfrac{6}{5} = 6 : 5$

75. (b) Let the number be x.

According to the question,

$\therefore \qquad \dfrac{x + 12}{6} = 112 \Rightarrow x + 12 = 672$

$\Rightarrow \qquad x = 672 - 12 = 660$

$\therefore$ Correct answer $= \dfrac{660}{6} + 12 = 110 + 12 = 122$

76. (d) Here, total cost price of the wheat $= 45 \times 30$

$= ₹ \, 1350$

Now, 40% of the total quantity $= 30 \times \dfrac{40}{100} = 12$ kg

$\therefore$ Selling price $= 12 \times 50 = ₹ \, 600$

Now, to get 25% overall profit.

Total selling price $= \left(\dfrac{100 + \text{profit} \, \%}{100}\right) \times \text{CP}$

$= \dfrac{100 + 25}{100} \times 1350 = ₹ \, 1687.5$

Rest S.P $= 1687.5 - 600 = ₹ \, 1087.5$

Rest quantity $= 30 - 12 = 18$ kg

$\therefore$ Price of the wheat per kg $= \dfrac{1087.5}{18} = 60.41 = ₹ \, 60$

77. (d) According to the question,

Amount of milk left after 3 operations

$= \left[40\left(1 - \dfrac{4}{10}\right)^3 \right] = \left(40 \times \dfrac{9}{10} \times \dfrac{9}{10} \times \dfrac{9}{10}\right) = 29.16$ L

78. (b) Let total number of votes recorded $= x$

Now, according to the question,

(60% of x) $-$ (40% of x) $= 298$

$\Rightarrow \qquad$ 20% of $x = 298$

$\Rightarrow \qquad x \times \dfrac{20}{100} = 298 \Rightarrow \dfrac{x}{5} = 298$

$\Rightarrow \qquad x = 5 \times 298$

$\therefore \qquad x = 1490$

79. (d) Given, $x - \dfrac{1}{x} = 2$

Now, on squaring both sides, we get

$\Rightarrow \qquad x^2 + \dfrac{1}{x^2} - 2 = 4$

$[\because (a - b)^2 = a^2 + b^2 - 2ab]$

$\Rightarrow x^2 + \dfrac{1}{x^2} = 4 + 2 \Rightarrow x^2 + \dfrac{1}{x^2} = 6$

80. (b) Let the height of tower $= 5\sqrt{3}x$

and distance of point $= 5x$

Let the angle of elevation $= \theta$

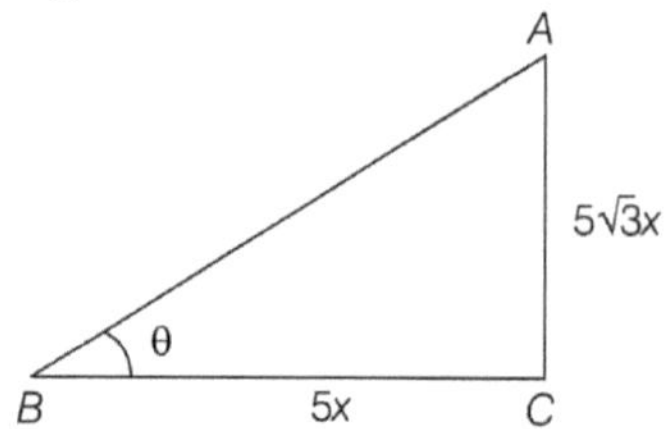

Then, In ΔABC,

$$\tan\theta = \dfrac{AC}{BC}$$

$\Rightarrow \qquad \tan\theta = \dfrac{5\sqrt{3}x}{5x} = \sqrt{3}$

$\Rightarrow \qquad \tan\theta = \sqrt{3} = \tan 60°$

$\Rightarrow \qquad \theta = 60°$

81. (d) $\because$ Average score of runs of 11 innings $= 63$

$\therefore$ Total score of runs of 11 innings $= 11 \times 63 = 693$

$\because$ Average score of runs of first 6 innings $= 60$

$\therefore$ Total score of runs of 6 innings $= 6 \times 60 = 360$

Now, average score of runs of last 6 innings $= 65$

$\therefore$ Total score of runs of last 6 innings

$= 6 \times 65 = 390$

Hence, total runs scored in sixth innings

$= 360 + 390 - 693 = 750 - 693 = 57$

82. (c) Let the average of 50 students be x and y is the weight of new student.

Then, sum of weights of all 50 students $= 50x$

According to the question,

$$50x - 50 + y = 50\left(x + \dfrac{1}{2}\right)$$

$\Rightarrow \qquad 50x - 50 + y = 50x + 25$

$\Rightarrow \qquad -50 + y = 25 \Rightarrow y = 75$ kg

83. (c) Given, $\angle C = 59° \approx 60°$

Here, $AB = 12$ cm, $BC = 8$ cm

By using cosine formula,

$$\cos C = \dfrac{AC^2 + BC^2 - AB^2}{2 \times AC \times BC}$$

$\cos 60° = \dfrac{AC^2 + (8)^2 - (12)^2}{2 \times AC \times 8}$

$\Rightarrow \dfrac{1}{2} = \dfrac{AC^2 + 64 - 144}{16 AC}$

$\Rightarrow 8AC = AC^2 - 80$

$\Rightarrow AC^2 - 8AC - 80 = 0$

$\Rightarrow AC = 4 \pm 4\sqrt{6}$

But AC being a side cannot be negative

$\therefore AC = 4 + 4\sqrt{6} = 13.79 \approx 14$ cm.

84. *(a)* Here, $r_1 = 20\%$, $r_2 = 10\%$ and marked price = ₹ 700

$\therefore$ SP of an item $= \text{MP}\left(1 - \dfrac{r_1}{100}\right)\left(1 - \dfrac{r_2}{100}\right)$

$= 700\left(1 - \dfrac{20}{100}\right)\left(1 - \dfrac{10}{100}\right) = 700 \times \dfrac{80}{100} \times \dfrac{90}{100}$

$= 7 \times 8 \times 9 = ₹ 504$

85. *(c)* Population after two years

$= 20000\left(1 + \dfrac{20}{100}\right)\left(1 + \dfrac{30}{100}\right) = 20000 \times \dfrac{120}{100} \times \dfrac{130}{100}$

$= 2 \times 120 \times 130 = 31200$

86. *(c)* Let, initial price of rice = ₹ x per kg

Now, a reduction of 20% in price.

$\therefore$ Reduced price of rice $= x \times \dfrac{80}{100} = ₹ \dfrac{4x}{5}$ per kg

Now, according to the question,

$$\dfrac{1200}{\dfrac{4x}{5}} - \dfrac{1200}{x} = 5$$

$\Rightarrow \quad \dfrac{6000}{4x} - \dfrac{1200}{x} = 5$

$\Rightarrow \quad \dfrac{1500}{x} - \dfrac{1200}{x} = 5$

$\Rightarrow \quad \dfrac{300}{x} = 5 \Rightarrow x = \dfrac{300}{5} = 60$

$\Rightarrow \quad x = ₹ 60$

$\therefore$ Reduced price of rice $= \dfrac{4x}{5} = \dfrac{4 \times 60}{5}$

$= ₹ 48$ per kg

87. *(a)* Let the income of a person = ₹ 100

$\because$ Spend on different expenses = ₹ 60

$\therefore$ Total saving $= 100 - 60 = ₹ 40$

Now, income after increment of 20%

$= \dfrac{120}{100} \times 100 = ₹ 120$

and expences after increment of 10%

$(60 + 10)\%$ of 120

$= 120 \times \dfrac{70}{100} = ₹ 84$

$\therefore$ New saving $= 120 - 84 = ₹ 36$

Now, percentage decrease is his saving

$= \left(\dfrac{40 - 36}{40}\right) \times 100$

$= \dfrac{4}{40} \times 100 = \dfrac{100}{10} = 10\%$

88. *(d)* Length of train = 150 m

Time = 12 s

$\because \quad \text{Speed} = \dfrac{\text{Distance}}{\text{Time}}$

$\therefore$ Speed of train $= \dfrac{150}{12}$ m/s $= \dfrac{150}{12} \times \dfrac{18}{5} = 45$ km/h

89. *(d)* Number $= 6P + 3$

Square of number $= (6P + 3)^2 = 36P^2 + 9 + 36P$

$\qquad = 36P^2 + 36P + 6 + 3$

$\qquad = 6(6P^2 + 6P + 1) + 3$

When, square of the number is divided by 6, we get remainder as 3.

90. *(b)* Total number of boys and girls = 256

$\therefore$ Number of girls $= \dfrac{7}{(9 + 7)} \times 256$

$\qquad = \dfrac{7 \times 256}{16} = 7 \times 16 = 112$

91. *(a)*

$A \xrightarrow{+12} M \xrightarrow{-10} C \xrightarrow{+12} \boxed{O}$

$E \xrightarrow{+12} Q \xrightarrow{-10} G \xrightarrow{+12} \boxed{S}$

$N \xrightarrow{+12} Z \xrightarrow{-10} P \xrightarrow{+12} \boxed{B}$

92. *(d)*

0   4   18   48 $\boxed{100}$ 180

$+4 \quad +14 \quad +30 \quad +52 \quad +80$

$+10 \quad +16 \quad +22 \quad +28$

$+6 \quad +6 \quad +6$

93. *(a)* As, the sound of Apes is known, as Gibber, similarly sound of camels is known as Grunt.

94. *(b)* As,

T S R $\longrightarrow$ F E D
$-1 \quad -1 \qquad -1 \quad -1$

Same as,

W V U $\longrightarrow$ M L K
$-1 \quad -1 \qquad -1 \quad -1$

95. *(c)* As,

$7 \longrightarrow 32$

$\times 4 + 4$

Same as,

$28 \longrightarrow \boxed{116}$

$\times 4 + 4$

96. *(b)* The given figure is embedded in the figure given in option (b).

97. *(a)*

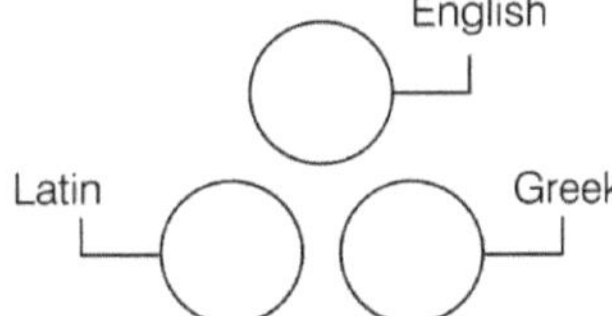

English, Greek and Latin are entirely different from one-another. All three are different language.

98. *(d)* Here, sign * implies division and sign @ implies multiplication

$4 \div 2 \times 3 = 6$, $18 \div 6 \times 4 = 12$

Therefore, $24 \div 3 \times 7 = \boxed{56}$

99. *(d)* According to the question,
$$32 \div 8 - 4 \times 12 + 4 = 32 + 8 \div 4 - 12 \times 4$$
$$= 32 + 2 - 12 \times 4 = 32 + 2 - 48 = -14$$

100. *(c)* Letters of the basic word are written in the coded word in such a way that last and first letters, second last and second letters, third last and third letters and so on are written together in the coded word.

As,   CARPET   NATIONAL

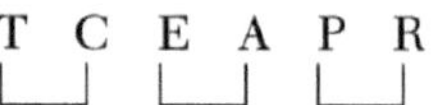 

101. *(a)* The arrangement according to dictionary is as follows

    Grease, Great, Greet, Grind, Growth
      (4)   (3)   (5)   (1)   (2)

102. *(d)* Option figure (d) will be complete the given question figure.

103 *(d)* The pattern of the given series is as follows.

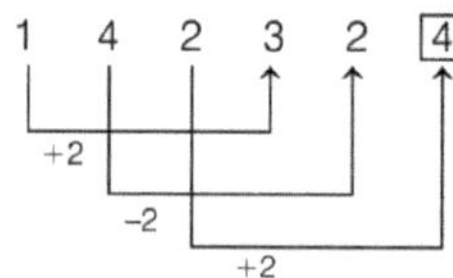

104. *(b)* As, $25 + 17 = 42 \Rightarrow \dfrac{42}{7} = 6$

and $38 + 18 = 56 \Rightarrow \dfrac{56}{7} = 8$

Same as, $89 + 16 = 105 \Rightarrow \dfrac{105}{7} = 15$

105. *(c)* On the basis of given statements, we could say that both assumptions I and II follow.

106. *(c)* Walking diagram of John is as follows

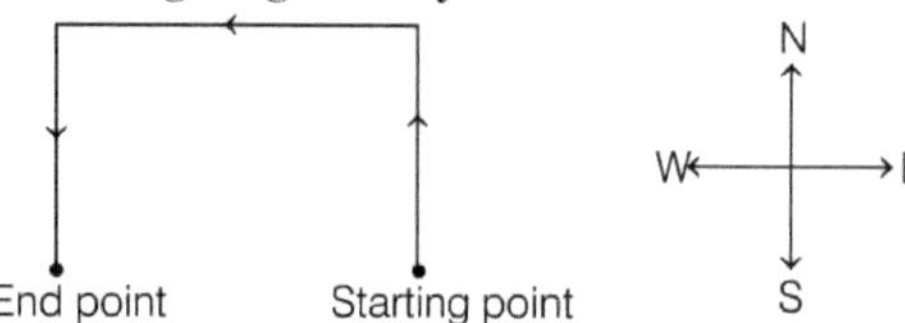

If is clear from diagram that john is in facing South direction now.

107. *(d)* As, $64 + 7 = 460$

$\Rightarrow$ $64 \times 7 + 12 = 460$

and $25 + 8 = 212$

$\Rightarrow$ $25 \times 8 + 12 = 212$

Same as, $43 + 8 = ?$

$\Rightarrow$ $43 \times 8 + 12 = 356$

$\therefore$ $? = 356$

108. *(c)* As,

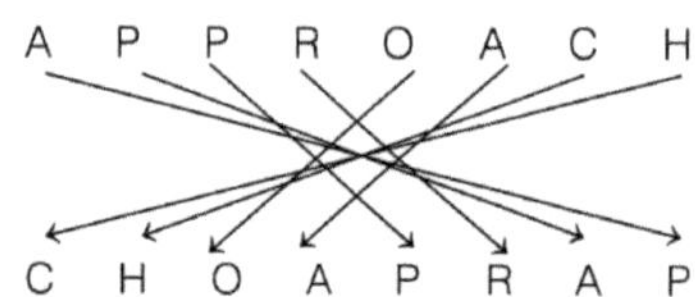

Same as,

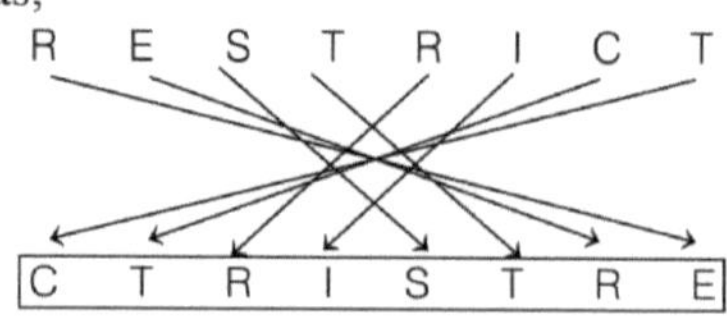

Sol. (Q. Nos. 109-111)

109. *(d)* The pattern is as follows,

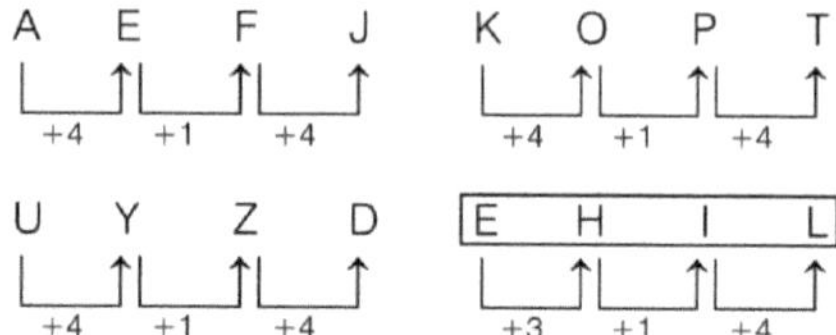

Hence option (d) is odd.

110. *(b)*
$$81 \xrightarrow{\times 3} 243 \ ; \quad 16 \xrightarrow{\times 4} 64$$
$$64 \xrightarrow{\times 3} 192 \ ; \quad 25 \xrightarrow{\times 3} 75$$

Hence, option (b) is odd.

111. *(a)* Except distinguish, all others are related to separation or segregation.

112. *(c)* Let us check all the option one by one.

From option (a) $8 \times 8 \div 1 + 7$
$$= 64 + 7 = 71 \neq 8$$

From option (b), $8 + 8 \div 1 \times 7$

$\Rightarrow$ $8 + 56 = 64 \neq 8$

From option (c), $8 \div 8 \times 1 + 7$
$$= 1 \times 1 + 7 = 8 = 8$$
         (True)

From option (d,) $8 + 8 \times 1 \div 7$

$\Rightarrow$ $8 + \dfrac{8}{7} = \dfrac{64}{7} \neq 8$

$\therefore$ Option (c) is correct.

113. *(a)* According to the question, the direction diagram can be drawn as,

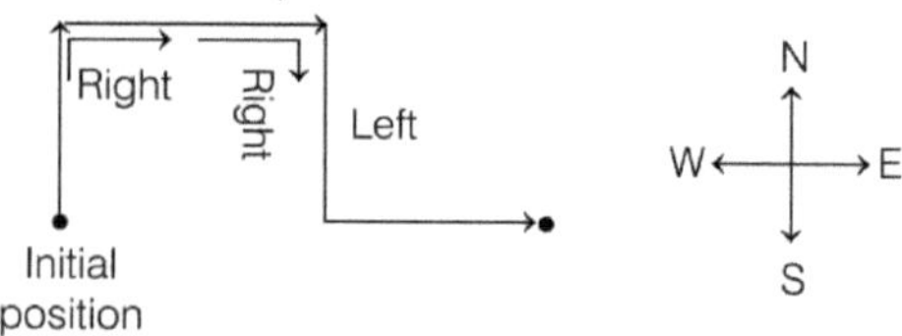

Clearly, Ritu is going towards East.

114. *(a)*

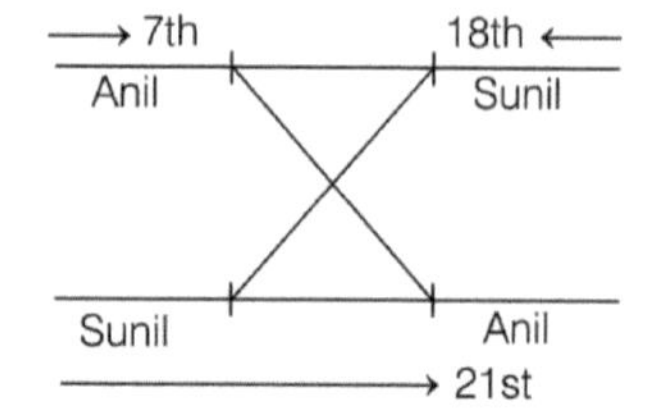

Total number of students $= (21 + 18 - 1) = 38$

115. *(b)* Since, the narrator has no brother or sister, his father's son means himself. So, the man who is talking is the father of the man in the photograph. Thus, the man in the photograph is his son.

116. *(c)* According to the statements, 80% of the total runs were made by spinners. So, I does not follow. Nothing about the opening batsmen is mentioned in the statement. So, statement II also does not follow.

117. *(a)* Clearly, I directly follows from the given statement. Also, it is mentioned that old ideas are replaced by new ones, as thinking changes with the progressing time. So, II does not follow.

118. *(a)* Arrangement according to the questions is as follows

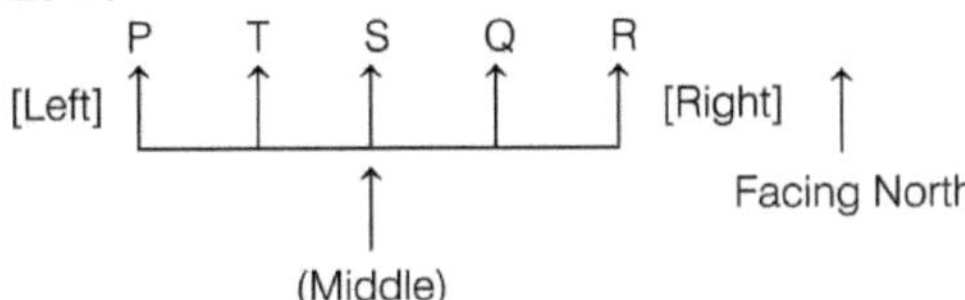

∴ S is in the middle of the row.

119. *(c)* In each successive step, one line is shifted from right to left. Hence, IIIIIX will come in place of question mark.

120. (a) Figure given in option (a) is the correct mirror image of the given question figure.

121. *(c)* The Speaker of Lok Sabha presides over the Joint Session of both the Houses of the Parliament in India. Hence, option (c) is the correct answer.

By virtue of power granted to President under Article 108, he may call the joint sitting of the Parliament. The joint meeting is presided over by the Speaker or in his absence, by the Deputy Speaker of the Lok Sabha or in their absence, the Deputy-Chairperson of the Rajya Sabha. Joint sitting of Parliament is a constitutional mechanism to break the deadlock between Rajya Sabha and Lok Sabha.

122. *(b)* Ocean currents are primarily cuased by wind blowing over the sea surface. Hence, option (b) is the correct answer.

Ocean currents are the continuous flow of the huge amount of water in a definite direction. Ocean currents can also be classified based on temperature as cold currents and warm currents.

123. *(b)* Fundamental duties of Indian citizens are provided by 42nd amendment. Hence, option (b) is the correct answer.

The Fundamental Duties were added to the Constitution by the 42nd Amendment in 1976, upon the recommendations of the Swaran Singh Committee. By the 42nd Constitution (Amendment) Act, 1976, a new Chapter IV-A containing Article 51-A was added to the Constitution. The Amendment added ten Fundamental Duties and the 11th fundamental duty was added by the 86th Constitutional Amendment.

124. *(b)* Production of goods and services is the basis for determining National Income. It is calculated by the total value of goods and services produced in the country. Hence, option (b) is the correct answer.

The sum of total income received for the services of labour, land or capital in a country is called National Income (NI). National Income can be calculated through three methods: Product method, Expenditure method and Income method.

Formula to calculate National Income

$$NI = C + G + I + X + F - D$$

Where,

C denotes the Consumption,

G denotes the Government expenditure,

I denotes the Investments,

X denotes the Net Exports (Exports minus Imports),

F denotes the National Resident's Foreign Production,

D denotes the Non-National Resident's Domestic Production

125. *(a)* MK Gandhi took the leadership of the National Movement (Khilafat Movement) in 1919-20. Hence, option (a) is the correct answer.

Mahatma Gandhi arrived India in 1915 from South Africa. At first, he spent a year exploring different places in India to understand the situation. Mahatma Gandhi's political activity began in the period of 1917-18, when he dealt with the issues of the Champaran Indigo Farmers (1917), the Ahmedabad Textile Workers (1918) and the Kheda Peasants (1918).

126. *(d)* The Moti Masjid was built by Shah Jahan at Agra in 1655. Hence, option (d) is the correct answer.

Shah Jahan (1628–58) was a Mughal emperor. He is also best remembered for his architectural achievements. He built Taj Mahal in Agra which was erected in the memory of his wife Mumtaz Mahal and he also built a famous Mosque Jama Masjid in Delhi. In 1648, he transferred his capital from Agra to Delhi and created the new city of Shahjahanabad.

127. *(d)* Hardwood trees like sal, teak, neem and shisham are found in Tropical deciduous forests. Hence, option (d) is correct. These trees are mainly used for making furniture, transport and construction material. Tropical deciduous forests are found in region which receives rainfall between 100-150 cm. The trees of this forest shed their leaves during dry season.

128. *(b)* The Reserve Bank of India was established on 1st April, 1935 in accordance with the Reserve Bank of India Act, 1934. Hence, option (b) is correct. It was nationalised in the year 1949. It acts as a banker to Central Government. It is also responsible for the issue and supply of the Indian rupee and the regulation of the Indian banking system.

129. *(a)* Global hectare is used to measure the ecological foot print as well as biocapacity of entire Earth. Hence, option (a) is correct. In terms of Ecological Footprint, one global hectare refers to average productive land and water that an individual, population or entity requires producing all the resources it consumes.

130. *(a)* Administration of Union Territories Part VIII of the Indian Constitution (Article 239 to 242). Hence, option (a) is the correct answer.

Administration of Union Territories has been provided under Article 239 of the Constitution of India. The Seventh Constitution Amendment Act of 1956 replaced the States in Part C and Territories in Part D of the First Schedule by the 'Union Territories'. At present, there are eight Union Territories in India.

131. *(a)* Shivaji was crowned as an independent king at Rajgarh, in 1674. Hence, option (a) is the correct answer.

Shivaji (1630-1680) was also known as Chhatrapati Shivaji Maharaj. He was an Indian Maratha ruler who challenged Mughals. He helped people who wanted to convert to Hinduism.

He also promoted Hindu and Sanskrit political traditions. Shivaji was known for Treaty of Purandar in 1665. He was also considered a master of the Guerrilla Warfare.

132. *(d)* The Battle of Plassey was fought one hundred years before the War of Independence (1857), where the destiny of India changed drastically. Hence, option (d) is the correct answer.

Battle of Plassey was fought on 23rd June, 1757, in Plassey on the banks of Hooghly river between British East India Company and the Nawab of Bengal, Siraj-ud Daulah and his French allies. It was fought under the leadership of Robert Clive. Britishers won the battle. The battle enabled the East India Company to take control of Bengal.

133. *(c)* Methane gas is produced by the decomposition of organic waste in an oxygen-free environment. Hence, option (c) is correct. The treatment and handling of waste water also produces methane.

134. *(c)* The larynx is another name for the voice box. Hence, option (c) is correct. It's a tube about 2 inches (5 cm) long in adults. It sits above the windpipe (trachea) in the neck and in front of the food pipe.

135. *(d)* Mycology is the branch of biology concerned with the study of fungi. Hence, option (d) is correct. It also includes their genetic and biochemical properties, their taxonomy and their use to humans as a source for tinder, medicine, food and entheogens, as well as their dangers, such as toxicity or infection.

136. *(b)* Chambal river is not a South-flowing river. Hence, option (b) is the correct answer.
Chambal river flows through Madhya Pradesh, Rajasthan and Uttar Pradesh. It originates at Janapav hills, South of Mhow (Madhya Pradesh)

and drains into the Yamuna river at Jalaun (Uttar Pradesh).
Damodar river is a South flowing river that originates in Jharkhand and drains into Hooghly river at Howrah (West Bengal). It is also referred as 'Sorrow of Bengal'.

The Kosi river originates at Triveni (Nepal) and flows southwards to drain into Ganga near Kursela (Bihar). It is known as 'Sorrow of Bihar'.

137. *(d)* Akash is an air to ground missile. Hence, option (d) is the correct answer.

Akash missile was built by Defense Research and Development Organisation (DRDO) under the Integrated Guided-Missile Development Programme (1983). It has a range of 50.80 km.

138. *(d)* The headquarters of INTERPOL is located in Lyon, France. Hence, option (d) is the correct answer.
INTERPOL (International Criminal Police Organisation) is an international organisation which supports police and law enforcement agencies and controls crime in the world. It was founded in 1923 by Johannes Schober, former Chancellor of Austria.

139. *(b)* Petroleum, a complex mixture of hydrocarbons that occur in Earth in liquid, gaseous or solid form. Hence, option (b) is correct.

The term is often restricted to the liquid form, commonly called crude oil, but, as a technical term, petroleum also includes natural gas and the viscous or solid form known as bitumen, which is found in tar sands.

140. *(a)* Graphite is also used as a dry lubricant. Hence, option (a) is correct. Dry lubricants are those materials that despite being in the solid phase, are able to reduce friction between two surfaces sliding against each other without the need for a liquid oil medium.

141. *(a)* As per the Doppler's effect, when the distance between the source and the listener decreases, the apparent frequency increases. Hence, option (a) is correct. It means the apparent frequency is more than the actual frequency of sound.

142. *(b)* Andhra Pradesh is the first state to have been formed on linguistic basis to safeguard the rights of the Telugu people of Madras state. Hence, option (b) is the correct answer.

After the creation of Andhra Pradesh, the Fazl Ali Commission (1953) was formed under the chairmanship of Fazl Ali. The Commission's recommendations were focused on the reorganisation of the state on the basis of linguistic criteria.

The state Andhra Pradesh was formed on 1st November, 1956. It is the seventh largest state in India. The official language of Andhra Pradesh is Telegu. It borders Odisha to the North-East, Telangana to the North-West, Karnataka to the West, Chhattisgarh to the North, Bay of Bengal to the East and Tamil Nadu to the South.

143. *(b)* Equality before law and equal protection of law is dealt with/in Article 14 of the Indian Constitution. Hence, option (b) is the correct answer.

Article 14 provides that the State shall not deny to any person equality before the law or the equal protection of the laws within the Territory of India.

Article 13 states that laws which are consistent with or in derogation of the Fundamental Rights shall be void.

Article 15 prohibits discrimination on grounds of religion, race, caste, sex or place of birth.

Article 16 provides equal opportunity in matters of public employment.

144. *(a)* The Mahadeo hills are a range of sandstone hills located in Central India. Hence, option (a) is correct. These hills are located in the Northern part of Satpura range. Hence, option (a) is the correct answer.

The cave shelters found in the Mahadeo hills contains some of the earliest evidence of rock paintings in India. Dhupgarh is the highest point in the Mahadeo hills with a height of 1352 meters.

145. *(d)* Union Minister of Heavy Industries and Public Enterprises Prakash Javadekar on 29th June, 2021 inaugurated NATRAX- the High-Speed Track (HST) for automobiles in Indore. Hence, option (d) is correct. The track is the longest such track in Asia and the world's fifth-longest.

146. *(c)* Chloe Zhao won the Oscar for Best Director for the film Nomadland at the 93rd Annual Academy Awards on 25th April, 2021. Hence, option (c) is correct. She became the first woman of colour, first Chinese woman and second woman ever to win the award.

147. *(c)* Singapore has become the first country to complete the official process for ratification of the Regional Comprehensive Economic Partnership (RCEP) agreement. Hence, option (c) is correct.

148. *(c)* The largest fish-exporting region of the world is North-West Pacific Region. Hence, option (c) is the correct answer.

This region is also called as Cascadia. It is a geographic region in Western-North America bounded by the Pacific Ocean to the West and Rocky Mountains on the East.

149. *(a)* Aspirin is effective in relieving skeletal pain such as that due to arthritis and in reducing fever (antipyretic). Hence, option (a) is correct. Because of its anti-blood clotting action, aspirin finds use in the prevention of heart attacks.

150. *(c)* The electromagnetic spectrum when arranged from longest wavelength to shortest includes radio waves, microwaves, infrared, optical, ultraviolet, X-rays and gamma-rays. Hence, option (c) is correct.

151. *(b)* If any one starts a new business and has little savings and few employees then she/he has to figure out what business/activity they should start.

152. *(d)* A football match is going on and a person likes one team but his group favours the other one. In this scenario, that person should stick to his/her favourite team.

153. *(b)* While returing home from a far away place if anyone's pocket has been picked. Then, they should hire a taxi and pay on reaching home.

154. *(d)* The newspaper hawker comes late in the morning and therefore, a person has to go to work without reading the newspaper. In this case, a person should apprise him about his/her problem.

155. *(a)* In order to get respect and reputation in the society, a person need to develop friendly relationship with all the persons.

156. *(c)* As I get up late in the morning and my neighbour utilises this opportunity to read newspaper. Then, I would tell him that he should read the newspaper and return it me.

157. *(c)* If one of my close friends does not look after his old parents who stay with him. Then, I will tell my friend that what he is doing is not quite correct.

158. *(b)* When a new person joins my department in the office, in this condition, I should go and meet him and help him, if he needs any help.

159. *(c)* While having a walk along the sea-shore, if I notice a man drowning and shouting for help, then I will go immediately into the water, as I know swimming.

160. *(b)* While walking on the road, I found an envelope which contains an Aadhar Card. Then, I will post the Aadhar Card to the address of its owner as it does not involve expenditure of very high amount.

161. *(a)* For efficient guest relations executive must have a pleasant personality and skills of courteus behaviour.

162. *(c)* If someone involves me in an argument. Then, I will try to learn a lesson or two from the person who is arguing.

163. *(d)* While expressing my views on an important subject, I will look for opinions expressed by other people, then speak.

164. *(d)* If a person is not capable of taking his/her decision, then one should take suggestion or advice from parents, friends and close relatives.

165. *(b)* Being a member of the sports team of my college, if due to some misunderstanding other players of team have stopped talking with me, then I will go forward and try to find out the problem and sort out it.

166. *(c)* If a person gets less marks than expected in the examination, which has jeopardised his/her chances for further studies. Then, one should try to take up a job and go for further studies through correspondence course.

167. *(a)* A friend of mine, who stays along with me, has the habit of remaining awake late in the night. Due to his habit, my sleep is disturbed. In this situation, I will motivate him to sleep early.

168. *(b)* The responsibility of hospitality of the guest or looking after their smooth and enjoyable stay in a hotel lies on the shoulder of guest relations executive.

169. *(b)* In an interview if a person is asked to describe him/herself. Then one should go ahead with full steam and give all the relevant information.

170. *(b)* Whenever anyone joins a group. Then, it will take some time to understand people.

171. *(c)* As a manager I will engage in 2 way communication with stress on feedback.

172. *(d)* Due to urgent piece of work, if my father is not able to send money on time. Then, I will arrange money from another source and carry on my work.

173. *(d)* If any person tries to obstruct my work time and again then I will ask him the reason for obstructing and give him suitable reply.

174. *(a)* If my favourite player is found to be guilty of match fixing, then I would like a ban to be imposed on him.

175. *(c)* In the examination hall if I found that question paper is too tough to be answered satisfactorily by me. Then, I will attempt those questions about which I know something.

176. *(d)* In case of breaking out of a fire in my neighbourhood then I will reach the site and do my best to help the victims.

177. *(a)* An infection or contagious disease has been break out spread in my city then, I will inform the health centres to take necessary action.

178. *(c)* While working as a primary school teacher, I found a student is not able to pay his tuition fee. In this scenario, I will find out the reason for non-payment of fee and then personally help the boy, if needed.

179. *(c)* If I see some smoke coming out of building of my office and come to know that there is fire somewhere. Then, I will inform the fire brigade in no time.

180. *(c)* If a person is getting late for a meeting and on the way to office if he/she witness an accident. In this situation, ignore the meeting and help the injured.

181. *(a)* If I have been sent on a visit to rural area on a project to educate the local children. I will take part in the project whole heartedly and try to put in my maximum effort.

182. *(c)* Amongst the given options, option (c) reflect the correct attitude toward adolescent son. One shall conduct an open discussion with the son and let him make his own decisions.

183. *(c)* If my colleague tell me that I often show short tempered behaviour, then, I will take it sportingly and look for some ways to control my temper.

184. *(c)* In this scenario, I will return the extra money immediately to the employer. It will improve my credibility.

185. *(c)* If any guest in the hotel has suddenly become unwell, as a manager, I will meet the guest and then urgently call the doctor and help the patient as required.

186. *(d)* While travelling in a train if my co-passenger is not able to catch a train while the train has started moving. Then, I will get up and pull the chain.

187. *(c)* If a guy slipped and fell in front of me while walking through the college corridor and my friends started laughing. In this condition, I will help him and ask my friends not to laugh.

188. *(a)* If I am in a bus which meets with an accident. Then, I would ask and motivate others to help out people who are hurt.

189. *(c)* In this scenario, I will try and help him as much as I could using a sign language.

190. *(d)* While watching a movie in a theatre, a small child starts crying. Then, I will ask the child's parents if everything is ok with the child and if there is any help, I will give to them.

191. *(a)* To work efficiently in the service sector, a person should be decisive or quick in decision making.

192. *(d)* I will try to get used to the new work environment and adjust.

193. *(c)* In this scenario, I will change the mode of the presentation as few hours are left for meeting. In such a short period new presentation cannot be created.

194. *(c)* If a stranger comes to you asking about an address while I am waiting for someone. Then, I will explain him properly and repeatedly until he understands the direction properly.

195. *(a)* I will flatly refuse the offer as paying bribe is not a good option.

196. *(c)* On visiting my relative home I found that he is not well and is unable to give proper welcome. In this situation, I will stay and help him.

197. *(b)* In this situation, I will call my neighbour and politely tell him that perhaps by mistake he has parked his car in my slot. Hence, problem can be solved in a smooth manner.

198. *(d)* In a park, I see two boys fighting and beating each other. Then, I will go and ask them politely to stop fighting and resolve the issue by talking and discussing.

199. *(b)* After finishing chocolate, if I didn't find any dustbin around to dispose off the wrapper then I will keep it with myself until-find a dustbin.

200. *(d)* To make the environment of my work place more and more congenial and worth working, I will take all the given steps.

NCHMCT

Hotel Management

National Council for Hotel Management and Catering Technology

Solved Paper 2020

Instructions

- There are Five (A-E) Sections in this Solved Paper.
- For every correct attempt, the student will be awarded **1 mark**.
- All the questions are in MCQs form and each having four options.

Marks : 200

Time : 3 hrs

Section A : Numerical Ability And Scientific Aptitude

1. Which of the following number is divisible by 3?
(a) 5967013   (b) 541326
(c) 585412   (d) 534230

2. The sum of four consecutive even numbers A, B, C and D is 180. What is the sum of the set of next four consecutive even numbers?
(a) 214   (b) 204   (c) 196   (d) 212

3. Sunil can do a piece of work in 2 days, while Saurav can do it in 3 days. They work together for a day and rest of the work is done by Sachin in 1 day. They get ₹ 1800 for the whole work. Find out the wage of Sachin, if wages are paid in proportion to work done.
(a) ₹ 150   (b) ₹ 400   (c) ₹ 250   (d) ₹ 300

4. The simple interest on a sum of money is equal to the principal and the number of year is equal to the rate per cent per annum. The rate per cent is
(a) 25%   (b) 100%   (c) 10%   (d) 12%

5. What will be the simple interest for 1 yr and 4 months on the sum of ₹ 25800 at the rate of 14% per annum?
(a) ₹ 4816   (b) ₹ 2580
(c) ₹ 4818   (d) ₹ 4518

6. Simple interest on ₹ 800 for 4 yr and on ₹ 800 for 2 yr combined together is ₹ 192. Find the rate of interest.
(a) 5%   (b) 4%   (c) 5.8 %   (d) 6.5%

7. Father is nine times as old as his son and the mother is eight times as old as the son. The sum of the father's and the mother's age is 51 yr. What is the age of the son?
(a) 7 yr   (b) 5 yr   (c) 4 yr   (d) 3 yr

8. The ratio between the present ages of Simran and Smriti is 3 : 7 respectively. After 4 yr Smriti's age will be 39 yr. What was Simran's age 4 yr ago?
(a) 12 yr   (b) 13 yr   (c) 19 yr   (d) 11 yr

9. The difference between the ages of two persons is 10 yr. Fifteen years ago the elder one was twice as old as the younger one. The present age of the elder person is
(a) 35 yr   (b) 25 yr   (c) 55 yr   (d) 45 yr

10. The average of 7 consecutive numbers is 20. The largest of these numbers is
(a) 20   (b) 22   (c) 23   (d) 24

11. A man bought number of oranges half at ₹ 3 per piece and other half at ₹ 2 per piece. At what price per dozen should he sell them to make a profit of 20%?
(a) ₹ 30/dozen   (b) ₹ 36/dozen
(c) ₹ 40/dozen   (d) ₹ 42/dozen

12. A trader marks his goods 20% above the cost price and allows a discount of 15% on it. Find out the gain per cent.
(a) 1%   (b) 5%   (c) 2%   (d) 6%

13. The average runs scored by a batsman in 15 innings is 48. After 16th innings his average runs become 50. How many runs does the batsman scored in 16th inning?
(a) 70   (b) 80   (c) 90   (d) 100

14. On the day of independence, sweets were to be equally distributed amongst 300 children, but on the day 50 children were absent, so each child got one extra sweet. How many sweets were distributed?
(a) 1450   (b) 1700   (c) 1650   (d) 1500

15. The average of marks of a student in 7 subjects is 75. His average marks in 6 subjects excluding Science is 72. How many marks did he score in Science?
(a) 84   (b) 87   (c) 90   (d) 93

16. If the price of the petrol is increased by 30%, by how much per cent a car owner must reduce his consumption in order to maintain the same budget?
(a) 21%   (b) $21\frac{1}{3}\%$ (c) $23\frac{1}{13}\%$ (d) 23%

17. Two candidates fought an election. One of them got 55% of the total votes and won by 432 votes. What is the total number of votes polled ?
(a) 4000   (b) 4120   (c) 4200   (d) 4320

18. In a school 10% of boys are equal to the one-fourth of the girls. What is the ratio of the boys and girls in that school?
(a) 3 : 2   (b) 5 : 2   (c) 2 : 1   (d) 4 : 3

19. The price of a chair is 60% of a table. The price of a stool is 15% of the table. The stool cost is what percentage of the chair?
(a) 15%   (b) 20%
(c) 25%   (d) 30%

20. The angles of a triangle are in the ratio of 1 : 2 : 3. The largest angle of the triangle is
(a) 30°   (b) 60°   (c) 90°   (d) 120°

21. If one star equals four circles and three circles equal four diamonds, then what is the ratio of star to diamond?
(a) 1 : 3   (b) 3 : 4
(c) 16 : 3   (d) 4 : 3

22. If the ratio of two numbers is 5 : 6 and their LCM is 480, then their HCF is
(a) 20   (b) 16   (c) 6   (d) 5

23. The HCF of 2923 and 3239 is
(a) 37   (b) 47   (c) 73   (d) 79

24. The product of two numbers is 4025 and their LCM is 25. Find their HCF.
(a) 161   (b) 165
(c) 175   (d) 180

Directions (Q. Nos. 25-27) *Study the following bar graph carefully and answer the questions that follow*

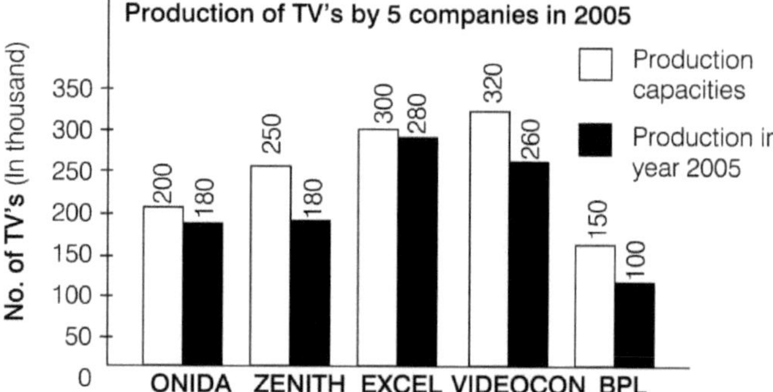

25. In year 2005, which company had the maximum percentage of unutilised capacity?
(a) Onida   (b) Zenith
(c) Excel   (d) BPL

26. In year 2005, which company had the minimum percentage of unutilised capacity?
(a) Onida   (b) Excel
(c) Videocon   (d) BPL

27. The TV's produced by 'Excel' form what percentage of the total production?
(a) 25%   (b) 30%
(c) 28%   (d) 26%

28. $\dfrac{\sqrt{81}}{11} \times \dfrac{\sqrt{121}}{9} =$

(a) 3 (b) 5 (c) 1 (d) 7

29. A gardner plants 17956 tress in such a way that there are as many rows as there are trees in a row. How many rows are there?

(a) 136 (b) 144 (c) 134 (d) 154

30. A general of army wants to create a formation of square from 36562 army men. After arrangement he found some army men remained unused. The number of army men remained unused is

(a) 36
(b) 65
(c) 81
(d) 97

Section B : Reasoning and Logical Deduction

Directions (Q. Nos. 31-33) *Complete the series by replacing question marks (?)*

31. CD, FGH, ?, OPQRS, UVWXYZ.

(a) HIJK (b) KLMN (c) IJKL (d) JKLM

32. 1 YO, 6 VQ, 13 SS, 22PU, ?

(a) 22 MV (b) 33 MW
(c) 33 NW (d) 44 OV

33. 1, 10, ?, 52, 85, 126

(a) 17 (b) 27
(c) 29 (d) 37

Directions (Q. Nos. 34 and 35) *Find out the alternative which will replace the question mark.*

34. CARS : VOLVO : : FURNITURE : ?

(a) FWD (b) TATA (c) IKEA (d) ITC

35. AIRLINE : AIRINDIA : : BANK : ?

(a) ICICI (b) HDFC (c) SBI (d) IDFC

36. In the following question, certain pairs of words are given, out of which the words in all pairs except one bear a certain common relationship. Choose the pair in which the words are differently related.

(a) Earth : Planet (b) Moon : Satellite
(c) Sun : Star (d) Rocket : Sky

37. Find out the odd among the four.

(a) Crab (b) Oyster
(c) Alligator (d) Tortoise

38. Which of the one is different from the rest ?

(a) Earth (b) Mars (c) Neptune (d) Moon

39. In the following number series, only one number is wrong. Find out the wrong number.

125, 126, 124, 127, 123, 129

(a) 126 (b) 124 (c) 123 (d) 129

Directions (Q. Nos. 40-42) *Each of these questions consists of two sets. Figures (1), (2), (3) and (4) are set of question figures and figures (a), (b), (c) and (d) constitute the set of answer figures. There is a definite relationship among figures (1), (2), (3) and (4). Select a suitable figure from the answer figures (a), (b), (c) and (d) which establishes a similar relationship.*

40.

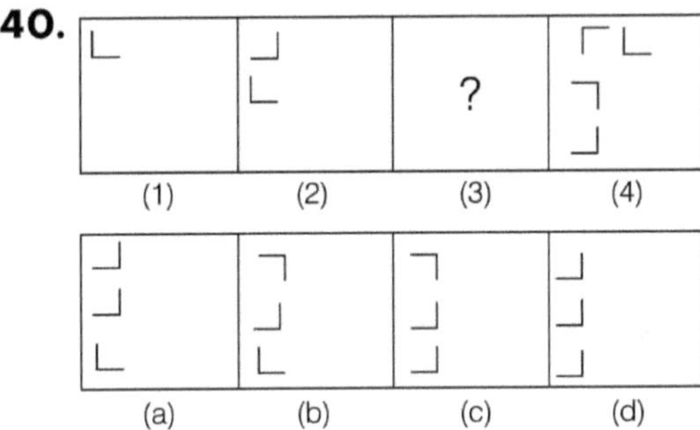

41.

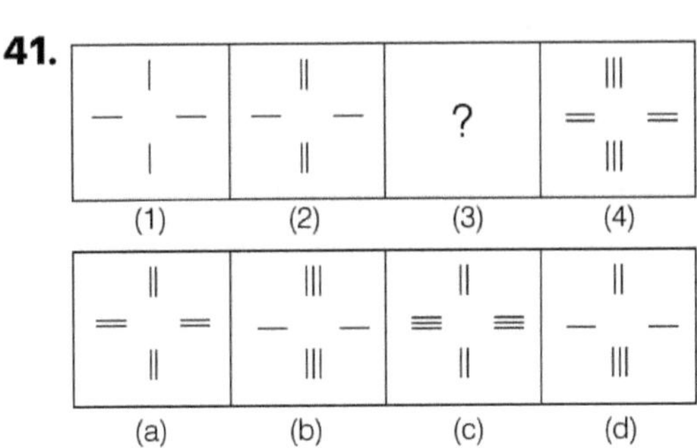

42.

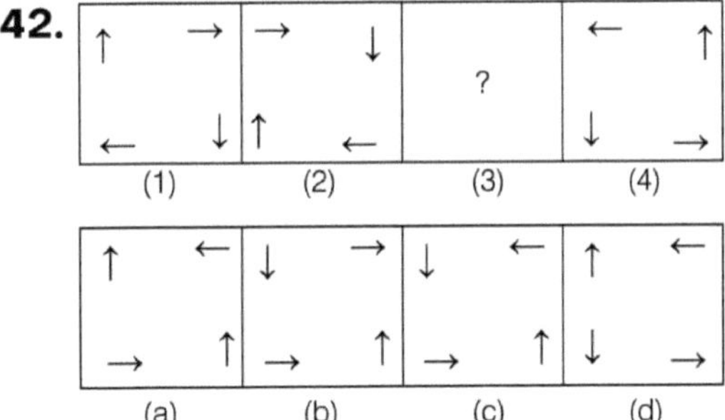

Directions (Q. Nos. 43-45) *Using the diagram below and answer the following questions.*

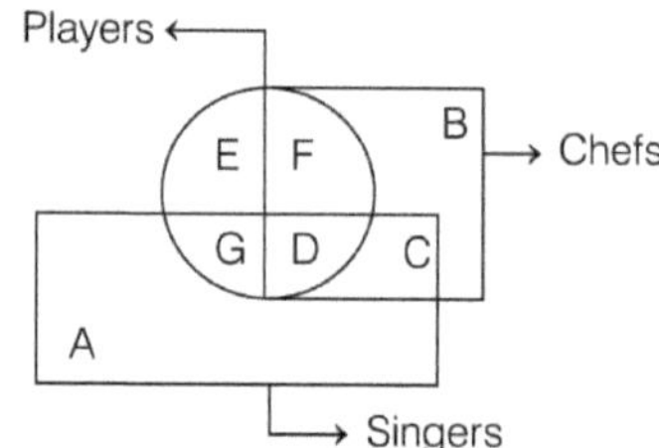

43. Which space represents chefs who are only singers?

(a) A   (b) B   (c) C   (d) D

44. Which space in the figure represents chefs who are singers and players?

(a) A   (b) B   (c) C   (d) D

45. Which space represents chefs who are only players?

(a) F   (b) E   (c) D   (d) A

Directions (Q. Nos. 46 and 47) *In each question below are given two statements followed by two conclusions numbered (I) and (II). You have to take the given statements to be true even if they seem to be at variance from commonly known facts. Read the conclusion and then decide which of the given conclusions logically follows from the two given statements, disregarding commonly known facts.*

(a) If only conclusion (I) follows
(b) If only conclusion (II) follows
(c) If either conclusion (I) or (II) follow
(d) If neither conclusion (I) nor (II) follow

46. Statements No women teacher can play.
Some women teachers are athletes.

Conclusions

I. Male athletes can play.
II. Some athletes can play.

47. Statements All trucks fly.
All scooters fly.

Conclusions

I. All trucks are scooters.
II. Some scooters do not fly.

Directions (Q. Nos. 48-50) *Each of these questions has an Assertion (A) and a Reason (R). Mark answer as*

(a) If both (A) and (R) are true and (R) is the correct explanation of (A)
(b) If both (A) and (R) are true, but (R) is not the correct explanation of (A)
(c) If (A) is true, but (R) is false
(d) If (A) is false, but (R) is true

48. Assertion (A) A person with blood group 'O' is considered a universal recipient.
Reason (R) Type 'O' blood doesn't contain any antigens.

49. Assertion (A) Indian President is the head of the state.
Reason (R) Indian Parliament consists of the President, Lok Sabha and Rajya Sabha.

50. Assertion (A) Earth is the only planet known to have life.
Reason (R) Earth has an atmosphere which is a mixture of oxygen, nitrogen and carbon dioxide.

51. In a certain code language APPLAUSE is written as PAPLUASE. How will SPLENDID be written in that code?

(a) SEPLNDDI   (b) PSLEDNID
(c) ELNDIDSP   (d) PSLEDNDI

52. Swati is 7 ranks ahead of Raju, who ranks 36 in a class of 60. What is Swati's rank from the last?

(a) 41   (b) 32   (c) 31   (d) 45

53. Answer the given question based on the following English alphabet :
A, B, C, D, E, F, G, H, I, J, K, L, M, N, O, P, Q, R, S, T, U, V, W, X, Y, Z.
If all the vowels are removed from the alphabet, which letter will be the fourth to the left of the sixteenth letter from the right?

(a) X   (b) B   (c) D   (d) C

54. Introducing Ankita to guests, Basker said "Her father is the only son of my father". How is Ankita related to Basker?

(a) Mother   (b) Sister   (c) Daughter (d) Niece

55. A woman said to a man, "The only brother of your sister is my father". How is that woman related to that man?

(a) Wife   (b) Sister   (c) Mother   (d) Daughter

56. If the son of the old person is the uncle of my son, then the old person is related to me as

(a) Father   (b) Grand father
(c) Father-in-law   (d) Son

Directions (Q. Nos. 57-60) *Study the following information carefully and answer the questions given below.*

A, B, C, D, E, F and G are the seven members of the family. There are three females among them. There are two married couples in the family. Each of them has a different profession from Architect, Lawyer, Doctor,

Teacher, Engineer, General Manager of a Hotel and Musician, not necessary in the same order. B is the Lawyer and he is married of F, the General Manager of a Hotel. A is brother of G, who is the Architect. C is the Doctor and is an unmarried lady. D is the Teacher and the sister of G. E is not an Engineer.

57. Which of the following pairs represent a married couple?
(a) BG   (b) ED   (c) AC   (d) DC

58. What is A's profession?
(a) Engineer (b) Musician (c) Lawyer (d) Teacher

59. What is E's profession?
(a) Doctor   (b) Musician (c) Teacher (d) Architect

60. Which of the following combinations represents the husbands of the two married couples?
(a) B and G   (b) A and F
(c) B and E   (d) D and C

Section C : General Knowledge and Current Affairs

61. Who was the first Indian woman to Climb Mt. Everest?
(a) Reita Faria   (b) Karnam Malleswari
(c) Bachendri Pal   (d) Aarti Saha

62. Which of the following is the National Airline of Germany?
(a) Cathay Pacific   (b) Quantas
(c) Luifthansa   (d) Garuda

63. Who was the first Indian woman to get an Olympic medal?
(a) Aarti Saha   (b) Karnam Malleswari
(c) P.T. Usha   (d) Sania Mirza

64. Myanmar was known by which name?
(a) Rangoon (b) Burma   (c) Peking (d) Formosa

65. The highest commissioned rank of Naval Services in India is
(a) Admiral   (b) Chief Marshal
(c) General   (d) Wing Commander

66. Washington DC is situated on the bank of river
(a) Potomac (b) Thames   (c) Danube (d) Nile

67. Babur defeated __________ in the first battle of Panipat on 21st April, 1526.
(a) Sher Shah   (b) Bairam Khan
(c) Hasan Khan   (d) Ibrahim Lodhi

68. The famous "C.K. Naidu" Trophy is associated with which sport?
(a) Cricket   (b) Lawn Tennis
(c) Badminton   (d) Hockey

69. What is the present name of the National Park which was established in 1931 with the aim to protect the wildlife of Karnataka and was named as 'Venugopala Wildlife Park'?
(a) Sundarban National Park
(b) Bandipur National Park
(c) Gir National Park
(d) Jim Corbett National Park

70. IPL stands for
(a) Indian Players League
(b) International Premier League
(c) Indian Premier League
(d) Indo-Pakistan League

71. 'NITI' in NITI Aayog stands for
(a) National Integration Tribunal of India
(b) National Index for Travel Institutions
(c) National Institutions for Transforming India
(d) National Institute for Tourism in India

72. The lowest temperature at which an oil gives sufficient vapours to form an explosive mixture with air is known as
(a) Smoke Point   (b) Flash Point
(c) Explosive Point   (d) Acidic Flux

73. Who is also known by the name 'Frontier Gandhi' ?
(a) Subhash Chandra Bose
(b) Jawaharlal Nehru
(c) Bal Gangadhar Tilak
(d) Abdul Gaffar Khan

74. Two smallest continents of the world are
(a) Australia and Antarctica
(b) Antarctica and Europe
(c) Australia and Europe
(d) Australia and South America

75. Who was popularly known as the 'Lady with the Lamp'?
(a) Indira Gandhi   (b) Queen Elizabeth
(c) Florence Nightingale   (d) Mother Teresa

76. The two largest denomination notes demonetised on 08th November, 2016 in India were
(a) 100 and 500   (b) 500 and 2000
(c) 500 and 1000   (d) 50 and 100

77. 'Higgs Boson' is also known as the
 (a) Sand Particle (b) God Particle
 (c) Electron (d) Neutron

78. 'The God of Small Things' is written by
 (a) Uma Shankar Joshi (b) Taslima Nasreen
 (c) Marget Thatcher (d) Arundhati Roy

79. Which city is known as 'Gateway of India' ?
 (a) Delhi (b) Goa
 (c) Mumbai (d) Hyderabad

80. Which is the largest planet in our solar system?
 (a) Earth (b) Saturn (c) Pluto (d) Jupiter

81. Who won the 'Women Singles' title in the U.S. Open Tennis Tournament 2018?
 (a) Serena Williams (b) Anastasija Sevastova
 (c) Naomi Oska (d) Elena Vesnina

82. Who amongst the following was the first Woman Chief-Minister of U.P. State?
 (a) Mayawati (b) Sucheta Kriplani
 (c) Sarojini Naidu (d) Kiran Bedi

83. Which is the capital of South Korea?
 (a) Seoul (b) Pyong Yang
 (c) Hong Kong (d) Dublin

84. Which is the device used to detect and measure small electric current in a circuit?
 (a) Galvanometer
 (b) Thermometer
 (c) Transformer
 (d) Electromagnetic Induction

85. Which part of our body gets affected by Tuberculosis?
 (a) Liver (b) Blood
 (c) Lungs (d) Eyes

86. Indentify the communication service founded in 2009 by Jan Koum and Brian Action who were former employees of Yahoo and was acquired by Facebook in 2014?
 (a) Twitter (b) Instagram
 (c) Hangout (d) Whatsapp

87. Who is the mother of 'Mahatma Gandhi'?
 (a) Kasturba (b) Putlibai
 (c) Archana Gandhi (d) Supriya Gandhi

88. Which state in India has the lowest literacy rate?
 (a) Kerala (b) Punjab
 (c) Assam (d) Bihar

89. Which was the first living creature sent in space?
 (a) Rat (b) Monkey
 (c) Cat (d) Dog

90. What do Dr. C.V. Raman. Dr. Zakir Hussain, Satyajit Ray and Mother Teresa have in common?
 (a) Pulitzer Prize (b) Magsaysay Award
 (c) Nobel Prize (d) Bharat Ratna

Section D : English Language

Directions (Q. Nos. 91-95) *Each of these questions consists of a sentence which is divided into four parts numbered a to d. Identify the part which contains an error.*

91. (a) I can show you
 (b) The place where the accident occurred
 (c) and caused him
 (d) to lost his right eye

92. (a) Monika and Leena
 (b) is going
 (c) to the book fair
 (d) today evening

93. (a) It is a misfortune
 (b) That you could not do anything
 (c) To help him
 (d) When he were in trouble

94. (a) I know you helped him
 (b) Yet I am not angry
 (c) With you
 (d) For he is yours friend

95. (a) Pants of his father
 (b) Was cut short
 (c) By two inches
 (d) So that he could use them

Directions (Q. Nos. 96-100) *In each of the following questions, out of the given alternatives, choose the one which is nearest in meaning to the underlined word in the sentence.*

96. Your master will like you if you are <u>diligent</u>.
 (a) Conscientious (b) Obedient
 (c) Meticulous (d) Hard working

97. Govt. ID cards are the only way to <u>authenticate</u> one's identity in airports.
(a) Validate   (b) Displayed
(c) Supporting   (d) Immigrate

98. He had the <u>nerve</u> to suggest that I was cheating.
(a) strength   (b) capacity
(c) audacity   (d) courage

99. Nisha looked beautiful and elegant in a <u>classy</u> pink dress, she wore for her sister's wedding.
(a) Majestic   (b) Important
(c) Simple   (d) Huge

100. We <u>cherish</u> the good memories of the festive season.
(a) Treasure   (b) Cheer
(c) Harmonise   (d) Praise

Directions (Q. Nos. 101-105) *In each of the following questions, out of the given alternatives, choose the one which is most nearly opposite in meaning to the underlined word in the sentence.*

101. At his success in examination he felt <u>elated</u>.
(a) excellent   (b) dejected
(c) resting   (d) jubilant

102. <u>Complicated</u> instructions in a question paper leads to confusion.
(a) Complex   (b) Slow   (c) Tough   (d) Simple

103. Indian Institute of Management is an <u>autonomous</u>, organisation, responsible for the finance, exams and administration.
(a) Magnanimous   (b) Ambiguous
(c) Operational   (d) Dependent

104. A character without a <u>blemish</u> is a virtue of a leader.
(a) shame   (b) disgrace
(c) decoration   (d) blot

105. The sweet shop in M block market serves <u>delicious</u> 'desserts'.
(a) Tasteful   (b) Appetizing
(c) Distasteful   (d) Appealing

Directions (Q. Nos. 106-110) *In each of the following questions, choose the option which can be substituted for the given words/sentence.*

106. A person, who takes no intoxicating drugs or drinks.
(a) Truant   (b) Teetotaller
(c) Topper   (d) Tyrant

107. Stealing from writing of others.
(a) Reproducing   (b) Reframing
(c) Copying   (d) Plagiarism

108. Yearly celebration of a date as an event.
(a) Centenary   (b) Jubilee
(c) Anniversary   (d) Birthday

109. A person pretending to be somebody he is not.
(a) Imposter   (b) Liar
(c) Rogue   (d) Magician

110. A person, who dies for a noble cause
(a) Mercenary   (b) Misanthrope
(c) Martyr   (d) Namesake

Directions (Q. Nos. 111-115) *Choose the word/phrase nearest in meaning to the underlined part.*

111. My colleague decided to <u>back me up</u> in the meeting.
(a) criticise   (b) appreciate
(c) support   (d) follow

112. The <u>fair and square</u> policy of the Chief Minister has made him very popular in his state.
(a) Clever and deceitly   (b) Honest
(c) Ambiguous   (d) Relevant and practical

113. All the students <u>turned a deaf ear</u> to their teachers during dance party.
(a) listened attentively
(b) behaved obediently
(c) started hooting
(d) did not pay attention to

114. You have to rush from <u>pillar to post</u>, but you have no chance of getting what you want without a bribe.
(a) Be very busy   (b) Go to post office
(c) Made to run around   (d) Stand near a pillar

115. His arrogant behaviour with others has left him <u>high and dry</u>.
(a) To be penniless   (b) To be very sick
(c) To be very famous   (d) Isolated

Directions (Q. Nos. 116-120) *In the following questions, four words are given. One word is spelt correctly while three words are wrongly spelt. Choose the correctly spelt word.*

116. (a) Gaurantee   (b) Gurantee
(c) Guarantee   (d) Garantee

117. (a) inconvinience   (b) inconvenience
(c) inconveneince   (d) inconveniense

118. (a) Vacum　　(b) Vaacum
(c) Vacuum　　(d) Vacumm

119. (a) Preservarance　　(b) Preserverence
(c) Perseverence　　(d) Perseverance

120. (a) Receipt　　(b) Reciept
(c) Raceipt　　(d) Reecipt

Directions (Q.Nos. 121-125) *In each of the following four words, one word has been spelt wrongly. Choose the wrongly spelt word.*

121. (a) Homogenious　　(b) Honorarium
(c) Honourable　　(d) Hoarding

122. (a) Companion　　(b) Compaign
(c) Community　　(d) Competitive

123. (a) Ballistic　　(b) Bullock
(c) Bulletin　　(d) Baloon

124. (a) Passenger　　(b) Instructor
(c) Conquer　　(d) Grammer

125. (a) Boredom　　(b) Implicit
(c) Explicit　　(d) Bruchure

Directions (Q. Nos. 126-135) *Fill in the blanks with the appropriate option given below.*

126. During the lecture the teacher enlarged .... the importance of the topic in our daily life.
(a) about　　(b) for　　(c) upon　　(d) on

127. The visit of PM has been advanced .... four days.
(a) for　　(b) by　　(c) to　　(d) with

128. He is a man .... humble origin.
(a) for　　(b) with　　(c) of　　(d) over

129. The cricket team with more number of all rounders, has an advantage .... the opponent team.
(a) at　　(b) over
(c) above　　(d) on

130. The old school teacher was kind .... the weak students.
(a) for　　(b) at　　(c) on　　(d) to

131. Some strange customs have .... from earlier times.
(a) suspended　　(b) survived
(c) desiccated　　(d) disarranged

132. Ram is the .... boy in the class.
(a) strongest and very tall　　(b) strongest and tallest
(c) weakest and short　　(d) weak and shortest

133. Ants and Bees work together in large members, ... they do so in a rigid manner and .... with close relatives.
(a) if, but　　(b) only, but　　(c) but, only　　(d) and, only

134. To .... yourself from .... wear warm clothes.
(a) prohibit heat　　(b) protect; cold
(c) save; cold　　(d) suffer; cold

135. The crew of the boat .... after its collision.
(a) drowned　　(b) seized　　(c) bound　　(d) sink

Directions (Q. Nos. 136-140) *Read the following passage carefully to answer the questions that follow.*

Graduation is only a milestone in life journey. It does not mark the end of education road. In a very real sense it is the commencement time, the beginning of a new journey which will test the toughness of your mental and moral fibre, the efficiency of your university training. The new experiences, the new problems and the new situations will demand from you the exercise of qualities for the fostering of which the university functions. In a new and Independent India the future will give powers and responsibilities to you. The historic role of the large educated classes in the building up of free India cannot be over estimated. If a leader is one who knows where he is going, who has a firm grasp of the insights and institutions which have made our civilisation so enduring and who can harness them for every aspect of life, it is on the university that can train men for leadership.

The universities are more than institutions for higher learning and professional training. They are called upon to educate, younger generation, form character and create new type of intellectual leadership.

136. The suitable title for the above passage is
(a) becoming a graduate　　(b) High school
(c) University education　　(d) Intellectual leadership

137. Graduation is
(a) Just a degree
(b) The end of education
(c) The beginning of a new journey
(d) New problem route

138. Toughness of your mental and moral fibre means
(a) Strength of your mental and moral qualities
(b) Greatness
(c) Power of being educated
(d) Character

139. Which of the following words is closest in meaning to the word FOSTER?
(a) Encourage　　(b) Disregard
(c) Discourage　　(d) Disrespect

140. Which of the following words is closest in meaning to the word <u>commencement</u> as used in the passage?
   (a) Begin   (b) Close
   (c) Stop   (d) Continue

Directions (Q. Nos. 141-145) *Read the following passage carefully to answer the questions that follow.*

Street theatre in India is a well established ancient art form, despite the proliferation of modern means of entertainment and communication, street theatre continues to flourish in India. Street theatre as a channel of communication has for centuries been propagating reforms, by highlighting social, economic and political issues present in the society.

Unlike in the olden days, its performance is no longer restricted to villages or small localities of the city. Today, small groups of performers, including students, would stage performances to mobilise public opinion or to help create or raise awareness over an issue of particular public importance.

141. According to the passage, what is a well established art form, that is also ancient.
   (a) Cinema   (b) Music
   (c) Street theatre   (d) Classical dance

142. Which is an important issue that street theatre does NOT deal with (as in passage)?
   (a) Social   (b) Religious
   (c) Economic   (d) Political

143. In olden days, where were street theatre performances mostly done.
   (a) In colleges   (b) In city centre
   (c) In villages   (d) In schools

144. Which group has joined the street theatre art form in modern times?
   (a) Office workers   (b) Housewives
   (c) Students   (d) Government servants

145. When street theatre mobilise public opinion over an important issue, they
   (a) Raise awareness   (b) Raise income
   (c) Raise anger   (d) Raise hatred

Directions (Q. Nos. 146-150) *Read the following passage carefully to answer the questions that follow.*
The Team India Cricket Shop opened with the Smashing of a cocount on the morning of 29th April, 2000. All our immediate families had come. My mother and Omi's family were visibly happy while Ish's parents were silent. They still visualised Ish as an army officer, not a shopkeeper in Balrampur.

'May Laxmi shower all blessings on you hardworking boys,' Omi's mother said before she left.

Soon, it was just us in our twenty-feet-by-ten-feet shop.

'Move the counter in, the shutter won't close,'. Ish screamed at Omi. Omi's forehead broke into sweat as he lifted the bulky countertop yet again to move it back an inch.

I stepped out of the shop and crossed the road for the tenth time to look at the board. It was six feet wide and two feet tall. We had painted it blue.

The colour of the Indian Cricket team. In the centre, we had the letters 'Team India Cricket Shop' in the colours of the Indian flag. The excited painter from Shahpur had thrown in the faces of Tendulkar and Ganguly for free. Ganguly had a squint and Tendulkar's lips looked bee-stung, but it all added to the charm.

146. Where is the 'Team India Cricket Shop' located?
   (a) New Delhi   (b) Shahpur
   (c) Belrampur   (d) MCG Ground

147. Apart from the author, names of other two partners of the shop are
   (a) Ish and Omi
   (b) Tendulkar and Ganguly
   (c) Ish and Chetan
   (d) Omi and Bhagat

148. The word 'squint' means
   (a) Wrinkled forehead
   (b) Eye glasses
   (c) Eyes that look in different direction
   (d) Grumpy face

149. Why Ish's parents were silent?
   (a) They did not like the name of the shop.
   (b) They were feeling uncomfortable due to heat.
   (c) They wanted Ish to become an army officer.
   (d) The counter was creating problem in the shop.

150. What were the colours of the letters on the board of the shop?
   (a) Blue-Indian cricket team
   (b) Dark black
   (c) Saffron, white and green
   (d) Blue and black

Section E : Aptitude For Service Sector

151. You are in an elevator with two other strangers and the electricity goes off in between. What would you do?

(a) Panic and scream in the elevator.

(b) Let the other people decide the course of action while you stand there and watch.

(c) Try to break open the elevator.

(d) Keep calm and try and ring the emergency alarm to seek help.

152. Annual day function is to be organised in your school, the responsibility of this has been assigned to you would

(a) try to get rid of this responsibility.

(b) try to organise it with the help of your batchmates.

(c) avoid all your responsibilities.

(d) delegate it to someone else.

153. What do you do when you reach late for your class?

(a) Quietly try to sneak into the class without being noticed by the teacher.

(b) Do not attend the class only.

(c) Admit your reason for being late in the class and whole heartedly accept the teacher's decision.

(d) Make up excuses to convince the teacher.

154. In an examination hall, you find that your question paper is too tough. The best thing you can do is

(a) try cheating from your neighbouring student.

(b) leave the paper and walk out.

(c) try attempting those questions first, of which you know the answers.

(d) write irrelevant matter to just fill in the pages.

155. While working in a group, you tend to

(a) adjust with other members, but as per your convenience.

(b) Be a bit hesitant.

(c) Not involved with the group activity.

(d) Extend full cooperation to the other group members.

156. You are transferred to a section in your school where you do not have any friends, you would

(a) sit in one corner of the class and not take interest in anything.

(b) cry, for you do not like your surroundings.

(c) try and make new friends in the new section.

(d) ignore, everything and just concentrate on your studies.

157. You find a lady entering your restaurant carrying a lot of bags in hand, you will

(a) rush to open the door and help her with her bags.

(b) not bother about the same.

(c) be agitated due to shortage of space in the restaurant.

(d) ask her to leave her bags outside

158. As a manager you notice there has been repeated customer complaints against a subordinate, you will

(a) reprimand him and give him a deadline to improve.

(b) fire him from the job.

(c) ask other colleagues to warn him about the same.

(d) try to find out the problem and give him a remedial training.

159. Only a hard working person can move ahead in life. What is your opinion?

(a) Hard working people are not always successful.

(b) Hard working people are never successful.

(c) A hard working person will definitely succeed, sooner or later.

(d) It all depends on your luck.

160. One of your roommate has the habit of speaking loudly over the phone which disturbs you while studying. Despite your repeated requests, his habit seems to be getting worse. You

(a) start speaking loudly when your roommate is studying to teach him a lesson.

(b) fight with your roommate.

(c) complain about your roommate to the hostel warden.

(d) have an open discussion with your roommate about your problem and try to solve it amicably.

161. In the class you are delivering a speech when a classmate of yours is continuously interrupting you with several queries, you would

(a) not pay attention to him.

(b) start speaking at a faster pace than before.

(c) stop the speech and let him speak.

(d) politely let him know that all his queries will be addressed at the end.

162. There has been a sudden death in the family recently and you are still grieving. However you have your annual examination round the corner and for that you have to catch up with a lot of studies. What would you do?

(a) You will get back to studying after you get over your grief.

(b) You will ignore your examination and continue grieving.

(c) You will motivate yourself to get back to studying as only grieving will not do any good to you.

(d) You will run away from everything.

163. If an argument starts with someone, then I invariably
  (a) listen to the viewpoint of that person carefully and then speak what is in my mind.
  (b) state my view at the very outset.
  (c) start saying whatever comes to my mind.
  (d) be confused and perplexed.

164. Your neighbour is continuously throwing garbage in your premise despite repeated warnings. You would
  (a) go to their house and engage into a fight with them.
  (b) inform the police about this incident.
  (c) take the garbage and throw it back in their premise.
  (d) ask them the reason for their action and sternly yet politely ask them to stop this nuisance.

165. Your close relative has gifted you a birthday present, which you did not like much. You will
  (a) openly express your dislike.
  (b) request him to exchange the item.
  (c) respect the feelings of the person and use the gift appropriately.
  (d) give a hint that the gift is not to your liking.

166. You observe that you are burdened with extra work in your workplace compared to your other colleagues. You would
  (a) continue doing the work in spite of increasing stress levels.
  (b) revolt outright.
  (c) politely reason out the situation with your supervisor.
  (d) gain sympathy of others.

167. You are never in limelight or focus inspite of your efficiency at work. You would
  (a) lower your performance level.
  (b) continue working and wait for the moment of recognition.
  (c) keep silent regarding your grievances.
  (d) openly publicise your efficiency and proclaim that your are the best.

168. A typical airline flight might have about 150 passengers served by 4 flight attendants. Upon getting this information
  (a) you start wondering about the work pressure.
  (b) vouch never to work as a flight attendant.
  (c) you ignore as you are not interested in aviation industry.
  (d) you wonder how challenging and thrilling the job of a flight attendant must be.

169. Your supervisor repeatedly criticises you in front of your subordinates. You feel insulted. You would
  (a) speak to other colleagues regarding this and consider leaving the job.
  (b) ignore the situation but feel very angry and hurt by his words.
  (c) hit back harshly and make him gulp his own words.
  (d) approach him directly and explain your feelings to him.

170. You have observed lately that one of your colleague at work place has taken you for granted and often tries to pass off his responsibilities to you. You would
  (a) tolerate for some more time and then counter fiercely.
  (b) shout at him in front of every one.
  (c) discuss the matter with him in one to one mode
  (d) stay normal and ignore, although you don't like it.

171. You accidently over hear a colleague talking negatively about you to your boss you would
  (a) storm-in straight away to deny the charges.
  (b) calmly step in and establish logic for your behaviour and actions.
  (c) start fighting with your colleague in front of the boss.
  (d) ignore and walk away.

172. You have been instructed to do a job by your supervisor. You have not understood a part of the instructions. You would
  (a) seek clarification again before you commence the job.
  (b) plunge into the job and clarify only when stuck.
  (c) confidently go ahead without bothering about the consequences of mistake.
  (d) keep your supervisor informed that some future clarification may be needed.

173. You as a class monitor have been asked to select a team for accomplishing a job. You would select students
  (a) only those who are close to you.
  (b) only those who would do something when asked.
  (c) only those who are ready to adapt to any situation they may come across.
  (d) those who are close to you, those who would do something when asked and those who are ready to adapt to any situation they may come across.

174. Your friends have invited you for a gathering. You accept that and on returning home you are informed that there is a family get together on the same day. You would
  (a) flatly refuse to attend the family gathering.
  (b) blame your friends for holding the gathering on the same day.
  (c) decide to attend none of the functions.
  (d) very politely refuse to go to one of the places.

175. Your neighbour's daughter is getting married and on the day of the wedding, a fire breaks out. You would
(a) panic and run away
(b) secure the children and the aged people first before you try to help others
(c) go to a safe distance and watch what is happening.
(d) come back home and relax.

176. You were going through your younger brother's maths exam copy which was checked and returned by the class teacher. You noticed a correct answer marked wrong. You would
(a) straight away place a written complaint to the principal of the school.
(b) blame you brother rudely saying that he should have taken it to the concerned teacher.
(c) go and speak to the concerned teacher yourself without creating a fuss.
(d) put up a quarrel with the concerned teacher.

177. How would you ensure that you become the focal point in a group discussion?
(a) By aggressive gestures and words
(b) Logical talking with appropriate humour.
(c) Snubbing others while they want to speak.
(d) Trying to stop aggressive outburst of others.

178. The welfare society of your locality is organising a Blood Donation Camp. You would
(a) express only verbal desire to support such an initiative.
(b) refrain from going to the venue
(c) get irritated as you do not have time for such activities.
(d) show full enthusiasm and ensure that you are present on the day of the event.

179. Which of the following is not a part of a well groomed individual?
(a) Streaked hair   (b) Well kept nails
(c) Ironed shirt   (d) Formal shoes

180. Two of your close friends are having a strained relationship. You would
(a) leave them to handle the situation on their own.
(b) allow time to naturally heal up the relationship.
(c) take initiative and try to find out the root cause of the strained relationship.
(d) sever your friendship with both of them.

181. If your batchmate confides his secrets, you would
(a) use the information shared to your advantage.
(b) tell them to few of your other friends.
(c) discuss them with your parents.
(d) discuss the secrets only with the batchmate, if required.

182. A new member joins the cricket team of which you are the captain. A day after his joining, he gives a suggestion to you. You would
(a) snap at him, saying that his suggestions are not required at such an early stage of joining.
(b) advice him to understand how the team works.
(c) think about the suggestions and judge their relevance.
(d) listen to it and forget about it.

183. You are attending a class and suddenly, your mobile phone rings loudly. You would
(a) try to hide so that it would be difficult to locate the source
(b) own up and apologise to the teacher
(c) quickly switch off the mobile phone
(d) give excuses for keeping your phone in the 'ring' mode.

184. You are seated in an aircraft at the window seat. A little boy comes and requests you for the window seat and tells you to take the middle seat. You would
(a) explain him politely that it is illegal.
(b) give up your seat on request.
(c) flatly refuse.
(d) offer a chocolate and deny the little boy the window seat.

185. As a team leader, you find one of your team members is not performing up to the mark. You would
(a) shout at him in front of everybody.
(b) arrange for a counselling session.
(c) give a poor appraisal to him straight away.
(d) ignore thinking that he would develop with time.

186. Your manager calls you in his cabin and points out some deficiencies in you performance. You would
(a) consider the manager as 'over analytical'.
(b) consider the manager as a person who wants you to improve.
(c) consider the manager as a 'dominating' person.
(d) listen and judge nothing.

187. Your team has failed to win a final match. As the captain of the team
(a) take all blame on yourself for the defeat.
(b) blame your team members for the defeat.
(c) try to find out reasons of defeat by discussing with the team members.
(d) resign from the captaincy.

188. You are carrying two heavy bags and waiting at a railway station. The train arrives. You struggle with your bags and manage to board the train. Just then, you see an old lady trying hard to lift her bag. You will

(a) advice her to call a porter.
(b) try to find your own seat thinking you can help her after wards.
(c) help her to lift her bag.
(d) tell a passer-by to help her.

189. You are in crowded railway station. Suddenly you spot a little girl all alone and looking confused. You would
(a) hand her over to the Railway Police for further help.
(b) ask her if she is lost and ask her to look for her parents or relatives.
(c) take no action
(d) take her to your house for further assistance.

190. You have visited your uncle's place. At the middle of the night your uncle suffers a 'heart attack'. You will
(a) ignore and go back to sleep.
(b) wake up immediately and call for an ambulance.
(c) google some medicines for him.
(d) wait till somebody instructs you for some action.

191. You have visited a place of tourist interest. You see a group of people littering on the road. You would
(a) politely tell them that there is a dustbin nearby.
(b) shout at them for such a behaviour.
(c) express your displeasure with a stern look.
(d) ignore and walk away.

192. A customer has booked a room in your hotel but at the time of arrival, room is not available. You will
(a) take him to your residence.
(b) regret and tell him that hotel is sold out.
(c) regret and arrange the room in another comparable category of hotels.
(d) provide him the list of other hotels in the city.

193. A technique that might be used by an active listener is to
(a) describe a situation.
(b) express anxiety.
(c) paraphrase the speakers words.
(d) offer a point of view when in conversation.

194. An old lady, slipped and fell in the lobby of the hotel while walking and she starts shouting. You would
(a) tell her its her fault
(b) look for a lady staff to help her
(c) help and make her comfortable
(d) nothing can be done as incident has already taken place.

195. A co-worker tells you in confidence that she plans to call in sick while she is actually taking a week's vacations, you will
(a) inform the authorities
(b) ignore the information
(c) advise her to be honest at the work place
(d) take all her responsibilities and encourage her to go for the vacation

196. While travelling in a train, you see a purse lying on the seat next to you, you will
(a) pocket the cash and throw the purse.
(b) ignore as it you did not notice.
(c) change your seat to avoid touching that purse.
(d) take the purse and hand over to Police or Railway officer on duty.

197. While working as a school teacher, you find a child is unable to understand the lesson always. You will
(a) take him to the Principal for strict action.
(b) discuss with the parents of the child and do the needful.
(c) ignore him in the class.
(d) ask him to take private tuitions from you.

198. What would you do if you realise at the last moment that the assignment you have done is not up to the mark?
(a) Presume that the teacher may not notice it.
(b) Ask the teacher for an extension and promise an up to the mark submission in future.
(c) Ignore what feacher says after checking.
(d) Give excuses for not doing the task up to the mark.

199. At your school, your friend asks your opinion about an issue, you will
(a) present your honest opinion as you are an expert of that particular subject.
(b) give wrong answer purposely.
(c) rely on other's opinion.
(d) avoid the questions stating that you are busy.

200. Your-boss doesn't pay attention to what you have just said, as he was busy at his computer, you will
(a) speak loudly to make yourself heard.
(b) wait for sometime to talk.
(c) leave his office and stop talking in future.
(d) tell everyone about this incident.

Answers

1. (b)	2. (d)	3. (d)	4. (c)	5. (a)	6. (b)	7. (d)	8. (d)	9. (a)	10. (c)
11. (b)	12. (c)	13. (b)	14. (d)	15. (d)	16. (c)	17. (d)	18. (b)	19. (c)	20. (c)
21. (c)	22. (b)	23. (d)	24. (a)	25. (d)	26. (b)	27. (c)	28. (c)	29. (c)	30. (c)
31. (d)	32. (b)	33. (b)	34. (c)	35. (c)	36. (d)	37. (c)	38. (d)	39. (d)	40. (b)
41. (a)	42. (c)	43. (c)	44. (d)	45. (a)	46. (d)	47. (d)	48. (d)	49. (b)	50. (b)
51. (b)	52. (b)	53. (d)	54. (c)	55. (d)	56. (a)	57. (b)	58. (a)	59. (b)	60. (c)
61. (c)	62. (c)	63. (b)	64. (b)	65. (a)	66. (a)	67. (d)	68. (a)	69. (b)	70. (c)
71. (c)	72. (b)	73. (d)	74. (c)	75. (c)	76. (c)	77. (b)	78. (d)	79. (c)	80. (d)
81. (c)	82. (b)	83. (a)	84. (a)	85. (c)	86. (d)	87. (b)	88. (d)	89. (d)	90. (d)
91. (d)	92. (b)	93. (d)	94. (d)	95. (b)	96. (d)	97. (a)	98. (c)	99. (a)	100. (a)
101. (b)	102. (d)	103. (d)	104. (c)	105. (c)	106. (b)	107. (d)	108. (c)	109. (a)	110. (c)
111. (c)	112. (b)	113. (d)	114. (c)	115. (d)	116. (c)	117. (b)	118. (c)	119. (d)	120. (a)
121. (a)	122. (b)	123. (d)	124. (d)	125.. (d)	126. (c)	127. (b)	128. (c)	129. (b)	130. (d)
131. (b)	132. (b)	133. (c)	134. (b)	135. (a)	136. (c)	137. (c)	138. (a)	139. (a)	140. (a)
141. (c)	142. (b)	143. (c)	144. (c)	145. (a)	146. (c)	147. (a)	148. (c)	149. (c)	150. (c)
151. (d)	152. (b)	153. (a)	154. (c)	155. (d)	156. (c)	157. (a)	158. (d)	159. (c)	160. (d)
161. (d)	162. (c)	163. (a)	164. (d)	165. (c)	166. (c)	167. (b)	168. (d)	169. (d)	170. (c)
171. (b)	172. (a)	173. (c)	174. (d)	175. (b)	176. (c)	177. (b)	178. (d)	179. (a)	180. (c)
181. (d)	182. (c)	183. (b)	184. (b)	185. (b)	186. (b)	187. (c)	188. (c)	189. (a)	190. (b)
191. (b)	192. (c)	193. (c)	194. (c)	195. (c)	196. (d)	197. (b)	198. (b)	199. (a)	200. (b)

Hints & Solutions

1. (*b*) We know that, a number is completely divisible by 3, when sum of its digit is completely divisible by 3.

Checking options,

(a) 5967013

$$5 + 9 + 6 + 7 + 0 + 1 + 3 = 31$$

It is not divisible by 3.

(b) 541326

$$5 + 4 + 1 + 3 + 2 + 6 = 21$$

∴ It is divisible by 3.

(c) 585412

$$5 + 8 + 5 + 4 + 1 + 2 = 25$$

It is not divisible by 3.

(d) 534230

$$5 + 3 + 4 + 2 + 3 + 0 = 17$$

It is not divisible by 3.

So, 541326 is completely divisible by 3.

Hence, option (b) is correct.

2. (*d*) Let the four consecutive even numbers are

$A = x$, $B = x + 2$, $C = x + 4$ and $D = x + 6$.

According to the question,

$$x + x + 2 + x + 4 + x + 6 = 180$$

$\Rightarrow \quad 4x + 12 = 180$

$\Rightarrow \quad 4x = 180 - 12$

$\Rightarrow \quad x = \dfrac{168}{4}$

$$= 42$$

Then, the next four consecutive even numbers are

$$x + 8, x + 10, x + 12, x + 14$$

$\Rightarrow \quad 42 + 8, 42 + 10, 42 + 12, 42 + 14$

$\Rightarrow \quad 50, 52, 54, 56$

∴ The sum of next four consecutive even numbers

$$= 50 + 52 + 54 + 56 = 212$$

3. (*d*) ∵ One day work of Sunil $= \dfrac{1}{2}$

One day work of Saurav $= \dfrac{1}{3}$

∴ (Sunil + Saurav)'s one day work $= \left(\dfrac{1}{2} + \dfrac{1}{3} \right) = \dfrac{5}{6}$

Rest of work $= 1 - \dfrac{5}{6} = \dfrac{1}{6}$

∴ Sachin's 1 day's work $= \dfrac{1}{6}$

$\therefore$ Ratio of Sunil, Saurav and Sachin's 1 day's work
$$= \frac{1}{2} : \frac{1}{3} : \frac{1}{6}$$
$$= 3 : 2 : 1$$
$\because$ $\qquad$ Total wages = ₹ 1800

$\therefore$ The wage of Sachin $= 1800 \times \dfrac{1}{3 + 2 + 1}$
$$= 1800 \times \frac{1}{6}$$
$$= ₹ 300$$

4. (*c*) Let the principal be ₹ P.
According to the question,
Simple interest = ₹ P
and Time = R yr

We know that, $\text{SI} = \dfrac{P \times R \times T}{100}$

$\Rightarrow \qquad R = \dfrac{\text{SI} \times 100}{P \times T}$

$\Rightarrow \qquad R = \dfrac{P \times 100}{P \times R}$

$\Rightarrow \qquad R^2 = 100$

$\therefore \qquad R = \sqrt{100}$
$$= 10\%$$

5. (*a*) Given,
$P = ₹ 25800$
$R = 14\%$ per annum
$T = 1$ yr 4 months
$$= 1 + \frac{4}{12}$$
$$= 1 + \frac{1}{3}$$
$$= \frac{4}{3} \text{ yr}$$
We know, that
$$\text{SI} = \frac{P \times R \times T}{100}$$
$$= \frac{25800 \times 14 \times \dfrac{4}{3}}{100}$$
$$= 258 \times 14 \times \frac{4}{3}$$
$$= ₹ 4816$$

6. (*b*) Let the rate of interest be $R\%$ per annum.
According to the question,
$$\frac{800 \times R \times 4}{100} + \frac{800 \times R \times 2}{100} = 192$$
$\Rightarrow \qquad 32R + 16R = 192$
$\Rightarrow \qquad 48R = 192$
$\therefore \qquad R = \dfrac{192}{48}$
$$= 4\%$$

7. (*d*) Let the age of son = x year
Then, age of father = $9x$ yr
and age of mother = $8x$ yr
According to the question,
$$9x + 8x = 51$$
$\Rightarrow \qquad 17x = 51$
$\Rightarrow \qquad x = \dfrac{51}{17} = 3$
$\therefore$ Age of son = 3 yr

8. (*d*) Let the present ages of Simran and Smriti be $3x$ yr and $7x$ yr, respectively.
Then, after 4 yr, age of Smriti $= (7x + 4)$ yr
According to the question,
$$7x + 4 = 39$$
$\Rightarrow \qquad 7x = 39 - 4$
$\Rightarrow \qquad 7x = 35$
$\Rightarrow \qquad x = 5$
So, present age of Simran $= 3 \times 5$
$$= 15 \text{ yr}$$
$\therefore$ Simran's age 4 yr ago = 15 − 4
$$= 11 \text{ yr}$$

9. (*a*) Let the present ages of two persons be x yr and y yr,
such that $x > y$
According to the question,
$$x - y = 10$$
$\Rightarrow \qquad x = 10 + y \qquad \qquad \text{...(i)}$
and $\qquad (x - 15) = 2(y - 15)$
$\Rightarrow \quad y + 10 - 15 = 2y - 30 \qquad$ [by Eq. (i)]
$\Rightarrow \quad 30 - 15 + 10 = 2y - y$
$\therefore \qquad y = 25 \text{ yr}$
On putting the value of y in Eq. (i), we get
$$x = 35 \text{ yr.}$$
$\therefore$ Present age of the elder person = 35 yr.

10. (*c*) Let the seven consecutive numbers are
$x, x + 1, x + 2, x + 3, x + 4, x + 5$ and $x + 6$.

We know that, average $= \dfrac{\text{Sum of numbers}}{\text{Total numbers}}$

$$\frac{x + x + 1 + x + 2 + x + 3 + x + 4 + x + 5 + x + 6}{7} = 20$$

$\Rightarrow \qquad 7x + 21 = 7 \times 20$
$\Rightarrow \qquad 7x = 140 - 21 = 119$
$\Rightarrow \qquad x = \dfrac{119}{7} = 17$

$\therefore$ Largest number $= x + 6$
$$= 17 + 6 = 23$$

11. (*b*) Given, profit% = 20%

According to question,
Cost price of 1 dozen oranges $= 6 \times 3 + 6 \times 2 = ₹ 30$

We know that, profit $\% = \left(\dfrac{\text{SP} - \text{CP}}{\text{CP}} \right) \times 100$

$$\Rightarrow \qquad 20 = \left(\frac{SP - 30}{30}\right) \times 100$$

$$\Rightarrow \qquad SP - 30 = \frac{20 \times 30}{100}$$

$$\Rightarrow \qquad SP - 30 = 6$$

$$\therefore \qquad SP = 30 + 6 = ₹\ 36$$

12. (*c*) Let the cost price (CP) = ₹ x

Then, marked price (MP) $= x \times \left(\dfrac{100 + 20}{100}\right)$

$$= \frac{120x}{100}$$

$$= ₹\ \frac{6x}{5}$$

Given, discount (r) = 15%

We know that, $SP = \left(\dfrac{100 - r}{100}\right) \times MP$

$$= \frac{100 - 15}{100} \times \frac{6x}{5}$$

$$= \frac{85}{100} \times \frac{6x}{5}$$

$$= \frac{₹\ 51x}{50}$$

$$\therefore \quad \text{Gain \%} = \frac{SP - CP}{CP} \times 100$$

$$= \frac{\dfrac{51x}{50} - x}{x} \times 100$$

$$= \frac{51x - 50x}{50x} \times 100$$

$$= \frac{x}{50x} \times 100$$

$$= 2\%$$

13. (*b*) Given, average run scored in 15 innings = 48

Then, total runs scored in 15 innings $= 15 \times 48$
$$= 720$$

After 16th inning, the average runs = 50

Then, total runs scored in 16 innings $= 16 \times 50$
$$= 800$$

$\therefore$ Score of batsman in 16th inning
$$= 800 - 720 = 80$$

14. (*d*) Let the number of sweets distributed be x.

According to question,

$$\frac{x}{250} - \frac{x}{300} = 1$$

$$\Rightarrow \qquad \frac{6x - 5x}{1500} = 1$$

$$\Rightarrow \qquad \frac{x}{1500} = 1$$

$$\therefore \qquad x = 1500$$

15. (*d*) Given, average marks of student in 7 subjects = 75

Then, total marks of student in 7 subjects
$$= 75 \times 7 = 525$$

and total marks of student in 6 subjects
excluding Science $= 6 \times 72 = 432$

$\therefore$ Score in Science $= 525 - 432 = 93$

16. (*c*) Here, $a = 30\%$

According to the formula,

$$\text{Reduction in consumption} = \left(\frac{a}{100 + a}\right) \times 100\%$$

$$= \frac{30}{100 + 30} \times 100\%$$

$$= \frac{30}{130} \times 100\% = \frac{300}{13}\ \%$$

$$= 23\frac{1}{13}\ \%$$

17. (*d*) Let the total number of votes polled be x.

According to the question,

$$x \times \frac{55}{100} - x \times \frac{(100 - 55)}{100} = 432$$

$$\Rightarrow \qquad \frac{55x}{100} - \frac{45x}{100} = 432$$

$$\Rightarrow \qquad \frac{10x}{100} = 432$$

$$\therefore \qquad x = 4320$$

18. (*b*) Let the number of boys and girls be x and y, respectively.

According to the question,

$$\frac{10}{100} \times x = \frac{y}{4}$$

$$\therefore \qquad \frac{x}{y} = \frac{100}{4 \times 10} = \frac{5}{2} = 5 : 2$$

19. (*c*) Let the price of the chair, table and stool be ₹ x, ₹ y and ₹ z, respectively.

According to the question,

$$x = \frac{60}{100} \times y$$

$$\Rightarrow \qquad y = ₹\ \frac{10x}{6} \qquad \qquad \text{...(i)}$$

and $$z = \frac{15}{100} \times y$$

$$\Rightarrow \qquad z = \frac{15}{100} \times \frac{10x}{6} \qquad \text{[by Eq. (i)]}$$

$$\Rightarrow \qquad z = \frac{x}{4}$$

$$\therefore \text{Required per cent} = \frac{\dfrac{x}{4}}{x} \times 100 = \frac{x}{4x} \times 100 = 25\%$$

$\therefore$ Stool cost is 25% of chair cost.

20. (*c*) Let the angles of the triangle are $x°$, $2x°$ and $3x°$.

Then, $x° + 2x° + 3x° = 180°$

[by the angle sum property]

$\Rightarrow \quad 6x° = 180°$

$\Rightarrow \quad x° = \dfrac{180°}{6} = 30°$

$\therefore$ Largest angle $= 3x° = 3 \times 30° = 90°$

21. (*c*) According to the question,

$\qquad$ 1 star = 4 circles $\qquad\qquad$ ...(i)

and $\qquad$ 3 circles = 4 diamonds

$\Rightarrow \qquad$ 1 circle $= \dfrac{4}{3}$ diamonds

On putting this value in Eq. (i), we get

$\qquad$ 1 star $= 4 \times \dfrac{4}{3}$ diamond

$\Rightarrow \qquad \dfrac{\text{star}}{\text{diamond}} = \dfrac{16}{3}$

$\therefore$ star : diamond $= 16 : 3$

22. (*b*) Let the two numbers be $5x$ and $6x$.

Given, LCM of the two numbers = 480

and LCM of $5x$ and $6x = 30x$

According to the question,

$\Rightarrow \qquad 30x = 480$

$\Rightarrow \qquad x = \dfrac{480}{30} = 16$

$\therefore$ The numbers are $5 \times 16 = 80$ and $6 \times 16 = 96$

$\because \qquad 80 = 2 \times 2 \times 2 \times 2 \times 5$

and $\qquad 96 = 2 \times 2 \times 2 \times 2 \times 2 \times 3$

$\therefore$ HCF of 80 and 96 $= 2 \times 2 \times 2 \times 2 = 16$

23. (*d*) As, $\quad 2923 = 79 \times 37$

and $\qquad 3239 = 79 \times 41$

$\therefore$ HCF of 2923 and 3239 = 79

24. (*a*) Here, LCM = 25 and product of two numbers

$\qquad\qquad\qquad\qquad\qquad\qquad = 4025$

We know that,

HCF $\times$ LCM = product of two numbers

$\therefore$ HCF $= \dfrac{\text{Product of two numbers}}{\text{LCM}}$

$\qquad = \dfrac{4025}{25} = 161$

25. (*d*) Percentage of unutilised capacity

$\qquad = \dfrac{\text{Production capacity} - \text{Production}}{\text{Production capacity}} \times 100$

$\therefore$ Percentage of unutilised capacity of company

ONIDA $= \dfrac{200 - 180}{200} \times 100 = 10\%$

ZENITH $= \dfrac{250 - 180}{250} \times 100 = 28\%$

EXCEL $= \dfrac{300 - 280}{300} \times 100 = \dfrac{20}{3}\% = 6\dfrac{2}{3}\%$

VIDEOCON $= \dfrac{320 - 260}{320} \times 100$

$\qquad\qquad = \dfrac{75}{4}\%$

$\qquad\qquad = 18\dfrac{3}{4}\%$

BPL $= \dfrac{150 - 100}{150} \times 100$

$\qquad = \dfrac{50}{150} \times 100$

$\qquad = \dfrac{100}{3}$

$\qquad = 33\dfrac{1}{3}\%$

Hence, BPL had the maximum percentage of unutilised capacity.

26. (*b*) According to the previous solution,

EXCEL had the minimum percentage $6\dfrac{2}{3}\%$ of unutilised capacity.

27. (*c*) Total TV production

$\qquad = 180 + 180 + 280 + 260 + 100$

$\qquad = 1000$

and TV production by Excel = 280

$\therefore$ Required percentage $= \dfrac{280}{1000} \times 100$

$\qquad\qquad = 28\%$

28. (*c*) $\dfrac{\sqrt{81}}{11} \times \dfrac{\sqrt{121}}{9} = \dfrac{9}{11} \times \dfrac{11}{9} = 1$

29. (*c*) Total number of rows $= \sqrt{17956}$

$\qquad\qquad = \sqrt{2 \times 2 \times 67 \times 67}$

$\qquad\qquad = \sqrt{(2)^2 \times (67)^2}$

$\qquad\qquad = 2 \times 67 = 134$

30. (*c*) First, we have to find out the square root of 36562

	191
1	$3\,6\,\overline{5}\,\overline{2}\,\overline{6}$
	1
29	26562
	261
381	462
	381
	81

Here, the remainder is 81.

$\therefore$ The number of army men remained unused = 81

31. (*d*) The pattern is as follows,

C D $\qquad$ F G H $\qquad$ J K L M $\qquad$ O P Q R S $\qquad$ U V W X Y Z

$\quad$ +2 $\qquad\quad$ +2 $\qquad\qquad$ +2 $\qquad\qquad$ +2

H + 2 = J and M + 2 = O

Hence, the missing term will be 'JKLM'.

32. (*b*) The pattern is as follows

1YO, 6VQ, 13SS, 22 PU, 33MW

For the number sequence pattern is

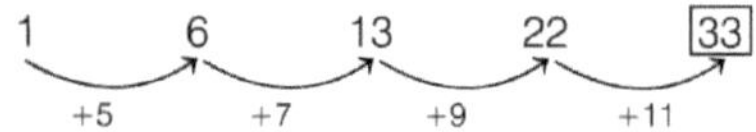

For the alphabetic sequence pattern is

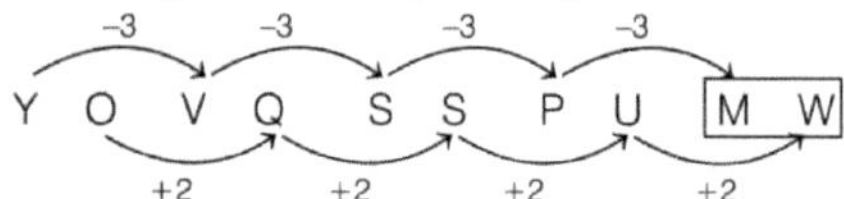

Hence, the missing term will be '33 MW'.

33. (*b*) The pattern is as follows

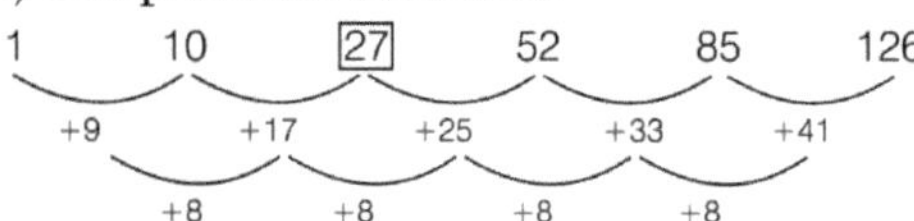

The difference between the numbers in this series is increased by '8'. So, $10 + 17 = 27$.

Hence, the missing term will be '27'.

34. (*c*) As 'VOLVO' is the company of the 'CARS', in the same way 'IKEA' is the company of the 'FURNITURE'.

35. (*c*) As 'AIRINDIA' is the flag carrier government body of AIRLINE of India. In the same way 'SBI' is the government 'BANK' of India.

36. (*d*) Except Rocket : Sky, all are related to each other in same way.

37. (*c*) All except Alligator have protective shells.

38. (*d*) Except 'Moon' all are planets while moon is a natural satellite.

39. (*d*) The pattern is as follows

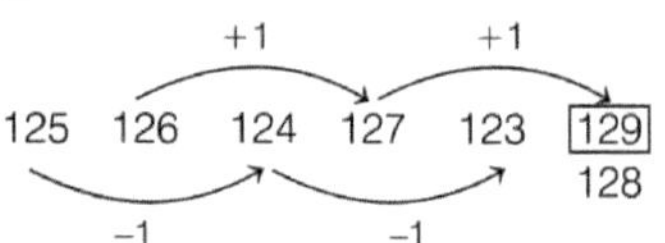

Hence, the wrong number will be 129.

40. (*b*) The 'L' shaped element at the top left corner is rotating 90° in anti-clockwise direction with each step and one such element is added with 90° rotation in clockwise direction. So, the missing figure will be option (b).

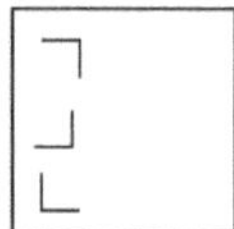

41. (*a*) The number of lines increased by + 1 in each step vertically and horizontally in alternative way. So, the missing figure will be option (a) .

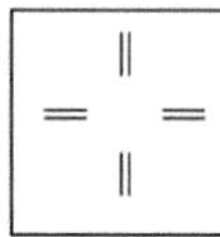

42. (*c*) Arrows given in the figures are rotating in clockwise direction in each step.

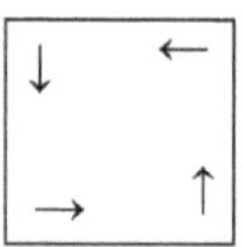

Sol. (Q. Nos. 43-45)

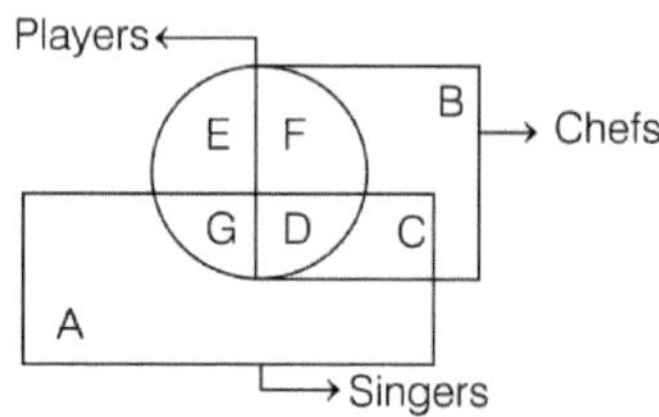

43. (*c*) 'C' represents Chefs who are only Singers.

44. (*d*) 'D' represents Chefs who are Singers and Players both.

45. (*a*) 'F' represents Chefs who are only Players.

Sol. (Q. Nos. 46 and 47)

46. (*d*)

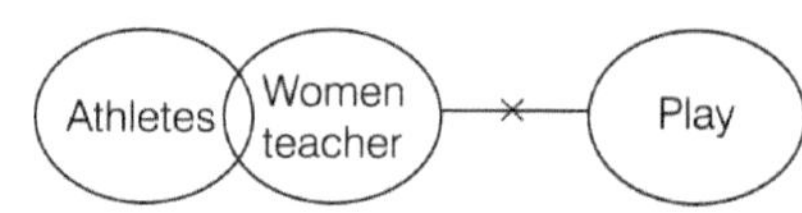

Conclusions

      I. Male athletes can play.   (False)

      II. Some athletes can play.   (False)

Hence, neither Conclusions I nor II follows.

47. (*d*)

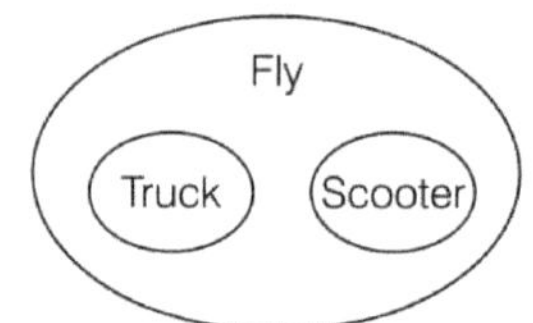

Conclusions

      I. All truck are scooter.   (False)

      II. Some scooters do not fly.   (False)

Hence, neither conclusion I nor II follows.

48. (*d*) Blood group 'AB' is a universal recipient and group 'O' is a universal donar due to absence of both A and B antigen in the group 'O'. So, the correct answer is (d). (A) is false but (R) is true.

49. (*b*) Both (A) and (R) are true and R is not the correct explanation of (A).

50. (*b*) Both (A) and (R) are true, but (R) is not the correct explanation of (A).

51. (*b*) As,

Similarly,

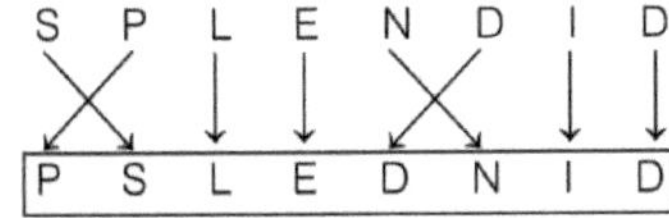

52. (*b*) According to the question,

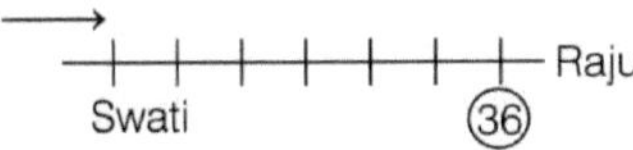

Raju's rank from the last = 60 − 36 + 1
$$= 24 + 1 = 25$$
(As total number of student = 60)
∴ Swati's rank from the last = 25 + 7 = 32

53. (*d*) If all the vowels are removed from the alphabetic sequence, we get,
B, C, D, F, G, H, J, K, L, M, N, P, Q, R, S, T, V, W, X, Y, Z.
Letter which is fourth to the left of the sixteenth letter from the right will be twentieth letter from the right i.e. 'C'.
Letter (4th left + 16th right = 20th letter right) = C

54. (*c*)

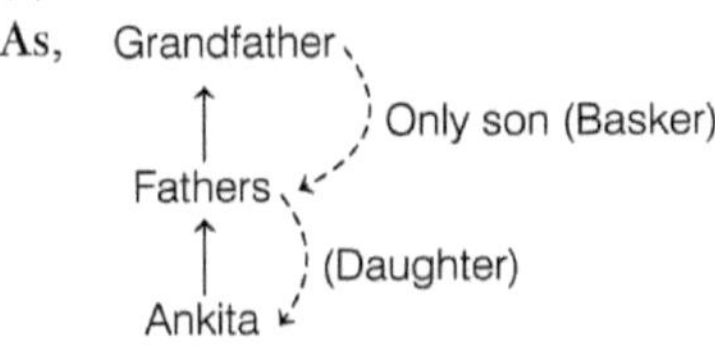

Hence, Ankita is the daughter of Basker.

55. (*d*)

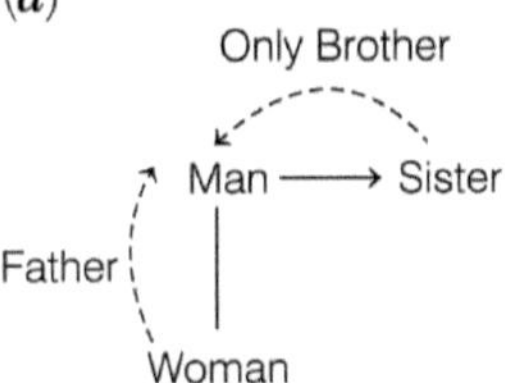

Here, woman is the daughter of the man.

56. (*a*)

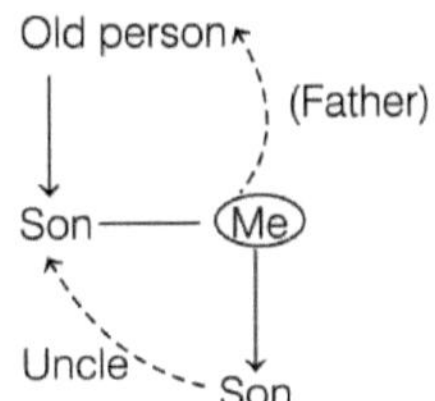

Hence, the old person is father of me.

Sol. (Q. Nos. 57-60) *According to the given information*

Member of the family	Profession	Gender	Relation
A	Engineer	Male	Brother of D and G
B	Lawyer	Male	Married to F
C	Doctor	Female	Unmarried
D	Teacher	Female	Sister of A and G
E	Musician	Male	Married to D
F	General Manager	Female	Married to B
G	Architect	Male	Brother of A and D
—	—	—	—

57. (*b*) 'ED' is the married couple.

58. (*a*) A is an Engineer.

59. (*b*) E is a musician.

60. (*c*) B and E are the husbands of F and D respectively.

91. (*d*) Part (d) contains the error. The given sentence is in present tense; hence, the verb should also be in present tense. Replace 'lost' with 'lose' to make the sentence grammatically correct.

92. (*b*) Part (b) contains the error. The subject of the sentence i.e., Monika and Leena is in plural form; hence, the verb should also be in plural form. Replace 'is going' with 'are going' to make the sentence grammatically correct.

93. (*d*) Part (d) contains the error. A singular subject takes a singular verb. Hence, replace 'were' with 'was' to make the sentence grammatically correct.

94. (*d*) Part (d) contains the error. The word 'yours' is incorrectly used as an adjective in the sentence. 'Yours' is a possessive pronoun and 'your' is a possessive adjective. Hence, replace 'yours' with 'your' to make the sentence error free.

95. (*b*) Part (b) contains the error. 'Pants' is a plural noun; hence, the verb should also be in plural form. Replace 'was' with 'were' to make the sentence grammatically correct.

96. (*d*) 'Hard working' is nearest in meaning to 'diligent'. Both words mean 'working in a careful and thorough manner'.

97. (*a*) 'Validate' is nearest in meaning to 'authenticate'. Both words mean 'to prove or show something to be genuine or valid'.

98. (*c*) 'Audacity' is nearest in meaning to 'nerve'. Both words mean 'courage or confidence that other people find rude or shocking'.

99. (*a*) 'Majestic' is nearest in meaning to 'classy'. Both words mean 'stylish, fashionable and causing great admiration and respect'.

100. (*a*) 'Treasure' is nearest in meaning to 'cherish'. Both words mean 'to hold something very dear'.

101. (*b*) 'Dejected' is the opposite of 'elated'. 'Elated' means ecstatically happy and 'dejected' means sad and depressed.

102. (*d*) 'Simple' is the opposite of 'complicated'. 'Complicated' means involving many different and confusing aspects and 'simple' means plain, basic and presenting no difficulty.

103. (*d*) 'Dependent' is the opposite of 'autonomous'. 'Autonomous' means having the freedom to act independently and 'dependent' means requiring someone or something for support.

104. (*c*) 'Decoration' is the opposite of 'blemish'. 'Blemish' means a flaw that spoils the appearance of something and 'decoration' means the art of decorating or making something appear beautiful.

105. (*c*) 'Distasteful' is the opposite of 'delicious'. 'Delicious' means very pleasant to taste and 'distasteful' means disagreeable or unpleasant tasting.

111. (*c*) 'Back up' means to provide support. Hence, option (c) 'support' is nearest in meaning to 'back up'.

112. (*b*) 'Fair and square' means honestly and straightforwardly. Hence, option (b) 'honest' is nearest in meaning to 'fair and square'.

113. (*d*) 'Turn a deaf ear' means to refuse to listen or respond to a statement or request. Hence, option (d) 'did not pay attention to' is nearest in meaning to 'turn a deaf ear'.

114. (*c*) 'From pillar to post' means to move from one place to another needlessly. Hence, option (c) 'made to run around' is nearest in meaning to 'from pillar to post'.

115. (*d*) 'High and dry' means left alone in a difficult situation. Hence, option (d) 'isolated' is nearest in meaning to 'high and dry'.

139. (*a*) 'Encourage' is closest in meaning to 'foster'. Both words mean 'promoting the development of something desirable'.

140. (*a*) 'Begin' is closest in meaning to 'commencement'. Both words mean 'the start of something.'

Solved Paper 2019

Instructions

- There are Five (A-E) Sections in this Solved Paper.
- For every correct attempt, the student will be awarded **1 mark**.
- All the questions are in MCQs form and each having four options.

Marks : 200

Time : 3 hrs

Section A : English Language

Directions (Q. Nos. 1-5) *Each of these questions consists of a sentence which is divided into four parts labelled (a) to (d). Identify the part which contains an error.*

1. (a) We should always
   (b) Side with those who
   (c) are true and unselfish
   (d) and work for other

2. (a) Not only the doctor   (b) but also the nurses
   (c) is very kind   (d) to the patients

3. (a) A great many student has
   (b) been declared
   (c) Successful
   (d) In the class

4. (a) Just when Alfred Nobel's discoveries
   (b) Which were to make him one of the richest man
      of his day
   (c) Were beginning to bring him rewards
   (d) An Anti-Nobel campaign was started in France

5. (a) Anxious to hear of his illness,
   (b) I went to visit him
   (c) But was relieved to see that
   (d) He was more better

Directions (Q. Nos. 6-10) *In each of the following questions, out of the given alternatives, choose the one which is nearest in meaning to the underlined word in the given sentence.*

6. The flat has been <u>refurbished</u> recently.
   (a) Constructed   (b) Renovated
   (c) Damaged   (d) Plastered

7. During medical emergencies, when a delay of even one minute can cause the death of a patient, the doctor has to be <u>decisive</u>.
   (a) Deliberate (b) Cruel   (c) Clever   (d) Firm

8. Graduation day is a <u>momentous</u> day for most students.
   (a) Sad   (b) Important
   (c) Lactic   (d) Disastrous

9. The food served in that restaurant is <u>not fresh</u>.
   (a) Rotten   (b) Old
   (c) Decayed   (d) Stale

10. For a lot of boys in India, becoming a successful cricket star has become an <u>obsession</u>. Earlier, it was a hobby and sometimes, passion.
   (a) Preoccupation   (b) Suspicion
   (c) Frustration   (d) Failure

Directions (Q. Nos. 11-15) *In each of the following questions, out of the given alternatives, choose the one which is most nearly opposite in meaning to the underlined word.*

11. The <u>ferocious</u> ruler ruled autocratically, when in power.
(a) gentle
(b) barbarous
(c) fierce
(d) dangerous

12. A <u>stubborn</u> professional finds it difficult to survive for longer period of time in his/her job.
(a) flexible
(b) adamant
(c) obdurate
(d) determined

13. <u>Clarity</u> in speech is helpful for employees of hotel industry because guests can then understand them easily.
(a) boasting
(b) candour
(c) reserve
(d) confusion

14. A class in schools of the metropolitan cities, like Delhi and Mumbai, has <u>heterogeneous</u> type of students.
(a) colourful
(b) standard
(c) homogeneous
(d) different

15. He was asked to <u>accelerate</u> the pace of work.
(a) Rapid
(b) Control
(c) Slacken
(d) Supervise

Directions (Q. Nos. 16-20) *In each of the following questions, choose the option which can substitute the given words/sentence.*

16. A person who does not express himself freely.
(a) Insolvent
(b) Invincible
(c) Introvert
(d) Impostor

17. One who specialises in the study of birds.
(a) Naturalist
(b) Zoologist
(c) Ornithologist
(d) Biologist

18. A person who always looks at the dark or negative side of life.
(a) Pessimist
(b) Philatelist
(c) Pedestrian
(d) Philistine

19. A person who regards the whole world as his country.
(a) Contemporaries
(b) Cosmopolitan
(c) Cynosure
(d) Cynic

20. A professional rider in horse races.
(a) Coach
(b) Jockey
(c) Horse cruiser
(d) Rider

Directions (Q. Nos. 21-25) *Out of four alternatives given for idioms/phrases underlined in the following sentences, choose the one which best expresses the meaning of given idiom/phrase.*

21. All the residents of the colony <u>painted the town red</u> on the eve of festival.
(a) To whitewash buildings
(b) To celebrate noisily in public places
(c) To create nuisance
(d) To renovate buildings

22. The teacher <u>turned a blind eye</u> to the mischievous activities of all notorious students in his/her class.
(a) punished severely
(b) pretended not to notice
(c) acknowledged
(d) appreciated and loved

23. The Chairman <u>pulled a long face</u> when the house did not accept the suggestion put forth by him.
(a) to get annoyed
(b) to be agitated
(c) to make a quarrel
(d) to look disappointed

24. He is very rich, so helping him with money is like <u>carrying coals to Newcastle</u>.
(a) to send something where it is plentiful
(b) it will be helpful
(c) not asked for
(d) a donation

25. Rohan is so spontaneous that he always replies at <u>the spur of the moment</u>.
(a) without thinking
(b) after few moments
(c) without delay
(d) after finding logical reason

Directions (Q. Nos. 26-30) *In the following questions, four words are given, one word is spelt correctly, while three words are wrongly spelt. Choose the correctly spelt word.*

26. (a) Accommodation
(b) Accomodotion
(c) Acommodation
(d) Acomodation

27. (a) Commetee
(b) Comittee
(c) Committee
(d) Commitee

28. (a) Beurocracy
(b) Beurocrasy
(c) Buerocrasy
(d) Bureaucracy

29. (a) Ocurencee
(b) Ocurrence
(c) Occurence
(d) Occurrence

30. (a) Sattellite
(b) Satelite
(c) Sattelite
(d) Satellite

Directions (Q. Nos. 31-35) *In each of the following questions, four words are given, three of which are spelt correctly while one is misspelt. Choose the misspelt word.*

31. (a) Defence   (b) Defeciency
     (c) Deficient   (d) Defensive

32. (a) Mystique   (b) Mutten
     (c) Myth   (d) Mysterious

33. (a) Ankel   (b) Anxiety
     (c) Accommodation   (d) Allergy

34. (a) Messenger   (b) Misterious
     (c) Miniature   (d) Millennium

35. (a) Encyclopedia   (b) Endenger
     (c) Endeavour   (d) Endurance

Directions (Q. Nos. 36-45) *Fill in the blank with the appropriate option given below.*

36. She was beaten ……… a bat.
     (a) on   (b) with
     (c) to   (d) of

37. The little girl was scared ……… crossing the busy road alone.
     (a) on   (b) in   (c) at   (d) of

38. The little boy stood ……… the tree.
     (a) within   (b) under   (c) from   (d) off

39. Democracy in any country demands discipline and ……… to the rules.
     (a) follow   (b) adherence
     (c) agreement   (d) obligation

40. Columbus ……… America.
     (a) invented   (b) discovered
     (c) created   (d) found

41. Fifty rupees ……… a large amount fifty years ago.
     (a) were   (b) was
     (c) have   (d) are

42. A second theory about homosapiens agrees that our ……… language evolved as a means of sharing information about the world.
     (a) fancy   (b) unique
     (c) expert   (d) melodious

43. The glass ……… into small pieces.
     (a) disintegrated   (b) dissolved
     (c) crumbled   (d) shattered

44. He was in a hurry and just glanced ……… the letter.
     (a) through   (b) over   (c) by   (d) at

45. Can you finish the task …… tomorrow?
     (a) in   (b) by   (c) with   (d) on

Directions (Q. Nos. 46-50) *Read the following passage carefully to answer the questions that follow.*

Dusk had fallen by the time we all came out of the movie theatre. We ate a few samosas and drank a cup of tea each from a nearby restaurant, after which my friends dropped me off at the bus stop. I was the only one who had to catch a bus to get back home. They left when I was able to find the bus that I was supposed to board.

It had been a great day for me, my first outing with my friends in Sambalpur! I was happy and excited. However, unlike other days, on that evening, I was boarding a late bus. Usually, by that time, I would be at home. That evening I expected to reach home only by dinner time.

There were only a handful of people inside the bus. Most of the seats were empty. As the first few rows were not so good for long-distance travel, I found myself a seat at the rear of the bus. It was on the right side of the aisle, next to the window. I slid open the window pane to let the fresh air in, and started to look outside.

The street lights were on and so were the lights in the small shops. Inside the bus, it was close to dark. There were lights installed on the roof of the bus, but since the insides of the lamp shades were full of dirt and dead insects, most of the light was getting blocked, creating a faint glimmer.

46. Where was the author dropped by his friends after the movie and snacks?
     (a) Sambalpur   (b) Close to movie theatre
     (c) Near to his house   (d) At the bus stop

47. What did the author and his friends have after the movie show?
     (a) Samosas and tea   (b) Popcorn and cold drinks
     (c) Samosa and coffee   (d) Popcorn

48. By what time did the author expect to reach home?
     (a) By evening   (b) By dinner time
     (c) Late night   (d) Before Dusk

49. "Dusk has fallen by the time" what is the meaning of 'Dusk'?
     (a) Night
     (b) Darker stage of twilight
     (c) Dinty surface
     (d) Dust

50. What do you understand by the word 'aisle'?
     (a) Seat behind the driver
     (b) Next to window
     (c) Area between rows of seats
     (d) Rear row

Directions (Q. Nos. 51-55) *Read the following passage carefully to answer the questions that follow.*

Everybody wants success, but not all achieve it. One of the reasons is that there are people who do not exert themselves, but depend on others. But self-interest is the best incentive to work. If this interest does not prompt us to do our own work for our own good, we cannot expect others to sacrifice their interests to bring that good to us. Moreover, a work done for others is not generally done so well as a work done by a person for himself. Besides, dependence on others destroys self-confidence and does not allow the faculties to develop. The result is that we fail in life. Indeed, no God or Goddess will come to our help if we do not help ourselves.

51. What do you consider to be the central idea of this passage?
(a) Self-help is best
(b) Be kind
(c) Be religious
(d) Be carefree

52. What is one of the reasons, according to the passage, that people do not achieve success?
(a) Not taking help from others
(b) Not praying regularly
(c) Not making self-motivated efforts
(d) Being over-confident

53. What is the best incentive to work?
(a) Government Schemes
(b) Self-interest
(c) Sacrifice of others
(d) Inherited property

54. Why can we not expect others to sacrifice their interests to bring good things for us?
(a) Government is responsible
(b) People are stupid
(c) People have their own interests
(d) God is responsible

55. Select the word nearest in meaning to the word 'exert' as used in the passage.
(a) work hard
(b) help others
(c) want
(d) demand

Directions (Q. Nos. 56-60) *Read the following passage carefully to answer the questions that follow.*

Organised retail has fuelled new growth categories like liquid hand wash, breakfast cereals and pet food in the consumer goods industry, accounting for almost 50% of their sales, said data from market research firm Nielsen. The figures showed some of these new categories got more than 40% of their business from modern retail outlets. The data also suggests how products in these categories reach the neighbourhood Kirana stores after they have established themselves in modern trade.

While grocers continue to be an important channel, for the new and evolving categories we saw an increased presence of high-end products in modern trade. for e.g. premium products in laundry detergents, dishwashing, car air freshner and surface care.

56. 'Organised retail' refers to
(a) Petrol pumps
(b) Multiplex
(c) Grocery store
(d) Shopping malls

57. An example of a premium product, that is not found in the passage is
(a) Dishwashing
(b) Laundry detergent
(c) Car air freshner
(d) Designer clothes

58. An example of a new type of retail product that reaches local Kirana store after selling well in organised retail business is
(a) Only breakfast cereal
(b) Only pet food
(c) Only liquid handwash
(d) Liquid handwash, breakfast cereal and pet food

59. According to Nielsen, what percent of total sales for organised retail come from new growth categories?
(a) Not mentioned in the passage
(b) 40%
(c) 100%
(d) 50%

60. What does that phrase 'high-end' in the passage mean?
(a) Tall
(b) Cheap
(c) Expensive
(d) Useful

Section B – Numerical Ability and Analytical Aptitude

61. Mayank can do a piece of work in 3 days. Sanjay can do the same work in 4 days. The wage for full work is ₹ 350. If both work together to complete the work, then find out the earning of Sanjay if the wages are paid in proportion to work done.
(a) ₹ 160
(b) ₹ 180
(c) ₹ 140
(d) ₹ 150

62. If the selling price of 50 articles is equal to the cost price of 40 articles, then the loss or gain % is
(a) 25% gain
(b) 20% gain
(c) 20% loss
(d) 25% loss

63. What fraction of an hour is a second?

(a) $\dfrac{1}{24}$ (b) $\dfrac{1}{3600}$ (c) $\dfrac{1}{60}$ (d) $\dfrac{1}{120}$

64. The value of $\sqrt{10+\sqrt{24+\sqrt{131+\sqrt{153+\sqrt{256}}}}}$ is

(a) 8 (b) 4
(c) 6 (d) 12

65. The ratio between two numbers is 3 : 4 and their sum is 490. The numbers are

(a) 220 and 270 (b) 210 and 280
(c) 230 and 260 (d) 200 and 290

66. Calculate the simple interest on ₹ 7200 at $12\dfrac{3}{4}\%$ per annum for 9 months.

(a) ₹ 650.5 (b) ₹ 680.5
(c) ₹ 688.5 (d) ₹ 678.5

67. The mean marks obtained by 300 students in a subject are 60. The mean of top 100 students was found to be 80 and the mean of last 100 students was found to be 50. The mean marks of the remaining 100 students is

(a) 60 (b) 65 (c) 70 (d) 50

68. The average salary per month of 30 employees in a company is ₹ 4000. If the manager's salary is added, the average salary increases to ₹ 4300, what is the salary of the manager?

(a) ₹ 10000 (b) ₹ 13000
(c) ₹ 12000 (d) ₹ 13300

69. Find the average of all prime numbers between 30 and 50.

(a) 39.8 (b) 39.2
(c) 39.6 (d) 39.4

70. If $a:b=3:4$, $b:c=4:7$, then $\dfrac{a+b+c}{c}$ is equal to

(a) 7 (b) 1 (c) 3 (d) 2

71. 90% of the students were present in a school and 20 students were absent. The total number of students in a school are

(a) 400 (b) 200
(c) 100 (d) 300

72. At an election there are two candidates in the contest. The candidate who gets 62% of the votes declared winner by 144 votes. Find the total number of votes polled. Assume that none of the votes polled was invalid.

(a) 700 (b) 600 (c) 550 (d) 750

73. A number less than 100, when divided by 2, 3, 4 and 5 leaves remainder 1 in each case. The number is

(a) 61 (b) 81 (c) 71 (d) 91

74. A sum of ₹ 549 is to be divided among Priya, Preeti and Sonu in such a way that 3 times Priya's share, 4 times Preeti's share and 7 times Sonu's share are all equal. What is the share of Priya?

(a) ₹ 189 (b) ₹ 279 (c) ₹ 252 (d) ₹ 108

75. 1000 persons are taking a dip into a cuboidal pond which is 80 m long and 50 m broad. What is the rise of water level in the pond, if the average displacement of the water by a person is $0.4\ \text{m}^3$?

(a) 10 cm (b) 40 cm (c) 20 cm (d) 30 cm

76. Find the number which is nearest to 457 and is exactly divisible by 11.

(a) 462 (b) 451 (c) 450 (d) 460

77. Find the lowest common multiple of 24, 36 and 40.

(a) 240 (b) 480 (c) 120 (d) 360

78. A vendor bought 5 buttons for a rupee. How many for a rupee must be sell to gain 25%?

(a) 3 (b) 2 (c) 5 (d) 4

79. What approximate value should come in place of the question mark ?

23% of $6783+57\%$ of $8431=?$

(a) 6366 (b) 6520 (c) 6460 (d) 6420

80. Seven years ago, the ratio of the ages of Sonu and Suresh was 3 : 4 respectively. 9 yr hence, the ratio of their ages will be 7 : 8 respectively. What is the present age of Suresh?

(a) 28 yr (b) 23 yr (c) 19 yr (d) 16 yr

81. The LCM of two numbers is 198 and their HCF is 2. If first number is 18, then find the second number.

(a) 16 (b) 24 (c) 22 (d) 20

82. The simple interest on a certain sum of money for 3 yr at 15% per annum is ₹ 125 less than the simple interest on the same sum for 5 yr at 10% per annum. Find the sum.

(a) ₹ 2200 (b) ₹ 2300
(c) ₹ 2400 (d) ₹ 2500

83. A person's salary has increased from ₹ 12500 to ₹ 14375. What is the percentage increase in his salary?

(a) 15% (b) 13% (c) 14% (d) 12%

84. A sum of ₹ 10000 was taken on loan. This is to be repaid into five equal annual installments. If the rate by simple interest be 20% annually, then the value of each installment is ....
(a) ₹ 7000   (b) ₹ 2856   (c) ₹ 6000   (d) ₹ 4000

85. A laser printer is sold for ₹ 12000 for a loss of 20%. What is the cost price of the laser printer?
(a) ₹ 13000   (b) ₹ 16000
(c) ₹ 15000   (d) ₹ 14000

86. If $\sqrt{18 \times 14 \times x} = 168$, then x is equal to
(a) 112   (b) 113   (c) 115   (d) 117

87. A man's present age is 8 times of his son. After 10 yr, he will be thrice the age of his son. How old is son at present?
(a) 4 yr   (b) 16 yr   (c) 12 yr   (d) 8 yr

88. A motorist travels to place 150 km away at an average speed of 50 km/h and returns at 30 km/h. Find out the average speed for whole journey.
(a) 32.5 km/h   (b) 39.5 km/h
(c) 35.5 km/h   (d) 37.5 km/h

89. $\dfrac{\sqrt{50} + \sqrt{98}}{\sqrt{18}} = ?$
(a) $3\sqrt{2}$ (b) 4
(c) 5   (d) $2\sqrt{3}$

90. The difference between ages of two men is 8 yr. 16 yr ago, their ages were in the ratio 3 : 2. The present age of elder is
(a) 24 yr   (b) 16 yr
(c) 32 yr   (d) 40 yr

Section C : Reasoning and Logical Deduction

91. Find the missing term in the series.
AK, EO, IS, ..., QA, UE
(a) MW   (b) NX   (c) IW   (d) IV

Directions (Q. Nos. 92 and 93) *There is a certain relation between two given words on one side of : : and one word is given on another side of : : while another word is to be found from the given alternatives, having the same relation with this word as the given pair has. Select the best alternative.*

92. Anaemia : Blood : : Cataract : ?
(a) Throat   (b) Eye
(c) Ear   (d) Skin

93. Horse : Neigh : : Jackal : ?
(a) Bray   (b) Howl   (c) Squeak   (d) Chatter

94. Find out the odd among the four.
(a) Dehradun   (b) Bhopal
(c) Lucknow   (d) Pune

95. What is the next term in the series?
DCXW, FEVU, HGTS, ...
(a) LKPO   (b) LMRS   (c) ABYZ   (d) JIRQ

Direction (Q. No. 96) *There is a certain relation between two given words on one side of : : and one word is given on another side of : : while another word is to be found from the given alternatives, having the same relation with this word as the given pair has. Select the best alternative.*

96. Melt : Liquid : : Freeze : ?
(a) Solid   (b) Ice
(c) Condense   (d) Crystal

97. Complete the series by choosing one number from the four given alternatives.
6, 25, 62, 123, 214, 341, ?
(a) 510   (b) 511   (c) 398   (d) 459

98. In the given series, choose the incorrect number.
6, 14, 24, 36, 50, 66, 84, 103, 126
(a) 66   (b) 36   (c) 126   (d) 103

99. By looking in a mirror, it appears that it is 6:30 in the clock. What is the real time?
(a) 5:30   (b) 11:00
(c) 6:30   (d) 1:00

Directions (Q. Nos. 100-102) *Each of these questions consist of two sets. Figure (A), (B), (C) and (D)/(E) are set of question figures and figures (a), (b), (c) and (d) constitute the set of answer figures. There is a definite relationship among figures (a), (b), (c) and (d)/(e). Select a suitable figure from the answer figures (a), (b), (c) and (d) which establishes a similar relationship.*

100.

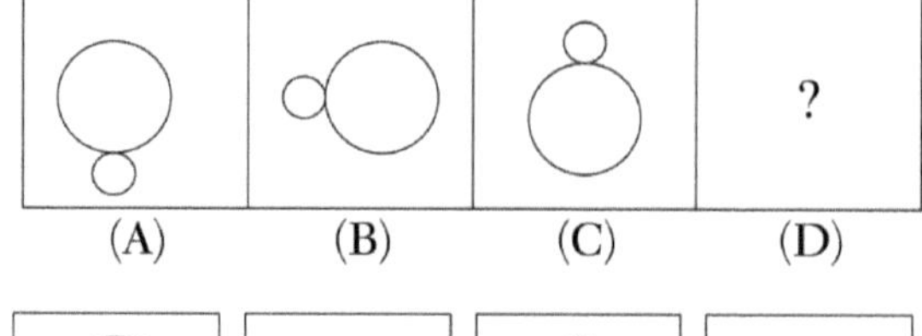

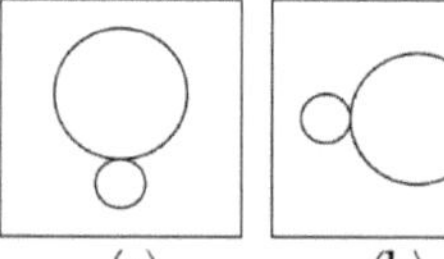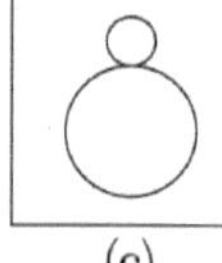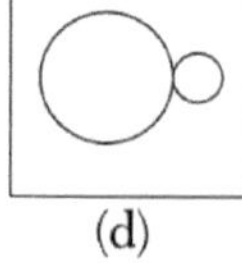

101.

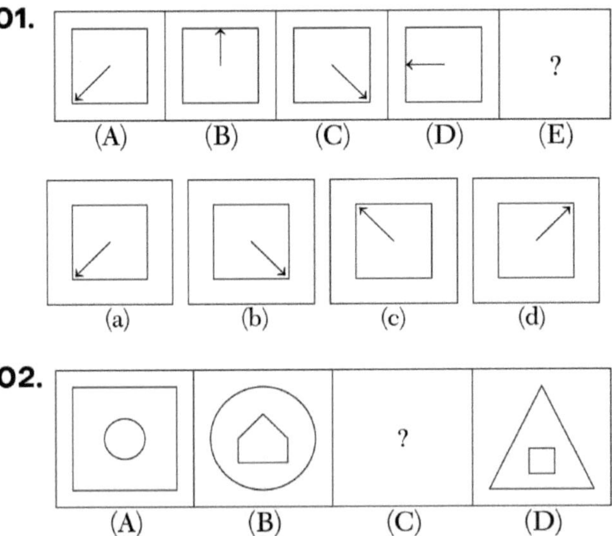

102.

Directions (Q. Nos. 103-105) *Using the diagram below, answer the following question.*

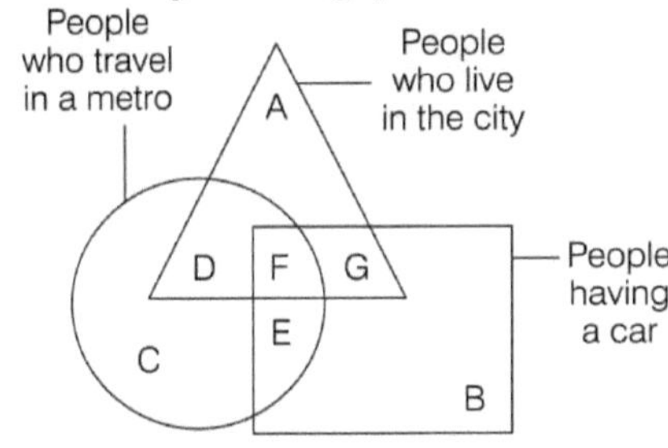

103. Which space represents people who do not live in the city but travel by metro and also have a car?

(a) B   (b) E   (c) G   (d) C

104. Which space represent people who live in the city and have a car?

(a) D   (b) F
(c) F and G   (d) E and F

105. Which space represents people living in the city having a car and still travelling in a metro?

(a) F   (b) E   (c) D   (d) G

Directions (Q. Nos. 106-108) *In each question below are given two statements followed by two conclusions numbered I and II. You have to take the given two statements to be true even if they seem to be at variance from commonly known facts. Read the conclusion and then decide which of the given conclusions logically follows from the two given statements, disregarding commonly known facts.*

Give Answer
(a) If only Conclusion I follows
(b) If only Conclusion II follows
(c) If either Conclusion I or II follows
(d) If neither Conclusion I nor II follows

106. Statements
All water is divine.
All temples are divine.
Conclusions
  I. All water is temple.
  II. All temples are water.

107. Statements
Most teachers are boys.
Some boys are students.
Conclusions
  I. Some students are boys.
  II. Some teachers are students.

108. Statements
Some doctors are fools.
Some fools are rich.
Conclusions
  I. Some doctors are rich.
  II. Some rich are doctors.

Directions (Q. Nos. 109-111) *Each of these questions has an Assertion (A) and a Reason (R).*

Mark answer as
(1) if both (A) and (R) are true and (R) is the correct explanation of (A)
(2) if both (A) and (R) are true but (R) is not the correct explanation of (A)
(3) if (A) is true but (R) is false
(4) if (A) is false but (R) is true

109. Assertion (A) On the equinoxes, the day and night are equal all over the globe.

Reason (R) On the equinoxes, the position of earth with respect to the sun is such that neither pole is inclined towards the sun.

(a) 2   (b) 1   (c) 4   (d) 3

110. Assertion (A) Uranium undergoes nuclear fusion reaction.

Reason (R) It has a big, unstable nucleus.

(a) 4   (b) 1   (c) 3   (d) 2

111. Assertion (A) No food material normally enters the wind pipe during swallowing.

Reason (R) When we swallow, the back portion of our tongue covers the opening of the wind pipe.

(a) 4   (b) 1   (c) 2   (d) 3

112. In a certain code, COMMUNICATION is written as OITACINUMMOCN. How is DETERMINATION written in the same code?
(a) NOITANIMRETED
(b) OITANIMRETEDN
(c) INATIONDETERM
(d) OITANMIREDETN

113. Saturday was a holiday for Republic Day. 14th of the next month is again a holiday because of Valentine's day. What was it on the 14th?
(a) Thursday   (b) Wednesday
(c) Monday   (d) Friday

114. In a class of 45 students, where girls are twice that of boys, Ravi is ranked 11th from top. If there are 5 girls ahead of Ravi, how many boys are after him in Rank?
(a) 9   (b) 10
(c) 15   (d) 11

115. Rahul told Anand "Yesterday I defeated the only brother of the daughter of my grandmother". Whom did Rahul defeat?
(a) Brother   (b) Son
(c) Cousin   (d) Father

116. Introducing Rekha to the guest, Priya said, "Her mother is the only daughter of my Father." How is Rekha related to Priya?
(a) Niece   (b) Mother
(c) Daughter   (d) Sister

117. If 2 days after tomorrow is Saturday, what day was 4 days before yesterday?
(a) Friday   (b) Sunday
(c) Saturday   (d) Thursday

Directions (Q. Nos. 118-120) *Study the following information to answer the given questions.*

P, Q, R, S, T, U, V and W are eight friends sitting around a circle facing towards the center.
(i) W is on the immediate left of P but is not the neighbour of T or S.
(ii) U is on the immediate right of Q and V is the neighbour of T.
(iii) R is between T and U.

118. What is the position of S?
(a) On the immediate left of Q
(b) On the immediate left of P
(c) Between Q and U
(d) Second to the right of U

119. What is the position of V?
(a) Third to the right of U
(b) Between T and R
(c) Second to the left of S
(d) On the immediate right of W

120. Which of the following statement is true?
(a) V is between W and T.
(b) U is the neighbour of V.
(c) T is between U and Q.
(d) W is between P and S.

Section D : General Knowledge and Current Affairs

121. Which of the following is the National game of Australia?
(a) Cricket   (b) Baseball
(c) Kabaddi   (d) Hockey

122. Which Mughal emperor had imprisoned his Father Shah Jahan and become the Mughal emperor after killing his brothers?
(a) Aurangzeb   (b) Akbar
(c) Humayun   (d) Babur

123. Kaziranga National Park is in which State of India?
(a) Uttar Pradesh   (b) Kerala
(c) Assam   (d) Maharashtra

124. Who was the first Chinese visitor to India?
(a) Tenzing Norgay   (b) Junko Tabei
(c) Fahien   (d) Hiuen Tsang

125. The amount of blood in the human body is generally equivalent to ...... per cent of body weight.
(a) 7   (b) 18
(c) 25   (d) 2

126. Barometer is used to measure which of the following?
(a) Atmospheric pressure   (b) Purity of milk
(c) Temperature   (d) Altitude

127. ...... Revolution is the increase of oil seed production.
(a) Yellow   (b) White
(c) Green   (d) Blue

128. The enzymes Pepsin and Renin are found in
(a) Mouth   (b) Stomach
(c) Intestine   (d) Pancreas

129. If the pH of a solution is greater than 7, the property of the solution is
(a) Suspension   (b) Acidic
(c) Neutral   (d) Basic

130. What was the capital of Vijayanagara Empire?
(a) Bodhgaya   (b) Kannauj
(c) Hampi   (d) Amaravati

131. Out of the following, who was also popularly known as the 'Fuhrer'?
(a) Adolf Hitler   (b) Napoleon Bonaparte
(c) William Shakespeare   (d) Mahatma Gandhi

132. Who won the 'Golden Ball' Award in FIFA World Cup 2018?
(a) Danijel Subasic   (b) Harry Kane
(c) Kylian Mbappe   (d) Luka Modric

133. Which planet in the Solar System has the most circular orbit?
(a) Mercury (b) Venus (c) Earth (d) Jupiter

134. The number of Union Territories in India
(a) 7   (b) 9   (c) 6   (d) 5

135. The capital of Sikkim is
(a) Gangtok (b) Agartala (c) Imphal (d) Shillong

136. In which country will you find the Lord's, Oval and Leeds stadiums?
(a) United States of America (b) Spain
(c) Britian   (d) West Indies

137. The first General Post Office (GPO) in India was established in the year 1774. In which city it was established?
(a) Kolkata (b) Mumbai (c) Delhi (d) Chennai

138. Night blindness is caused by the deficiency of
(a) Vitamin C   (b) Vitamin E
(c) Vitamin B   (d) Vitamin A

139. The study of inter-relationship between living and their environment is called
(a) Etiology   (b) Embryology
(c) Exobiology   (d) Ecology

140. QANTAS is a popular airline of
(a) Australia   (b) Netherlands
(c) Korea   (d) Japan

141. Which city is hosting the 2020 Olympics?
(a) Rio de Janeiro (Brazil)
(b) Tokyo (Japan)
(c) Los Angeles (USA)
(d) Paris (France)

142. Who was the first Indian to win the Nobel Prize in Literature?
(a) Sarojini Naidu   (b) Vijaylakshmi Pandit
(c) Rabindranath Tagore   (d) Mihir Sen

143. Regulatory body 'TRAI' associated with which of the following?
(a) Telecom   (b) Technical Education
(c) Tourism   (d) Transport

144. Heathrow Airport is located in
(a) Stockholm   (b) London
(c) Paris   (d) Madrid

145. Junk e-mail is also called
(a) Spam (b) Spool (c) Spoof (d) Sniffer

146. In which city 'National Gandhi Museum and Library' is located?
(a) Chennai   (b) Ahmedabad
(c) New Delhi   (d) Bengaluru

147. The term 'Deuce' is used in which sports?
(a) Golf   (b) Badminton
(c) Hockey   (d) Baseball

148. The famous Physicist 'Stephen William Hawking' was born in which country?
(a) England (b) Japan (c) America (d) Russia

149. H_2SO_4 stands for
(a) Sulphur Dioxide   (b) Sulphuric Acid
(c) Mercuric Oxide   (d) Sodium Nitrate

150. The minimum age required to contest for Presidentship of India is
(a) 30   (b) 23   (c) 20   (d) 35

Section E : Aptitude for Service Sector

151. Your class has been given a group task by your faculty and members of group assigned to you are not known to you.
(a) Don't participate with enthusiasm in the task.
(b) Request your faculty to change your group.
(c) You take this as an opportunity to learn things in the new group.
(d) On your own decide to change the group and start working with a known group.

152. You are preparing for your 10 + 2 final exams. Your neighbour's children make a lot of noise while playing and that disturbs you. You will
(a) go and shout at the children.
(b) tell other neighbours about these children and the fact that they were such rowdy kids.
(c) ignore the whole situation.
(d) request to the parents of these children to stop them from creating such disturbances.

153. At times despite your best efforts, you still fail to impress your superiors with quality of your work, you
(a) blame your fate for this.
(b) continue doing the same quality of work as it doesn't affect you.
(c) lose interest in your work.
(d) discuss with superiors and try again till you succeed

154. You meet a motorist with a flat tyre. You will
(a) help him by calling a mechanic.
(b) stop and try to change the tyre even though you don't have the expertise.
(c) help him park his car on one side of the road.
(d) ignore the situation and drive on.

155. You are staying in a hostel and sharing room with fellow mates. When you leave the room to go to college, you
(a) always put all things at their right places.
(b) expect your roommates to clean up the room.
(c) be bossy and ask others to clean it up for you.
(d) leave the room in complete mess.

156. You have to prepare for a vital examination as well as an important project at the same time. You will
(a) prepare a time table allocating the required time to each and follow it.
(b) you will start panicking and as a result will not be able to do anything satisfactorily.
(c) you will prepare for any one of them.
(d) prepare for the examination and get your project done by your sibling.

157. While dining at a reputed restaurant you ordered vegetarian soup but you have been served with non-vegetarian soup. You will
(a) call the server and shout at him/her.
(b) call the manager and complain to him/her.
(c) leave the restaurant immediately.
(d) forget the incident and do nothing about it.

158. You have planned a day trip with your friends and you are leading the group. One of your friend from other town who is in your town and staying in a hotel, calls up that he needs your help as he is not feeling well. You will
(a) ask him to wait till you come back from the trip.
(b) ask him to call someone else.
(c) re-schedule the whole day trip.
(d) call some other friend and ask him to help the sick friend of yours.

159. A farewell party is to be organised at your college by group of students. You
(a) try to make another group and challenge the same.
(b) volunteer for the group.
(c) not be bothered about it.
(d) let others organise it themselves.

160. A new role for leaders is to take on responsibility as
(a) overseer
(b) mentors only
(c) coaches only
(d) both coaches and mentors

161. You are a cashier at the cash counter of a hospital. There is no one waiting at the window to pay. You will
(a) go and help a co-worker.
(b) quit your seat, go behind the office and relax.
(c) remain seated at your counter and be attentive to anybody requiring help.
(d) stay at the counter but listen to the mobile phone music through a pair of earphones.

162. If someone criticises you for your mistakes, you will
(a) fight with the person.
(b) start talking to others about his mistakes.
(c) not pay any attention to it.
(d) listen to him and take it as feedback for improvement.

163. You are the leader of a group and new member joins it. How would you make the member comfortable?
(a) Giving him a complicated task.
(b) Giving him a complete set of instructions to study and leave him alone.
(c) Ignore him and do your business.
(d) By making the job interesting to him and by praising him when he does well.

164. You have been sent to a Historical Monument for a cleanliness project and to educate the locals over the same. You know that there will not be any supervision there, you
(a) will ask your younger brother to go there and do it for you.
(b) show no enthusiasm and just complete the project.
(c) whole-heartedly participate in the project and try to put in your best efforts.
(d) will not go there, at all.

165. Whenever any new assignment, which is out of your routine comfort, is given to you, you will
(a) eagerly take up such assignments.
(b) try to sick to your comfort zone only.
(c) take up the assignment and make excuses for the delayed submission.
(d) never initiate the same.

166. You are working in a hotel and staying along with other staff in the official accommodation provided by the company. One day you fall sick. In your opinion
(a) you apply for leave as per company policy.
(b) you expect your friends to apply for the leave on your behalf.
(c) expect your boss to grant your leave.
(d) you don't need to apply for leave as everyone is aware.

167. A park in your locality has an open drain. You will
(a) request your neighbours to pool money to convert that to a closed drain.
(b) inform the local councillor.
(c) put up a signage to highlight the condition of the drain and ask people to be careful.
(d) expect your friends to cover it up.

168. While working as a manager in a hotel, you are informed that one guest in the hotel has suddenly fallen ill. You will
(a) call a doctor and send him to the guest.
(b) let the guest handle things on his/her own.
(c) meet the guest and then urgently call the doctor and help the patient as required.
(d) ask your junior manager to deal with it.

169. You are in a crowded city bus when you see an old person and a lady with an infant get on to the bus. What would you do?
(a) Ignore the situation and keep sitting in your seat.
(b) Offer your seat to one and ask someone else to vacate their seat for the other.
(c) Judge the situation and offer the seat to the appropriate person.
(d) Offer your seat to the lady with the infant and direct the old person to the senior citizen seat.

170. You have secured a management job in an organisation. Upon joining, you realised that the environment is overbearing. Your reaction would be
(a) to isolate yourself from the environment and keep blaming the staff.
(b) carry on and do nothing about it.
(c) leave the job.
(d) to talk to staff, take them into your confidence and then initiate the process of rectification.

171. You are a sincere and dedicated manager of a well established hotel. Your company wants you to go and handle a property which is not doing well in business. You will
(a) leave the job and take another job.
(b) crib about the new assignment.
(c) try to convince the superiors to send someone else, instead of you.
(d) you accept the challenge and go ahead with the assignment.

172. One of your team member always tries to obstruct your work, repeatedly. You will
(a) not do anything.
(b) start interfering in his tasks, too.
(c) take these exerts seriously.
(d) try to discuss with him about his obstructing behaviour.

173. To work efficiently and effectively in the service industry, which of the following you think is/are the essential ability (ies)/qualities?
(a) Being introvert.
(b) Being responsible only.
(c) Being helpful and outgoing only.
(d) Both being responsible and being helpful and outgoing.

174. In the examination hall you find that your question paper is too tough to be answered. The best thing you can do is
(a) complain to the Examiner to change the question paper.
(b) try to cheat.
(c) leave the paper and walk out of the Examination hall.
(d) try to attempt the questions you know first.

175. One of your team mates is repeatedly failing to score in cricket matches despite being talented and skilled. You will
(a) collect money from other team mates and send him to a coaching school.
(b) ignore and drop him, making room for other extra player.
(c) do not give him a chance to play.
(d) organise a coaching and practice sessions with all your team mates and ensure he succeeds.

176. If all of a sudden your maid becomes seriously ill at night, you would
(a) not care for the situation.
(b) ask someone else to help and leave from there.
(c) take her to the nearest hospital.
(d) wait for the morning to contact a doctor.

177. You receive calls from customer care continuously for the same matter. What will you do?
(a) Don't receive the call.
(b) Put your phone in silent mode and ignore the calls.
(c) Put costomer care number on block list.
(d) Receive the call but instruct them about not continuing with the calls.

178. You are going to cinema hall to watch a movie. You have some edible items in your bag. The cinema hall does not allow eatables inside.

HM 2019

Watchman asks if you are carrying any food items in your bag

(a) you will hand over the food items.

(b) you will argue with the watchman and insist on carrying the food items.

(c) gather a crowd and create a scene in the cinema hall.

(d) you will not tell him anything.

179. You have got an assignment from your boss. Before you execute it, the plan is to be made and discussed. In your opinion

(a) planning is half the task done.

(b) planning is sheer waste of time.

(c) planning is only a personal opinion.

(d) planning is not required at all.

180. While working as a restaurant supervisor in a hotel, one of your guests asks you to send food from the buffet to his room as he is hosting a party. This practice is totally against the hotel policy. You will

(a) inform him about the policy and refuse politely.

(b) still send the food to his room.

(c) will ask for money in lieu of the food service.

(d) refuse him the food service, rudely.

181. If you happen to see someone getting hit by a car and getting badly injured, you would

(a) run away from the place in fear of getting involved in a police case.

(b) immediately try and help the victim.

(c) try to chase the car to get hold of the driver.

(d) run and call the police.

182. You are preparing for the final examination scheduled on the next day, but your neighbour plays loud music and you are getting disturbed. What will you do?

(a) You also start playing music louder than your neighbour.

(b) Request your neighbour and inform him about your exmination.

(c) Inform the local police and complain.

(d) Ignore and try to concentrateon your preparation.

183. You are busy in a departmental store in the children's clothing section. You find an old lady looking for help in the packaged food section. You will

(a) ignore the situation.

(b) excuse yourself from your own customers and quickly help the lady in the other section.

(c) inform the appropriate sales staff to attend to her.

(d) pretend to be busy at your own counter.

184. The entrance path of your college is littered with paper and plastic on a daily basis. You will

(a) criticise the sweeper of that area.

(b) leave it as it is and do nothing.

(c) think that this is college responsibility.

(d) make a group of like-minded friends and create awareness in the college.

185. You are on you way to appear for a job interview and while walking down the road, your dress is spoilt by a vehicle passing by on the road. You will

(a) pick up a stone and throw at the vehicle and start an argument.

(b) you decide to drop the interview and go back home.

(c) you clean up your clothes as much as you can and keep your mind focused on the interview.

(d) you will click a photograph of the car number and inform the traffic police about the incident.

186. One of your classmates has lost his mobile and you know that one of your good friends has found the same mobile. You will

(a) ignore the whole incident.

(b) ask your friend to return it to the owner.

(c) tell your classmate which of your friends has stolen it.

(d) suggest your friend not to return the mobile.

187. According to you, what should you do to control the ill-effects of stress of modern day life.

(a) Only sufficient relaxation and rest.

(b) Only diet control.

(c) Only physical exercise.

(d) Diet control, sufficient relaxation and rest and physical exercise.

188. You have stomach ache and nausea and you have some very urgent work lined up at office. You feel that it is

(a) necessary to attend work just to complete the urgent work.

(b) not necessary to attend office but you need to inform them about not being present.

(c) not required to visit office if you are unwell.

(d) not necessary to bother about work and no need to inform office as well.

189. One of your junior staff who has been working with you for a long time, now does not take his job seriously and even replies to you. You will

(a) try to transfer him to some other department.

(b) shout at him and ask him to behave.

(c) talk to him and try to understand his problem and then act.

(d) shift his tasks to other staff members.

190. A classmate of yours has become addicted to some vile habits, you have been noticing changes in his behaviour, you will
(a) start avoiding him.
(b) punish him.
(c) not do anything.
(d) counsel him and assist him to overcome the addiction.

191. A guest is not satisfied with the service of the department you are heading and you come to know about this from another colleague
(a) approach the guest and try to find out the situation and act accordingly.
(b) tell the other person to take care of this.
(c) do nothing about it.
(d) immediately inform yor boss.

192. Your maid's son met with an accident and needs blood immediately. You will
(a) collect money and give it to the maid to pay for the blood.
(b) gather some of your friends to donate the blood and refrain from donating yourself.
(c) volunteer to donate spontaneously.
(d) be indifferent and totally neglect the situation.

193. A fight takes place between two of your best friends. What will you do?
(a) You also involve yourself in fighting .
(b) Try to convince both to stop fighting and try to find a solution to the problem.
(c) Ignore them and leave the scene.
(d) Take side of one of the friends, who you think is right.

194. You are part a group assignment in your school. You will
(a) shall agree with the ideas of others and not participate much.
(b) dominate with your ideas over the others.
(c) share your ideas with others.
(d) shall be generating your own ideas after listening to the other people's ideas.

195. On the way back home from office after a very tiring day, you see an old lady standing in the bus next to where you are seated and requesting for the seat from you. You will

(a) shout at the lady for riding in a crowded bus.
(b) offer your seat to the lady.
(c) tell her that you are also very tired and can't offer the seat.
(d) ignore the request.

196. You are driving a car without fastening the seat belt. You are stopped by the traffic police. You will
(a) you stop the car and start arguing with the traffic police.
(b) immediately stop the car and follow the instructions given by the traffic police.
(c) increase the speed of your car and try to escape.
(d) you take away your hands off the car steering and try to put on your seat belt.

197. Imagine a colleague of yours whom you don't get along with well, needs your help on an important assignment given to him. When he approaches you, you will
(a) ignore him completely.
(b) welcome him and assist, to the best of your ability.
(c) misguide him and enjoy his failure.
(d) ask him to seek help from others.

198. You friend has become angry with you without any apparent reason. You
(a) will try to please him.
(b) will criticise him among your other friends.
(c) will not talk to him at all.
(d) will sort out the misunderstanding by talking to him.

199. One of your classmate with whom you don't get along very well slips and falls down in front of you in the college corridor and your friends started laughing. You will
(a) just sit and watch.
(b) join your friends in laughter.
(c) help him and ask your friends not to laugh.
(d) walk away from the scene.

200. A new year party is to be arranged in your office. You will
(a) sit back and wait for the invitation.
(b) try to organise it on your own.
(c) organise by taking help of your colleagues.
(d) let someone else take the lead.

HM 2019

Answers

1. *(d)*	2. *(c)*	3. *(a)*	4. *(b)*	5. *(d)*	6. *(b)*	7. *(d)*	8. *(b)*	9. *(d)*	10. *(a)*
11. *(a)*	12. *(a)*	13. *(d)*	14. *(c)*	15. *(c)*	16. *(c)*	17. *(c)*	18. *(a)*	19. *(b)*	20. *(b)*
21. *(b)*	22. *(b)*	23. *(d)*	24. *(a)*	25. *(a)*	26. *(a)*	27. *(c)*	28. *(d)*	29. *(d)*	30. *(d)*
31. *(b)*	32. *(b)*	33. *(a)*	34. *(b)*	35. *(b)*	36. *(b)*	37. *(d)*	38. *(b)*	39. *(b)*	40. *(b)*
41. *(b)*	42. *(b)*	43. *(d)*	44. *(a)*	45. *(b)*	46. *(d)*	47. *(a)*	48. *(b)*	49. *(b)*	50. *(c)*
51. *(a)*	52. *(c)*	53. *(b)*	54. *(c)*	55. *(a)*	56. *(c)*	57. *(d)*	58. *(d)*	59. *(d)*	60. *(c)*
61. *(d)*	62. *(c)*	63. *(b)*	64. *(b)*	65. *(b)*	66. *(c)*	67. *(d)*	68. *(d)*	69. *(a)*	70. *(d)*
71. *(b)*	72. *(b)*	73. *(a)*	74. *(c)*	75. *(a)*	76. *(a)*	77. *(d)*	78. *(d)*	79. *(a)*	80. *(b)*
81. *(c)*	82. *(d)*	83. *(a)*	84. *(d)*	85. *(c)*	86. *(a)*	87. *(a)*	88. *(d)*	89. *(b)*	90. *(d)*
91. *(a)*	92. *(b)*	93. *(b)*	94. *(d)*	95. *(d)*	96. *(a)*	97. *(a)*	98. *(d)*	99. *(a)*	100. *(d)*
101. *(d)*	102. *(b)*	103. *(b)*	104. *(c)*	105. *(a)*	106. *(d)*	107. *(a)*	108. *(d)*	109. *(b)*	110. *(a)*
111. *(b)*	112. *(b)*	113. *(a)*	114. *(a)*	115. *(d)*	116. *(c)*	117. *(a)*	118. *(a)*	119. *(a)*	120. *(a)*
121. *(a)*	122. *(a)*	123. *(c)*	124. *(c)*	125.. *(a)*	126. *(a)*	127. *(a)*	128. *(b)*	129. *(d)*	130. *(c)*
131. *(a)*	132. *(d)*	133. *(b)*	134. *(a)*	135. *(a)*	136. *(c)*	137. *(a)*	138. *(d)*	139. *(d)*	140. *(a)*
141. *(b)*	142. *(c)*	143. *(a)*	144. *(b)*	145. *(a)*	146. *(c)*	147. *(b)*	148. *(a)*	149. *(b)*	150. *(d)*
151. *(c)*	152. *(d)*	153. *(d)*	154. *(c)*	155. *(a)*	156. *(a)*	157. *(b)*	158. *(d)*	159. *(b)*	160. *(d)*
161. *(c)*	162. *(d)*	163. *(d)*	164. *(c)*	165. *(a)*	166. *(a)*	167. *(b)*	168. *(c)*	169. *(d)*	170. *(d)*
171. *(d)*	172. *(d)*	173. *(d)*	174. *(d)*	175. *(d)*	176. *(d)*	177. *(d)*	178. *(a)*	179. *(a)*	180. *(a)*
181. *(b)*	182. *(b)*	183. *(c)*	184. *(d)*	185. *(c)*	186. *(b)*	187. *(d)*	188. *(b)*	189. *(c)*	190. *(d)*
191. *(a)*	192. *(c)*	193. *(b)*	194. *(c)*	195. *(b)*	196. *(b)*	197. *(b)*	198. *(d)*	199. *(c)*	200. *(c)*

Hints & Solutions

1. *(d)* Part (d) contains the error, the sentence contains incorrect use of 'other' because plural form of 'other' should be used to denote a number of people. Hence, replace 'other' with 'others' to make the sentence error free.

2. *(c)* Part (c) contains the error. The sentence contains the plural subject (nurses); hence, plural form of verb should be used. Replace 'is' with 'are' to make the sentence grammatically correct.

3. *(a)* The phrase 'a great many' means 'a large number of'. It is used with plural noun which will be followed by a plural verb. Hence, replace 'student has' with 'students have' to make the sentence grammatically correct.

4. *(b)* The phrase of 'one of the' is followed by a plural noun. Hence, 'man' will be replaced by 'men' to make the sentence error free.

5. *(d)* The given sentence uses double comparative adjectives which is incorrect. 'Better' is a comparative degree of 'good' and hence, will not use 'more'. Remove more to make the sentence grammatically correct.

6. *(b)* The word 'refurbished' means to renovate or redecorate something, especially a building. Hence, option (b) 'renovated' is nearest in meaning to the word 'refurbished'.

7. *(d)* The word 'decisive' means having an ability to make decisions quickly. Hence, option (d) 'firm' is the nearest in meaning to the word 'decisive'.

8. *(b)* The word 'momentous' means 'of great significance especially having a bearing on future events.'

Hence option (b) 'important' is nearest in meaning to the word 'momentous'.

9. *(d)* 'Stale' is nearest in meaning to the word 'not fresh.' 'Stale' means 'no longer fresh or unpleasant to eat'.

10. *(a)* The word 'obsession' means an idea or thought that continually preoccupies or intrudes a person's mind. Hence option (a) 'preoccupation' means the state of being preoccupied with something' is nearest in meaning of 'obsession'.

11. *(a)* 'Ferocious' means savagely fierce, cruel or violent. Hence, 'gentle' is its correct opposite.

12. *(a)* 'Stubborn' means unreasonably or perversely unyielding. Hence, 'flexible' meaning ready to change to adapt to different circumstances. Hence, 'flexible' is opposite in meaning to 'stubborn.

13. *(d)* The word 'clarity' means 'the quality of being explicit or coherent.

Hence, 'confusion' means when one is not clear or when one is doubtful or uncertain is the correct answer.

14. *(c)* The word 'heterogenous' means assorted or different.

Hence, 'homogeneous is its correct antonym of the underlined word. Similar or equivalent is opposite in meaning to the given word.

15. *(c)* The word 'accelerate' means to gain speed or happen at a faster rate. Hence, 'slacken' meaning to slow down or to decrease the speed is its correct antonym.

61. *(d)* Mayank can do a piece of work in 3 days.

$\therefore$ 1 day work of Mayank $= \dfrac{1}{3}$

Similarly, 1 day work of Sanjay $= \dfrac{1}{4}$

$\therefore$ Ratio of wages of Mayank and Sanjay $= \dfrac{1}{3} : \dfrac{1}{4}$

$$= 4 : 3$$

Now, total wages $= ₹\ 350$

$\therefore$ Sanjay's earning $= \left(\dfrac{3}{4+3}\right) \times 350 = ₹\ 150$

62. *(c)* Let the selling price of one article be $₹\ 1$.

Then, selling price of 50 articles is $₹\ 50$.

$\therefore$ Cost price of 40 articles $= ₹\ 50$

Cost price of 1 article $= ₹\ \dfrac{50}{40} = ₹\ \dfrac{5}{4}$

Here, $\text{CP} > \text{SP}$

$\therefore$ Loss $\% = \dfrac{\text{CP} - \text{SP}}{\text{CP}} \times 100$

$$= \dfrac{\left(\dfrac{5}{4} - 1\right)}{\left(\dfrac{5}{4}\right)} \times 100 = \dfrac{1}{4} \times \dfrac{4}{5} \times 100$$

$$= 20\%$$

63. *(b)* We know that, $1\ \text{h} = 3600\ \text{s}$

$\therefore$ Required fraction $= \dfrac{1\ \text{s}}{1\ \text{h}} = \dfrac{1\ \text{s}}{3600\ \text{s}} = \dfrac{1}{3600}$

64. *(b)* $\sqrt{10 + \sqrt{24 + \sqrt{131 + \sqrt{153 + \sqrt{256}}}}}$

$$= \sqrt{10 + \sqrt{24 + \sqrt{131 + \sqrt{153 + 16}}}}$$

$$= \sqrt{10 + \sqrt{24 + \sqrt{131 + \sqrt{169}}}}$$

$$= \sqrt{10 + \sqrt{24 + \sqrt{131 + 13}}}$$

$$= \sqrt{10 + \sqrt{24 + \sqrt{144}}} = \sqrt{10 + \sqrt{24 + 12}}$$

$$= \sqrt{10 + \sqrt{36}} = \sqrt{10 + 6} = \sqrt{16} = 4$$

65. *(b)* Let the two numbers be $3x$ and $4x$, respectively.

According to the question,

$$3x + 4x = 490$$

$$\Rightarrow \qquad 7x = 490$$

$$\Rightarrow \qquad x = 70$$

$\therefore$ Required numbers are

$$3x = 3 \times 70 = 210$$

and $\qquad 4x = 4 \times 70 = 280$

66. *(c)* Given, Principal $(P) = ₹\ 7200$

Time $(T) = 9$ months $= \dfrac{9}{12} = \dfrac{3}{4}$ yr

Rate $(R) = 12\dfrac{3}{4}\% = \dfrac{51}{4}\%$ per annum

We know that, Simple Interest (SI) $= \dfrac{P \times R \times T}{100}$

$$= \dfrac{7200 \times 51 \times 3}{4 \times 4 \times 100}$$

$$= ₹\ 688.5$$

67. *(d)* Total marks obtained by 300 students $= 300 \times 60$

$$= 18000$$

Total marks obtained by top 100 students $= 100 \times 80$

$$= 8000$$

Total marks obtained by last 100 students $= 100 \times 50$

$$= 5000$$

$\therefore$ The mean marks of remaining 100 students

$$= \dfrac{18000 - (8000 + 5000)}{100}$$

$$= \dfrac{18000 - 13000}{100} = \dfrac{5000}{100} = 50$$

68. *(d)* Let the manager's salary be $₹\ x$.

$\because$ Average salary of 30 employees $=\ 4000$

$\therefore$ Total salary of 30 employees

$$= ₹\ (30 \times 4000)$$

$$= ₹\ 120000$$

According to the question,

$$\Rightarrow \quad \dfrac{120000 + x}{31} = 4300$$

$$\Rightarrow \quad 120000 + x = 133300$$

$$\Rightarrow \qquad x = 133300 - 120000$$

$$\therefore \qquad x = ₹\ 13300$$

69. *(a)* There are 5 prime numbers between 30 and 50. They are 31, 37, 41, 43, 47.

$\therefore$ Required average $= \dfrac{\text{Sum of terms}}{\text{Number of terms}}$

$$= \dfrac{31 + 37 + 41 + 43 + 47}{5}$$

$$= \dfrac{199}{5} = 39.8$$

70. *(d)* $a : b = 3 : 4,\ b : c = 4 : 7$

$\therefore \quad a : b : c = 3 : 4 : 7$

Now, let $a = 3k$

$$b = 4k$$

$$c = 7k$$

$\therefore \dfrac{a+b+c}{c} = \dfrac{3k + 4k + 7k}{7k} = \dfrac{14k}{7k} = 2$

71. *(b)* Let the total number of students in school be x.

$\therefore$ Absent students $= 20$

According to the question,

$$x - \frac{90}{100}x = 20$$

$$\Rightarrow \qquad \frac{10}{100}x = 20$$

$$\Rightarrow \qquad x = \frac{20 \times 100}{10}$$

$$\therefore \qquad x = 200$$

72. *(b)* Let the total number of votes be x.

Votes got by winning candidate $= \dfrac{62}{100}x$

Votes got by loosing candidate $= \left(\dfrac{100 - 62}{100}\right)x$

$$= \frac{38}{100}x$$

According to the question,

$$\frac{62}{100}x - \frac{38}{100}x = 144$$

$$\Rightarrow \quad \frac{62x - 38x}{100} = 144 \Rightarrow \frac{24x}{100} = 144$$

$$\Rightarrow \qquad x = \frac{144 \times 100}{24}$$

$$\therefore \qquad x = 600$$

$\therefore$ Total number of votes $= 600$

73. *(a)* LCM $(2, 3, 4, 5)$

2	2, 3, 4, 5
2	1, 3, 2, 5
3	1, 3, 1, 5
5	1, 1, 1, 5
	1, 1, 1, 1

$\therefore$ LCM $= 2 \times 2 \times 3 \times 5 = 60$

$\therefore$ The least number below 100 which on dividing by 2, 3, 4 and 5 leaves remainder 1 in each case $= 60 + 1 = 61$

74. *(c)* Let the share of Priya, Preeti and Sonu be x, y and z respectively.

$$\therefore \qquad 3x = 4y = 7z$$

Now, let $\quad 3x = 4y = 7z = k$

$$\therefore \qquad x = \frac{k}{3}, \, y = \frac{k}{4}, \, z = \frac{k}{7}$$

According to the question,

$$x + y + z = 549$$

$$\Rightarrow \qquad \frac{k}{3} + \frac{k}{4} + \frac{k}{7} = 549$$

$$\Rightarrow \quad \frac{28k + 21k + 12k}{84} = 549 \Rightarrow \frac{61}{84}k = 549$$

$$\Rightarrow \qquad k = \frac{549 \times 84}{61}$$

$$\therefore \qquad k = 756$$

$$\therefore \quad \text{Priya's share} = x = \frac{k}{3} = \frac{756}{3} = ₹\ 252$$

75. *(a)* Total displacement $= 0.4 \times 1000 = 400 \text{ m}^3$

Let the rise of water level $= h$ m

Total displacement $=$ Total volume of cuboidal pond

$$\therefore \qquad 400 = 80 \times 50 \times h$$

$$\Rightarrow \qquad h = \frac{400}{80 \times 50}$$

$$\Rightarrow \qquad h = 0.1 \text{ m}$$

$$\therefore \qquad h = 10 \text{ cm} \qquad [\because 1 \text{ m} = 100 \text{ cm}]$$

76. *(a)*

$$\begin{array}{r} 11)\overline{457}(41 \\ \underline{44} \\ 17 \\ \underline{11} \\ 6 \end{array}$$

The number which nearest 457 and exactly divisible by $11 = 457 - 6 + 11 = 462$

77. *(d)* LCM of 24,36 and 40

2	24, 36, 40
2	12, 18, 20
2	6, 9, 10
3	3, 9, 5
	1, 3, 5

$\therefore$ LCM of 24, 36 and $40 = 2 \times 2 \times 2 \times 3 \times 3 \times 5 = 360$

78. *(d)* Cost Price (CP) of 1 button $= ₹\ \dfrac{1}{5}$, Gain $= 25\%$

$\therefore$ Selling Price (SP) of 1 button

$$= \left(\frac{100 + \text{Gain}\%}{100}\right) \times \text{CP}$$

$$= \left(\frac{100 + 25}{100}\right) \times \frac{1}{5} = \frac{125}{100 \times 5} = ₹\ \frac{1}{4}$$

Required number of buttons

$$= \frac{1}{1/4} = 4 \text{ buttons}$$

79. *(a)* 23% of $6783 + 57\%$ of $8431 = ?$

$$\Rightarrow \qquad ? = \frac{23}{100} \times 6783 + \frac{57}{100} \times 8431$$

$$\Rightarrow \qquad ? = 1560.09 + 4805.67$$

$$\Rightarrow \qquad ? = 6365.76$$

$$\Rightarrow \qquad ? \approx 6366$$

80. *(b)* Let the ages of Sonu and Suresh 7 yr ago be $3x$ and $4x$, respectively.

$\therefore$ Sonu's present age $= (3x + 7)$ yr

and Suresh's present age $= (4x + 7)$ yr

According to the question,

$$\frac{3x + 7 + 9}{4x + 7 + 9} = \frac{7}{8} \Rightarrow \frac{3x + 16}{4x + 16} = \frac{7}{8}$$

$$\Rightarrow \qquad 24x + 128 = 28x + 112$$

$\Rightarrow \quad 28x - 24x = 128 - 112$

$\Rightarrow \qquad 4x = 16 \Rightarrow x = 4$

$\therefore$ Suresh's present age $= 4 \times 4 + 7 = 23$ yr

81. *(c)* Let the second number be x.

$\qquad$ HCF $(18, x) = 2$

$\qquad$ LCM $(18, x) = 198$

We know that,

HCF $\times$ LCM $=$ Product of numbers

$\qquad 2 \times 198 = 18 \times x \Rightarrow \quad x = \dfrac{2 \times 198}{18}$

$\therefore \qquad\qquad x = 22$

82. *(d)* Let the sum of money be P.

According to the question,

$\therefore \quad \dfrac{P \times 5 \times 10}{100} - \dfrac{P \times 3 \times 15}{100} = 125 \left[\because SI = \dfrac{P \times t \times r}{100}\right]$

$\Rightarrow \qquad P\left[\dfrac{50}{100} - \dfrac{45}{100}\right] = 125$

$\Rightarrow \qquad\qquad P \times \dfrac{5}{100} = 125$

$\therefore \qquad\qquad\qquad P = ₹\ 2500$

83. *(a)* Required percentage increase

$= \left[\dfrac{\text{New salary} - \text{Old salary}}{\text{Old salary}}\right] \times 100$

$= \left(\dfrac{14375 - 12500}{12500}\right) \times 100 = 15\%$

84. *(d)* Total amount to be repaid $= P + \dfrac{P \times R \times T}{100}$

$= 10000 + \dfrac{10000 \times 20 \times 5}{100}$

$= 10000 + 10000 = ₹\ 20000$

Each installment $= \dfrac{20000}{5} = ₹\ 4000$

85. *(c)* Given, SP of laser printer $= ₹\ 12000$

$\qquad\qquad$ Loss $= 20\%$

CP of laser printer $= \left(\dfrac{100}{100 - \text{Loss}\%}\right)$ SP

$= \left(\dfrac{100}{100 - 20}\right) \times 12000$

$= \dfrac{100}{80} \times 12000$

$= ₹\ 15000$

86. *(a)* $\sqrt{18 \times 14 \times x} = 168$

On squaring both sides, we get

$\qquad 18 \times 14 \times x = 168 \times 168$

$\therefore \qquad\qquad x = \dfrac{168 \times 168}{18 \times 14}$

$\qquad\qquad\qquad x = 112$

87. *(a)* Let the age of son be x yr.

$\therefore \quad$ Age of man $= 8x$ yr

According to the question,

$\qquad\qquad (8x + 10) = 3(x + 10)$

$\Rightarrow \qquad\qquad 8x + 10 = 3x + 30$

$\Rightarrow \qquad\qquad\qquad 5x = 20$

$\qquad\qquad\qquad\qquad x = 4$

$\therefore \quad$ Present age of son $= 4$ yr

88. *(d)* Since, the distance travelled is constant and the respective speeds are $x = 50$ km/h and $y = 30$ km/h.

$\therefore$ According to the formula,

Average speed $= \dfrac{2xy}{x + y} = \dfrac{2 \times 50 \times 30}{50 + 30}$

$= \dfrac{3000}{80} = 37.5$ km/h

89. *(b)* $\dfrac{\sqrt{50} + \sqrt{98}}{\sqrt{18}} = ?$

$\Rightarrow \dfrac{\sqrt{2 \times 5 \times 5} + \sqrt{2 \times 7 \times 7}}{\sqrt{3 \times 3 \times 2}} = ?$

$\Rightarrow \qquad\qquad\qquad ? = \dfrac{5\sqrt{2} + 7\sqrt{2}}{3\sqrt{2}}$

$\Rightarrow \qquad\qquad\qquad ? = \dfrac{12\sqrt{2}}{3\sqrt{2}}$

$\therefore \qquad\qquad\qquad ? = 4$

90. *(d)* Let the age of younger man be x yr and the age of elder man be $(x + 8)$ yr.

According to the question,

$\qquad\qquad \dfrac{x + 8 - 16}{x - 16} = \dfrac{3}{2}$

$\Rightarrow \qquad\qquad \dfrac{x - 8}{x - 16} = \dfrac{3}{2}$

$\Rightarrow \qquad 3x - 48 = 2x - 16 \Rightarrow x = 32$

$\therefore \qquad$ Age of elder man $= 32 + 8 = 40$ yr

91. *(a)* The pattern of the series is

$A \xrightarrow{+4} E \xrightarrow{+4} I \xrightarrow{+4} \boxed{M} \xrightarrow{+4} Q \xrightarrow{+4} U$

$K \xrightarrow{+4} O \xrightarrow{+4} S \xrightarrow{+4} \boxed{W} \xrightarrow{+4} A \xrightarrow{+4} E$

$\therefore$ The missing term is **MW**.

92. *(b)* As, Anaemia is a disease related to blood. Similarly, Cataract is a disease related to eye.

93. *(b)* Neigh is the sound produced by Horse. Similarly, Howl is the sound produced by Jackal.

94. *(d)* Except Pune, all other are capitals of Indian States.

95. *(d)* The pattern of the series is,

$D \xrightarrow{+2} F \xrightarrow{+2} H \xrightarrow{+2} \boxed{J}$

$C \xrightarrow{+2} E \xrightarrow{+2} G \xrightarrow{+2} \boxed{I}$

$X \xrightarrow{-2} V \xrightarrow{-2} T \xrightarrow{-2} \boxed{R}$

$W \xrightarrow{-2} U \xrightarrow{-2} S \xrightarrow{-2} \boxed{Q}$

$\therefore$ **JIRQ** will be the next term in the series.

96. (*a*) As, liquid state results from the process of melting. Similarly, solid state results from the process of freezing.

97. (*a*) The pattern of the series is,
$$(2)^3 - 2 = 6 \ , (3)^3 - 2 = 25$$
$$(4)^3 - 2 = 62 \ , \qquad (5)^3 - 2 = 123$$
$$(6)^3 - 2 = 214 \ , \qquad (7)^3 - 2 = 341$$
$$(8)^3 - 2 = \boxed{510}$$

98. (*d*) The pattern of the series is,

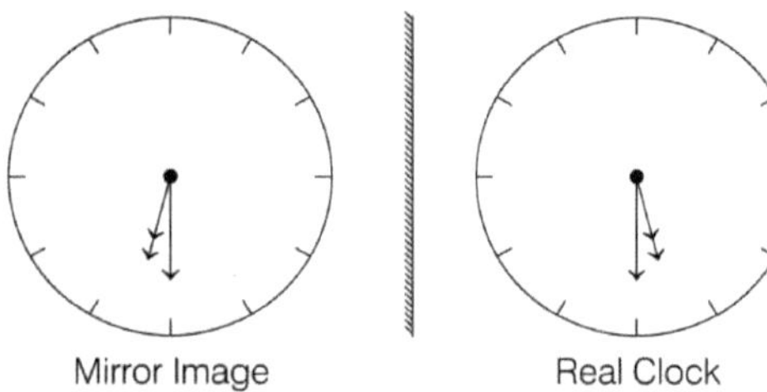

$\therefore$ 103 is the wrong term.

99. (*a*)

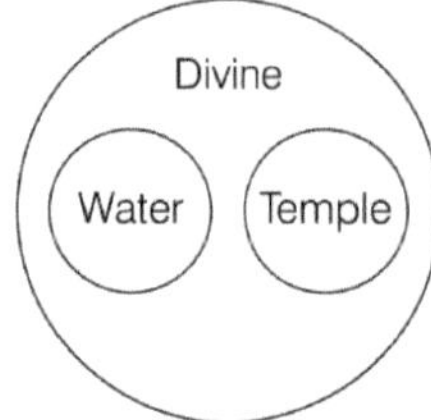

Mirror Image   Real Clock

Hence, real time $= 5 : 30$

100. (*d*) In each subsequent figure, the main figure rotates $90°$ in clockwise direction. So, option figure (d) will replace the question mark.

101. (*d*) In each subsequent figure, the arrow rotates $135°$ in clockwise direction. So, option figure (d) will replace the question mark.

102. (*b*) In each subsequent figure, the inner figure becomes outer and a new figure appears inside the outer figure.

So, option figure (b) will replace the question mark.

103. (*b*) Region E represents people who do not live in the city but travel by metro and also have a car.

104. (*c*) F and G represents people who live in the city and have a car.

105. (*a*) Region F represents people who live in a city, have a car and still travel in a metro.

106. (*d*) From the given statements,

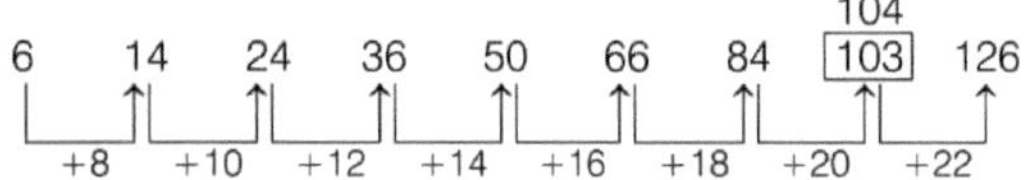

Conclusions I. (✗)   II. (✗)

So, neither Conclusion I nor II follows.

107. (*a*) From the given statements,

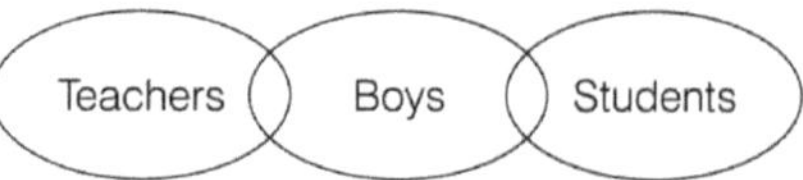

Conclusions I. (✓)   II. (✗)

So, only Conclusion I follows.

108. (*d*) From the given statements,

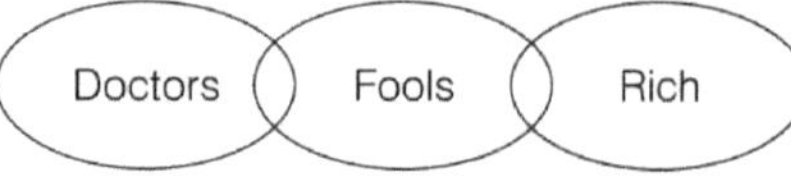

Conclusions I. (✗)   II. (✗)

So, neither Conclusion I nor II follows.

109. (*b*) Both (A) and (R) are true as, on equinoxes, the day and night are equal all over the globe and on the equinoxes, the position of earth with respect to the sun is such that neither pole is inclined towards the sun.

$\therefore$ (R) is the correct explanation of (A).

110. (*a*) 'A' is false as Uranium doesn't undergo fusion reaction, Uranium always undergo fission reaction.

'R' is true as Uranium has big and unstable nucleus.

111. (*b*) 'A' is true as no food material normally enters the wind pipe during swallowing.

'R' is true as when we swallow the back portion of our tongue covers the opening of the wind pipe and 'R' is the correct explanation of 'A'.

112. (*b*)

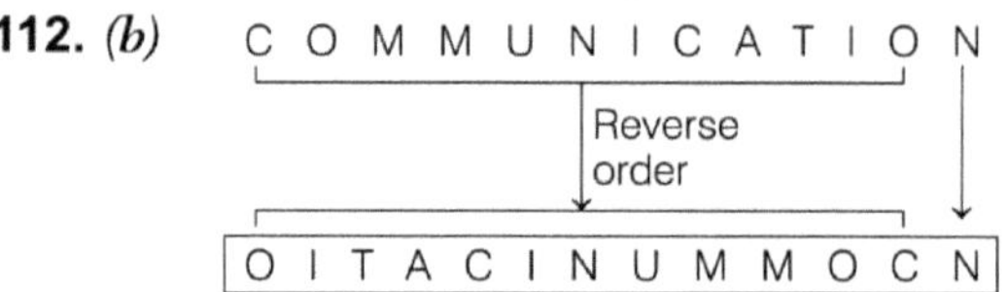

Similarly,

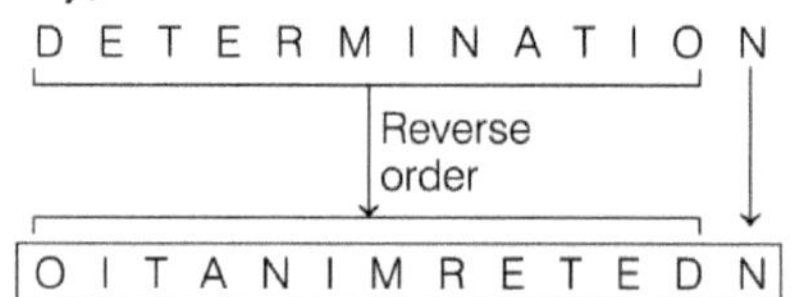

113. (*a*) Day on Republic Day i.e. 26 January = Saturday
Number of days between 26 January and 14 February $= 5 + 14 = 19$
$$= 2 \text{ weeks} + 5 \text{ odd days}$$
$\therefore$ Day on 14th February = Saturday $+ 5$ days
$$= \text{Thursday}$$

114. (*a*) Total students $= 45$
Let number of boys be 'a'.
$\therefore$ Number of girls $= 2a$
$\therefore \qquad a + 2a = 45$
or $\qquad a = \dfrac{45}{3} = 15$

Hence, number of boys $= 15$
Now, Ravi is ranked 11th from top and 5 girls are ahead of Ravi.
$\therefore$ Number of boys ahead of Ravi $= (10 - 5) = 5$
Hence, number of boys after Ravi in rank
$$= 15 - 5 - 1 = 9$$

115. *(d)* Daughter of grand mother is aunt of Rahul and only brother of Rahul's aunt is Rahul's father. So, Rahul defeated his father.

116. *(c)* Only daughter of Priya's father is Priya herself. So, Priya is mother of Rekha, or Rekha is daughter of Priya.

117. *(a)* 2 days after tomorrow $=$ Saturday
$\therefore$ Today $=$ Saturday $- 3$ days $=$ Wednesday

and 4 days before yesterday $=$ Wednesday $- 5$ days
$$= \text{Friday}$$

Sol. (Q. Nos. 118-120) *From the given information,*

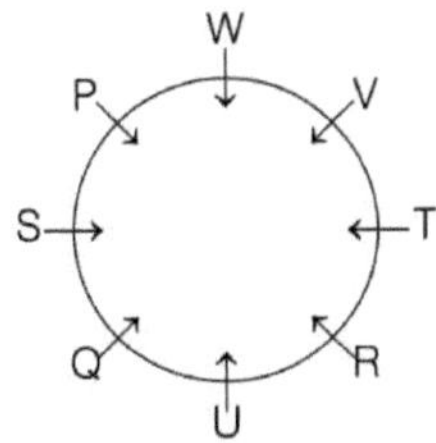

118. *(a)* Clearly, S is on the immediate left of Q.

119. *(a)* Clearly, V is third to the right of U.

120. *(a)* Clearly, V is between W and T.

National Council for Hotel Management and Catering Technology

Solved Paper 2018

Instructions

- There are Five (A-E) Sections in this Solved Paper.
- For every correct attempt, the student will be awarded **1 mark**.
- All the questions are in MCQs form and each having four options.

Marks : 200

Time : 3 hrs

Section A : Numerical Ability And Scientific Aptitude

1. The largest natural number by which the product of three consecutive even natural numbers is always divisible, is
  (a) 16   (b) 24   (c) 48   (d) 96

2. The least perfect square number which is divisible by 3, 4, 5, 6 and 8, is
  (a) 900   (b) 1200   (c) 2500   (d) 3600

3. The HCF and LCM of two numbers are 44 and 264 respectively. If the first number is divided by 2, the quotient is 44. The other number is
  (a) 33   (b) 66   (c) 132   (d) 264

4. By how much is 12% of 24.2 more than 10% of 14.2 ?
  (a) 0.1484   (b) 14.84   (c) 1.484   (d) 2.762

5. Sapan was asked to find $\dfrac{7}{9}$ of a fraction. But he made a mistake of dividing the given fraction by $\dfrac{7}{9}$ and got an answer which exceeded the correct answer by $\dfrac{8}{21}$. The correct answer is ......
  (a) $\dfrac{3}{7}$ (b) $\dfrac{7}{12}$ (c) $\dfrac{2}{21}$ (d) $\dfrac{1}{3}$

6. Bhuwan earns twice as much in January as in each of the other months. What part of his annual earnings he earns in that month?
  (a) $\dfrac{2}{13}$ (b) $\dfrac{1}{10}$ (c) $\dfrac{5}{7}$ (d) $\dfrac{1}{5}$

7. If $\sqrt{24} = 4.899$, then the value of $\sqrt{\dfrac{8}{3}}$ is ......
  (a) 0.544   (b) 2.666   (c) 1.633   (d) 1.333

8. By how much is 30% of 80 greater than $\dfrac{4}{5}$ th of 25?
  (a) 2   (b) 4   (c) 10   (d) 15

9. Out of three numbers, the first is twice the second and is half of the third. If the average of the three numbers is 56, then three numbers in order are
  (a) 48, 96, 24   (b) 48, 24, 96
  (c) 96, 24, 48   (d) 96, 48, 24

10. Three utensils contain equal mixtures of milk and water in the ratio 6 : 1, 5 : 2, and 3 : 1 respectively. If all the solutions are mixed together, find the ratio of milk and water in the final mixture.
  (a) 65 : 19   (b) 2 : 1   (c) 4 : 3   (d) 45 : 23

11. Sandeep lost 20% by selling a bicycle for ₹ 1536. What per cent shall he gain or lose by selling it for ₹ 2000?

(a) 2.25% (b) $4\dfrac{1}{6}\%$

(c) $\dfrac{6}{5}\%$ (d) $5\dfrac{3}{7}\%$

12. A can do a piece of work in 10 days, while B alone can do it in 15 days. They work together for 5 days and the rest of the work is done by C in 2 days. If they get ₹ 450 for the whole work, then how much amount should C get?

(a) ₹ 75 (b) ₹ 150 (c) ₹ 175 (d) ₹ 225

13. Two pipes A and B can fill a tank in 24 min and 32 min respectively. If both the pipes are opened simultaneously, after how much time pipe B should be closed so that the tank is full in 18 min?

(a) 6 min (b) 9 min (c) 8 min (d) 12 min

14. A man cycles from A to B, a distance of 21 km in 1 h 40 min. The road from A is level for 13 km and then it is uphill to B. The man's average speed on level is 15 km/h. Find his average uphill speed.

(a) 9 km/h (b) 10 km/h
(c) 11 km/h (d) 12 km/h

15. A person sees a train passing over 1 km long bridge. The length of the train is half that of bridge. If the train clears the bridge in 2 min, the speed of the train is

(a) 50 km/h (b) 45 km/h
(c) 60 km/h (d) 30 km/h

16. In a stream running at 2 km/h, a motor boat goes 10 km upstream and back again to the starting point in 55 min. Find the speed of motor boat in still water.

(a) 18 km/h (b) 20 km/h
(c) 22 km/h (d) 24 km/h

17. The difference between the ages of two persons is 10 yr. 15 yr ago, the elder one was twice as old as the younger one. The present age of the elder person is

(a) 25 yr (b) 35 yr (c) 45 yr (d) 55 yr

18. A lent ₹ 600 to B for 2 yr and ₹150 to C for 4 yr and received altogether from both ₹ 90 as simple interest. The rate of interest is ....

(a) 4% (b) 5% (c) 10% (d) 12%

19. A sum of ₹ 550 was taken as a loan. This is to be repaid in two equal annual installments. If the rate of interest be 20% compounded annually, then the value of each installment is ....

(a) ₹ 421 (b) ₹ 396
(c) ₹ 360 (d) ₹ 350

20. A butler stole wine from a butt of sherry which contained 40% of spirit and he replaced what he had stolen by wine containing only 16% spirit. The butt was then of 24% strength only. How much of the wine did he steal?

(a) $\dfrac{2}{3}$ (b) $\dfrac{1}{3}$

(c) $\dfrac{1}{2}$ (d) $\dfrac{1}{4}$

Directions (Q. Nos. 21-25) *The following table shows the number of new employees added to different categories of employees in a company and also the number of employees from these categories who left the company every year since the foundation of the company in 2012.*

Year	Managers New	Managers Left	Technicians New	Technicians Left	Operators New	Operators Left	Accountants New	Accountants Left	Peons New	Peons Left
2012	760	–	1200	–	880	–	1160	–	820	–
2013	280	120	272	120	256	104	200	100	184	96
2014	179	92	240	128	240	120	224	104	152	88
2015	148	88	236	96	208	100	248	96	196	80
2016	160	72	256	100	192	112	272	88	224	120
2017	193	96	288	112	248	144	260	92	200	104

21. During the period between 2012 and 2017, the total number of operators who left the company is what per cent of the total number of operators who joined the company?

(a) 20% (b) 23%
(c) 29% (d) 31%

22. For which of the following categories, the percentage increase in the number of employees working in the company from 2012 to 2017 was the maximum?

(a) Peons (b) Managers
(c) Accountants (d) Technicians

23. What is the difference between the total number of Technicians added to the company and the total number of Accountants added to the company during the years 2013 to 2017 ?

(a) 88 (b) 93
(c) 110 (d) 118

24. What was the total number of Peons working in the company in the year 2016?
(a) 912 (b) 1192
(c) 1244 (d) 1292

25. What is the pooled average of the total number of employees of all categories in the year 2014?
(a) 1115 (b) 1155
(c) 1195 (d) 1235

Directions (Q. Nos. 26-30) *Study the following graph to answer these questions.*

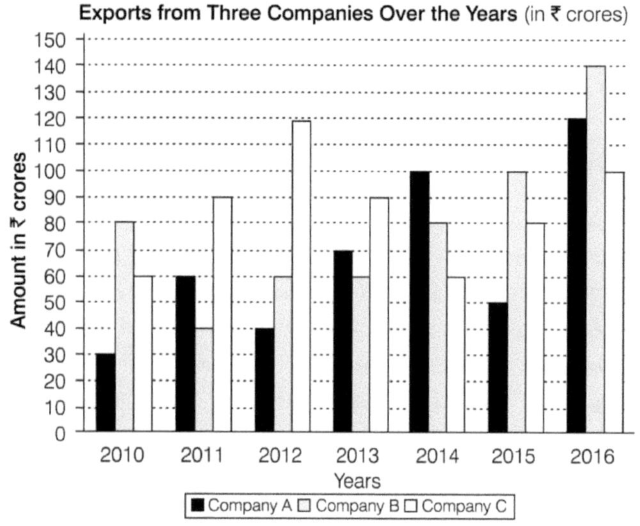

26. Average annual exports during the given period for Company B is approximately what per cent of the average annual exports for Company C ?
(a) 86.10% (b) 88.62%
(c) 90.45% (d) 93.33%

27. In how many of the given years, were the exports from Company C more than the average annual exports over the given years?
(a) 3 (b) 4
(c) 5 (d) 6

28. What was the difference between the average exports of the three Companies in 2010 and the average exports in 2015?
(a) ₹ 16.12 crore (b) ₹ 17.75 crore
(c) ₹ 20.00 crore (d) ₹ 21.80 crore

29. In which year was the difference between the exports from Companies A and B the minimum?
(a) 2011 (b) 2013
(c) 2014 (d) 2015

30. For which of the following pairs of years, the total exports from the three Companies together are equal?
(a) 2012 and 2013 (b) 2013 and 2015
(c) 2014 and 2015 (d) 2012 and 2015

Section B : Reasoning and Logical Deduction

Directions (Q. Nos. 31-33) *Each of the following questions is based on the following information.*
(i) 'P × Q' means 'P is the father of Q'.
(ii) 'P – Q' means 'P is the sister of Q'.
(iii) 'P + Q' means 'P is the mother of Q'.
(iv) 'P ÷ Q' means 'P is the brother of Q'.

31. Which of the following represent 'R is the niece of M'?
(a) M ÷ K × T – R (b) M – J + R – N
(c) R – M × T ÷ W (d) K ÷ M × R + T

32. In the expression B + D × M ÷ N, how is M related to B?
(a) Granddaughter (b) Daughter
(c) Grandson (d) Son

33. Which of the following represents 'J is the son of F'?
(a) J ÷ R – T × F (b) J + R – T × F
(c) J ÷ M – N × F (d) None of these

Directions (Q. Nos. 34-36) *Each of the following questions is based on the information given below.*
A, B, C, D, E, F, G and H are sitting around a circle facing at the centre. G is fourth to the right of A who is second to the right of D. E is second to the right of C who is not an immediate neighbour of G. B is second to the right of F.

34. Which of the following is sitting third to the right of H?
(a) A (b) D
(c) B (d) F

35. What is F's position with respect to C?
(A) Fourth to the left
(B) Fifth to the left
(C) Fourth to the right
(D) Third to the right
Choose the correct option.
(a) Only (A) (b) Only (D)
(c) (A) and (C) (d) (B) and (C)

36. In which of the following pairs is the first person sitting to the immediate right of the second person?

(a) BD   (b) EG

(c) GF   (d) HE

Directions (Q. Nos. 37-39) *Complete the series by replacing '?'.*

37. 1, 3, 6, 11, '?', 37, 70

(a) 3   (b) 37

(c) 11   (d) 20

38. Q1F, S2E, U6D, W21C, '?'

(a) Y66B   (b) Y44B

(c) Y88B   (d) Z88B

39. WFB, TGD, QHG, NIK, '?'

(a) PJL   (b) KJP

(c) NIJ   (d) KJH

Directions (Q. Nos. 40-42) *In each of these questions, choose the incorrect term.*

40. 7, 12, 19, 28, 35, 52, 67, 84, 103

(a) 19   (b) 35

(c) 67   (d) 103

41. 42, 40, 36, 34, 30, 28, 26, 22, 18, 16

(a) 26   (b) 40

(c) 18   (d) 34

42. 5, 9, 11, 33, 65, 129, 257

(a) 5   (b) 65

(c) 11   (d) 129

Directions (Q. Nos. 43-45) *In each of the following questions, find out the alternative which will replace the question mark.*

43. Indolence : Work : : Taciturn : ?

(a) Act   (b) Speak   (c) Cheat   (d) Observe

44. Chef : Restaurant : : Druggist : ?

(a) Pharmacy   (b) Medicine

(c) Chemist   (d) Store

45. Cringe : Fear : : Yawn : ?

(a) Delighted   (b) Worry

(c) Boredom   (d) Anger

Directions (Q. Nos. 46-48) *Each of these questions consists of two sets. Figures (1), (2), (3), (4) and (5) constitute the set of Question Figures and figures (a), (b), (c) and (d) constitute the set of Answer Figures. There is a definite relationship among figures (1), (2), (3), (4) and (5). Select a suitable figure from the answer figures (a), (b), (c), (d) which establishes a similar relationship after figure (5).*

46. Question Figures

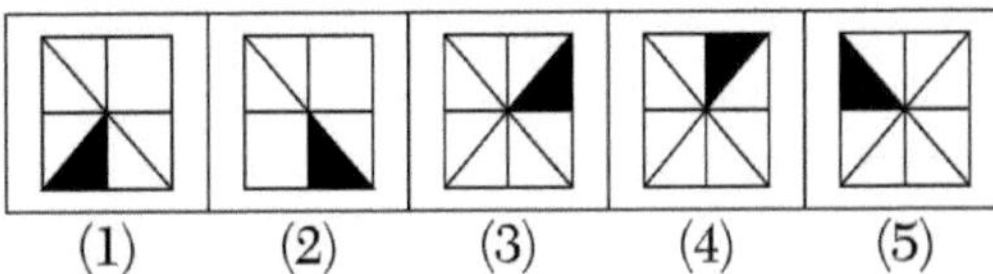

Answer Figures

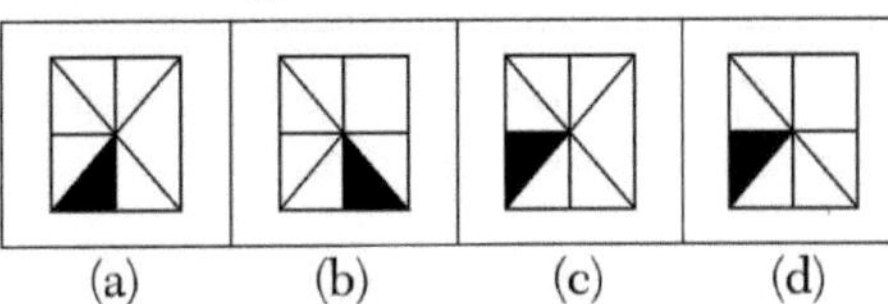

47. Question Figures

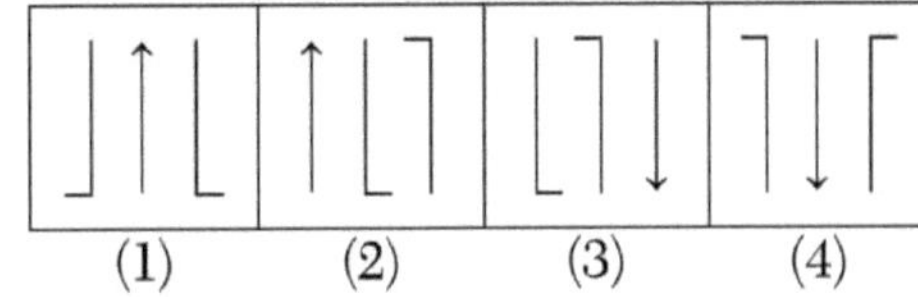

Answer Figures

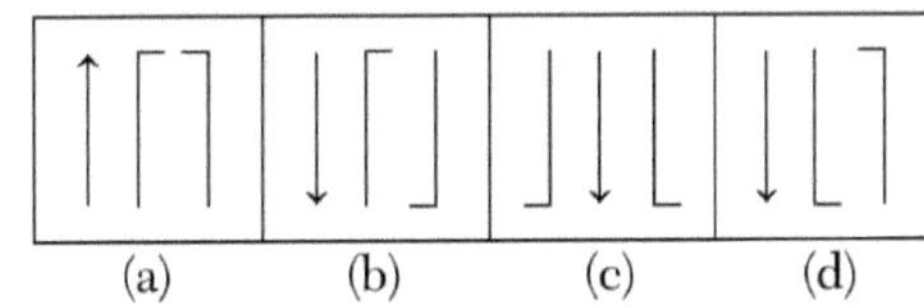

48. Question Figures

○	□	S	△□	‖	C	S‖	↑
△	×	○	□S	△□	‖	C	S
(1)		(2)	(2)		(4)		(5)

Answer Figures

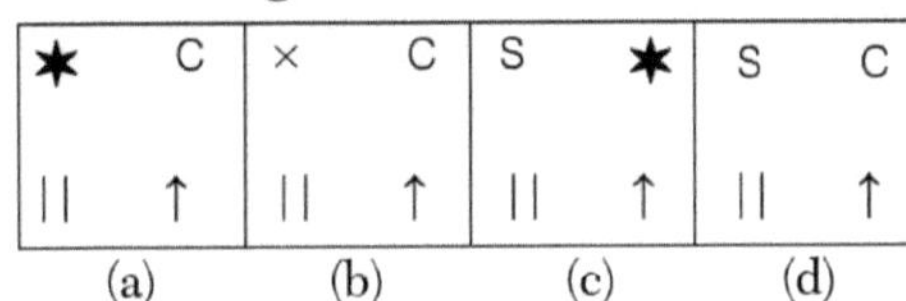

Directions (Q. Nos. 49-51) *Study the following figure to answer these questions.*

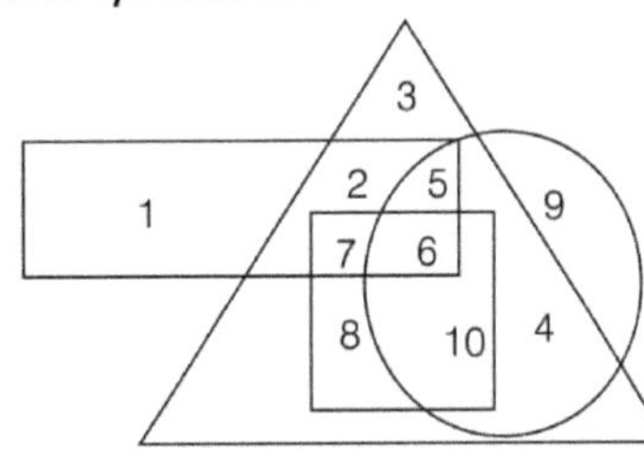

The rectangle represents government employees, the triangle represents urban people, the circle represents graduates and the square represents clerks.

49. Which of the following numbers represents clerks who are government employees and urban?

(a) 2   (b) 6   (c) 7   (d) 11

50. Which of the following statements is true?

(a) All government employees are graduates
(b) Some urban people are not graduates
(c) No clerk is urban
(d) None of the above

51. Which of the following numbers represents urban people who are graduates but neither government employees nor clerks?

(a) 4   (b) 5   (c) 6   (d) 9

Directions (Q. Nos. 52-54) *In each of the following questions, a conclusion is followed by Statements* I *and* II. *Mark answer as*

(a) if the Statement I alone in needed to draw the conclusion
(b) if the Statement II alone is needed to draw the conclusion
(c) if both the Statements I and II are needed to draw the conclusion
(d) if both the Statements I and II are not sufficient to draw the conclusion

52. Most villagers are uneducated and therefore superstitious.

I. Education increases rationality.
II. Villagers do not go to schools.

53. Detergents should be used to clean clothes.

I. Detergents form more lather.
II. Detergents help to dislodge grease and dirt.

54. Vegetable prices are soaring in the market.

I. Vegetables are becoming a rare commodity.
II. People cannot eat vegetables.

Directions (Q. Nos. 55-57) *Each of these questions has an Assertion* (A) *and a Reason* (R).
Mark answer as

(a) if both (A) and (R) are true and (R) is the correct explanation of (A)
(b) if both (A) and (R) are true but (R) is not the correct explanation of (A)
(c) if (A) is true but (R) is false
(d) if (A) is false but (R) is true

55. **Assertion** (A) When the bus suddenly starts, the person inside it falls backward.

Reason (R) The bus pushes the persons forward.

56. **Assertion** (A) Increase in carbon dioxide would melt polar ice.

Reason (R) Global temperature would rise.

57. **Assertion** (A) Water kept in earthen pots gets cooled in summer.

Reason (R) Evaporation causes cooling.

58. In a certain code language, DISTANCE is written as IDTUNADF and DOCUMENT is written as ODDVEMOU. How is THURSDAY written in that language?

(a) HTVSYTEB   (b) DTVSETZB
(c) HTVSDSBZ   (d) DTTQYRBE

59. Pointing to a person, Ashish said, "His only brother is the father of my daughter's father". How is the person related to Ashish?

(a) Father   (b) Brother-in-law
(c) Brother   (d) Uncle

60. Ramesh is 7 ranks ahead of Khan in a class of 39. If Khan's rank is seventeenth from the last, what is Ramesh's rank from the start?

(a) 11th   (b) 13th
(c) 16th   (d) 18th.

Section C : General Knowledge and Current Affairs

61. In India, the Tropic of Cancer does not pass through which of the following states?

(a) Rajasthan   (b) Chhattisgarh
(c) Mizoram   (d) Meghalaya

62. In which district of Karnataka is the historic place 'Hampi' located?

(a) Bijapur   (b) Bellary
(c) Gulbarga   (d) Raichur

63. The most famous musician at the court of Mughal Emperor Akbar was Tansen. His original name was

(a) Baz Bahadur   (b) Mukund Pandey
(c) Ram Chand   (d) Ramtanu Pandey

64. The Reserve Bank of India has recently introduced ₹ 50 denomination banknotes in the Mahatma Gandhi Series with motif of .... on the reverse.

(a) Qutub Minar   (b) Konark Sun Temple
(c) Hampi with Chariot   (d) Charminar

65. At what temperature does water have the highest density?

(a) – 1°C   (b) 0°C   (c) 4°C   (d) 100°C

66. Who among the following Mughal emperors initiated Din-I-Ilahi?
(a) Shah Jahan (b) Aurangzeb
(c) Akbar (d) Jahangir

67. From which country's Constitution has the Constitution of India borrowed the principle of 'Concurrent List'?
(a) England (b) U.S.A.
(c) Australia (d) Germany

68. The study of heavenly bodies is known as ....
(a) Astrology (b) Astronautics
(c) Astronomy (d) Astrophysics
Ans. (c)

69. The boundary line between India and China is called ....
(a) Radcliffe Line (b) Durand Line
(c) McMahon Line (d) 20th Parallel

70. The world famous 'Khajuraho' sculptures are located in .....
(a) Gujarat (b) Maharashtra
(c) Odisha (d) Madhya Pradesh

71. Which of the following musical instruments is said to have been invented by Amir Khusrau?
(a) Sarangi (b) Sarod
(c) Sitar (d) Veena

72. Who has become the new Chairman of Indian Space Research Organisation (ISRO) in January 2018?
(a) K. Sivan (b) A.S. Kiran Kumar
(c) K. Radhakrishnan (d) None of these

73. Where does the one of the largest ice and snow festivals in the world 'Harbin International Ice and Snow Sculpture Festival' take place annually?
(a) Canada (b) Russia
(c) China (d) Norway

74. Which one of the following after 'Yoga' and 'Nouroz' has been recently listed as an intangible Cultural Heritage under UNESCO?
(a) Jagannath Rath Yatra (b) Kumbh Mela
(c) Pushkar Mela (d) Puri Rath Yatra

75. Which of the following personalities has never served as President of India?
(a) Pratibha Patil
(b) Zakir Hussain
(c) Shankar Dayal Sharma
(d) Jawaharlal Nehru

76. Which part of our body gets affected by jaundice?
(a) Kidney (b) Liver
(c) Lung (d) Brain

77. India celebrated its .... Republic Day on 26th January, 2018.
(a) 67th (b) 68th (c) 69th (d) 70th

78. Popular 'Real Fruit Juice' belongs to which of the following companies?
(a) Nestle (b) Britannia
(c) Parle (d) Dabur

79. Shubhankar Sharma is an Indian sportsperson associated with
(a) archery (b) golf
(c) table tennis (d) wrestling

80. The famous 'The Leela Palaces, Hotels and Resorts' is founded by
(a) Jamshedji N Tata (b) Capt. C.P.K. Nair
(c) M.S. Oberoi (d) Lalit Suri

81. What is the name of the India's fastest and first multi-petaflops supercomputer recently installed at IITM, Pune in January 2018?
(a) Vardhan (b) Prayaag
(c) Harsh (d) Pratyush

82. 'Swiggy', a food ordering and delivery company is from
(a) USA (b) India
(c) Switzerland (d) Singapore

83. Which Indian cricketer has recently released his autobiography 'A Century Is Not Enough'?
(a) Sourav Ganguly (b) Rahul Dravid
(c) Sachin Tendulkar (d) Anil Kumble

84. 'Wok to Walk' is a fast food takeaway restaurant chain specialised in wok stir-fried Asian cuisine which served in oyster pails is from.......
(a) China (b) Canada
(c) Australia (d) Netherlands

85. Justin Trudeau, who came to India in February 2018 along with his/her family for a 7-day visit is the Prime Minister of ....
(a) Cambodia (b) Sri Lanka
(c) Canada (d) Kenya

86. Where did Amazon test drives Food Retail Venture in India in February 2018 to become first foreign e-commerce company to stock and sell food items directly to consumers?
(a) Gurugram (b) Bhopal
(c) Kolkata (d) Pune

87. Which female gymnast has created history in February 2018 when she became the India's first World Cup medal winner with a bronze?
(a) Dipa Karmakar   (b) Aruna Reddy
(c) Sakshi Malik   (d) Babita Kumari

88. The Indian Hotels Company (IHCL) and its subsidiaries, are collectively known by the name
(a) The Lalit Hotels
(b) The Park Hotels
(c) The Taj Group
(d) The ITC Group

89. 'Himalayan', the popular mineral water is from the house of
(a) Reliance   (b) Tata
(c) Adani   (d) PepsiCo

90. In February 2018, Turkmenistan, Afghanistan, Pakistan and India have ceremonially broke ground on ..... section of ambitious, multi-billion dollar TAPI gas pipeline connecting central Asia with South Asia covering 1840 km.
(a) Turkmenistan   (b) Afghanistan
(c) Pakistan   (d) India

Section D : Aptitude For Service Sector

91. A park in front of your house has hardly any trees. Your neighbours have often expressed their desire to plant trees in the park. You will
(a) not be interested in the matter since it is a community work.
(b) expect some neighbour to take initiative and start the project.
(c) ask some neighbour to start planting trees with others help.
(d) take initiative yourself and start the work, while also asking others to help.

92. A family staying nearby your house has a kid who is a child with special needs. Most people in your locality avoid any interactions with the family. You will
(a) request family staying next door to help the family, if possible.
(b) try and ignore the family like many others.
(c) visit them and render whatever help you could render.
(d) keep contact with them regularly and ask others to visit them and provide assistance as needed.

93. Pollution levels in the metro town you stay have reached dangerous proportions. People discuss this subject all the time. You will
(a) ask your friends to do something about the matter.
(b) think that this is to be dealt by the government only.
(c) criticise the government all the time for creating this situation.
(d) reduce the usage of your own car to the minimum and utilise public transport to the maximum.

94. Your close friend expresses a desire to organise a 'Blood Donation Camp' to collect blood for a local hospital. You will
(a) expect your friend to seek help from others and not disturb you.
(b) take active part in the project and get fully involved.
(c) tell him that it is not his job and you cannot help him in this venture.
(d) take limited interest and request others to help in the task.

95. To work efficiently in a social sector, which of the following personality traits is considered most significant?
(a) Perseverance and hard work
(b) Helping attitude
(c) Higher academic achievements
(d) Good looks

96. According to you, efforts made by our government to facilitate movements of handicapped people to reach public places is considered
(a) quite inadequate
(b) much more than needed
(c) needing considerable improvement
(d) highly adequate

97. If you are earning adequately from your business
(a) you need not give any money for charity, because you have earned it.
(b) you should regularly give money for charity.
(c) you may give some money for charity.
(d) you should give money for charity, if others are also giving.

98. If your servant is feeling too unwell and asks for leave, you will
(a) insist on his/her coming.
(b) ask her/him to arrange for some substitute.
(c) give him/her leave but deduct money as a punishment.
(d) understand her/his problem and grant leave.

99. In case your childhood friend wants to borrow some money from you, you will
(a) tell him that on principle, you do not lend money.
(b) ignore his request and avoid discussion on this subject.
(c) ask your friend to ask somebody else to help him out.
(d) spare the money he wants and help him out.

100. A person staying opposite to your house parks his car in your parking slot almost everyday. You will
(a) shout at him and create a scene to embarrass him.
(b) bring this to the notice of other neighbours and tell him that he is doing a wrong thing.
(c) ignore this development but look for an opportunity to talk to him.
(d) politely tell him to avoid parking his car in your area.

101. While travelling in a train, you notice an old man standing in a reserved compartment. You will
(a) ask him to leave the reserved compartment.
(b) tell him he should not have entered the compartment.
(c) try and ignore him and mind your business.
(d) make space for him and let him sit down for the time being.

102. According to you, which of the following is the main reason due to which people in India hesitate to take road accident victims to hospitals to save lives?
(a) People hate to help.
(b) People are very busy.
(c) People are scared of interaction with the police.
(d) Nobody wants to take extra burden/effort.

103. Which of the following is considered to be one of the most desirable quality for a person working in service sector?
(a) Good health
(b) Team work
(c) Helping attitude
(d) Patience

104. While going on the road, you see two young boys shouting at each other and may even hit each other anytime. You will
(a) also shout even louder and ask them to behave properly.
(b) ask them to calm down and resolve the matter amicably.
(c) mind your own business and carry on.
(d) expect some other person to intervene and resolve the issue between them.

105. You love to talk on your mobile phone and talk to your friends for a long time everyday. Your wife and children often tell you that they get disturbed by such noise of your talking. You will
(a) shout at them and ask them to shut up.
(b) realise your mistake and talk less and also softly.
(c) not bother about what they say.
(d) ask them to go to some other room when you are talking on phone.

106. A person staying across your house often installs loudspeakers and plays religious music loudly, which disturbs everybody a great deal. You will
(a) try and ignore the issue.
(b) go and pick up a fight with him to stop this music.
(c) discuss the issue with other neighbours and ask their opinion.
(d) politely request him to play the music softly so that it does not disturb others unnecessarily.

107. You observe a lady in your neighbourhood everyday in the night feeds stray dogs with milk and bread. You feel
(a) dogs and stray animals should find their own food.
(b) giving them food is not appropriate as it should be consumed by human beings only.
(c) human beings should share some food with stray animals as well.
(d) we may give animals some food, if it is spare.

108. A very large number of Non-Governmental Organisations (NGOs) are active in our country. Some take government funds and others raise their own funds. You feel
(a) some NGOs are really doing a very good job to serve the society.
(b) most NGOs are misappropriating funds and not doing their assigned job.
(c) the concept of NGOs is a hopeless concept.
(d) most NGOs are doing a good work.

109. Near your house there is a huge slum. Whenever you pass through this area, you feel
(a) people who stay in this slum should be asked to shift elsewhere.
(b) government should provide them alternate accommodation to shift out.
(c) people who stay in this slum must be forced to shift elsewhere.
(d) this slum should be burnt as it has no business to be there.

110. While working in a hotel as an Assistant Manager, you find a guest too demanding and even misbehaved with you. You will
(a) tell him firmly that he is too demanding.

HM 2018

(b) inform your superior and politely explain to him what you are doing to help him.

(c) ignore the guest and mind your business.

(d) shout at him and ask him to behave properly.

111. With a large number of young men and young women working abroad, their old parents feel neglected in India and need old age care urgently. You feel

(a) the problem is not significant for the society.

(b) young people abroad must make some arrangements for their parents.

(c) since a lot of old people are affected, government should build old age homes.

(d) they must look after themselves as this situation is their own creation.

112. In big towns, a large number of very good schools are coming up. But due to high fee structure, only rich can send their kids to such schools. You feel

(a) some seats should be reserved for the poor as well.

(b) rich and poor kids studying together is not desirable.

(c) admission should be given to all based on merit.

(d) poor children should not dream to study in such schools.

113. While you are starting your car to go to office, your neighbour suddenly approaches you, seeking your help to take his mother to hospital, as she is not well. You will

(a) excuse yourself by saying that you were getting late for office.

(b) ask him to take help of some other neighbours.

(c) willingly escort the patient to the hospital yourself.

(d) get irritated and quickly proceed to your office.

114. Recently, statistical data revealed by the government shows that in India rich are getting richer, while poor are becoming more poor. You feel

(a) rich should share their wealth with poor by doing social work.

(b) we must accept the present situation, as nothing can be done about it.

(c) government must, create more jobs and employment opportunities for the poor on the highest priority.

(d) poor should not dream to become rich.

115. In the recent past, it has been reported that private hospitals have been running hospitals as a business venture and at the same time, showing carelessness towards patients. You feel

(a) that government must step into stop exploitation of patients by private hospitals.

(b) patients have no business to question hospitals as to what they charge and what care they provide to patients.

(c) private hospitals must charge reasonably to all patients.

(d) they are quite justified to charge more as they also provide modern facilities to the patients.

116. An assistant working under you does not turn up for work for three days without informing you. On his return, he informs that his son had to be taken to hospital. You will

(a) cut his salary for three days and warn him sternly.

(b) explain to him that he should have informed you about his problem and should not repeat this mistake again.

(c) ignore this lapse and counsel him appropriately.

(d) shout at him and initiate steps to sack him from the job.

117. When a blind man approaches you to help him with some money, you will

(a) ask him to approach somebody else.

(b) ignore him and move away from him.

(c) help him with whatever money you can spare.

(d) get angry and ask him to work and earn some money himself.

118. Your close friend, who is also a social worker, plans to organise a free medical check up for the poor people of your area. He approaches you to help him in this task, you will

(a) tell your friend bluntly that you are very busy with your work presently.

(b) try and find some time to assist him.

(c) be glad to help him and request other friends to also help him.

(d) think it is a sheer waste of time for you and will try and ignore your friend for a few days.

119. In the recent past, treatment of patients by reputed private hospitals has been much in the news. According to you presently patient care by these hospitals

(a) is highly satisfactory.

(b) is much beyond expectations.

(c) is just about satisfactory.

(d) needs much improvement.

120. During the last few years law and order situation in your colony has been deteriorating substantially. You will

(a) plan to shift to some other locality.

(b) try and manage with the existing situation.

(c) discuss with people of your colony and take the issue with concerned agencies / authorities.

(d) expect others to do the needful but apprise others of the prevailing condition.

121. During the past few years, tourism industry has progressed considerably. During this period, availability of hotel rooms desirable facilities and reasonable charges has
(a) decreased drastically (b) remained the same
(c) decreased marginally (d) increased somewhat

122. In your opinion, medical facilities in rural India are considered
(a) just about adequate
(b) highly satisfactory
(c) quite inadequate
(d) excellent and commendable

123. Your maid servant has been working for you for more than 5 years now. Suddenly she informs you that owing to some family issues, she wants to quit the job. You will
(a) get angry and tell her that she could not do so suddenly.
(b) give her salary and ask her to get out.
(c) ask her to complete the month and then leave by the month end.
(d) give her a patient hearing and then decide accordingly.

124. The airlines with whom you have booked your ticket suddenly informs you one day prior, that the flight is cancelled due to some technical reason. You will
(a) ask them to cancel your ticket and refund your money immediately.
(b) get angry and pick-up a fight with the airlines staff.
(c) lodge a complaint against the airlines with the concerned authority.
(d) book your ticket as per options offered by the same airlines on the same date.

125. While working in hotel industry as an executive, which of the following personality traits you think is most significant to deal with an angry and unreasonable customer?
(a) Good looks
(b) Higher intelligence
(c) Patience and tact
(d) Hard working attitude

126. While going on your scooter, you happen to slightly hit a cyclist inadvertently and cause him a minor injury. You will
(a) try to run away from the place of accident.
(b) get angry and abuse the cyclist for not driving carefully.
(c) hit the cyclist at the earliest and blame him fully for the accident.
(d) talk to the cyclist nicely and help him to go to the nearest clinic for treatment of his injury.

127. Your good friend one day suddenly gets angry and tries to misbehave with you. You will
(a) feel extremely bad and tell him that you did not expect this from him.
(b) tell him that you want to break up with him immediately.
(c) not feel bad but talk to him patiently and try to understand as to why did he behave in that fashion.
(d) also shout at him and tell him to behave properly.

128. While you are making a project and working in a group, you tend to
(a) dominate over other members of the team.
(b) do your very best to look after the project and help yourself as well.
(c) enjoy cooperating with other team members.
(d) lose interest in the project.

129. Your boss does not appreciate your work and continues to ignore you. You will
(a) get angry and ask your boss to behave properly.
(b) ask him politely as to why is he not happy and then try to adjust with what he tells you was the problem.
(c) ignore your boss and continue doing your duty.
(d) look for another job.

130. When your boss assigns you a big task, you tend to
(a) jump into it without any preparation.
(b) get annoyed and prefer to take long leave.
(c) prepare yourself adequately and then accept it.
(d) avoid it somehow by politely declining it.

131. You suddenly decide to visit your nephew and enjoy your holiday with him. On reaching his house, you realise that he is not keeping well and he did not extend the warmth you were expecting. You will
(a) tell him that you were highly disappointed with his behaviour.
(b) leave his house after a few hours, being badly hurt.
(c) stay with him and since he is not well, try and help him in whatever way you can.
(d) lose your cool and leave his house immediately after telling him that you will never see him again.

132. Your close relative has gifted you a birthday present, which you did not like much. You will
(a) openly express your dislike.
(b) request him to exchange the item.
(c) respect the feelings of the person and use the gift appropriately.
(d) give a hint that the gift is not of your liking.

133. While you went abroad on an official tour, on reaching your destination, you realise that your luggage has not arrived and it may take 3 to 4 days before you would receive it.
You will
(a) ignore the incident and forget about the luggage.
(b) lodge an official complaint with airlines and demand compensation for causing such terrible inconvenience.
(c) get extremely annoyed and go and pick up a fight with the airlines staff for such careless behaviour.
(d) request the airlines to deliver the luggage at the earliest possible.

134. The shopping complex near your house is not handicap friendly. Due to which old and people with special needs find it difficult to shop for their daily needs. You will
(a) take the subject with local authorities with the help of other people of your area.
(b) expect people with special needs to shop elsewhere.
(c) wait patiently for the concerned authorities to take some action to remedy the present situation.
(d) try and ignore this situation as it exists now.

135. The medicine you purchased from the nearby medical store is not curing your disease. You suspect the medicine to be spurious and not genuine. You will
(a) try and ignore the incident.
(b) ask other neighbours, if they had similar experience and if yes, then take up the matter with consumer court/other agencies.
(c) tell the medical store to change the medicine.
(d) ask others to take up the matter, if they also suspect that medicines sold by that medical store are not considered genuine.

136. In a recent direction by the Supreme Court of India, the court has directed that police should not harass people who bring victims of road accidents to hospitals. You feel this direction will
(a) not make any difference in the attitude of police personnel.
(b) discourage people to help road accident victims.
(c) encourage people to help road accident victims.
(d) encourage police people to harass people who are helping others.

137. Since two schools are located near your house, everyday both in the morning and afternoon, when schools open and close, there is complete road blockage due to so many vehicles, which causes tremendous inconvenience to all residents of the area. You will
(a) ask other residents of the area to do something about it.
(b) consider shifting out of the colony where you are presently staying.
(c) accept it as your fate and try to forget about it.
(d) take up the issue with police/other authorities through your Resident's Welfare Association (RWA) after taking other residents into confidence.

138. While staying in a reputed hotel room, you ordered your vegetarian food, but to your surprise, you see that you have been served a non-vegetarian dish as well. You will
(a) call the waiter who served the food and shout at him.
(b) vacate room of the hotel and stay elsewhere immediately.
(c) call the manager room-service and lodge a written complaint.
(d) inform the waiter and try and forget about the incident.

139. While you are functioning as a manager in a hotel, one of your senior staff members has started coming late for work and also misbehaved with other employees frequently. You will
(a) get angry and warn him verbally as well as in writing.
(b) not take it seriously and try and ignore his changed behavioural pattern.
(c) call him and counsel him to assess his problem and then try and help him as needed.
(d) initiate disciplinary action against him at the earliest to correct him.

140. While travelling in a Metro train you observe that a number of seats are reserved for ladies, old people and handicapped. You feel
(a) there is so much rush in Metro train, this reservation is highly inappropriate.
(b) this facility be avoided in all compartments and may be provided in a few.
(c) it is desirable since people in general do not care much for the old and the handicapped.
(d) this can be a reason for fights and arguments among people who are travelling, therefore should be avoided.

Section E : English Language

Directions (Q. Nos. 141-160) *Read the following passages carefully to answer the questions that follow.*

PASSAGE 1

It is a commonly held belief that quality and productivity are a function of technology or a set of new equipment. No doubt these are essential, but they alone are not sufficient for bringing about improvements in productivity or quality. It is the men and women behind the machines and the people who manage the technology who are critical in bringing about these improvements.

It has been a strange paradox of India's economic development that even though people are our most abundant resource, they have so far either been neglected or treated as liabilities rather than as assets. Part of the reason for this has been outdated labour laws which have been a deterrent for industrialists and employers, leading them to establish capital-intensive rather than labour-intensive operations.

The other reason has been a confrontationist attitude, both on the part of labour as well as managements. A change must come about in both of these factors, outside representation and leadership of unions, etc. need to change.

At the same time, the attitude of confrontation must change to one of cooperation and active collaboration.

141. Which of the following arguments has been emphasised in the paragraph?
(a) Only technology or a new set of equipment can improve quality and productivity.
(b) Only management behind any type of machines can improve quality and productivity.
(c) By managing the new technology, labour can bring about improvements in quality and productivity.
(d) Indian labour and management is neither quality nor productivity conscious.

142. India's strange contradiction of development is
(a) people are resourceful but new equipment is not given to them.
(b) people are resourceful but they are neglected.
(c) labour is not earnest and therefore it is no longer a liability.
(d) labour is inefficient but still it is pampered.

143. Capital-intensive operations can lead to
(a) strict labour laws   (b) new labour laws
(c) too many labour laws   (d) irrelevant labour laws

144. The opposite of 'deterrent' as used in the passage is
(a) help   (b) non-interference
(c) influence   (d) patronage

145. Labour-intensive operations can lead to
(a) better relations between labour and management
(b) fear of unemployment
(c) industrial process needing to employ many people
(d) None of the above

PASSAGE 2

Since the world has become industrialised, there has been an increase in the number of animal species that have either become extinct or are nearing extinction. Bengal tigers, for instance, which once roamed in the jungles in vast numbers, now number only 2,300 and by the year 2025 their population is estimated to go down to zero.

What is **alarming** about the case of the Bengal tiger is that this extinction will have been caused almost entirely by poachers who according to some sources, are not interested in material gain but in personal gratification.

This is an example of the callousness that is part of what is causing the problem of extinction. Animals like the Bengal tiger, as well as other endangered species, are a valuable part of the world's ecosystem. International laws protecting these animals must be enacted to ensure their survival and the survival of our planet.

Countries around the world have begun to deal with this problem in various ways. Some countries, in order to circumvent the problem, have allocated large amounts of land to animal reserves. They then, charge admission fee to help defray the costs of maintaining the parks and often must also depend on world organisations for support.

When they get the money, they can invest in equipment and patrols to protect the animals. Another solution that is an attempt to **stem the tide** of animal extinction is an international boycott of products made from endangered species. This seems fairly effective, but it will not by itself prevent animals from being hunted and killed.

146. What is the author's main concern in the passage?
(a) Problems of industrialisation
(b) The Bengal tiger
(c) Endangered species
(d) Callousness of man

147. According to the passage, poachers kill for
(a) material gain
(b) personal satisfaction
(c) Both (a) and (b)
(d) None of the above

148. Which of the following words is closest in meaning to the word **'alarming'**?
(a) Serious   (b) Dangerous
(c) Distressing   (d) Frightening

149. Certain species are becoming extinct because of
  - (a) industrialisation
  - (b) poaching
  - (c) love of products made from them
  - (d) All of the above

150. The phrase 'stem the tide' means
  - (a) save
  - (b) stop
  - (c) touch
  - (d) spare

PASSAGE 3

According to the research findings of a team of American scientists published recently, the sea waves contain as much energy as the world is consuming at present. Scientists have found that through the application of two major devices called land-based systems and offshore devices, this source of energy can provide huge amount of electricity without cooling towers and pollution.

Land-based systems include tapered channels and fixed Oscillation Water Column (OWC) devices whereas offshore devices include floating OWC devices, buoys, etc. Through these devices the mechanical energy of ocean waves is absorbed and converted into electrical energy.

The wave power potential depends on numerous factors such as the device's capability to harness long wavelengths, period of waves and depth of water where they arise.

Compared to conventional power stations which require greater space and are difficult to maintain in critical situations, wave power devices are highly modular, cost effective and easier to upgrade.

As the recent findings suggest, sea wave energy has much greater potential to be used for electricity generation than the hitherto known sources of renewable energy.

Moreover, most of the renewable energy systems require hundreds of square acres of useful land for their installation. But in case of wave energy devices, 'space crunch' can never be a serious problem.

151. Harnessing energy from sea waves
  - (a) undermines ecological balance
  - (b) requires huge capital
  - (c) requires high technical expertise
  - (d) results in saving of useful land area

152. Which one of the following statements is correct?
  - (a) Wind energy is converted into mechanical power.
  - (b) Mechanical energy of ocean waves is converted into electrical energy.
  - (c) Conventional power stations are easy to maintain in critical situation.
  - (d) None of the above

153. Which one of the following statements is correct?
  - (a) Fixed as well as floating oscillating water column devices are required to harness ocean wave energy.
  - (b) Fixed oscillating water column devices are required for offshore based system.
  - (c) Floating oscillating water column devices are required for land-based.
  - (d) Electricity generated from oceans is independent of the depth of water where waves arise.

154. The capacity of system to generate electricity from ocean waves
  - (a) can be increased only at exorbitant cost.
  - (b) can be easily upgraded.
  - (c) can be increased but it requires a great space.
  - (d) is only a few megawatts.

155. Which one of the following statements is not correct?
  - (a) Conventional power stations require cooling towers.
  - (b) Power generation from ocean waves also adds to pollution like conventional power stations.
  - (c) Ocean wave energy can meet all the present energy of the world.
  - (d) Period of waves is one of the relevant factors in power generation from ocean waves.

PASSAGE 4

It is said that once three old men set out on a journey together. One of them was bald, the second was a philosopher and the third was a barber. At nightfall they decided that each one of them should keep a vigil turn by turn.

The barber was to keep watch first of all, the philosopher after that and the bald man last of all. So, the philosopher and the bald man went to sleep and the barber was on watch. For sometime he kept awake but in the end, he felt tired and he thought of some diversion as otherwise it was difficult for him to pass time.

Then he took out the razor from his box and shaved the head of the philosopher. At the fixed time, he woke up the philosopher and went to sleep. When the philosopher got up and felt his head all over, he was startled and said in surprise, "It was my turn but this wretched fellow has awakened the bald man."

156. Why did the philosopher get up?
  - (a) He realised that his head was being shaved off.
  - (b) It was his turn to keep watch.
  - (c) He was awakened by the barber.
  - (d) He had a bad dream.

157. Who went to sleep first?
    (a) The philosopher and the barber.
    (b) The barber and the bald man.
    (c) The bald man and the philosopher.
    (d) The barber.

158. Why did the barber shave off the head of the philosopher?
    (a) The barber was jealous of the philosopher.
    (b) The barber wanted to indulge in some fun.
    (c) The barber wanted the philosopher to keep watch.
    (d) The barber was feeling drowsy.

159. Which one of the following is the correct sequence decided upon the three to keep watch turn by turn?
    (a) Barber – bald man – philosopher
    (b) Bald man – philosopher – barber
    (c) Barber – philosopher – bald man
    (d) Bald man – barber – philosopher

160. Which one of the following statements is not correct?
    (a) All the three men decided to keep watch one by one.
    (b) The barber woke up the bald man.
    (c) The head of the philosopher was shaved off.
    (d) The philosopher was startled on feeling his head all over.

Directions (Q. Nos. 161-166) *Fill in the blanks.*

161. If you had followed the rules, you .... disqualified.
    (a) will not be   (b) would not be
    (c) will not have been   (d) would not have been

162. .... she is clever, she often makes mistakes.
    (a) Despite   (b) Since
    (c) Although   (d) Yet

163. Tables are usually made .... wood.
    (a) from   (b) of
    (c) with   (d) by

164. She has been supporting her family .... her husband's death.
    (a) on   (b) at
    (c) from   (d) since

165. Smallpox has been eradicated .... India.
    (a) in   (b) from
    (c) within   (d) out of

166. Did the child .... from the chair?
    (a) fell   (b) fallen
    (c) falling   (d) fall

Directions (Q. Nos. 167-172) *Each of these questions consists of a sentence which is divided into four parts, numbered (a) to (d). Identify the part which contains an error.*

167. (a) My observation is
    (b) that between
    (c) Sudhakar and Shashi
    (d) Shashi is the most intelligent

168. (a) You had better
    (b) to stop
    (c) your work for sometime and listen
    (d) to what I say

169. (a) You can accomplish
    (b) a great deal more
    (c) in a day if one gets up
    (d) early in the morning

170. (a) No sooner did
    (b) the bus arrived at the bus stand
    (c) than the passengers
    (d) rushed towards it to get a seat

171. (a) Through careful
    (b) practice in writing
    (c) one eventually learns to express
    (d) themselves effectively

172. (a) We can't hardly believe that the
    (b) situation is so serious as
    (c) to justify such precautions
    (d) as you have taken

Directions (Q. Nos. 173-184) *In each of the following passage some numbered blank spaces are given. For each numbered blank space answer choices are given. Pick out the one which is the most appropriate for that blank space. Keep the trend of the passage in mind.*
Patriotism is one of the qualities that touches the hearts of the ...(173).... countrymen. When a soldier fights and dies in saving his country from the enemy, his sacrifice in this way is termed as ...(174)... and attains the ....(175)... worthy of worship. Thus, in a war the soldier gets ...(176)... without surrendering, by which he ...(177)... saved his life, ...(178)... the hearts of his fellow being. This situation is true not only in ...(179).... an enemy but for anyone who struggles to achieve a ...(180).... aim without surrendering and ... (181).... his life. He ...(182)... succeeded but he leaves a ...(183).... for others to follow who will definitely win and attain victory ..... (184).... their adversaries.

173. (a) humble   (b) rustic
    (c) fellow   (d) sophisticated

174. (a) intelligent   (b) virtuous
    (c) supreme   (d) courageous

175. (a) death   (b) martyrdom
    (c) end   (d) goal

176. (a) vanquished   (b) vanguard
    (c) reward   (d) award

177. (a) would have had   (b) would be able to
    (c) would have   (d) could have

178. (a) attracting   (b) winning
    (c) taking   (d) getting

179. (a) struggling   (b) killing
    (c) winning   (d) fighting

180. (a) esteemed   (b) high
    (c) patriotic   (d) laudable

181. (a) offers   (b) sacrifices
    (c) lays   (d) present

182. (a) could have   (b) could not have
    (c) may have   (d) may not have

183. (a) trail   (b) trial
    (c) goal   (d) situation

184. (a) upon   (b) over
    (c) on   (d) against

Directions (Q. Nos. 185-190) *Choose the word/phrase nearest in meaning to the underlined part.*

185. She was not able to <u>make up her mind</u> in selecting a college.
(a) be prepared
(b) make someone happy
(c) make a decision
(d) criticise someone

186. The girl didn't say anything, but her mother could tell by <u>reading between the lines</u> that something is wrong.
(a) understanding the hidden meaning
(b) have good sight
(c) learn quickly
(d) be intelligent

187. She penned her feelings in a letter and posted it to him. Now, <u>the ball was in his court</u>.
(a) final decision rests on him
(b) her letter has reached him
(c) he had nothing to say
(d) he was caught in a trap

188. When he heard that he had once again not been selected, he <u>lost heart</u>.
(a) felt sad   (b) became unwell
(c) became angry   (d) became discouraged

189. Dowry is <u>a burning question</u> of the day.
(a) widely debated issue   (b) relevant solution
(c) irrelevant issue   (d) dying issue

190. There is no <u>hard and fast rule</u> regarding the dress to be worn in the party.
(a) rule that is fast changing
(b) rule that cannot be broken or modified
(c) rule that can be broken or modified
(d) rule that is difficult

Directions (Q. Nos. 191-196) *In each of the following questions, choose the option which can be substituted for the given words/sentence.*

191. A disease which spreads by contact.
(a) Incurable   (b) Infectious
(c) Contagious   (d) Fatal

192. An intense and unreasonable fear or dislike of a particular thing or situation.
(a) Horror   (b) Scare
(c) Phobia   (d) Fright

193. The feeling inside you which tells you what is right and what is wrong.
(a) Conscience   (b) Fear
(c) Consciousness   (d) Cleverness

194. Having juicy or fleshy and thick tissues.
(a) Succulent   (b) Translucent
(c) Dissolvent   (d) Dissident

195. An excessively morbid desire to steal
(a) Stealomania   (b) Kleptomania
(c) Cleftomania   (d) Keptomania

196. One who thinks or speaks too much of himself.
(a) Imposter   (b) Enthusiast
(c) Egotist   (d) Optimist

Directions (Q. Nos. 197-200) *In the following questions, out of the four alternatives, choose the one that best expresses the meaning of the given word.*

197. OBSTINATE
(a) Stubborn   (b) Pretty   (c) Silly   (d) Clever

198. ALERT
(a) Hostile   (b) Watchful
(c) Brave   (d) Quick

199. ACCEDE
(a) Consent   (b) Access
(c) Assess   (d) Proceed

200. AVARICE
(a) Envy   (b) Generosity
(c) Greed   (d) Hatred

Answers

1. (c)	2. (d)	3. (c)	4. (c)	5. (b)	6. (a)	7. (c)	8. (b)	9. (b)	10. (a)
11. (b)	12. (b)	13. (c)	14. (b)	15. (b)	16. (c)	17. (b)	18. (b)	19. (b)	20. (a)
21. (c)	22. (b)	23. (a)	24. (b)	25. (c)	26. (d)	27. (b)	28. (c)	29. (b)	30. (a)
31. (b)	32. (c)	33. (d)	34. (c)	35. (c)	36. (d)	37. (d)	38. (c)	39. (b)	40. (b)
41. (a)	42. (c)	43. (b)	44. (a)	45. (c)	46. (d)	47. (d)	48. (a)	49. (c)	50. (b)
51. (a)	52. (a)	53. (b)	54. (d)	55. (c)	56. (a)	57. (a)	58. (c)	59. (d)	60. (c)
61. (d)	62. (b)	63. (d)	64. (c)	65. (c)	66. (c)	67. (c)	68. (c)	69. (c)	70. (d)
71. (c)	72. (a)	73. (c)	74. (b)	75. (d)	76. (b)	77. (c)	78. (d)	79. (b)	80. (b)
81. (d)	82. (b)	83. (a)	84. (d)	85. (c)	86. (d)	87. (b)	88. (c)	89. (b)	90. (b)
91. (d)	92. (d)	93. (d)	94. (b)	95. (b)	96. (a)	97. (b)	98. (d)	99. (d)	100. (d)
101. (d)	102. (c)	103. (c)	104. (b)	105. (b)	106. (d)	107. (c)	108. (d)	109. (b)	110. (b)
111. (b)	112. (c)	113. (c)	114. (a)	115. (a)	116. (c)	117. (c)	118. (c)	119. (d)	120. (c)
121. (a)	122. (c)	123. (d)	124. (d)	125.. (c)	126. (d)	127. (c)	128. (b)	129. (b)	130. (c)
131. (c)	132. (c)	133. (d)	134. (a)	135. (b)	136. (c)	137. (d)	138. (d)	139. (c)	140. (c)
141. (c)	142. (b)	143. (d)	144. (d)	145. (a)	146. (c)	147. (b)	148. (c)	149. (d)	150. (b)
151. (d)	152. (b)	153. (a)	154. (b)	155. (b)	156. (c)	157. (c)	158. (b)	159. (c)	160. (b)
161. (d)	162. (c)	163. (b)	164. (d)	165. (b)	166. (d)	167. (d)	168. (b)	169. (c)	170. (b)
171. (d)	172. (a)	173. (c)	174. (b)	175. (b)	176. (a)	177. (d)	178. (b)	179. (d)	180. (d)
181. (b)	182. (d)	183. (a)	184. (b)	185. (c)	186. (a)	187. (a)	188. (d)	189. (a)	190. (b)
191. (c)	192. (c)	193. (a)	194. (a)	195. (b)	196. (c)	197. (a)	198. (b)	199. (a)	200. (c)

Hints & Solutions

1. (c) Let the three consecutive even natural numbers be $2x$, $2x + 2$ and $2x + 4$, respectively.

$\therefore$ Its product $= 2x(2x + 2)(2x + 4)$

If $x = 1$, the product $= 48$

If $x = 3$, the product $= 480$

$\therefore$ The largest natural number by which the product of three consecutive even natural numbers is always divisible, is 48.

2. (d) LCM of 3, 4, 5, 6 and 8 = 120

Now, 120 is not a perfect square and it must be multiplied with 30

$\therefore$ Required number $= 120 \times 30$

$= 3600$

$\therefore$ The least perfect square number which is divisible by 3, 4, 5, 6 and 8 is 3600.

3. (c) As, HCF and LCM of two numbers are 44 and 264, respectively.

According to the question,

One number is $44 \times 2 = 88$

$\therefore$ Other number $= \dfrac{HCF \times LCM}{One\ number}$

$= \dfrac{44 \times 264}{88} = 132$

4. (c) Required difference $= 12\%$ of $24.2 - 10\%$ of 14.2

$= \dfrac{12 \times 24.2}{100} - \dfrac{10 \times 14.2}{100}$

$= \dfrac{2904}{1000} - \dfrac{1420}{1000} = \dfrac{1484}{1000}$

$= 1.484$

5. (b) Let the required fraction be $\dfrac{x}{y}$.

Then, correct answer $= \dfrac{7}{9} \times \dfrac{x}{y} = \dfrac{7x}{9y}$

and Incorrect answer $= \dfrac{x}{y} \div \dfrac{7}{9} = \dfrac{9x}{7y}$

$\therefore$ According to the question,

$\dfrac{9x}{7y} - \dfrac{7x}{9y} = \dfrac{8}{21}$

$\Rightarrow \quad \dfrac{81x - 49x}{63y} = \dfrac{8}{21}$

$\Rightarrow \quad \dfrac{32x}{63y} = \dfrac{8}{21}$

$$\therefore \qquad \frac{x}{y} = \frac{8 \times 63}{21 \times 32} = \frac{3}{4}$$

$$\therefore \qquad \text{Correct answer} = \frac{7x}{9y} = \frac{7 \times 3}{9 \times 4} = \frac{7}{12}$$

6. (*a*) Suppose Bhuwan earns ₹ x in each of the 11 months,

Then, earning in January = ₹ $2x$

$\therefore$ Total income $= 11x + 2x = 13x$

$\therefore$ Part of the total earning in January $= \dfrac{2x}{13x} = \dfrac{2}{13}$

7. (*c*)
$$\sqrt{\frac{8}{3}} = \sqrt{\frac{8 \times 3}{3 \times 3}} = \frac{\sqrt{24}}{3}$$

$$= \frac{4.899}{3} \qquad [\because \sqrt{24} = 4.899]$$

$$= 1.633$$

8. (*b*) Required difference $= \dfrac{30}{100} \times 80 - \dfrac{4}{5} \times 25$

$$= 24 - 20 = 4$$

9. (*b*) Let the second number be x.

Then, the first number $= 2x$

$\therefore$ The third number $= 4x$

$$\text{Average of three numbers} = \frac{\text{Sum of three numbers}}{3}$$

$$= \frac{x + 2x + 4x}{3} = \frac{7x}{3}$$

Now, according to the question,

$$\frac{7x}{3} = 56 \quad \Rightarrow \quad x = \frac{56 \times 3}{7}$$

$$\therefore \qquad\qquad x = 24$$

Second number $= 24$

$\therefore$ First number $= 24 \times 2 = 48$

Third number $= 24 \times 4 = 96$

$\therefore$ The three numbers in order are 48, 24 and 96.

10. (*a*) Let each vessel contain L of mixture

$\therefore$ Total quantity of milk $= \dfrac{6}{7} + \dfrac{5}{7} + \dfrac{3}{4}$

$$= \frac{24 + 20 + 21}{28} = \frac{65}{28}$$

$\therefore$ Total quantity of water $= \dfrac{1}{7} + \dfrac{2}{7} + \dfrac{1}{4}$

$$= \frac{4 + 8 + 7}{28} = \frac{19}{28}$$

$\therefore$ Required ratio $= \dfrac{\frac{65}{28}}{\frac{19}{28}} = \dfrac{65}{19} = 65 : 19$

11. (*b*) Selling price of the bicycle = ₹ 1536

Loss% = 20%

We know that, $\text{CP} = \dfrac{100}{100 - \text{Loss}\%} \times \text{SP}$

$$\therefore \qquad \text{CP} = \frac{100}{100 - 20} \times 1536 = ₹\ 1920$$

Now, SP = ₹ 2000

$$\text{Gain\%} = \frac{\text{SP} - \text{CP}}{\text{CP}} \times 100 = \frac{2000 - 1920}{1920} \times 100$$

$$= \frac{25}{6} = 4\frac{1}{6}\%$$

12. (*b*) 1 day work of $A = \dfrac{1}{10}$

1 day work of $B = \dfrac{1}{15}$

$\therefore (A + B)$'s 1 day work $= \dfrac{1}{10} + \dfrac{1}{15}$

$$= \frac{3 + 2}{30} = \frac{5}{30} = \frac{1}{6}$$

$(A + B)$'s 5 days work $= 5 \times \dfrac{1}{6} = \dfrac{5}{6}$

Remaining work $= 1 - \dfrac{5}{6} = \dfrac{1}{6}$

Now, according to the question,

2 day's work of $C = \dfrac{1}{6}$

$\therefore$ 1 day work of $C = \dfrac{1}{12}$

$\therefore$ C can do the whole work in 12 days.

Ratio of work of A, B and $C = \dfrac{1}{10} : \dfrac{1}{15} : \dfrac{1}{12} = 6 : 4 : 5$

Amount that C gets $= \dfrac{5}{(6 + 4 + 5)} \times 450$

$$= ₹\ 150$$

13. (*c*) Part filled by pipe A in 1 min $= \dfrac{1}{24}$

Part filled by pipe A in 18 min $= \dfrac{18}{24} = \dfrac{3}{4}$

The remaining part $= 1 - \dfrac{3}{4} = \dfrac{1}{4}$

Time taken by B to fill the remaining part $= \dfrac{\frac{1}{4}}{\frac{1}{32}}$

$$= \frac{1}{4} \times \frac{32}{1} = 8 \text{ min}$$

$\therefore$ After 8 min, pipe B should be closed.

14. (*b*) According to the question,

Time taken to cover 13 km $= \dfrac{13}{15}$ h

$$= \frac{13}{15} \times 60 = 52 \text{ min}$$

Total time $= 1$ h $+$ 40 min

$$= 60 \text{ min} + 40 \text{ min} = 100 \text{ min}$$

Remaining time $= 100 - 52 = 48$ min

and remaining distance $= 21 - 13 = 8$ km

$\therefore$ Required speed $= \dfrac{8\ \text{km}}{\dfrac{48}{60}\ \text{h}} = \dfrac{8 \times 60}{48}$

$= 10\ \text{km/h} \left[\because \text{Speed} = \dfrac{\text{Distance}}{\text{Time}} \right]$

15. (b) Given, length of train $= 1$ km

Then, length of bridge $= \dfrac{1}{2}$ km

$\therefore$ Total distance $= 1\ \text{km} + \dfrac{1}{2}\ \text{km} = \dfrac{3}{2}\ \text{km}$

and Time taken $= 2\ \text{min} = \dfrac{2}{60}\ \text{h} = \dfrac{1}{30}\ \text{h}$

Speed of the train $= \dfrac{\text{Distance}}{\text{Time}}$

$= \dfrac{\dfrac{3}{2}}{\dfrac{1}{30}} = \dfrac{3}{2} \times \dfrac{30}{1} = 45\ \text{km/h}$

16. (c) Let the speed of the motor boat $= x$ km/h

Speed of the stream $= 2$ km/h

Then, speed upstream $= (x - 2)$ km/h

Speed downstream $= (x + 2)$ km/h

According to the question,

$\dfrac{10}{x - 2} + \dfrac{10}{x + 2} = \dfrac{55}{60}$

$\Rightarrow \dfrac{10\,(x + 2) + 10\,(x - 2)}{(x - 2)\,(x + 2)} = \dfrac{11}{12}$

$\Rightarrow \dfrac{20x}{x^2 - 4} = \dfrac{11}{12}$

$\Rightarrow 11x^2 - 240x - 44 = 0$

$\Rightarrow (x - 22)\,(11x + 2) = 0$

$\therefore x = 22 \text{ or } -\dfrac{2}{11}$

$\therefore$ Speed of the motor boat $= 22$ km/h

17. (b) Let the present age of elder person be x yr.

Present age of younger person $= y$ yr.

15 yr ago, age of elder person $= (x - 15)$ yr

and age of younger person $= (y - 15)$ yr

$\therefore$ According to the question,

and $x - y = 10$

$(x - 15) = 2\,(y - 15)$

$\Rightarrow x - 15 = 2y - 30$

$\Rightarrow x - 15 = 2\,(x - 10) - 30$

$\Rightarrow x = 50 - 15 = 35$ yr

$\therefore$ Present age of elder person $= 35$ yr.

18. (b) Let the rate of interest be $R\%$.

Then, according to the question,

$\dfrac{600 \times R \times 2}{100} + \dfrac{150 \times R \times 4}{100} = 90$

$\Rightarrow 12R + 6R = 90$

$\Rightarrow 18R = 90$

$\therefore R = 5\%$

19. (b) Given, $P = ₹\,550$, $R = 20\%$

and total number of installments $= 2$

According to the formula,

$\text{Amount} = P \left(1 + \dfrac{R}{100} \right)^n$

$= 550 \left(1 + \dfrac{20}{100} \right)^2 = 550 \left(\dfrac{120}{100} \right)^2$

$= 550 \times \dfrac{36}{25} = ₹\,792$

$\therefore$ The value of each installment $= 396$

20. (a) According to the rule of alligation,

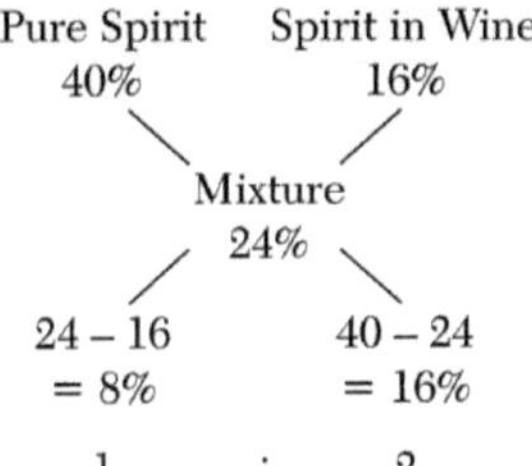

Thus, 24% of spirit's mixture contains $\dfrac{1}{3}$rd part of 40% spirit.

So, he stole $\left(1 - \dfrac{1}{3} \right) = \dfrac{2}{3}$ part of the wine.

21. (c) Total number of operator who left the company

$= 104 + 120 + 100 + 112 + 144 = 580$

Total number of operator who joined the company

$= 880 + 256 + 240 + 208 + 192 + 248 = 2024$

Let required percentage be $x\%$.

$\therefore$ According to the question,

$580 = x\% \text{ of } 2024$

$\Rightarrow 580 = \dfrac{x}{100} \times 2024$

$\Rightarrow x = \dfrac{580 \times 100}{2024}$

$\therefore x = 28.65\% \cong 29\%$

22. (b) Number of managers working in the company in 2012 $= 760$

In 2017 $= (760 + 280 + 179 + 148 + 160 + 193)$
$- (120 + 92 + 88 + 72 + 96)$

$= 1252$

$\therefore$ Percentage increase in the number of manager

$= \dfrac{1252 - 760}{760} \times 100 = 64.74\%$

Number of technicians working in the company in 2012 $= 1200$

In 2017 $= (1200 + 272 + 240 + 236 + 256 + 288)$
$- (120 + 128 + 96 + 100 + 112)$

$= 1936$

∴ Percentage increase in the number of technicians

$$= \frac{1936 - 1200}{1200} \times 100 = 61.33\%$$

Number of operators working in the company in 2012 = 880

In 2017 = $(880 + 256 + 240 + 208 + 192 + 248)$
$$- (104 + 120 + 100 + 112 + 144)$$
$$= 1444$$

∴ Percentage increase in the number of operators

$$= \frac{1444 - 880}{880} \times 100 = 64.09\%$$

Number of Accountants working in the company in 2012 = 1160

In 2017 = $(1160 + 200 + 224 + 248 + 272 + 260)$
$$- (100 + 104 + 96 + 88 + 92)$$
$$= 1884$$

∴ Percentage increase in the number of

Accountants = $\dfrac{1884 - 1160}{1160} = 62.14\%$

Number of Peons working in the company in 2012 = 820

In 2017 = $(820 + 184 + 152 + 196 + 224 + 200)$
$$- (96 + 88 + 80 + 120 + 104)$$
$$= 1288$$

∴ Percentage increase in the number of Peons

$$= \frac{1288 - 820}{820} \times 100 = 57.07\%$$

Clearly, the percentage increase is maximum in case of managers.

23. (a) According to the given table,

Total number of technicians added to the company from the year 2013 to 2017
$$272 + 240 + 236 + 256 + 288 = 1292$$

Total number of Accountants added from 2013 to 2017 $= 200 + 224 + 248 + 272 + 260 = 1204$

∴   Required difference = $1292 - 1204 = 88$

24. (b) Total number of peons working in the company in the year 2016
$$= (820 + 184 + 152 + 196 + 224)$$
$$- (96 + 88 + 80 + 120)$$
$$= 1576 - 384 = 1192$$

25. (c) Required average

$$= \frac{1007 + 1464 + 1152 + 1380 + 972}{5}$$

$$= \frac{5975}{5} = 1195$$

26. (d) According to the given graph,

Total export for company B
$$= 80 + 40 + 60 + 60 + 80 + 100 + 140$$
$$= ₹ 560 \text{ crores}$$

∴ Average export for company B = $\dfrac{560}{7}$ crores

Total export for Company C
$$= 60 + 90 + 120 + 90 + 60 + 80 + 100 = 600$$

∴ Average export for company C = ₹ $\dfrac{600}{7}$ crores

Let the required percentage be $x\%$.

Then, $\dfrac{560}{7} = \dfrac{x}{100} \times \dfrac{600}{7}$

∴ $x = \dfrac{56 \times 100}{60}$

$$= \frac{560}{6} = \frac{280}{3} = 93.33\%$$

27. (b) According to given graph,

Export of Company C in
$$2011 = ₹ 90 \text{ crore}$$
$$2012 = ₹ 120 \text{ crore}$$
$$2013 = ₹ 90 \text{ crore}$$
$$2016 = ₹ 100 \text{ crore}$$

∴ Average annual export of company C
$$= \frac{600}{7} \text{ crores}$$
$$= 85.71 \text{ crores}$$

∴ Required number of years more than average export of company, C = 4

28. (c) According to the question,

Average exports of the three companies in 2010
$$= \frac{30 + 80 + 60}{3} = \frac{170}{3} \text{ crore}$$

Average exports of the three company in 2015
$$= \frac{50 + 100 + 80}{3} = ₹ \frac{230}{3} \text{ crore}$$

∴ Required difference = $\left(\dfrac{230}{3} - \dfrac{170}{3} \right)$ crore

$$= \frac{60}{3} = ₹ 20 \text{ crores}$$

29. (b) The difference in year $2010 = (80 - 30) = ₹ 50$ crore
The difference in year $2011 = (60 - 40) = ₹ 20$ crore
The difference in year $2012 = (60 - 40) = ₹ 20$ crore
The difference in year $2013 = (70 - 60) = ₹ 10$ crore
The difference in year $2014 = (100 - 80) = ₹ 20$ crore
The difference in year $2015 = (100 - 50) = ₹ 50$ crore
The difference in year $2016 = (140 - 120) = ₹ 20$ crore

∴ In 2013, the difference between the exports from company A and B was minimum.

30. (a) Total export in $2010 = 30 + 80 + 60 = ₹ 170$ crores
Total export in $2011 = 60 + 40 + 90 = ₹ 190$ crores
Total export in $2012 = 40 + 60 + 120 = ₹ 220$ crores
Total export in $2013 = 70 + 60 + 90 = ₹ 220$ crores
Total export in $2014 = 100 + 80 + 60 = ₹ 240$ crores
Total export in $2015 = 50 + 100 + 80 = ₹ 230$ crores
Total export in $2016 = 120 + 140 + 100 = ₹ 360$ crores

∴ In 2012 and 2013, the total exports from the three companies together are equal.

31. (*b*) From option (a),

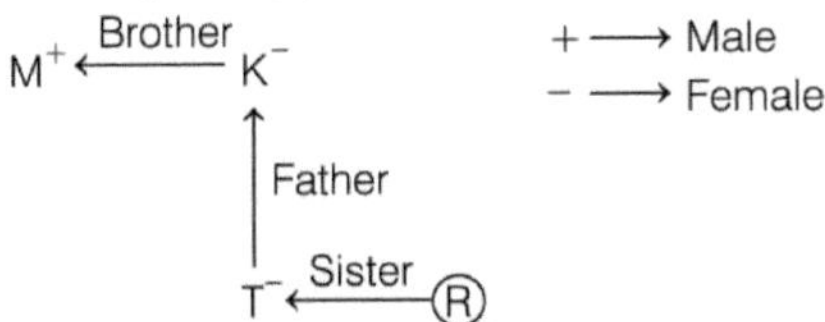

We cannot defined the gender of R.
So, option (a) is false.
From option (b),

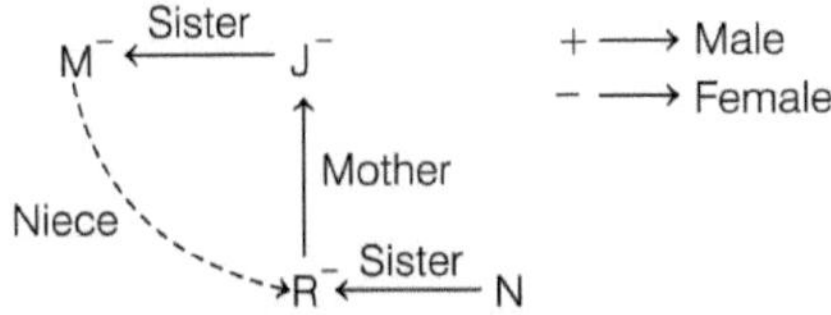

Hence, from option (b) it is clear 'R' is the Niece

of M.

32. (*c*) According to the expression,

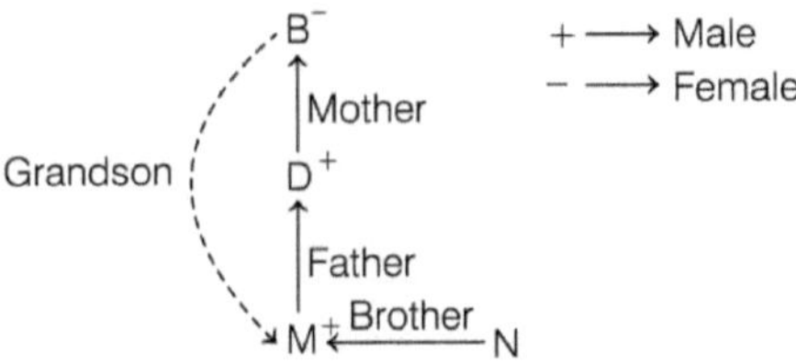

It is clear 'M' is the grandson of B.

33. (*d*) The blood relation diagram for all the given option is as
From option (a),

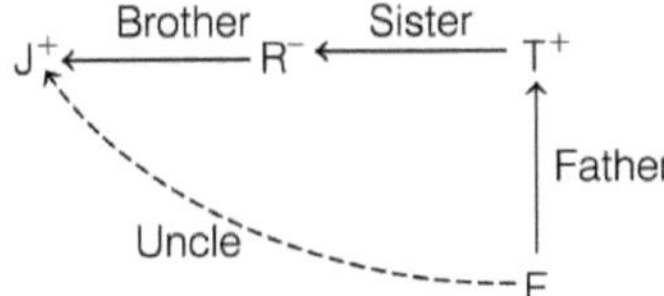

Here, J is the uncle of F.
From option (b),

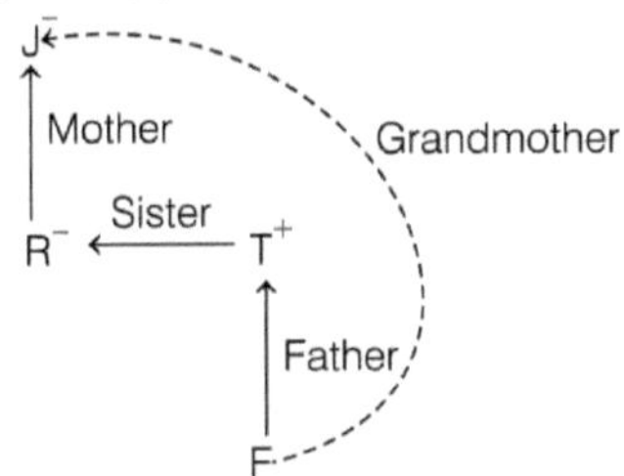

Here, J is the grandmother of F.
From option (c),

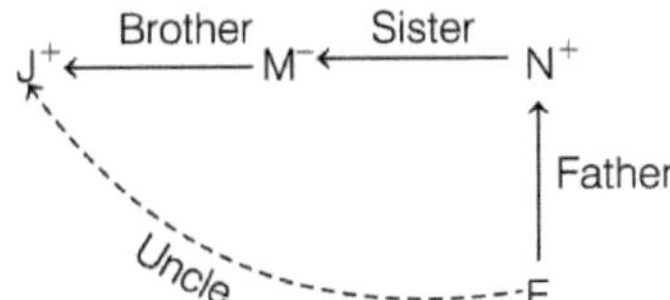

Here, J is the uncle of F.
Hence, all the given options are not defined 'J is the son of F'.
So, option (d) is the correct answer.

Sol. (Q. Nos. 34-36) *According to the given information.*

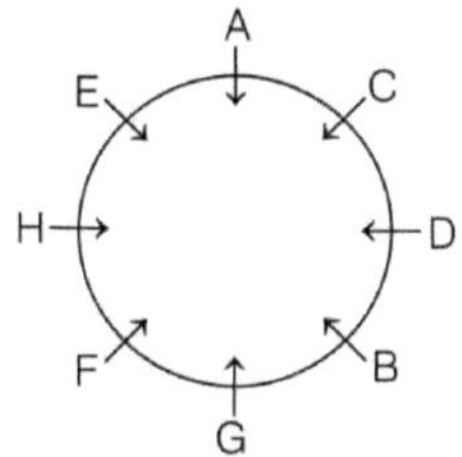

34. (*c*) 'B' is sitting third right of H.

35. (*c*) 'F' is fourth to the left of 'C' and fourth to the right of 'C'.

So our answer will be option (c).

36. (*d*) 'H' is sitting immediate right of 'E'.
Hence, option (d) is correct.

37. (*d*) The pattern is as follows,

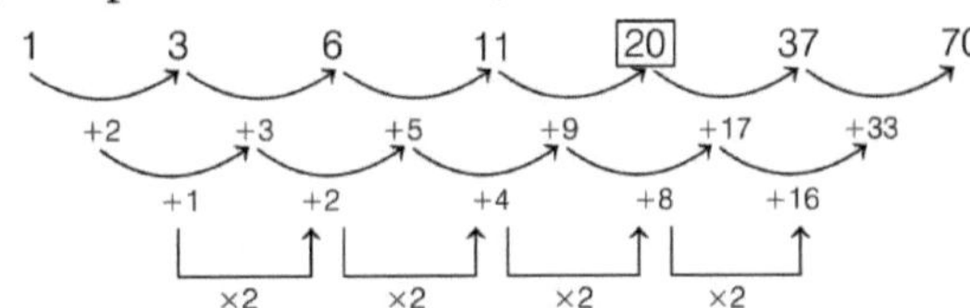

Hence, the missing number will be 20.

38. (*c*) The pattern is as follows

Q 1 F S 2 E U 6 D W 21 C Y 8 8 B

For numerical sequence,

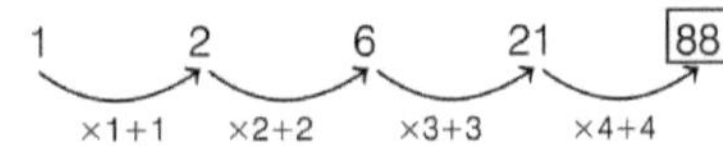

For alphabetical sequence,

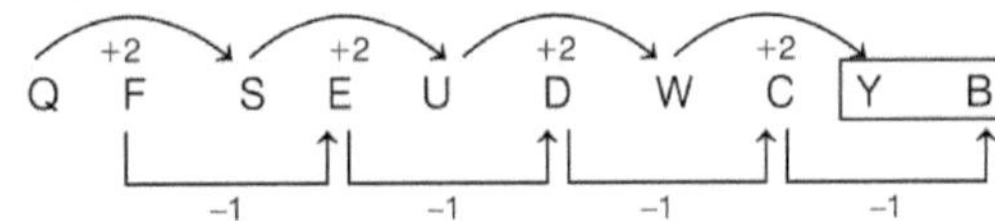

Hence, the missing term will be 'Y88B'.

39. (*b*) The pattern is as follows

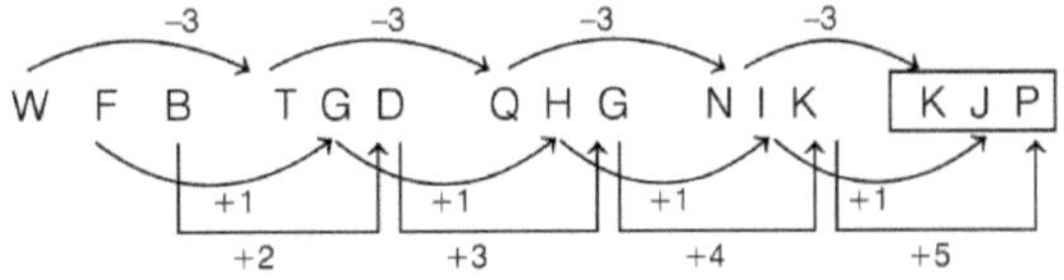

The missing term will be KJP.
Hence, option (b) is correct.

40. (*b*) The pattern is as follows,

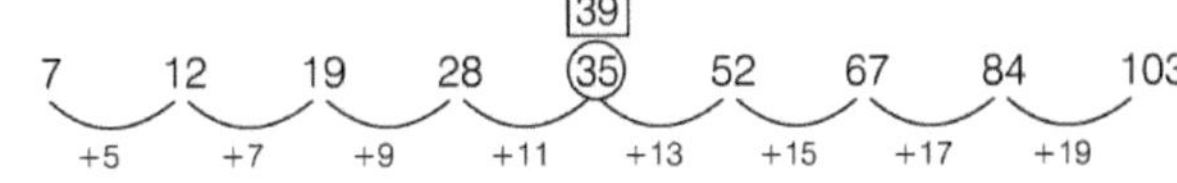

Hence, the wrong number is 35.

41. (*a*) The pattern is as follows,

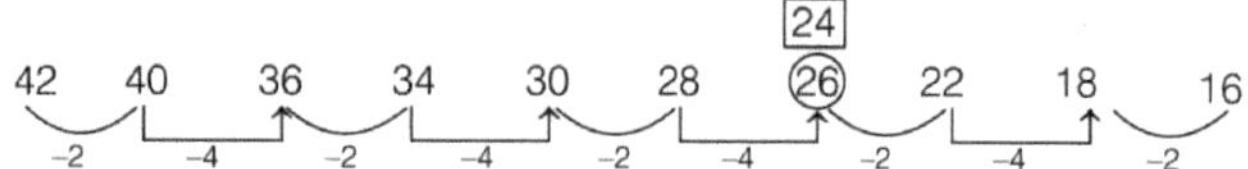

Hence, the wrong number is 26.

42. (*c*) The pattern is as follows,

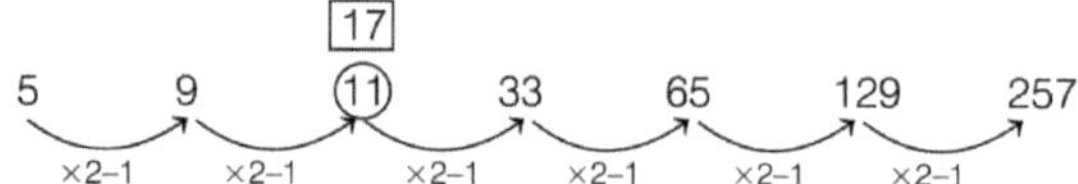

Hence, the wrong term is '11'.

43. (*b*) As, 'Indolence' and 'Work' are opposite to each other. In the same way, 'Taciturn' and 'Speak' are opposite to each other.

44. (*a*) A Chef works in a restaurant. Similarly, a Druggist works in a pharmacy.

45. (*c*) As 'Cringe' is the sign of 'Fear', in the same way 'Yawn' is the sign of Boredom.

46. (*d*) The shaded region is moving in anti-clockwise direction in each step. So, the next figure will be

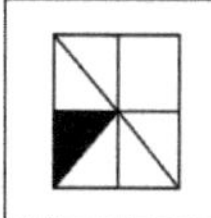

Hence, option (d) is correct.

47. (*d*) In every step 3, 2, 3 and 2 upper figures are deleted and 4, 3, 4 and 3 figures are deleted from lower figures.

48. (*a*) To understand the pattern of the figure we have to draw the rotation of the figure.

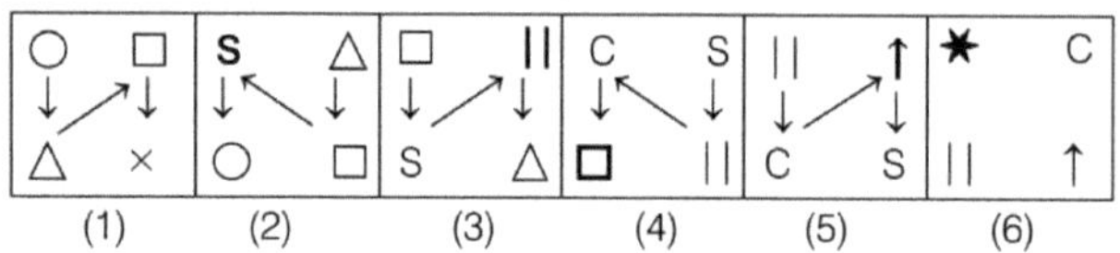

In each step a new element is added to replace a old one.

Hence, option (a) is correct.

Sol. (Q. Nos. 49-51)

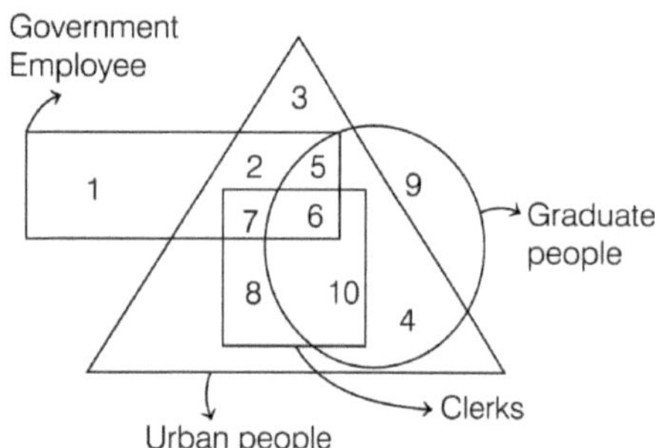

49. (*c*) '7' represents clerks who are government employees and urban.

50. (*b*) Some urban people are not graduates.

51. (*a*) '4' represents urban people who are graduates but neither government employees nor clerks.

52. (*a*) Only Statement I is draw. Superstition is not the only reason of people being uneducated. Even educated people can be superstitious.

The given facts can't be completely acceptable because education increases not only rationality but it also makes us self dependent and provides us knowledge, dignity etc.

According to the IInd statement, villagers do not go to schools, therefore they are uneducated. This is not true in all conditions because one can get an education anywhere and anytime.

53. (*b*) Only Statement II is draw alone. Nothing is mentioned about lather formation by detergent. So, I is not drawn. Also, detergents should be used as they clean clothes better and easily. So, Statement II can be drawn.

54. (*d*) The availability of vegetables is not mentioned in the given statements. So, Statement I can't be drawn. Also Statement II is not directly related to the conclusion and so it also can't be drawn.

Hence, both the Statements I and II are not sufficient to draw the conclusion.

55. (*c*) (A) is true but (R) is false.

When the bus starts, the person inside it falls backward because the bus moves forward but due to the law of inertia, the man tends to be in the initial position of rest. Hence, option (c) is correct.

56. (*a*) The carbon-dioxide envelope in earth's atmosphere traps the heat with increase in the proportion of carbon-dioxide, therefore the global temperature would rise, thus causing the polar ice to melt.

Hence, both(A) and (R) are true and (R) is the correct explanation of (A).

Hence, option (a) is correct.

57. (*a*) Earthen pot become cool in summer because during summer evaporation increase. So it evaporates taking latent heat and removal of latent heat cause pots gets cooled.

This phenomenon is called evaporation. Hence, both (A) and (R) are true and (R) is the correct explanation of (A).

Hence, option (a) is correct.

58. (*c*) In a certain code language,

As,

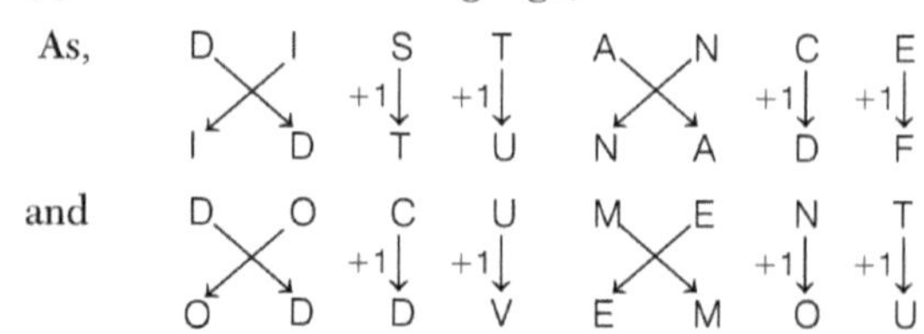

Similarly,

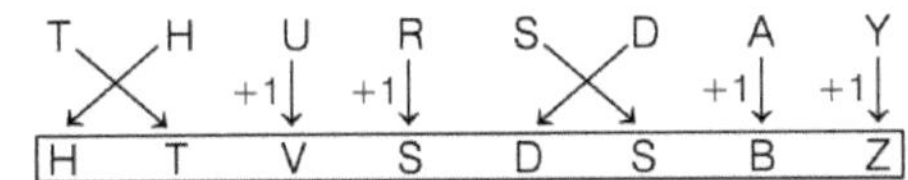

Hence, 'THURSDAY' will written as 'HTVSDSBZ'.

59. (*d*)

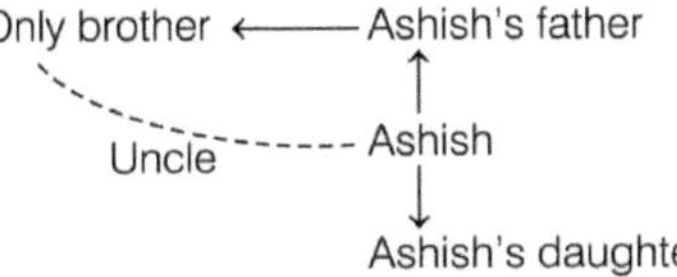

Father of Ashish's daughter's father → Ashish's father.

Hence, the person is the brother of Ashish's father.

Therefore, the person is the uncle of Ashish.

60. (*c*) According to the question,

Khan's rank from the last = 17th

Ramesh is 7th rank ahead of Khan. It means there are '6' students between them.

Total number of students from the last to Ramesh

$$= 17 + 6 = 23$$

Now, $39 - 23 = 16$

Hence, Ramesh's rank from the start will be 16th.

144. (*d*) 'Patronage' is the opposite of 'deterrent' as used in the passage. 'Deterrent' means something that discourages someone from doing something while 'patronage' means to support or encourage someone.

148. (*c*) 'Distressing' is closest in meaning to 'alarming'. Both words mean 'worrying or disturbing'.

150. (*b*) The phrase 'stem the tide' means to stop a prevailing trend.

Hence, 'stop' is the correct answer.

167. (*d*) Part D contains the error. The sentence is making a comparison between Sudhakar and Shashi, hence, the adjective used should be in comparative degree. Replace 'the most' with 'more' to make the sentence grammatically correct.

168. (*b*) Part B contains the error. Preposition 'to' is incorrectly used in the sentence. Remove 'to' to make the sentence grammatically correct.

169. (*c*) Part C contains the error. Replace 'one gets up' with 'you get up' to make the sentence grammatically correct.

170. (*b*) Part B contains the error. As 'did' is already used in part A, past tense verb 'arrived' will not be used. Hence, replace 'arrived' with 'arrive' to make the sentence grammatically correct.

171. (*d*) Part D contains the error, 'Oneself' is the correct reflexive pronoun to be used with 'one'. Replace 'themselves' with 'oneself' to make the sentence grammatically correct.

172. (*a*) Part A contains the error. 'Cant' should not be used with 'hardly'.

Hence, replace 'can't' with 'can' to make the sentence grammatically correct.

185. (*c*) 'Make up her mind' means to make a decision.

186. (*a*) 'Reading between the lines' means to look for the implied meaning.

Hence option (a) 'understanding the hidden meaning' is nearest in meaning to 'reading between the lines'.

187. (*a*) 'The ball was in his court' means that it was up to him to make the final move. Hence, option (a) 'final decision rests on him' is nearest in meaning to 'the ball was in his court'.

188. (*d*) 'Lost heart' means became discouraged.

189. (*a*) 'Burning question' means an urgent or crucial issue under discussion. Hence, option (a) 'widely debated issue' is nearest in meaning to 'burning question'.

190. (*b*) 'Hard and fast rule' means a strict rule that is not to be tampered with. Hence, option (b) 'rule that cannot be broken or modified' is nearest in meaning to 'hard and fast rule'.

197. (*a*) 'Obstinate' means determined to act in a particular way. Hence, 'stubborn' is its correct meaning.

198. (*b*) 'Alert' means quick to notice an unusual or dangerous situation. Hence, 'watchful' is its correct meaning.

199. (*a*) 'Accede' means to agree to a demand, request or treaty. Hence, 'consent' is its correct meaning.

200. (*c*) 'Avarice' means excessive desire for wealth or gain. Hence, 'greed' is its correct meaning.

NCHMCT
Hotel Management

National Council for Hotel Management and Catering Technology

Solved Paper 2017

Instructions

- There are Five (A–E) Sections in this Solved Paper.
- For every correct attempt, the student will be awarded **1 mark**.
- All the questions are in MCQs form and each have four options.

Marks : 200

Time : 3 hrs

Section A : Numerical Ability And Analytical Aptitude

Directions (Q. Nos. 1-5) *The bar graph shown below gives the data of the production of cement (in lakh tonnes) by three different companies A, B and C over five years. Study the graph and answer the questions that follow.*

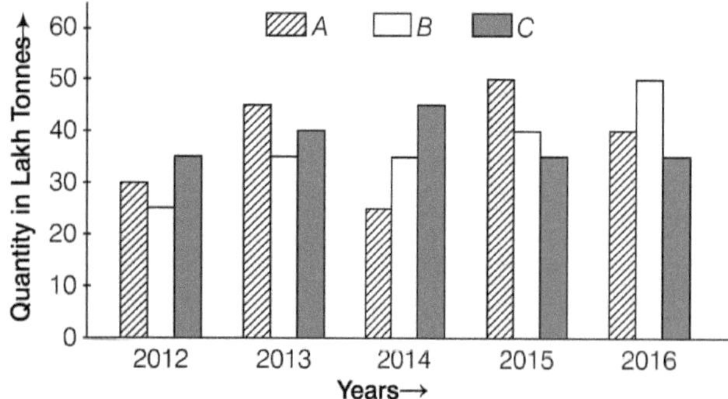

1. What is the ratio of the average production of Company *A* in the period 2014-2016 to the average production of Company *B* in the same period?

(a) 1 : 1   (b) 15 : 17   (c) 23 : 25   (d) 27 : 29

2. What is the percentage increase in the production of Company *B* from 2012 to 2015?

(a) 30%   (b) 45%
(c) 50%   (d) 60%

3. The average production for five years was maximum for which Company(ies)?

(a) *A*
(b) *B*
(c) *C*
(d) Both *A* and *C*

4. For which of the following years, the percentage rise/fall in production from the previous year is the maximum for Company *B*?

(a) 2013
(b) 2014
(c) 2015
(d) 2016

5. In which year was the percentage of production of Company *C* to the production of Company *B* the maximum?

(a) 2012   (b) 2013
(c) 2014   (d) 2015

Directions (Q. Nos. 6-10) *Study the following pie-chart and table to answer the questions based on them.*

Proportion of Population of Seven Villages in 2014

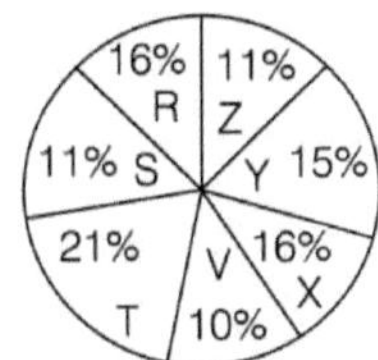

Village	% Population Below Poverty Line
X	38
Y	52
Z	42
R	51
S	49
T	46
V	58

6. Find the population of village S, if the population of village X below poverty line in 2014 is 12160.
(a) 18500   (b) 20500   (c) 22000   (d) 26000

7. The ratio of population of village T below poverty line to that of village Z below poverty line in 2014 is ………… .
(a) 11 : 23   (b) 13 : 11
(c) 23 : 11   (d) 11 : 13

8. If the population of village R in 2014 is 32000, then what will be the population of village Y below poverty line in that year?
(a) 14100   (b) 15600
(c) 16500   (d) 17000

9. If in 2015, the population of villages Y and V increase by 10% each and the percentage of population below poverty line remains unchanged for all the villages, then find the population of village V below poverty line in 2015, given that the population of village Y in 2014 was 30000.
(a) 11250   (b) 12760   (c) 13140   (d) 13780

10. If in 2016, the population of village R increases by 10% while that of village Z reduces by 5% compared to that in 2014 and the percentage of population below poverty line remains unchanged for all the villages, then find the approximate ratio of population of village R below poverty line to the ratio of population of village Z below poverty line for the year 2016.
(a) 2 : 1   (b) 3 : 2   (c) 4 : 3   (d) 5 : 4

11. The LCM of two numbers is 48. The numbers are in the ratio 2 : 3. The sum of the numbers is
(a) 28   (b) 32
(c) 40   (d) 64

12. The difference of the squares of two consecutive odd integers is divisible by which of the following integers?
(a) 3   (b) 6   (c) 7   (d) 8

13. When 0.36 is written in simplest fractional form, the sum of the numerator and the denominator is ……… .
(a) 34   (b) 45
(c) 114   (d) 135

14. A crate of mangoes contains one bruised mango for every 30 mangoes in the crate. If 3 out of every 4 bruised mangoes are considered unsalable, and there are 12 unsalable mangoes in the crate, then how many mangoes are there in the crate?
(a) 360   (b) 480
(c) 520   (d) 430

15. Nine persons went to a hotel for taking their meals. Eight of them spent ₹ 12 each on their meals and the ninth spent ₹ 8 more than the average expenditure of all the nine. What was the total money spent by them?
(a) ₹ 115   (b) ₹ 116
(c) ₹ 117   (d) ₹ 108

16. A number is as much greater than 36 as is less than 86. Find the number.
(a) 61   (b) 50
(c) 65   (d) 67

17. Abhay's age after six years will be three-seventh of his father's age. Ten years ago, the ratio of their ages was 1 : 5. What is Abhay's father's age at present?
(a) 52 yr   (b) 50 yr   (c) 54 yr   (d) 48 yr

18. If $2^{n+4} - 2^{n+2} = 3$, then n is equal to
(a) 0   (b) 2
(c) -1 (d) -2

19. Due to a reduction of $6\frac{1}{4}\%$ in the price of sugar, a man is able to buy 1 kg more for ₹ 120. Find the reduced rate of sugar.
(a) ₹ 7.25 per kg   (b) ₹ 7.50 per kg
(c) ₹ 8.00 per kg   (d) ₹ 7.75 per kg

20. What per cent of 7 is 84?
(a) 300%   (b) 120%
(c) 1200%   (d) 12%

HM 2017

21. *A, B* and *C* started a business by investing ₹ 120000, ₹ 135000 and ₹ 150000, respectively. Find the share of *C* out of an annual profit of ₹ 56700.

(a) ₹ 16800   (b) ₹ 18900
(c) ₹ 21000   (d) ₹ 23000

22. If 15 men, working 9 h a day, can reap a field in 16 days, in how many days will 18 men reap the field, working 8 h a day?

(a) 14 days   (b) 15 days
(c) 13 days   (d) 16 days

23. *A* and *B* undertake to do a piece of work for ₹ 600. *A* alone can do it in 6 days while *B* alone can do it in 8 days. With the help of *C*, they finish it in 3 days. Find the share of *C*.

(a) ₹ 100   (b) ₹ 150   (c) ₹ 75   (d) ₹ 125

24. Two pipes can fill a tank in 10 h and 12 h, respectively while a third pipe empties the full tank in 20 h. If all the three pipes operate simultaneously, in how much time will the tank be filled?

(a) 6 h 45 min   (b) 7 h 30 min
(c) 7 h 15 min   (d) 7 h 45 min

25. A man travelled from the village to the post-office at the rate of 25 km/h and walked back at the rate of 4 km/h. If the whole journey took 5 h 48 min, find the distance of the post-office from the village.

(a) 20 km   (b) 22 km
(c) 24 km   (d) 26 km

26. A train 150 m long is running with a speed of 68 km/h. In what time will it pass a man who is running at 8 km/h in the same direction in which the train is going?

(a) 12 s   (b) 11 s   (c) 9 s   (d) 10 s

27. A man can row $7\frac{1}{2}$ km/h in still water. If in a river running at 1.5 km/h, it takes him 50 min to row to a place and back, how far is the place?

(a) 4 km   (b) 3 km   (c) 5 km   (d) 7 km

28. In what ratio must water be mixed with milk to gain 20% by selling the mixture at cost price?

(a) 1 : 2   (b) 1 : 3   (c) 1 : 5   (d) 1 : 6

29. A sum at simple interest at $13\frac{1}{2}$% per annum amounts to ₹ 2502.50 after 4 yr. Find the sum.

(a) ₹ 1575   (b) ₹ 1605   (c) ₹ 1625   (d) ₹ 1655

30. Find the compound interest on ₹ 16000 at 20% per annum for 9 months, compounded quarterly.

(a) ₹ 2512   (b) ₹ 2522
(c) ₹ 2372   (d) ₹ 2462

Section B : Reasoning And Logical Deduction

Directions (Q. Nos. 31 and 32) *Some statements are followed by two Conclusions I and II. Decide which of the conclusions follows from the statements.*

Mark answer as
(a) if only Conclusion I follows
(b) if only Conclusion II follows
(c) if neither Conclusions I nor II follows
(d) if both Conclusions I and II follow

31. Statements
1. Some scooters are trucks.
2. All trucks are trains.
Conclusions
I. Some scooters are trains.
II. No truck is a scooter.

32. Statements
1. Some players are singers.
2. All singers are tall.
Conclusions
I. Some players are tall.
II. All players are tall.

Directions (Q. Nos. 33 and 34) *In each of the following questions, two statements numbered I and II are given. There may be cause and effect relationship between the two statements. These two statements may be the effect of the same cause or independent causes. These statements may be independent causes without having any relationship. Read both the statements in each question and mark your answer as*

(a) if Statement I is the cause and Statement II is its effect.
(b) if Statement II is the cause and Statement I is its effect.
(c) if both the Statements I and II are effects of independent causes.
(d) if both the Statements I and II are effects of some common cause.

33. Statement I There is sharp decline in the production of oilseeds this year.

Statement II The Government has decided to increase the import quantum of edible oil.

34. Statement I The Reserve Bank of India has recently put restrictions on few small banks in the country.

Statement II The small banks in the private and co-operative sector in India are not in a position to withstand the competitions of the bigger banks in the public sector.

Directions (Q. Nos. 35-37) *Read the following information carefully to answer these questions.*

Prashant Arora has three children - Sangeeta, Vimal and Ashish. Ashish married Monika, the eldest daughter of Mr. and Mrs. Roy. Mr. Roy married their youngest daughter to the eldest son of Mr. and Mrs. Sharma, who had two children named Amit and Shashi. Mr. and Mrs. Roy have two more children, Roshan and Vandana, both elder to Veena. Sameer and Ajay are sons of Ashish and Monika. Rashmi is the daughter of Amit.

35. How is Sameer related to Monika's father?
   (a) Grandson   (b) Son
   (c) Cousin   (d) Son-in-law

36. What is the surname of Sameer?
   (a) Roy   (b) Sharma
   (c) Arora   (d) None of these

37. How is Mrs. Roy related to Ashish?
   (a) Aunt   (b) Mother-in-law
   (c) Mother   (d) Sister-in-law

Directions (Q. Nos. 38-40) *Study the following information carefully to answer these questions.*

A Business School with six Professors L, M, N, O, P and Q, has decided to implement a new scheme of course management. Each Professor has to coordinate one course and support another course. This semester, O's support course is Finance, while three others have it in coordinator's role. P and Q have Marketing as one of their subjects. Q coordinates Operations, which is a support course for both N and P. Finance and IT are L's subjects. Both L and O have same subjects. Strategy is a support course for only one of the Professors.

38. Who coordinates the IT course?
   (a) L   (b) N
   (c) O   (d) None of these

39. Which course is supported by M?
   (a) Operations   (b) IT
   (c) Finance   (d) Strategy

40. Who among the following are coordinating the Finance course?
   (a) L, M and N   (b) L and N
   (c) N and O   (d) M, N and O

Directions (Q. Nos. 41 and 42) *Examine the route diagram given below to answer these questions.*

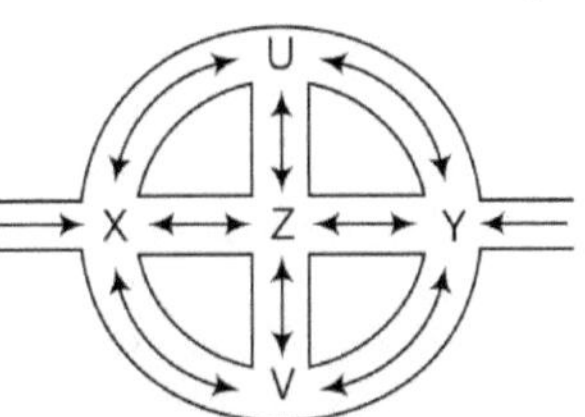

The arrows indicate directions of possible movement.

41. Which is the most crowded junction, assuming that each arrow denotes equal traffic?
   (a) U   (b) X
   (c) Y   (d) Z

42. What is the maximum number of bus routes possible from X to Y such that the bus does not come to one junction more than once in a route?
   (a) 4   (b) 6
   (c) 8   (d) 9

Directions (Q. Nos. 43 and 44) *The following figure represents the flow of natural gas through pipelines across major cities A, B, C, D and E. Assume that supply equals demand.*

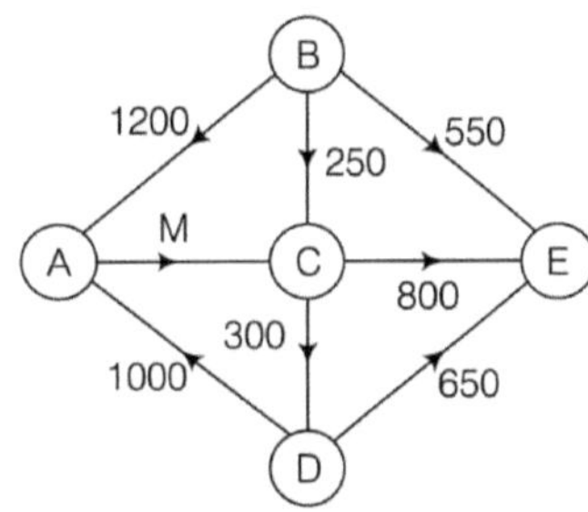

43. If the number of units demanded in C is 225, what is the value of M?
   (a) 775   (b) 850
   (c) 875   (d) 1075

44. If the total demand in E is 80% of the demand in A, what is the demand in A?
   (a) 2400 units
   (b) 2500 units
   (c) 4500 units
   (d) None of the above

45. A is B's sister. C is B's mother. D is C's father. E is D's mother. Then, how is A related to D?
   (a) Grandfather
   (b) Grandmother
   (c) Daughter
   (d) Granddaughter

46. Pointing out to a lady, a girl said, "She is the daughter-in-law of the grandmother of my father's only son." How is the lady related to the girl?
  (a) Sister-in-law   (b) Mother
  (c) Aunt   (d) Cannot be determined

47. In a row of boys, A who is 10th from the left and B who is 9th from the right interchange their positions, A becomes 15th from the left. How many boys are there in the row?
  (a) 23   (b) 31   (c) 27   (d) 28

48. In a certain code language, '134' means 'good and tasty'; '478' means 'see good pictures' and '729' means 'pictures are faint'. Which of the following digits stands for 'see'?
  (a) 9   (b) 2   (c) 1   (d) 8

49. If ROSE is coded as 6821, CHAIR is coded as 73456 and PREACH is coded as 961473, what will be the code for SEARCH?
  (a) 246173   (b) 214673   (c) 214763   (d) 216473

50. A man has a certain number of small boxes to pack into parcels. If he packs 3, 4, 5 or 6 in a parcel, he is left with one over; if he packs 7 in a parcel, none is left over. What is the number of boxes, he may have to pack?
  (a) 106   (b) 301   (c) 309   (d) 400

Directions (Q. Nos. 51-53) *Complete the series.*

51. 2Z5, 7Y7, 14X9, 23W11, 34V13, '?'
  (a) 47U15   (b) 47V14   (c) 45U15   (d) 27U24

52. 1, 2, 3, 10, '?', 9802
  (a) 99   (b) 199
  (c) 299   (d) 999

53. Z, S, W, O, T, K, Q, G, '?', '?'
  (a) N, D   (b) N,C
  (c) O,D   (d) O,C

Directions (Q. Nos. 54-56) *Choose the odd one out.*

54. 2, 5, 10, 50, 500, 5000
  (a) 5000   (b) 500   (c) 10   (d) 50

55. 3, 8, 15, 24, 34, 48, 63
  (a) 15   (b) 24
  (c) 34   (d) 48

56. 380, 188, 92, 48, 20, 8, 2
  (a) 20   (b) 48
  (c) 92   (d) 2

Directions (Q. Nos. 57 and 58) *The questions given below have a statement followed by two Assumptions I and II. Decide which of the assumptions is implicit from the statement.*
  Mark answer as
  (a) if only Assumption I is implicit
  (b) if only Assumption II is implicit
  (c) if neither Assumption I nor II is implicit
  (d) if both Assumptions I and II are implicit

57. Statement Most people who stop smoking gain weight.
  Assumptions
    I. If one stops smoking, one will gain weight.
    II. If one does not stop smoking, one will not gain weight.

58. Statement Postal rates have been increased to meet the deficit.
  Assumptions
    I. The present rates are very low.
    II. If the rates are not increased, the deficit cannot be met.

Directions (Q. Nos. 59 and 60) *From the four logical diagrams, select the one which best illustrates the relationship among the three given classes in the questions.*

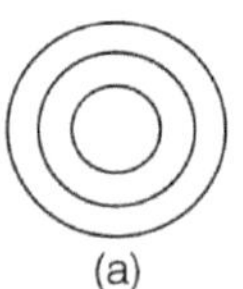 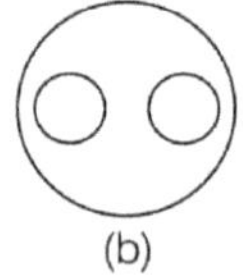 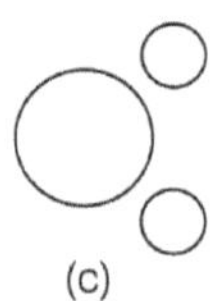 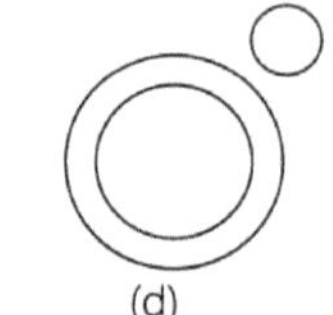

  (a)   (b)   (c)   (d)

59. Judge, Thief, Criminal

60. Square, Rectangle, Polygon

Section C : General Knowledge And Current Affairs

61. Which one of the following hotels in India is called one of the "ten romantic hotels in the world" according to a Chic French lifestyle magazine and is also regarded as a perfect example of an inn of the British colonial era, "a jewel of the Raj"?
(a) The Windamere Hotel, Darjeeling
(b) Woodville Palace Hotel, Shimla
(b) The Elgin Hotel, Darjeeling
(d) Hotel Fairhavens, Nainital

62. The 250 year old heritage hotel "Ahilya Fort" is located in which part of India?
(a) Udaipur, Rajasthan
(b) Maheshwar, Madhya Pradesh
(c) Kangra, Himachal Pradesh
(d) Jhansi, Uttar Pradesh

63. Which city of Madhya Pradesh is having famous destinations like MP Tourism's Yacht Club, Upper and Lower Lakes, "Van Vihar" (Safari Park)?
(a) Bhopal   (b) Gwalior   (c) Indore   (d) Ujjain

64. Domino's Pizza is world famous pizza restaurant chain from :
(a) Italy   (b) USA   (c) UK   (d) France

65. Who invented the clinical thermometer?
(a) Alexander Fleming   (b) Gabriel D Fahrenheit
(c) Edward Jenner   (d) Louis Pasteur

66. Vasco da Gama was the first European to find a sea route to India and landed at :
(a) Surat   (b) Calcutta   (c) Pondicherry   (d) Calicut

67. Which Wildlife National Park of the Karnataka is also known by the name Rajiv Gandhi National Park?
(a) Bandipur National Park
(b) Bhadra Wildlife Sanctuary
(c) Dandeli Wildlife Sanctuary
(d) Nagarhole National Park

68. The .... is the former palace residence of the Maharajas, and has been carefully and meticulously restored was designed and built by Maharaja Pratap Singh in 1910.
(a) Lalit Laxmi Vilas Palace, Udaipur
(b) Lalit Ashok, Bengaluru
(c) Lalit Temple View, Khajuraho
(d) Lalit Grand Palace, Srinagar

69. Which of the following statements is/are true about 'The Darjeeling Himalayan Railway'?
(a) The train goes via Kurseong.
(b) It is a UNESCO World Heritage site.

(c) The toy train runs between New Jalpaiguri and Darjeeling.
(d) All of the above

70. How many members of Rajya Sabha, the Upper House of Parliament of India retire in every two years?
(a) One-third   (b) One-fourth
(c) One-fifth   (d) One-sixth

71. In which year, Mahatma Gandhi launched the Quit India Movement?
(a) 1930   (b) 1939   (c) 1942   (d) 1945

72. Which one of the following hill stations in Himachal Pradesh is built on five hills-Kathlog, Patreyn, Tehra, Bakrota and Balun?
(a) Chamba   (b) Khajjiar
(c) Dalhousie   (d) Shimla

73. When was the United Nations (UN) formed?
(a) 14th February, 1942   (b) 24th, October, 1945
(c) 24th January, 1947   (d) 07th March, 1949

74. Maggi Noodles is from the house of :
(a) Lotte India Ltd   (b) Parle Agro
(c) Nestle India Ltd   (d) Cadbury India Ltd

75. Greenland is the largest island in the world and is a self-governing province of :
(a) Denmark   (b) Iceland
(c) Canada   (d) Norway

76. The longitude running through the old Royal Observatory at Greenwich near London is marked 0° and is called as the :
(a) Tropic of Cancer   (b) Tropic of Capricorn
(c) Equator   (d) Prime Meridian

77. India played with .... and won 4:1 in the Asia-Oceania Group One Davis Cup in February 2017.
(a) Japan   (b) South Korea
(c) China   (d) New Zealand

78. The Goa Legislative Assembly has how many seats?
(a) 40   (b) 59
(c) 70   (d) None of these

79. The area on both sides of the Equator, between the Tropic of Cancer and the Tropic of Capricorn is called the :
(a) Temperate Zone
(b) Frigid Zone
(c) Torrid Zone
(d) None of the above

80. "Ginger Hotels", the popular chain of budget hotels is owned by the :
(a) Oberoi Group　　(b) Tata Group
(c) Ambassador Hotels　　(d) Park Hotels

81. Deficiency of which one of the following vitamins causes swelling and bleeding of gums due to scurvy in human beings?
(a) Vitamin A　　(b) Vitamin B
(c) Vitamin C　　(d) Vitamin D

82. Which Indian shuttler has attained the Junior World No.1 spot as per the Badminton World Federation (BWF) ranking announced in February 2017?
(a) Yuzvendra Chahal　　(b) Vishnu Vardhan
(c) Lakshya Sen　　(d) Saketh Myneni

83. Which company has introduced its tea brand 'Teavana', in India in January 2017?
(a) Starbucks　　(b) Nescafe
(c) Costa Coffee　　(c) Gloria Jean's

84. … has been recently announced as the best actress in the 64th National Film Awards for the year 2016.
(a) Surabhi Lakshmi　　(b) Zaira Wasim
(c) Kangana Ranaut　　(d) Tanvi Azmi

85. Which planet of the Solar System has two moons, named as 'Phobos' and 'Deimos'?
(a) Venus　　(b) Mars　　(c) Jupiter　　(d) Saturn

86. Which of the following belong(s) to the Oberoi Group of Hotels and Resorts?
(a) The Motor Vessel Vrinda, Kerala
(b) The Nile Cruisers
(c) The Trident Hotels
(d) All of the above

87. Which company has unveiled low calorie beverage brand 'Aquarius' in India in December 2016?
(a) PepsiCo　　(c) Parle Agro
(c) Coca Cola　　(d) Bisleri

88. 'Four Seasons Hotels Ltd' is an international luxury hospitality company, which owns more than 100 hotels worldwide and has its headquarters in :
(a) New York　(b) London　(c) Tokyo　(d) Toronto

89. The Incredible India calendar 2017 is having a picture of —— for the month of January.
(a) Gulmarg, Jammu & Kashmir
(b) Shree Jagannath Temple, Odisha
(c) Khajuraho, Madhaya Pradesh
(d) Charminar, Telangana

90. The 2017 Yes Chef Conclave has taken place in India on 11th and 12th April 2017 in :
(a) New Delhi
(b) Mumbai
(c) Bengaluru
(d) Bhubaneswar

Section D : Aptitude For Service Sector

91. Which of the following do you consider as the most important quality of social worker?
(a) Helping attitude　　(b) Hard working nature
(c) Adequate motivation　　(d) All of these

92. When you are going on your motorcycle, you happen to meet with a minor accident involving a scooter. You will
(a) try to avoid the scene and get away.
(b) park your motorcycle and shout at the scooterist blaming him.
(c) park your motorcycle and hit the scooterist at the earliest.
(d) help the scooterist to get up and tender an apology for the inadvertent accident.

93. A small park in front of your house usually remains dirty and you have been observing this situation for a long time now. You will
(a) expect others to do something about it.
(b) try and ignore it, as it does not directly concern you.
(c) ask you neighbours to do something about it.
(d) take initiative to clean the park and request others to helpout as well.

94. When some representative of a well known old age home approaches you for some monetary help, you will
(a) ask him to get away and not waste your time.
(b) feel that people like this are quite dishonest and deserve no help.
(c) try and ignore him by looking busy in something else.
(d) spare whatever money you can and donate.

95. While working as a member of a team, due to a mistake by a team member, your task is not completed and your boss gets quite angry. You will
(a) go to the boss and tell him what has happened.
(b) blame your team member for the lapse and embarrass him.
(c) take the blame on the entire team and say sorry.
(d) fight and abuse the team member in front of all others.

96. While you are talking to your friend on the road, one man asks you an address in your colony. You will
(a) bluntly tell him that you are not there to guide people.
(b) tell him the general direction where he could find the address.
(c) guide him adequately so that he understands.
(d) ask him to take somebody else's help.

97. While travelling in a crowded metro, you are busy talking on your mobile when your co-passengers object as they are getting disturbed. You will
(a) quickly finish your call and say sorry.
(b) continue with your call as if nothing has happened.
(c) raise your voice and pickup a fight.
(d) tell them that you have nothing to do with them and they should mind their own business.

98. One of your colleagues in the office is facing some financial problem and seeks your help. You will
(a) tell him bluntly that he needs to manage his finance in a much better fashion.
(b) spare some money and try to help him.
(c) politely tell him that you do not believe in such financial transactions.
(d) ask some other colleague to help him if he can.

99. While travelling in Shatabdi Express, you see the passenger in front of your seat has forgotten to take off the charger he was using. You will
(a) quietly remove the charger and keep in your bag.
(b) ignore the charger and mind your own business.
(c) tell the passenger who is the owner of the charger to keep it with him.
(d) pick up an argument to claim it is your charger.

100. Being the leader of a team to complete a project to take important decisions, you would
(a) let others decide without seeking your opinion.
(b) decide first and then let others know of it subsequently.
(c) seek others opinion and then take a decision.
(d) ask some other members of the team to decide on your behalf.

101. While you are out of your house, you realise that there has been a theft in your house and a number of costly items have been stolen. You will
(a) talk to your neighbours and try to hold them responsible, since they were at home when the theft occurred.
(b) feel extremely bad and curse your luck.
(c) start searching for a new house to shift there.
(d) try to forget the incident and be more careful in the future.

102. While working in an office which has public dealings on a day when a number of employees are absent, you will
(a) also take leave and go home.
(b) tell your superior to arrange more manpower.
(c) just perform your share of work and refuse other work.
(d) try to do extra work and help deal with other matters to help public.

103. While working in a corporate, suddenly you receive transfer orders to work in another office on a different location, you will
(a) take long leave and avoid going there.
(b) try and adjust with new environment of work as usual.
(c) lose interest in your work and just carry on.
(d) avoid working at the new place and try changing your transfer orders.

104. While dealing with an angry customer in a hotel, you will
(a) ask to meet your senior and refuse to talk to him.
(b) consult your senior and try to resolve the issue at the earliest.
(c) shout back at him and tell him he has no business to show his temper.
(d) ignore him totally and mind your business.

105. While functioning in your office if you commit a mistake, you will
(a) try and blame others for the same.
(b) try to cover up the issue somehow.
(c) accept your fault and say sorry.
(d) just try to rectify your mistake by putting extra work.

106. While driving your scooter you inadvertently hit a woman and she gets injured. You will
(a) outrightly blame her for the accident.
(b) try to runaway from the accident scene.
(c) accept your mistake and take her to the nearest hospital.
(d) ask others on the road to help her.

107. In your office an employee working under you comes late for work often. You will
(a) take steps to remove him from his job.
(b) call him and severally warn him to become punctual.
(c) speak to him personally and try to find reasons for such behaviour and counsel him.
(d) ignore him and let him come late.

108. In your office, your boss finds fault with your work often and does not appreciate the good work done by you, you will
(a) ignore him and mind your own business.
(b) pick up a fight with him and argue on small issues.
(c) ask your colleagues to speak to your boss on your behalf.
(d) talk to your boss and try to find out the real issue and subsequently initiate corrective action.

109. Your immediate neighbour often parks his car in the slot meant for you in front of your office. You will
(a) tell your friends in your neighbourhood about the stupidity of your neighbour.
(b) pickup a fight with him on the issue.
(c) politely tell him to park his car in his slot and not yours.
(d) park your car in such a fashion that he cannot take out his car.

110. A family in your neighbourhood often plays music loudly causing tremendous disturbance to all in the area. You will
(a) try and forget about it.
(b) go and request your neighbour not to disturb you.
(c) tell your other neighbours about this repeated disturbance.
(d) pick up a fight with the neighbour, who plays loud music.

111. While you leave your office in the evening, you will
(a) personally see that all lights and fans are switched off.
(b) feel that this is certainly not your job.
(c) expect your lower staff to do it.
(d) ask yor subordinates to ensure this.

112. While travelling in a train, you purchase and drink a bottle of mineral water. After that, you will
(a) leave the empty bottle in the train.
(b) throw the bottle out of the running train.
(c) keep the bottle with you and after twisting it throw it in a dustbin.
(d) expect your co-passenger to throw the bottle in a dustbin.

113. While you ordered a shirt for yourself online, you realise that the shirt received does not fit the size you had ordered. You will
(a) shout at the delivery boy and tell him that he did not know his job.
(b) refuse to take the delivery of the shirt.
(c) take the delivery and contact the company online to exchange the shirt.
(d) never order any item online.

114. In the night you hear shouts of panic in your neighbourhood, perhaps there could be a theft. You will
(a) ignore the incident and think others should help.
(b) wake up your other neighbours and ask them to help.
(c) feel it is none of your job to interfere.
(d) go to the house concerned and offer help as required.

115. While travelling by air, you see the passenger sitting next to you is not feeling too well and needs help. You will
(a) change your seat immediately and shift to a vacant seat near you.
(b) ignore him completely and mind your own business.
(c) call the air hostess and ask her to help the person.
(d) help him physically and at the same time call the air hostess also.

116. A member of your team often behaves awkwardly and also does not complete the share of work assigned to him. You will
(a) take steps to remove him from the team.
(b) tell other members to speak to him to mend his ways.
(c) pickup a fight with him and threaten him that he would be dropped from the team.
(d) talk to him patiently and understand his problems and then motivate him to take part in the team effort more enthusiastically.

117. If you have just been denied promotion and your junior has been selected, what should you do?
(a) Leave the organisation.
(b) Abuse the junior for manipulation and protest against the management.
(c) Move to the court.
(d) Talk to your boss, bring out your contribution and ask for reconsideration.

118. While selecting a candidate for a service industry job, you will go for a candidate who is
(a) highly academic
(b) social and helpful
(c) quiet and an introvert
(d) responsible

119. While working in a group, you tend to be
(a) a bit assertive.
(b) cooperating with others.
(c) adjusting with other members, but as it suits you.
(d) not getting much involved with group activities.

120. When you meet a very angry customer, you
  (a) must tell him not to show his temper.
  (b) tell him to cool down and try to resolve his problem.
  (c) tell him you would refer the issue to your seniors.
  (d) tell him that there is not much you could do about the problem.

121. On coming across a very demanding and dominating customer, one should
  (a) tell him that he has no business to behave like that.
  (b) shout back at him and tell him that he is unreasonable.
  (c) politely tell him that he is unreasonable.
  (d) try and resolve his problem or inform your seniors.

122. If you mistakenly occupy a wrong berth in the train, on arrival of the rightful passenger, you would .
  (a) quietly vacate the berth.
  (b) apologise and then vacate the berth.
  (c) tell the passenger that you would vacate after you get a berth.
  (d) vacate but tell the passenger that nothing much has happened and he should not make a fuss.

123. If you had a fight with one of your close friends due to a communication gap, what would you do?
  (a) Break up with the person for ever.
  (b) Make efforts to become friends again.
  (c) Purposely avoid meeting the person.
  (d) Make efforts to have a working relationship.

124. Your colleague on his own gives you negative feed back about your work, you will
  (a) tell him it is none of his business.
  (b) tell him that no one is perfect.
  (c) tell your boss about all this.
  (d) take it sportingly and thank him for the feedback.

125. In service industry, handling difficult people and tense situations with diplomacy and tact is considered a
  (a) very important ability.
  (b) fairly significant quality.
  (c) not very important ability.
  (d) quality which can be ignored.

126. You don't like a few habits of one of your close friends, you would
  (a) tell him so and ask him to change his habits.
  (b) start ignoring him since you cannot change him.
  (c) accept him as he is.
  (d) tell him bluntly that you did not like those habits.

127. If you are a manager and one of your employees is not working properly, as a manager you would
  (a) try to develop his abilities and interest in another job.
  (b) give him two weeks to improve.
  (c) fire him.
  (d) talk to him and try to find out his problem.

128. You are a leader of a group and the group members have a problem with your style of working. How would you manage the situation ?
  (a) Continue with your style of working.
  (b) Talk to your team members and come to a solution.
  (c) Change your style of working.
  (d) Leave the team.

129. The front office in the organisation has a very uncomfortable physical set-up to work in, you would
  (a) launch a campaign to set things right.
  (b) complain to seniors regarding it.
  (c) manage somehow with reluctance.
  (d) ignore everything and concentrate on your job.

130. You find that some people in your office do not have much work, so you will endeavour
  (a) to get rid of them somehow.
  (b) to train them and make them fit for promotion to higher grade.
  (c) to shift them to other sections where there is shortage of people.
  (d) not to think much about it as the responsibility lies with others.

131. If you notice some of your colleagues cheating the organisation, and making money by huge embezzlements. you would
  (a) never tell the owners because your relations with those colleagues will be strained.
  (b) tell the owners on the condition that your name should be kept secret.
  (c) blackmail the culprits by threatening to tell the owners.
  (d) ask for your share in the money they are making.

132. Your colleague in the office is a heart patient and often does not feel well. He at times finds it difficult to finish his task and seeks help from others. You will
  (a) think that he must finish his assigned job, if he can.
  (b) try to avoid him.
  (c) ask other colleagues to help him.
  (d) go over to him and offer help.

133. While going to your office. you see an accident taking place on the road. You will
(a) observe whether others are helping or not.
(b) help if others are helping.
(c) volunteer help alongwith others.
(d) ignore the accident and proceed further.

134. Your immediate neighbour seeks your help for going to hospital as some one in their family has suffered a heart attack. You will
(a) tell them that you are terribly busy and could not help.
(b) drive them to the hospital and offer necessary assistance.
(c) ask them to call an ambulance themselves.
(d) ask other neighbour to help.

135. Which of the following human qualities you value most in your mind?
(a) Being extremely rich and selfish.
(b) Having tall and good looking personality.
(c) Being kind hearted and helpful.
(d) Being self centered and having egos.

136. While you are getting ready to go to market with your family, your close friend drops in to spend sometime with you. You will
(a) feel extremely angry by this development but feel you have no option.
(b) feel happy to receive him and go to market some other time.
(c) receive him but think to send him away at the earliest.
(d) inform him that you would see him some other time as you were going out.

137. Welfare society of your colony is organising a camp to plant trees in your neighbourhood. You will
(a) feel angry as you have no spare time for such activities.
(b) like participating, but could not go due to some sudden family commitment.
(c) show your face by going there but come back at the earliest opportunity.
(d) enthusiastically participate and plant as many trees as you could.

138. To work efficiently in service sector, you must be
(a) highly confident   (b) compassionate
(c) caring   (d) hard working

139. While boarding a bus, you notice that the person ahead of you has dropped his purse on the road. You will
(a) keep the purse, since you have found it.
(b) over look it.
(c) collect the purse and hand over the owner.
(d) expect somebody else to collect the purse and give it to the owner.

140. Your close friend requests you to join him in organising blood donation camp to collect a large quantity of blood to give to a major hospital of your city. You will
(a) feel that this is certainly not your job.
(b) tell him that you have no spare time.
(c) request your other friends to take part, since you have no spare time.
(d) rearrange your schedule and go and help your friend.

Section E : English Language and Comprehension

Directions (Q. Nos. 141-146) *Choose the word which best expresses the meaning of the underlined word in the given sentence.*

141. The tour was cancelled on account of <u>incessant</u> rain.
(a) constant   (b) heavy
(c) intermittent   (d) unexpected

142. Seeds need moisture, air and warmth to <u>germinate</u>.
(a) cease   (b) reproduce
(c) breed   (d) sprout

143. The militant was <u>nabbed</u> at the airport.
(a) caught   (b) liberated (c) traced   (d) beaten

144. Drinking is a <u>vice</u> which ultimately ruins a person.
(a) habit   (b) kindness
(c) purity   (d) evil

145. Some people try to spread <u>anarchy</u> in the country.
(a) lawfulness   (b) calm
(c) harmony   (d) lawlessness

146. <u>Frantic</u> efforts were made to save the drowning child.
(a) Hopeless (b) Desperate (c) Sincere (d) Careful

Directions (Q. Nos. 147-152) *Choose the word which is closest to the opposite in meaning of the underlined word in the given sentence.*

147. We must realize the <u>futility</u> of wars.
(a) urgency   (b) importance
(c) value   (d) usefulness

148. He is a <u>valiant</u> young man.
(a) fearless   (b) cowardly
(c) assertive   (d) sluggish

149. The new boss is well known for his <u>rigid</u> approach to all problems.
  (a) flexible   (b) quick
  (c) sympathetic   (d) logical

150. His transfer order was <u>revoked</u> yesterday.
  (a) renounced   (b) approved
  (c) cancelled   (d) proposed

151. The Indian cricketers put up a <u>dismal</u> performance in Australia.
  (a) bleak   (b) doleful   (c) desolate   (d) cheerful

152. He looked <u>agitated</u> when he arrived.
  (a) enthusiastic   (b) disturbed
  (c) roused   (d) calm

Directions (Q. Nos. 153-158) *In each of the following questions, four words are given, three of which are spelt correctly while one is mis-spelt. Choose the mis-spelt word.*

153. (a) Tolerance   (b) Benevolence
   (c) Independance   (d) Occurrence

154. (a) Leisure   (b) Trasure
   (c) Pleasure   (d) Cashier

155. (a) Meditation   (b) Conversion
   (c) Ambition   (d) Confesion

156. (a) Believe   (b) Decieve
   (c) Perceive   (d) Conceive

157. (a) Magnificient   (b) Efficient
   (c) Deficient   (d) Sufficient

158. (a) Innovation   (b) Varification
   (c) Excavation   (d) Purification

Directions (Q. Nos. 159-164) *In each of the following questions, an idiomatic expression is followed by four alternatives. Choose the one which best expresses the meaning of the given idiom.*

159. To worship the rising Sun
   (a) To honour the promising people
   (b) To honour a man who is coming to power
   (c) To indulge in flattery
   (d) To welcome the coming events

160. French leave
   (a) Long absence
   (b) Leave on the pretext of illness
   (c) Absence without permission
   (d) Casual leave

161. To pull strings
   (a) To exert hidden influence
   (b) To speed up
   (c) To start something
   (d) To tease someone

162. A green horn
   (a) An envious person
   (b) A trainee
   (c) An inexperienced person
   (d) A short-tempered person

163. To take somebody for a ride
   (a) To entertain someone   (b) To deceive someone
   (c) To keep company   (d) To ridicule someone

164. Sitting on the fence
   (a) Lazy and idle
   (b) Being stubborn
   (c) Uncomfortable
   (d) Hesitating between two opinions

Directions (Q. Nos. 165-170) *In each of the following questions, choose the most suitable word for the given expression.*

165. An animal story with a moral
   (a) Fable   (b) Tale
   (c) Anecdote   (d) Parable

166. One who cannot die
   (a) Invulnerable   (b) Perpetual
   (c) Immortal   (d) Perennial

167. Special words used by a profession or group that are difficult for others to understand.
   (a) Rhetoric   (b) Jargon
   (c) Pedantic   (d) Verbatim

168. A young person with exceptional qualities or abilities
   (a) Scholar   (b) Diligent
   (c) Freak   (d) Prodigy

169. Line at which the earth or sea and sky appear to meet
   (a) Horizon   (b) Zenith
   (c) Fringe   (d) Plinth

170. Large scale departure of people
   (a) Migration   (b) Emigration
   (c) Immigration   (d) Exodus

Directions (Q. Nos. 171-176) *In each of the following questions, a sentence is given, part of which has been underlined. Three possible substitutes for the underlined part are suggested as alternatives. Choose the alternative which can most appropriately replace the underlined part to make the sentence grammatically correct. However, if you think the sentence is correct as it is, choose 'No change required' as your answer.*

171. I advise you to <u>call upon</u> the doctor for consultation.
  (a) call in   (b) call to
  (c) call at   (d) No change required

172. The article should not <u>exceed more than</u> a hundred words.
  (a) exceed beyond   (b) exceed
  (c) exceed than   (d) No change required

173. He <u>shook hand with me</u> after receiving the prize.
  (a) shook hands with me
  (b) shook my hands
  (c) shook my hand
  (d) No change required

174. We are <u>looking forward to seeing</u> you soon.
  (a) looking forward towards seeing
  (b) looking forward for seeing
  (c) looking forward to see
  (d) No change required

175. He prefers <u>to walk than to ride</u>.
  (a) walking then riding
  (b) to walk over riding
  (c) walking to riding
  (d) No change required

176. He drives as if the road <u>belongs</u> to him.
  (a) belonged
  (b) has belonged
  (c) is belonging
  (d) No change required
Ans. (d) No change is required.

Directions (Q. Nos. 177-180) *Fill in the blanks.*

177. We felt it was a movement unable to be resisted for ....
  (a) more time
  (b) much longer
  (c) any more
  (d) any length

178. It was easy to guess what they had been doing ....
  (a) from living   (b) so as to live
  (c) for a living   (d) to live

179. She was so shy .... all invitations.
  (a) that to refuse   (b) as refusing
  (c) for refusing   (d) as to refusing

180. .... can't always be the best.
  (a) None   (b) Every one
  (c) One   (d) No one

Directions (Q. Nos. 181-200) *Read the following passages carefully to answer the questions that follow.*

PASSAGE 1

The first step is for us to realise that a city need not be a frustrater of life; it can be among other things, a mechanism for enhancing life, for producing possibilities of living which are not to be realized except through cities. But, for that to happen, deliberate and drastic planning is needed. Towns as much as animals, must have their systems of organs-those for transport and circulation are an obvious example. What we need now are organ systems for recreation, leisure, culture, community expression. This means abundance of open space, easy access to un-spoilt nature, beauty in parks and in fine buildings, gymnasia and swimming baths and recreation grounds in plenty, central spaces for celebrations and demonstrations, halls for citizens' meetings, concert halls and theatres and cinemas that belong to the city. And the buildings must not be built anyhow or dumped down anywhere; both they and their groupings should mean something important to the people of the place.

181. According to the author, the function of a city is to
  (a) provide adequate community expression.
  (b) make available centres of recreation and public gatherings.
  (c) facilitate traffic and communication.
  (d) raise the tone of life and make it more meaningful.

182. The opening sentence of the passage implies that
  (a) the possibilities of living a decent life cannot be found in a city.
  (b) only a city can provide the means to lead a full life.
  (c) among other places, a city can also help man to lead a successful life.
  (d) a city provides better opportunities for good living than a village.

183. "A city need not be a frustrater of life" means that
  (a) one does not expect fulfillment of all life's requirements from a city.
  (b) city life provides all the essential needs of life.
  (c) a city does not necessarily lift man's standard of living.
  (d) a city should not defeat the fulfilment of life's aspirations and aims.

184. "The building must not be built anyhow or dumped down anywhere" .... the statement implies that building should be .
 (a) built with suitable material.
 (b) constructed, according to some suitable design, not indiscriminately.
 (c) scattered to provide for more of open space.
 (d) built to enable citizens to enjoy nature.

185. Cities can be made to provide full facilities for life, only if
 (a) these can be mechanically developed.
 (b) proper transport system is introduced.
 (c) cinemas, theatres and concert halls are established there.
 (d) these are thoughtfully and vigorously designed to serve people's needs

PASSAGE 2

What is immediately needed today is the establishment of a World Government or an International Federation of Mankind. It is the utmost necessity of the world today, and all those persons who wish to see all human beings happy and prosperous naturally feel it keenly. Of course, at times, we all feel that many of our problems of political, social and cultural life would come to an end if there were one Government all over the world.

Travellers, businessmen, seekers of knowledge and teachers of righteousness know very well that great impediments and obstructions are faced by them when they pass from one country to another, exchange goods, get information, and make an effort to spread their good gospel among their fellow-men. In the past, religious sects divided one set of people against another, colour of the skin or construction of the body set one against the other.

But, today when philosophical light has exploded the darkness that was created by religious differences, and when scientific knowledge has falsified the theory of social superiority and when modern inventions have enabled human beings of all religious views and of all races and colours to come in frequent contact with one another, it is the governments of various countries that keep people of one country apart from those of another.

They create artificial barriers, unnatural distinctions, unhealthy isolation, unnecessary fears and dangers in the minds of the common men who by their nature want to live in friendship with their fellowmen. But all these evils would cease to exist if there were one Government all over the world.

186. Which of the following problems has not been mentioned in the passage as likely to be solved with the establishment of world Government?
 (a) Social problems　　(b) Political problems
 (c) Cultural problems　　(d) Economic problems

187. What divides people of one country against another?
 (a) Different languages.
 (b) Different social and political systems of different people.
 (c) Material advancement of a few nations with imperialistic leanings.
 (d) Governments of various countries.

188. What was the factor that set one man against another, in the past?
 (a) Material prosperity of certain people in the midst of grinding poverty.
 (b) Superior physical strength of some persons.
 (c) Colour of the skin or construction of the body.
 (d) Some people being educated and other illiterate.

189. What will the world Government be expected to do?
 (a) It will bring about universal happiness and prosperity.
 (b) It will end all wars for all time to come.
 (c) It will bring about a moral regeneration of mankind.
 (d) It will arrange for interplanetary contacts.

190. What is the urgent need of the world today?
 (a) The establishment of an international economic order.
 (b) The establishment of a world government.
 (c) The creation of a cultured international social order.
 (d) The raising of an international spiritual army.

PASSAGE 3

True, it is the function of the army- to maintain law and order in abnormal times. But in normal times there is another force that compels citizens to obey the laws and to act with due regard to the rights of others. The force also protects the lives and the properties of law abiding men. Laws are made to secure the personal safety of its subjects and to prevent murder and crimes of violence. They are made to secure the property of the citizens against theft and damage to protect the rights of communities and castes to carry out their customs and ceremonies, so long as they do not conflict with the rights of others. Now the good citizen, of his own free will obey these laws and take care that everything he does is done with due regard to the rights and well-being of others.

But the bad citizen is only restrained from breaking these laws by fear of the consequence of his actions. And the necessary steps to compel the bad citizen to act as a good citizen are taken by this force. The supreme control of law and order in a State is in the hands of a minister who is responsible to the State Assembly and acts through the Inspector General of Police.

191. Which of the following statements expresses most accurately the idea contained in the first sentence?
  (a) It is the job of the army to ensure internal peace at all times.
  (b) It is the police that should always enforce law and order in the country.
  (c) Army and the police ensure people's security through combined operations.
  (d) It is in exceptional circumstances that the army has to ensure peace in the country.

192. The last sentence of the passage implies that
  (a) the Inspector General of Police is the sole authority in matters of law and order.
  (b) in every State, maintenance of public peace is under the overall control of the responsible minister.
  (c) a minister and a responsible State Assembly exercise direct authority in matters pertaining to law and order.
  (d) the Inspector General of Police is responsible to the State Assembly for maintaining law and order.

193. According to the writer of this passage, which one of the following is not the responsibility of the police?
  (a) To protect the privileges of all citizens.
  (b) To check violent activities of citizens.
  (c) To ensure peace among citizens by safeguarding individual rights.
  (d) To maintain peace during extraordinary circumstances.

194. Which of the following reflects the main thrust of the passage?
  (a) It deals with the importance of the army in maintaining law and order.
  (b) It highlights role of the police as superior to that of the army.
  (c) It discusses the roles of the army and the police in different circumstances.
  (d) It points to the responsibility of the Minister and the Inspector General of Police.

195. "They are made to secure the property of citizens against theft and damage" means that the law

  (a) safeguards people's possessions against being stolen or lost.
  (b) assists the citizens whose property has been stolen or destroyed.
  (c) initiates process against offenders of law.
  (d) helps in recovering the stolen property of the citizens.

PASSAGE 4

Management education in India has an intense magnetic effect on students and parents alike. The placement figures often tend to drive the community to flock towards acquiring a post-graduate degree in management in search of a bright future. As compared to the other professional courses in engineering, medicine, etc the role of management education has moved beyond transfer of academic knowledge for professional excellence to creating and transforming personality of students demonstrating confidence with character.

The expectation from managesment graduates extends beyond concepts and includes skill-sets which are contextual and application oriented. A two year exposure is expected to convert a studious student into a confident communicator, knowledgeable manager and ethical citizen. Companies too are focusing on skill-sets such as communication, team management and general awareness, behavioural compatibility, domain knowledge, emotional quotient and intelligence quotient. The programmes offered by B-schools, therefore, must project the same by enabling an interactive system of pedagogy, opportunity for expression, varying evaluation from a subjective and descriptive approach to an application oriented assessment system and provide opportunity for enhancing written and spoken communication skill.

This would entail a change in approach to teaching from a teacher driven top-down approach in a student driven bottoms-up approach and adoption of Socratic methods of discussion. A concern for community and commitment to society needs to be instilled, hence socially relevant programmes need to be part of the curriculum. For management schools, it in not just about admissions, teaching and placement, it is also about creating lifelong alliances with students and a bonding that becomes irrevocable.

196. What is the most important aspect sought to be conveyed by the author in this passage?
- (a) Students who undergo management courses get good placements.
- (b) Management is better than medicine or engineering.
- (c) Parents want their children to study management.
- (d) Programmes offered by B-schools must enable student fulfil the expectations of the environment.

197. What, according to the author, is the suggested approach B-schools need to adopt?
- (a) Character building
- (b) Student centric
- (c) Application oriented
- (d) All of the above

198. Which of the following statements is NOT true as per the passage?
- (a) Academic knowledge of management subjects alone is adequate to do well
- (b) Companies are looking towards employing individuals with an all-round capability and wholesome personality

- (c) Knowledgeable students who express their views clearly and display pragmatism are likely to be more successful
- (d) None of the above

199. What is the paradigm shift B-schools need to follow as per the author?
- (a) Admission of students and trying for their placements subsequently is sufficient.
- (b) Establishing and nurturing a long standing meaningful and beneficial association between the student and the institution is critical.
- (c) Providing the required infrastructure and facilities necessary for students to study is their only responsibility.
- (d) Inviting appropriate guest faculty to interact with students.

200. The two year curriculum in B-schools should provide students with
- (a) domain knowledge and skill sets required to enable correct decision-making.
- (b) oral and written communication skills to convey their views confidently and to contribute to team goals.
- (c) adequate exposure and inputs to undertake their social responsibilities ethically and professionally.
- (d) All of the above

Answers

1. (c)	2. (d)	3. (d)	4. (a)	5. (a)	6. (c)	7. (c)	8. (b)	9. (b)	10. (a)
11. (c)	12. (d)	13. (a)	14. (b)	15. (c)	16. (a)	17. (b)	18. (d)	19. (b)	20. (c)
21. (c)	22. (b)	23. (c)	24. (b)	25. (a)	26. (c)	27. (b)	28. (c)	29. (c)	30. (b)
31. (a)	32. (a)	33. (a)	34. (b)	35. (a)	36. (c)	37. (b)	38. (c)	39. (d)	40. (a)
41. (d)	42. (b)	43. (d)	44. (b)	45. (d)	46. (b)	47. (a)	48. (d)	49. (b)	50. (b)
51. (a)	52. (a)	53. (b)	54. (a)	55. (c)	56. (b)	57. (a)	58. (c)	59. (d)	60. (a)
61. (a)	62. (b)	63. (a)	64. (b)	65. (b)	66. (d)	67. (d)	68. (d)	69. (d)	70. (a)
71. (c)	72. (c)	73. (b)	74. (c)	75. (a)	76. (d)	77. (d)	78. (d)	79. (c)	80. (b)
81. (c)	82. (c)	83. (a)	84. (a)	85. (b)	86. (c)	87. (c)	88. (d)	89. (b)	90. (b)
91. (a)	92. (d)	93. (d)	94. (d)	95. (c)	96. (c)	97. (a)	98. (c)	99. (c)	100. (c)
101. (d)	102. (d)	103. (b)	104. (b)	105. (c)	106. (c)	107. (c)	108. (d)	109. (c)	110. (b)
111. (a)	112. (c)	113. (c)	114. (d)	115. (d)	116. (d)	117. (d)	118. (d)	119. (b)	120. (b)
121. (c)	122. (b)	123. (b)	124. (d)	125.. (a)	126. (a)	127. (d)	128. (b)	129. (d)	130. (c)
131. (b)	132. (d)	133. (c)	134. (b)	135. (c)	136. (b)	137. (d)	138. (a)	139. (c)	140. (d)
141. (a)	142. (d)	143. (a)	144. (d)	145. (d)	146. (b)	147. (d)	148. (b)	149. (a)	150. (b)
151. (d)	152. (d)	153. (c)	154. (b)	155. (d)	156. (b)	157. (a)	158. (b)	159. (b)	160. (c)
161. (a)	162. (c)	163. (b)	164. (d)	165. (a)	166. (c)	167. (b)	168. (d)	169. (a)	170. (d)
171. (a)	172. (b)	173. (a)	174. (d)	175. (c)	176. (d)	177. (c)	178. (c)	179. (d)	180. (c)
181. (d)	182. (b)	183. (d)	184. (b)	185. (d)	186. (d)	187. (d)	188. (c)	189. (a)	190. (b)
191. (d)	192. (b)	193. (d)	194. (c)	195. (a)	196. (d)	197. (b)	198. (a)	199. (b)	200. (d)

Hints & Solutions

1. (*c*) Average production of company *A*

$$= \frac{25 + 50 + 40}{3} \text{ lakh tonnes}$$

$$= \frac{115}{3} \text{ lakh tonnes}$$

Average production of company *B*

$$= \frac{35 + 40 + 50}{3} \text{ lakh tonnes}$$

$$= \frac{125}{3} \text{ lakh tonnes.}$$

∴ Required ratio $= \dfrac{115}{3} : \dfrac{125}{3}$

$$= 23 : 25$$

2. (*d*) Required percentage increase $= \dfrac{40 - 25}{25} \times 100\%$

$$= \frac{15}{25} \times 100\%$$

$$= 60\%$$

3. (*d*) Average production of company *A*

$$= \frac{30 + 45 + 25 + 50 + 40}{5}$$

$$= \frac{190}{5} \text{ lakh tonnes}$$

Average production of company *B*

$$= \frac{25 + 35 + 35 + 40 + 50}{5}$$

$$= \frac{185}{5} \text{ lakh tonnes}$$

Average production of company *C*

$$= \frac{35 + 40 + 45 + 35 + 35}{5}$$

$$= \frac{190}{5} \text{ lakh tonnes}$$

∴ The average production for five years was maximum for both Companies *A* and *C*.

4. (*a*) Percentage rise in 2013 $= \dfrac{35 - 25}{25} \times 100\%$

$$= 40\%$$

Percentage rise in 2014 $= \dfrac{35 - 35}{35} \times 100\%$

$$= 0\%$$

Percentage rise in 2015 $= \dfrac{40 - 35}{35} \times 100\%$

$$= 14\frac{2}{7}\%$$

Percentage rise in 2016 $= \dfrac{50 - 40}{40} \times 100\%$

$$= 25\%$$

∴ The percentage rise in production was maximum in the year 2013.

5. (*a*) Percentage of production of Company *C* to the production of Company *B*

in 2012 $= \dfrac{35}{25} \times 100\% = 140\%$

in 2013 $= \dfrac{40}{35} \times 100\% = 114\frac{2}{7}\%$

in 2014 $= \dfrac{45}{35} \times 100\% = 128\frac{4}{7}\%$

in 2015 $= \dfrac{35}{40} \times 100\% = 87\frac{1}{2}\%$

∴ The percentage was maximum in the year 2012.

6. (*c*) Let the total population of villages be *x*.

∴ 38% of 16% of $x = 12160$

$$\Rightarrow \quad \frac{38}{100} \times \frac{16}{100} \times x = 12160$$

$$\Rightarrow \quad x = \frac{12160 \times 10000}{38 \times 16} = 200000$$

∴ Population of $S = 11\%$ of $200000 = 22000$

7. (*c*) Let the total population be *x*.

∴ Required ratio $= \dfrac{46\% \text{ of } 21\% \text{ of } x}{42\% \text{ of } 11\% \text{ of } x}$

$$= \frac{46 \times 21}{42 \times 11} = 23 : 11$$

8. (*b*) Let the total population be *x*.

Now, according to the question,

$$16\% \text{ of } x = 32000$$

$$\therefore \quad x = \frac{32000 \times 100}{16}$$

$$= 200000$$

∴ Population of *Y* below poverty line

$$= 52\% \text{ of } 15\% \text{ of } 200000$$

$$= \frac{52}{100} \times \frac{15}{100} \times 200000$$

$$= 52 \times 15 \times 20$$

$$= 15600$$

9. (*b*) Let the total population be *x*.

Then, 15% of $x = 30000$

$$\Rightarrow \quad x = \frac{30000 \times 100}{15}$$

$$= 200000$$

Population of *V* in 2014 $= 200000 \times \dfrac{10}{100} = 20000$

Now, population of *V* in 2015

$$= 20000 \times \frac{110}{100}$$

$$= 22000$$

$\therefore$ Population of V below poverty line in 2015

$$= 58\% \text{ of } 22000$$
$$= \frac{58}{100} \times 22000$$
$$= 12760$$

10. (a) Population of R in 2016 $= 110\%$ of 16% of x

[where, x = total population in 2014]

Population of Z in 2016 $= 95\%$ of 11% of x

$\therefore$ Required ratio $= \dfrac{51\% \text{ of } 110\% \text{ of } 16\% \text{ of } x}{42\% \text{ of } 95\% \text{ of } 11\% \text{ of } x}$

$$= \frac{51 \times 110 \times 16}{42 \times 95 \times 11}$$
$$= 272 : 133 \approx 2 : 1$$

11. (c) Let the numbers be $2x$ and $3x$.

Then, $\text{HCF} = x$

We know that,

Product of two numbers $= \text{HCF} \times \text{LCM}$

$\Rightarrow \quad 2x \times 3x = x \times 48$

$\Rightarrow \qquad 6x = 48$

$\Rightarrow \qquad x = 8$

$\therefore$ Sum of the numbers $= 2x + 3x$
$$= 5x = 5 \times 8$$
$$= 40$$

12. (d) Let the two consecutive odd integers be $(2n + 1)$ and $(2n + 3)$.

Then, $(2n + 3)^2 - (2n + 1)^2$
$$= 4n^2 + 9 + 12n - 4n^2 - 1 - 4n$$
$$= 8 + 8n \text{ which is divisible by 8.}$$

13. (a) $0.36 = \dfrac{36}{100} = \dfrac{9}{25}$

$\therefore$ Required sum $= 25 + 9 = 34$

14. (b) Let the total mangoes be x.

Total bruised mangoes $= \dfrac{x}{30}$

Total unsalable mangoes $= \dfrac{x}{30} \times \dfrac{3}{4}$
$$= \frac{3x}{120}$$

Now, according to the question,

$$\frac{3x}{120} = 12$$

$\Rightarrow \qquad x = \dfrac{12 \times 120}{3}$

$$= \frac{1440}{3} = 480$$

15. (c) Let the expenditure of 9th person $= ₹\, x$

Expenditure of eight persons $= 12 \times 8 = ₹\, 96$

Average expenditure $= \dfrac{96 + x}{9}$

According to the question,

$\therefore \qquad \dfrac{96 + x}{9} + 8 = x$

$\Rightarrow \qquad 96 + x + 72 = 9x$

$\Rightarrow \qquad 168 = 8x$

$\Rightarrow \qquad x = 21$

$\therefore$ Total money spent $= 96 + 21 = ₹\, 117$

16. (a) Let the number be x.

According to the question,

$$x - 36 = 86 - x$$

$\Rightarrow \qquad 2x = 122$

$\Rightarrow \qquad x = 61$

17. (b) Let the present age of Abhay's father be x yr and the present age of Abhay be y yr.

According to the question,

$$y + 6 = \frac{3}{7}(x + 6)$$

$\Rightarrow \qquad 7y + 42 = 3x + 18$

$\Rightarrow \qquad 3x - 7y = 24 \qquad \ldots\text{(i)}$

and $\qquad \dfrac{y - 10}{x - 10} = \dfrac{1}{5}$

$\Rightarrow \qquad 5y - 50 = x - 10$

$\Rightarrow \qquad x - 5y = -40 \qquad \ldots\text{(ii)}$

On solving Eqs. (i) and (ii), we get

$$y = 18 \text{ yr}, \ x = 50 \text{ yr}$$

$\therefore$ Abhay's father age is 50 yr.

18. (d) $\qquad 2^{n+4} - 2^{n+2} = 3$

$\Rightarrow \qquad 2^{n+2}(2^2 - 1) = 3$

$\Rightarrow \qquad 2^{n+2} = 1$

$\Rightarrow \qquad 2^{n+2} = 2^0$

$\Rightarrow \qquad n + 2 = 0$

$\Rightarrow \qquad n = -2$

19. (b) Let the price of sugar before reduction be x per kg.

Price after reduction $= x - 6\dfrac{1}{4}\%$ of x
$$= x - \frac{25x}{400} = \frac{375x}{400}$$

According to the question,

$$\frac{120}{\frac{375x}{400}} - \frac{120}{x} = 1$$

$\Rightarrow \qquad \dfrac{120 \times 400}{375x} - \dfrac{120}{x} = 1$

$\Rightarrow \qquad \dfrac{48000 - 45000}{375x} = 1$

$\Rightarrow \qquad 3000 = 375x$

$\Rightarrow \qquad x = \dfrac{3000}{375} = 8$

Rate of sugar after reduction
$$= 8 \times \frac{375}{400} = ₹\, 7.50 \text{ kg}$$

20. (*c*) Required per cent $= \dfrac{84}{7} \times 100\% = 1200\%$

21. (*c*) Ratio of profits of A, B and C = Ratio of investment of A, B, C = $120000 : 135000 : 150000$

$$= 120 : 135 : 150$$
$$= 24 : 27 : 30$$
$$= 8 : 9 : 10$$

$\because$ Annual profit $= ₹56700$

$\therefore$ Share of $C = 56700 \times \dfrac{10}{27} = ₹\ 21000$

22. (*b*) Let the number of days be x.

Then, $15 \times 9 \times 16 = x \times 18 \times 8$

$$\Rightarrow \qquad x = \dfrac{15 \times 9 \times 16}{18 \times 8} = 15 \text{ days}$$

23. (*c*) Work done by A in one day $= \dfrac{1}{6}$

Work done by B in one day $= \dfrac{1}{8}$

Let work done by C in one day $= \dfrac{1}{x}$

According to the question,

$$\Rightarrow \qquad \dfrac{1}{6} + \dfrac{1}{8} + \dfrac{1}{x} = \dfrac{1}{3}$$
$$\Rightarrow \qquad \dfrac{4+3}{24} + \dfrac{1}{x} = \dfrac{1}{3}$$
$$\Rightarrow \qquad \dfrac{1}{x} = \dfrac{1}{3} - \dfrac{7}{24}$$
$$\Rightarrow \qquad x = 24$$

Now, ratio of share of A, B and C

$$= \dfrac{1}{6} : \dfrac{1}{8} : \dfrac{1}{24} = 4 : 3 : 1$$

$\therefore$ Share of $C = \dfrac{600 \times 1}{8} = ₹\ 75$

24. (*b*) Part filled in 1 h $= \dfrac{1}{10} + \dfrac{1}{12} - \dfrac{1}{20}$

$$= \dfrac{6+5-3}{60}$$
$$= \dfrac{8}{60} = \dfrac{2}{15}$$

$\therefore$ Time taken to fill the tank $= \dfrac{15}{2}$ h

$$= 7 \text{ h } 30 \text{ min}$$

25. (*a*) Let the distance of the post-office from the village be x km.

According to the question,

$$\dfrac{x}{25} + \dfrac{x}{4} = 5 + \dfrac{48}{60}$$
$$\Rightarrow \qquad \dfrac{4x + 25x}{100} = \dfrac{29}{5}$$
$$\Rightarrow \qquad \dfrac{29x}{100} = \dfrac{29}{5}$$

$$\Rightarrow \qquad x = \dfrac{100}{5} = 20 \text{ km}$$

26. (*c*) Given, length of the train $= 150$ m

Relative speed $= 68 - 8 = 60$ km/h

$$= 60 \times \dfrac{5}{18} = \dfrac{150}{9} \text{ m/s}$$

$\therefore$ Required time $= \dfrac{150}{\frac{150}{9}} = 9 \text{ s} \quad \left[\because \text{Time} = \dfrac{\text{Distance}}{\text{Speed}}\right]$

27. (*b*) Let the distance be x km.

Given, speed in still water $= 7\dfrac{1}{2}$ km/h

and speed of stream $= 1.5$ km/h

$\therefore$ Downstream speed $= 7\dfrac{1}{2} + 1.5$

$$= 7.5 + 1.5 = 9 \text{ km/h}$$

Upstream speed $= 7\dfrac{1}{2} - 1.5$

$$= 7.5 - 1.5 = 6 \text{ km/h}$$

According to the question,

$$\dfrac{x}{9} + \dfrac{x}{6} = \dfrac{50}{60}$$
$$\Rightarrow \qquad \dfrac{2x + 3x}{18} = \dfrac{5}{6}$$
$$\Rightarrow \qquad \dfrac{5x}{18} = \dfrac{5}{6}$$
$$\Rightarrow \qquad x = 3 \text{ km}$$

28. (*c*) Let the cost price of the milk be ₹ 1 per litre.

$\therefore$ SP of 1L of mixture $= ₹\ 1$; gain% $= 20\%$

$\therefore$ CP of 1L of mixture $= \left(\dfrac{100}{100 + \text{gain}\%}\right) \times \text{SP}$

$$= \dfrac{100}{(100 + 20)} \times 1$$
$$= ₹\ \dfrac{5}{6}$$

According to the rule of alligation,

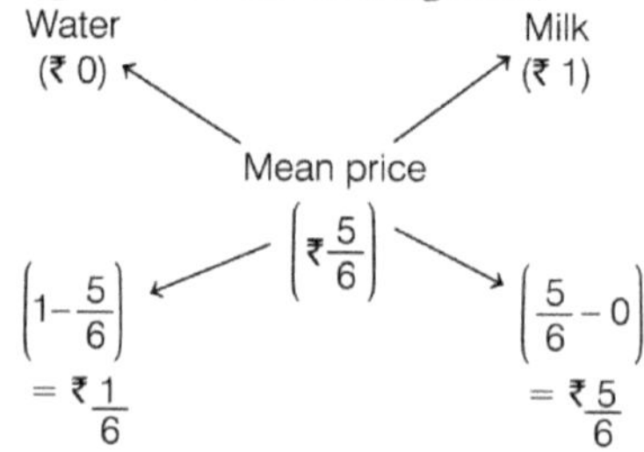

$\therefore$ Required ratio $= \dfrac{1}{6} : \dfrac{5}{6} = 1 : 5$

29. (*c*) Let the sum be ₹ P.

According to the formula,

$$A = \dfrac{P \times R \times T}{100} + P$$

$$\Rightarrow \quad 2502.50 = \frac{P \times 27 \times 4}{2 \times 100} + P$$

$$\Rightarrow \quad 2502.50 = P\left(1 + \frac{27}{50}\right)$$

$$\Rightarrow \quad 2502.50 = P \times \frac{77}{50}$$

$$\Rightarrow \quad P = \frac{2502.50 \times 50}{77} = ₹\ 1625$$

30. (*b*) Since, the interest is compounded quarterly.

$$\therefore \text{Rate of interest } (R) = \frac{20}{4} = 5\%$$

and time period $(n) = \dfrac{9}{12} \times 4 = 3$

$$\therefore \quad CI = P\left[\left(1 + \frac{R}{100}\right)^n - 1\right]$$

$$= 16000\left[\left(1 + \frac{5}{100}\right)^3 - 1\right]$$

$$= 16000\left[\left(\frac{21}{20}\right)^3 - 1\right]$$

$$= 16000\left[\frac{9261 - 8000}{8000}\right]$$

$$= \frac{16000 \times 1261}{8000}$$

$$= ₹\ 2522$$

31. (*a*)

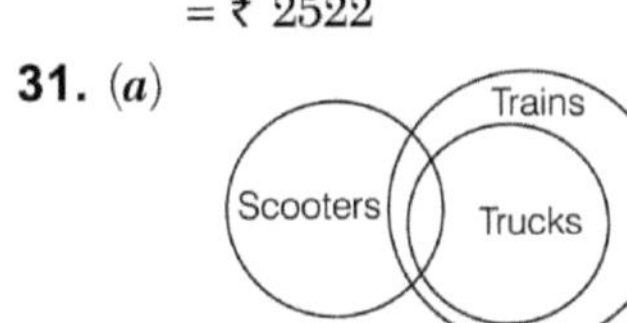

Conclusions I. (✔)   II. (✘)
Hence, only Conclusion I follows.

32. (*a*)

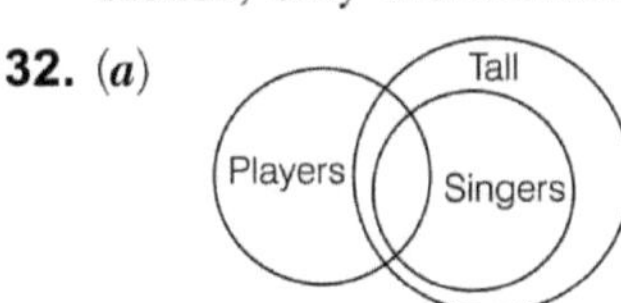

Conclusions I. (✔)   II. (✘)
Hence, only Conclusion I follows.

33. (*a*) A sharp decline in oilseed production is bound to reduce oil supply and import of oil is the only means to restore the essential supply.

34. (*b*) The inability of the small banks to compete with bigger banks shall not ensure security and good service to the customers, which is an essential concomitant that has to be looked into by the Reserve Bank.

Sol. (Q. Nos. 35–37) *According to information,*

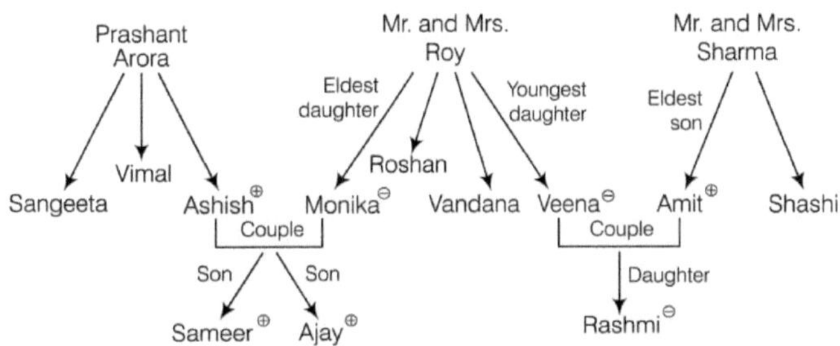

35. (*a*) Sameer is the grandson of Monika's father.

36. (*c*) Sameer's surname is Arora.

37. (*b*) Mrs. Roy is the mother-in-law of Ashish.

Sol. (Q. Nos. 38-40) *According to information,*

	Support	Coordinate
L	IT	Finance
M	Strategy	Finance
N	Operations	Finance
O	Finance	IT
P	Operations	Marketing
Q	Marketing	Operations

38. (*c*) O coordinates the IT course.

39. (*d*) Strategy is supported by M.

40. (*a*) L, M and N are coordinating the finance course.

41. (*d*) Z is the most crowded junction with traffic coming from four directions.

42. (*b*) There are 6 possible routes from X to Y.

43. (*d*) Since, supply equals demand.

$$\therefore \quad 250 + M = 800 + 300 + 225$$

$$\Rightarrow \quad M = 1325 - 250$$

$$= 1075 \text{ units}$$

44. (*b*) Total demand in E $= 550 + 800 + 650$

$$= 2000$$

$$\therefore \text{Demand in A} = 2000 \times \frac{100}{80} = 2500 \text{ units}$$

45. (*d*)

A is granddaughter of D.

46. (*b*)

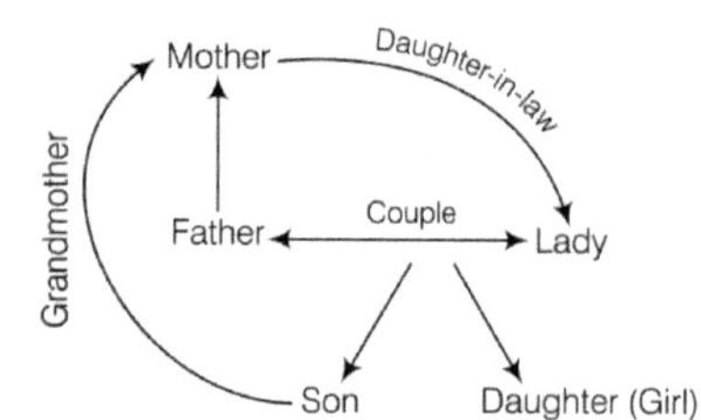

Lady is the mother of the girl.

47. (*a*)

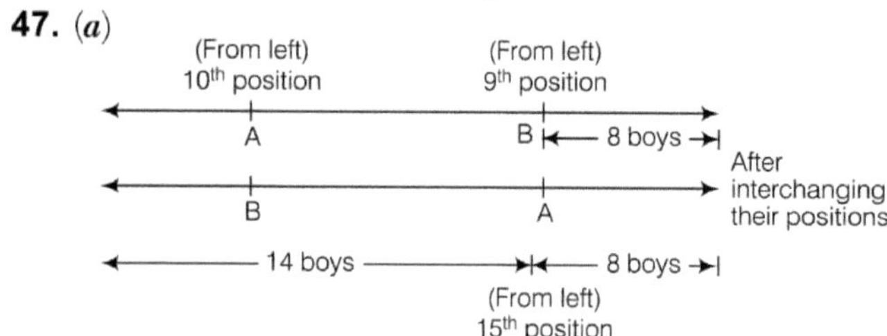

∴ Total number of boys in the row

$$= 14 + 1 + 8 = 23$$

48. (*d*)

good and tasty $\longrightarrow$ 1 3 **4**   …(i)

See good pictures $\longrightarrow$ **4** 7 8   …(ii)

Pictures are faint $\longrightarrow$ 7 2 9   …(iii)

From Eqs. (i) and (ii), good $\longrightarrow$ 4

From Eqs. (ii) and (iii), pictures $\longrightarrow$ 7

From Eq. (ii)   see $\longrightarrow$ 8

∴ '8' digit stands for 'see'.

49. (*b*)

R	O	S	E,	C	H	A	I	R,	P	R	E	A	C	H
6	8	2	1	7	3	4	5	6	9	6	1	4	7	3

From the above codes, we get

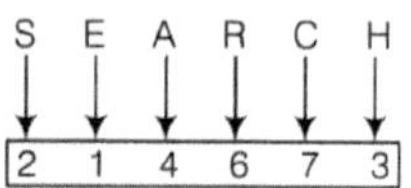

S	E	A	R	C	H
2	1	4	6	7	3

Code for SEARCH is 214673.

50. (*b*) LCM of 3, 4, 5 and 6 $= 2 \times 2 \times 3 \times 5 = 60$

2	3,	4,	5,	6,
2	3,	2,	5,	3,
3	3,	1,	5,	3,
5	1,	1,	5,	1,
	1,	1,	1,	1,

Total number of boxes

$$= n \times (\text{LCM of 3, 4 5 and 6}) + 1$$

(with also it is divisible by 7)

$$= n \times 60 + 1$$

$$= 5 \times 60 + 1 \qquad [n = 5, \text{ for divisible by 7}]$$

Hence, total number of boxes $= 300 + 1 = 301$

51. (*a*)

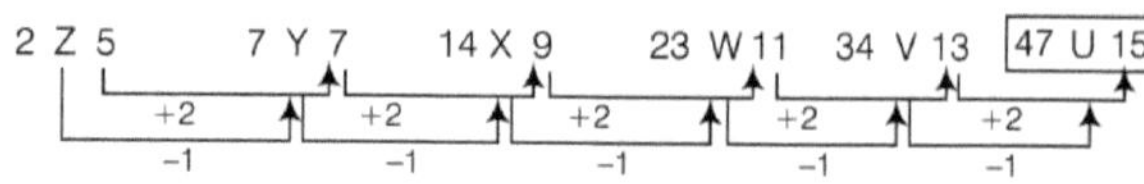

Also, $2 + 5 = 7$ $23 + 11 = 34$

          $7 + 7 = 14$ $34 + 13 = 47$

         $14 + 9 = 23$

∴ ? = 47U15

52. (*a*)

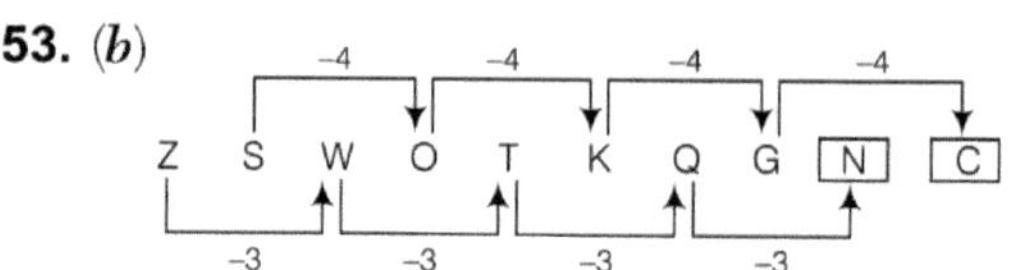

∴ ? = 99

53. (*b*)

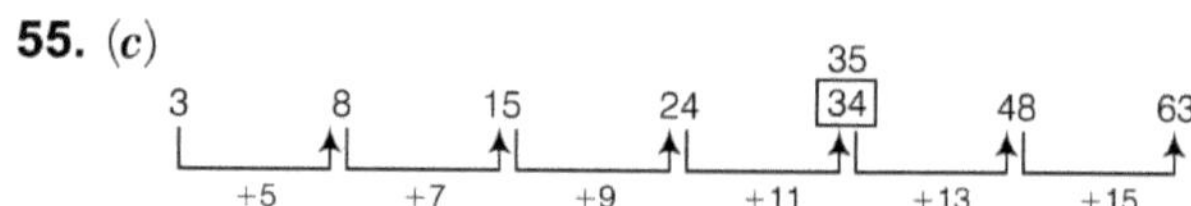

∴ ?, ? = N, C

54. (*a*) Each term of the sequence is the product of preceeding two terms. So, 5000 is wrong and must be replaced by $500 \times 50 = 25000$.

55. (*c*)

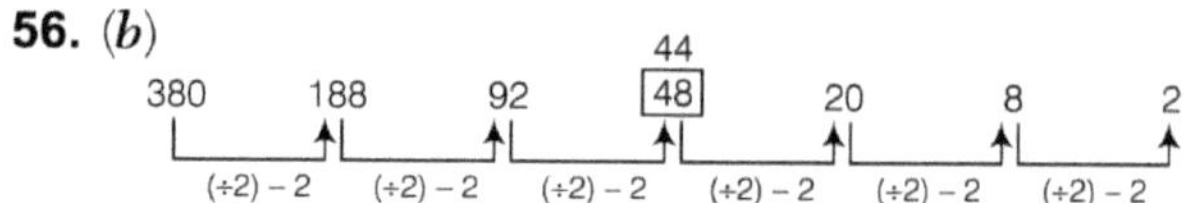

∴ 34 is the odd one out.

56. (*b*)

∴ 48 is the odd one out.

57. (*a*) Only Assumption I is implicit as smoke quitting will lead to gain weight but it cannot be assumed that those who do not quit smoking will not gain weight.

58. (*c*) Neither of the two assumptions is implicit as it is not certain that present rates are very low. Also, we can't say that increasing rates is the only way to meet deficit.

59. (*d*) A thief is a criminal but a judge cannot be a criminal or a thief.

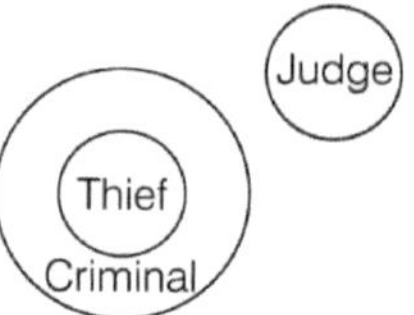

60. (*a*) All squares are rectangles and all rectangles are polygons.

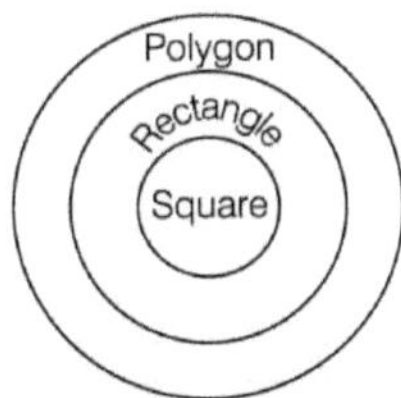

141. (*a*) The word 'incessant' means continuing or following without interruption. So, 'constant' is its correct synonym.

142. (*d*) Germinate means to begin to grow and put out shoots after a period of dormancy. So, 'sprout' is its correct similar meaning word.

143. (*a*) 'Nabbed' means to catch (someone) doing something wrong. So, 'caught' is the correct answer.

144. (*d*) 'Vice' means immoral, wicked or evil habit, action or trait. So, 'evil' is its correct synonym.

145. (*d*) Anarchy' means absence of government or a state of disorder and lawlessness. Hence, option (d) is the correct answer.

146. (*b*) 'Frantic' means conducted in a hurried, excited and disorganised way. Hence, 'desperate' meaning last-chance or last attempt is its correct synonym.

148. (*b*) 'Valiant' means fearless, brave. So, 'cowardly' is closest to the opposite in meaning of 'valiant'.

149. (*a*) 'Rigid' means unable to bend or not flexible. Hence, 'flexible' is closest to the opposite in meaning of 'rigid'.

150. (*b*) 'Revoked' means to disapprove. So, 'approved' is closest to the opposite in meaning of 'revoked'.

151. (*d*) Dismal means pitifully or disgracefully bad. So, 'cheerful' is closest to the opposite in meaning of 'dismal'.

152. (*d*) 'Agitated' means feeling or appearing troubled ; or upset. Hence, 'calm' meaning feeling free from anger or any other strong emotions is its correct antonym.

Solved Paper 2016

National Council for Hotel Management and Catering Technology

Instructions
- There are Five (A–E) Sections in this Solved Paper.
- For every correct attempt, the student will be awarded **1 mark**.
- All the questions are in MCQs form and each having four options.

Marks : 200
Time : 3 hrs

Section A : Numerical Ability And Analytical Aptitude

1. A library has an average of 510 visitors on Sundays and 240 on other days. The average number of visitors per day in a month of 30 days beginning with a Sunday is
(a) 250   (b) 276   (c) 280   (d) 285

2. A number when divided by 6 leaves a remainder 3. When the square of the number is divided by 6, then the remainder is
(a) 0   (b) 1   (c) 2   (d) 3

3. Find the sum of all even natural numbers less than 75.
(a) 1410   (b) 1406   (c) 1408   (d) 1412

4. Six bells commence tolling together and toll at intervals of 2, 4, 6, 8, 10 and 12 s, respectively. In 30 min, how many times do they toll together?
(a) 4   (b) 10   (c) 15   (d) 16

5. Mr. Bhaskar in on tour and he has ₹ 360 for his expenses. If he exceeds his tour by 4 days, he must cut down his daily expenses by ₹ 3. For how many days is Mr. Bhaskar on tour?
(a) 18   (b) 19   (c) 21   (d) 20

6. If $\dfrac{5+2\sqrt{3}}{7+4\sqrt{3}} = a+b\sqrt{3}$, then
(a) $a=-11, b=-6$ (b) $a=-11, b=6$
(c) $a=11, b=-6$ (d) $a=6, b=11$

7. Three-fifth of the square of a certain number is 126.15. What is the number?
(a) 14.5   (b) 75.69
(c) 145   (d) 210.25

8. The HCF of two number is 8. Which one of the following can never be their LCM?
(a) 24   (b) 48
(c) 56   (d) 60

9. Simplify $\dfrac{5.32 \times 56 + 5.32 \times 44}{(7.66)^2 - (2.34)^2}$.
(a) 7.2   (b) 8.5
(c) 10   (d) 12

10. If $1.5x = 0.04y$, then the value of $\left(\dfrac{y-x}{y+x}\right)$ is
(a) $\dfrac{730}{77}$ (b) $\dfrac{73}{77}$ (c) $\dfrac{7.3}{77}$ (d) None of these

11. In measuring the sides of a rectangle, one side is taken 5% in excess and other 4% in deficit. Find the error per cent in the area calculated from these measurements.
(a) 1%
(b) 0.9%
(c) 0.8%
(d) 0.85%

12. In a two-digit number, the digit in the unit's place is four times the digit in ten's place and sum of the digits is equal to 10. What is the number?
(a) 14
(b) 41
(c) 82
(d) None of these

13. When the numerator of a fraction increases by 4, the fraction increases by 2/3. The denominator of the fraction is
(a) 2
(b) 3
(c) 4
(d) 6

14. The ratio between the present ages of P and Q is $6 : 7$. If Q is 4 yr older than P, what will be the ratio of the ages of P and Q after 4 yr?
(a) $3 : 4$
(b) $3 : 5$
(c) $4 : 3$
(d) None of these

15. If the cost of x m of wire is ₹ d, then what is the cost of y m of wire at the same rate?
(a) ₹$\left(\dfrac{xy}{d} \right)$
(b) ₹(xd)
(c) ₹(yd)
(d) ₹$\left(\dfrac{yd}{x} \right)$

16. Two pipes A and B can fill a tank in 24 min and 32 min, respectively. If both the pipes are opened simultaneously, after how much time B should be closed, so that the tank is full in 18 min?
(a) 7
(b) 8
(c) 9
(d) 10

17. In a stream running at 2 km/h, a motorboat goes 6 km upstream and back again to the starting point in 33 min. Find the speed of the motorboat in still water.
(a) 21 km/h
(b) 22 km/h
(c) 24 km/h
(d) 23 km/h

18. If the sales tax be reduced from $3\dfrac{1}{2}\%$ to $3\dfrac{1}{3}\%$, then what difference does it make to a person who purchases an article with marked price of ₹ 8400?
(a) ₹ 13
(b) ₹ 12
(c) ₹ 14
(d) ₹ 15

19. A man bought a horse and a carriage for ₹ 3000. He sold the horse at a gain of 20% and the carriage at a loss of 10%, thereby gaining 2% on the whole. Find the cost of the horse.
(a) ₹ 1100
(b) ₹ 1200
(c) ₹ 1250
(d) ₹ 1150

20. Two numbers are in the ratio $3 : 5$. If 9 is subtracted from each, the new numbers are in the ratio $12 : 23$. The smaller number is
(a) 27
(b) 33
(c) 49
(d) 55

Directions (Q. Nos. 21-25) *The bar graph given below shows the foreign exchange reserves of a country (in million US $) from 2008-09 to 2015-16. Answer the questions based on this graph.*

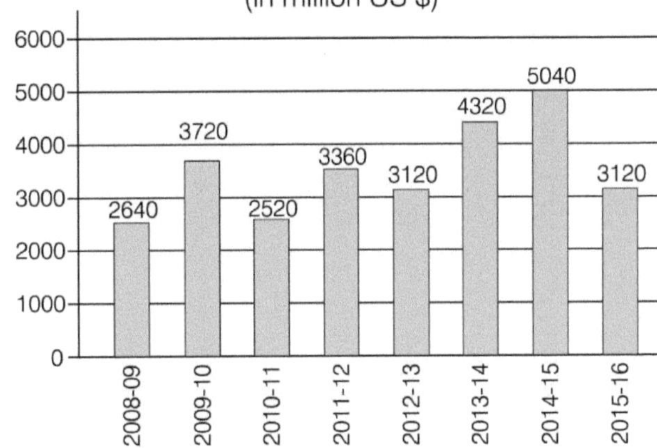

21. The ratio of the number of years in which the foreign exchange reserves are above the average reserves to those in which the reserves are below the average reserves is
(a) $2 : 6$
(b) $3 : 5$
(c) $4 : 4$
(d) $5 : 3$

22. The foreign exchange reserves in 2014-15 was how many times that in 2011-12?
(a) 0.7
(b) 1.2
(c) 1.4
(d) 1.5

23. What was the percentage increase in the foreign exchange reserves in 2014-15 over 2010-11?
(a) 100%
(b) 150%
(c) 200%
(d) 620%

24. For which year, the per cent increase of foreign exchange reserves over the previous year is the highest?
(a) 2009-10
(b) 2010-11
(c) 2011-12
(d) 2013-14

25. The foreign exchange reserves in 2013-14 were approximately what per cent of the average foreign exchange reserves over the period under review?
(a) 95%
(b) 110%
(c) 115%
(d) 125%

Directions (Q. Nos. 26-30) *The following table gives the percentage of marks obtained by seven students in six different subjects in an examination. Study the table and answer the questions based on it. The numbers in the brackets show the maximum marks in each subject.*

Students	Maths (150)	Chemistry (130)	Physics (120)	Geography (100)	History (60)	Computer Science (40)
Aditi	90	50	90	60	70	80
Aman	100	80	80	40	80	70
Sapan	90	60	70	70	90	70
Rahul	80	65	80	80	60	60
Mukesh	80	65	85	95	50	90
Tanvi	70	75	65	85	40	60
Sanjay	65	35	50	77	80	80

26. In which subject is the overall percentage the best?
(a) Maths   (b) History
(c) Physics   (d) Chemistry

27. What was the aggregate of marks obtained by Sapan in all the six subjects?
(a) 409   (b) 419   (c) 429   (d) 449

28. What is the overall percentage of Sanjay?
(a) 52.5%   (b) 55%
(c) 60%   (d) 64.5%

29. What are the average marks (approx.) obtained by all the seven students in Physics?
(a) 77.26   (b) 89.14
(c) 91.37   (d) 96.11

30. The number of student (s) who obtained 60% and above marks in all the subjects is
(a) one   (b) two
(c) three   (d) None of these

Section B : Reasoning and Logical Deduction

Directions (Q. Nos. 31 and 32) *Find the odd one out.*

31. 3, 8, 18, 46, 100, 210, 432
(a) 5   (b) 18
(c) 46   (d) 100

32. 4, 5, 15, 49, 201, 1011, 6073
(a) 5   (b) 15
(c) 49   (d) 201

Directions (Q. Nos. 33 and 34) *Each of these questions has a statement followed by two Conclusions I and II. Consider the statement and the following conclusions. Decide which of the conclusions follows from the statement.*

Give answer
(a) if Conclusion I follows
(b) if Conclusion II follows
(c) if neither Conclusion I nor II follows
(d) if both Conclusions I and II follow

33. **Statement** The best way to escape from a problem is to solve it.

Conclusions
I. Your life will be dull if you don't face a problem.
II. To escape from problems, you should always have some solutions with you.

34. **Statement** India's economy is dependent mainly on forests.
Conclusions
I. Trees should be preserved to improve the Indian economy.
II. India wants only maintenance of forests to improve economic conditions.

Directions (Q. Nos. 35 and 36) *Each of these questions has an Assertion (A) and Reason (R).*
Give answer
(a) if both A and R are true and R is the correct explanation of A
(b) if both A and R are true but R is not the correct explanation of A
(c) if A is true but R is false
(d) if A is false but R is true

35. **Assertion** (A) Baking soda creates acidity in the stomach.
Reason (R) Baking soda is alkaline.

36. **Assertion** (A) Cut fruits and vegetables should not be kept in open for long.
Reason (R) Their vitamin content is ruined.

37. In a certain code, TOGETHER is written as RQEGRJCT. In same code, PAROLE will be written as
(a) NCPQJG   (b) NCQPJG
(c) RCPQJK   (d) RCTQNG

38. If 'cinto baoli tsi nzro' means 'her village is Sarurpur'; 'mhi cinto keep tsi oind' means 'her first love is literature' and 'oind geit tsi cinto pki' means 'literature collection is her hobby', which word would mean 'literature'?
(a) cinto
(b) baoli
(c) oind
(d) geit

39. Pointing to a photograph, a woman says, "This man's son's sister is my mother-in-law". How is the woman's husband related to the man in the photograph?
(a) Grandson
(b) Son
(c) Son-in-law
(d) Nephew

40. Four girls are sitting on a beach to be photographed. Shikha is to the left of Reena. Manju is to the right of Reena. Rita is between Reena and Manju. Who would be second from the left in the photograph?
(a) Reena
(b) Shikha
(c) Manju
(d) Rita

41. A child is looking for his father. He went 90 m in the East before turning to his right. He went 20 m before turning to his right again to look for his father at his uncle's place 30 m from this point. His father was not there. From here, he went 100 m to the North before meeting his father in a street. How far did the son meet his father from the starting point?
(a) 80 m
(b) 100 m
(c) 140 m
(d) 260 m

42. One morning after sunrise, Reeta and Kavita were talking to each other face to face at Tilak Square. If Kavita's shadow was exactly to the right of Reeta, which direction Kavita was facing?
(a) North
(b) South
(c) East
(d) None of these

43. Nitin was counting down from 32. Sumit was counting upwards the numbers starting from 1 and he was calling out only the odd numbers. What common number will they call out at the same time, if they were calling out at the same speed?
(a) 19
(b) 21
(c) 22
(d) They will not call out the same number

44. In a class of 60, where girls are twice that of boys, Kamal ranked seventeenth from the top. If there are 9 girls ahead of Kamal, how many boys are after him in rank?
(a) 3
(b) 7
(c) 12
(d) 23

45. There are twenty people working is an office. The first group of five works between 8 : 00 am and 2 : 00 pm. The second group of ten works between 10 : 00 am and 4 : 00 pm. And the third group of five works between 12 noon and 6 : 00 pm. There are three computers in the office which all the employees frequently use. During which of the following hours the computers are likely to be used most?
(a) 10:00 am - 12 noon
(b) 12 noon - 2:00 pm
(c) 1:00 pm - 3:00 pm
(d) 2:00 pm - 4:00 pm

46. At the end of business conference, all the ten people shake hands present with each other once. How many handshakes will there be altogether?
(a) 20
(b) 45
(c) 55
(d) 90

47. In a caravan, in addition to 50 hens, there are 45 goats and 8 camels with some keepers. If the total number of feet be 224 more than the number of heads in the caravan, the number of keepers is
(a) 5
(b) 8
(c) 10
(d) 15

48. In a 500 m race, the ratio of the speeds of two contestants A and B is 3 : 4. If A has a start of 140 m, then A win by.
(a) 60 m
(b) 40 m
(c) 20 m
(d) 10 m

49. Two dices are tossed. What is the probability that the total score is a prime number?
(a) 1/6
(b) 5/12
(c) 1/2
(d) 7/9

50. How many words can be formed by using all the letters of the word 'DAUGHTER', so that the vowels always come together?
(a) 720
(b) 1440
(c) 2460
(d) 4320

51. What will be the difference between the sum of the odd digits and the sum of the even digits in the number 857423?
(a) Zero
(b) One
(c) Two
(d) None of these

Directions (Q. Nos. 52-54) *Study the following information to answer these questions.*

A cube is coloured red on two opposite faces, blue on two adjacent faces and yellow on the two remaining faces. It is then cut into two halves along the plane parallel to the red faces. One piece is then cut into four equal cubes and the other one into 32 equal cubes.

52. How many cubes do not have any coloured face?
(a) 0
(b) 2
(c) 4
(d) 8

53. How many cubes do not have any red face?
(a) 8   (b) 16
(c) 20   (d) 24

54. How many cubes have atleast two coloured faces?
(a) 20   (b) 24   (c) 28   (d) 32

Directions (Q. Nos. 55-57) *The following questions are based on the given diagram in which the triangle represents female graduates, small circle represents self-employed females and the big circle represents self-employed females with bank loan facility. Numbers are shown in the different sections of the diagram. On the basis of these numbers, answer the following questions.*

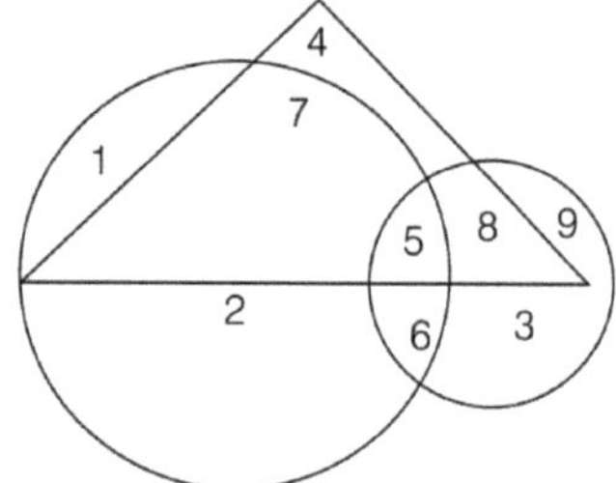

55. How many female graduates are self-employed?
(a) 12   (b) 13   (c) 15   (d) 20

56. How many female graduates are not self-employed?
(a) 4   (b) 10   (c) 12   (d) 15

57. How many non-graduate females are self-employed?
(a) 9   (b) 11
(c) 12   (d) 21

Directions (Q. Nos. 58-60) *Read the following information carefully to answer these questions.*

There are six teachers A, B, C, D, E and F in a school. Each of the teachers teaches two subjects, one compulsory subject and the other optional subject. D's optional subject was history while three others have it as compulsory subject. E and F have physics as one of their subjects. F's compulsory subject is mathematics which is an optional subjects of both C and E. History and English are A's subjects but in terms of compulsory and optional subjects, they are just reverse of those D's. Chemistry is an optional subject of only one of them. The only female teacher in the school has English as her compulsory subject.

58. What is C's compulsory subject?
(a) History   (b) Physics
(c) English   (d) Chemistry

59. Who is the female member in the group?
(a) A   (b) B
(c) C   (d) D

60. Who among the following has same compulsory and optional subject as those of F's?
(a) D   (b) B
(c) A   (d) None of these

Section C : General Knowledge and Current Affairs

61. The International Fleet Review (IFR) 2016, a ceremonial and stately inspection of naval warships by President of India has taken place in February 2016 in
(a) Vishakhapatnam   (b) Kolkata
(c) Mumbai   (d) Cochin

62. Which one of the following popular fast food chain companies has recently opened its 1000 th restaurant/store in India?
(a) McDonald   (b) KFC
(c) Domino's Pizza   (d) Pizza Hut

63. 'Neermahal', a former Royal Palace constructed by King Bir Bikram Kishore Debbarman in 1930 is a famous tourist place in
(a) Tripura
(b) Arunachal Pradesh
(c) Assam
(d) West Bengal

64. Which one of the following nations has won the men's football gold medal in the recently concluded South Asian Games 2016?
(a) India   (b) Nepal
(c) Bangladesh   (d) Maldives

65. Which among the following cities is placed first as the cleanest among all state capitals and cities with million plus population as per the Swachh Sarvekshan Report released by Government of India in February 2016?
(a) Chandigarh   (b) Tiruchirappalli
(c) Gangtok   (d) Mysuru

66. In which one of the following Indian cities, the grand finale of World's Second Young Chef Olympiad (YCO) 2016 has taken place in February 2016?
(a) Mumbai
(b) Kolkata
(c) Bengaluru
(d) New Delhi

67. Which Pakistan province has recently become first to adopt Hindu Marriage Bill, 2015 in order to allow the minority community to register their marriages?
(a) Sindh
(b) Punjab
(c) Balochistan
(d) None of the above

68. 'Taj Falaknuma Palace', a luxurious hotel by Taj Group of Hotels is located in
(a) Jaipur
(b) Lucknow
(c) Bhopal
(d) Hyderabad

69. Which one of the fast food MNCs in India has partnered with PepsiCo India in February 2016 as its new exclusive beverage and snack provider?
(a) McDonald
(b) Subway
(c) Pizza Hut
(d) Domino's Pizza

70. Which one of the following universities founded by freedom fighter Pandit Madan Mohan Malviya, is celebrating 100 years of its establishment in February 2016?
(a) Banaras Hindu University
(b) Allahabad University
(c) Deendayal Upadhyaya Gorakhpur University
(d) Guru Nanak Dev University

71. Which among the following food and edible oil companies recently launched 'Fortune VIVO', India's first diabetes care oil?
(a) Adani Wilmar Limited
(b) Cargill
(c) Agro Tech Foods Limited
(d) Marico

72. Which company has launched 'SKINN', a fine French perfume in February 2016?
(a) ITC
(b) Raymond
(c) Titan
(d) None of these

73. 'The GiG Carnival', the three-day entertainment, food and design festival as part of Incredible India initiative has taken place in February 2016 in
(a) Lucknow
(b) Delhi
(c) Chandigarh
(d) Jaipur

74. The popular heritage hotel 'Taragarh Palace Hotel' is located in which part of India?
(a) Kangra, Himachal Pradesh
(b) Nainital, Uttarakhand
(c) Jodhpur, Rajasthan
(d) Udaipur, Rajasthan

75. 'Maharaja Express', the luxury train covers Delhi-Agra-Ranthambore-Jaipur-Delhi route under the 4 days journey named as
(a) Gems of India
(b) Treasures of India
(c) The Indian Panorama
(d) The Heritage of India

76. Where did the 'Make in India', a week-long event take place in February 2016?
(a) New Delhi
(b) Mumbai
(c) Ahmedabad
(d) Bengaluru

77. Who has been chosen as the first recipient of the First World Sanskrit Award in 2016 given by Government of India?
(a) Maha Chakri Sirindhorn
(b) Raghuveer Chaudhari
(c) Khadga Prasad Sharma Oli
(d) Aneerood Jugnauth

78. 'Zahra' and 'Philae' are the two Nile cruisers in Egypt owned by which group of hotels from India?
(a) ITC Group
(b) Oberoi Hotels
(c) Tata Group
(d) Ashok Group

79. 'Umaid Bhawan Palace, Jodhpur' which has been named the world's best hotel of 2016 by the TripAdvisor's 2016 Travellers' Choice Awards, is a world famous luxury hotel owned by
(a) Tata Group
(b) Jaypee Group
(c) The Leela Group
(d) Clarks Group

80. Which former Indian cricketer has been appointed as a member of the new Anti-Corruption Oversight Group?
(a) Anil Kumble
(b) Sourav Ganguly
(c) Javagal Srinath
(d) Rahul Dravid

81. Boutros Boutros-Ghali, the former sixth United Nations (UN) Secretary-General who has recently passed away at the age of 93 was the politician and diplomat from
(a) South Africa
(b) Brazil
(c) Indonesia
(d) Egypt

82. In which of the following places, Intercontinental Hotels Group (IHG), one of the world's leading hotel companies, has unveiled its 5000th hotel 'The Hotel Indigo' in February 2016?
(a) Mumbai
(b) Dubai
(c) New York
(d) London

83. Which one of the famous chefs from India started the 'My Yellow Table Season 2', a television show on NDTV Good Times in January 2016?
(a) Kunal Kapoor
(b) Sanjeev Kapoor
(c) Vikas Khanna
(d) Shipra Khanna

84. Which one of the following companies has launched an Ayurveda product 'Ratnaprash SugarFree' in December 2015?
(a) Patanjali Ayurveda Limited
(b) Hindustan Unilever Limited
(c) Dabur India Limited
(d) Emami Limited

85. In which one of the following cities is the Simhasth Kumbh Mahaparv (Holy Dip) 2016 taking place?
(a) Haridwar   (b) Ujjain
(c) Allahabad   (d) Nashik

86. Which one of the following popular film stars is the brand ambassador of online grocery store 'BigBasket'?
(a) Deepika Padukone   (b) Ranbir Kapoor
(c) Shah Rukh Khan   (d) Jacqueline Fernandez

87. Which one of the following companies has launched ready to drink flavoured milk beverage brand 'VIO' in India?
(a) PepsiCo   (b) Parle
(c) Coca-Cola   (d) Dabur

88. Which one of the following iconic hotels of Delhi is being shut down for facelift for 2 years from April 2016 till April 2018?
(a) The Imperial
(b) The Ambassador
(c) The Taj Mahal
(d) The Oberoi

89. Who is the writer of the recently released book 'Life Mantras'?
(a) Shatrughan Sinha   (b) Subrata Roy Sahara
(c) Vijay Mallya   (d) Ratan Tata

90. 'CREAM CRACKER' and 'DIGESTIVE MARIE' are the popular range of biscuits from
(a) Britannia   (b) ITC
(c) Nestle   (d) Parle

Section D : Aptitude For Service Sector

91. While driving your car in the market, you inadvertently met with a minor accident involving a cyclist. You will
(a) angrily abuse the cyclist and tell him it was his fault
(b) try and run away from the scene of the accident
(c) help the cyclist get up and apologise for the mistake involving both of you
(d) get out of your car and hit the cyclist and create a scene

92. When you observe a cluster of slums in the heart of a modern city, you feel
(a) there is absolutely no place for such poor people in a modern city
(b) the government must give these poor people some alternative space and then shift them without force
(c) these slums must be immediately removed forcibly and area should be cleared
(d) these poor people should be given a notice of one month to shift to some other place

93. While you are studying for your examination, your neighbour's children make lot of loud noise while playing and disturb you a great deal. You will
(a) ignore the whole thing and try to focus on your studies
(b) tell other neighbours about these children and the fact they were such rowdy kids
(c) go and shout at the children and threaten them that you will beat them if they make loud noise
(d) go and request the parents of the children to stop them from making such disturbances

94. While you are walking in the park in front of your house, you observe there are very few good trees in the park. You will
(a) expect other residents to do something about it
(b) plant some trees yourself and request others also to do the same
(c) discuss the situation with other residents and plan some action
(d) try and forget about it

95. While travelling in a bus, you drink a bottle of Coke and will then
(a) push the empty bottle under the luggage of a co-passenger
(b) carry the bottle with you till you find a waste disposal place
(c) throw the empty bottle on the road
(d) look for some lonely place to throw the empty bottle

96. While travelling on a long journey in a train, you notice a co-passenger not keeping too well and was looking for some help. You will
(a) ask other passenger to assist him as required
(b) change your seat and avoid him
(c) ask other passengers if somebody was a doctor and yourself assist him in whatever way you could
(d) tell him that you were not a doctor so could not help him

97. While working as a primary school teacher, you find a poor student is not able to pay his tuition fee. You will
(a) take him to the Principal for strict action
(b) speak to his parents and ask them to pay fee
(c) find the reason for non-payment of fee and then personally help the boy, if needed
(d) punish him severely in front of the whole class

98. When a new person joins your department in the office, you feel
  (a) your boss should call you and introduce him to you
  (b) you should go and meet him and help him, if he needs any help
  (c) you must ignore him totally
  (d) he must come and introduce himself to you

99. Your driver, who has worked for you for more than 10 years honestly, wants to quit his job, you will
  (a) pay him off immediately and ask him to leave
  (b) talk to him nicely and try to find his problem and then act
  (c) ask him to leave by the month end
  (d) shout at him and call him a cheat

100. In your office, one of your colleagues often takes credit for jobs that you have done, you will
  (a) tell him bluntly that he is a dishonest man
  (b) inform your boss as to what kind of a man he is
  (c) speak to him politely and tell him that such things do not help
  (d) tell other colleagues about it to bring his image down

101. While shopping in a busy market, one 10 years old child approaches you and says that he is lost. You will
  (a) ask the child to approach somebody else, as you are busy
  (b) request some shopkeeper to help him, if he can
  (c) talk to the child and hand him over to the police
  (d) ignore him and continue your shopping.

102. When you are having a walk along the sea-shore, you notice a man drowning and shouting for help. You will
  (a) draw the attention of others and keep on walking
  (b) not like to get involved and continue your walk
  (c) go into the water to help him, as you know swimming
  (d) raise an alarm and request some other swimmer to help him

103. While walking on the road, you find an envelope which contains an Aadhar Card. You will
  (a) leave the envelope there only and move on
  (b) post the Aadhar Card to the address of its owner
  (c) give the envelope to your friend and ask him to deal with it
  (d) curse the owner of the card and call him extremely careless

104. The office you own, has recently acquired a new software and some employees are not able to work with it efficiently. You will
  (a) sack these employees and recruit trained persons
  (b) give them a short notice to get trained or leave the job
  (c) organise a short training program for these employees
  (d) accept some inefficiency and let them continue working

105. While receiving your salary, you discover that your employer has paid extra money. You will
  (a) not give the money even after employer feels he has paid extra money to you
  (b) think that your are lucky and keep the money
  (c) return the money immediately to the employer
  (d) keep the money, but plan to return the money at a later date

106. While working as a manager in a hotel, you are informed that one of your guest has suddenly become very unwell. You would
  (a) ask the guest to go to some doctor
  (b) call a doctor and send him to the guest
  (c) meet the guest and then urgently call the doctor and help the patient as required
  (d) ask your subordinate to deal with it and need not bother you

107. Truly speaking, who among the following do you admire most?
  (a) Charles Shobhraj   (b) Kapil Dev
  (c) Sooraj Pancholi   (d) Mother Teresa

108. You are waiting at the bus-stop for your bus when a passerby comes towards you and enquired about an address nearby. You will
  (a) inform him bluntly that you are not there to guide everybody around
  (b) guide him generally in the direction only
  (c) try and explain the route patiently so that he understands
  (d) tell him to ask somebody else about it

109. While you are working in your office, one colleague asks you to help him complete his urgent assignment. You will
  (a) tell him that you are busy with your work and it was not feasible to help him also
  (b) quickly finish your work and help him as best as you can
  (c) tell him that could not he see that you were engrossed with your work
  (d) tell him that you would try and help him if possible

110. When waiting to board a train, you notice an old man struggling with his luggage. You will
  (a) ask the old man to seek somebody's help
  (b) wait for somebody else to come forward and help him
  (c) willingly go to him and help him with his luggage
  (d) look the other way and ignore him

111. After having a cup of coffee in a plastic disposable cup at the railway platform, you are unable to see a dustbin around. You will
(a) leave it on the platform and move away
(b) find a place where some muck is lying and throw the cup there
(c) keep it with you till you find a dustbin nearby
(d) throw it on the railway tracks

112. While you are rushing to your office, your immediate neighbour requests you to drop his cheque in the bank, which is located about 500 yards from your office. You will
(a) tell him that it may not be possible immediately, but you may do so in a day or two
(b) take his cheque and drop during the lunch break
(c) tell him that you are not there for these kind of jobs
(d) frankly tell him that it won't be possible for you to do so

113. When travelling in a train, one of your co-passengers suddenly realises that he has lost his purse and mobile phone. You will
(a) wait for other passengers to react
(b) console him and offer some minor help that you can
(c) ask him to take the help of other passengers
(d) change your seat to avoid him

114. While you are having a walk on the road with your dog, suddenly your dog barks and injures a man on the road. You will
(a) tell the man that you have no control over your dog
(b) tell the man that you are sorry
(c) console that man and offer him to take him to the nearby hospital
(d) try to run away from the scene

115. Your next door neighbour does not care for his old parents and constantly ignores them. You will
(a) tell other neighbours to do something and help the old parents
(b) discuss this with other neighbours and try to find some way out
(c) politely discuss the topic with the neighbour and offer your help as needed
(d) not bother about it

116. While you are working as a manager in the house-keeping department of a 5-star hotel, one day one of your guests gets extremely angry and shouts at the staff for minor lapse. You will
(a) inform him that mistakes can be made by anyone and there is no reason for him to behave like that
(b) tell him to contact your boss and sort the matter out

(c) apologise on behalf of the staff and make amends to satisfy him
(d) tell the guest that you could shout louder than him and he must behave properly

117. While you are busy preparing yourself for a job interview after two days, your younger sister requests you to help her solve a Maths question. You will
(a) ask her to contact some friends and seek their help
(b) ask your mother to help her since you have no time to spare
(c) while having your dinner, you will find sometime and help her
(d) bluntly tell her that it is just not possible for you to spare sometime for her

118. You are going to meet your friend in the evening when your neighbour calls to help him as he is feeling unwell. You will
(a) request him to call somebody else
(b) ask your another neighbour to help him
(c) change your programme to meet your friend and instead help the neighbour
(d) ask him to wait till your return

119. You are travelling in a reserved compartment on a journey from Delhi to Lucknow, when an old man approaches you to help him as he had no reservation, but had to travel due to an emergency. You will
(a) ask him to request some other passenger to help him
(b) request the rail authorities in the train to help him out
(c) tell him that it is none of your business to accommodate him
(d) agree to share your berth with the man, if needed

120. When your preparations for board exams of class 12th are in progress, one of your friends asks you to help him out solve a few questions. You will
(a) tell him that since you have to revise so much, you have no time
(b) request him to check with some other friend and go to him
(c) adjust your timing in such a way that you can also help him
(d) avoid talking to him

121. You and your brother are staying in a joint family. Your brother wishes to stay away from your parents. You will
(a) request your brother not to separate, as you both have to look after your parents in their old age
(b) continue to stay with your parents even if your brother separates

(c) ask some other close relatives to convince your brother not to separate

(d) opt yourself to stay separately before your brother separates

122. Which of the following is considered to be one of the most desirable quality for a person working in service sector?

(a) Good health   (b) Team work

(c) Helping attitude   (d) Patience

123. While working as a teacher, you find one student is not able to cope with the lessons. You will

(a) take him to the Principal

(b) tell his parents to deal with him

(c) speak to him separately and find out his problem

(d) punish him severely in front of the whole class

124. While travelling in a train, you observe a co-passenger drops a hundred rupee not. You will

(a) ignore the incident and mind your business

(b) take the note and handover to the passenger who dropped it

(c) keep the note in your pocket as if you had found it

(d) make a noise and tell the passenger that he had dropped the note

125. While you are about to cross a major crossing, you notice a blind man struggling to cross the road. You will

(a) ask a young boy to help him cross the road

(b) go and catch his hand and help him cross the road

(c) curse the blind man and say why should he come to such busy roads

(d) continue to go your way and ignore him

126. When you reach your home after your office in the evening, you find your immediate neighbour has parked his car in the slot earmarked for you. You will

(a) call him and shout at him to make him realise his mistake

(b) call him and politely tell him that perhaps by mistake he has parked his car in your slot

(c) park your car in such a way that he cannot take out his car

(d) tell your other neighbours that how stupid is your immediate neighbour and that he has no manners

127. While you work sincerely in your office and deliver goods, your boss never appreciates your work. You will

(a) confront your boss and tell him infront of others that he is very unfair

(b) stop working and look for another job

(c) continue to work hard and perform your duty to show better results

(d) meet him separately and tell him that you are doing your work to the best of your ability

128. Everyday morning when you leave your room for your office, you

(a) leave your room in a mess and go to office

(b) tell your younger brother to arrange your room

(c) always put all things at their right places

(d) expect other family members to organise your room

129. You observe two of your neighbours are having a heated argument in front of your house. You will

(a) go to your immediate neighbour and ask him to intervene

(b) tell your other neighbours how stupid are the people who are fighting

(c) remain indoors and close your main door

(d) go and ask them to cool down and resolve the matter in an amicable manner

130. In the market, you observe a boy is driving his car rashly and hits a poor labourer, who is going on his cycle. Subsequently, the boy starts hitting the labourer blaming him. You will

(a) start shouting and hitting the boy to save the labourer

(b) ignore the accident and mind your business

(c) stop the boy from hitting the labourer and ask him to pay some money to get his cycle repaired and arrange medical aid

(d) also join the boy to abuse and humiliate the labourer

131. Your company asks you to work in another department of company, which you do not like. You will

(a) perform most inefficiently to show your disgust

(b) try to go back to your old department

(c) start avoiding your work and ask for leave frequently

(d) try to get used to the new work environment and adjust

132. In case, your colleagues tell you that you are often short tempered, you will

(a) listen to it but tell them that almost everybody loses his temper, so there is nothing serious about it

(b) tell them to mind their own business and need not comment about others

(c) take sportingly and look for some ways to control temper

(d) argue with them and assert that they are wrong

133. While dealing with a customer who is very upset about some services provided by your hotel, which of the following you need most?

(a) Cleverness

(b) Politeness

(c) Logic

(d) Patience

134. You observe one of your close friends is often unfair with you. You will
   (a) tell other friends about it
   (b) tell your friend how you feel and that this situation is not acceptable to you
   (c) continue to be friendly with him and let him realise his mistake
   (d) start avoiding meeting him

135. Your maid servant, who has been working for you for the past 2 years, now does not take the job so seriously and even replies you back. You will
   (a) shout at her loudly and tell her that you would not tolerate all this
   (b) ask her to mend her ways sternly
   (c) talk to her and try to understand her problem and then act
   (d) remove her from the job immediately

136. One of your old friends wants to borrow ₹ 20000 from you, you will
   (a) tell him that you do not like anybody borrowing any money from you
   (b) make efforts not to interact with him any more
   (c) tell others that he is so poor in managing his finances
   (d) tell him to return the money before a stipulated time but give him money

137. In case you are allotted substantial additional work in your office, you would
   (a) request your boss to provide you additional manpower
   (b) try and do your best to cope with the additional load of work

   (c) tell all others that your boss has been very unfair with you
   (d) tell your boss that you just cannot handle this much of work

138. While you are locking your flat to go somewhere, you will
   (a) expect some family member to switch off all lights and fans
   (b) ask somebody younger to you to do it
   (c) personally ensure that it is done
   (d) think that this is none of your concern

139. When your are paying him money, the old rickshaw puller requests you for little extra money than what you normally give, you would
   (a) shout at him loudly and insult him for asking little extra money
   (b) not give him any money and ask him to do whatever he felt like
   (c) give him the extra bit of money without much fuss
   (d) tell him that you would only give him what you normally give and nothing extra

140. When some old and handicapped beggar approaches you begging for money, you think that
   (a) we should not encourage begging at all costs
   (b) government should make provision for beggars so that they do not beg
   (c) begging must be declared an offence and beggars should be put in jails
   (d) you must help such people in whatever way you can and give some money or help

Section E : English Language and Comprehension

Directions (Q. Nos. 141-145) *Fill in the blank.*

141. They were disappointed to see the armed guards. It ……… them from doing anything disruptive.
   (a) inspired   (b) prevented
   (c) encouraged   (d) irritated

142. The ……… politician thought that all bureaucrats should be polite to him.
   (a) insolent   (b) merciless
   (c) civilised   (d) docile

143. Paula was ……… as a child, accepting without a question, everything she was told.
   (a) reticent   (b) taciturn
   (c) recalcitrant   (d) credulous

144. The route between the two cities has always been known to wind its ……… way through steep mountain passes and coarse terrain.
   (a) easy   (b) smooth   (c) elusive   (d) tortuous

145. As there were not enough seats to ……… so many people at the venue of the meeting, they had to put up a big tent outside.
   (a) entertain   (b) ascertain
   (c) welcome   (d) accommodate

Directions (Q. Nos. 146-149) *Identify the best way of writing the sentence in the context of the correct usage of standard written English.*

146. (a) New words could be used, if required, to express the full force of exclamation.
   (b) If necessary, new words should be used to express the full force of exclamation.
   (c) To express the full force of exclamation, if necessary, new words will be used.
   (d) New words are used, if required, to express the full force of exclamation.

147. (a) Neither he come nor he writes a letter now.
   (b) Neither does he come nor he write a letter now.

(c) Neither he comes nor does he writes a letter now.
(d) Neither does he come nor does he write a letter now.

148. (a) Emily but saw him turning again to the papers and she stopped hastily retiring.
(b) Emily was hastily retiring; but she saw him turn again to the papers and she stopped.
(c) Emily stopped retiring; but she saw him turn again to the papers.
(d) She saw him turning again to the papers and she stopped, and went again to retire.

149. (a) At first, the jury was divided in opinion, but finally it returned a unanimous verdict.
(b) At first the jury were divided in opinion, but finally it returned a unanimous verdict.
(c) At first the jury was divided, in opinion, but finally they returned a unanimous verdict.
(d) At first the jury were divided in opinion, but finally they returned a unanimous verdict.

Directions (Q. Nos. 150-154) *In each of the following questions, out of the given group of words, choose the mis-spelt word.*

150. (a) Goverment   (b) Professional
(c) Grammar   (d) Introduction

151. (a) Cureable   (b) Currency
(c) Campaign   (d) Chronicle

152. (a) Heritage   (b) Ecstasy
(c) Glimpse   (d) Discription

153. (a) Numismatics   (b) Nuisence
(c) Nucleus   (d) Numerous

154. (a) Retreive   (b) Rheumatism
(c) Reprieve   (d) Reverberate

Directions (Q. Nos. 155-159) *Choose the word which is opposite in meaning to the underlined word.*

155. <u>Nourishing</u> food is a necessity for a pregnant woman.
(a) Unwholesome   (b) Poor
(c) Undercooked   (d) Heavy

156. A feeling of brotherhood should be <u>propagated</u> amongst the masses.
(a) Disseminated   (b) Suppressed
(c) Dissipated   (d) Crushed

157. We must realise the <u>futility</u> of wars.
(a) Urgency   (b) Usefulness
(c) Value   (d) Importance

158. His punctuality and regularity <u>propitiates</u> everyone with whom he deals.
(a) Depresses   (b) Excites
(c) Enrages   (d) Appeases

159. The problem of dowry in our country has assumed <u>gargantuan</u> proportions.
(a) Negligible   (b) Bearable
(c) Minute   (d) Minimal

Directions (Q. Nos. 160-164) *In each of the following questions, choose the option which can be substituted for the given words/sentence.*

160. One who plays a game for pleasure and not professionally
(a) Veteran   (b) Player
(c) Connoisseur   (d) Amateur

161. A light sailing boat built especially for racing
(a) Dinghy   (b) Canoe
(c) Yacht   (d) Frigate

162. A house for storing grains
(a) Cellar   (b) Store
(c) Godown   (d) Granary

163. The place where bricks are baked
(a) Foundry   (b) Mint
(c) Cemetery   (d) Kiln

164. A person pretending to be somebody he is not
(a) Imposter   (b) Liar
(c) Rogue   (d) Magician

Directions (Q. Nos. 165-169) *In each of the following questions, find out which part of the sentence has an error. If there is no mistake, the answer is 'No error'.*

165. <u>Walking in the park one spring afternoon,</u> <u>a dog came running from behind</u> <u>and bit him in the right leg.</u>
      (A)   (B)   (C)
<u>No error</u>
(D)
(a) A   (b) B   (c) C   (d) D

166. <u>During their trial in the lower court,</u> <u>it was proved that the five accused</u>
      (A)   (B)
<u>did not carry any espionage activity.</u>   <u>No error.</u>
       (C)   (D)
(a) A   (b) B   (c) C   (d) D

167. <u>The Minister had requested for booking only two rooms</u>   <u>one on the third floor for his staff</u>
(A)   (B)

<u>and the other on the ground floor for himself.</u>   <u>No error.</u>
(C)   (D)

(a) A   (b) B   (c) C   (d) D

168. <u>Do you want</u>   <u>that I come with you</u>   <u>or do you want to go alone?</u>   <u>No error</u>
(A)   (B)   (C)   (D)

(a) A   (b) B   (c) C   (d) D

169. <u>Unemployment is very high at the moment</u>   <u>and it's very difficult</u>   <u>for the people to find work.</u>   <u>No error.</u>
(A)   (B)   (C)   (D)

(a) A   (b) B   (c) C   (d) D

Directions (Q. Nos. 170-174) *Choose the correct order of the sentences marked A, B, C and D to form a logical paragraph.*

170. A. Its aim was to remove from dance any external associations, so that the dancers could concentrate on pure movement and pure pattern.

      B. Abstract dance was the name of a specific style of ballet, devised in the 1920s and developed at the bahaus.

      C. Ballroom dancing, for example, is concerned with the pleasure the movement and pattern-making give to the dancers and not with some external 'programme'.

      D. In the wider sense, a great deal of dance is 'abstract'.

      (a) DBCA   (b) BADC   (c) BDCA   (d) BDAC

171. A. In those countries where the ideals of liberty and equality have received the greatest devotion and particularly in America, the political Constitution has been framed with the precise object of making impossible too great a concentration of power.

      B. A philosophy that emphasises the likeness of all men will be averse from recognising those exceptional qualities in any individual which place him so clearly above his fellows that he may justly claim to lead and influence them.

      C. A different though related strand of thought is equalitarian.

      D. Further, when circumstances make it necessary for a particular individual to display qualities of leadership in a very high degree, his position is under constant and bitter attack on the score of dictatorship, and it is necessary for him to conceal his qualities, consciously, behind a facade of 'ordinariness'.

      (a) CBAD   (b) CABD   (c) CDAB   (d) DCAB

172. A. It has removed many of the material obstacles to the pursuit of the good life from the majority of mankind in those countries at a high level of technical development.

      B. But it has exposed us to new dangers, not the obvious dangers of new weapons of destruction, but the much more serious ones of a purely materialist view of life.

      C. The growth of science and technology has conferred obvious and immense benefits upon the community.

      D. It has also, as we too often forget, made possible new and daring adventures of the mind.

      (a) CADB   (b) ABDC   (c) ACBD   (d) CDBA

173. A. There are manifest dangers in the persuasive aspect of leadership.

      B. It is alarming, for example, to reflect how great a part the power to speak well has acquired in an age of broadcasting.

      C. It is quite possible for men to feel that they are freely giving their allegiance to a leader, when actually they are simply slaves of his techniques of propaganda.

      D. At its lowest, the technique of persuasion may involve all those devices of suggestion and propaganda which are so freely available to the unscrupulous in a scientific age.

      (a) ABDC
      (b) ACBD
      (c) CDBA
      (d) ADBC

174. A. The leader should possess high intelligence.

   B. The reasons for this frequent neglect of intelligence as a prerequisite of leadership are complex.

   C. It is certainly true to say that this is more commonly underrated than any other aspect of leadership.

   D. There is first, a very general misunderstanding of such a phrase as 'of very high intelligence'.

   (a) ABCD   (b) ACBD   (c) DABC   (d) DBAC

Directions (Q. Nos. 175-179) *Choose the word/phrase nearest in meaning to the underlined part.*

175. The operation was <u>touch and go</u> as new complications arose and were solved.

   (a) safe   (b) risky
   (c) easy   (d) quick

176. My friend <u>got the sack</u> from his first job.

   (a) got tired   (b) was demoted
   (c) resigned   (d) was dismissed

177. In these days of rising prices, we are <u>paying through our nose</u>.

   (a) paying dearly
   (b) reducing our purchases
   (c) buying on credit
   (d) paying in instalments

178. The police fired <u>at random</u> at the violent crowd and several persons lost their lives.

   (a) pointedly   (b) aimlessly
   (c) unwillingly   (d) intentionally

179. He resigned the post <u>on his own accord</u>.

   (a) according to his judgement
   (b) which he liked
   (c) voluntarily and willingly
   (d) according to his convenience

Directions (Q. Nos. 180-184) *Choose the word which is nearest in meaning to the underlined word.*

180. We arrived safely at the <u>quay</u> and went ashore.

   (a) peninsula   (b) wharf
   (c) target   (d) island

181. Editors are known to be <u>pernickety</u> about grammar.

   (a) spiteful   (b) careless
   (c) fussy   (d) ignorant

182. I rather like the <u>quaint</u> little house at the end of the street.

   (a) old   (b) quiet
   (c) haunted   (d) unusual

183. Some of the discoveries of modern science are simply <u>marvellous</u>.

   (a) praiseworthy
   (b) commendable
   (c) amazing
   (d) admirable

184. The football coach had a sympathetic presence, <u>albeit</u> a commanding one.

   (a) although   (b) furthermore
   (c) because   (d) not only

Directions (Q. Nos. 185-200) *Read the passages given below to answer the questions that follow.*

PASSAGE 1

The composer Wolfgang Amadeus Mozart's remarkable musical talent was apparent even before most children can sing a simple nursery rhyme. Wolfgang's older sister Maria Anna (who the family called Nannerl) was learning the clavier, an early keyboard instrument, when her 3-year old brother took an interest in playing. As Nannerl later recalled, "Wolfgang often spent much time at the clavier picking out thirds, which he was always striking, and his pleasure showed that it sounded good."

Their father Leopold, an assistant concert master at the Salzburg, recognised his children's unique gifts and soon devoted himself to their musical education. Born in Salzburg, Austria, on 27th January, 1756, Wolfgang had composed his first original work by age five. Leopold planned to take Nannerl and Wolfgang on tour to play before the European courts. Their venture was to nearby Munich where the children played for Maximillian III Joseph, elector of Bavaria.

Leopold soon set his sights on the capital of the Hapsburg Empire, Vienna. On their way Vienna, the family stopped in Linz, where Wolfgang gave his first public concert. By this time; Wolfgang was not only a virtuoso harpsichord player, but he had also mastered the violin. The audience at Linz was stunned by the 6 year old, and word of his genius soon travelled to Vienna. In a much anticipated concert, the Mozart children appeared at the Schonbrunn Palace on 13th October, 1762. They utterly charmed the Emperor and Empress.

Following this success, Leopold was inundated with invitations for the children to play for a fee. Leopold seized the opportunity and booked as many concerts as possible at courts throughout Europe.

A concert could last 3 hours, and the child played at least 2 in a day. Today, Leopold might be considered the worst kind of stage parent, but at the time, it was not uncommon for prodigies to make extensive concert tours. Even so, it was an exhausting schedule for a child who just past the age of needing an afternoon nap.

185. According to the passage, Wolfgang became interested in music because
    (a) his father thought it would be profitable
    (b) he had a natural talent
    (c) he saw his sister learning to play an instrument
    (d) he came from a musical family

186. What was the consequence of Wolfgang's first public appearance?
    (a) He charmed the Emperor and Empress of Hapsburg
    (b) Word of Wolfgang's genius spread to the capital
    (c) Leopold set his sights on Vienna
    (d) Invitations for the miracle children to play poured in

187. Each of the following statements about Wolfgang Mozart is directly supported by the passage except
    (a) Mozart's father, Leopold, was instrumental in shaping his career
    (b) Maria Anna was a talented musician in her own right
    (c) Wolfgang's childhood was devoted to his musical career
    (d) Wolfgang preferred the violin than other instruments

188. According to the passage, during Wolfgang's early years, child prodigies were
    (a) few and far between
    (b) accustomed to extensive concert tours
    (c) expected to spend at least 6 hours in a day practising their music
    (d) expected to play for courts throughout Europe

189. Based on information found in the passage, Mozart can best be described as
    (a) a child prodigy
    (b) a workaholic
    (c) the greatest composer of the 18th century
    (d) a victim of his father's ambition

PASSAGE 2

Book clubs are a great way to meet new friends or keep in touch with old ones, while keeping up on your reading and participating in lively and intellectually stimulating discussions. If you're interested in starting a book club, you should consider the following options and recommendations.

The first thing you'll need is members. Before recruiting, think carefully about how many people you want to participate and also what the club's focus will be. e.g. some book clubs focus exclusively on fiction, others read non-fiction.

Some are even more specific, focusing only on a particular genre such as mysteries, science fiction or romance. Others have a more flexible and open focus. All of these possibilities can make of a great club, but it is important to decide on a focus at the outset so the guidelines will be clear to the group and prospective members.

After setting the basic parameters, recruitment can begin. Notify friends and family, advertise in the local newspaper, and hang flyers on bulletin boards in local stores, colleges, libraries, and bookstores. When enough people express interest, schedule a kick-off meeting during which decisions will be made about specific guidelines that will ensure that the club runs smoothly.

This meeting will need to establish where the group will meet (rotating homes or a public venue such as a library or coffee shop); how often the group will meet, and on what day of the week and at what time; how long the meetings will be; how books will be chosen and by whom, who will lead the group (if anyone); and whether refreshments will be served and if so, who will supply them. By the end of this meeting, these guidelines should be set and a book selection and date for the first official meeting should be finalised.

Planning and running a book club is not without challenges, but when a book club is run effectively, the experience can be extremely rewarding for everyone involved.

190. Which of the following organisational patterns is the main one used in the passage?
    (a) Chronological   (b) Hierarchical
    (c) Comparison contrast   (d) Cause and effect

191. According to the passage, when starting a book club, the first thing a person should do is to
    (a) hang flyers in local establishments
    (b) put an ad in a local newspaper
    (c) decide on the focus and size of the club
    (d) decide when and where the group will meet

192. Which of the following would not be covered during the book club's kick-off meeting?
    (a) Deciding on whether refreshments will be served.
    (b) Discussing and/or appointing a leader
    (c) Choosing the club's first selection
    (d) Identifying what kind of books or genre will be the club's focus

193. A good title for this passage would be
    (a) Book Clubs: A Great Way to Make New Friends
    (b) Starting a Successful Book Club : A Guide
    (c) Five Easy Steps to Start a Successful Book Club
    (d) Reading in Groups Sharing Knowledge, Nurturing Friendships

194. Which of the following is not something that successful book clubs should do?
    (a) Focus exclusively on one genre
    (b) Have guidelines about where and when to meet
    (c) Have a focus
    (d) Decide how to choose and who will choose book selections

195. Which of the following inferences can be drawn from the passage?
    (a) Smaller groups are better for a variety of reasons.
    (b) The social aspect of book clubs is more important than the intellectual.
    (c) Starting your own book club is better than joining an existing one.
    (d) When starting and running a book club, a casual approach is risky.

PASSAGE 3

Today, the import duty on a complete machine is 35% for all practical purposes, whereas the import duty on the raw materials and components range from 40%-85%. The story does not end here. After paying such high duties on components, once a machine is made; it is subjected to excise duty from 5%-10%. At the time of sale, the machine tools are subjected to further taxation, i.e., Central sales taxes and State sales taxes which range from 4%-16%. This much for the tax angle. Another factor which pushes the cost of manufacturing of machine tools is the very high rate of interest payable to banks ranging up to 16%, as against 4%-7% prevailing in other advanced countries. The machine tools industry in India has an enviable record of very quick technology absorption, assimilation and development.

There are a number of success stories about how machine tool builders were of help to the most critical times. It will be a pity, in fact a tragedy, if we allow this industry to die and disappear from the scene. It may be noted that India is at least 6000 km away from any dependable source of supply of machine tools. The Government of India has always given a great deal of importance to the development of small scale and medium scale industries.

This industry has also performed pretty well. Today, they are in need of help from India's machine tool industry to enable them to produce quality components at reduced costs. Is it anybody's case that the needs of the fragile sector will be met from a distance of 6000 km? Then, what is it that the industry expects from the Government? It wants a level playing field. In fact, all of us must have a deep introspection and recognise the fact that the machine tool industry has a very special place in the country from the point of strategic and vital interests of the nation.

196. Consider the following statements.
    1. The machine tool industry has a very meagre role to play in India.
    2. The performance of the small scale industry can be further improved with the help from the Indian machine tool industry.

Which of the statements given above is/are correct?
    (a) Only 1　　　　(b) Only 2
    (c) Both 1 and 2　　　(d) Neither 1 nor 2

197. Which of the following best explains the sentence "It wants a level playing field?

The machine tool industry in India
    (a) needs liberalised policy to import the desired components at a low cost
    (b) needs land at subsidised rate
    (c) needs electricity at subsidised rate
    (d) wants to adopt novel marketing strategies for sales promotion

198. Which one of the following is the correct statement?
    (a) The Government of India has taken due notice of the problems of the machine tool industry.
    (b) The Government of India has not taken sufficient measures to help the machine tool industry.
    (c) India should not waste its precious resources on the production of machine tools.
    (d) Banks in other countries are running in loss owing to a low interest rate.

199. According to the passage, all the following factors are responsible for high cost of machine tools in India, except
    (a) sales tax　　　　(b) excise duty
    (c) higher duty on components
    (d) high profit margin of the manufacturers

200. Why do small and medium scale industries look for help from India's machine tool industry?
    1. To compete with the IT sector.
    2. To produce components at lower cost without sacrificing quality.

Select the correct answer using the codes given below
    (a) Only 1　　　　(b) Only 2
    (c) Both 1 and 2　　　(d) Neither 1 nor 2

Answers

1. (d)	**2.** (d)	**3.** (b)	**4.** (d)	**5.** (d)	**6.** (c)	**7.** (a)	**8.** (d)	**9.** (c)	**10.** (b)
11. (c)	**12.** (d)	**13.** (d)	**14.** (d)	**15.** (d)	**16.** (b)	**17.** (b)	**18.** (c)	**19.** (b)	**20.** (b)
21. (b)	**22.** (d)	**23.** (a)	**24.** (a)	**25.** (d)	**26.** (a)	**27.** (d)	**28.** (c)	**29.** (b)	**30.** (b)
31. (b)	**32.** (a)	**33.** (b)	**34.** (a)	**35.** (d)	**36.** (b)	**37.** (a)	**38.** (c)	**39.** (a)	**40.** (a)
41. (b)	**42.** (a)	**43.** (d)	**44.** (c)	**45.** (b)	**46.** (b)	**47.** (d)	**48.** (c)	**49.** (b)	**50.** (d)
51. (b)	**52.** (c)	**53.** (b)	**54.** (b)	**55.** (d)	**56.** (a)	**57.** (d)	**58.** (a)	**59.** (d)	**60.** (d)
61. (a)	**62.** (c)	**63.** (a)	**64.** (b)	**65.** (d)	**66.** (b)	**67.** (c)	**68.** (d)	**69.** (b)	**70.** (a)
71. (a)	**72.** (c)	**73.** (b)	**74.** (a)	**75.** (b)	**76.** (b)	**77.** (a)	**78.** (b)	**79.** (a)	**80.** (d)
81. (d)	**82.** (c)	**83.** (a)	**84.** (c)	**85.** (b)	**86.** (c)	**87.** (c)	**88.** (d)	**89.** (b)	**90.** (a)
91. (c)	**92.** (b)	**93.** (d)	**94.** (b)	**95.** (b)	**96.** (c)	**97.** (c)	**98.** (b)	**99.** (b)	**100.** (c)
101. (c)	**102.** (c)	**103.** (b)	**104.** (c)	**105.** (c)	**106.** (c)	**107.** (d)	**108.** (c)	**109.** (b)	**110.** (c)
111. (c)	**112.** (b)	**113.** (b)	**114.** (c)	**115.** (c)	**116.** (c)	**117.** (c)	**118.** (c)	**119.** (d)	**120.** (c)
121. (a)	**122.** (c)	**123.** (c)	**124.** (b)	**125..** (b)	**126.** (b)	**127.** (c)	**128.** (c)	**129.** (d)	**130.** (c)
131. (d)	**132.** (c)	**133.** (b)	**134.** (c)	**135.** (c)	**136.** (d)	**137.** (b)	**138.** (c)	**139.** (c)	**140.** (d)
141. (b)	**142.** (a)	**143.** (d)	**144.** (d)	**145.** (d)	**146.** (b)	**147.** (d)	**148.** (b)	**149.** (b)	**150.** (a)
151. (a)	**152.** (d)	**153.** (b)	**154.** (a)	**155.** (a)	**156.** (b)	**157.** (b)	**158.** (c)	**159.** (c)	**160.** (d)
161. (c)	**162.** (d)	**163.** (d)	**164.** (a)	**165.** (a)	**166.** (c)	**167.** (a)	**168.** (b)	**169.** (c)	**170.** (b)
171. (a)	**172.** (a)	**173.** (d)	**174.** (b)	**175.** (b)	**176.** (d)	**177.** (a)	**178.** (b)	**179.** (c)	**180.** (b)
181. (c)	**182.** (d)	**183.** (c)	**184.** (a)	**185.** (c)	**186.** (b)	**187.** (d)	**188.** (b)	**189.** (a)	**190.** (a)
191. (c)	**192.** (c)	**193.** (b)	**194.** (d)	**195.** (b)	**196.** (b)	**197.** (a)	**198.** (b)	**199.** (d)	**200.** (b)

Hints & Solutions

1. (d) A 30 days month beginning with Sunday has 5 Sunday.

$\therefore$ Required average $= \dfrac{510 \times 5 + 240 \times 25}{30}$

$= \dfrac{2550 + 6000}{30}$

$= \dfrac{8550}{30} = 285$

2. (d) Let the number be x.

According to the question,

$$x = 6q + 3$$
$$\Rightarrow \quad x^2 = (6q + 3)^2$$
$$= 36q^2 + 9 + 36q$$
$$= 36q^2 + 36q + 6 + 3$$
$$= 6(6q^2 + 6q + 1) + 3$$

Hence, the remainder is 3.

3. (b) The even natural numbers less than 75 are

$$2, 4, 6, 8, \ldots, 74.$$

i.e., $\quad 2(1, 2, 3, 4, \ldots, 37)$

$\therefore$ Required sum $= 2\left[\dfrac{n(n+1)}{2}\right]$

$= 2\left[\dfrac{37(37+1)}{2}\right]$ $\quad$ [here, $n = 37$]

$= 37 \times 38$

$= 1406$

4. (d) Time after which bells toll together

$= \text{LCM } (2, 4, 6, 8, 10, 12) = 120 \text{ s}$

$= 2 \text{ min}$

In 30 min, the bells will toll together $= \left(\dfrac{30}{2} + 1\right)$

$= 16 \text{ times}$

5. (d) Let the number of tour days be x

and daily expense be ₹ y.

According to the question,

$$xy = 360$$

and $\quad (x + 4)(y - 3) = 360$

$$\Rightarrow \quad xy + 4y - 3x - 12 = 360$$
$$\Rightarrow \quad 4y - 3x = 12 \quad [\because xy = 360]$$
$$\Rightarrow \quad 4\left(\dfrac{360}{x}\right) - 3x = 12$$
$$\Rightarrow \quad 1440 - 3x^2 = 12x$$

$\Rightarrow \qquad 3x^2 + 12x - 1440 = 0$

$\Rightarrow \qquad x^2 + 4x - 480 = 0$

$\Rightarrow \qquad x^2 + 24x - 20x - 480 = 0$

$\Rightarrow \qquad x(x + 24) - 20(x + 24) = 0$

$\Rightarrow \qquad (x + 24)(x - 20) = 0$

$\therefore \qquad x = 20 \qquad [\because x \neq -24]$

6. (c) Given, $\dfrac{5 + 2\sqrt{3}}{7 + 4\sqrt{3}} = a + b\sqrt{3}$ ...(i)

$$\dfrac{5 + 2\sqrt{3}}{7 + 4\sqrt{3}} = \dfrac{5 + 2\sqrt{3}}{7 + 4\sqrt{3}} \times \dfrac{7 - 4\sqrt{3}}{7 - 4\sqrt{3}}$$

$$= \dfrac{(5 + 2\sqrt{3})(7 - 4\sqrt{3})}{7^2 - (4\sqrt{3})^2}$$

$$[\because a^2 - b^2 = (a + b)(a - b)]$$

$$= \dfrac{35 - 20\sqrt{3} + 14\sqrt{3} - 24}{49 - 48}$$

$$= 11 - 6\sqrt{3}$$

$$11 - 6\sqrt{3} = a + b\sqrt{3} \qquad [\text{from Eq. (i)}]$$

$$\therefore \qquad a = 11, b = -6$$

7. (a) Let the number be x.

According to the question,

$$\dfrac{3}{5}x^2 = 126.15$$

$$\Rightarrow \qquad x^2 = 126.15 \times \dfrac{5}{3}$$

$$\Rightarrow \qquad x^2 = 210.25$$

$$\therefore \qquad x = 14.5$$

8. (d) Given, HCF of two numbers = 8

We know that, HCF is always a factor of LCM.

$\therefore$ Among the given options, 60 cannot be the LCM of the numbers.

9. (c) We have,

$$\dfrac{5.32 \times 56 + 5.32 \times 44}{(7.66)^2 - (2.34)^2}$$

$$= \dfrac{5.32(56 + 44)}{(7.66 + 2.34)(7.66 - 2.34)}$$

$$= \dfrac{5.32 \times 100}{10 \times 5.32} = 10$$

10. (b) We have, $1.5x = 0.04y$

$$\Rightarrow \qquad \dfrac{x}{y} = \dfrac{0.04}{1.5}$$

$$= \dfrac{4}{150} = \dfrac{2}{75}$$

$$\therefore \qquad \left(\dfrac{y - x}{y + x}\right) = \dfrac{y\left(1 - \dfrac{x}{y}\right)}{y\left(1 + \dfrac{x}{y}\right)} = \dfrac{1 - \dfrac{x}{y}}{1 + \dfrac{x}{y}}$$

$$= \dfrac{1 - \dfrac{2}{75}}{1 + \dfrac{2}{75}} = \dfrac{73}{77}$$

11. (c) Let the original length be l and breadth be b of a rectangle.

Original area of rectangle = lb

Then, new length = $\dfrac{105}{100}l$

New breadth = $\dfrac{96}{100}b$

New area = $\dfrac{105}{100} \times \dfrac{96}{100}lb$

$$\therefore \text{ Percentage error } = \left|\dfrac{\dfrac{105}{100} \times \dfrac{96}{100}lb - lb}{lb}\right| \times 100$$

$$= \dfrac{10080\, lb - 10000\, lb}{10000\, lb} \times 100$$

$$= \dfrac{80}{100} = 0.8\%$$

12. (d) Let two-digit number be $10x + y$.

According to the question,

$$y = 4x \text{ and } x + y = 10$$

$$\Rightarrow \qquad x + 4x = 10 \Rightarrow x = \dfrac{10}{5} = 2$$

$$\therefore \qquad y = 4x = 8$$

Hence, the required number is 28.

13. (d) Let the original fraction be $\dfrac{x}{y}$.

According to the question,

$$\dfrac{x + 4}{y} = \dfrac{x}{y} + \dfrac{2}{3}$$

$$\Rightarrow \qquad \dfrac{x + 4}{y} - \dfrac{x}{y} = \dfrac{2}{3}$$

$$\Rightarrow \qquad \dfrac{x + 4 - x}{y} = \dfrac{2}{3}$$

$$\Rightarrow \qquad \dfrac{4}{y} = \dfrac{2}{3}$$

$$\Rightarrow \qquad y = \dfrac{4 \times 3}{2} = 6$$

Hence, the denominator is 6.

14. (d) Let the age of P and Q be $6x$ and $7x$, respectively.

According to the question,

$$7x = 6x + 4$$

$$\Rightarrow \qquad x = 4$$

$$\therefore \qquad \text{Age of } P = 6x$$

$$= 6 \times 4$$

$$= 24 \text{ yr}$$

and age of $Q = 7x$
$$= 7 \times 4 = 28 \text{ yr}$$
$\therefore$ Ratio of ages after 4 yr $= \dfrac{24 + 4}{28 + 4}$
$$= \dfrac{28}{32} = \dfrac{7}{8}$$

15. (*d*) Given, cost of x m of wire $= ₹\, d$

$\therefore$ Cost of 1 m of wire $= ₹\, \dfrac{d}{x}$

So, cost of y m of wire $= ₹\, \dfrac{dy}{x}$

16. (*b*) Part of tank filled by A in 1 min $= \dfrac{1}{24}$

Part of tank filled by B in 1 min $= \dfrac{1}{32}$

Let pipe B should be used for x min.
$$\Rightarrow \quad \dfrac{18}{24} + \dfrac{x}{32} = 1$$
$$\Rightarrow \quad \dfrac{x}{32} = 1 - \dfrac{18}{24}$$
$$= \dfrac{6}{24}$$
$$\Rightarrow \quad x = \dfrac{6}{24} \times 32$$
$$= 8 \text{ min}$$
So, pipe B should be closed after 8 min.

17. (*b*) Given, speed of stream = 2 km/h

Total time $= 33$ min $= \dfrac{33}{60}$ h

Let speed of boat in still water $= x$ km/h
$\therefore$ Downstream speed $= (x + 2)$ km/h
and upstream speed $= (x - 2)$ km/h
According to the question,
$$\dfrac{6}{x + 2} + \dfrac{6}{x - 2} = \dfrac{33}{60}$$
$$\Rightarrow \dfrac{6x - 12 + 6x + 12}{x^2 - 4} = \dfrac{33}{60}$$
$$\Rightarrow \quad 12x = 33\left(\dfrac{x^2 - 4}{60}\right)$$
$$\Rightarrow \quad \dfrac{12x \times 60}{33} = x^2 - 4$$
$$\Rightarrow \quad \dfrac{240x}{11} = x^2 - 4$$
$$\Rightarrow \quad 11x^2 - 240x - 44 = 0$$
$$\Rightarrow \quad 11x^2 - 242x + 2x - 44 = 0$$
$$\Rightarrow \quad 11x(x - 22)x + 2(x - 22) = 0$$

$$\Rightarrow \quad (x - 22)(11x + 2) = 0$$
$$\therefore \qquad x = 22 \qquad \left[\because x \neq \dfrac{-2}{11}\right]$$

Hence, speed of boat in still water is 22 km/h.

18. (*c*) Given, marked price $= ₹\, 8400$

Reduction in sales tax $= 3\dfrac{1}{2}\% - 3\dfrac{1}{3}\%$
$$= \left(\dfrac{7}{2} - \dfrac{10}{3}\right)\% = \dfrac{1}{6}\%$$
$\therefore$ Required difference $= 8400 \times \dfrac{1}{6 \times 100}$
$$= ₹\, 14$$

19. (*b*) Let the cost of horse be $₹x$.

Then, cost of carriage $= ₹\,(3000 - x)$

Now, SP of horse at 20% gain $= \dfrac{120}{100}x$

and SP of carriage at 10% loss $= \dfrac{90}{100}(3000 - x)$

$\therefore$ Total SP $= \dfrac{120}{100}x + \dfrac{90}{100}(3000 - x)$
$$= \dfrac{120x - 90x + 270000}{100}$$
$$= \dfrac{30x + 270000}{100}$$
$$= 2700 + 0.3x$$
Total CP $= ₹\, 3000$

$\because$ Gain per cent $= \dfrac{SP - CP}{CP} \times 100$
$$\Rightarrow \dfrac{(2700 + 0.3x) - 3000}{3000} \times 100 = 2$$
$$\Rightarrow \dfrac{0.3x - 300}{3000} \times 100 = 2$$
$$\Rightarrow \quad 0.3x - 300 = 60$$
$$\Rightarrow \quad x = \dfrac{60 + 300}{0.3}$$
$$= \dfrac{360 \times 10}{3} = 1200$$
So, cost of horse is $₹\, 1200$.

20. (*b*) Let the number be $3x$ and $5x$, respectively.
According to the question,
$$\dfrac{3x - 9}{5x - 9} = \dfrac{12}{23}$$
$$\Rightarrow \quad 23(3x - 9) = 12(5x - 9)$$
$$\Rightarrow \quad 69x - 207 = 60x - 108$$
$$\Rightarrow \quad 9x = 99$$
$$\Rightarrow \quad x = 11$$
Hence, smaller numbers is $3x = 33$.

21. (*b*) Average foreign exchange reserves over the period

$$= \frac{2640 + 3720 + 2520 + 3360 + 3120 + 4320 + 5040 + 3120}{8}$$

$$= \frac{27840}{8} = 3480 \text{ million US \$}$$

∴ Number of years in which the foreign exchange reserves are above the average reserves = 3

and number of years in which the foreign exchange reserves are below the average reserves = 5

∴ Required ratio $= \dfrac{3}{5} = 3:5$

22. (*d*) Foreign Exchange reserves in 2014-15 = 5040 million US $

Foreign Exchange reserves in 2011-12 = 3360 million US $

∴ Required answer $= \dfrac{5040}{3360} = 1.5$

23. (*a*) Foreign exchange reserve in 2014-15
$= 5040$ million US $

Foreign exchange reserve in 2010-11
$= 2520$ million US $

∴ Required increase in percentage

$$= \frac{5040 - 2520}{2520} \times 100$$

$$= \frac{2520}{2520} \times 100$$

$$= 100\%$$

24. (*a*) Percentage increase over the previous year

in 2009-10 $= \dfrac{3720 - 2640}{2640} \times 100 = 40.9\%$

in 2010-11 = Percentage has decreased

in 2011-12 $= \dfrac{3360 - 2520}{2520} \times 100$

$$= 33.33\%$$

in 2013-14 $= \dfrac{4320 - 3120}{3120} \times 100$

$$= 38.46\%$$

Hence, the highest increase was in the year 2009-10.

25. (*d*) ∵ Foreign exchange reserve in 2013-14
$= 4320$ million US $

Average foreign exchange over the period
$= 3480$ million US $

∴ Required percentage $= \dfrac{4320}{3480} \times 100$

$$= 125\%$$

26. (*a*) The overall percentage with respect to

Maths $= \dfrac{1}{7}(90 + 100 + 90 + 80 + 80 + 70 + 65)$

$$= \frac{1}{7} \times 575 = 82.14\%$$

History $= \dfrac{1}{7}(70 + 80 + 90 + 60 + 50 + 40 + 80)$

$$= \frac{1}{7} \times 470 = 67.14\%$$

Physics $= \dfrac{1}{7}(90 + 80 + 70 + 80 + 85 + 65 + 50)$

$$= \frac{1}{7} \times 520 \approx 74.29\%$$

Chemistry $= \dfrac{1}{7}(50 + 80 + 60 + 65 + 65 + 75 + 35)$

$$= \frac{1}{7} \times 430 \approx 61.43\%$$

Hence, the overall percentage is best in Maths.

27. (*d*) Aggregate marks obtained by Sapan

$$= 90\% \text{ of } 150 + 60\% \text{ of } 130 + 70\% \text{ of } 120 + 70\% \text{ of } 100 + 90\% \text{ of } 60 + 70\% \text{ of } 40$$

$$= 135 + 78 + 84 + 70 + 54 + 28$$

$$= 449$$

28. (*c*) Aggregate marks obtained by Sanjay

$$= 65\% \text{ of } 150 + 35\% \text{ of } 130 + 50\% \text{ of } 120 + 77\% \text{ of } 100 + 80\% \text{ of } 60 + 80\% \text{ of } 40$$

$$= 97.5 + 45.5 + 60 + 77 + 48 + 32$$

$$= 360$$

Total marks $= 150 + 130 + 120 + 100 + 60 + 40$
$$= 600$$

∴ Required percentage $= \dfrac{360}{600} \times 100 = 60\%$

29. (*b*) Required average $= \dfrac{1}{7}[90\% \text{ of } 120 + 80\% \text{ of } 120 + 70\% \text{ of } 120 + 80\% \text{ of } 120 + 85\% \text{ of } 120 + 65\% \text{ of } 120 + 50\% \text{ of } 120]$

$$= \frac{1}{7} \times 120 \; [90\% + 80\% + 70\% + 80\% + 85\% + 65\% + 50\%]$$

$$= \frac{1}{7} \times 120 \times \frac{520}{100} = 89.14\%$$

30. (*b*) From the table, it is clear that Sapan and Rahul obtained 60% and above marks in all the subjects.

Hence, the number of students who obtained 60% and above marks in all subjects is two.

31. (*b*) The pattern is

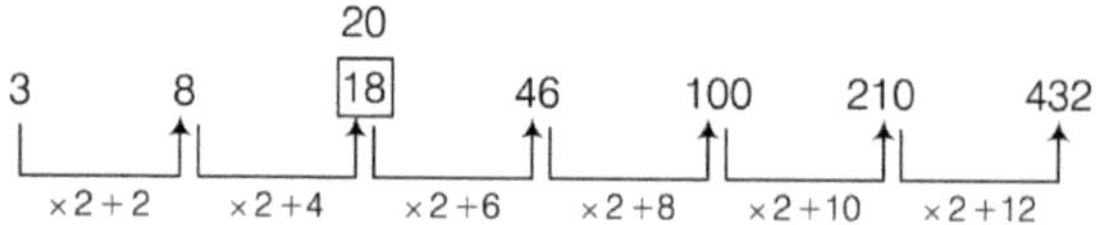

32. (*a*) The pattern is

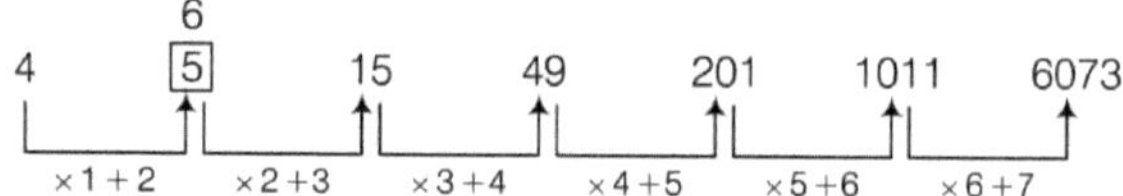

33. (*b*) Only Conclusion II follows. As, the given statement does not tell anything about life. It tells only about problems and the way to escape from them. Hence, conclusion II follows.

34. (*a*) Only Conclusion I follows. As, preservation of forest is necessary. Because tree is a part of forest and Conclusion II is not correlated with the statement. So, option (a) is correct.

35. (*d*) Assertion (A) is false but reason (R) is true. As, Baking soda is alkaline and cannot create acidity in the stomach.

36. (*b*) Both A and R are true but R is not the correct explanation of A. As, when we cut fruits and vegetables are kept in open, the vitamins in them get oxidised and remain of no use. Hence, option (b) is correct.

37. (*a*) As,

$$\begin{array}{cccccccc} T & O & G & E & T & H & E & R \\ -2\downarrow & +2\downarrow & -2\downarrow & +2\downarrow & -2\downarrow & +2\downarrow & -2\downarrow & +2\downarrow \\ R & Q & E & G & R & J & C & T \end{array}$$

Similarly,

$$\begin{array}{cccccc} P & A & R & O & L & E \\ -2\downarrow & +2\downarrow & -2\downarrow & +2\downarrow & -2\downarrow & +2\downarrow \\ N & C & P & Q & J & G \end{array}$$

38. (*c*)

cinto baoli tsi nzro → her village is Sarurpur.

mni cinto keep tsi oind → her first love is literature.

oind geit tsi cinto pki → literature collection is her hobby.

∴ Code of literature is oind.

39. (*a*)

Man in Photograph
↓
Son ⟶ Sister
↑
Mother-in-law
Woman

∴ Woman's husband is the grandson of the man in the photograph.

40. (*a*)

Left ├────┼────┼──── Right
　　Shikha　Reena　　Manju （Rita above）

Reena is second from the left in the photograph.

41. (*b*) According to the question,

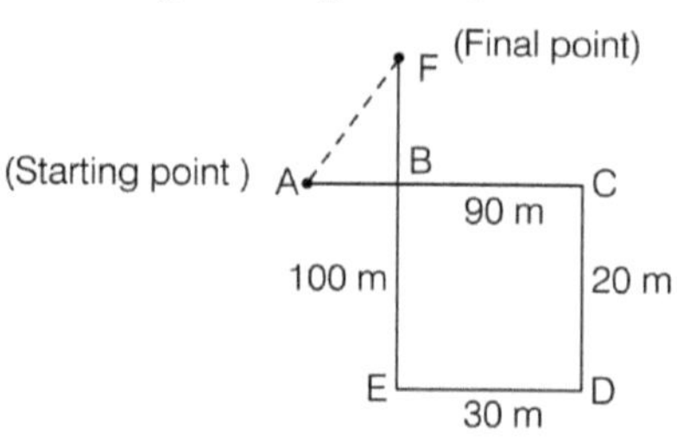

Here,　AB = 60 m, BF = 80 m

∴　　　$AF = \sqrt{60^2 + 80^2}$

　　　　$= \sqrt{3600 + 6400}$

　　　　$= \sqrt{10000}$

　　　　$= 100$ m

42. (*a*) According to the question,

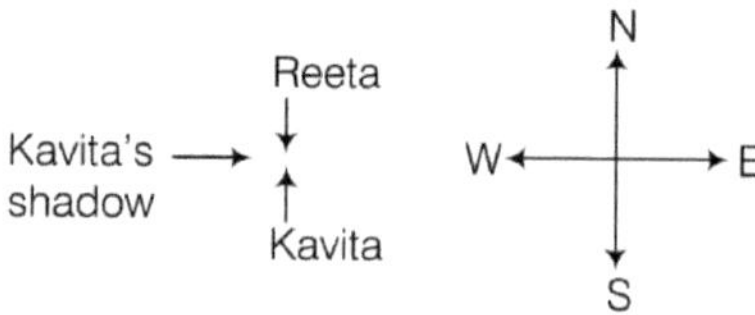

∴　Kavita was facing North.

43. (*d*) Nitin　: 32　31　30　29　28　27　26　25　24　23　22
　　　Sumit : 1　3　　5　7　　9　11　13　15　17　19　21 ...

Clearly, they will never call out the same number.

44. (*c*) Since, girls are twice that of boys.

∴　Number of girls = 40

and number of boys = 20

9 girls,　7 boys　Kamal　　12 boys
├─────── 16 ───────┼ 17 ┼── 43 ──┤

So, there are 12 boys ranked after Kamal.

45. (*b*) First group = 8 : 00 am - 2 : 00 pm

Second group = 10 : 00 am - 4 : 00 pm

Third group = 12 : 00 pm - 6 : 00 pm

So, the computers are likely to be used most during 12 noon to 2 : 00 pm

46. (*b*) Total number of handshakes $= \dfrac{n(n-1)}{2}$

$$= \dfrac{10(10-1)}{2} = 45$$

47. (*d*) Let total number of keepers be k.

∴　Number of heads $= k + 103$

and number of feet

$$= 50 \times 2 + 45 \times 4 + 8 \times 4 + 2 \times k$$

$$= 312 + 2k$$

According to the question,

$$312 + 2k = 224 + (k + 103)$$

$\Rightarrow$　　　$312 + 2k = 327 + k$

$\Rightarrow$　　　　　$k = 327 - 312 = 15$

48. (*c*) Let the speed of A and B be $3x$ and $4x$, respectively.

According to the question,

Time taken by A to cover 360 m $= \dfrac{360}{3x}$

$\Rightarrow$ Distance covered by B in $\dfrac{360}{3x} = \dfrac{360}{3x} \times 4x$

$$= 480 \text{ m}$$

$\therefore$ A win by $= (500 - 480)$ m

$$= 20 \text{ m.}$$

49. (*b*) Number of total outomes $= 6 \times 6 = 36$

Number of favourablte outcomes
$= (1,2), (1,2), (1,4), (1,6), (2,1), (2,3), (2,5), (3,2), (3,4),$
$(4,1), (4,3), (5,2), (5,6), (6,1), (6,5)$ i.e. 15.

$\therefore$ Required probability $= \dfrac{15}{36}$

$$= \dfrac{5}{12}$$

50. (*d*) Required number of ways $= 6! \times 3!$

$$= 6 \times 5 \times 4 \times 3 \times 2 \times 3 \times 2$$

$$= 4320$$

51. (*b*) Sum of odd digits $= 5 + 7 + 3$

$$= 15$$

Sum of even digits $= 8 + 4 + 2$

$$= 14$$

$\therefore$ Required difference $= 15 - 14$

$$= 1$$

52. (*c*) Consider a 4 inch cube.

The top half is cut into four equal cubes. All of them have atleast one painted face. The bottom half is cut into 32 equal cubes. The central four cubes in the top layer are paintless.

53. (*b*) Since, the top and bottom faces are coloured red, so the middle layer of 16 cubes will not have any red coloured face.

54. (*b*) 24 cubes have atleast two coloured faces.

Sol. (Q. Nos. 55-57)

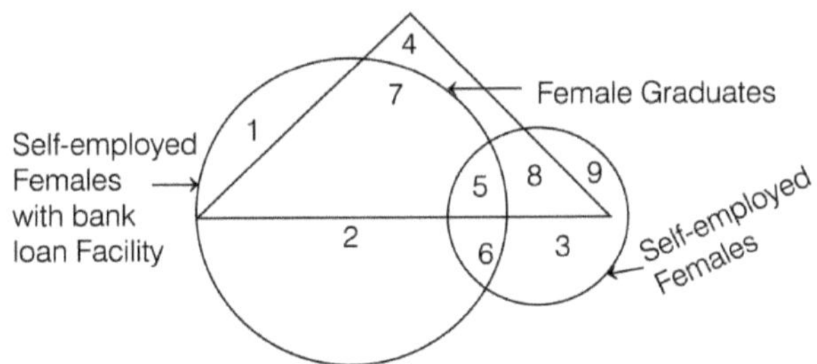

55. (*d*) Self-employed female graduates are
$$5 + 8 + 7 = 20$$

56. (*a*) 4 female graduates are not self-employed.

57. (*d*) Non-graduate females who are self-employed are
$$9 + 3 + 6 + 2 + 1 = 21$$

Sol. (Q. Nos. 58-60) *According to the given information,*

		Compulsory	Optional
(Male) A	$\rightarrow$	History	English
(Male) B	$\rightarrow$	History	Chemistry
(Male) C	$\rightarrow$	History	Mathematics
(Female) D	$\rightarrow$	English	History
(Male) E	$\rightarrow$	Physics	Mathematics
(Male) F	$\rightarrow$	Mathematics	Physics

58. (*a*) C's compulsory subject is History.

59. (*d*) D is the female member in the group.

60. (*d*) None of these

146. (*b*) The sentence given in option (b) contains the correct modal verb 'should' and has the correct positioning of the 'if clause'; hence, it is the correct answer.

147. (*d*) The sentence given in option (d) has used the form of inversion. In such sentences, the auxiliary verb is placed before the subject. Hence, option (d) is the correct answer.

148. (*b*) The sentence given in option (b) contains the proper structure and the correct use of the conjunction 'but'; hence, it is the correct answer.

149. (*b*) When 'jury' is divided, it is considered to be plural and takes a plural verb, but when 'jury' is in union, then we take it as singular and a singular verb is used. So, option (b) is the correct answer.

155. (*a*) 'Nourishing' refers to food that contains substances necessary for growth and good health. Hence, 'unwholesome' meaning not beneficial to health is its correct antonym.

156. (*b*) 'Supressed' is opposite in meaning to 'Propagate'. Propagate means to spread or carry forward and 'suppressed' means to forcibly put an end to.

157. (*b*) 'Futility' means 'having no use'. So, 'usefulness' is its correct antonym.

158. (*c*) 'Propitiate' means to appease someone or to win someone's favour by doing something that pleases them. Hence, 'enrages' meaning to make someone angry is opposite in meaning to 'propitiate'.

159. (*c*) 'Gargantuan' means 'very big in size' or 'colossal' or 'huge'. Hence, its correct opposite is 'minute' which means 'tiny' or 'very small'.

165. (*a*) The given sentence requires the use of the conjunction 'while' to make it grammatically correct. Hence, add 'while' before 'walking' to make the sentence error free.

166. (*c*) The phrase 'carry out' means to perform or execute a task.

When two actions of past are mentioned in a sentence, the action that occurred first should be mentioned in past perfect tense.

Hence, replace 'did not carry' with 'had not carried out' to make the sentence error free and grammatically correct.

167.(*a*) The given sentence has the incorrect use of 'for booking'. Hence, replace it with 'to book' to make the sentence error free and grammatically correct.

168.(*b*) The given sentence contains the incorrect pronoun 'I'. Hence, replace 'that I' with 'me to' to make the sentence error free.

169.(*c*) The given sentence contains the incorrect use of the article 'the'. Hence, remove it to make the sentence error free and grammatically correct.

170.(*b*) BADC

171.(*a*) CBAD

172.(*a*) CADB

175.(*b*) The phrase 'touch and go' means refers to something that is uncertain and risky. Hence, option (b) is the correct answer.

177.(*a*) 'Paying through one's nose' means to pay an excessive amount for something. Hence, option (a) is the correct answer.

180.(*b*) 'Quay' refers to the platform used for loading and unloading ships. Hence, 'wharf' meaning dock is the nearest in meaning to 'quay'.

181.(*c*) 'Pernickety' means placing too much emphasis on trivial or minor details. Hence, 'fussy' is the nearest in meaning to 'pernickety'.

182.(*d*) 'Quaint' means old-fashioned or unusual and option (a) 'old' does not fit the definition completely. Hence, 'usual' is the nearest in meaning to 'quaint'.

183.(*c*) 'Marvellous' means something that causes great wonder or is extra ordinary. Hence. 'amazing' is the nearest in meaning to 'marvellous'.

184.(*a*) 'Albeit' means 'although'. Hence, option (a) is the correct answer.

189.(*a*) Based on the information found in the passage, Mozart can be described as a victim of his father's ambition.

Hotel Management

National Council for Hotel Management and Catering Technology

Solved Paper 2015

Instructions
- There are Five (A-E) Sections in this Solved Paper.
- For every correct attempt, the student will be awarded **1 mark**.
- All the questions are in MCQs form and each have four options.

Marks : 200

Time : 3 hrs

Section A : Numerical Ability and Scientific Aptitude

1. What is the radius of a cylinder's base if it is formed by melting a sphere of radius 7 cm when the height of the cylinder is $\dfrac{28}{3}$ cm?

(a) 14 cm   (b) 7 cm
(c) 28 cm   (d) None of these

2. Fifty silver coins of diameter 4 cm and thickness 1 mm are melted to draw a wire of 2 mm diameter. What will be the length of the wire?

(a) 22 m   (b) 20 m
(c) 50 m   (d) 5 m

3. The sides of a triangle are 9 cm, 10 cm, 11 cm. If the smallest side of a similar triangle is 18 cm, what is the perimeter of this triangle?

(a) 30 cm   (b) 60 cm
(c) 90 cm   (d) None of these

4. Bucket A is twice as big as bucket B. Tank T can be filled by bucket A in 50 turns. If the empty tank T can be filled in 20 turns by bucket A, how many turns A and B together require filling rest of the tank?

(a) 15   (b) 10   (c) 30   (d) 20

5. A, B, C respectively can complete a work in 12, 15, 20 days. A does the work for 2 days, then B does it for 3 days and then C does for 4 days. If D completes the rest of the work in 13 days, in how many days can D do the complete work alone?

(a) 18 days   (b) 24 days
(c) 30 days   (d) None of these

6. 3 yr ago, Puja was one-fourth as old as Sunita was. 3 yr hence their ages will be in the ratio of $7 : 22$. Find the present age of Sunita?

(a) 81 yr   (b) 63 yr   (c) 18 yr   (d) 45 yr

7. Kamal is 5 yr older than Raj who is thrice as old as Arun. If sum of their ages is 40, how old is Raj?

(a) 5 yr   (b) 10 yr
(c) 15 yr   (d) 20 yr

8. A sum of ₹ 125 doubles in 5 yr, the interest being compounded annually. In how many more years will it get additional interest of ₹ 250?

(a) 5   (b) 10
(c) 15   (d) None of these

9. Train A of length 120 m is running at a speed of 60 km/h. Train B of length 150 m, running in the same direction, crosses train A in 64.8 sec. What is the speed of train B?
(a) 75 km/h   (b) 135 km/h
(c) 15 km/h   (d) None of these

10. A boat covers certain distance upstream in 5 h and same distance downstream in 2 h. What is the ratio of speeds of boat to the speed of the stream?
(a) 7 : 3   (b) 3 : 7   (c) 10 : 3   (d) 10 : 7

11. P and Q together have ₹ 1519. If 4/ 9 of P's share is equal to 13/25 share of Q, how much amount does P has?
(a) ₹ 819   (b) ₹ 700
(c) ₹ 719   (d) ₹ 619

12. Ram purchased a house for ₹ 35 lakh and spent 20% of its cost on its repairs. What sale price should he fix in order to have a gain of 20%?
(a) ₹ 49 lakh   (b) ₹ 50 lakh
(c) ₹ 50.4 lakh   (d) ₹ 42 lakh

13. A shopkeeper mixes 15 kg of rice purchased at the rate of ₹ 30/kg with 25 kg of rice purchased at the rate of ₹ 40/kg. What should be his selling price per kg in order to make a profit of 20%?
(a) ₹ 40.5   (b) ₹ 41.5
(c) ₹ 42.5   (d) ₹ 43.5

14. HCF of two numbers is 13. If the other factors of their LCM are 7 and 3, what is the smaller number of the two?
(a) 273   (b) 39
(c) 91   (d) 130

15. Find the least number which should be added to 3587 to make it divisible by 30, 42 and 105?
(a) 113   (b) 93
(c) 103   (d) 193

16. A train goes 400 km at an average speed of 50 km/h and returns at an average speed of 40 km/h. Find the average speed of the train for the whole journey?
(a) 45 km/h   (b) 40 km/h
(c) 44.44 km/h   (d) 55.55 km/h

17. A and B started a business by investing ₹ 25 lakh and ₹ 30 lakh respectively. After 2 months A withdrew ₹ 5 lakh while C joined the business by investing ₹ 10 lakh. B withdrew after another 3 months. If ₹ 9 lakh was the profit at the end of 1 year, what is the profit of B?
(a) ₹ 2.7 lakh   (b) ₹ 1.8 lakh
(c) ₹ 5.4 lakh   (d) ₹ 4.5 lakh

18. Solve for a; 2.7% of 300 + 0.03% of 400 − a = 12.2% of 10
(a) 8.44   (b) 7   (c) 0.81 %   (d) 0.7

19. In how many ways can we select a group of 5 persons having at least two women from a group of 6 men and 6 women?
(a) 96   (b) 396
(c) 696   (d) None of these

20. In a hall, there are 10 persons each of blood group A, B, AB and O. If one person is called, what is the probability of having them from blood group A or B?
(a) $\dfrac{1}{10}$ (b) $\dfrac{1}{4}$
(c) $\dfrac{1}{6}$ (d) None of these

21. If $a^2 + b^2 = 73$ and $a - b = 5$, find the value of a, where $a > 0$.
(a) 8   (b) 3
(c) 11   (d) − 3

22. Simplify $\dfrac{(13 - 7 \times 9 - 2)}{(23 \times 5 - 2 \times 5 - 41 \times 7)}$,
(a) $\dfrac{7}{18}$ (b) $\dfrac{-2}{7}$ (c) $\dfrac{49}{162}$ (d) $\dfrac{2}{7}$

Directions (Q. Nos. 23-25) *Answer the questions based on the information given. The rate of taxation has the following slabs in India.*

Taxable Income (₹)	Tax Rate
0 − 50,000	Exempt
50,000 − 60,000	10%
60,000 − 1,50,000	20%
1,50,000 +	30%

For salaried employees having salaries below ₹ 1,50,000 p.a., a standard deduction of ₹ 30,000 is available, which is reduced from the total income. Besides, a rebate is available on investments in various saving schemes like Provident Fund, Infrastructure Bonds, Post Office Savings etc. The rebate is calculated at 20% of the total investment in these savings instruments. Thus, if a person has invested ₹ 10000 in some saving instruments, he gets ₹ 2,000 rebate on his net tax liability.

However, if the salary increases above ₹ 150000 p.a, the standard deduction is reduced to ₹ 25000 and the rebate on investments is calculated at the rate of 15% of the total investment. Thus, a person saving ₹ 20000 will get a rebate of ₹ 3000 on his liability. Besides, a tax surcharge of 10% is added on the total tax liability for all tax payers. Also, working women have a further rebate of ₹ 5000 available to them on their total tax liability.

23. What will be the total tax liability of Mr. Rajiv Srivastava, who has a salary of ₹ 150000 p.a. (Assume he saved ₹ 40000 in the year)?
(a) ₹ 5000 (b) ₹ 5500
(c) ₹ 1000 (d) Data insufficient

24. Mrs. Shruti Srivastava who works in the same firm, earns a salary of ₹ 150000 p.a. How much must she save to pay no tax for the year?

(a) ₹ 41000   (b) ₹ 40000   (c) ₹ 30000   (d) ₹ 60000

25. Prakash Purti has a salary income of ₹ 144000. Besides he has earned ₹ 35000 as consultancy income. He has saved ₹ 70000 for the year in tax savings instruments. How much tax will he have to pay?
(a) ₹ 18800 (b) ₹ 14800
(c) ₹ 4800 (d) None of these

Section B : Reasoning and Logical Deduction

Directions (Q. Nos. 26-30) *Read the information given below and answer the questions that follow.*

(i) There is a group of seven persons A, B, C, D, E, F and G.

(ii) There are four males, three females, two married couples and three unmarried persons in the group.

(iii) The seven persons are seated in a row on the bench.

(iv) Their professions are engineer, teacher, doctor, psychologist, businessman, architect and student.

(v) B keep it as before is not married and another person, the psychologist is the most intelligent.

(vi) The engineer is married to the teacher, who is the least intelligent of the group.

(vii) D is an architect. He is sitting on the leftmost corner.

(viii) The student is sitting on the rightmost corner of the bench.

(ix) The doctor is married to C. C is the second most intelligent of the group followed by her husband.

(x) The least intelligent of the group is sitting on the immediate right of D, followed by the most intelligent.

(xi) There are as many more intelligent persons than the engineer as there are less intelligent.

(xii) On the bench followed by D, there are three females sitting in succession.

(xiii) The psychologist is a female.

(xiv) The student is more intelligent than the architect, who is more intelligent than only one person F.

(xv) Neither A nor G is a female.

26. Who is sitting on the immediate right of D?
(a) F (b) E (c) C (d) Can't say

27. Which two are sitting together?
(a) D and E
(b) E and A
(c) Teacher and businessman
(d) Engineer and doctor

28. The engineer is not more intelligent than
(a) student (b) architect
(c) teacher (d) businessman

29. Which of these cannot be a married couple?
(a) A - F
(b) A - C
(c) G - F
(d) None of the above

30. Which of these represents the correct order of intelligence (in the decreasing sequence)?
(a) EBF (b) CDF
(c) ECB (d) None of these

Directions (Q. Nos. 31-33) *Study the following information to answer the given questions.*

(i) Eight friends A, B, C, D, E, F, G and H are seated in a circle facing the centre.

(ii) D is between B and G and F is between A and H.

(iii) E is second to the right of A.

31. Which of the following is A's position?
(a) Left of F
(b) Right of F
(c) Between E and F
(d) None of the above

32. Which of the following information are not required to ascertain the position of C?
(a) (i)
(b) Either (ii) or (iii)
(c) (iii)
(d) All are required

33. Which of the following is C's position?
(a) Between E and F
(b) Between A and E
(c) Second to the left of B
(d) None of the above

Directions (Q. Nos. 34-36) *Find the missing term in each of the following series.*

34. 2, 4, 8, 16, 32, ..., 128
(a) 64 (b) 65 (c) 66 (d) 67

35. $\dfrac{1}{24}, \dfrac{1}{12}, \dfrac{1}{4}, 1, 5, \ldots$
(a) 30 (b) 35 (c) 40 (d) 45

36. 4, 7, 5, 9, ..., 11, 7, 13
   (a) 6   (b) 8   (c) 9   (d) 3

Directions (Q. Nos. 37 and 38) *Find the missing character '?' from among the given alternatives.*

37.

K	B
G	?

   (a) C   (b) D   (c) E   (d) F

38.

B	15	?
3	N	21

   (a) T   (b) S
   (c) R   (d) U

39. Sonam is walking facing West, then turns 90° in clockwise direction, and then turns 90° in clockwise direction again. In which direction is she finally moving?
   (a) South   (b) North
   (c) East   (d) West

40. What are the directions of the route from A to D?

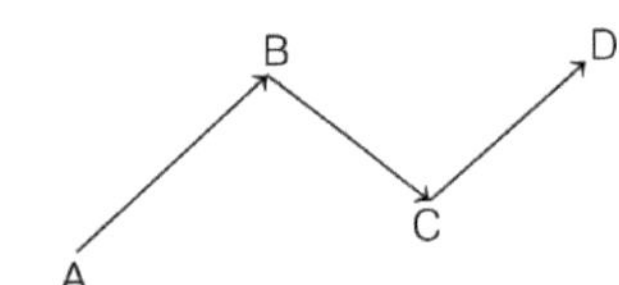

   (a) NW, SW, NW
   (b) SE, NE, SW
   (c) NE, SE, NE
   (d) SE, NE, SE

41. Kamal drives his bike and goes to college. He comes back following the same route. He again drives from his house towards North and reaches the market. What is the direction of his house with respect to market?
   (a) South   (b) Can't be determined
   (c) North-East   (d) East

42. Showing a photograph to a friend, Ravi says, "She is the grand daughter of the elder brother of my father". How is this girl related to Ravi?
   (a) Niece   (b) Sister
   (c) Aunt   (d) Sister-in-law

43. A family consists of a husband and wife, their three sons and two daughters, three wives of three sons. How many females are in this family?
   (a) 5   (b) 6
   (c) 7   (d) None of these

44. L is the father of N and P. P is the son of L but N is not the son of L. How is N related to L?
   (a) Daughter   (b) Son-in-law
   (c) Mother   (d) Niece

Directions (Q. Nos. 45-47) *Choose from the given four diagrams (1) to (4) the one that best illustrates a relationship among the three given classes in the questions below.*

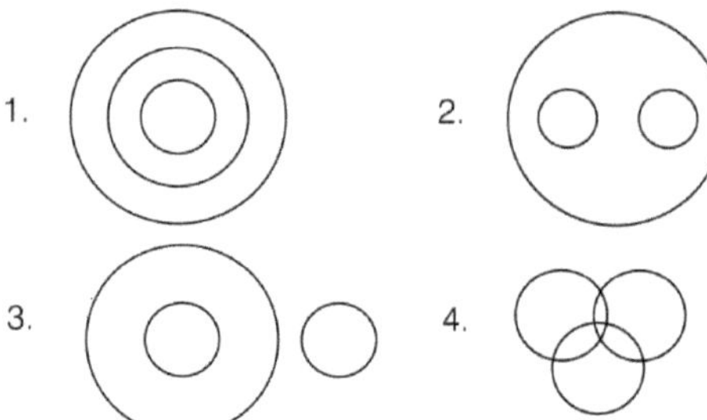

45. Eatables, Chicken, fish
   (a) 1   (b) 2   (c) 3   (d) 4

46. Students, Teachers, Wives
   (a) 1   (b) 2   (c) 3   (d) 4

47. Sweet, Rasgulla, Shirt
   (a) 1   (b) 2   (c) 3   (d) 4

Directions (Q. Nos. 48-51) *There are two pairs, the first pair follows some relationship. Use the same relationship to find the second analogy of the second pair.*

48. FG : BC : : RI : ?
   (a) EN   (b) NE   (c) MF   (d) ST

49. EDC : RQP : : MLK : ?
   (a) XYZ   (b) PQR   (c) ZYX   (d) NOP

50. L : O : : D : ?
   (a) W   (b) X   (c) Y   (d) Z

51. TZW : 28 : : QYS : ?
   (a) 35   (b) 160   (c) 38   (d) 158

Directions (Q. Nos. 52-54) *Complete the given series of figures by replacing '?' from the answer figures.*

52. Question Figures

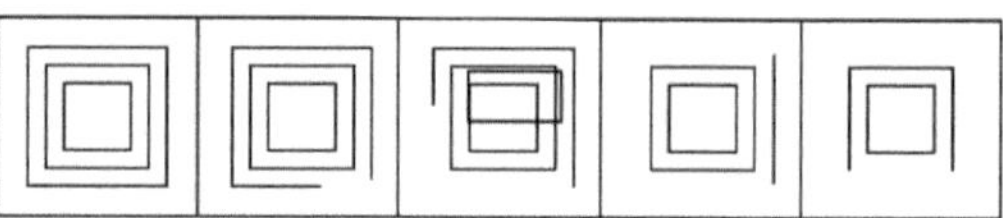

Answer Figures

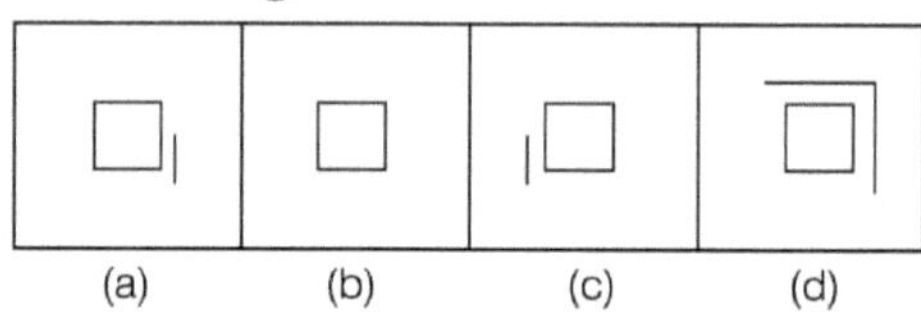

53. Question Figures

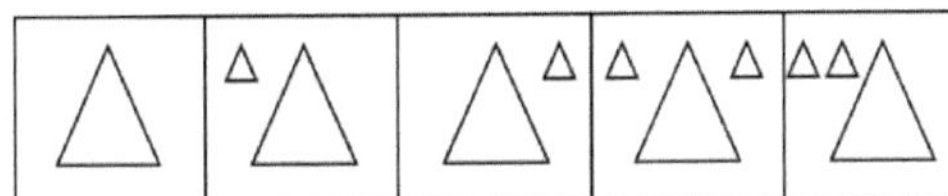

Answer Figures

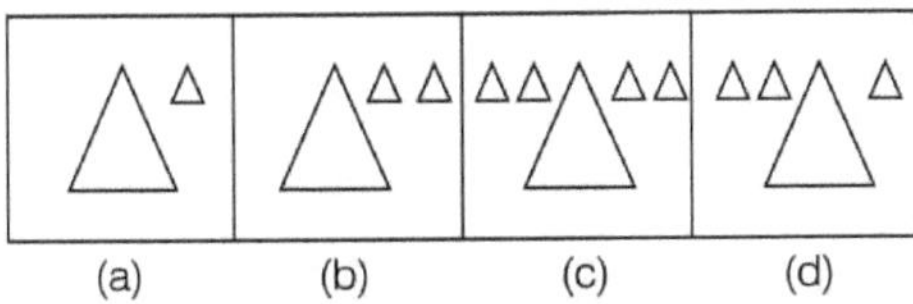

   (a)   (b)   (c)   (d)

54. Question Figures

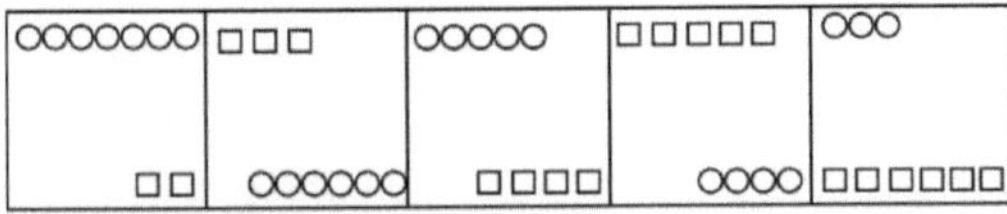

Answer Figures

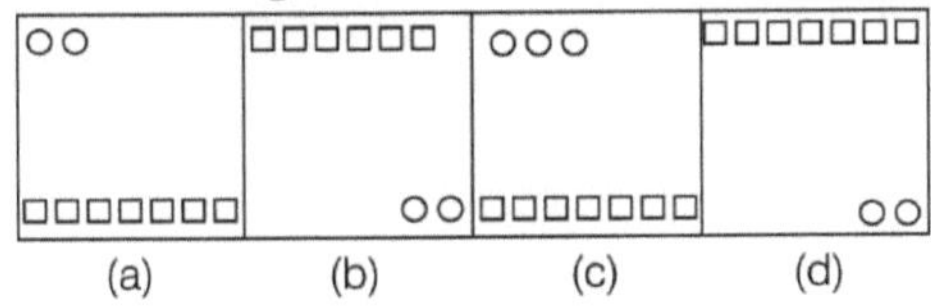

   (a)   (b)   (c)   (d)

55. In a certain code, 'this is the tree' is written as 2153, 'the green tree' is written as 573 and 'tree of life' is written as 309. Which symbol stands for 'the'?

(a) 2   (b) 3   (c) 5   (d) 0

56. If in a certain language, POPULAR is coded as QPQVMBS, then which word would be coded as GBNPVT?

(a) EAMOSU   (b) FAMOUS
(c) FASOUM   (d) FASAUM

57. If white is called blue, blue is called red, red is called yellow, yellow is called green, green is called black, black is called violet and violet is called orange, then what would the colour of human blood be?

(a) Red   (b) Green   (c) Yellow   (d) Violet

Directions (Q. Nos. 58-60) *Each of these questions has an inference based on the passage. Read the passage and mark your answer.*

(a) If the inference is 'definitely true'
(b) If the inference is 'probably true'
(c) If the 'data provided is inadequate'
(d) If the inference is 'definitely false'

In the commodities business size does matter. This is common wisdom.

The Indian sugar industry is the second largest in the world after Brazil, has traditionally been fragmented, which led to widespread sickness and large number of mills going bankrupt, a situation exacerbated by a slew of government controls, which are, meaningfully getting diluted since August 1998. Its now been more than fourteen-and-a-half years since the industry was delicensed.

No official permission is required either to build a new factory or for brown field expansion plan, except that there must not be any violation of command area norms. Even then, there aren't many who have the capacity to play the volumes game at the cyclic sugar business:

58. India has not yet been able to consolidate its firm stand in the international sugar market.

59. At present, the Indian sugar industry has been made considerably free from government controls.

60. Prior to 1998, Indian sugar industry was considerably lower in the world ranking of large nations.

Section C : General Knowledge

61. Who is the Chairman of Central Board of Film Certification (CBFC) in India?

(a) Prasoon Joshi   (b) Leela Samson
(c) Sharmila Tagore   (d) None of these

62. Which Indian company announced the creation of $250 million 'Innovate in India Fund' to give a boost to start-ups?

(a) Reliance Industries   (b) Infosys
(c) TCS   (d) Wipro

63. In Cricket World Cup tournament, India played against Pakistan on 15th February, 2015 in which Australian city?

(a) Perth   (b) Adelaide
(c) Sydney   (d) Melbourne

64. Which among the following is a Public Sector Bank?

(a) HDFC Bank
(b) ICICI Bank
(c) IDBI Bank
(d) Federal Bank

65. World Cancer Day is held on .... every year to raise awareness of cancer.

(a) 4th February   (b) 4th March
(c) 4th April   (d) 4th May

66. 35th National Games were held from 31st January, 2015 to 14th February, 2015 in

(a) Gujarat   (b) Kerala
(c) Karnataka   (d) Goa

67. Which country is going to host International Cricket Council (ICC) World Twenty 20 in 2016?
(a) India   (b) Sri Lanka
(c) South Africa   (d) England

68. In February 2015, Indian American Composer Ricky Kej won the Grammy Award in which category?
(a) Best New Artist   (b) Best Children's Album
(c) Best New Age Album   (d) Best Pop Vocal Album

69. Mr. Naresh Goyal is the Founder Chairman of which airline in India?
(a) Indigo   (b) Go Air
(c) Jet Airways   (d) None of these

70. Whom did Serena Williams defeat in the final to win the Australian Open 2015 Women's Singles title?
(a) Venus Williams   (b) Maria Sharapova
(c) Ekaterina Makarova   (d) None of these

71. Which day of the year is celebrated as World Radio day?
(a) 13th February   (b) 15th February
(c) 13th March   (d) 15th March

72. Which technology giant became the first company to reach a market value of $700 billion?
(a) Microsoft   (b) Google
(c) Apple   (d) Facebook

73. Recently, Indian government released set of .... Commemorative Postage Stamps on Swachh Bharat Mission (Clean India Mission).
(a) Four   (b) Three
(c) Two   (d) None of these

74. Vitamin B12 helps in fighting against
(a) Goiter   (b) Rickets
(c) Anemia   (d) None of these

75. Which online retailer has acquired luxury fashion portal Exclusively.com?
(a) Flipkart.com   (b) Amazon.com
(c) Snapdeal.com   (d) Ebay.com

76. Which movie won the Oscar in the best picture category in the 87th Academy Awards?
(a) The Theory of Everything
(b) Glory
(c) Still Alice
(d) Birdman

77. Indian Government has announced setting up of a new IIT in
(c) Karnataka   (b) Gujarat
(c) Kerala   (d) Punjab

78. IRCTC has partnered with which e-commerce portal for online shopping?
(a) Snapdeal   (b) Flipkart
(c) Amazon   (d) Jabong

79. World's first humanoid robot staffed hotel is set to open in which country in July 2015?
(a) China   (c) Japan
(c) South Korea   (d) None of these

80. Advance ticket booking facility for railway passengers is available .... days before the start of the journey.
(a) 60   (b) 90
(c) 120   (d) None of these

81. Insurance Laws (Amendment) Bill 2015 hiked Foreign Direct Investment (FDI) cap in the insurance sector to 49 percent from present .... percent.
(a) 20   (b) 26   (c) 30   (d) 38

82. Which state government has launched Bhagyashree scheme for girl child?
(a) Bihar   (b) Uttar Pradesh
(c) Haryana   (d) Maharashtra

83. .... has won silver prize in the prestigious Golden Gate Award at the Internationale Tourismus-Borse Berlin (ITB-Berlin)-2015.
(a) Kerala Tourism
(b) Goa Tourism
(c) Madhya Pradesh Tourism
(d) Rajasthan Tourism

84. Acid used in Car battery is
(a) Hydrochloric acid   (b) Boric acid
(c) Sulphuric acid   (d) Carbonic acid

85. Which is the most abundant mineral in human body?
(a) Iron   (b) Calcium
(c) Magnesium   (d) Sodium

86. McMohan line is the border between
(a) India and Nepal   (b) India and Pakistan
(c) India and China   (d) India and Myanmar

87. Who among the following is known as the Metro man of India?
(a) Rajendran   (b) E. Sridharan
(c) N. Mishra   (d) K.S. Rao

88. Carolina Marin Martin of .... has won the prestigious Women's Singles Title in the All England Open Badminton Championships 2015.
(a) Denmark   (b) Spain
(c) Malaysia   (d) England

89. National Youth Day is celebrated in India on the birthday of
(a) Swami Dayananda　　(b) Swami Vivekananda
(c) Rajiv Gandhi　　(d) None of these

90. The Maze Tower in which city has been recognised by Guinness World Records as representing the largest vertical maze?
(a) Shanghai　　(b) Dubai
(c) Hong Kong　　(d) New York

Section D : Aptitude For Service Sector

91. While walking on the road, you find a man accidently dropping his wallet and walking away unaware, you will
(a) pick up the wallet and hand it over to him.
(b) leave it as it is none of your business.
(c) shout out and tell him he has dropped his wallet.
(d) pick up the wallet and keep it with you as you found it.

92. You have to go shopping while your friend calls you for help as he is ill. You will
(a) postpone your shopping and go to help your friend.
(b) ask him to call someone else.
(c) call another friend and ask him to help the ill friend.
(d) ask him to hang on while you return from your shopping.

93. You finished your chocolate, and now you can't find any dustbin around to dispose of the wrapper. You
(a) will throw it anywhere.
(b) keep it with you until you find a dustbin.
(c) find a heap of trash where other people are throwing their garbage and you do the same.
(d) try and stuff it in someone else's luggage.

94. A stranger comes to you asking about an address while you are waiting for someone. You will
(a) ask him to ask someone else.
(b) direct him casually without being too precise about the address.
(c) explain him properly and repeatedly until he understands the directions properly.
(d) tell him that you are not standing there to direct people.

95. One of your friends arrives to your house unannounced while you are preparing to go out with your family. You
(a) would feel disappointed.
(b) are happy to see him and postpone your outing and welcome him.
(c) would welcome him but keep thinking how to get rid of him quickly.
(d) would tell him that you will see him later because you are going out right now.

96. A guy slipped and fell in front of you while walking through the college corridor and your friends started laughing. You will
(a) join your friends in the laughter.
(b) add some comment to increase the fun.
(c) help him and ask your friends not to laugh.
(d) just sit and watch.

97. One of your relatives invites you to visit them. Reaching there you find that he is not well and is unable to give a proper welcome. You would
(a) get angry and return.
(b) stay there but feel disappointed.
(c) stay and help him.
(d) not react at all.

98. You are getting late for a meeting and while driving, you witness an accident. You would
(a) ignore the meeting and help the injured.
(b) ignore it and rush for the meeting.
(c) try and ask someone else to help him.
(d) curse others for not helping and rush for the meeting.

99. You are travelling in a train and one of your co-passengers is left on a platform while the train starts moving. You would
(a) not bother.
(b) look around waiting for someone to react.
(c) ask others to do something.
(d) get up and pull the chain.

100. While travelling in an airline, you ordered something and there is some delay in your request for which air hostess apologizes to you. You
(a) would not consider the apology.
(b) get angry and start fighting.
(c) would accept the apology and request them to process your request as quickly as possible.
(d) would get disappointed and say nothing.

101. You are talking on your phone while travelling in a public transport while your co-passengers are getting disturbed. You
(a) will start fighting.
(b) would ask them to mind their own business.

    (c) would continue talking on your phone and ignore them.

    (d) would hang up and apologize.

102. While doing a transaction with a shopkeeper, he accidently returned you more amount than he was supposed to. You realize this when you get back home. You

    (a) won't tell him and keep the extra amount.

    (b) keep the money thinking you got lucky.

    (c) return the extra amount immediately telling that he made a mistake.

    (d) keep the money thinking that you will return it later.

103. A foreign tourist approaches you for some help but you don't share any common-language. You

    (a) would waive him off telling that you don't understand his language.

    (b) would try and arrange a translator in order to help him.

    (c) try and help him as much as you could using sign language.

    (d) try making fun of him.

104. One of your friends is in distress and needs some financial help but is too shy to ask. You

    (a) will go to him and help him saying he can return the money whenever he can.

    (b) will cash this chance to make fun of him.

    (c) would wait for him to ask for your help.

    (d) do not intend to help him.

105. There are some bad characters influencing the living conditions of people in your community. You

    (a) will gather people around you and oppose them

    (b) will manage with the condition.

    (c) would wait for some help from others.

    (d) would leave the community.

Ans. (a)

106. There has been a death in a family in your community. At the same time some other family is planning a celebration. You, being the representative of your community

    (a) will ask the other family to delay the celebration.

    (b) won't interrupt in the matter.

    (c) will ask members of the community to come together for the first family and then congratulate the other family but ask them to postpone their celebration.

    (d) will join the celebration as well.

107. There is a function in your close relation and they need your assistance. You

    (a) would tell them that you are too busy to help.

    (b) would help them with great enthusiasm.

    (c) would tell about this to other relatives and ask them to help.

    (d) will take it like a burden.

108. You have been sent on a visit to a rural area on a project to educate the local children. You

    (a) whole heartedly take part in the project and try to put in your maximum effort.

    (b) start complaining about the mismanagement.

    (c) show no enthusiasm but anyhow complete your project.

    (d) bailout of the project.

109. There is a function in your school/college and the management requests your participation but you are also busy with some other project. You

    (a) deny your participation saying you are too busy.

    (b) express your apologies and try to contribute as much as possible.

    (c) start feeling annoyed with such requests.

    (d) participate whole heartedly in the event and manage your project as well.

110. You see water running from a tap at any public place while no one is using it. You

    (a) walk away without bothering.

    (b) close the tap properly and ensure no water is wasted.

    (c) attract attention of other people toward it.

    (d) also leave the water funning after using taps.

111. After exiting your room in your house. You

    (a) switch off all the electrical appliances that are not required.

    (b) leave the lights and fans as they were.

    (c) expect someone else to do this for you.

    (d) forget to do these things but follow whenever you remember.

112. In your house you

    (a) keep littering here and there expecting others to clean it.

    (b) keep your things properly and don't care for others.

    (c) arrange everything and dry to maintain hygiene everywhere.

    (d) make such a mess making life of others miserable too.

113. There is plenty of rain clogging in your society creating problems in communication. You would

    (a) face the difficulty every day without complaining.

    (b) report the matter in the local municipal office.

    (c) gather people and try to resolve the problem yourself.

    (d) motivate other people to resolve the problem.

114. During summers, on a very sunny day, you come across a poor person who is very thirsty and dehydrated. You
   - (a) buy him some water and juice from the market.
   - (b) tell him to stay at home when the weather is so hot.
   - (c) ask him to go to a dharmshala for help.
   - (d) buy him juice and ask him to pay.

115. While watching a movie in a theatre, a small child starts crying.
   - (a) You yell at his/her parents for disturbing you in between the movie.
   - (b) You try to ignore but instead pass comments on the child.
   - (c) You ask their parents humbly to take their child out of the theatre.
   - (d) You ask their parents if everything is ok with the child and if there is any help you can give to them.

116. While buying ticket in a bus, the conductor asks for change since you gave a large amount of note, you
   - (a) shout at him, that he should have change and won't buy the ticket.
   - (b) ask him to give you the ticket, keep the money and give change when he gets it:
   - (c) get down from the bus and wait for the next one.
   - (d) keep looking at other passengers until someone offers you change.

117. While standing in a queue at railway station, you see an illiterate person at the counter filling the form for a ticket. You
   - (a) tell him to move out of the line and fill the form as you are in hurry.
   - (b) tell him to go back from where he came, since he does not know even how to fill a form.
   - (c) go and offer him help in filling the form and buying the ticket.
   - (d) ask the attendant at the counter to help him to fill the form.

118. In a park, you see two boys fighting and beating each other. You
   - (a) go and start beating both of them.
   - (b) ignore and walk away.
   - (c) tell other people in the park that the fight should be stopped.
   - (d) go to them and ask them politely to stop fighting and resolve the issue by talking and discussing.

119. While eating at a restaurant, you are left with food. You
   - (a) leave the food there as it is.
   - (b) eat all of it even though you are not able to, which might result in bad health for you.
   - (c) ask them to pack it so that you can have it with your next meal.
   - (d) ask them to pack it so that you can give it to anyone who is in need of food.

120. In the hostel after taking a bath, you remember that you left the geyser ON. You
   - (a) go back to the hostel to turn it OFF.
   - (b) ask your friends in the hostel to switch it off.
   - (c) ignore, thinking that it is not your concern.
   - (d) do it again deliberately.

121. You are listening to loud music on your birthday night; your neighbour who has her exam tomorrow, comes to you to request you to slow down the volume. You
   - (a) ask her to go to someone else's place to study.
   - (b) tell her that you will slow down the volume but you don't do it.
   - (c) turn off the music.
   - (d) turn off the music and ask her if there is something that you can teach her for tomorrow's exam or may be clear any doubts that she has.

122. If you happen to be in a bus which meets with an accident you would
   - (a) ask and motivate others to help out people who are hurt.
   - (b) try and get away from the scene at the earliest.
   - (c) extend physical help to people who need such help.
   - (d) inform district authorities and police.

123. While you are away on a holiday, you have a theft in your house and you lose some jewellery and cash, you would
   - (a) plan to shift to another house.
   - (b) feel absolutely devastated and go into a depression.
   - (c) be more security conscious and try and forget it.
   - (d) blame your neighbours and have a fight with them.

124. Being a member of team while reaching a decision, you would
   - (a) let others decide.
   - (b) take a decision and inform others.
   - (c) consult others and then decide.
   - (d) let the matter be pending and later impose your decision.

125. To work efficiently and effectually in a service industry, which of the following you think is the most essential ability/quality?
   - (a) Being responsible
   - (b) Being an introvert
   - (c) Being helpful and outgoing
   - (d) Being highly academically qualified

126. One of your team members generally behaves in a selfish and clever manner quite often, you will
 (a) tell him about it in front of everyone.
 (b) tell him that this is not the way to behave.
 (c) counsel him separately after taking him into confidence.
 (d) ignore him as a member of the team.

127. A lot of the products of your company are defective but you come to know about it only after the products have been sold and customers start complaining of it. You would
 (a) issue a general information to all regarding defects in the product and advise them to get it exchanged for a defect-free product from the outlet.
 (b) ignore the complaints.
 (c) blame the customers for complaints.
 (d) do nothing.

128. If you want to computerise your office to make it more and more efficient and modern you would
 (a) get rid of the old staff and arrange new staff who are well-versed in operating computers.
 (b) get the whole staff trained accordingly.
 (c) expel some of the employees due surplus workers.
 (d) adjust the surplus workers at some other place for which they are fit.

129. What is the best quality in a person?
 (a) Ability to please others (b) Ability to work hard
 (c) Sincerity   (d) Cordiality

130. Whenever you do some work you commit a lot of errors and mistakes which are always noticed by someone. You then
 (a) get irritated about your own-self.
 (b) curse your fate and get angry easily on the other person.
 (c) try to keep quiet at that moment and wait for the opportunity to find fault in other person.
 (d) decide that to err is human.

131. What will be your response to an angry customer who wants to see the senior manager with a complaint?
 (a) You would be patient and try to cool him down.
 (b) Tell him it is very difficult to see the manager.
 (c) Talk to him yourself.
 (d) Try to solve his problem by consulting seniors.

132. If you are transferred to a place you do not like, you would
 (a) forget about your choice and work whole-heartedly.
 (b) try your best to get transferred to your favourite place.
 (c) not take interest in work.
 (d) take long leave.

133. The responsibility of hospitality of the guest or looking after their smooth and enjoyable stay in a hotel lies on the shoulders of
 (a) General Manager (b) Guest Relations Executive
 (c) Floor Supervisor (d) Front Office Manager

134. If on a tough day, you are the only person available to handle the customer, you should
 (a) just do your part of the work.
 (b) try and work to the maximum of your ability to satisfy customers.
 (c) take leave and go back home.
 (d) ask for additional help from the boss.

135. You see some smoke coming out of the building of your office and come to know that there is fire somewhere. First of all you would
 (a) go out of the building without considering the consequences thereof.
 (b) make a noise and inform all.
 (c) phone the fire brigade in no time.
 (d) first use the fire-fighting equipment or do something else to extinguish the fire.

136. Public dealings require
 (a) quick decisions   (b) good listening
 (c) politeness   (d) punctuality

137. Which of the following statements reflects your opinion about yourself?
 (a) I am not certain of my self-confidence.
 (b) I am even today as confident as before.
 (c) My self-confidence is declining day-by-day.
 (d) I have never been self-confident at all.

138. You are perplexed and find yourself in a fix when you are asked to
 (a) speak something from the stage.
 (b) do as others do.
 (c) listen and argue.
 (d) be among strangers.
 Ans. (a)

139. What would you do if you get late in the morning due to bus timings?
 (a) Let it be as it is.
 (b) Take the consent of management.
 (c) Do not do anything.
 (d) Make some alternative arrangement.

140. If you are wrongly accused of something, you would
 (a) not even try to rebut the accusation, as it would be of no use.
 (b) be able to convince others of your innocence easily.
 (c) try to convince others, but without any hope of doing so.
 (d) try your best to convince others and hope that you succeed.

Section E : English Language

Directions (Q. Nos. 141-144) *Choose the word which best expresses the meaning of the underlined word in the given sentence.*

141. The operator was commended for his <u>dexterity</u>.
  (a) cooperation (b) courtesy
  (c) punctuality (d) skill

142. Many species of animals have become <u>extinct</u> during the last hundred years.
  (a) feeble (b) aggressive
  (c) scattered (d) non-existent

143. The community is <u>agog</u> with speculation about the fate of the money collected.
  (a) excited (b) worried
  (c) depressed (d) annoyed

144. Few teachers have been spared the problem of an <u>obstreperous</u> pupil in the class.
  (a) awkward (b) lazy
  (c) hostile (d) cheerful

Directions (Q. Nos. 145-148) *Choose the word which is opposite in meaning of the underlined word in the given sentence.*

145. He <u>urges</u> to learn everything.
  (a) desires (b) advises
  (c) supports (d) opposes
  ↪ 'Oppose' is opposite in meaning to 'urges'. 'Urges' means to persuade someone to do something or recommend while 'oppose' means to prevent someone from doing something.

146. A <u>serene</u> mind can never be the pioneer of a great revolution.
  (a) nervous (b) jocular
  (c) earnest (d) agitated

147. Matter <u>expands</u> on heating.
  (a) shrinks (b) reduces
  (c) diminishes (d) contracts

148. He climbed up a <u>stationary</u> wagon.
  (a) moving (b) static
  (c) shunting (d) standing

Directions (Q. Nos. 149-153) *Choose the option that is the plural form of the given word.*

149. Sheep
  (a) sheep's (b) sheeps
  (c) sheepes (d) sheep

150. Alumnus
  (a) alumni (b) alumnus
  (c) alumnuses (d) alumnus

151. Toe
  (a) toes (b) toss (c) tows (d) toe's

152. Brake
  (a) brakes (b) break
  (d) braks (c) brake's

153. Thief
  (a) thiefs (b) thievs
  (c) thief's (d) thieves

Directions (Q. Nos. 154-159) *In each of these questions, choose the option which can be substituted for the given words.*

154. One who despises persons of lower social position
  (a) Prim (b) Snob
  (c) Prig (d) Aristocrat

155. One who is determined to exact full vengeance for wrongs done to him
  (a) Vindicator (b) Usurer
  (c) Vindictive (d) Virulent

156. An associate in an office or institution
  (a) Companion (b) Ally
  (c) Colleague (d) Accomplice

157. The art of cutting trees and bushes into ornamental shapes
  (a) Horticulture (b) Bonsai
  (c) Pruning (d) Topiary

158. A formal written charge against a person for some crime or offence
  (a) Rancor (b) Indictment
  (c) Animosity (d) Acrimony

159. To act in a fussy, uncertain way and not achieving much
  (a) Fain (b) Faff
  (c) Trouble-maker (d) Annoying

Directions (Q. Nos. 160-165) *Choose the option which best expresses the meaning of the underlined idiom/phrase in the sentence.*

160. You must not <u>mince matters</u>; tell the truth.
  (a) cut short (b) conceal facts
  (c) tell with frankness (d) comply with

161. I am afraid, the two brothers are at <u>cross purposes</u>.
  (a) quarrel with each other
  (b) dislike each other
  (c) against each other
  (d) misunderstanding each other

162. Some people have the habit of <u>wearing their heart on their sleeve</u>.
   (a) avoiding being friendly with others
   (b) saying something which is not to be taken seriously
   (c) exposing their innermost feelings to others
   (d) wasting their time on unnecessary details

163. The sight of the accident <u>made my flesh creep</u>.
   (a) worried me
   (b) frightened me
   (c) confused me
   (d) drew my attention

164. She was received by her friends <u>with open arms</u>.
   (a) indifferently
   (b) warmly
   (c) casually
   (d) coldly

165. There was a job for me <u>to cut my teeth on</u>.
   (a) to try
   (b) to gain experience
   (c) to sharpen my wits
   (d) to earn a decent salary

Directions (Q. Nos. 166-170) *A word has been written in four different ways out of which only one is correctly spelt. Choose the correctly spelt word.*

166. (a) grametic
   (b) grammetic
   (c) grammatic
   (d) gramatic

167. (a) distilry (b) distillry (c) distillery (d) distilery

168. (a) sustinence
   (b) sustenance
   (c) sustenense
   (d) sustinance

169. (a) achievment
   (b) acheivment
   (c) achievement
   (d) achievemant
   Ans. (c)

170. (a) coreander
   (b) coriander
   (c) corriandar
   (d) coreandor

Directions (Q. Nos. 171-175) *A sentence has been broken into four parts. Choose the part that has an error.*

171. (a) My brother went to church at
   (b) the Foundling Hospital on the morning,
   (c) still in ignorance of what
   (d) had happened on the previous night.

172. (a) Any further cylinders that fell,
   (b) it was hoped, could be destroyed
   (c) at once by high explosives,
   (d) which was being rapidly manufactured and distributed.

173. (a) It was the first time that a grave
   (b) had opened in my road of life,
   (c) and the gape it made in the
   (d) smooth ground was wonderful.

174. (a) He disappeared into his bedroom
   (b) and returned in a few minutes
   (c) as the character of a amiable
   (d) and simple-minded non-conformist clergyman.

175. (a) As it pulled on, one of the loafing man at the corner
   (b) dashed forward to open the door in the hope of earning
   (c) a copper, but was elbowed away by another loafer,
   (d) who had rushed up with the same intention.

Directions (Q. Nos. 176-200) *Read the passages below and answer the questions that follow each passage.*

PASSAGE I

The collapse in the price of oil has come as a big shock not only to the Russian economy, but also to its political system. As the price falls from its peak earlier in the year of $115 a barrel to below $50, the government faces some harsh choices. Fifty-two percent of Russia's budget revenues are derived from the energy sector.

And even though the energy sector comprises only 27% of its total economy, the crisis has deflated much of Russia's self-confidence, and will in the immediate term force the adoption of some drastic economic measures. In the long term, it may set Russia on a new political path. Sanctions and the downward momentum of oil prices have inflicted powerful economic damage on Russia.

Government actions halted the slide, notably pumping capital into the banking system and ruling out capital controls. This maintained confidence in the banks and prevented panic withdrawals by depositors. Yet if interest rates were kept at 17%, the economy would be ruined. Investment, already low, would fall further. The oligarch class is deeply opposed to the imposition of capital controls, but the government may well soon be running out of other options.

The so-called policy of 'deoffshorisation' and nationalisation of the elites has been at the heart of Putin's third-term presidency, and it is now accelerated by the sanctions and the economic crisis as a whole. The likelihood of a potential split between Putin and the economic-elite is low, yet we know that when a bank run starts, it is almost impossible to stop. Putin has done his best to not to let it show in personal appearances. In his annual address in December, Putin outlined the key challenges facing

Russia. He indicated that rather than intensifying state controls, the crisis would force Russia to liberalise and to develop a more dynamic small and medium business sector.

Above all, he suggested that Russia would not turn to the past for models of its future. The speech was a surprisingly measured response to the challenges at that time. It refused to accept that Russia was isolated, and it outlined a surprisingly liberal trajectory for Russian's development - at a time where many in the west were expecting Putin to tighten the screws and isolate itself further.

The system, however, is built to sustain inertia, and operates within the framework of balancing the various factions. The crisis may precisely force a breakout from the economic dead end and political stalemate to achieve a meaningful rejuvenation of the polity and the economy. Putin is a master at the unexpected feint and demarche, and as a result of this crisis, he may well surprise us yet.

176. As a result of the current oil crises, Putin
  (a) must ignore these developments and move on.
  (b) estimates that it would not impact Russia much.
  (c) would be pushed to shake things up.
  (d) None of the above

177. In the recent past, Putin has indicated that
  (a) he would reduce controls.
  (b) he would encourage medium and small sector business.
  (c) Russia needs to look at its future.
  (d) All of the above

178. To overcome the current economic crisis in Russia, the government has
  (a) withdrawn money from all banks.
  (b) gone for huge capital controls.
  (c) put more money in banks.
  (d) approached rich nations of world to seek loans.

179. As per the paragraph, which of the following statements is not true?
  (a) Putin may be able to overcome the current economic crisis.
  (b) Fall in oil prices has not much affected Russian economy.
  (c) Putin feels that Russia has not been concerned by other world powers.
  (d) None of the above

PASSAGE II

The Rajapaksa government was insensitive towards India. The new Lankan government will have its own set of priorities but it should also understand India's worries. For example, India is concerned about the increasing Chinese presence in Sri Lanka.

While we should have close relations with China, we must also assuage India's fears. In addition, we need better people-to-people contact between the two countries. It should not be very difficult to ensure our shared culture and the fact that most professionals in both countries speak the same language.

We also need to work harder to secure more private Indian investment and make better use of India's financial assistance. Instead of using funds only for construction, Sri Lanka must use India's experience in HRD too. Sri Lanka's high commissioner in New Delhi has been working on improving relations between the two business communities but we should also move swiftly on the Free Trade Agreement, which has been held up for years.

This does not mean ignoring the concerns of Lankan businessmen who sometimes have got a raw deal from Indian state governments. But such matters should be discussed frankly and solutions must be found to facilitate the economic partnerships that the region needs. Sri Lanka could also establish a special relationship with India, which will bring SAARC on a par with other regional groups.

This region has problems because of the traditional rivalry between India and Pakistan. Sri Lanka which is in a position to win the trust or both countries, should take the lead in suggesting cooperation on education cultural engagement and disaster management.

A synergistic attitude on these issues could be productive for the whole region. India's expertise can also help strengthen Sri Lanka's independent institutions. By voting out Rajapaksa, the electorate has made it clear that it is tired of an over mighty executive. But we should not make the mistake of thinking that a change of guard will solve the problem. To avoid a recurrence, we must strengthen alternative repositories of authority.

We must ensure that norms prevalent in other parliaments are implemented here too. For example, we must have more effective consultative committees and prevent members of the executive from chairing these or financial oversight committees.

180. After defeating Rajapaksa, the people of Sri Lanka should
  (a) celebrate this change and relax now.
  (b) plan and try to bring Rajapaksa back in the next election.

    (c) learn a lesson and be on guard to ensure that a person like Rajapaksa does not come to head Sri Lanka again.

    (d) None of the above

181. The new government in Sri Lanka needs to ensure that they

    (a) have good relations with China on priority.

    (b) maintain good relations with India even at the cost of China.

    (c) have good relations with India and China both.

    (d) ignore both India and China.

182. In the past, businessmen from Sri Lanka

    (a) have been warmly welcomed in India.

    (b) have not been interested in doing much business with India.

    (c) were not treated well in India.

    (d) did not make attempts to do business in India.

183. As per the paragraph, which of the following statements is not true?

    (a) People to people contact must be encouraged by India as well as Sri Lanka.

    (b) Rajapaksa government made good attempts to improve relations with India.

    (c) Owing to strained relations between India and Pakistan, SAARC has not been much effective.

    (d) None of the above

PASSAGE III

Gold imports have skyrocketed despite the global price of the yellow metal weakening. That signals that gold has not lost its sheen as an investment choice. The government is worried that the surge in gold imports could undermine the country's balance of payments position.

The worry is not misplaced. India's current account deficit is within limits of prudence, due to the sharp drop in global crude prices, but splurging foreign exchange on imported gold will negate these gains. Anecdotal evidence suggests that people are using their unaccounted money to buy jewellery and bullion, shunning financial instruments that create audit trails.

So, the need is to establish audit trails of these transactions. One way would be for the Centre to impose a nominal 1% excise duty on jewellery, to create audit trails and curb the use of black money to fund gold purchases. Jewellery purchases in cash of over ₹ 5 lakh is captured under the Annual Information Returns (AIR) that identify potential taxpayers by examining their expenditure patterns. AIR creates an audit trail too, but there are no trails for cash purchases below ₹ 5 lakh. The import surge is being attributed to a relaxation of the 80 : 20 scheme-at least one-fifth of every lot of imported gold is exclusively made available for exports, and the balance for domestic use-for star and premier trading houses.

However, the government should desist from any attempt to restrict the demand for gold through quantitative restrictions or impose higher import duties, as it would only encourage smuggling. Investors will dump gold when the economy grows, and they regain confidence that financial instruments would yield decent returns. The government should also be persistent in marketing alternative financial instruments such as inflation-indexed bonds, and restore people's faith in financial instruments.

Implementation of the goods and service tax and direct tax reform to lower rates and widen the base would also curtail black money and the demand for gold in which to store black money.

184. Which of the following actions of the government may create new and more smugglers in India?

    (a) By increasing duties on import of gold.

    (b) By reducing demand for gold through checking entry of gold into India.

    (c) Both (a) and (b)

    (d) None of the above

185. In the recent past, due to increase in gold imports, India

    (a) has been able to save considerable foreign exchange.

    (b) did not save much foreign exchange.

    (c) has wasted considerable foreign exchange.

    (d) has not been much effected.

186. The government fears that excessive imports of gold will

    (a) ultimately reduce generation of black money.

    (b) certainly increase circulation of black money.

    (c) not be impacting creation unaccounted money.

    (d) None of the above

187. As per the paragraph, which of the following statements is not true?

    (a) With reduction of gold prices, imports of gold have reduced.

    (b) As our economy grows, people would like to buy more gold.

    (c) In the recent past, crude prices have been increasing globally.

    (d) All of the above

PASSAGE IV

Online marketplace Snapdeal.com is seeking to acquire a significant stake in a logistics company or form a joint venture with one to overcome the delivery challenges in India's fast growing e-commerce market, two people familiar with the matter said.

Snapdeal is flushed with funds, having raised $627 million (about ₹ 3,845 crore at the then exchange rate) from Japanese internet, media and telecom conglomerate Soft Bank in October. "They are keen to have something of their own but it is too late to build a network from scratch," one of the people quoted above said on condition of anonymity. "They are considering all options, including a significant stake buy or a joint venture to have some control on quality."

The second person, who also declined to be named, said Snapdeal is most interested to start with a minority stake with a right to buy the remaining stake later. "They want a company with a pan-India network with a significant presence in tier-II and III cities. They also want the company to have a good reverse logistics capability," this person said. Snapdeal declined-comment on queries related to their plan to get into logistics.

But people close to the development said the thought is that once it takes over a significant minority stake, Snapdeal will invest in IT and synchronise it with its own platform over a period of time. Snapdeal does not want to run the company immediately as logistics is not its primary business and it also lacks service relationship in the unorganised logistics market, these people said.

According to them, founder and CEO is driving the process. Snapdeal remains the only big e-tailer in India that does not have a captive delivery arm and relies completely on third-party logistics. Flipkart has e-kart and Jabong has GoJavas, which handle a significant portion of their total shipments, GoJavas has now been spun-off but still works for Jabong's deliveries. Amazon is also investing to build its own logistics network.

188. Currently, Snapdeal is facing which of the following problems?
   (a) Need to raise funds to make the company viable in expanding business.
   (b) Recruiting dedicated and professional manpower.
   (c) Issues in delivery of items to customers.
   (d) None of the above

189. Most leading e-commerce companies in India
   (a) have issues with delivering items to customers.
   (b) do not have much problems in delivering items.
   (c) do not require dedicated delivery arms.
   (d) depend on third party logistics.

190. To meet its delivery challenges, Snapdeal plans to
   (a) purchase a minority stake in a logistics company with option to have a major stake subsequently.
   (b) avoid getting into logistics but for a JV.
   (c) deal with logistics company which has network spreading all over India.
   (d) All of the above

191. As per the paragraph, which of the following statements is not true?
   (a) Snapdeal is not keen to run its own logistics company.
   (b) Snapdeal has adequate funds presently.
   (c) Soft Bank of Japan has invested in Snapdeal.
   (d) Snapdeal is not interested in reverse delivery capability.

PASSAGE V

Minister for Agriculture on the occasion of World Fisheries Day informed that the Government is focused to usher in a Blue Revolution meaning increase in fish production and productivity in the country on the occasion of World Fisheries Day.

National Fisheries Development Board under Ministry of Agriculture organised celebrations on World Fisheries Day at Pragati Maidan. The Minister informed that India ranks world number two in fish production and also the second highest aquaculture country in the world.

India with a fishermen population of 14.5 million and a coastal line of 8,118 kilometers can rise to be a major player in the world fisheries. India also has a fleet of 200,000 fishing vessels and last year has exported fish worth 5 billion US dollars. The Minister informed that India has a vast area of unutilised and untapped Inland water resources and is short of quality fish seed and formulated fish feed and government will focus on filling the critical gaps.

He informed that the Government has announced a new scheme 'Blue Revolution-Inland Fisheries' in the last budget session and the Government is likely to launch very soon a programme to usher in Blue Revolution in the country.

Even though, the per capita income consumption in the world for fish is 18 kilograms per annum, India stands at 8 kilograms. India currently produces 9.58 million metric tonnes of fish out of which 64% of production is Inland and 36% is from marine sources. The Minister also informed that the fisheries can be an engine of growth due to high growth rates of 7.9% in Inland fisheries last year. He also informed that Fisheries sector in our country is a small scale nature with vast majorities of stakeholders along the value chain from production to consumption.

In India, fisheries is recognised as a powerful income and employment generator as it stimulates growth of a number of subsidiary sectors. Fisheries in both inland and marine waters have been contributing as in important source of livelihood and supplies nutritious protein for the growing population.

In fact, with exponential increase in human populations, the food demand, shrinkage of cultivable land and decline in the agricultural productivity, role of fisheries sector to fulfill the growing demand for food is of paramount importance for nutritional security. From a mere traditional activity years ago, the fisheries sector has transformed into a significant commercial enterprise with an impressive growth in recent times.

As per the latest FAG statistics released in 2014 (The State of World Fisheries and Aquaculture 2014), the global fish production has reached to 158 million tonnes, with food fish supply increasing at an average annual rate of 3.2 percent, outpacing world population growth at 1.6 percent.

192. Government plans to encourage fish production due to
(a) increase in food demand.
(b) reduction in yield of agriculture.
(c) reduction in availability of land for cultivation.
(d) All of the above

193. We need to launch Blue Revolution, as fisheries sector can
(a) provide more employment
(b) encourage other linked sectors
(c) improve income standards
(d) All of the above

194. Looking at global level, fish production in India is considered
(a) extremely low   (b) below the average
(c) just about adequate   (d) quite substantial

195. As per the paragraph, which of the following statements is not true?
(a) Production of fish from marine sources is more than Inland in India.
(b) India has tremendous potential to increase fish production.

(c) Fisheries has not become a huge commercial venture.
(d) None of the above

PASSAGE VI

Public sector Coal India's trade unions pose a political challenge to the Narendra Modi government's desire to reform the economy. The manner in which government deals with the striking unions, which represent employees of a company that extracts about 80% of India's coal, will signal its resolve in tackling status quo elements who hold back development.

Coal India's unions, including Sangh Parivar-affiliated Bharatiya Mazdoor Sangh oppose the entry of private coal miners. This is an unfair position on both economic and ethical grounds-these unions are exploiting Coal India's near monopoly to feather their own nest. Coal is India's largest source of primary commercial energy supply and the power sector's performance is closely linked to it.

India's nationalisation drive four decades ago brought coal mining within its ambit and left mining largely in the hands of Coal India group. Since then, other sources of energy such as oil and gas have been opened up to private players as there is no economic rationale for the state to allocate its scarce resources to mining which can be done better by others. Areas such as healthcare and education should have priority on state fund as they are the most effective means to provide equality of opportunity.

Yet, Coal India's unions have blocked three successive governments from allowing in professional miners. The unions obstinacy has extracted an economic price. Profitable and cash-rich Coal. India has in the recent past been unable to meet domestic demand. Consequently, India's coal imports have galloped in the last three years, pushing up costs which are eventually borne by citizens.

Also, ironically, while the unions have opposed private mining in India, they don't seem to have a problem with private miners abroad supplying about one-fourth of India's coal consumption. If that coal could be mined in India, more jobs would be created at home and the technology to carry out environmentally less destructive underground mining could be introduced on a larger scale.

Coal India's unions have taken an untenable position. Their recalcitrance has cost India dear over the last decade and it is important for the government to bring them around. Far too often, economic reforms have been stalled by different interest groups who have cloaked partisan interests under the garb of national interest. It shouldn't happen again.

196. Unions of Coal India
    (a) should be allowed to continue their strike.
    (b) must have a major say in economic reforms.
    (c) should not be permitted to hold economic reforms to ransom.
    (d) have a major grievances/which must be addressed at the earliest.

197. Coal India's Unions are presently
    (a) badly against private mining.
    (b) not opposed to import of coal to India.
    (c) Both (a) and (b)
    (d) None of the above

198. During the past few years, performance of Coal India to meet domestic demand of coal has been
    (a) excellent and commendable.
    (b) quite satisfactory to meet our requirements.
    (c) not at all satisfactory.
    (d) None of the above

PASSAGE VII

Myntra, recently acquired by Flipkart, is seeking bigger discounts from retailers and brands by virtue of its increased sway in the fashion e-commerce space, in a move that's being likened by vendors to Amazon's pressure on book publishers. Brands that were already giving higher margins to Myntra said the No. 1 online fashion retailer is asking apparel makers for more.

'Earlier margins varied between 28% to 32%. Now, they have increased it outright to 36-38% and some weaker players are even asked to give 40% margins,' said a retail consultant who works with many brands. Several apparel, footwear, fashion and lifestyle vendors ET spoke with echoed this. Most of them say margins at brick-and-mortar franchises are generally pegged at 30-35%.

Companies said online retailers are engaged in a difficult balancing act of offering deep discounts to consumers on the one hand and trying to make a profit on the other hand. In the process, vendors get squeezed further, they said. A lot of manufacturers are hooked to the volume drug.

Now, Myntra is saying give us bigger discounts otherwise we won't do volumes from you or even block

your products, said the head of a large apparel brand asking not to be named, 'For more and more companies, their businesses are dependent on them. It earlier happened to small electronic manufacturers from e-commerce companies. Now, fashion apparel companies are getting hammered.' Joint MD of Mandhana Industries, which markets Salman Khan's Being Human Lifestyle brand, said online retailers are focusing not just on acquiring customers but also turning profitable.

"They have realised that they have become the largest selling platform," he said, adding that almost 15% of Being Human's revenue currently comes from e-commerce sites and almost half of this from Myntra alone. "So obviously they are pressurising (retailers) and they themselves are under pressure as e-commerce companies are burning cash by giving discounts.

In order to save some margins for themselves they are pushing brands to give better margins." E-commerce companies need to achieve profitability by creating efficiencies in their supply chain, besides reducing their skyrocketing marketing and staff costs and not by asking for more discounts from brands. CEO of Arvind Lifestyle Brands, which sells labels including US Polo Association and Nautica, on Myntra, said the e-commerce company did not approach him for bigger margins.

'We are only concerned they don't undervalue our brands by discounting. We ensure that doesn't happen and it is part of our agreement,' he said. In the US, Amazon.com has been accused by some vendors publishers of using its clout to put pressure on them. The consultant cited above said the acquisition of Myntra by Flipkart could lead to a similar situation in India as well.

199. From small retailers, Myntra is now asking
    (a) very less margins
    (b) more margins
    (c) no margins
    (d) None of the above

200. Currently, online commerce companies are involved in
    (a) offering substantial discounts to customers.
    (b) make profits themselves.
    (c) Both (a) and (b)
    (d) None of the above

Answers

1. *(b)*	2. *(b)*	3. *(b)*	4. *(d)*	5. *(c)*	6. *(b)*	7. *(c)*	8. *(a)*	9. *(d)*	10. *(a)*
11. *(a)*	12. *(c)*	13. *(d)*	14. *(b)*	15. *(d)*	16. *(c)*	17. *(a)*	18. *(b)*	19. *(c)*	20. *(d)*
21. *(a)*	22. *(d)*	23. *(b)*	24. *(b)*	25. *(d)*	26. *(a)*	27. *(d)*	28. *(d)*	29. *(d)*	30. *(d)*
31. *(b)*	32. *(d)*	33. *(b)*	34. *(a)*	35. *(a)*	36. *(a)*	37. *(b)*	38. *(a)*	39. *(c)*	40. *(c)*
41. *(a)*	42. *(a)*	43. *(b)*	44. *(a)*	45. *(b)*	46. *(d)*	47. *(c)*	48. *(b)*	49. *(c)*	50. *(a)*
51. *(b)*	52. *(a)*	53. *(b)*	54. *(d)*	55. *(c)*	56. *(b)*	57. *(c)*	58. *(a)*	59. *(b)*	60. *(c)*
61. *(a)*	62. *(b)*	63. *(b)*	64. *(c)*	65. *(a)*	66. *(b)*	67. *(a)*	68. *(c)*	69. *(c)*	70. *(b)*
71. *(a)*	72. *(c)*	73. *(b)*	74. *(c)*	75. *(c)*	76. *(d)*	77. *(c)*	78. *(c)*	79. *(b)*	80. *(c)*
81. *(b)*	82. *(d)*	83. *(a)*	84. *(c)*	85. *(b)*	86. *(c)*	87. *(b)*	88. *(b)*	89. *(b)*	90. *(b)*
91. *(a)*	92. *(a)*	93. *(b)*	94. *(c)*	95. *(b)*	96. *(c)*	97. *(c)*	98. *(a)*	99. *(d)*	100. *(c)*
101. *(d)*	102. *(c)*	103. *(b)*	104. *(a)*	105. *(a)*	106. *(c)*	107. *(b)*	108. *(a)*	109. *(d)*	110. *(b)*
111. *(a)*	112. *(c)*	113. *(b)*	114. *(a)*	115. *(d)*	116. *(b)*	117. *(c)*	118. *(d)*	119. *(d)*	120. *(b)*
121. *(d)*	122. *(c)*	123. *(c)*	124. *(c)*	125.. *(a)*	126. *(c)*	127. *(a)*	128. *(d)*	129. *(c)*	130. *(d)*
131. *(d)*	132. *(a)*	133. *(b)*	134. *(b)*	135. *(d)*	136. *(c)*	137. *(b)*	138. *(a)*	139. *(d)*	140. *(b)*
141. *(d)*	142. *(d)*	143. *(a)*	144. *(c)*	145. *(d)*	146. *(d)*	147. *(d)*	148. *(a)*	149. *(d)*	150. *(a)*
151. *(a)*	152. *(a)*	153. *(d)*	154. *(b)*	155. *(c)*	156. *(c)*	157. *(d)*	158. *(b)*	159. *(b)*	160. *(b)*
161. *(d)*	162. *(c)*	163. *(b)*	164. *(b)*	165. *(b)*	166. *(c)*	167. *(c)*	168. *(b)*	169. *(c)*	170. *(b)*
171. *(b)*	172. *(d)*	173. *(c)*	174. *(c)*	175. *(a)*	176. *(c)*	177. *(d)*	178. *(c)*	179. *(b)*	180. *(d)*
181. *(c)*	182. *(c)*	183. *(b)*	184. *(c)*	185. *(c)*	186. *(b)*	187. *(d)*	188. *(c)*	189. *(b)*	190. *(d)*
191. *(a)*	192. *(d)*	193. *(d)*	194. *(d)*	195. *(a)*	196. *(c)*	197. *(c)*	198. *(c)*	199. *(b)*	200. *(c)*

Hints & Solutions

1. (*b*) Let the radius of cylinder and sphere be r_c cm and r_s cm, respectively.

According to the question,

Volume of the cylinder = Volume of sphere

$$\pi r_c^2 h = \frac{4}{3}\pi r_s^3$$

$$\Rightarrow \quad \pi \times r_c^2 \times \frac{28}{3} = \frac{4}{3} \times \pi \times (7)^3$$

$$\left[\because n = \frac{28}{3} \text{ cm and } r_s = 7 \text{ cm, given }\right]$$

$$\Rightarrow \quad r_c^2 = \frac{4}{3} \times (7)^3 \times \frac{3}{28} \Rightarrow r_c^2 = 7^2$$

$$\therefore \qquad r_c = 7 \text{ cm}$$

2. (*b*) Given, thickness of each coin = 1 mm

Then, total height of 50 coins $= 50 \times 1 = 50$ mm

$\because$ diameter of coin = 4 cm

Then, $r = 2$ cm

$$= 2 \times 10 \text{ mm} \qquad [\because 1 \text{ cm} = 10 \text{ mm}]$$

$$= 20 \text{ mm}$$

Diameter of wire = 2 mm $\Rightarrow$ radius = 1 mm

Let, h = length of wire

According to the question,

Volume of 50 coins = Volume of the wire

$$\Rightarrow \quad \pi \times (20)^2 \times 50 = \pi \times (1)^2 \times h$$

$$[\because \text{ when we use 50 coins, the shape is as like cylinder}]$$

$$\Rightarrow \quad (20)^2 \times 50 = 1\, h$$

$$\therefore \qquad h = 20000 \text{ mm}$$

$$= \frac{20000}{1000} \text{ m } \left[\because 1 \text{ mm} = \frac{1}{1000} \text{ m}\right]$$

$$= 20 \text{ m}$$

3. (*b*) Let the two similar triangles are $\triangle ABC$ and $\triangle DEF$.

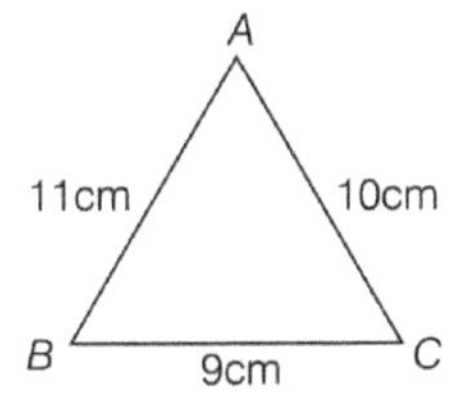
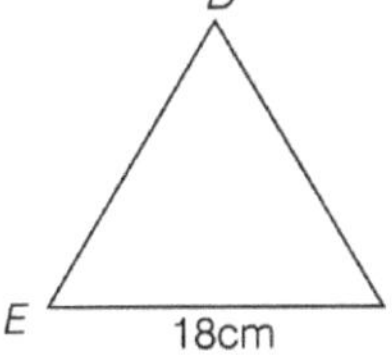

As, $\triangle ABC \sim \triangle DEF$

$$\therefore \qquad \frac{AB}{DE} = \frac{BC}{EF} = \frac{AC}{DF}$$

$$\Rightarrow \quad \frac{BC}{EF} = \frac{9}{18} = \frac{1}{2}$$

$$\therefore \qquad \frac{AB}{DE} = \frac{1}{2}$$

$$\Rightarrow \qquad DE = 2 \times AB$$

$$= 2 \times 11 = 22 \text{ cm}$$

and $$\frac{AC}{DF} = \frac{1}{2}$$

$$\Rightarrow \qquad DF = 2 \times AC$$

$$= 2 \times 10 \text{ cm}$$

$$= 20 \text{ cm}$$

$\therefore$ The perimeter of $\triangle DEF = DE + EF + FD$

$$= 22 + 18 + 20$$

$$= 60 \text{ cm}$$

4. (*d*) According to the question,

Let the capacity of bucket $B = x$ L

Then, capacity of bucket $A = 2x$ L

$\therefore$ Total capacity of tank $T = 50 \times 2x = 100x$ L

Tank T filled by bucket $A = 20 \times 2x = 40x$ L

Remaining part of tank $T = 100x - 40x = 60x$ L

Total capacity of the tank A and $B = x + 2x = 3x$

$\therefore$ Number of turns required by A and B together to fill the remaining part of tank $= \dfrac{60x}{3x} = 20$

Or

(*d*) Number of turns of bucket A to fill tank $T = 50$

Then, part of tank filled in 1 turn by bucket $A = \dfrac{1}{50}$

Part of tank filled in 20 turns by bucket $A = \dfrac{20}{50} = \dfrac{2}{5}$

Part remaining to be filled $= 1 - \dfrac{2}{5} = \dfrac{3}{5}$

Given, capacity of bucket $A = 2 \times$ capacity of bucke B

$\therefore$ Part of tank filled by bucket B in 1 turn $= \dfrac{1}{100}$

So, part of tank filled by bucket A and B together in 1 turn $= \dfrac{1}{100} + \dfrac{1}{50} = \dfrac{3}{100}$

$\therefore$ Number of turns required to fill remain $\dfrac{3}{5}$ part

$$= \frac{3}{5} \times \frac{100}{3} = 20 \text{ turns}$$

5. (*c*) A's one day work $= \dfrac{1}{12}$

$\therefore A$'s 2 days work $= 2 \times \dfrac{1}{12} = \dfrac{1}{6}$

B's one day work $= \dfrac{1}{15}$

$\therefore B$'s 3 days work $= 3 \times \dfrac{1}{15} = \dfrac{1}{5}$

C's one day work $= \dfrac{1}{20}$

$\therefore C$'s 4 days work $= 4 \times \dfrac{1}{20} = \dfrac{1}{5}$

Work done by A, B and C together $= \dfrac{1}{6} + \dfrac{1}{5} + \dfrac{1}{5}$

$$= \dfrac{17}{30}$$

$\therefore$ Remaining work $= 1 - \dfrac{17}{30} = \dfrac{13}{30}$

$\therefore \dfrac{13}{30}$ work is done by D in 13 days.

Hence, D can do the whole work in

$$= 13 \times \dfrac{30}{13} = 30 \text{ days}$$

6. (**b**) Let the present age of Sunita be x yr.

and the present age of Puja be y yr.

3 yr ago, age of Sunita $= (x - 3)$ yr and age of Puja $= (y - 3)$ yr

$\therefore$ According to the question,

$$(y - 3) = \dfrac{1}{4}(x - 3)$$

$\Rightarrow \quad 4y - 12 = x - 3$

$\Rightarrow \quad 4y - x = 9 \qquad \qquad ...(i)$

After 3 yr,

age of Sunita $= (x + 3)$ yr and age of Puja $= (y + 3)$ yr

Now, $\quad \dfrac{y + 3}{x + 3} = \dfrac{7}{22}$

$\Rightarrow \quad 22y + 66 = 7x + 21$

$\Rightarrow \quad 22y - 7x = -45 \qquad \qquad ...(ii)$

On solving Eqs. (i) and (ii), we get

$$y = 18 \text{ and } x = 63$$

$\therefore$ Present age of Sunita $= 63$ yr.

7. (**c**) Let age of Arun $= x$ yr

Then, age of Raj $= 3x$ yr

$\therefore$ Age of Kamal $= (3x + 5)$ yr

According to the question,

Sum of their ages $= 40$

$\Rightarrow \quad x + 3x + (3x + 5) = 40$

$\Rightarrow \quad 7x + 5 = 40$

$\Rightarrow \quad x = \dfrac{35}{7} = 5$

Hence, age of Raj $= 3 \times 5 = 15$ yr.

8. (**a**) Given, $P = ₹ 125$

Then, $A = 2 \times 125 = ₹ 250$ and $t = 5$ yr

$\therefore$ CI $= A - P = 250 - 125 = ₹ 125$

We know, that $A = P\left(1 + \dfrac{r}{100}\right)^t$

$\Rightarrow \quad 250 = 125\left(1 + \dfrac{r}{100}\right)^5$

$\Rightarrow \quad 2 = \left(1 + \dfrac{r}{100}\right)^5 \qquad \qquad ...(i)$

Let the more years be t yr.

According to the question,

$$\text{CI} + 250 = P\left[\left(1 + \dfrac{r}{100}\right)^{5 + t} - 1\right]$$

$\Rightarrow 125 + 250 = 125\left[\left(1 + \dfrac{r}{100}\right)^5 \times \left(1 + \dfrac{r}{100}\right)^t - 1\right]$

$$\text{[by Eq. (ii)]}$$

$\Rightarrow \quad \dfrac{375}{125} = \left[2 \times \left(1 + \dfrac{r}{100}\right)^t - 1\right] \quad \text{[by Eq. (i)]}$

$\Rightarrow \quad 3 = 2\left(1 + \dfrac{r}{100}\right)^t - 1$

$\Rightarrow \quad \dfrac{4}{2} = \left(1 + \dfrac{r}{100}\right)^t$

$\Rightarrow \quad 2 = \left(1 + \dfrac{r}{100}\right)^t \qquad \qquad ...(iii)$

Now, comparing Eqs. (i) and (iii), we get

$$\left(1 + \dfrac{r}{100}\right)^t = \left(1 + \dfrac{r}{100}\right)^5$$

$\therefore \qquad t = 5 \text{ yr}$

9. (**d**) Length of the train $A = 120$ m

Speed of the train $A = 60$ km/h

Length of train $B = 150$ m

Let the speed of the train $B = x$ km/h

Then, the speed of the train A relative to B

$$= (60 - x) \text{ km/h}$$

$$= (60 - x) \times \dfrac{5}{18} \text{ m/s}$$

$$= \dfrac{300 - 5x}{18} \text{ m/s}$$

We know that, Time $= \dfrac{\text{Distance}}{\text{Speed}}$

$\Rightarrow \quad \dfrac{(150 + 120)}{\left(\dfrac{300 - 5x}{18}\right)} = 64.8$

$\Rightarrow \quad \dfrac{270}{\left(\dfrac{300 - 5x}{18}\right)} = 64.8$

$\Rightarrow \quad 270 \times 18 = 64.8\,(300 - 5x)$

$\Rightarrow \quad 4860 = 19440 - 324x$

$\Rightarrow \quad 324x = 14580$

$\Rightarrow \quad x = \dfrac{14580}{324} = 45 \text{ m/s}$

$\Rightarrow \quad x = 45 \times \dfrac{18}{5} \text{ km/h} = 162 \text{ km/h}$

10. (a) Let the certain distance be d km.

Speed of the boat $= x$ km/h

and the speed of the stream $= y$ km/h

Then, upstream speed $= (x - y)$ km/h

and downstream speed $= (x + y)$ km/h

As, the time taken to travel downstream is 2 h.

$$\frac{d}{x + y} = 2 \qquad \left[\because \text{Time} = \frac{\text{Distance}}{\text{Speed}} \right]$$

$$\Rightarrow \qquad 2x + 2y = d \qquad \text{...(i)}$$

And the time taken to travel upstream $= 5$ h

$$\frac{d}{x - y} = 5 \qquad \left[\because \text{Time} = \frac{\text{Distance}}{\text{Speed}} \right]$$

$$\Rightarrow \qquad 5x - 5y = d \qquad \text{...(ii)}$$

From Eqs. (i) and (ii), we get

$$2x + 2y = 5x - 5y$$

$$\Rightarrow \qquad 5y + 2y = 5x - 2x$$

$$\Rightarrow \qquad 7y = 3x$$

$$\Rightarrow \qquad \frac{x}{y} = \frac{7}{3}$$

$$\therefore \qquad x : y = 7 : 3$$

11. (a) Let the share of P be ₹ x and the share of Q be ₹ y.

Then, $x + y = 1519$

$$\Rightarrow \qquad x = 1519 - y \qquad \text{...(i)}$$

According to the question,

$$\frac{4}{9} \text{ of } x = \frac{13}{25} \text{ of } y$$

$$\Rightarrow \qquad \frac{4x}{9} = \frac{13y}{25}$$

$$\Rightarrow \qquad 100x = 117y$$

$$\Rightarrow \qquad 100\,(1519 - y) = 117y \qquad \text{[from Eq. (i)]}$$

$$\Rightarrow \qquad 151900 - 100y = 117y$$

$$\Rightarrow \qquad 117y + 100y = 151900$$

$$\Rightarrow \qquad 217y = 151900$$

$$\Rightarrow \qquad y = \frac{151900}{217} = ₹\ 700$$

$$\therefore \qquad x = 1519 - 700 = ₹\ 819$$

Hence, share of $P = ₹\ 819$

12. (c) Given, cost price of house $= ₹\ 3500000$

After repairing, the new cost price of house

$$= 3500000 \times \left(\frac{100 + 20}{100} \right)$$

$$= 3500000 \times \frac{120}{100}$$

$$= ₹\ 4200000$$

Given, gain% $= 20\%$

We know that, gain% $= \dfrac{\text{SP} - \text{CP}}{\text{CP}} \times 100$

$$\Rightarrow \qquad \frac{20}{100} = \frac{\text{SP} - 4200000}{4200000}$$

$$\Rightarrow \qquad \frac{4200000}{5} = \text{SP} - 4200000$$

$$\Rightarrow \qquad \text{SP} - 4200000 = 840000$$

$$\therefore \qquad \text{SP} = 840000 + 4200000$$

$$= ₹\ 5040000$$

$$= ₹\ 50.4 \text{ lakh}$$

13. (d) According to question,

Total cost price of rice $= 15 \times 30 + 25 \times 40$

$$= 450 + 1000 = ₹\ 1450$$

Profit $= 20\%$

We know, that SP $= \left(\dfrac{100 + \text{Profit}\%}{100} \right) \times \text{CP}$

$$\Rightarrow \qquad \text{SP} = \frac{(100 + 20)}{100} \times 1450$$

$$= \frac{120}{100} \times 1450$$

$$= ₹\ 1740$$

$$\therefore \quad \text{SP of 1 kg rice} = \frac{1740}{(15 + 25)}$$

$$= \frac{1740}{40} = ₹\ 43.5$$

14. (b) Given, HCF of two numbers $= 13$

Then, the numbers are $13 \times 7 = 91$ and $13 \times 3 = 39$

$\therefore$ Smaller of the two numbers $= 39$

15. (d) Here, $30 = 2 \times 3 \times 5$

$$42 = 2 \times 3 \times 7$$

$$105 = 5 \times 3 \times 7$$

$\therefore$ LCM of 30, 42 and $105 = 2 \times 3 \times 5 \times 7 = 210$

When 3587 is divided by 210, then remainder $= 17$

$\therefore$ Required number $= 210 - 17 = 193$

16. (c) Here, $x = 50$ km/h and $y = 40$ km/h

According to the formula,

Average speed $= \dfrac{2xy}{x + y}$

$$\therefore \text{Average speed} = \frac{2 \times 50 \times 40}{50 + 40}$$

$$= \frac{2 \times 50 \times 40}{90}$$

$$= 44.44 \text{ km/h}$$

17. (a) According to the question,

Total investment of $A = (25 \times 2 + 20 \times 10)$ lakh

$$= (50 + 200) \text{ lakh}$$

$$= ₹\ 250 \text{ lakh}$$

Total investment of $B = 30 \times 5$

$$= ₹\ 150 \text{ lakh}$$

Total investment of $C = 10 \times 10$

$$= ₹\ 100 \text{ lakh}$$

Now, ratio of investment of A, B and C

$$= 250 : 150 : 100 = 5 : 3 : 2$$

$\because$ Total profit at the end of 1 year $= ₹\ 9$ lakh

$\therefore$ The share of B in the profit $= \left(\dfrac{3}{10} \times 9\right)$ lakh

$$= \left(\dfrac{27}{10}\right) \text{ lakh}$$

$$= ₹2.7 \text{ lakh}$$

18. (*b*) 2.7% of $300 + 0.03\%$ of $400 - a = 12.2\%$ of 10

$\Rightarrow \dfrac{2.7}{100} \times 300 + \dfrac{0.03}{100} \times 400 - a = \dfrac{12.2}{100} \times 10$

$\Rightarrow \qquad 2.7 \times 3 + 0.03 \times 4 - a = 1.22$

$\Rightarrow \qquad 8.1 + 0.12 - 1.22 = a$

$\therefore \qquad\qquad\qquad a = 7$

19. (*c*) There are 4 possible cases of selecting a group of 5 persons.

We may have

(2 women and 3 men), (3 women and 2 men),

(4 women and 1 man), (5 women only)

$\therefore$ Required number of ways

$= {}^6C_2 \times {}^6C_3 + {}^6C_3 \times {}^6C_2 + {}^6C_4 \times {}^6C_1 + {}^6C_5$

$= \dfrac{6!}{2!\,4!} \times \dfrac{6!}{3!\,3!} + \dfrac{6!}{3!\,3!} \times \dfrac{6!}{2!\,4!} + \dfrac{6!}{4!\,2!} \times \dfrac{6!}{1!\,5!} + \dfrac{6!}{5!\,1!}$

$= \dfrac{6 \times 5}{2} \times \dfrac{6 \times 5 \times 4}{3 \times 2} + \dfrac{6 \times 5}{2} \times \dfrac{6 \times 5 \times 4}{3 \times 2} + \dfrac{6 \times 5}{2} \times 6 + 6$

$$\left[\because {}^nC_r = \dfrac{n!}{r!\,n-r!}\right]$$

$= 15 \times 20 + 15 \times 20 + 90 + 6$

$= 300 + 300 + 90 + 6$

$= 696$

20. (*d*) Number of persons in each blood group (A, B, AB, O) is 10.

Total number of persons present in the hall

$$= 4 \times 10$$

$$= 40$$

Probability of blood group A $= \dfrac{{}^{10}C_1}{{}^{40}C_1} = \dfrac{10}{40} = \dfrac{1}{4}$

Probability of blood group B $= \dfrac{{}^{10}C_1}{{}^{40}C_1} = \dfrac{10}{40} = \dfrac{1}{4}$

$\therefore$ Required probability of blood group A or B

$$= \dfrac{1}{4} + \dfrac{1}{4} = \dfrac{2}{4} = \dfrac{1}{2}$$

21. (*a*) Given, $\quad a^2 + b^2 = 73 \qquad$ ...(i)

and $\qquad\qquad a - b = 5 \qquad$ ...(ii)

On squaring both sides, we get

$$(a - b)^2 = 5^2$$

$\Rightarrow \quad a^2 + b^2 - 2ab = 25 \quad [\because (x-y)^2 = x^2 + y^2 - 2xy]$

$\Rightarrow \qquad 73 - 2ab = 25 \qquad$ [From Eq. (i)]

$\Rightarrow \qquad\qquad 2ab = 73 - 25$

$\Rightarrow \qquad\qquad ab = \dfrac{48}{2} = 24 \qquad$ ...(iii)

Now, $(a + b)^2 = (a - b)^2 + 4ab$

$\qquad\qquad = (5)^2 + 4 \times 24 \qquad$ [by Eqs. (ii) and (iii)]

$\qquad\qquad = 25 + 96$

$\qquad\qquad = 121$

$\qquad (a + b) = 11 \qquad$ ...(iv)

Now, on solving Eqs. (ii) and (iv), we get

$$a = 8 \text{ and } b = 3$$

22. (*d*) $\dfrac{(13 - 7 \times 9 - 2)}{(23 \times 5 - 2 \times 5 - 41 \times 7)} = \dfrac{13 - 63 - 2}{115 - 10 - 287}$

$$= \dfrac{-52}{-182}$$

$$= \dfrac{2}{7}$$

23. (*b*) Given, Mr. Rajiv salary $= ₹\ 150000$

After standard deduction income

$$= 150000 - 30000$$

$$= ₹\ 120000$$

From the table, income upto $₹\ 50000$ have no tax.

Then, remaining amount $= 120000 - 50000$

$$= ₹\ 70000$$

Again from the table, 10% tax on income from $₹\ 50000$ to $₹\ 60000$.

Then, tax $= 10000 \times \dfrac{10}{100} = ₹\ 1000$

and tax on income from $₹\ 60000$ to $₹\ 150000$ is 20%.

Then, tax $= 60000 \times \dfrac{20}{100} = ₹\ 12000$

Total tax $= 1000 + 12000 = ₹\ 13000$

Given, Mr. Rajiv savings $= ₹\ 40000$

Saving tax $= 40000 \times \dfrac{20}{100} = ₹\ 8000$

Remaining tax $= 13000 - 8000 = ₹\ 5000$

Given, a tax surcharge of 10% is added on the total tax.

$\therefore$ Total tax paid by Mr. Rajiv $= 5000 \left(\dfrac{100 + 10}{100}\right)$

$$= 5000 \times \dfrac{110}{100}$$

$$= ₹\ 5500$$

24. (*b*) Given, salary of Mrs. Shruti $= ₹\ 150000$

By above solution it is clear that, if she saves $₹\ 40000$ her total tax becomes $₹\ 5000$ and as per question as additional rebate of $₹\ 5000$ is available for working women. Hence, net tax for the year become zero.

Hence, option (b) is correct.

25. (*d*) According to the question,

Prakash salary $= 144000 + 35000 = ₹\ 179000$

After standard deduction income

$$= 179000 - 25000$$
$$= ₹\ 154000$$

From the table till ₹ 50000 have no tax.

The remaining amount $= 154000 - 50000$
$$= ₹\ 104000$$

Again from the table 10% tax on ₹ 50000 to ₹ 60000.

Then, tax $= 10000 \times \dfrac{10}{100} = ₹\ 1000$

And 20% tax on ₹ 60000 to ₹ 150000.

Then tax $= 94000 \times \dfrac{20}{100} = ₹\ 18800$

Given, Mr. Prakash saving $= ₹\ 70000$

Saving tax $= 70000 \times \dfrac{15}{100} = ₹\ 10500$

Remaining tax $= 18800 + 1000 - 10500$
$$= ₹\ 9300$$

Given, a tax surcharge of 10% is added on the tax

$\therefore$ Prakash paid total tax $= 9300 \times \left(\dfrac{100 + 10}{100} \right)$

$$= 9300 \times \dfrac{110}{100} = ₹\ 10230$$

Sol. (Q. Nos. 26-30) *According to the question,*

Most intelligent Least intelligent

$\text{E} > \text{C} > \text{A/G} > \text{G/A} > \text{B} > \text{D} > \text{F}$

$\Rightarrow$ Psychologist > Businessman > Doctor/Engineer > Engineer/Doctor > Student > Architect > Teacher

Sitting
Arrangement

$\overset{+}{\text{D}}$	$\overset{-}{\text{F}}$	$\overset{-}{\text{E}}$	$\overset{-}{\text{C}}$	$\overset{++}{\text{A/G}}$	$\overset{++}{\text{G/A}}$	$\overset{+}{\text{B}}$
Architect	Teacher	Psychologist	Business Man	Engineer/ Doctor	Engineer/ Doctor	Student

$$\left[\begin{array}{l} + \to \text{Male} \\ - \to \text{Female} \end{array} \right]$$

Married couples $=$ (A/G) Engineer and (F) Teacher
$\Rightarrow$ (A/G) Doctor and (C) Businessman

26. (*a*) F is sitting immediate right of D.

27. (*d*) Engineer and Doctor are sitting together.

28. (*d*) Here, the position of Engineer and Doctor are not confirmed but engineer is not more intelligent than businessman.

29. (*d*) Since, the condition of A and G is not clear. So all three given couples can be possible.

30. (*d*) No one shows the correct order of intelligence.

Sol. (Q. Nos. 31-33) *According to the question,*

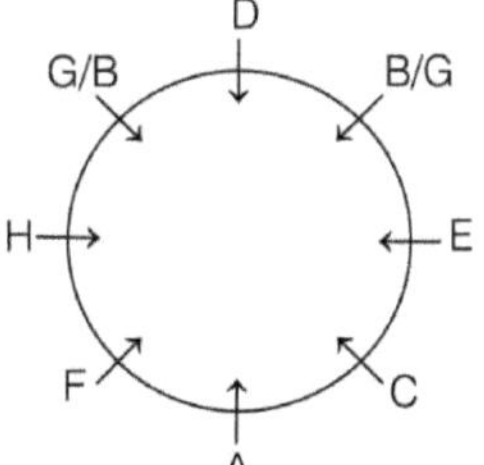

31. (*b*) A's position is the right of F.

32. (*d*) All the given information are required to ascertain the position of C.

33. (*b*) 'C' is sitting between A and E.

34. (*a*) The pattern is as follows

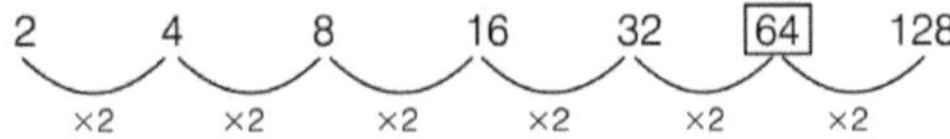

Hence, '64' will be the missing term.

35. (*a*) The pattern is as follows

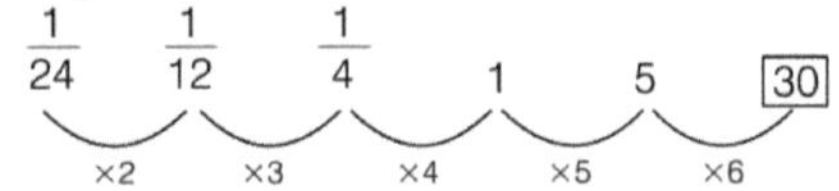

Hence, the missing term will be '30'.

36. (*a*) The pattern is as follows

4   7   5   9   6   11   7   13

$+1$ $+2$ $+1$ $+2$ $+1$ $+2$

Hence, the missing term will be '6'.

37. (*b*) The pattern is as follows,

K   G   Ⓓ   B

-4 -3 -2

Hence, the missing term will be 'D'.

38. (*a*) The pattern is as follows,

B's position $= 2 = 2 + 1$
$$= 3$$

N's position $= 14 = 14 + 1$
$$= 15$$

T's position $= 20 = 20 + 1 = 21$

Hence, the missing term will be 'T'.

39. (*c*) According to the question,

Hence, it is clear she finally moving in East direction.

40. (*c*) The directions of the route from A to D will be NE, SE, NE.

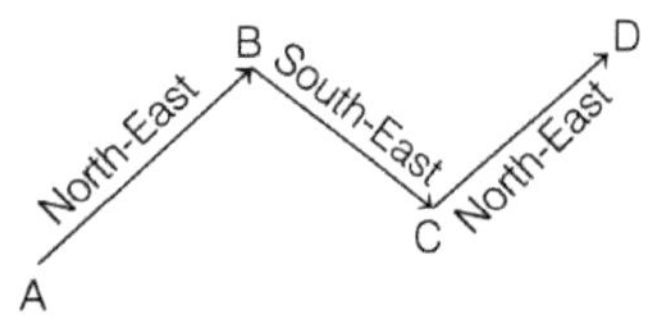

41. (*a*) According to the question,

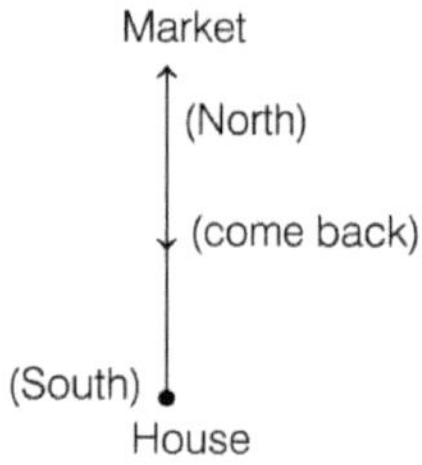

Hence, it is clear the direction of his house with respect to market is 'South'.

42. (*a*) According to the question,

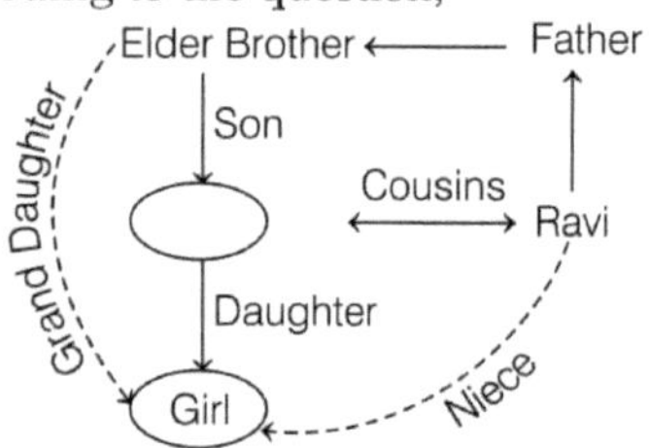

It is clear from the diagram the girl is the niece of Ravi.

43. (*b*) According to the question,
Family consists Husband = 1
Wife = 1
All sons = 3
All daughters = 2
All daughter-in-law = 3
Hence, total number of females in the family will be '6'.

44. (*a*) According to the question,

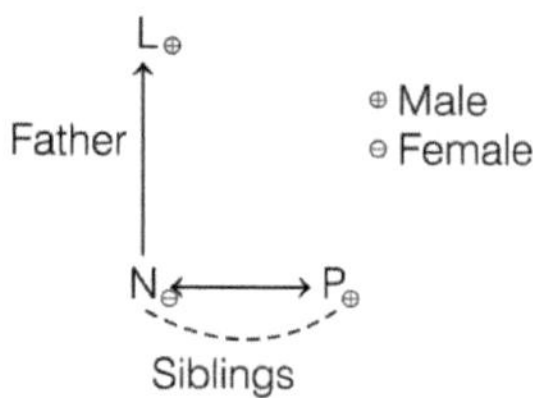

Hence, it is clear 'N' is the daughter of 'L'.

45. (*b*) The correct Venn diagram is

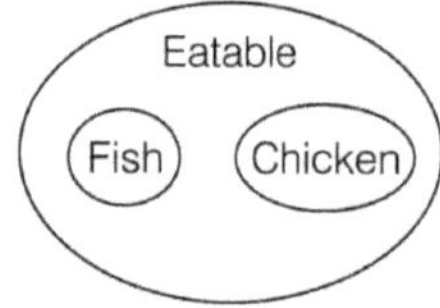

Chicken and Fish both are eatable dishes.
Hence, option (b) is correct.

46. (*d*) The correct Venn diagram is

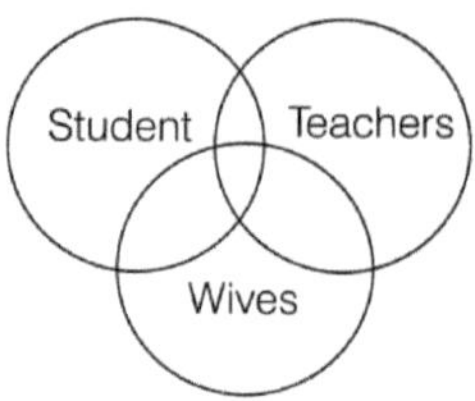

Some wives may be teacher or student and its *vice-versa* is also a possibility.
Hence, option (d) is correct answer.

47. (*c*) The correct Venn diagram is

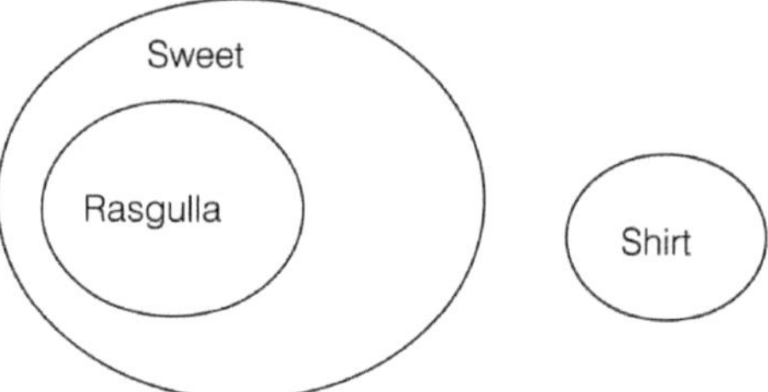

All Rasgulla are sweet but no sweet is shirt.
Hence, option (c) is correct.

48. (*b*) The pattern is as follows
As,

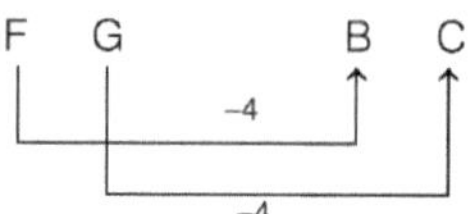

Similarly,

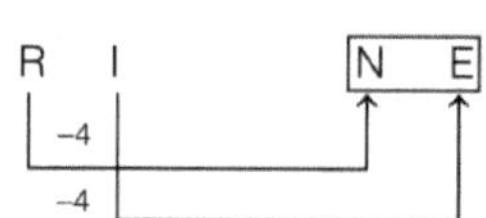

Hence, 'NE' will come on the place of question mark.

49. (*c*) The pattern is as follows
As,

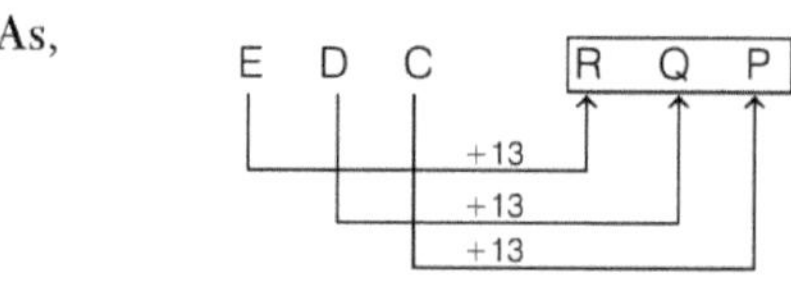

Similarly,

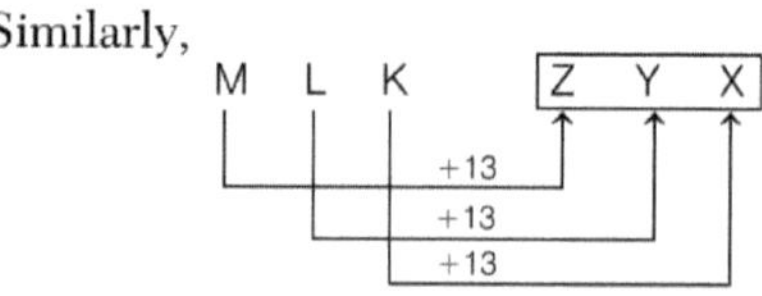

Hence, 'ZYX' will come on the place of question mark.

50. (*a*) The pattern is as follows,

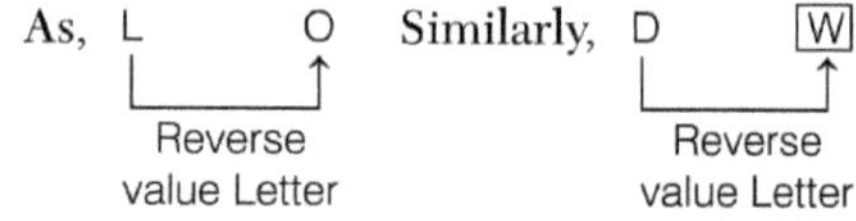

Hence, option (a) is correct.

51. (*b*) The pattern is as follows
As,

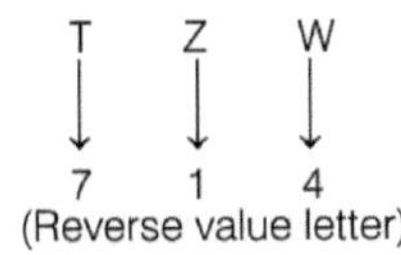

$\therefore 7 \times 1 \times 4 = 7 \times 4 = 28$

Similarly,

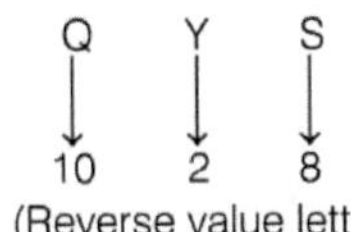

$\therefore 10 \times 2 \times 8 = 20 \times 8 = \boxed{160}$

52. (*a*) In every step, number of lines breaking from outmost figure in the following sequence $\dfrac{1}{2}, 1, \dfrac{3}{2}, 2, \dfrac{5}{2}, 3, \ldots$

So, the next figure will be

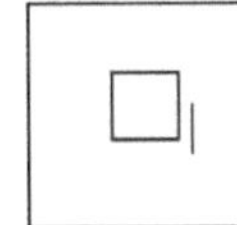

53. (*b*) In each step a small triangular shape is added top of the left corner and right corner alternatively. So, the next figure will be

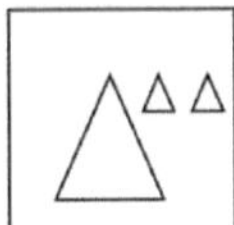

54. (*d*) In each step a circle is decrease and the group of circles shift top to bottom alternatively and on the other hand a square is increase and group of squares shift top to bottom alternatively.

So, the next figure will be

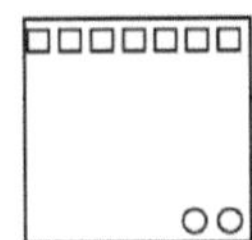

55. (*c*) According to the given code,

this	is	the	{tree}	⇒	2	1	5	{3}
the		green	{tree}	⇒	5		7	{3}
{tree}		of	life	⇒	{3}		0	9

Hence, from the above coding the code for 'the' will be '5'.

56. (*b*) As,

P O P U L A R
+1↓ +1↓ +1↓ +1↓ +1↓ +1↓ +1↓
Q P Q V M B S

Similarly,

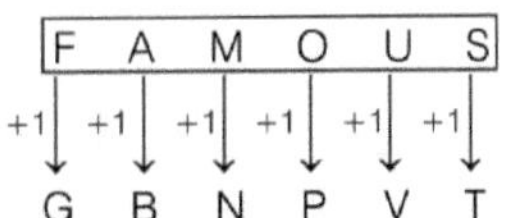

F A M O U S
+1↓ +1↓ +1↓ +1↓ +1↓ +1↓
G B N P V T

Hence, option (*b*) is correct.

57. (*c*) As, we know the colour of human blood is red and here 'red' is called 'yellow', so, yellow would be the colour of human blood.

58. (*a*) If we go through the passage, then we find it is the real concern of the passage. Hence, we can infer, India has not yet been able to consolidate its firm stand in the international sugar market. So, the inference is definitely true.

59. (*b*) According to the passage, since August 1998 government control on sugar mills is getting diluted. But we do not know how much the government control has been diluted. So, the inference is probably true.

60. (*c*) There is no such information regarding the position of Indian sugar industry in the world ranking of large nation prior to August 1998. So, the data provided is inadequate.

141. (*d*) 'Dexterity' means the ability to perform a difficult action quickly. Hence, 'skill' best expresses the meaning of 'dexterity'.

142. (*d*) 'Extinct' refers to something that is no longer in existence. Hence, 'non-existent' best expresses the meaning of 'extinct'.

143. (*a*) 'Agog' means very eager to curious to hear or see something. Hence, 'excited' best expresses the meaning of 'agog'.

144. (*c*) 'Obstreperous' means stubbornly resistant to control. Hence, 'hostile' best expresses the meaning of 'obstreperous'.

145. (*d*) 'Oppose' is opposite in meaning to 'urges'. 'Urges' means to persuade someone to do something or recommend while 'oppose' means to prevent someone from doing something.

146. (*d*) 'Agitated' is opposite in meaning to 'serene'. 'Serene' means calm and composed while 'agitated' means to feel troubled or nervous.

147. (*d*) 'Contracts' is opposite in meaning to 'expand'. 'Expand' means to become larger while 'contract' means to decrease in size, number or range.

148. (*a*) 'Moving' is opposite in meaning to 'stationary'. 'Stationary' means motionless or not intended to be moved.

160. (*b*) 'Mince matters' means to restrain one's language to avoid giving offense. Hence, option (*b*) 'conceal facts' best expresses the meaning of 'mince matters'.

161. (*d*) 'Cross purposes' means failure to understand each other. Hence, option (*d*) 'misunderstanding each other' best expresses the meaning of 'cross purposes'.

162. (*c*) 'Wearing their heart on their sleeve' means exposing their innermost feelings to others.

163. (*b*) 'Made someone's flesh creep' means to scare someone or make them feel disgusted. Hence, option (b) 'frightened me' best expresses the meaning of 'made my flesh creep'.

164. (*b*) 'With open arms' means with great affection or enthusiasm. Hence, option (b) 'warmly' best expresses the meaning of 'with open arms'.

165. (*b*) 'To cut my teeth on' means to get your first experience by doing something. Hence, option (b) 'to gain experience' best expresses the meaning of the idiom 'to cut my teeth on'.

171. (*b*) Part (b) contains the error. Preposition 'on' is incorrectly used in the sentence. Replace 'on' with 'in' to make the sentence grammatically correct.

172. (*d*) Part (d) contains the error. 'Explosives' is a plural noun hence, the verb used with it, should be in plural form. Replace 'was' with 'were' to make the sentence grammatically correct.

173. (*c*) Part (c) contains the error. 'Gape' means to stare and 'gap' means space. Hence, replace 'gape' with 'gap' to make the sentence grammatically correct.

174. (*c*) Part (c) contains the error. 'Amiable' starts with a vowel sound hence, article 'a' should be replaced by 'an' to make the sentence grammatically correct.

175. (*a*) Part (a) contains the error. Plural form of nouns and pronouns are used with 'one of the'. Hence, replace 'man' with 'men' to make the sentence grammatically correct.

Hotel Management

National Council for Hotel Management and Catering Technology

Solved Paper 2014

Instructions

- There are Five (A–E) Sections in this Solved Paper.
- For every correct attempt, the student will be awarded **1 mark**.
- All the questions are in MCQs form and each have four options.

Marks : 200
Time : 3 hrs

Section A : Numerical Ability and Scientific Aptitude

1. The gas associated with the greenhouse effect is
(a) carbon dioxide
(b) oxygen
(c) nitrogen dioxide
(d) sulphur dioxide

2. The force which prevents us from slipping while walking on the road is
(a) muscular force of our body
(b) friction force
(c) gravitational pull by earth
(d) balanced forces of nature

3. Fly ash is produced by
(a) petroleum
(b) natural gas
(c) coal
(d) All of these

4. 'Orion' is the name of a
(a) star
(b) planet
(c) galaxy
(d) constellation

5. The part that protects the human eye is called
(a) cornea
(b) choroid
(c) retina
(d) blind spot

6. Which of the following is good conductor of electricity?
(a) Tap water
(b) Distilled water
(c) Sea water
(d) Rain water

7. Acid rain is caused by
(a) deforestation
(b) carbon dioxide
(c) carbon monoxide
(d) oxides of sulphur and nitrogen

8. A mountain climber experiences a nose bleed due to
(a) decrease in atmospheric pressure
(b) increase in atmospheric pressure
(c) more gravitational pull
(d) effect of high altitude

9. The ENT doctor generally uses a
(a) convex mirror
(b) convex lens
(c) plane mirror
(d) concave mirror

10. One horse power is equal to
(a) 736 watts
(b) 756 watts
(c) 748 watts
(d) 746 watts

11. The filament of an incandescent light bulb is made of
(a) tungsten
(b) silver
(c) iron
(d) graphite

12. Which one of the following power sources is not a non-conventional source of power?
(a) Wind energy
(b) Natural gas
(c) Solar energy'
(d) Tidal energy

13. Which layer of the earth is made up of iron and nickel?
(a) Core
(b) Crust
(c) Mantle
(d) Lithosphere

14. Mercury, which is used in thermometers, is a liquid at room temperature and is a
(a) non-metal   (b) metal
(c) acid   (d) alkali

15. Which part of the food is most helpful in the process of digestion?
(a) Vitamins   (b) Proteins
(c) Fats   (d) Fibres

16. In a race of 600 m, A can beat B by 60 m and in a race of 500 m, B can beat C by 50 m. By how many metres will A beat C in a race of 400 m?
(a) 76 m   (b) 80 m
(c) 70 m   (d) 84 m

17. A man travelled a distance of 80 km in 7 h partly on foot at the rate of 8 km/h and partly on bicycle at 16 km/h. Find the distance travelled on foot.
(a) 26 km   (b) 32 km
(c) 30 km   (d) 28 km

18. If 20 men can build a wall 112 m long in 6 days, what length of a similar wall can be built by 25 men in 3 days?
(a) 65 m   (b) 52 m
(c) 70 m   (d) 78 m

19. If the compound interest on a certain sum of money for 3 yr at 10% per annum be ₹ 993, what would be the simple interest?
(a) ₹ 880   (b) ₹ 890
(c) ₹ 895   (d) ₹ 900

20. What annual installment will discharge a debt of ₹ 4600 due in 4 yr at 10% simple interest?
(a) ₹ 1000   (b) ₹ 1030
(c) ₹ 1100   (d) None of these

21. A number whose fifth part increased by 5 is equal to, its fourth part diminished by 5, is
(a) 160   (b) 180   (c) 200   (d) 220

22. Two numbers are such that the ratio between them is 3 : 5, but if each is increased by 10, the ratio between them becomes 5 : 7. The numbers are
(a) 3, 5   (b) 7, 9
(c) 13, 22   (d) 15, 25

23. A man rows downstream 30 km and upstream 18 km, taking 5 h each time. What is the velocity of the stream (current)?
(a) 1.2 km/h   (b) 1.5 km/h
(c) 2.5 km/h   (d) 1.8 km/h

24. A train 125 m long is running at 50 km/h. In what time will it pass a man running at the rate of 5 km/h in the same direction in which the train is going?
(a) 25 sec   (b) 10 sec
(c) 20 sec   (d) 15 sec

25. A is twice as fast as B and B is thrice as fast as C is. The journey covered by C in 42 min, will be covered by A in
(a) 11 min   (b) 14 min
(c) 7 min   (d) 17 min

26. A pipe can fill a tank in 15 h. Due to a leak in the bottom, it is filled in 20 h. If the tank is full, how much time will the leak take to empty it? .
(a) 30 h   (b) 40 h
(c) 50 h   (d) 60 h

27. A can build a wall in 30 days, which B alone can build in 40 days. If they build it together and get a payment of ₹ 700, what is B's share?
(a) ₹ 300   (b) ₹ 400
(c) ₹ 375   (d) ₹ 425

28. A vendor bought a number of bananas at 3 for a rupee and sold them at 2 for a rupee. Find his gain per cent.
(a) 35%   (b) 50%
(c) 25%   (d) 12.5%

29. A tradesman allows a discount of 15% on the marked price. How much above the cost price must he mark his goods to gain 19%?
(a) 34%   (b) 40%
(c) 25%   (d) 30%

30. In a mixture of 35 L, the ratio of milk and water is 4 : 1. Now, 7 L of water is added to the mixture. Find the ratio of milk and water in the new mixture.
(a) 1 : 2   (b) 2 : 1
(c) 1 : 4   (d) 4 : 1

Section B : Reasoning and Logical Deduction

Directions (Q. Nos. 31-35) *Complete the series by replacing '?'*

31. 8, 24, 12, 36, 18, 54, '?'
- (a) 27
- (b) 108
- (c) 68
- (d) 72

32. 2, 4, 12, 48, 240, '?'
- (a) 960
- (b) 1440
- (c) 1080
- (d) 1920

33. 71, 76, 69, 74, 67, 72, '?'
- (a) 77
- (b) 80
- (c) 65
- (d) 76

34. DWE, GUH, JSK, '?', POQ
- (a) MQN
- (b) NMQ
- (c) NQM
- (d) OPQ

35. AA '?' A '?' B '?' A '?' A '?' B
- (a) ABBAA
- (b) AABBB
- (c) ABABA
- (d) BAABA

Directions (Q. Nos. 36-40) *Find the odd one out.*

36. 3, 8, 15, 24, 34, 48, 63
- (a) 15
- (b) 24
- (c) 48
- (d) 34

37. 253, 136, 352, 460, 324, 631, 244
- (a) 136
- (b) 324
- (c) 352
- (d) 631

38. 41, 43, 47, 53, 61, 71, 73, 81
- (a) 61
- (b) 71
- (c) 73
- (d) 81

39. GLQ, OTY, AFL, DIN, CHM, EJO
- (a) OTY
- (b) AFL
- (c) DIN
- (d) EJO

40. BFD, MQO, RVT, EJG, PTR, CGE
- (a) RVT
- (b) PTR
- (c) EJG
- (d) CGE

41. If in a certain code language the word 'FLOWER' is written as 'GNRAJX', how will the word 'SAND' be coded in the same language?
- (a) TDPZ
- (b) OQPS
- (c) TCRI
- (d) TCQH

42. Mohan is taller than Shyam but shorter than Ramesh. Ramesh is taller than Rajat but shorter than Gautam. If Shyam is taller than Rajat, who is the shortest among all?
- (a) Gautam
- (b) Rajat
- (c) Shyam
- (d) Ramesh

43. The average age of A, B and C is 18 yr. If B is two years older than A and five years younger than C, then what is the age of C?
- (a) 22 yr
- (b) 19 yr
- (c) 15 yr
- (d) 17 yr

44. If in a certain code language 'RJI' means 'GIVE ME FOOD' and 'NPQR' means 'I LOVE GOOD FOOD' and 'SBN' means 'LOVE YOUR COUNTRY'. Find out the meaning of the letter 'N'.
- (a) GOOD
- (b) YOUR
- (c) LOVE
- (d) COUNTRY

45. Pointing to a person, a man said to a woman, "His mother is the only daughter of your father". How is the woman related to that person?
- (a) Wife
- (b) Daughter
- (c) Sister
- (d) Mother

46. Ravi starts from his house and walks straight towards East. After walking 75 m he turns left and walks 25 m. Again he turns left and walks 25 m. Once again, he turns left and walks 25 m. How far is he now from his house?
- (a) Zero m
- (b) 50 m
- (c) 150 m
- (d) None of these

Directions (Q. Nos. 47-50) *Each of these questions consists of two words which have a relationship followed by four pairs of words. Choose the pair which is related to each other in the same way as the words in the original pair.*

47. Sachin Tendulkar : Cricket
- (a) Saina Nehwal : Tennis
- (b) Mary Kom : Weightlifting
- (c) Sunil Chhetri : Football
- (d) Sushil Kumar : Boxing

48. Rajasthan : Jaipur
- (a) Mizoram : Aizawl
- (b) Tripura : Silvassa
- (c) Tamil Nadu : Trivandrum
- (d) Uttarakhand : Lucknow

49. India : Asia
- (a) USA : South America
- (b) Brazil : North America
- (c) Spain : Europe
- (d) Israel : Africa

50. Bihu : Assam
- (a) Lavani : Gujarat
- (b) Bharatanatyam : Kerala
- (c) Garba : Maharashtra
- (d) Kuchipudi : Andhra Pradesh

Directions (Q. Nos. 51-53) *Read the following information carefully to answer these questions.*

Six members of a family G, H, I, J, K and L are an Accountant, Clerk, Lawyer, Jeweller, Doctor and Engineer, but not in the same order. Doctor is the grandfather of L who is an Accountant. Clerk J is married to G. I, who is a Jeweller, is married to the Lawyer. H is the mother of L and K. There are two married couples in the family.

51. What is the profession of K?
   (a) Doctor   (b) Clerk
   (c) Engineer   (d) Accountant

52. How many male members are there in the family?
   (a) Two   (b) Three
   (c) Four   (d) Cannot be determined

53. How is G related to K?
   (a) Wife   (b) Father
   (c) Grandmother   (d) Grandfather

Directions (Q. Nos. 54-57) *In the following diagram, the circle represents College Professors, the triangle stands for Surgical Specialists, and medical specialists are represented by the rectangle.*

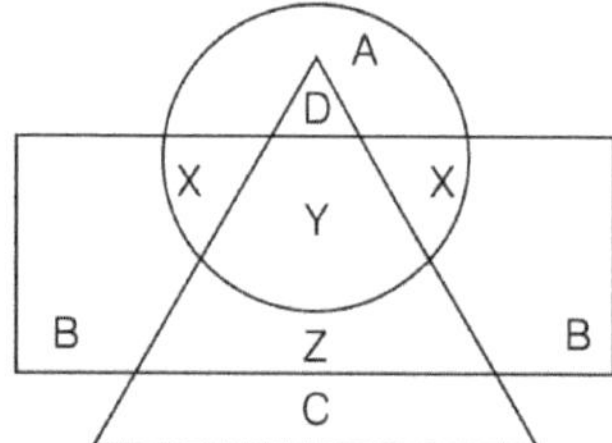

54. College Professors who are also Surgical Specialists are represented by
   (a) A   (b) B
   (c) C   (d) D

55. Surgical Specialists who are also Medical Specialists but not Professors are represented by
   (a) B   (b) C
   (c) X   (d) Z

56. What does C represent?
   (a) Medical Specialists
   (b) College Professors
   (c) Surgical Specialists
   (d) Medical and Surgical Specialists

57. What does B represent?
   (a) Professors who are neither Medical nor Surgical Specialists
   (b) Professors who are not Surgical Specialists
   (c) Medical Specialists who are neither Professors nor Surgical Specialists
   (d) Professors who are not Medical Specialists

Directions (Q. Nos. 58-60) *Each of these questions consists of two sets. Figures* (1), (2), (3) *and* (4) *constitute the set of Question Figures and figures* (a), (b), (c) *and* (d) *constitute the set of Answer Figures. There is a definite relationship between figures* (1) *and* (2). *Establish a similar relationship between figures* (3) *and* (4) *by selecting a suitable figure from the Answer Figures to replace* ?' *in figure* (4).

58. Question Figures

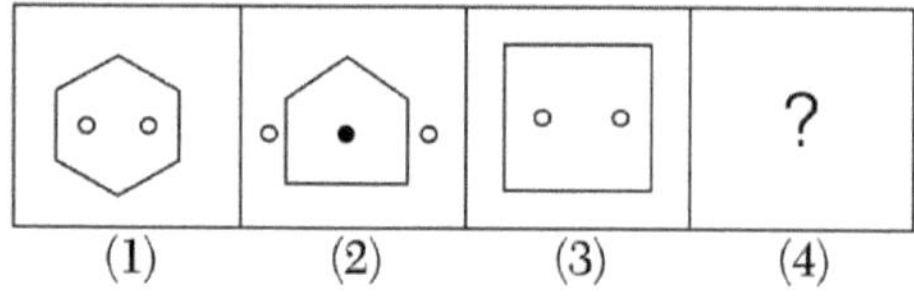

Answer Figures

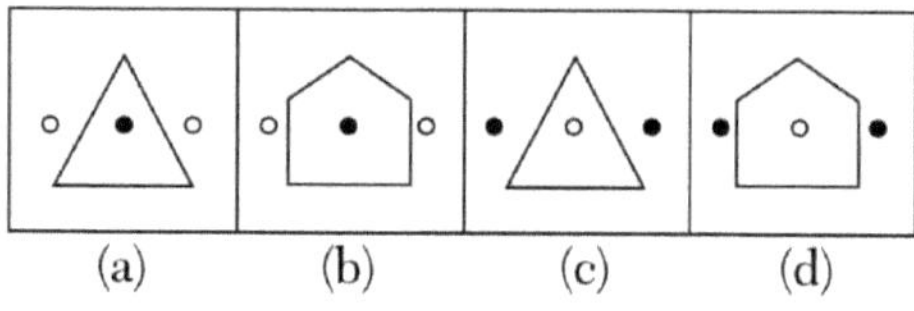

59. Question Figures

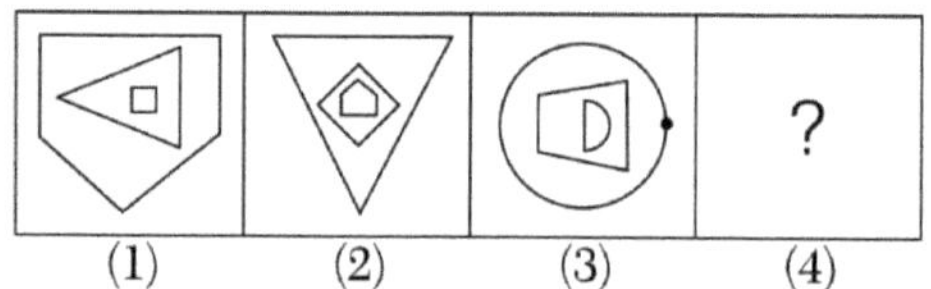

Answer Figures

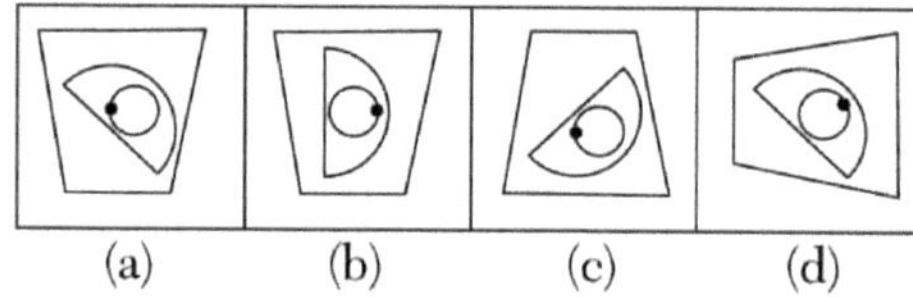

60. Question Figures

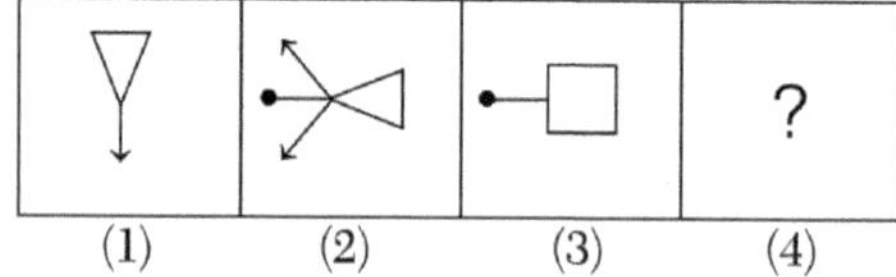

Answer Figures

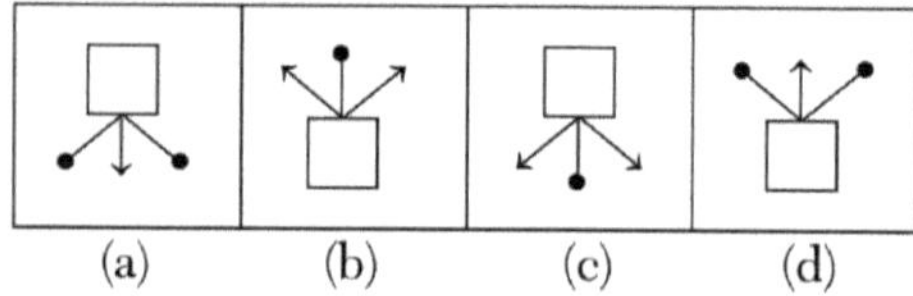

Section C : General Knowledge and Current Affairs

61. 'Bisleri' is a brand bottled water company belongs to which country?
(a) India
(b) The USA
(c) The UK
(d) Australia

62. The Wildflower Hall, Shimla, is a famous luxury hotel/resort belongs to
(a) Hilton Group
(b) Oberoi Group
(c) ITDC
(d) Hyatt Group

63. The Maharajas' Express, the luxury train of India offers .... itinerary of 4 days/3 nights to the travellers to the wondrous circuit of 'Golden Triangle'.
(a) The Indian Splendour
(b) Treasures of India
(c) The Heritage of India
(d) The Indian Panorama

64. The Nobel Peace Prize is awarded by
(a) Sweden
(b) Denmark
(c) Britain
(d) Norway

65. 'The Lalit', a luxury hotel brand belongs to which group of hotels?
(a) ITDC
(b) Hyatt Group
(c) Hilton Group
(d) Bharat Hotels

66. 'World AIDS Day' is observed every year on
(a) 24th October
(b) 1st December
(c) 15th March
(d) 11th July

67. Adventure Tour Operators Association of India (ATOAI) offering/offered 777 days of the Incredible Indian Himalaya tour of ...... states.
(a) six
(b) seven
(c) eight
(d) nine

68. Heena Siddhu is a famous Indian female ....
(a) Badminton player
(b) Archer
(c) Shooter
(d) Wrestler

69. The 'Oberoi Vanyavilas' is a luxury jungle resort located adjacent to the
(a) Jim Corbett National Park
(b) Ranthambhore Tiger Reserve
(c) Kanha National Park
(d) Kaziranga National Park

70. Who is the CMD of 'Bhartiya Mahila Bank' (BMB)?
(a) Arundhati Bhattacharya
(b) Usha Ananthasubramanian
(c) V. R. Iyer
(d) Archana S. Bhargava

71. 'Emmental', 'Gouda', 'Edam', 'Cheddar' are popular international varieties of
(a) Wine
(b) Olive Oil
(c) Cheese
(d) Sauce

72. Who is the present Air Chief Marshal of the Indian Air Force (IAF)?
(a) Arup Raha
(b) N. A. K. Browne
(c) Bikram Singh
(d) None of these

73. The famous 'Lalitha Mahal Palace Hotel' situated just outside the Mysore city belongs to which group of hotels?
(a) ITC
(b) IHCL
(c) Oberoi
(d) The Ashok

74. 'Sochi', the venue of the 2014 winter Olympics Games is located in
(a) China
(b) Russia
(c) Japan
(d) Austria

75. Which famous hotel has won the National Tourism Award 2012-13 for the 'Best Eco-Friendly Hotel' in March 2014?
(a) ITC Maurya
(b) Hyatt Place
(c) Le Meridien
(d) Taj Mansingh

76. Who is fondly known as 'Madiba'?
(a) Mahatma Gandhi
(b) Aung San Suu Kyi
(c) Nelson Mandela
(d) Dalai Lama

77. The International Tourism Mart was organised in which one of the following states of India in October 2013?
(a) Assam
(b) Manipur
(c) Arunachal Pradesh
(d) Meghalaya

78. The Archaeological Survey of India and .... jointly launched a unique initiative to take India's heritage sites online in October 2013.
(a) Google
(b) MSN
(c) Yahoo
(d) Bing

79. The 'Real Fruit Juice', a branded packed fruit juice belongs to which one of the following companies?
(a) Parle
(b) PepsiCo
(c) Coke
(d) Dabur

80. Francois Englert and Peter W. Higgs were awarded the Nobel Prize 2013 in the field of
(a) Medicine
(b) Literature
(c) Economics
(d) Physics

81. Which Indian luxury hotel chain discontinued its 25 year old branding alliance with the German hotel group 'Kempinski' in late 2013?
(a) Oberoi Group
(b) Taj Group
(c) Leela Group
(d) ITC Group

82. Who among the following has won the men's singles title of the Australian Open Tennis Grand Slam 2014?
(a) Roger Federer
(b) Rafael Nadal
(c) Stanislas Wawrinka
(d) Tomas Berdych

83. Which of the following hill forts of Rajasthan have been added in the UN World Heritage list in 2013?

   1. Amber   2. Chittorgarh
   3. Gagron   4. Jaisalmer
(a) 1 and 2   (b) 1, 2 and 4
(c) 2, 3 and 4   (d) All of these

84. Who among the following football players was crowned FIFA Ballon d'Or winner for the year 2013?

(a) Cristiano Ronaldo   (b) Franck Ribery
(c) Xavi Hernandez   (d) Lionel Messi

85. 'JIVA', the complete Indian and all-natural 'Spas' is offered by which group of hotels in India?

(a) Hyatt Group   (b) Taj Group
(c) The Leela Group   (d) Le Meridien Group

86. 'Fusilli, 'Spaghetti', 'Penne' and 'Fettuccine are various types of popular

(a) Sauces   (b) Pepper
(c) Pastas   (d) None of these

87. Who among the following, scientists, was presented the Bharat Ratna in February 2014?

(a) K. Radhakrishnan
(b) Chintamani N. R. Rao
(c) Rajagopala Chidambaram
(d) K. Kasturirangan

88. Who is the France's celebrated pastry chef described by Vogue magazine as 'The Picasso of Pastry', who visited Delhi in March 2013?

(a) Pierre Herme
(b) Didier Lombard
(c) Henrik Scharfe
(d) Jack Sim

89. 'Hotel Padmini Nivas', Chevron Fairheavens' and 'Snow View Retreat' are the popular Heritage hotels located in

(a) Himachal Pradesh   (b) Sikkim
(c) Jammu and Kashmir   (d) Uttarakhand

90. 'St James Court', London, (The UK) is famous luxury hotel belongs to

(a) ITDC   (b) Le Meridien
(c) Taj Group   (d) Oberoi Group

Section D : Aptitude for Service Sector

91. According to the dictionary, the word 'hospitality' implies, friendly and generous reception of

(a) guests
(b) strangers
(c) new ideas
(d) All of the above

92. To work efficiently in the service sector, you should be

(a) decisive or quick in decision-making
(b) extremely courteous
(c) firm in your ideas
(d) punctual

93. If you happen to meet a very demanding customer, you should

(a) tell him that it is impossible to meet all his demands.
(b) inform him that you cannot do much for him.
(c) tell him that you would refer his issues to your seniors.
(d) try to resolve his issues to the best of your ability.

94. To become a good executive in the service sector, you should have

(a) reasonably good organising abilities
(b) a good academic background
(c) polite mannerisms
(d) an ability to control your staff

95. In the society, you want to be known as a

(a) fairly extrovert person
(b) truthful and wise man/woman
(c) self-centred individual
(d) strong and healthy person

96. On being assigned a new project, you

(a) tend to hesitate before starting
(b) plan sufficiently prior to starting
(c) jump on it with much vigour
(d) tend to decline the offer

97. If your job requires you to travel to different places, you

(a) would refuse the job   (b) seek others help
(c) ask your seniors
(d) make out a strategy to meet the job requirement

98. While coping with difficult circumstances, you

(a) focus more carefully on the task at hand.
(b) tend to give up and feel helpless.
(c) maintain your cool, but work slowly.
(d) lose self confidence.

99. When handling maximum transactions during your work schedule, you

(a) feel totally tired.
(b) get fed up with your work content.
(c) want to collect yourself to deal with the work.
(d) continue to remain active.

100. Which of the following do you consider as most significant in your life?
   (a) Name and popularity
   (b) Wealth and prosperity
   (c) Luxurious life pattern
   (d) Respect in society

101. When you are taking part in a team work, you tend to
   (a) avoid such activities
   (b) be fairly assertive
   (c) cooperate with team members
   (d) help others while looking after your interests as well

102. In case your boss does not give you a good assessment, as you thought he would, you would
   (a) confront the boss and pick up an argument.
   (b) feel terribly upset.
   (c) try and improve your performance.
   (d) start ignoring your boss thereafter.

103. According to you, which of the following is the most significant method to bring about some changes in the behavioural pattern of your subordinates?
   (a) Offer detailed suggestions/advice.
   (b) Removal from the existing place of work.
   (c) Hold a comprehensive discussion.
   (d) Ignore the subordinate altogether.

104. In your routine life, to which of the following do you give greater emphasis?
   (a) Maintaining your principles of morality and idealism.
   (b) Resolving your personal issues.
   (c) Helping others to solve their problems.
   (d) Assisting your family members.

105. In case you are not earning adequate money for your family, you would
   (a) adopt any means to earn more money.
   (b) try to ignore the need to earn more money.
   (c) borrow money from friends to meet the need.
   (d) plan to work harder to earn more.

106. On being allotted a time-bound project, you feel
   (a) highly stressed out.
   (b) confident/capable of solving the problem.
   (c) this kind of stress is quite uncalled for.
   (d) you are likely to make a lot of mistakes.

107. Having adequate social relations means to you that you have how many close-friends?
   (a) A very large number
   (b) Around 10 or 20
   (c) Only a few
   (d) May not be any one

108. According to you, in the service sector, reservation should depend upon
   (a) social backwardness
   (b) economic status
   (c) gender
   (d) religion

109. While expressing your views on an important subject, you
   (a) want to avoid expressing your opinion.
   (b) convey a truthful answer but in a diplomatic way.
   (c) express what comes to your mind at the spur of the moment.
   (d) look for opinions expressed by other people and then speak.

110. As per your opinion, which of the following do you find most attractive?
   (a) Taking calculated risks.
   (b) Living under secured conditions.
   (c) Staying with luxuries of life.
   (d) Avoiding taking any kind of risks.

111. Which of the following do you consider as the most significant personality attribute, to work in the service sector?
   (a) Being responsible.
   (b) Withdrawn and keeping to himself/herself.
   (c) Keen to help and be social.
   (d) High academic achievements.

112. According to you, what should you do to control the ill-effects of stress of modern day life?
   (a) Diet control
   (b) Sufficient relaxation and rest
   (c) Physical exercise
   (d) All of the above

113. If you wish to be friendly with some person, how much time would you take to open up to him?
   (a) Do not open up easily and keep hesitating.
   (b) Do not feel like opening up for quite some time.
   (c) Take a bit of time but open up thereafter.
   (d) Tend to open up rather quickly.

114. Your good friend misbehaves with you due to a misunderstanding, you would
   (a) misbehave with him also.
   (b) first try to clear the misunderstanding.
   (c) avoid meeting him thereafter.
   (d) wait for him to come to you to clear the misunderstanding.

115. Which of the following do you think is the most admirable quality of a person?
   (a) Friendly nature
   (b) Sincerity
   (c) Hard working nature
   (d) Pleasant manners

116. According to you, to execute routine jobs of life, a person needs to be
(a) highly overconfident
(b) slightly overconfident
(c) confident of himself
(d) under confident of himself

117. In case you are required to arrive at a decision on behalf of a team of people, you should
(a) wait for others to take a decision.
(b) take a decision yourself and subsequently inform others.
(c) find some means to take others opinion and then decide.
(d) impose your ideas on other members of the team

118. Your father happens to suffer from a heart attack, when you are alone at home, you would
(a) ask for neighbour's help.
(b) feel extremely nervous and panicky.
(c) call your brother, who is staying 2 kms away.
(d) take your father to the nearest hospital or call a doctor.

119. As per you, an effective leader of a team, should
(a) function according to his/her own style and need not bother about others' opinions.
(b) always give candid instructions and remain firm.
(c) go always by what others say or suggest.
(d) listen to others and then act according to the situation.

120. Generally speaking, while facing a difficult problem or a situation, you
(a) tend to become somewhat disappointed.
(b) become less efficient.
(c) like to acquire more self confidence.
(d) ask others to help you out.

121. In case, some known-person logically criticises some of your actions, you will consider him
(a) an opponent
(b) a person who lacks manners
(c) a well-wisher
(d) someone who should be ignored

122. People who know you think, that you are
(a) honest and rigid
(b) helpful and friendly
(c) self centred and secluded
(d) bad tempered and selfish

123. If you happen to witness a tragic road accident, you would
(a) avoid the scene of accident at any cost.
(b) try and help the injured and inform the police.
(c) tell others on the road to help.
(d) think why people are so careless as to meet with accidents.

124. When you see a handicapped person on the road, you think
(a) such people are a burden on society.
(b) you should try and avoid any contact with such persons.
(c) such people are a part of every society in the world.
(d) you must do your bit to help such people.

125. While working in a hotel if you come across a customer who tries to misbehave with you, you would
(a) keep your cool and tell him/her that you would do your best to help them out.
(b) tell him/her that they have no business to misbehave in that fashion.
(c) inform your superiors accordingly and wait for their instructions.
(d) call the police and report the matter to them.

126. Generally speaking, you feel that medical facilities in rural India are
(a) more than adequate
(b) fairly inadequate
(c) what our people deserve
(d) just about sufficient

127. It has been reported that India has eradicated polio for the past three consecutive years. You feel
(a) it should have happened 10 yrs back.
(b) it is a great achievement for our nation.
(c) it is satisfying for the country.
(d) people of the country do not desrve this.

128. Which of the following qualities of a person attracts you the most?
(a) Mental abilities
(b) Good looks
(c) Compassion
(d) Self confidence

129. According to you, what should a poor man do?
(a) Try to forget his poverty and live life as such.
(b) Curse his luck everyday.
(c) Put in more work to earn more money.
(d) Earn money adopting any means.

130. When you hear the news of a soldier getting killed on the borders, you feel
(a) he is paid by the Government to die for the country.
(b) is a part of his duty to sacrifice his life.
(c) such soldiers must be honoured by us.
(d) all of us must do something for our country.

131. When you pass through a slum area, you feel
(a) slums should never be allowed near cities, as they spread dirt and crime.
(b) slums should be far away from cities and should be ignored by us.

(c) people who stay in slums are also a part of our society and we must do our bit to improve their lot.

(d) our Government is not doing enough to improve conditions of living in such areas.

132. If one of your close friends does not look after his old parents who stay with him, you would

(a) feel that old people have got to live on their own.

(b) feel that it may not be possible for your friend to do the needful for his parents due to certain problems.

(c) tell your friend strongly that what he is doing is not quite correct.

(d) like to tell your friend casually about this, issue.

133. You prefer to work in the service sector as

(a) you think the job is well paid.

(b) you feel it is a prestigious job.

(c) you really like the job content.

(d) there is plenty of leisure time your disposal.

134. In your opinion, you consider a person as a good friend if

(a) he praises you most of the time.

(b) he lends you money often.

(c) he helps you under adverse circumstances.

(d) he mostly remains with you.

135. In case your company switches over to a new technology for modernisation; you would

(a) make arrangements to train the entire staff as per the new requirement.

(b) remove all the staff who are not familiar with the new technology.

(c) get rid of some employees whom you think are surplus.

(d) try to adjust some employees at other places in the company whom you feel are surplus.

136. Some of your friends drink and they also ask you to join them in their drinking sessions, you would

(a) love to join them and drink.

(b) get angry and tell them you would never do it.

(c) tell them that drinking is injurious to health.

(d) inform them about all the ill effects of drinking and why you hate to drink.

137. Your boss has just retired and a new boss has just taken over, you

(a) tell the new boss how good your old boss was and that nobody can be so good.

(b) extend him a warm welcome and observe his conduct.

(c) would go around him to please him since you know he will be of some help to you in future.

(d) will ignore him altogether.

138. You prefer your friends who

(a) are smart and clever

(b) always praise you

(c) are sincere and thoughtful

(d) are well mannered and polite

139. While working in your office/factory, if a fault of your co-worker puts you in trouble and causes embarrassment to you, you would

(a) pick up a big fight with him and tell him never to make such a mistake in future.

(b) inform your superiors immediately.

(c) tackle the problem with patience and tell him about the problem at a later date.

(d) feel terribly upset and tell him nothing about it.

140. While getting ready to go to office, you slip in your bathroom and sustain a minor injury on your hand, you would

(a) inform your boss that you are badly hurt and cannot come to office.

(b) feel that it is not quite essential to go to office under such circumstances.

(c) go to office to finish the pending work or to deal with immediate problems only.

(d) feel that somebody will attend to your work and you need not bother about it.

Section E : English Language

Directions (Q. Nos. 141-145) *Choose the word which best expresses the meaning of the **bold** word in the sentence.*

141. He is quite **meticulous** in his dealings with others.

(a) reserved   (b) haughty

(c) indifferent   (d) careful

142. His **judicious** handling of the matter saved the situation from going out of control.

(a) nervous   (b) sensible

(c) helpful   (d) cautious

143. The host looked quite **jaded** by the time the party was over.

(a) miserable   (b) cheerful

(c) inspiring   (d) exhausted

144. It was an **ignominious** defeat for the team.

(a) shameful   (b) admirable

(c) unaccountable   (d) worthy

145. His **conjecture** was better than mine.

(a) guess   (b) fact

(c) surprise   (d) doubt

Directions (Q. Nos. 146-150) *Choose the word which is opposite in meaning of the **bold** word in the sentence.*

146. **Ambiguity** of thoughts can prove disastrous.
    (a) rigidity   (b) clarity
    (c) certainty   (d) rationality

147. A **severe** mind can never be the pioneer of a great revolution.
    (a) nervous   (b) jocular
    (c) earnest   (d) agitated

148. Only an **agile** person can be a successful sportsman.
    (a) brisk   (b) sluggish
    (c) feeble   (d) weak

149. Renu did not heed the **disdain** she had to bear at the hands of her step-mother.
    (a) penitence   (b) humility
    (c) pride   (d) admiration

150. His friends liked everything about him except his **frugality**.
    (a) short temper   (b) extravagance
    (c) shabbiness   (d) punctuality

Directions (Q. Nos. 151-155) *Choose the option which best expresses the meaning of the **bold** idiom/phrase in the sentence.*

151. He **looks down upon** his poor cousins.
    (a) despises   (b) praises openly
    (c) neglects   (d) cares a lot

152. Since things are progressing well, you need not do anything to **rock the boat**.
    (a) agitate against   (b) conspire against
    (c) upset the balance   (d) create difficulties

153. He (is) **cut out** (for) a sailor.
    (a) not suitable   (b) looks like
    (c) specially suited to be   (d) behaving like

154. Whenever I meet him, he **pulls a long face**.
    (a) looks angry   (b) looks cheerful
    (c) looks gloomy   (d) looks indifferent

155. I did not mind what he was saying as he was only **talking through his hat**.
    (a) talking insultingly   (b) talking irresponsibly
    (c) talking ignorantly   (d) talking nonsense

Directions (Q. Nos. 156-160) *A word has been written in four different ways out of which only one is correctly spelt. Choose the correctly spelt word.*

156. (a) Collaboration   (b) Collaberation
    (c) Colaboration   (d) Coleberation

157. (a) Etiquete   (b) Ettiquete
    (c) Etiquette   (d) Ettiquette

158. (a) Entreprenuer   (b) Entrepraneur
    (c) Entrepreneur   (d) Entreapreneur

159. (a) Soveriegnty   (b) Sovereignty
    (c) Sovereignity   (d) Soveriegnity

160. (a) Gaurantee   (b) Guarantee
    (c) Garuntee   (d) Guaruntee

Directions (Q. Nos. 161-165) *In each question, choose the word which can be substituted for the given sentence/words.*

161. One who is unable to pay one's debt.
    (a) Loanee   (b) Borrower
    (c) Bankrupt   (d) Payee

162. A cure for all diseases.
    (a) Panacea   (b) Antidote
    (c) Antiseptic   (d) Fatal

163. One who knows everything.
    (a) Omnipotent   (b) Intelligent
    (c) Omniscient   (d) Genius

164. One who lives on others.
    (a) Stoic   (b) Parasite
    (c) Stupid   (d) Awkward

165. A funny imitation of a poem.
    (a) Parody
    (b) Caricature
    (c) Sonnet
    (d) Counterfeit

Directions (Q. Nos. 166-170) *In each of these questions, choose the best option to complete the sentence.*

166. He tames animals because he
    (a) is afraid of them
    (b) hates them
    (c) is fond of them
    (d) wants to set them free

167. He has no money now
    (a) because he was very rich earlier.
    (b) as he has given up all his wealth.
    (c) because he spends money with much care.
    (d) because he had received huge donations.

168. She always stammers in public meetings, but her speech today
    (a) could not be understood properly.
    (b) was fairly audible to everyone present in the hall.
    (c) was not received satisfactorily.
    (d) was surprisingly fluent.

169. The doctor warns him that unless he gives up
smoking,
   (a) he will not suffer.
   (b) his health will soon be recovered.
   (c) he will not recover.
   (d) will he be able to recover.

170. George is so lazy that he
   (a) can't depend upon others for getting his work
      done.
   (b) can seldom complete his work on time.
   (c) always extends help to others to complete their
      work.
   (d) always completes his work on time.

Directions (Q. Nos. 171-175) *Fill in the blanks.*

171. Mary .... in the crowd because of her height
and flaming red hair.
   (a) stood by (b) stood off (c) stood out (d) stood up

172. He was an .... person who was fond of
weird pets.
   (a) emotional   (b) eccentric
   (c) ambitious   (d) amiable

173. Family planning is essential for curbing the
rapid .... in population.
   (a) increase   (b) decline
   (c) spread   (d) spurt

174. There was adequate grazing area for the herds
since the land was .... populated.
   (a) densely   (b) disproportionately
   (c) inadequately   (d) sparsely

175. Beauty is to ugliness as adversity is to ....
   (a) happiness   (b) prosperity
   (c) cowardice   (d) misery

Directions (Q. Nos. 176-190) *Read the passages
below and answer the questions that follow each
passage.*

PASSAGE I

Management education in India has an intense
magnetic effect on students and parents alike. The
placement figures often tend to drive the community
to flock towards acquiring a post-graduate degree in
management in search of a bright future. As
compared to the other professional courses in
engineering, medicine, etc. the role of management
education has moved beyond transfer of academic
knowledge for professional excellence to creating and
transforming personality of students demonstrating
confidence with character.

The expectation from management graduates extend
beyond concepts and include skill-sets which are
contextual and application oriented. A two-year
exposure is expected to convert a studious student
into a confident communicator, knowledgeable
manager and ethical citizen.

Companies too are focusing on skill-sets such as
communication, team management and general
awareness, behavioural compatibility, domain
knowledge, emotional quotient and intelligence
quotient.

The programmes offered by B-schools, therefore,
must project the same by enabling an interactive
system of pedagogy, opportunity for expression,
varying evaluation from a subjective and descriptive
approach to an application oriented assessment
system and provide opportunity for enhancing written
and spoken communication skill.

This would entail a change in approach to teaching
from a teacher driven top-down approach is a student
driven bottoms-up approach and adoption of Socratic
methods of discussion concern for community and
commitment to society needs to he instilled, hence
socially relevant programmes need to be part of the
curriculum.

For management schools, it is not just about
admissions, teaching and placement, it is also about
creating lifelong alliances with students and a
bonding that becomes irrevocable.

176. What is the most important aspect sought to be
conveyed by the author in this passage?
   (a) Students who undergo management courses get
      good placements.
   (b) Management is better than medicine or
      engineering.
   (c) Parents want their children to study management.
   (d) Programmes offered by B-schools must enable
      student fulfil the expectations of the
      environment.

177. What, according to the author, is the suggested
approach B-schools need to adopt?
   (a) Character building   (b) Student centric
   (c) Application oriented   (d) All of these

178. Which of the following statements is not TRUE
as per the passage?
   (a) Academic knowledge of management subjects
      alone is adequate to do well.
   (b) Companies are looking towards employing
      individuals with an all-round capability and
      wholesome personality.

    (c) Knowledgeable students who express their views clearly and display pragmatism are likely to be more successful.

    (d) None of the above

179. What is the paradigm shift B-schools need to follow as per the author?

    (a) Admission of students and trying for their placements subsequently is sufficient.

    (b) Establishing and nurturing a long standing meaningful and beneficial association between the student and the institution is critical.

    (c) Providing the required infrastructure and facilities necessary for students to study is their only responsibility.

    (d) Inviting appropriate guest faculty to interact with students.

180. The two-year curriculum in B-schools should provide students with

    (a) domain knowledge and skill sets required to enable correct decision-making.

    (b) oral and written communication skills to convey their views confidently and to contribute to team goals.

    (c) adequate exposure and inputs to undertake their social responsibilities ethically and professionally.

    (d) All of the above

PASSAGE II

Global shipbreaking industry is expected to see about 20% reduction in business from its last year performance. The Indian story is no different. According to sources in shipbreaking industry based out of Alang in Gujarat, though India could hold on to its No. 1 position last year, it may find it difficult to do so this year given the ground realities.

"The industry is doing badly now due to low local demand as steel production has slowed down. More importantly, depreciation of the rupee against the dollar is also impacting the industry very badly", pointed out a leading player from Alang.

"It is too early to talk about how the industry would perform in 2014. It would all depend on what kind of Government is going to come to power and what their policies are," he added.

Meanwhile an environmental watchdog Robin des Bois (Robin Hood) said that the world market for ship demolition remains strong with India, Bangladesh and Pakistan together accounting for more than two-thirds of business. In 2013, 1,119 ships went to the world's breaker's yards, a decline of 16 per cent over 2012 which was an 'exceptional year' said the French monitoring group.

The figures confirm that the ship demolition sector is in good health. It is the second highest tally since 2006, when the group began compiling annual reports in an effort to boost transparency in a sector with a contested environmental record. In terms of number of ships demolished, the three South Asian countries accounted for 50 per cent of ships torn down in 2013. India, being the world leader, tore 343 ships or about 26 per cent of total ships demolished. Bangladesh and Pakistan stood third and fifth in the list with 210 and 104 ships or 16 and eight per cent respectively. In terms of tonnage, the three South Asian countries accounted for 71 per cent of the world's scrapped ships. India came in at the top with 2.8 million tonnes or 31 per cent of the total metal recycled globally.

181. In which of the following years were the largest number of ships broken down?

    (a) 2012   (b) 2013

    (c) 2006   (d) None of these

182. Which of the following statements is not TRUE as per the passage?

    (a) India was the world leader in ship-breaking in 2013.

    (b) India, Bangladesh and Pakistan accounted for 50% of the ships scrapped in 2013 in terms of tonnage.

    (c) Robin des Bois (Robin Hood) is an environmental watchdog from France.

    (d) Indian shipbreakers are not confident of holding on to their leading position in 2014.

183. The performance of the Indian shipbreaking industry in 2014 will depend upon

    (a) election results and policies of the new Government elected.

    (b) depreciation/appreciation of the rupee.

    (c) production of steel in India.

    (d) All of the above

184. In the passage, according to the author,

    (a) the watchdog started compiling annual records of ships broken since 2006 to provide information in the public domain.

    (b) shipbreaking has environmental connotations.

    (c) Robin des Bois is pessimistic about the shipbreaking sector doing well in 2014.

    (d) Both (a) and (b)

185. The contribution of Pakistan, India and Bangladesh in terms of number of ships demolished is

    (a) 26, 16 and 8 per cent respectively

    (b) 16, 8 and 26 per cent respectively

    (c) 8, 26 and 16 per cent respectively

    (d) None of the above

PASSAGE III

India on Monday test-fired its second-most ambitious nuclear missile in the making, the new-generation Agni-IV, with a strike range of 4000 km and promptly declared that it was ready for induction.

The over 5000 km Agni-V missile, in turn, will be tested the third time later this year. Both missiles are geared towards providing the country with some much-needed credible strategic deterrence against China, which can target any Indian city with its inter-continental ballistic missiles like the 11,200 km range Dong Feng 31 A.

"This third consecutively successful trial of Agni-IV, the last of its development launch, is significant. It takes India's level of strategic deterrence, its preparedness and effectiveness to newer heights," DRDO chief told Times of India. He said the Agni-IV was tested from Wheeler Island off the Odisha coast in its 'actual weapon configuration' in which it will be delivered to the Strategic Forces Command.

The almost one-tonne warhead was not nuclear. Chander, further, said the Agni-IV 'production line' should kick into operation by end-2014 or early-2015. "There will be two or three war trials. The missiles induction into SFC can begin simultaneously."

186. What is the strike range of Agni-IV missile?
   (a) 4000 km
   (b) > 5000 km
   (c) < 4000 km
   (d) None of the above

187. Which of the following statements is true?
   (a) The test was conducted with a nuclear warhead.
   (b) The Chinese inter-continental ballistic missiles have larger ranges than the Indian variants.
   (c) Agni-V will be produced by end 2014.
   (d) None of the above

188. Which organisation will receive these missiles once they are produced?
   (a) Indian Air Force
   (b) DRDO
   (c) Indian Navy
   (d) SFC

189. What do the words 'Much needed credible strategic deterrence' in the passage imply?
   (a) India's Nuclear Missile Development Programme is successful.
   (b) Our adversaries will be dissuaded from exercising the nuclear option.
   (c) We will be able to strike targets deep into the enemy territory.
   (d) All of the above

190. What is the connotation of the word 'induction' in the passage?
   (a) Starting of the production process.
   (b) Conduct user trials.
   (c) Made available for deployment by the organisation.
   (d) None of the above

Directions (Q. Nos. 191-194) *A sentence has been broken into four parts. One of the parts has a grammatical error. Identify the same.*

191. (a) To make the company commercially viable
   (b) their is an urgent need to prune the staff strength
   (c) and borrow money from the financial institutions
   (d) recommended by the consultant

192. (a) Some molecules contain two or more atoms of the same kind
   (b) a molecule of water, for example,
   (c) is make up two, atoms of the hydrogen
   (d) and one of oxygen

193. (a) Both teams played well,
   (b) but India's performance
   (c) was best when compared
   (d) with the West Indies.

194. (a) You will often find that
   (b) when you take your car
   (c) to Connaught Place
   (d) you has a parking problem

Directions (Q. Nos. 195-197) *In each of the following questions, choose the best option of the voice change.*

195. It is time to ring the bell.
   (a) It is time the bell rings.
   (b) It is being time to ring the bell.
   (c) It is time for the bell to ring.
   (d) It is time for the bell to be rung.

196. You must look into this matter.
   (a) This matter has been looked into by you.
   (b) This matter may be looked into by you.
   (c) This matter should be looked into by you.
   (d) This matter into looked by you.

197. Darjeeling grows tea.
   (a) Tea grows in Darjeeling.
   (b) Tea is grown in Darjeeling.
   (c) Let the tea be grown in Darjeeling.
   (d) Tea is being grown in Darjeeling.

Directions (Q. Nos. 198-200) *In each of the following questions, for the sentence given in Direct Speech, choose the correct Indirect Speech.*

198. He said, "I clean my teeth twice a day."
- (a) He said that he cleaned his teeth twice a day.
- (b) He said that he cleans his teeth twice a day.
- (c) He said that he used to clean his teeth twice a day.
- (d) He said that he is used to cleaning his teeth twice a day.

199. He said, "What a beautiful scene!"
- (a) He said that what a beautiful scene it was.
- (b) He wondered that it was a beautiful scene.
- (c) He exclaimed what a beautiful scene it was.
- (d) He exclaimed that it was a very beautiful scene.

200. He said to me, "Where is the post office?"
- (a) He wanted to know where the post office was.
- (b) He asked me that where the post office was.
- (c) He asked me where the post office was.
- (d) He asked me where was the post office.

Answers

1. (a)	2. (b)	3. (c)	4. (d)	5. (a)	6. (c)	7. (d)	8. (a)	9. (d)	10. (d)
11. (a)	12. (b)	13. (a)	14. (b)	15. (d)	16. (a)	17. (b)	18. (c)	19. (d)	20. (a)
21. (c)	22. (d)	23. (a)	24. (b)	25. (c)	26. (d)	27. (a)	28. (b)	29. (b)	30. (b)
31. (a)	32. (b)	33. (c)	34. (a)	35. (d)	36. (d)	37. (b)	38. (d)	39. (b)	40. (c)
41. (d)	42. (b)	43. (a)	44. (c)	45. (d)	46. (b)	47. (c)	48. (a)	49. (c)	50. (d)
51. (c)	52. (d)	53. (d)	54. (d)	55. (d)	56. (c)	57. (c)	58. (a)	59. (a)	60. (d)
61. (a)	62. (b)	63. (b)	64. (d)	65. (d)	66. (b)	67. (d)	68. (c)	69. (b)	70. (b)
71. (c)	72. (b)	73. (a)	74. (b)	75. (a)	76. (c)	77. (a)	78. (a)	79. (d)	80. (d)
81. (c)	82. (c)	83. (d)	84. (a)	85. (b)	86. (c)	87. (b)	88. (a)	89. (d)	90. (c)
91. (d)	92. (d)	93. (d)	94. (a)	95. (b)	96. (b)	97. (d)	98. (a)	99. (c)	100. (d)
101. (d)	102. (c)	103. (c)	104. (a)	105. (d)	106. (c)	107. (c)	108. (b)	109. (d)	110. (a)
111. (a)	112. (d)	113. (d)	114. (b)	115. (d)	116. (c)	117. (c)	118. (d)	119. (d)	120. (c)
121. (c)	122. (b)	123. (b)	124. (d)	125.. (a)	126. (b)	127. (b)	128. (c)	129. (c)	130. (c)
131. (c)	132. (d)	133. (c)	134. (c)	135. (d)	136. (d)	137. (b)	138. (d)	139. (c)	140. (a)
141. (d)	142. (b)	143. (d)	144. (a)	145. (a)	146. (c)	147. (b)	148. (b)	149. (d)	150. (b)
151. (a)	152. (d)	153. (c)	154. (c)	155. (d)	156. (a)	157. (c)	158. (c)	159. (b)	160. (b)
161. (c)	162. (a)	163. (c)	164. (b)	165. (a)	166. (c)	167. (b)	168. (d)	169. (c)	170. (b)
171. (c)	172. (b)	173. (a)	174. (d)	175. (b)	176. (d)	177. (d)	178. (a)	179. (b)	180. (d)
181. (a)	182. (b)	183. (d)	184. (d)	185. (c)	186. (a)	187. (b)	188. (d)	189. (b)	190. (c)
191. (b)	192. (c)	193. (c)	194. (d)	195. (d)	196. (c)	197. (b)	198. (b)	199. (c)	200. (c)

Hints & Solutions

16. (*a*) If A runs a race of 600 m

then, B runs $= 600 - 60 = 540$ m

Now, if A runs a race of 400 m then,

$$B \text{ runs } = \frac{540 \times 400}{600} = 360 \text{ m}$$

If B runs 500 m, then C runs $= (500 - 50)$ m

$$= 450 \text{ m}$$

$\therefore$ If B runs 360 m, then C runs $= \dfrac{450}{500} \times 360$

$$= 324 \text{ m}$$

Hence, A beats C by $(400 - 324)$ m $= 76$ m

17. (*b*) Let the journey on foot be x km.

Then journey on bicycle $= (80 - x)$ km

According to the question,

$$\frac{x}{8} + \frac{(80 - x)}{16} = 7$$

$\Rightarrow \qquad \dfrac{2x + 80 - x}{16} = 7$

$\Rightarrow \qquad x + 80 = 112$

$\therefore \qquad x = 32$ km

18. (*c*) Here, $M_1 = 20$, $D_1 = 6$, $W_1 = 112$

and $M_2 = 25$, $D_2 = 3$, $W_2 = ?$

According to the formula,

$$\frac{M_1 \times D_1}{W_1} = \frac{M_2 \times D_2}{W_2}$$

$\therefore \qquad W_2 = \dfrac{M_2 \times D_2}{M_1 \times D_1} \times W_1$

$$= \frac{25 \times 3}{20 \times 6} \times 112 = 70 \text{ m}$$

19. (*d*) Given, $R = 10\%$, Time $(n) = 3$ yr and

CI $= ₹ \, 993$

According to the formula,

$$CI = P\left\{\left(1 + \frac{R}{100}\right)^n - 1\right\}$$

$\Rightarrow \quad 993 = P\left\{\left(1 + \dfrac{10}{100}\right)^3 - 1\right\}$

$\Rightarrow \quad 993 = P\left\{\left(\dfrac{11}{10}\right)^3 - 1\right\}$

$\Rightarrow \quad 993 = P \times 0.331 \Rightarrow P = \dfrac{993}{0.331}$

$\Rightarrow \qquad P = ₹ \, 3000$

$\therefore$ Simple Interest $= \dfrac{P \times R \times T}{100}$

$$= \frac{3000 \times 10 \times 3}{100}$$

$$= ₹ \, 900$$

20. (*a*) Let each annual investment be $₹ \, x$.

According to the question,

$$\left(x + \frac{x \times 10 \times 3}{100}\right) + \left(x + \frac{x \times 10 \times 2}{100}\right) +$$

$$\left(x + \frac{x \times 10 \times 1}{100}\right) + x = ₹ \, 4600$$

$\Rightarrow \quad 4x + \dfrac{x \times 10}{100}(3 + 2 + 1) = ₹ \, 4600$

$\Rightarrow \quad 4x + \dfrac{6x}{10} = ₹ \, 4600 \Rightarrow 46x = ₹ \, 46000$

$\therefore x = ₹ \, \dfrac{46000}{46} = ₹ \, 1000$

$\therefore$ Required annual investment $= ₹ \, 1000$

21. (*c*) Let the required number be x.

According to the question,

$$\frac{x}{5} + 5 = \frac{x}{4} - 5$$

$\Rightarrow \qquad \dfrac{x}{4} - \dfrac{x}{5} = 10$

$\Rightarrow \qquad \dfrac{5x - 4x}{20} = 10$

$\therefore \qquad x = 200$

$\therefore$ The required number $= 200$

22. (*d*) Let the numbers be $3x$ and $5x$.

According to the question,

$$\frac{3x + 10}{5x + 10} = \frac{5}{7}$$

$\Rightarrow \qquad 21x + 70 = 25x + 50$

$\Rightarrow \qquad 4x = 20$

$\therefore \qquad x = 5$

Hence, the numbers are 15 and 25.

23. (*a*) Let the velocity of man in the river $= x$ km/h

and the velocity of the stream $= y$ km/h

Then,

downstream velocity $= (x + y)$ km/h

Upstream velocity $= (x - y)$ km/h

According to question,

$$x + y = \frac{30}{5} = 6 \qquad \ldots(\text{i})$$

and $\qquad x - y = \dfrac{18}{5} = 3.6 \qquad \ldots(\text{ii})$

On solving Eqs. (i) and (ii), we get

$$y = 1.2 \text{ km/h}$$

24. (*b*) According to the question,

Relative speed of train with respect to man

$$= (50 - 5) \text{ km/h} = 45 \text{ km/h}$$

$$= 45 \times \frac{5}{18} \text{ m/sec}$$

$$= 12.5 \text{ m/sec}$$

$$\therefore \text{Time taken to cross the man} = \frac{\text{Distance}}{\text{Speed}} = \frac{125}{12.5}$$
$$= 10 \text{ sec}$$

25. (*c*) Let the speed of $C = x$ km/h

Speed of $B = 3x$ km/h

$\therefore$ Speed of $A = 2 \times (3x) = 6x$ km/h

Time taken by C to cover a certain distance = 42 min

Then, distance covered by C = Speed × Time
$$= 42x \text{ km}$$

$\therefore$ Time taken by A to cover the same distance
$$= \frac{\text{Distance}}{\text{Speed}} = \frac{42x}{6x}$$
$$= 7 \text{ min}$$

26. (*d*) Let the time taken by the leak to empty the tank $= x$ h

According to the question,
$$\frac{1}{15} - \frac{1}{x} = \frac{1}{20}$$
$$\Rightarrow \quad \frac{1}{x} = \frac{1}{15} - \frac{1}{20} = \frac{4-3}{60} = \frac{1}{60}$$
$$\Rightarrow \quad x = 60 \text{ h}$$

Hence, time taken by the leak to empty the tank is 60 h.

27. (*a*) A's 1 day's work $= \dfrac{1}{30}$

B's 1 day's work $= \dfrac{1}{40}$

Ratio of the wages of A and $B = \dfrac{1}{30} : \dfrac{1}{40}$
$$= 4 : 3$$

$\therefore B$'s share $= 700 \times \dfrac{3}{3+4} = ₹\ 300$

28. (*b*) Given, SP of 2 banana $= ₹\ 1$

CP of 3 banana $= ₹\ 1$

Then, CP of 2 bananas $= 2 \times \dfrac{1}{3} = ₹\dfrac{2}{3}$

$$\therefore \text{ Gain \%} = \left(\frac{\text{SP} - \text{CP}}{\text{CP}}\right) \times 100\% = \frac{\left(1 - \frac{2}{3}\right)}{\frac{2}{3}} \times 100$$
$$= \frac{1}{3} \times \frac{3}{2} \times 100 = 50\%$$

29. (*b*) Let MP be $₹\ x$.

$$\therefore \quad \text{SP} = \text{MP}\left(\frac{100 - \text{discount}\%}{100}\right)$$
$$= x \times \frac{(100 - 15)}{100}$$
$$= \frac{85x}{100}$$

Now $\quad \text{CP} = \text{SP} \times \left(\frac{100}{100 + \text{Gain}\%}\right)$

$$= \frac{85x}{100} \times \left(\frac{100}{100 + 19}\right) = \frac{5}{7}x$$

$$\therefore \text{ Percentage increase in price} = \frac{\text{MP} - \text{CP}}{\text{CP}} \times 100$$
$$= \left(\frac{x - \frac{5}{7}x}{\frac{5}{7}x}\right) \times 100 = 40\%$$

30. (*b*) Given, total quantity of mixture = 35 L

Then, quantity of milk in the mixture $= \dfrac{4}{5} \times 35$ L
$$= 28 \text{ L}$$

and quantity of water in the mixture
$$= \frac{1}{5} \times 35 \text{ L} = 7 \text{ L}$$

Now, 7 L of water added in the mixture

$\therefore$ New ratio of milk and water
$$= 28 : (7 + 7) = 28 : 14 = 2 : 1$$

31. (*a*) Pattern of the series is as follows,

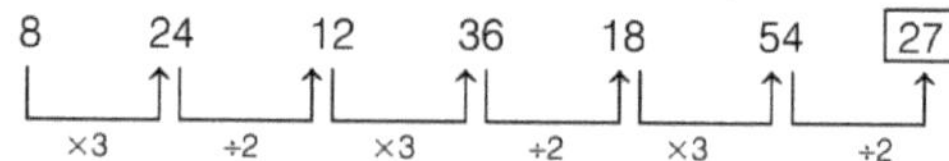

Hence, 27 is the missing number.

32. (*b*) Pattern of the series is as follows,

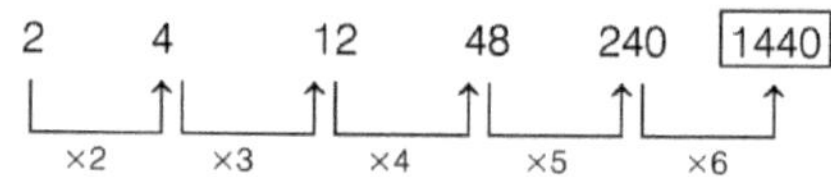

Hence, 1440 will come in place of ?.

33. (*c*) Pattern of the series is as follows,

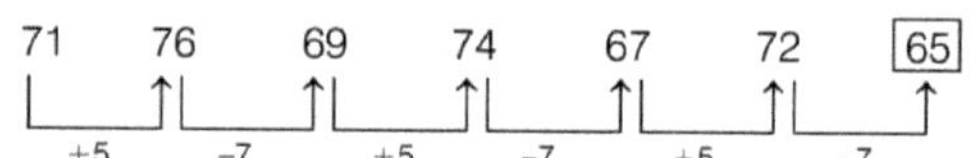

Hence, 65 will come in place of ?.

34. (*a*) Pattern of the series is as follows,

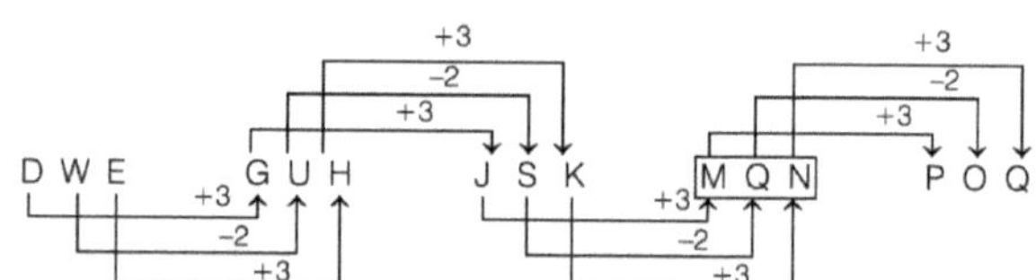

Hence, MQN will come in place of ?.

35. (*d*) A A B / A A B / A A B / A A B
$$\Rightarrow \text{BAABA}$$

36. (*d*) Pattern of the series is as follows,

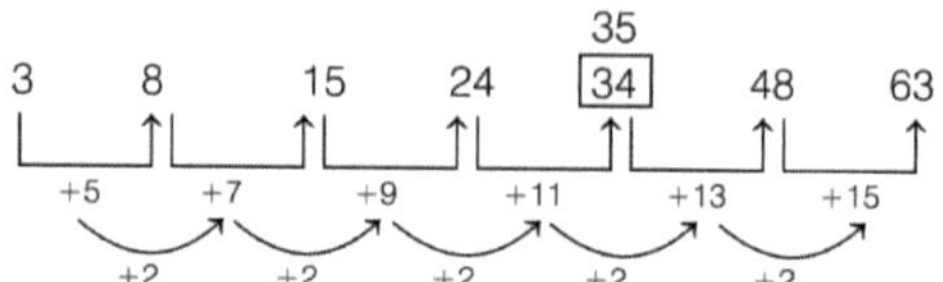

Hence, 34 is odd one here. 34 should be replaced with 35.

37. (*b*) Except 324, sum of the digits of the number is 10 in each case.

∴ 324 is odd one out.

38. (*d*) Except 81, all others are prime number.

39. (*b*)

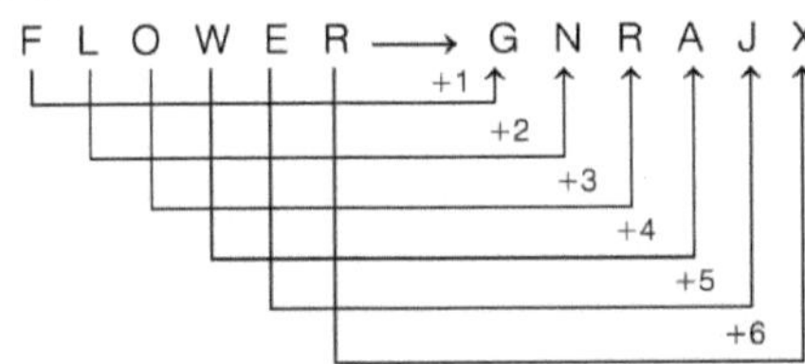

Hence, AFL is odd one out here.

40. (*c*)

Hence, EJG is odd one out.

41. (*d*) As,

∴ SAND is coded as TCQH.

42. (*b*) According to the question, the arrangement of height in decreasing order is as-

Gautam > Ramesh > Mohan > Shyam > Rajat

Hence, Rajat is shortest among all.

43. (*a*) Average of A, B and C is 18 yr

∴ Total sum of ages of A, B and C $= 18 \times 3 = 54$ yr

Let the age of B be y yr.

then, age of A $= (y - 2)$ yr and age of C $= y + 5$ yr

Then, $(y - 2) + y + (y + 5) = 54$

$\Rightarrow \quad 3y + 3 = 54 \quad \Rightarrow \quad y + 1 = 18 \quad \Rightarrow \quad y = 17$

∴ Age of C $= 17 + 5 = 22$ yr.

44. (*c*) According to the question,

RJI means GIVE ME FOOD

NPQR means I LOVE GOOD FOOD

and SBN means LOVE YOUR COUNTRY.

Hence, the meaning of the letter N is LOVE.

45. (*d*) According to the question,

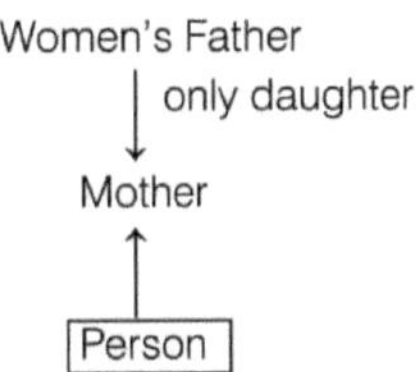

The only daughter of woman's father is the woman herself. The woman is the person's mother.

46. (*b*) According to the question,

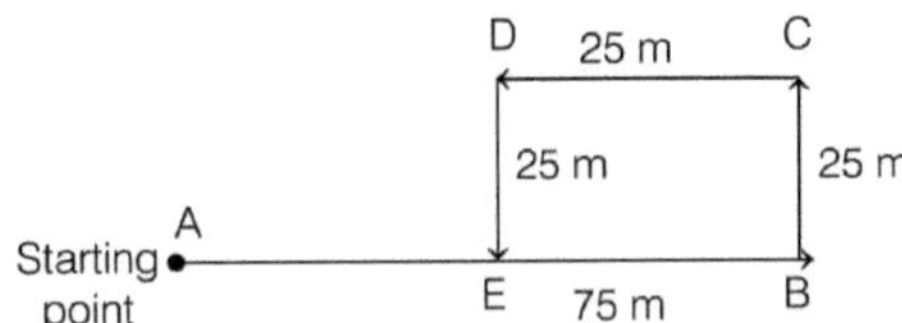

Required distance from the home $= AE = AB - BE$

$= 75 - 25 \qquad [\because EB = DC = 25 \text{ m}]$

$= 50$ m

Sol. (Q. Nos. 47-50)

47. (*c*) As, Sachin Tendulkar is a player of Cricket. Similarly, Sunil Chhetri is a player of Football.

48. (*a*) As, Jaipur is the capital of Rajasthan. Similarly, Aizawl is capital of Mizoram.

49. (*c*) As, India is a country in Asia. Similarly, Spain is a country in Europe.

50. (*d*) As, Bihu is the famous folk dance of Assam. In the same way Kuchipudi is the famous folk dance of Andhra Pradesh.

Sol. (Q. Nos. 51-53) According to the information,

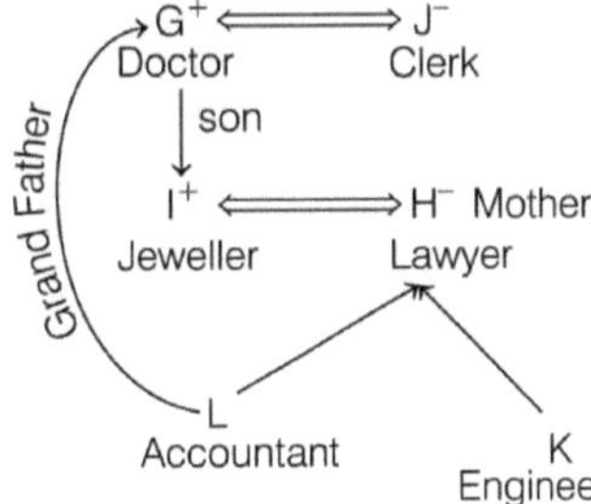

51. (*c*) K is an engineer.

52. (*d*) Here, the gender of L and K is not defined, so we cannot determined the number of male members are there in the family.

53. (*d*) Clearly, G is grandfather of K.

Sol. (Q. Nos. 54-57) According to the question,

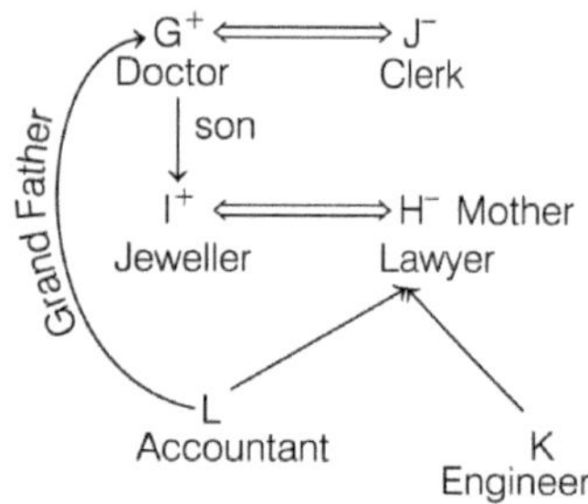

54. (*d*) Letter 'D' represent the college professors who are surgical specialists.

55. (*d*) Only Z represents surgical specialists and who are also medical specialists but not professors.

56. (*c*) As triangle represent surgical specialist.

Here, C is part of triangle only. Hence, C represent surgical specialists.

57. (*c*) As B is part of rectangle only which does not include the part of triangle and circle. Hence, B represent medical specialist who are neither professor nor surgical specialists.

58. (*a*) From figure (1) to figure (2), the outermost element reduces its side and the inner circles come out and a shaded circle comes inside the element.

In the same pattern, the figure (3) is related to figure (a).

59. (*a*) From figure (1) to figure (2), the outermost element after inverting in reverse direction converted to the innermost element of figure (2).

The middle element of figure (1) after rotation in 90° anti-clockwise direction converted to the outermost element of figure (2).

The innermost element of figure (1) after rotation of 45° converted to middle element of figure (2).

In the same pattern, the figure in option (a) analogous to the figure (3).

60. (*d*) From figure (1) to figure (2), the element moves in 90° clockwise direction. The number of given arrow becomes double, also a dotted arrow get attached in the middle.

In the same pattern figure (3) is analogous to figure in option (d).

141. (*d*) 'Meticulous' means to show great attention to detail. Hence, 'careful' best expresses the meaning of meticulous.

142. (*b*) 'Judicious' means having, showing or doing with good judgement or sense. Hence, 'sensible' best expresses the meaning of judicious.

143. (*d*) 'Jaded' means physically tired or weary. Hence, 'exhausted' best expresses the meaning of jaded.

144. (*a*) 'Ignominious' means deserving or causing public disgrace or shame. Hence, 'shameful' best expresses the meaning of ignominious.

145. (*a*) 'Conjecture' means a conclusion formed on the basis of incomplete information or a speculation. Hence, 'guess' best expresses the meaning of conjecture.

146. (*c*) 'Certainty' is opposite in meaning to 'ambiguity'. 'Ambiguity' means the quality of being open to more than one interpretation and 'certainty' means confidence or firm conviction that something is true.

147. (*b*) 'Jocular' is opposite in meaning to 'severe'. 'Severe' means serious or intense and 'jocular' means humorous or playful.

148. (*b*) 'Sluggish' is opposite in meaning to 'agile'. 'Agile' means the ability to move quickly and easily whereas 'sluggish' means slow-moving or inactive.

149. (*d*) 'Admiration' is opposite in meaning to 'disdain'. 'Disdain' means considered to be unworthy of one's consideration and 'admiration' means to respect and show warm approval.

150. (*b*) 'Extravagance' is opposite in meaning to 'frugality'. 'Frugality' means the quality of being economical with money or thriftiness and 'extravagance' means lack of restraint in spending money or using resources.

151. (*a*) The idiom 'look down upon' means to consider something lesser or inferior or to despise. Hence, option (a) is the correct answer.

152. (*d*) The idiom 'rock the boat' means to disturb a situation or to create problems and difficulties.

153. (*c*) The idiom 'cut out for' means to be naturally able or suited.

154. (*c*) The idiom 'pull a long face' means to look sad and gloomy.

155. (*d*) The idiom 'talking through one's hat' means to talk nonsense.

194. (*d*) Part (d) contains the error. The verb used with the pronoun 'you' is 'have', not 'has'. Hence, replace 'has' with 'have' to make the sentence grammatically correct.

Hotel Management

National Council for Hotel Management and Catering Technology

Solved Paper 2013

Instructions

- There are Five (A-E) Sections in this Solved Paper.
- For every correct attempt, the student will be awarded **1 mark**.
- All the questions are in MCQs form and each have four options.

Marks : 200
Time : 3 hrs

Section A : English Language

Directions (Q. Nos. 1-5) *In the following questions, choose the word which best expresses the meaning of the given word.*

1. VENUE
(a) Place   (b) Agenda   (c) Time   (d) Duration

2. STERILE
(a) Barren   (b) Arid   (c) Childless   (d) Dry

3. SYNOPSIS
(a) Index
(c) Summary
(b) Mixture
(d) Puzzle

4. GERMANE
(a) Responsible
(c) Possible
(b) Logical
(d) Relevant

5. PONDER
(a) Think
(c) Anticipate
(b) Evaluate
(d) Increase

Directions (Q. Nos. 6-10) *In the following questions choose the word which is the exact opposite of the given word.*

6. FLIMSY
(a) Frail   (b) Filthy   (c) Firm   (d) Flippant

7. BUSY
(a) Occupied
(c) Relaxed
(b) Engrossed
(d) Engaged

8. ADAPTABLE
(a) Adoptable
(c) Yielding
(b) Flexible
(d) Rigid

9. LOVE
(a) Villainy
(c) Compulsion
(b) Hatred
(d) Force

10. BALANCE
(a) Disbalance
(c) Debalance
(b) Misbalance
(d) Imbalance

Directions (Q. Nos. 11-15) *In each of the sentences given below a word is printed in bold. Below it four choices are given. Pick the one which is most nearly the same in meaning as the word printed in bold and can replace it without altering the meaning of the sentence.*

11. When youngsters do not have good role-models to **emulate**, they start searching for them amongst sportsmen or filmstars.
(a) imitate
(c) molify
(b) modify
(d) inhabit

12. The **aberration** in the India Economy can be attributed to short-sightedness of its political masters.
(a) procrastination (b) privilege
(c) deviation (d) steadfastness

13. The claims of students look hollow when they **attribute** their poor performance to difficulty of examination.
(a) infer (b) impute
(c) inhere (d) inundate

14. As soon as he finished his speech, there was **spontaneous** applause from the audience.
(a) well-timed (b) willing
(c) instinctive (d) instantaneous

15. The soldier proved his **mettle** in the battlefield.
(a) persistence (b) stamina and strength
(c) courage and endurance (d) heroism

Directions (Q. Nos. 16-20) *Each sentence below consists of a word which is bold. It is followed by four words given in options. Select the word which is OPPOSITE in meaning to the bold word.*

16. The atmosphere in that desolate place looked **ominous**.
(a) pleasant (b) encouraging
(c) auspicious (d) favourable

17. He spoke against corruption with **zeal**.
(a) indifference (b) calmness
(c) despair (d) passiveness

18. The story told by the teacher **amused** children in the class.
(a) frightened (b) jolted
(c) astonished (d) saddened

19. In a literary work, **obscurity** can be a virtue.
(a) clarity (b) precision
(c) definiteness (d) specificity

20. The managing director remarked that the secretary was an **asset** to the company.
(a) loss (b) liability
(c) drag (d) handicap

Directions (Q. Nos. 21-24) *Some proverbs/idioms are given below together with their meanings. Choose the correct meaning of the proverb/idiom.*

21. To play second fiddle
(a) To be happy, cheerful and healthy.
(b) To reduce importance of one's senior.
(c) To support the role and view of another person.
(d) To do back seat driving.

22. To set one's face against.
(a) To oppose with determination.
(b) To judge by appearance.
(c) To get out of difficulty.
(d) To look at one steadily.

23. To put one's hand to the plough
(a) To take up agricultural farming.
(b) To take a difficult task.
(c) To get entangled into unnecessary things.
(d) Take interest in technical work.

24. To join issue with
(a) To cooperate with others for a cause
(b) To join any voluntary organisation for good purpose
(c) To resolve dispute and restore peace
(d) To enter into argument over any issue

Directions (Q. Nos. 25-27) *In following questions, four alternatives are given for the idiom/phrase italicised in the sentence. Choose the alternative which best expresses the meaning of the idiom/phrase.*

25. How long will the people *put up with* the increasing economic hardships?
(a) welcome
(b) take easily
(c) remain satisfied with
(d) tolerate

26. Do not trust a man who *blows his own trumpet*.
(a) flatters (b) praises others
(c) admonishes others (d) praises himself

27. The dacoit murdered the man *in cold blood*.
(a) coldly (b) boldly
(c) ruthlessly (d) deliberately

Directions (Q. Nos. 28-43) *Read the following passages carefully and answer the questions given below each passage.*

PASSAGE I

Harold, a professional man who had worked in an office for many years, had a fearful dream. In it, he found himself in a land where small slug-like animals with slimy tentacles lived on people's bodies. The people tolerated the loathsome creatures because after many years they grew into elephants which then became the nation's system of transport, carrying everyone wherever they wanted to go. Harold suddenly realised that he himself was covered with these things and he woke up screaming. In a vivid sequence of pictures this dream dramatised for Harold what he had never been able to put into words; he saw himself as letting society feed on his-body in his early years so that it would carry him when he retired. He later threw off the "security bug" and took up freelance work.

28. Which one of the following phrases best helps to bring out the precise meaning of 'loathsome creatures' as given in the passage?
(a) Security bug and slimy tentacles
(b) Fearful dream and slug-like animals
(c) Slimy tentacles and slug-like animals
(d) Slug-like animals and security bug

29. Harold's dream was fearful because
(a) it brought him face to face with reality.
(b) it was full of vivid pictures of snakes.
(c) he saw huge elephants in it.
(d) in it he saw slimy creatures feeding on people's bodies.

30. In his dream, Harold found the loathsome creatures
(a) in his village   (b) in his own house
(c) in a different land   (d) in his office

31. The statement that 'he later threw off the security bug' means that
(a) Harold succeeded in overcoming the need for security.
(b) Harold stopped giving much importance to dreams.
(c) Harold started tolerating social victimisation.
(d) Harold killed all the bugs troubling him.

PASSAGE II

Laws of nature are not commands but statements of acts. The use of the word 'law' in this context is rather unfortunate. It would be better to speak of uniformities of nature. This would do away with the elementary fallacy that a law implies a law-giver. If a piece of matter does not obey a law of nature it is not punished. On the contrary, we say that the law has been incorrectly started.

32. Laws of nature differ from man-made laws because
(a) the former state facts of nature
(b) they must be obeyed
(c) they are natural
(d) unlike human laws, they are systematic

33. If a piece of matter violates nature's law, it is not punished because
(a) it is not binding to obey it.
(b) there is no superior being to enforce the law of nature.

(c) it cannot be punished.
(d) it simply means that the facts have not been correctly stated by the law.

34. The author is not happy with the word 'law' because
(a) it connotes rigidity and harshness
(b) it implies an agency which has made them.
(c) it does not convey the sense of nature's uniformity.
(d) it gives rise to false beliefs.

35. The laws of nature based on observation are
(a) conclusive about the nature of the universe.
(b) true and unfalsifiable.
(c) figments of the observer's imagination.
(d) subject to change in the light of new facts.

PASSAGE III

Courage is not only the basis of all virtue but also its expression. Faith, hope, charity and all the rest don't become virtues until it takes courage to exercise them. There are roughly two types of courage. The first, an emotional state which urges a man to risk injury or death, is physical courage. The second, a more reasoning attitude which enables him to take coolly his career, happiness, his whole future or his judgement of what he thinks either right or worthwhile, is moral courage.

I have known many men, who had marked physical courage, but lacked moral courage. Some of them were in high places, but they failed to be great in themselves because they lacked moral courage.

On the other hand, I have seen men who undoubtedly possessed moral courage but were very cautious about taking physical risks. But I have never met a man with moral courage who couldn't, when it was really necessary, face a situation boldly.

36. All virtues become meaningful because of
(a) faith   (b) charity   (c) courage   (d) hope

37. Physical courage is an expression of
(a) emotions   (b) deliberation
(c) uncertainty   (d) defiance

38. People with physical courage often lack
(a) mental balance   (b) capacity for reasoning
(c) emotional stability   (d) will to fight

39. A man with moral courage can
(a) defy his enemies
(b) overcome all difficulties
(c) face a situation boldly
(d) be very pragmatic

PASSAGE IV

In the world today we make health an end in itself. We have forgotten that health is really a means to enable a person to do his work and do it well. A lot of modern medicine–and this includes many patients as well as many physicians–pays very little attention to health but very much attention to those who imagine that they are ill.

Our great concern with health is shown by the medical columns in newspapers, the health articles in popular magazines and the popularity of the television programmes and all those books on medicine. We talk about health all the time. Yet for the most part the only result is more people with imaginary illness. The healthy man should not be wasting time talking about health: he should be using health for work.

40. Modern medicine is primarily concerned with
(a) promotion of good health.
(b) people suffering from imaginary illness.
(c) people suffering from real illness.
(d) increased efficiency in work.

41. Talking about health all the time makes people
(a) always suffer from imaginary illness.
(b) sometimes suffer from imaginary illness.
(c) rarely suffer from imaginary illness.
(d) often suffer from imaginary illness.

42. The passage suggests that
(a) health is an end in itself
(b) health is a blessing
(c) health is only means to an end
(d) we should not talk about health

43. The passage tells us
(a) how medicine should be manufactured
(b) what healthy man should or should not do
(c) what television programmes should be about
(d) how best to imagine illness

Directions (Q. Nos. 44-46) *Find the correctly spelt word.*

44. (a) Eflorescene   (b) Efllorescence
(c) Efflorescence   (d) Efflorascence

45. (a) Itinarery   (b) Itinerary
(c) ltenerary   (d) Itinarary

46. (a) Bouquete   (b) Bouquette
(c) Bouquet   (d) Boquet

Directions (Q. Nos. 47-49) *Read each sentence to find out whether there is any grammatical error in it. The error, if any, will be in one part of the sentence. The letter of that part is the answer. If there is no error, the answer is '(d)'. (Ignore the errors of punctuation, if any).*

47. (a) He wanted to work all right/(b) but we saw that he was completely worn/(c) and so we persuaded him to stop./(d) No error

48. (a) It is time/(b) we did something/(c) to stop road accidents./(d) No error

49. (a) At present juncture/(b) however, the super-computer/(c) would be a costly toy./(d) No error.

Directions (Q. Nos. 50-52) *In question below, each passage consists of six sentences. The first and the sixth sentences are given in the beginning. The middle four sentences in each have been removed and jumbled up. These are labelled P, Q, R and S. Find out the proper order for the four sentences.*

50. S_1 : Smoke oozed up between the planks.
S_6 : Most people bore the shock bravely.
P : Passengers were told to be ready to quit the ship.
Q : The rising gale fanned the smouldering fire.
R : Everyone now knew there was a fire on board.
S : Flames broke out here and there.
The proper sequence should be
(a) S R Q P   (b) Q P S R
(c) R S P Q   (d) Q S R P

51. S_1 : It was a dark moonless night.
S_6 : They all seemed to him to be poor and ordinary–mere childish words.
P : He turned over the pages, reading passages here and there.
Q : He heard them on the floor.
R : The poet took down his books of poems from his shelves.
S : Some of them contained his earliest writings which he had almost forgotten.
The proper sequence should be
(a) R P Q S   (b) R Q S P
(c) R S P Q   (d) R P S Q

52. S_1 : A noise started above their heads.
S_6 : Nearly two hundred lives were lost on the fateful day.
P : But people did not take it seriously.
Q : That was to show everyone that there was something wrong.
R : It was a dangerous thing to do.
S : For, within minutes the ship began to sink.

HM 2013

The proper sequence should be
(a) P Q S R   (b) P R Q S
(c) Q P R S   (d) Q P S R

Directions (Q. Nos. 53-60) *Pick out the most effective word(s) from the given words to fill in the blank to make the sentence meaningfully complete.*

53. I haven't seen you ...... a week.
(a) within   (b) since
(c) for   (d) from

54. Besides other provisions, that shopkeeper deals ...... cosmetics too.
(a) with   (b) in
(c) at   (d) for

55. That rule is applicable ...... everyone.
(a) to   (b) for
(c) about   (d) with

56. I shall take revenge ...... you.
(a) from   (b) with   (c) on   (d) at

57. She presented me a ...... of flowers.
(a) troup   (b) galaxy
(c) bouquet   (d) cluster

58. There was a ...... of eggs floating on the dirty water of the ditch.
(a) clump   (b) shoal
(c) clutch   (d) pile

59. A ..... of dancers was dancing an the stage.
(a) troupe   (b) galaxy
(c) herd   (d) clump

60. To save the drowning man, a ...... of sailors came out on the boats.
(a) troop   (b) crew
(d) band   (d) gang

Section B : Reasoning and Logical Deduction

Directions (Q. Nos. 61 and 62) *Read the following statements and answer the questions.*
S and R are brothers. T is the daughter of S. U is the spouse of R and mother of Q. P is the daughter of V, who is the spouse of T.

61. Who is the grandfather of P?
(a) U   (b) S
(c) R   (d) V

62. Who is the cousin of Q?
(a) T   (b) V
(c) R   (d) P

Directions (Q. Nos. 63-65) *Read the following information to answer questions given below.*
(a) A × B means 'A' is the brother of ' B'.
(b) A + B means 'A' is the mother of 'B'.
(c) A ÷ B means 'A' is the son of 'B'.
(d) A − B means 'A' is the husband of 'B'.

63. Which of the following would mean M is the father of N?
(a) M ÷ N + O   (b) M × O − N
(c) M + O ÷ N   (d) M − O + N

64. Which of the following is definitely true if N is the son of M?
(a) M + N × O   (b) M + N −O
(c) N ÷ M   (d) All of these

65. Which of the following would mean M is the Aunt of N?
(a) M + N − O   (b) M × O ÷ N
(c) N + O × M   (d) None of these

66. Neera is daughter of Mahendra. Mala, Achla's sister has a son Mohan and daughter Sushila. Kamla is maternal aunt of Sushila and mother of Krishna. Mohan is cousin of Krishna. Krishna is brother of Neera. How is Achla related to Mahendra?
(a) Cousin   (b) Sister-in-law
(c) Niece   (d) Daughter

67. Pointing to a woman, a man said, "Her husband's mother is the wife of my father's only son". How is the man related to that woman?
(a) Son   (b) Brother-in-law
(c) Uncle   (d) Father-in-law

Directions (Q. Nos. 68-72) *Read the following statements and answer the questions given below.*
Radha and Minnilal have two children Simmi and Divya, Divya is married to Anuj who is the son of Madhu and Jabbar. Resham is daughter of Anuj. Kiran who is Anuj's sister is married to Subodh and has two sons Tarun and Aman. Tarun is grandson of Madhu and Jabbar.

68. What is the relationship between Aman and Resham?
(a) Uncle-Niece   (b) Father-Daughter
(c) Husband-Wife   (d) Cousins

69. How is Subodh related to Jabbar?
(a) Son-in-law   (b) Son
(c) Brother   (d) Father-in-law

70. How is Resham related to Kiran?
(a) Niece   (b) Daughter
(c) Mother   (d) Aunt

HM 2013

71. How is Kiran related to Divya?
  (a) Aunt
  (b) Grandmother
  (c) Sister-in-law
  (d) Sister

72. Which of the following statement is definitely true?
  (a) Aman is the son of Simmi
  (b) Madhu is the mother-in-law of Subodh
  (c) Resham is the cousin of Kiran
  (d) All the three are true

73. Raj is walking towards West. He takes three turns while walking, all at an angle of 45° towards right, right and left. What direction is he facing now?
  (a) North-East   (b) South-East
  (c) East   (d) West

74. A and B start together from one point. They walk 10 km towards North. A turns left and covers 5 km whereas B turns right and covers 3 km. A turns left again and covers 15 km whereas B turns right and covers 15 km. How far is A from B?
  (a) 18 km   (b) 10 km
  (c) 5 km   (d) 8 km

Direction (Q. No. 75) *Which of the following groups of letters will complete the given series?*

75. xx-zzx-yzz-xyz-
  (a) xyzx   (b) zyxx
  (c) yxxy   (d) yxxz

Direction (Q. No. 76) *In the following question, select the number(s) from the given options for completing the given series.*

76. 2, 3, 5, 10, 20, 40, ?
  (a) 65   (b) 75
  (c) 60   (d) 80

Direction (Q. No. 77) *In the following question, four words are alike in some manner. Spot the odd one out.*

77. (a) Pond   (b) River
  (c) Stream   (d) Brook

Direction (Q. No. 78) *Three of the following four in the given question are alike in a certain way and so form a group. Select the group of letter that does not belong to that group.*

78. (a) FEUV   (b) DCXW
  (c) BAZY   (d) HGTS

Direction (Q. No. 79) *In the following question, there are four options. Three numbers, in these options are alike in certain manner, only one number does not fit in. Choose the one which is different from the rest.*

79. (a) 2553   (b) 1224
  (c) 7992   (d) 3885

Directions (Q. Nos. 80 and 81) *Which one figure can be made out of given paper cut-outs?*

80.

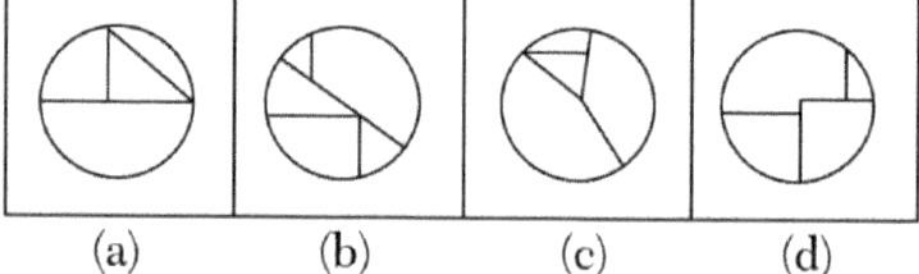

(a)   (b)   (c)   (d)

81.

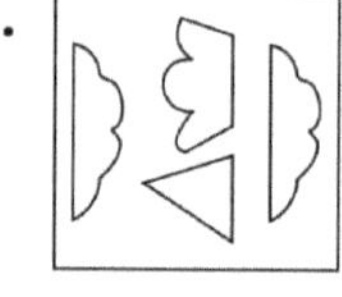

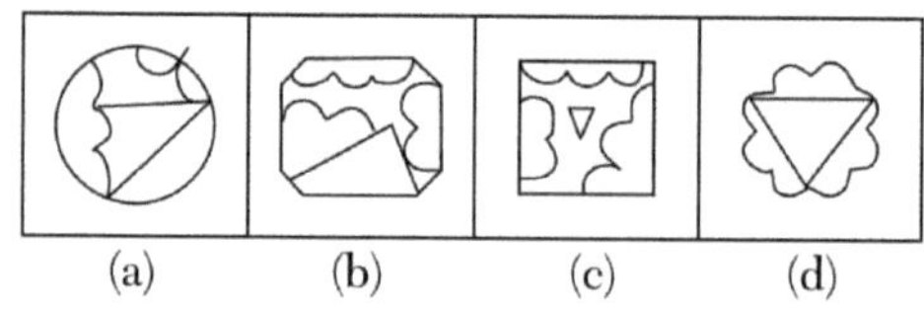

(a)   (b)   (c)   (d)

Direction (Q. No. 82) *In the following problem, a square transparent sheet with a pattern is given. Figure out from amongst the four alternatives as to how the pattern would appear when the transparent sheet is folded at the dotted line.*

82.

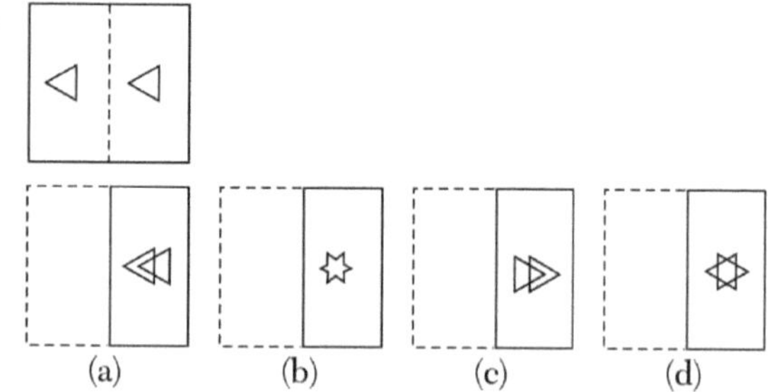

(a)   (b)   (c)   (d)

Directions (Q. Nos. 83 and 84) *In each question below are given two statements followed by two conclusions numbered I and II. You have to take the two given statements to be true even if they seem to be at variance from commonly known facts and then decide which of the given conclusions logically follows from the two given statements, disregarding commonly known facts. Read both the statements and*

Give Answer
(a) if only Conclusion I follows
(b) if only Conclusion II follows
(c) if either I or II follows
(d) if neither I nor II follows

83. Statements
1. Some dogs are pups.
2. All horses are pups.
Conclusions
I. Some dogs are horses.
II. Some horses are dogs.

84. Statements
1. Some toys are tables.
2. No table is black.
Conclusions
I. Some toys are black.
II. Some toys are not black.

Direction (Q. No. 85) *In the following question select the right option which indicates the correct code for the word or letter given in the question.*

85. If PHILOSOPHY is coded as HPLISOPOYH, ORNAMENTAL will be coded as
(a) ROANEMNTLA   (b) ONRAMNEALT
(c) ROANEMTNLA   (d) ROANEMNATL

Direction (Q. No. 86) *In the following question study the coded patterns and then select the right option from the given alternatives.*

86. In a certain code language.
1. 'Gor Paku' means 'Best Gift'
2. 'Mull Gor Sot' means 'Gift of Love'
3. 'Kot Mull Paku' means 'Best of Luck' and
4. 'Hed Sot Paku' means 'Love is Best'
Which of the following codes stand for the word 'Love'?
(a) Paku   (b) Hed
(c) Sot   (d) Mull

Direction (Q. No. 87) *The following question is based on the code pattern given below.*

Letters	X	S	M	A	P	E	D	L	W	T
Digits	1	6	9	8	3	5	0	2	4	7

Which of the given option has the correct coded form of the given letters?

87. XTDMSW
(a) 170946   (b) 179064   (c) 170964   (d) 176904

Directions (Q. Nos. 88-90) *In the diagram given below, the circle stands for 'educated', square for 'hard-working', triangle for 'urban people' and rectangle for 'honest'. The different regions of the diagram are numbered from 1 to 12. Study the diagram carefully and answer the questions.*

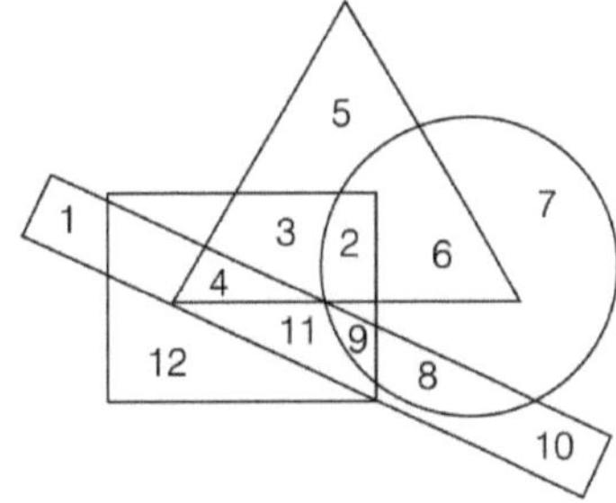

88. Non-urban people, who are honest, educated and hard-working are indicated by
(a) 11   (b) 10
(c) 8   (d) 9

89. Educated, hard-working and urban people are indicated by
(a) 7   (b) 2
(c) 3   (d) 4

90. Urban people who are hard-working and uneducated, but not honest are indicated by
(a) 6   (b) 2
(c) 3   (d) 4

Section C : Maths and Scientific Aptitude

91. If a man can row 30 km downstream and 18 km upstream, each in 3 h, what is the speed of boat in still water?
(a) 8 km/h   (b) 10 km/h
(c) 12 km/h   (d) 15 km/h

92. A man travels a certain distance at the rate of 10 km/h and returns the same point at rate of 15 km/h. His average rate for the whole journey is
(a) 12 km/h   (b) $12\frac{1}{2}$ km/h
(c) 13 km/h   (d) None of these

93. In a journey of 160 km, a train covers the distance 120 km at a speed of 80 km/h and the remaining distance at 40 km/h. The average speed of the train for the whole journey is
(a) 60 km/h   (b) 64 km/h
(c) 68 km/h   (d) 72 km/h

94. By selling a watch for ₹ 1056 at a loss of 12%. The cost price of the watch is
(a) ₹ 1250
(b) ₹ 1100
(c) ₹ 1150
(d) ₹ 1200

95. Surbhi sold a washing machine for ₹ 9499 at a gain of 15%. Find the cost price of the washing machine.
(a) ₹ 8000
(b) ₹ 8100
(c) ₹ 8260
(d) ₹ 8300

96. A man gave 35% of his sum of money to his son and 25% to his daughter, 50% of the remaining gave to a school. If he still has ₹ 2000 with him, find his total sum.
(a) ₹ 10000
(b) ₹ 12000
(c) ₹ 9000
(d) ₹ 8000

97. A candidate got 65% votes in an election and won by 3645 votes. Find the total number of votes polled if there were two candidates.
(a) 15100
(b) 15250
(c) 16300
(d) 12150

98. In a mixture of 60 L, the ratio of ethanol to ether is 4 : 1. The quantity of ether to be added to the mixture to make the ratio 2 : 1 will be
(a) 10 L
(b) 12 L
(c) 18 L
(d) 24 L

99. A tea merchants blends two types of tea costing ₹ 60 per kg and ₹ 80 per kg each respectively. To cost the resulting mixture ₹ 66 per kg, the two types of tea be mixed in the ratio of
(a) 3 : 7
(b) 7 : 3
(c) 4 : 5
(d) 5 : 4

100. The sum of the ages of son and father is 56 yr. After 4 yr the age of the father will be three times that of the son. Their ages respectively are
(a) 12 yr, 44 yr
(b) 16 yr, 42 yr
(c) 16 yr, 48 yr
(d) 18 yr, 36 yr

101. In 10 yr, A will be twice as old as B was 10 yr ago. If A is now 9 yr older than B, the present age of B is
(a) 19 yr
(b) 29 yr
(c) 39 yr
(d) 49 yr

102. The sum of the ages of father and son is 45 yr. Five years ago the product of their ages was 4 times the father's age at that time. The present ages of the father and son, respectively are
(a) 25 yr, 10 yr
(b) 36 yr, 9 yr
(c) 39 yr, 6 yr
(d) None of these

103. The surface area of cube is 726 m^2. Its volume is
(a) 1300 m^3
(b) 1331 m^3
(c) 1452 m^3
(d) 1542 m^3

104. The length of the diagonal of a cuboid 30 cm long, 24 cm broad and 18 cm high is
(a) 30 cm
(b) $15\sqrt{2}$ cm
(c) 60 cm
(d) $30\sqrt{2}$ cm

105. A cone is 8.4 cm high and the radius of its base is 2.1 cm. It is melted and recast into a sphere. The radius of a sphere is
(a) 2.2 cm
(b) 2.1 cm
(c) 2.4 cm
(d) 2 cm

106. The three dimensional photograph is prepared through
(a) holography
(b) photography
(c) photochromatic process
(d) radiography

107. If 10 bulbs of 100 watt remains switched on 1 h. daily then the total electricity consumed everyday would be
(a) 1 unit
(b) 100 kWh
(c) 10 unit
(d) 10 kWh

108. The rainbow appears
(a) due to dispersion
(b) due to refraction
(c) due to scattering
(d) Both (a) and (b)

109. The first law of thermodynamics confirms the concept of
(a) energy conservation
(b) temperature conservation
(c) mass conservation
(d) None of the above

110. The physical quantity obtained through the division of linear momentum of a body by its velocity
(a) velocity
(b) acceleration
(c) mass
(d) force

111. Which of the following is not a radioactive element?
(a) Astetin
(b) Franscium
(c) Titenium
(d) Zeronium

112. The substance (element) obtained after emission of a β-particle for $_{11}Na^{22}$.
(a) Mg
(b) Mn
(c) Ag
(d) Pb

113. Which of the following gas is utilised to fill up the balloon, specially when weather related prediction and reporting is to be done.
(a) O_2
(b) CO_2
(c) CH_2
(d) He

114. To prevent for knocking the substance employed in the car engine is
(a) ethyl alcohol
(b) butane
(c) lead tetraethyl
(d) white petrol

115. The gas produced through the pouring (passing) water on the calcium carbide is
(a) methane   (b) ethane
(c) ethylene   (d) acetylene

116. The water pollution in the rivers are measured by
(a) the amount of dissolved chlorine
(b) the amount of dissolved ozone
(c) the amount of dissolved nitrogen
(d) the amount of dissolved oxygen

117. Which of the following Human organ is affected by the consumption of a flatoxin food adulterent?
(a) Heart   (b) Lung
(c) Kidney   (d) Liver

118. The structure of the DNA was firstly outlined by
(a) Dr. Meghnath Saha
(b) Dr. Stefan Howking
(c) Watson and Crick
(d) Dr. Alexander Flemming

119. The phenomenon of genetic mutation occurs in
(a) DNA   (b) RNA
(c) Chromosome   (d) Ribosome

120. Which of the following has maximum protein?
(a) gram   (b) pea
(c) soyabean   (b) pigeon pea

Section D : General Awareness

121. A job shop is an example of a(n)
(a) repetitive process
(b) continuous process
(c) intermittent process
(d) specialised process

122. Three types of process strategies are
(a) goods, services and hybrids
(b) manual, automated and service
(c) process focus, repetitive focus and product focus
(d) modular, continuous and technological

123. Which of the following is **false** regarding repetitive processes?
(a) They use modules.
(b) They allow easy switching from one product to the other.
(c) They are the classic assembly lines.
(d) They have more structure and less flexibility than a job shop layout.

124. Mass customisation, when done correctly
(a) increases pressure on supply-chain performance.
(b) helps eliminate the guesswork that comes with sales forecasting.
(c) drives down inventories.
(d) All of the above

125. Service blueprinting
(a) provides the basis to negotiate prices with suppliers.
(b) mimics the way people communicate.
(c) determines the best time for each step in the process.
(d) focuses on the provider's interaction with the customer.

126. Strategies for improving productivity in services are
(a) separation, self-service, automation and scheduling
(b) lean production, strategy- driven investments, automation and process focus
(c) reduce inventory, reduce waste, reduce inspection and reduce rework
(d) high interaction mass customisation, service factory and just-in-time

127. Which of the following is **true** regarding vision systems?
(a) They are consistently accurate.
(b) They are modest in cost.
(c) They do not become bored
(d) All of the above are true.

128. "Automatic placement and withdrawal of parts and products into and from designated places in a warehouse" describes
(a) AGV   (b) CAD/CAM
(c) CIM   (d) ASRS

129. "Operators simply load new programs, as necessary, to produce different products" describes
(a) automated guided vehicles
(b) Flexible Manufacturing Systems (FMS)
(c) vision systems
(d) process control

130. Examples of the impact of technology on services include
(a) debit cards
(b) supermarket scanners
(c) electronic hotel key/lock systems
(d) All of the above

131. Which of the following is **true** regarding the concept of flexibility?
- (a) It is the ability to change production rates with little penalty in time, cost or customer value.
- (b) It can be accomplished with sophisticated electronic equipment.
- (c) It may involve modular, movable, even cheap equipment.
- (d) All of the above are true

132. The sport persons who are the new National Icons for Election Commission of India (ECI) are
- (a) Saina Nehwal and MC Mary Kom
- (b) Yogeshwar Dutt and Vijender Singh
- (c) Sushil Kumar and Gagan Narang
- (d) Sachin Tendulkar and Sania Mirza

133. 'Android' a Linux based operating system used in mobiles is created by which company?
- (a) BlackBerry
- (b) Apple
- (c) Google
- (d) None of these

134. Campaign against "Malnutrition in Child", an initiative of Ministry of Women and Child Development is done by which Indian film star?
- (a) Amitabh Bachchan
- (b) Akshay Kumar
- (c) Aamir Khan
- (d) None of these

135. Who wrote the book 'Discovery of India'?
- (a) Kuldeep Nayar
- (b) Jawaharlal Nehru
- (c) Mahatma Gandhi
- (d) Khushwant Singh

136. POSCO is a major steel of which country?
- (a) Korea
- (b) China
- (c) Indonesia
- (d) None of these

137. World Bank has recently appointed .... as its chief economist and senior Vice-President.
- (a) Montek Singh Ahluwalia
- (b) Kaushik Basu
- (c) Amartya Sen
- (d) C Rangarajan

138. Which state has the largest urban population in India?
- (a) Maharashtra
- (b) Kerala
- (c) Chhattisgarh
- (d) West Bengal

139. Mr. Hamid Ansari was re-elected as India's ...... Vice-President.
- (a) 13th
- (b) 14th
- (c) 12th
- (d) 11th

140. Which Insurance Company uses the tag line 'jiyo befikar'?
- (a) LIC
- (b) ICICI Prudential
- (c) TATA-AIG
- (d) Bajaj Allianz

141. Who became the first woman speaker of Lok Sabha in India?
- (a) Sarojini Naidu
- (b) Meira Kumar
- (c) Aruna Asaf Ali
- (d) Indira Gandhi

142. Which device is used for locating the submerged object under sea?
- (a) Sonar
- (b) Radar
- (c) Laser
- (d) Maser

143. The Sun reaches its maximum angular distance from the equator at the
- (a) Zenith
- (b) Solstice
- (c) Equinox
- (d) Noon time

144. When can one record the lowest temperature of air?
- (a) Just before sunrise
- (b) At midnight
- (c) At 3 a.m.
- (d) At sunrise

145. The most learned ruler of the Delhi Sultanate who was well versed in various branches of learning including Astronomy, Mathematics and Medicine was
- (a) Iltutmish
- (b) Alauddin Khalji
- (c) Muhammad Bin Tughlaq
- (d) Sikandar Lodhi

146. The 9th Postal Zone of India covers
- (a) Andhra Pradesh
- (b) Army Post Office
- (c) Goa
- (d) Andaman and Nicobar Islands

147. Who is responsible for the registration of voters in India?
- (a) Government
- (b) Voters
- (c) Political Parties
- (d) Election Commission

148. Which one of the following is the most effective carrier of communications?
- (a) Cables
- (b) Radio waves
- (c) Microwaves
- (d) Optical fibres

149. Name the Indian woman weight-lifter who in January 2013 won Maiden National Title in National Weightlifting Championship, 2013.
- (a) Binitha Devi
- (b) Amanpreet Kaur
- (c) Manpreet Kaur
- (d) Karnam Malleswari

150. Who is crowned as Pond's Femina Ms. India, 2013?
- (a) Zoya Afroz
- (b) Sobhita Dhulipala
- (c) Navneet Kaur Dhillon
- (d) Anukriti Gusain

Section E : Aptitude For Service Sector

151. You have been asked to complete your work but others plan to leave the work and enjoy themselves at the carnival
(a) You also start thinking the same way.
(b) You do your work as there is no fun in taking chances for such an important work.
(c) Ask your friends as well to do the work.
(d) Leave your friends thinking they have a non-serious attitude towards work.

152. For the past few weeks your neighbour has been repeatedly throwing his kitchen garbage and other things in your backyard. You are extremely upset about this and decide to
(a) Complain about it to the President of the colony.
(b) Present your complaint straightway to the neighbour in an informal manner.
(c) Hold a meeting with other neighbours.
(d) Remain quiet over the issue.

153. After practicing continuously for days, your football team has reached the finals. In the final match, your team has a good hold over the match. But things change completely when the two players upon whom the team relies get hurt and retire. You are now the last hope of the team.
(a) The pressure to win affects your concentration but you try to do your best.
(b) Be focused and give your best shot.
(c) Lose all hope of the winning.
(d) Think about your in capabilities and feel helpless.

154. Your elder brother criticises you in front of your parents. He does it repeatedly and this makes you feel insulted
(a) Talk to him openly about the way you have always felt and ask him not to do it any more.
(b) Go to the other members of your family rather than directly approaching him.
(c) Ignore the situation but feel angry and hurt by his words.
(d) Approach him several times but feel scared to complain to him.

155. On meeting an old classmate after a long gap, your reaction is
(a) You simply smile and get back to your work.
(b) Go up to her and start a conversation.
(c) Wait for her to take the initiative.
(d) Ignore her

156. While talking to your friend on the phone, you realise someone from the back is playing your favourite song
(a) Tell your friend that you are listening to the song.
(b) You are able to understand what your friend is saying and keep listening to the song along with the conversation.
(c) Try to do both the things together but cannot do either.
(d) Forget about the song and concentrate on your friend's voice.

157. You are going back quite late from your office and all of a sudden the car breaks down in the middle of a deserted road. You ring up at your place and your father says that he'll be there in half an hour. You cannot do nothing except waiting for him. You
(a) continue to sit in the car patiently and carefully and keep waiting for your father.
(b) feel a bit sacred.
(c) experience extreme panic as the waiting period increases.
(d) decide to get down from the car as it is getting more scary.

158. You are alone at home when one of your nieces hurts herself badly.
(a) You start feeling panicky.
(b) You ask for your neighbours' help.
(c) You call up your parents and ask them to come over as.
(d) You call the family doctor immediately and go and sit beside her to keep watch in the meantime.

159. You are with your friends on a school trip. You lot your way and you feel that you are lost. You
(a) start blaming the other person an start looking for ways to catch up with others.
(b) call up your parents.
(c) take out/buy a map and ask for directions.
(d) visit the shops.

160. You were discussing some important issue with one of your colleagues and you end up having a fight. You would
(a) ignore the whole situation and start chatting with others.
(b) blame her and move ahead.
(c) sit with her and try to clarify things to sort out the matter.
(d) promise to yourself that you will never talk to her in future.

161. You are sitting alone at the airport waiting for the flight. You are among strangers. You would
(a) chat only when others start.
(b) buy a magazine and keep yourself busy.
(c) start chatting with the person sitting next to you.
(d) sit idle and hope time passes fast.

162. You have joined a new company. People around you are quite friendly and helpful. What would you do to start a conversation with them
(a) Smile at everyone and say hello.
(b) Go right up to anyone who seems approachable and start talking animatedly.
(c) Take part in discussions that deal with work only.
(d) Behave very formally.

163. You take out your nephew and his friends to a mall. All of a sudden you realise that one of your nephew's friends is not there. You
(a) tell the children to be patient and report the matter to the officials.
(b) panic and take the group to a quiet corner being unsure of how to proceed.
(c) gather the rest of the children and take them along with you to the park officials who will then help you set about looking for the missing child while ensuring the safety to the rest out of the group.
(d) start looking out for the missing child and call his name.

164. In the examination hall, the teacher sees you talking to your friend. You were just asking for a pen but the teacher thinks that you were cheating and deducts your marks for that. You
(a) remain anxious throughout the paper but you continue writing.
(b) continue with the exam and once it is over go up to the teacher to explain the situation.
(c) immediately start protesting and insist that you have not been cheating.
(d) are not able to concentrate on the exam due to that incident.

165. If you have to prepare for your exam and at the same time prepare your project report
(a) Do one thing at a time and plan out a time table and work accordingly.
(b) Become anxious and impulsively do the tasks just for the sake of getting over with them.
(c) Try to do all the tasks at the same time.
(d) Keep crying without being able to work effectively at any task.

166. Your friend shouts at you due to some misunderstanding. She thinks that you have been creating problems in her personal life. You would
(a) shout back at her.
(b) tell others that she is in a habit of doing it.
(c) leave her and never talk to her.
(d) make the first move to clear the misunderstanding.

167. If you are sitting with your friends in a party and all of a sudden you see your old classmate after a long time was once your best friend in school. Would you
(a) leave your friends and stay with your classmate only.
(b) ignore your classmate for the sake of your friends.
(c) talk to your classmate for a while and then get back to your friends.
(d) introduce your classmate to your friends and make him/her feel comfortable with the whole group.

168. Your best friend has invited you for lunch but the same day you come to know about the interviews in the job placement cell of your college.
(a) Enjoy with your friend thinking that you will attend such interviews next time.
(b) Ring up your friend and explain the whole situation.
(c) You miss the interview's and leave for lunch.
(d) You keep grumbling and you are confused.

169. Your parents are going out for a few days. They ask you to pay the electricity bill on the due date but you lost the bill. Would you
(a) make sure that your parents don't come to know about it.
(b) you feel scared and keep calling your best friend as you are scared about the whole thing.
(c) ring up your parents to ask what can be done about it.
(d) decide to tell your parents that the maid is not careful with things and she must have thrown it.

170. When somebody asks your views regarding an issue,
(a) you fail to give a realistic and precise answer.
(b) your views are dependent on other people's views.
(c) you diplomatically answer the question in a very realistic and straight forward manner.
(d) you say anything that comes to your mind.

171. You are a member of a leading music group. During a performance, a judge asks you to step forward and sing alone as you are the main singer of the group
(a) You get distracted as the rest of the group is not with you.
(b) You concentrate on your singing to perform your level best.
(c) You form the opinion that you are going to be thrown out of the group.
(d) You keep thinking why you were asked to sing alone and remain confused throughout.

172. One of your colleagues who is very proud and haughty makes fun of you in front of others and laughs at you. You would
  (a) remain quite and tolerate everything.
  (b) tell her how you feel about it and ask her to avoid doing it.
  (c) try to change the topic of conversation.
  (d) keep blaming yourself for not being able to say anything.

173. Your sister was supposed to pick you up after a function in your college. But somehow she gets late. You don't have any source to contact her as she is not carrying her phone.
  (a) You keep waiting for her in the college.
  (b) You would pick up your bag and go to your friend's place.
  (c) You would go somewhere else to teach her a lesson.
  (d) You start shouting at her as soon as she reaches as you are fed up of waiting for her.

174. You are very tired and have to do some important work. You
  (a) keep thinking that you are tired and won't be able to work.
  (b) do the work whole heartedly.
  (c) would do it without thinking that you can make errors.
  (d) finish it off.

175. Your teacher tells you well in advance that a certain project needs to be completed within two week time. You would
  (a) do the work patiently and complete it within the given time.
  (b) leave the work for a while thinking that it'll be done later.
  (c) feel panicky and start devoting all your time to it.
  (d) ignore the work thinking that its just a day's job.

176. Which of the following statements best defines an open ended question?
  (a) Questions which ask for some written detail but have no determined set of available responses.
  (b) Questions which ask for some written detail and have a previously determined set of responses.
  (c) Short questions or statements which are followed by a number of options.
  (d) Questions which ask for some written detail and are followed by a number of options.

177. Which of the following questions types should be avoided when writing items for a scale?
  (a) Hypothetical questions
  (b) Unambiguous questions
  (c) Questions which have a closed format
  (d) Clear questions

178. Which of the following statements best defines a leading questions?
  (a) Questions that try to steer the respondent to a particular answer or in the direction of a particular answer.
  (b) Short questions or statements which have no determined set of responses.
  (c) Questions that place the individual in a situation they may never experience and ask them for their opinion on some issue.
  (d) Questions which ask for some written detail but have no determined set of responses.

179. Which of the following statements best defines the term test-retest reliability (consistency)?
  (a) Test-retest reliability assess reliability over time.
  (b) Test-retest reliability assesses whether there is a clear relationship between the construct at a theoretical level and the measure that has been developed.
  (c) Test-retest reliability refers to whether a test is measuring what we claim it is measuring.
  (d) Test-retest reliability refers to whether all the aspects of the psychometric test are generally working together to measure the same thing.

180. Which type of validity does the following statement refer to : "it assesses the extent to which it shows associations with measures that it should be related to"?
  (a) Concurrent   (b) Face validity
  (c) Convergent   (d) Discriminant

181. What type of validity is concerned with what the measure appears to measure?
  (a) Face validity   (b) Discriminant
  (c) Convergent   (d) Concurrent

182. Which of the following statements best defines factor analysis?
  (a) It is a multivariate data reduction statistical technique.
  (b) It is a univariate data reduction statistical technique.
  (c) It is a multivariate data enhancing statistical technique.
  (d) It is a univariate data enhancing statistical technique.

183. What is the function of a screen plot?
  (a) To plot the relationships between variables.
  (b) To plot the given values.
  (c) To plot the interaction between variables.
  (d) To plot the differences between variables.

184. Which of the following statements best defines orthogonal rotations?
  (a) Rotations that assume the each factors share no association and are unique of each other.

(b) Rotations that assume that each factor is correlated with another.

(c) Rotations that assume that each factor interacts with another.

(d) Rotations that assume that each factors share an association with each other.

185. Which of the following is a type of extraction procedure in exploratory factor analysis?

(a) Secondary component analysis

(b) Multi component analysis

(c) Principal component analysis

(d) Univariate component analysis

186. If you want to be successful, you should be

(a) grossly over confident   (b) confident

(c) under confident   (d) over confident

187. If you have just been denied promotion and your junior has been selected, what should you do?

(a) Leave the organisation.

(b) Abuse the junior for manipulation and protest against the management.

(c) Move the court.

(d) Talk to your boss, bring out your contribution and ask for reconsideration.

188. If you happen to on the spot of a road accident, where a person is injured, what should you do?

(a) Call the police.

(b) Inform the injured person's relative.

(c) Provide him first-aid, if you can.

(d) Avoid the scene of accident.

189. In case you get angry on some issue, you should

(a) display your anger by shouting and give vent to your anger.

(b) avoid the situation.

(c) try to reason and delay your reactions.

(d) distract your attention from the issue.

190. You would like to be friendly with a person who is

(a) clever and smart

(b) simple and honest

(c) extrovert and dominating

(d) quiet and withdrawn

191. While selecting a candidate for a service industry job, you will go for a candidate who is

(a) highly academic

(b) social and helpful

(c) quiet and an introvert

(d) responsible

192. If you happen to come across a girl child, who has unfortunately got separated from the parents in the crowd, you would

(a) enquire about her parents and help her as the need be.

(b) hand over the child to people around.

(c) inform the police .

(d) ignore to avoid any hassle.

193. In case you happen to witness a family quarrel in your immediate neighbourhood, you would

(a) ignore and forget.

(b) inform other neighbours and try to intervene.

(c) shout and tell them not to make noise inform police.

(d) inform police.

194. When you see a clustre of slums in your neighbourhood, what comes to your mind?

(a) Slums should be immediately removed to a far off place.

(b) Slums are a scar on our cities.

(c) Persons living in slums should also have a place to live.

(d) Try and ignore the issue.

195. On receipt of bad performance review, you would

(a) become extremely engry.

(b) be disappointed and frustrated.

(c) try and take criticism in stride and learn some lessons.

(d) go and fight with your boss.

196. A cuboid has six sides of different colours. The red side is opposite to black. The blue side is adjacent to white. The brown side is adjacent to blue. The red side is face down. Which one of the following would be the opposite to brown?

(a) Red   (b) Black   (c) White   (d) Blue

197. Half of the villagers of a certain village have their own houses. One-fifth of the villagers cultivate paddy. One-third of the villagers are literate. Four-fifth of the villagers are below twenty five. Then, which one of the following is certainly true?

(a) All the villagers who have their own houses are literate.

(b) Some villagers under twenty five are literate.

(c) A quarter of the villagers who have their own houses cultivate paddy.

(d) Half of the villagers who cultivate paddy are literate.

198. Six persons M, N, O, P, Q and R are sitting in two rows, three in each. Q is not at the end of any row. P is second to the left of R. O is the neighbour of Q and is sitting diagonally opposite to P. N is the neighbour of R. On the basis of above information, who is facing N?

(a) R   (b) Q

(c) P   (d) M

199. In a meeting, the map of a village was placed in such a manner that South-East becomes North, North-East becomes West and so on. What will South become?
(a) North
(b) North-West
(c) North-East
(d) West

200. Six persons A, B, C, D, E and F are standing in a row. C and D are standing close to each other alongside E. B is standing beside A only. A is fourth from F. Who are standing on the extremes?
(a) A and F
(b) B and D
(c) B and F
(d) None of the above

Answers

1. (a)	2. (b)	3. (c)	4. (d)	5. (a)	6. (c)	7. (c)	8. (d)	9. (b)	10. (d)
11. (a)	12. (c)	13. (b)	14. (c)	15. (c)	16. (c)	17. (a)	18. (d)	19. (a)	20. (b)
21. (c)	22. (a)	23. (b)	24. (b)	25. (d)	26. (d)	27. (c)	28. (c)	29. (a)	30. (c)
31. (a)	32. (a)	33. (b)	34. (a)	35. (d)	36. (c)	37. (a)	38. (b)	39. (c)	40. (b)
41. (d)	42. (c)	43. (b)	44. (c)	45. (b)	46. (c)	47. (b)	48. (d)	49. (a)	50. (a)
51. (d)	52. (c)	53. (c)	54. (b)	55. (a)	56. (c)	57. (c)	58. (c)	59. (a)	60. (b)
61. (b)	62. (a)	63. (d)	64. (c)	65. (d)	66. (b)	67. (d)	68. (d)	69. (a)	70. (a)
71. (c)	72. (b)	73. (a)	74. (d)	75. (d)	76. (d)	77. (a)	78. (a)	79. (b)	80. (a)
81. (d)	82. (d)	83. (d)	84. (b)	85. (c)	86. (c)	87. (c)	88. (d)	89. (b)	90. (c)
91. (a)	92. (a)	93. (b)	94. (d)	95. (c)	96. (a)	97. (d)	98. (b)	99. (b)	100. (a)
101. (c)	102. (b)	103. (b)	104. (d)	105. (b)	106. (a)	107. (a)	108. (d)	109. (a)	110. (c)
111. (d)	112. (a)	113. (d)	114. (c)	115. (d)	116. (d)	117. (d)	118. (d)	119. (c)	120. (c)
121. (d)	122. (c)	123. (b)	124. (d)	125.. (d)	126. (a)	127. (d)	128. (d)	129. (b)	130. (d)
131. (d)	132. (a)	133. (c)	134. (c)	135. (b)	136. (a)	137. (b)	138. (a)	139. (b)	140. (d)
141. (b)	142. (a)	143. (b)	144. (a)	145. (c)	146. (b)	147. (d)	148. (c)	149. (c)	150. (c)
151. (c)	152. (c)	153. (b)	154. (a)	155. (b)	156. (d)	157. (a)	158. (d)	159. (c)	160. (c)
161. (b)	162. (a)	163. (c)	164. (b)	165. (a)	166. (d)	167. (d)	168. (b)	169. (c)	170. (c)
171. (b)	172. (b)	173. (a)	174. (b)	175. (a)	176. (a)	177. (a)	178. (a)	179. (a)	180. (c)
181. (a)	182. (a)	183. (b)	184. (a)	185. (c)	186. (b)	187. (d)	188. (c)	189. (c)	190. (d)
191. (d)	192. (a)	193. (b)	194. (c)	195. (c)	196. (c)	197. (b)	198. (b)	199. (c)	200. (c)

Hints & Solutions

2. (*a*) 'Sterile' means not to be able to produce. Hence, 'barren' best expresses the meaning of sterile.

4. (*d*) 'Germane' means relevant to a subject under consideration. Hence, 'relevant' best expresses the meaning of germane.

5. (*a*) 'Ponder' means to consider or think about something carefully. Hence, 'think' best expresses the meaning of ponder.

6. (*c*) 'Firm' is the correct opposite of 'flimsy'. 'Flimsy' means weak, insubstantial or unconvincing and 'firm' means solid, strong and resilient.

8. (*d*) 'Rigid' is the correct opposite of 'adaptable'. 'Adaptable' means able to be modified or to adjust to new conditions and 'rigid' means inflexible or unable to be changed.

11. (*a*) 'Emulate' means to match or surpass someone by imitation. Hence, 'imitate' is the nearest in meaning to emulate.

12. (*c*) 'Aberration' means a departure from what is normal, usual or expected and 'deviation' means the same.

13. (*b*) 'Attribute' means to regard something as being caused by and 'impute' means the same.

14. (*c*) 'Spontaneous' means occurring without apparent external cause and 'instinctive' means when something is done without conscious thought. Hence, 'instinctive' is the nearest in meaning to 'spontaneous'.

15. (*c*) 'Mettle' means a person's ability to cope well with difficulties or valour. Hence, 'courage and endurance' are the nearest in meaning to mettle.

16. (*c*) 'Auspicious' is the correct opposite of 'ominous'. 'Ominous' means the possibility that something bad is going to happen and 'auspicious' means the possibility of successful future.

17. (*a*) 'Indifference' is the correct opposite of 'zeal'. 'Zeal' means great energy in pursuit of a cause and 'indifference' means lack of interest and concern.

19. (*a*) 'Clarity' is the correct opposite of 'obscurity'. 'Obscurity' means something which is unclear or difficult to understand.

20. (*b*) 'Liability' is the correct opposite of 'asset'. 'Asset' means a useful or valuable thing or person and 'liability' means a person or thing whose presence is likely to put one at a disadvantage.

47. (*b*) Part (b) contains the error. 'Worn out' means extremely tired or exhausted.

When an action is performed before another in the past, the action that takes place first should be in past perfect tense and the action that takes place second should be in simple past tense.

Hence, replace 'was completely worn' with 'had been completely worn out' to make the sentence grammatically correct.

49. (*a*) Part (a) contains the error. Article 'the' should be used before 'present' to make the sentence grammatically correct.

Sol. (*Q. Nos. 61 and 62*) *The given relation can be shown as,*

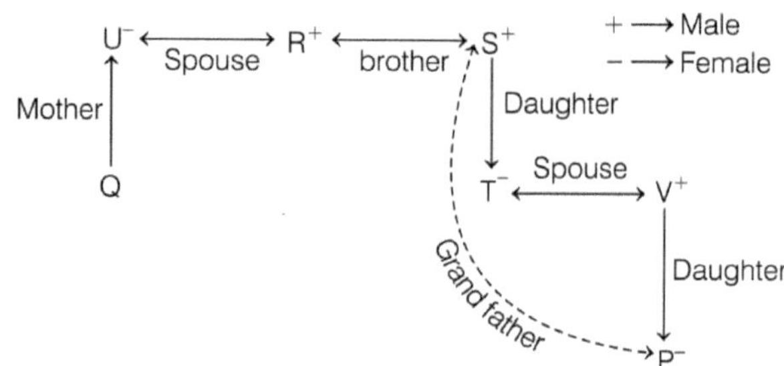

61. (*b*) S is the grandfather of P.

62. (*a*) T is the cousin of Q.

63. (*d*) According to the question, by using option (d),

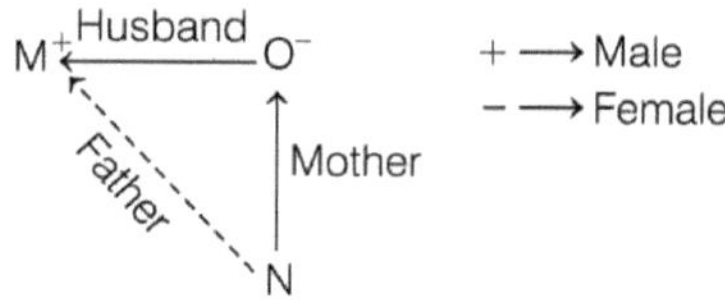

Clearly, M is the father of N. Hence, option (d) is correct.

64. (*c*) According to the question, by using option (c),

$$\begin{array}{c} M \\ \downarrow\; \text{Son} \\ N^+ \end{array}$$

Hence, option (c) is correct.

65. (*d*) According to the question, Option (a),

$$\begin{array}{c} M^- \\ \uparrow\; \text{Mother} \\ \;\;\;\; \text{Husband} \\ N^+ \longleftarrow O^- \end{array}$$

Here, M is mother of N not aunt, which is incorrect.

Option (b),

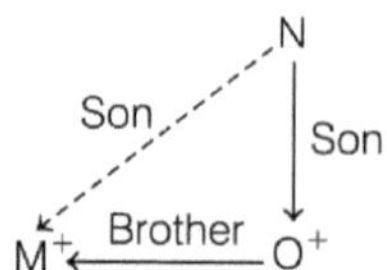

Here, M is son of N not Aunt. Which is incorrect.

Option (c),

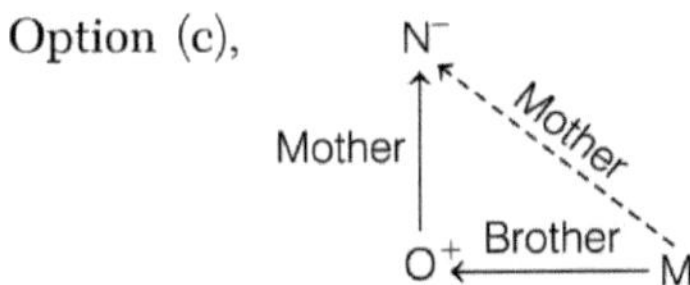

Here, M's gender is not defined. So, we cannot find any relation.

Clearly, no option shows the M is the aunt of N. Hence, option (d) is correct.

66. (*b*) According to the question,

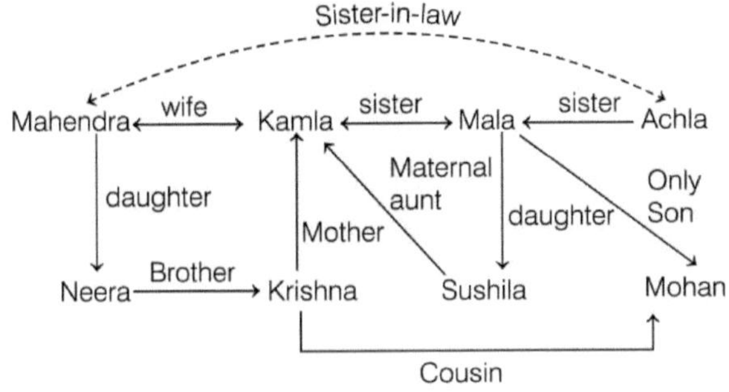

∴ Achla is sister-in-law of Mahendra.

67. (*d*) According to the question,

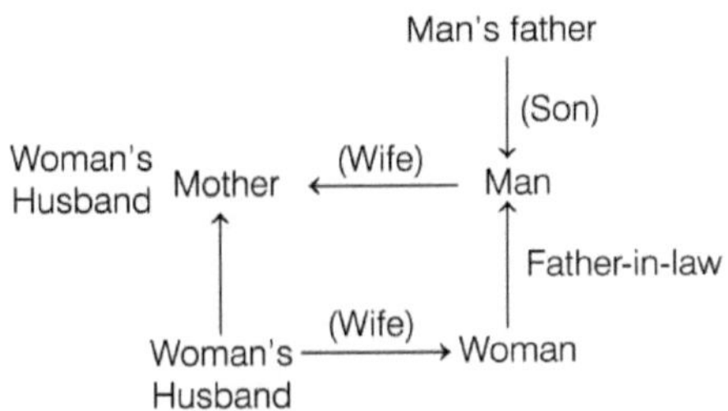

Hence, the man is the father-in-law of the woman.

Sol. (Q. Nos. 68-72) *According to the given statements the relationship can be shown as,*

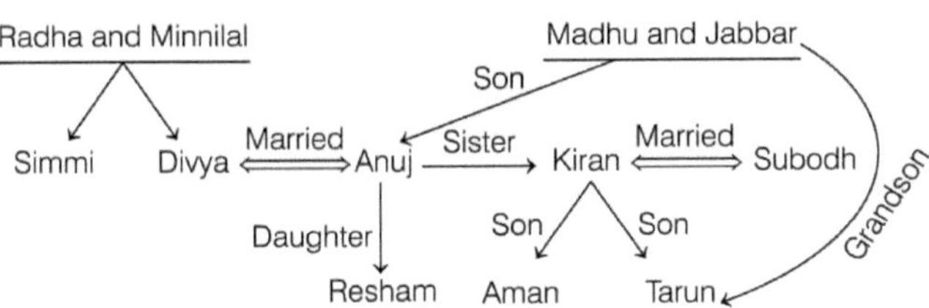

68. (*d*) From the above relationship chart, Aman and Resham are children of sister Kiran and brother Anuj respectively. Hence, Aman and Resham are cousins.

69. (*a*) According to above relationship chart, Subodh is husband of Kiran who is the daughter of Madhu and Jabbar. So, husband of Jabbar's daughter will be Jabbar's son-in-law.

70. (*a*) According to the above relationship chart, Resham is the daughter of Divya and Anuj while Kiran is sister of Anuj and aunt of Resham. Hence, Resham is niece of Kiran.

71. (*c*) Divya is the wife of Anuj and Kiran is sister of Anuj. As, brother's wife is sister-in-law. So, Kiran is sister-in-law of Divya.

72. (*b*) Kiran is the daughter of Madhu and wife of Subodh. So, Madhu is the mother-in-law of Subodh.

73. (*a*) According to the question,

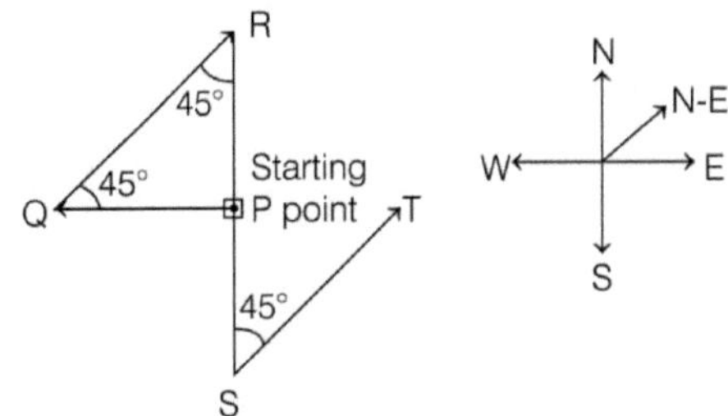

Hence, at the final point T, Raj is facing in the North-East direction.

74. (*d*) According to the question,

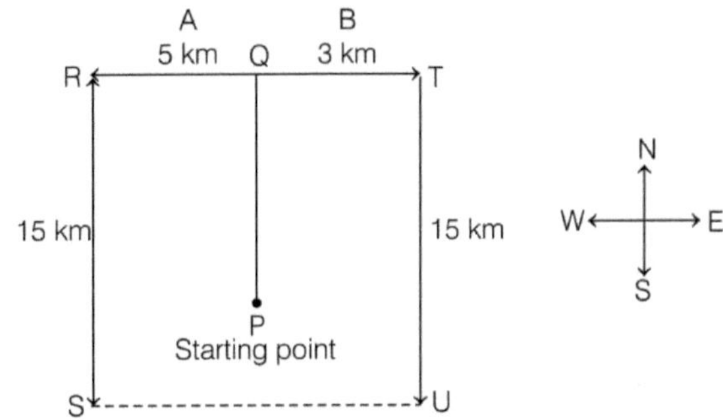

∴ Required distance = SU = RT = RQ + QT
$$= 5 + 3$$
$$= 8 \text{ km}$$

75. (*d*) xx<u>y</u>zz/x<u>x</u>yzz/<u>x</u>xyz<u>z</u> ⇒ yxxz

76. (*d*) Pattern of the series is as follows,

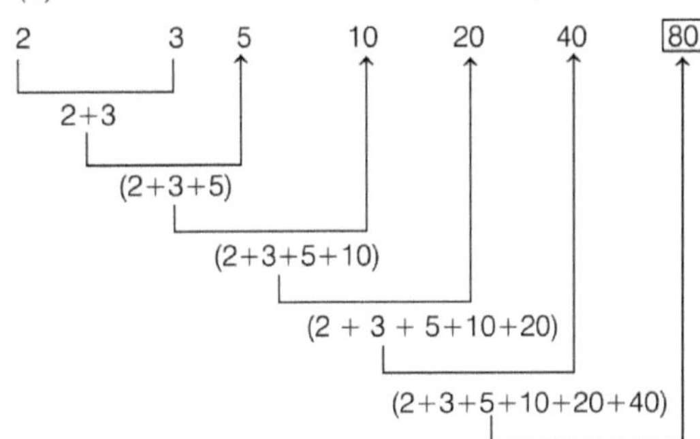

77. (*a*) Except Pond, all others are running form of water.

78. (*a*) Except FEUV, in all other opposite letter of first letter at fourth place and opposite letter of second letter at third place.

79. (*b*) Except in option (b), in all other numbers, the sum of numbers at first place and the fourth place is equal to the number at second and third place.

80. (*a*) After numbering and then adding the parts, the figure obtained is as shown below,

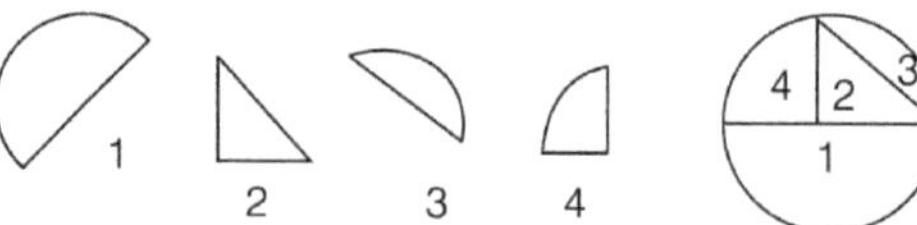

Hence, the figure given in option (a) can be made out of the given paper cut outs.

81. (*d*) After numbering and adding the parts the figure obtained is as shown below.

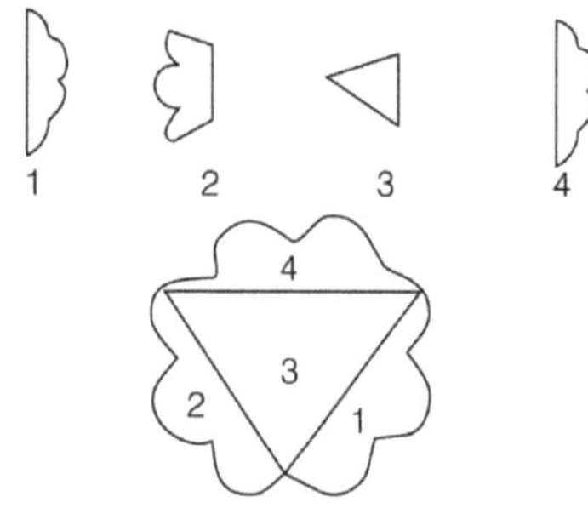

Hence, the figure in option (d) can be made out of the given paper cut outs.

82. (*d*) When the transparent sheet is folded at the dotted line it will form the pattern of star in the right direction as shown in figure of option (d).

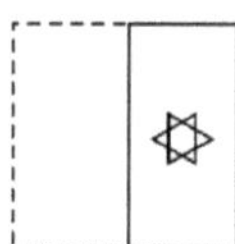

83. (*d*) According to the statements,

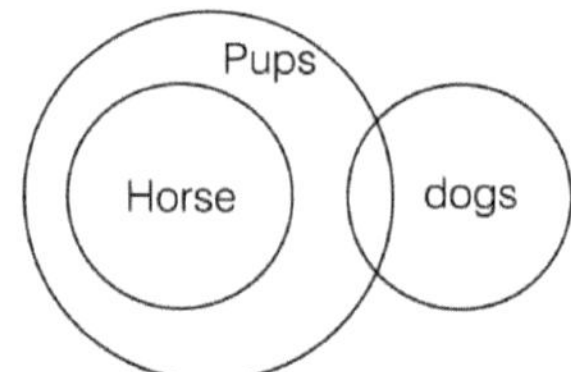

Conclusions I. (✗)   II. (✗)

84. (*b*) According to the statements,

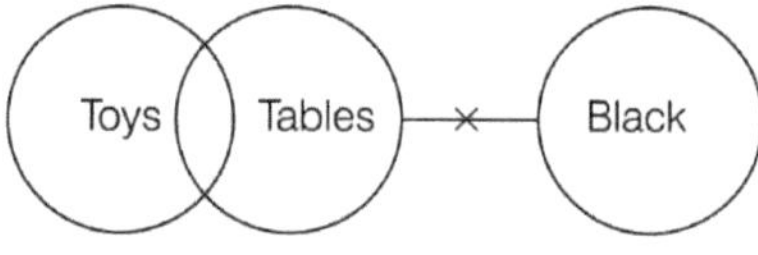

Conclusions I. (✗)   II. (✓)

85. (*c*) Here, the places of two consecutive letters in the word are interchanged to form the coded word.

As,

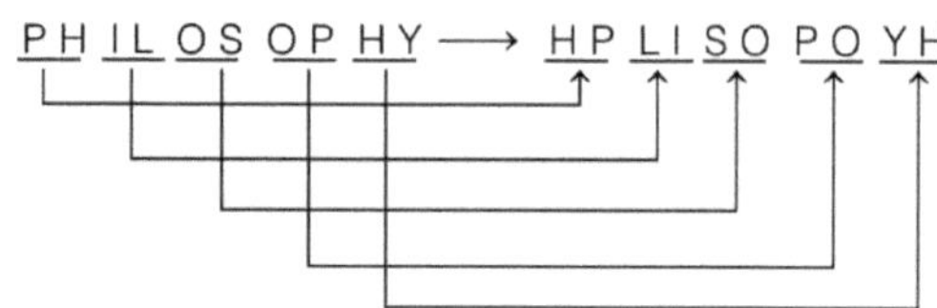

Similarly,

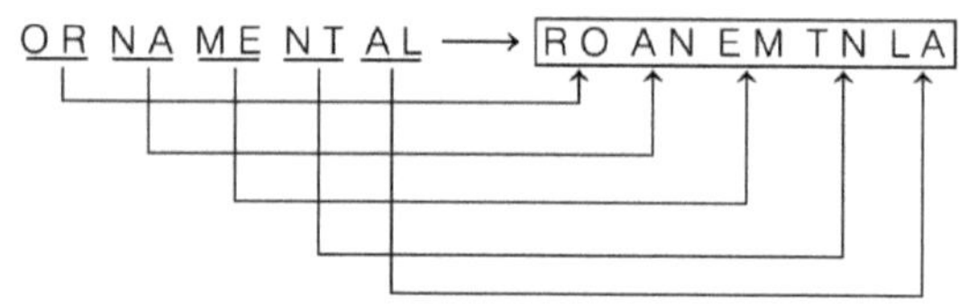

Hence, ORNAMENTAL is coded as ROANEMTNLA

86. (*c*) According to the question,

Gor Paku → Best Gift
Mull Gor Sot → Gift of Love
Kot Mull Paku → Best of Luck
Hed Sot Paku → Love is best

Clearly, code for Love → Sot

87. (*c*) According to the given coding pattern,

The code for XTD MSW is given as

∴ XTDMSW → 170964

Sol (Q. Nos. 88-90) According to the question,

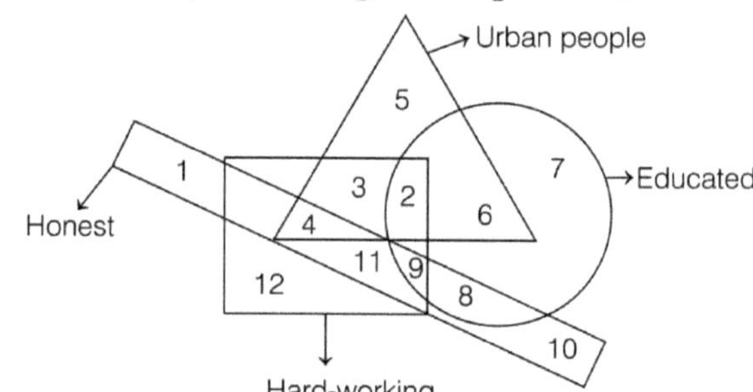

88. (*d*) Number '9' represent the non-urban people, who are honest, educated and hard-working.

89. (*b*) From the given diagram, the people who are educated, hard-working and urban people are indicated by 2.

90. (*c*) From the given diagram, the urban people who are hard-working and uneducated but not honest are indicated by 3.

91 (*a*) Let the speed of boat in still water be x km/h and the speed of the stream be y km/h.

Then, downstream speed = $(x + y)$ km/h
and upstream speed = $(x - y)$ km/h

∴ According to the question,

$$x + y = \frac{30}{3} = 10 \qquad \ldots(i)$$

and $$x - y = \frac{18}{3} = 6 \qquad \ldots(ii)$$

$$\left[\because \text{Speed} = \frac{\text{Distance}}{\text{Time}} \right]$$

From Eqs. (i) and (ii), we get
$$x = \frac{10 + 6}{2} = 8$$
and
$$y = \frac{10 - 6}{2} = 2$$

Hence, the speed of boat in still water = 8 km/h

92. (a) We know that, average speed $= \dfrac{2xy}{x + y}$

Here, $x = 10$ km/h and $y = 15$ km/h

$\therefore$ Average rate of the journey $= \dfrac{2 \times 10 \times 15}{10 + 15}$

$$= \frac{300}{25} = 12 \text{ km/h}$$

93. (b) According to the question,

Time taken to cover 120 m $= \dfrac{120}{80}$

$$\left[\because \text{Time} = \frac{\text{Distance}}{\text{Speed}} \right]$$

$$= \frac{3}{2} = 1.5 \text{ h}$$

Time taken to cover $(160 - 120)$ km i.e. 40 km

$$= \frac{40}{40} = 1 \text{ h}$$

$\therefore$ Average speed of the train $= \dfrac{\text{Total distance}}{\text{Total time}}$

$$= \frac{160}{1.5 + 1} = \frac{160}{2.5}$$

$$= 64 \text{ km/h}$$

94. (d) Given, SP = ₹ 1056, Loss = 12%

According to the formula,

$$CP = \frac{100}{(100 - \text{Loss}\%)} \times SP$$

$$\Rightarrow \quad CP = \frac{100}{(100 - 12)} \times 1056$$

$$= ₹ \left(\frac{100}{88} \times 1056 \right) = ₹ 1200$$

$\therefore$ The cost price of the watch = ₹ 1200

95. (c) Given, SP = ₹ 9499, Gain = 15%

According to the formula,

$$CP = \left(\frac{100}{100 + \text{gain}\%} \right) \times SP$$

$$= \frac{100}{100 + 15} \times 9499$$

$$= \frac{100}{115} \times 9499 = ₹ 8260$$

96. (a) Let the total sum of money be ₹ x.

According to the question,

$$\frac{35}{100} \times x + \frac{25}{100} \times x + \left[x - \left(\frac{35}{100}x + \frac{25}{100}x \right) \right] \times \frac{50}{100}$$
$$+ 2000 = x$$

$$\Rightarrow 0.35x + 0.25x + 0.4x \times 0.5 + 2000 = x$$

$$\Rightarrow \qquad 0.8x + 2000 = x$$

$$\Rightarrow \qquad 0.2x = 2000$$

$$\therefore \qquad x = 10000$$

$\therefore$ The total sum of money = ₹10000

97. (d) As winning candidate got 65%.

Then, losing candidate got $= (100 - 65)\% = 35\%$

Difference in votes percentage $= 65\% - 35\%$
$$= 30\%$$

When the difference is 30% then, the number of votes = 3645

When the difference is 100% then, the number of votes $= \dfrac{3645 \times 100}{30} = 12150$

Hence, the total number of votes polled = 12150.

98. (b) Given, total quantity of mixture = 60 L

Then, the quantity of ethanol $= \dfrac{4}{4 + 1} \times 60 = \dfrac{4}{5} \times 60$
$$= 48 \text{ L}$$

The quantity of ether $= \dfrac{1}{4 + 1} \times 60 = \dfrac{1}{5} \times 60 = 12$ L

Let the quantity of ether to be added be x L.

Then, according to the question,

$$\frac{48}{12 + x} = \frac{2}{1}$$

$$\Rightarrow \qquad 48 \times 1 = 2(12 + x)$$

$$\Rightarrow \qquad x = \frac{48 - 24}{2} = \frac{24}{2} = 12 \text{ L}$$

$\therefore$ The quantity of ether to be added = 12 L

99. (b) According to the rule of alligation,

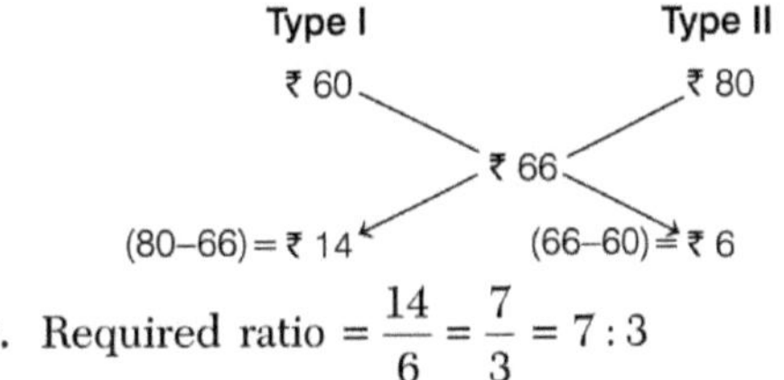

$\therefore$ Required ratio $= \dfrac{14}{6} = \dfrac{7}{3} = 7 : 3$

100. (a) Let the age of son be x yr.

Then, the age of father $= (56 - x)$ yr

According to the question,

$$(56 - x) + 4 = 3(x + 4)$$

$$\Rightarrow \qquad 60 - x = 3x + 12$$

$$\Rightarrow \qquad 4x = 48 \Rightarrow x = 12$$

Hence, the age of son = 12 yr

and the age of father $= (56 - 12) = 44$ yr

101. (c) Let the present age of B be x yr.

Then, the present age of $A = (x + 9)$ yr

According to the question,

$$(x + 9 + 10) = 2(x - 10)$$

$$\Rightarrow \qquad x + 19 = 2x - 20$$

$$\therefore \qquad x = 19 + 20 = 39 \text{ yr}$$

Hence, the present age of B = 39 yr.

102. (*b*) Let the present age of father = x yr

and the present age of son = $(45 - x)$ yr

According to the question,

$$(x - 5)(45 - x - 5) = 4 \times (x - 5)$$
$$\Rightarrow \quad (x - 5)(40 - x) = 4x - 20$$
$$\Rightarrow \quad 40x - x^2 - 200 + 5x = 4x - 20$$
$$\Rightarrow \quad -x^2 + 36x + 5x - 180 = 0$$
$$\Rightarrow \quad (x - 36)(x - 5) = 0$$
$$\therefore \quad x = 36 \text{ or } 5$$

$\therefore$ Father's age = 36 yr

and son's age = 45 − 36

$\qquad = 9$ yr

103. (*b*) Let the edge of the cube be a m.

We know that, surface area of the cube = $6a^2$

$$\Rightarrow \quad 6a^2 = 726$$
$$\Rightarrow \quad a^2 = \frac{726}{6} = 121$$
$$\therefore \quad a = 11 \text{ m}$$
$$\therefore \quad \text{Volume of the cube} = (a)^3$$
$$= (11)^3$$
$$= 1331 \text{ m}^3$$

104. (*d*) We know that,

length of diagonal = $\sqrt{l^2 + b^2 + h^2}$

Here, $l = 30$ cm

$\qquad b = 24$ cm and

$\qquad h = 18$ cm

$\therefore$ The length of the diagonal

$$= \sqrt{(30)^2 + (24)^2 + (18)^2}$$
$$= \sqrt{900 + 576 + 324}$$
$$= \sqrt{1800}$$
$$= 30\sqrt{2} \text{ cm}$$

105. (*b*) Let the radius of the sphere be x cm.

According to the question,

Volume of cone = Volume of sphere

$$\Rightarrow \quad \frac{1}{3} \times \pi \times (2.1)^2 \times 8.4 = \frac{4}{3} \times \pi \times x^3$$
$$\Rightarrow \quad (2.1)^2 \times 8.4 = 4 \times x^3$$
$$\Rightarrow \quad x^3 = (2.1)^3$$
$$\therefore \quad x = 2.1 \text{ cm}$$

$\therefore$ The radius of the sphere = 2.1 cm

196. (*c*) According to the question,

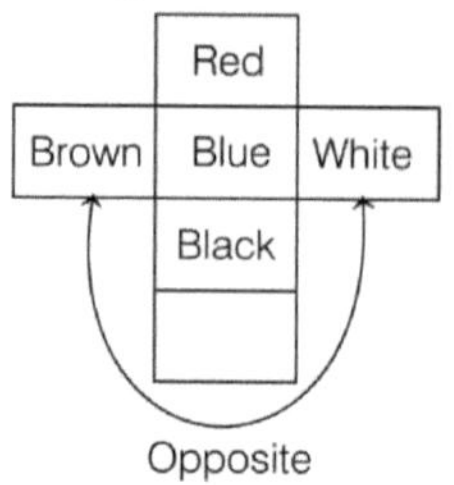

Hence, white be the opposite to brown.

197. (*b*) Let the total number of villagers = $100x$

Then, the number of villagers who have their own

houses = $100x \times \dfrac{1}{2} = 50x$

The number of villagers who cultivate paddy

$$= 100x \times \frac{1}{5} = 20x$$

The number of villagers who are literate

$$= 100x \times \frac{1}{3} = 33.33x$$

The number of villagers who are below 25

$$= 100x \times \frac{4}{5} = 80x$$

So, option (b) is correct because the number of villagers under twenty five are $80x$ and number of literate are $33.33x$.

198. (*b*) According to given information,

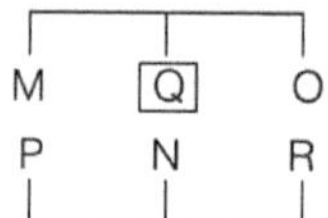

Hence, Q is facing N.

199. (*c*) According to the question,

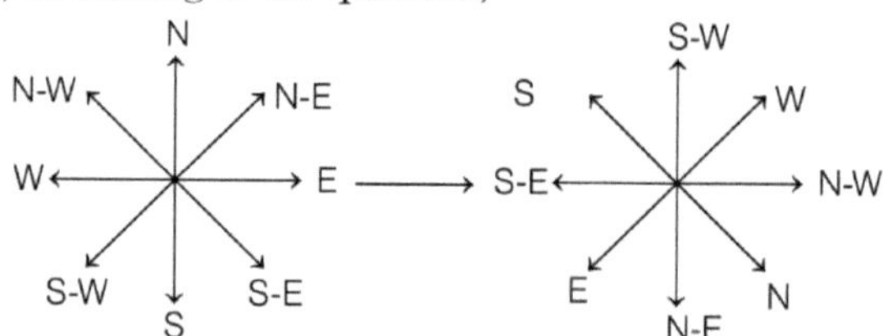

Hence, South becomes North-East.

200. (*c*) According to the given information,

Hence, B and F are standing on the extremes.

Solved Paper 2012

Instructions

- There are Five (A–E) Sections in this Solved Paper.
- For every correct attempt, the student will be awarded **1 mark**.
- All the questions are in MCQs form and each have four options.

Marks : 200
Time : 3 hrs

Section A : Numerical Ability and Scientific Aptitude

1. 70% of a number is equal to four-fifth of another number. If the difference between the two numbers is 100, what is the bigger number?
(a) 700 (b) 750
(c) 800 (d) None of these

2. Two cars A and B are running in the same direction. Car 'A' had already covered a distance of 60 km, when car 'B' started running. The cars meet each other in 3 h, after car 'B' started running. What was the speed of car 'A'?
(a) 40 km/h (b) 60 km/h
(c) 45 km/h (d) Cannot be determined

3. What quantity of water should be added to 3 L of 10% solution of salt, so that it becomes a 5% salt solution?
(a) 1.5 L (b) 2.7 L
(c) 3 L (d) None of these

4. A right circular cylindrical tank has the storage capacity of 38808 mL. If the radius of the base of the cylinder is three-fourth of the height, what is the diameter of the base?
(a) 28 cm (b) 56 cm
(c) 21 cm (d) 42 cm

5. A boat covers a distance of 30 km downstream in 2 h while it takes 6 h to cover the same distance upstream. If the speed of stream is half of the speed of the boat, then what is the speed of boat in km per hours?
(a) 15 km/h (b) 5 km/h
(c) 10 km/h (d) None of these

6. The ratio between the school ages of Neeta and Samir is 5 : 6 respectively. If the ratio between the one-third age of Neeta and half of the Samir's age is 5 : 9, then what is the school age of Samir?
(a) 30 yr
(b) 25 yr
(c) 36 yr
(d) Cannot be determined

7. The area of a rectangular field is $460\ m^2$. If the length is 15 per cent more than the breadth, what is breadth of the rectangular field?
(a) 15 m
(b) 26 m
(c) 34.5 m
(d) None of the above

8. A shopkeeper offered a discount of 15% on the labelled price. By selling an article for ₹ 340 after giving discount he earned a profit of $13\frac{1}{3}\%$. What would have been the per cent profit earned if no discount was offered?

(a) $28\frac{1}{3}$ (b) $30\frac{1}{3}$ (c) 27 (d) $33\frac{1}{3}$

9. Capacity of a cylindrical vessel is 25.872 L. If the height of the cylinder is three times the radius of its base, what is the area of the base in square cm?

(a) 336 (b) 1232
(c) 616 (d) None of these

10. Mr. Ramesh spends 25% of his monthly salary on household expenditure, 20% of the remaining on children's education and the remaining is equally invested in three different schemes. If the amount invested in each scheme is ₹ 5600, what was the monthly salary of Mr. Ramesh?

(a) ₹ 28000 (b) ₹ 21000
(c) ₹ 24000 (d) None of these

11. The profit earned after selling an article for ₹ 625 is the same as loss incurred after selling the article for ₹ 435. What is the cost price of the article?

(a) ₹ 530 (b) ₹ 520 (c) ₹ 540 (d) ₹ 550

12. A car covers the first 35 km of its journey in 45 min and covers the remaining 69 km in 75 min. What is the average speed of the car?

(a) 42 km/h (b) 50 km/h
(c) 52 km/h (d) 60 km/h

13. The ages of Samir and Tanuj are in the ratio of 8 : 15 respectively. After 9 yr, the ratio of their ages will be 11 : 18. What is the difference in years between their ages?

(a) 24 yr (b) 20 yr (c) 33 yr (d) 21 yr

14. The present ages of Vishal and Shekhar are in the ratio of 14 : 17 respectively. Six years from now, their ages will be in the ratio of 17 : 20 respectively. What is Shekhar's present age?

(a) 17 yr (b) 51 yr (c) 34 yr (d) 28 yr

15. A cask full of wine from which 8 L are drawn and is then filled with water. This operation is performed three more times. The ratio of quantity of wine left in the cask to that of the water is 16 : 65. How much wine did the cask hold originally?

(a) 42 L (b) 32 L
(c) 24 L (d) 18 L

16. Deficiency of iodine in diet leads to
(a) enlargement of hands and feet
(b) enlargement of liver
(c) enlargement of bones
(d) enlargement of neck region

17. Spinal cord is a part of
(a) CNS'
(b) SA node
(c) AV node
(d) Parasympathetic nervous system

18. Blood has no role in the transport of O_2 in
(a) earthworm (b) leech
(c) lung fishes (d) insects

19. Ozone Layer occurs in
(a) troposphere (b) ionosphere
(c) thermosphere (d) stratosphere

20. Which of the folowing is a renewable source of energy?
(a) Petroleum (b) Coal
(c) Natural gas (d) Trees

21. Chronometer is
(a) an instrument for comparing intensities of colours
(b) an instrument for changing or reversing the direction of electric current
(c) an instrument for measuring the direction and velocity of wind
(d) a clock for determining the longitude of a vessel at sea

22. The illumination of a surface is measured in the unit of
(a) Lux (b) Lumen
(c) Candela (d) Lux/m2

23. The kinetic energy of a particle continuously increases with time
(a) the resultant force on the particle must be at an angle less than 90° all the time
(b) the magnitude of its linear momentum is increasing continuously
(c) Both 'a' and 'b'
(d) Neither 'a' nor 'b'

24. Echo is the effect produced due to
(a) Refraction of sound
(b) Dispersion of sound
(c) Absorption of sound
(d) Reflection of sound

25. The photoelectric effect proves that
(a) velocity of light is infinite
(b) light is the form of quanta
(c) light travels in the form of transverse wave
(d) None of the above

26. Nitric acid does not react with
  (a) silver　　　　　　　　(b) gold
  (c) zinc　　　　　　　　　(d) None of these

27. Haemoglobin contains
  (a) iron　　　　　　　　　(b) aluminium
  (c) copper　　　　　　　　(d) None of these

28. Vitamin E is also called
  (a) tocopherol　　　　　　(b) riboflavin
  (c) ascorbic acid　　　　　(d) None of these

29. An ionic compound is made up of
  (a) atoms or groups of atoms carrying opposite electrical charges
  (b) electrically charged molecules
  (c) electrically charged atoms or groups
  (d) None of the above

30. A common metal used for the extraction of metals from their oxides by reduction is
  (a) copper　　　　　　　　(b) iron
  (c) aluminium　　　　　　(d) None of these

Section B : Reasoning and Logical Deduction

31. In a certain code JOINTLY is written as IPHOSMX. How is SERMON written in that code?
  (a) RFQNNO　　　　　　　(b) TFSNPO
  (c) TDQLNM　　　　　　　(d) RFQNMP

32. Three of the following four are alike in a certain way and so form a group. Which is the one that does not belong to that group?
  (a) 143　　　　　　　　　(b) 168
  (c) 224　　　　　　　　　(d) 37

Directions (Q. Nos. 33-35) *These questions are based on the following information.*

'P @ Q' means 'P is mother of Q'.
'P \$ Q' means 'P is husband of Q'.
'P # Q' means 'P is sister of Q'.
'P ★ Q' means 'P is son of Q'.

33. Which of the following indicates the relationship 'R is daughter of T'?
  (a) R#F★B@T　　　　　　(b) R#F★B\$T
  (c) T@B#R★F　　　　　　(d) T@B#F★R

34. M★H@D\$K, represents what relation of H with K?
  (a) Mother　　　　　　　　(b) Father
  (c) Father-in-law　　　　　(d) None of these

35. If F#J★T\$R@L, then which of the following is definitely true?
  (a) L is brother of F　　　　(b) F is sister of L
  (c) F is brother of J　　　　(d) L is brother of J

36. In a certain code '5 6 9' means 'nice little car', '8 3 5' means 'he is nice' and '9 3 7' means 'he has car', which of the following means 'has' in that code?
  (a) 3　　　　　　　　　　(b) 9
  (c) 7　　　　　　　　　　(d) 3 or 7

Directions (Q. Nos. 37 and 38) *In each questions below is given a statement followed by two assumptions is something supposed or taken for granted. You have to consider the statement and the following assumptions and decide which of the assumptions is implicit in the statements.*

Give answer
  (a) If only Assumption I is implicit
  (b) If only Assumption II is implicit
  (c) If either I or II is implicit
  (d) If neither I nor II is implicit

37. **Statements**　Ship was overturned.
　　　　　　　　　Captain was not traced.
  Conclusions
　I. Captain died in the accident.
　II. Captain is alive.

38. **Statements**　Some dedicated souls are angels.
　　　　　　　　　All social workers are angels.
  Conclusions
　I. Some dedicated souls are social workers.
　II. Some social workers are dedicated souls.

39. Three of the following four are alike in a certain way and so form a group. Which is the one that does not belong to that group?
  (a) Anxiety　　　　　　　(b) Worry
  (c) Inhibition　　　　　　(d) Curiosity

40. A and B standing at a distance of 20 km from each other on a straight East-West road. A and B start walking simultaneously, Eastwards and Westwards respectively, and both cover a distance of 5 km. Then A turns to his left and walks 10 km. 'B' turns to his right and walks 10 km at the same speed. Then both turn to their left and cover a distance of 5 km at the same speed. What will be the distance between them?
  (a) 10 km　　　　　　　　(b) 5 km
  (c) 20 km　　　　　　　　(d) 25 km

Directions (Q. Nos. 41-43) *Study the following information carefully to answer these questions.*

'A $ B' means 'A is wife of B'.

'A # B' means 'A is son of B'.

'A % B' means 'A is father of B'.

'A * B' means 'A is sister of B'.

41. Which of the following expressions represents the relationship 'T is brother of H'?
(a) H*T%K
(b) T*H%K
(c) H#K%T
(d) H*K%T

42. In H* T#F%L, how is H related to L?
(a) Cousin
(b) Brother
(c) Sister
(d) Cannot be determined

43. Which of the following expressions represent the relationship 'R is mother of J'?
(a) M*J#K$R
(b) M*J#R$K
(c) J#R#T
(d) R$K%M$J

44. In a certain code language EMPHASIS is written as NDIOBRJR. How will CREATURE be written in that code language?
(a) SBBDUTSD
(b) QBBDTUSD
(c) DSDBSTSF
(d) SBDBUTDS

Directions (Q. Nos. 45-47) *In the figure given below, there are three intersecting circles each representing certain section of people. Different regions are marked a to g. Read the statements in each of the following questions and choose the letter of the region which correctly represent the statements?*

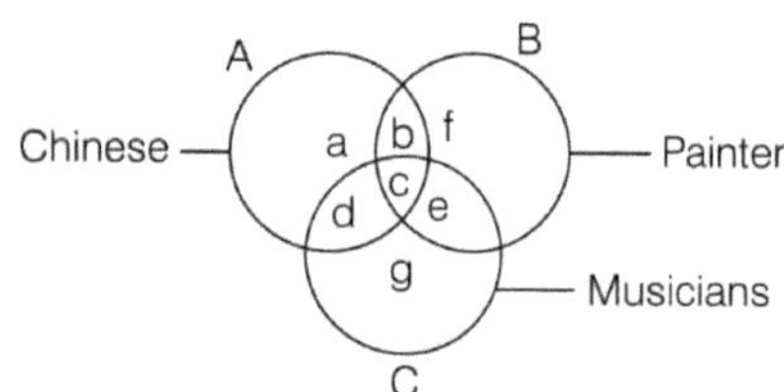

45. Chinese who are painters but not musicians.
(a) b
(b) c
(c) d
(d) g

46. Chinese who are musicians but not painters.
(a) d
(b) c
(c) b
(d) a

47. Painters who are neither chinese nor musicians.
(a) b
(b) c
(c) f
(d) g

Directions (Q. Nos. 48-50) *These questions are based on the following information. Study it carefully and answer the questions.*

(i) 'A × B' means 'A is father of B'.

(ii) 'A ÷ B' means 'A is daughter of B'.

(iii) 'A + B' means 'A is sister of B'.

(iv) 'A − B' means 'A is husband of B'.

48. In F ÷ R × H − L, how is H related to F?
(a) Father
(b) Brother
(c) Sister
(d) None of these

49. Which of the following indicates, 'N is mother of K'?
(a) K + L ÷ N × F
(b) K + L ÷ N − M
(c) H × L ÷ N
(d) N × F + K

50. In F − R + H ÷ T, how is F related to T?
(a) Son-in-law
(b) Daughter-in-law
(c) Son
(d) Daughter

51. Three of the following four are alike in a certain way and so form a group. Which is the one that does not belong to that group?
(a) Food : Hunger
(b) Water : Thirst
(c) Air : Suffocation
(d) Talent : Education

Direction (Q. No. 52) *In the number series given below only one is wrong. Find out that wrong number.*

52. 9 12 30 102 288 570 568
(a) 570
(b) 288
(c) 12
(d) 102

53. Arzan started walking towards East. He walked a distance of 5 km and then turned to his right and walked 10 km. He again turned to his right and walked another 15 km. Then he turned to his left and walked 5 km. In which direction is he in relation to his starting point?
(a) South
(b) South-East
(c) North-West
(d) South-West

54. Which of the following groups of letters should come in the place of the question mark (?) in the series formed by letter-groups of English alphabet given below?

AZB CYD EXF ? IVJ
(a) GUH
(b) GHU
(c) GWH
(d) GHW

Directions (Q. Nos. 55-57) *Read the following information carefully and answer the questions that follow.*
'A + B' means A is the father of B, 'A − B' means A is the wife of B, 'A × B' means A is the brother of B, 'A ÷ B' means A is the daughter of B.

55. If P − R × Q, which of the following is true?
(a) P is the sister of Q.
(b) Q is the husband of P.
(c) P is the sister-in-law of Q.
(d) Q is the son of P.

56. If P × R + Q, which of the following is true?
(a) P is the uncle of Q.
(b) P is the father of Q.
(c) P is brother-in-law of Q.
(d) P is grandfather of Q.

57. If P ÷ R + Q, which of the following is true?
(a) P is the father of Q
(b) P is the brother of Q
(c) P is the mother of Q
(d) P is the sister of Q

Directions (Q. Nos. 58-60) *In each of the questions given below which one of the four answer figures given below should come after the problem figures if the sequence were continued?*

58. Problem Figures

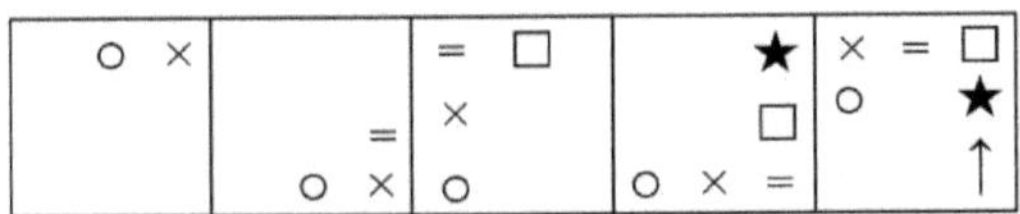

Answer Figures

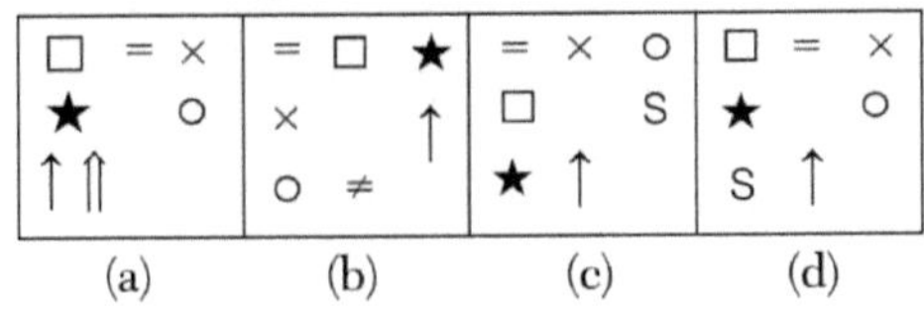

(a)   (b)   (c)   (d)

59. Problem Figures

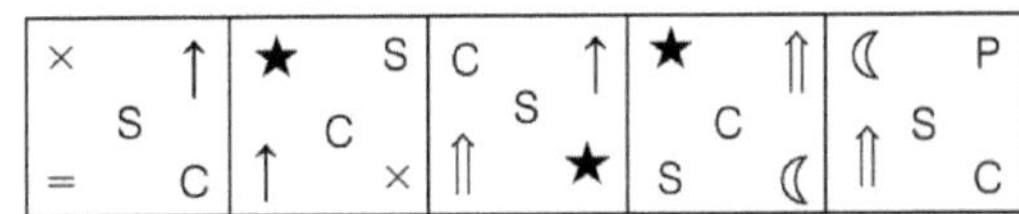

Answer Figures

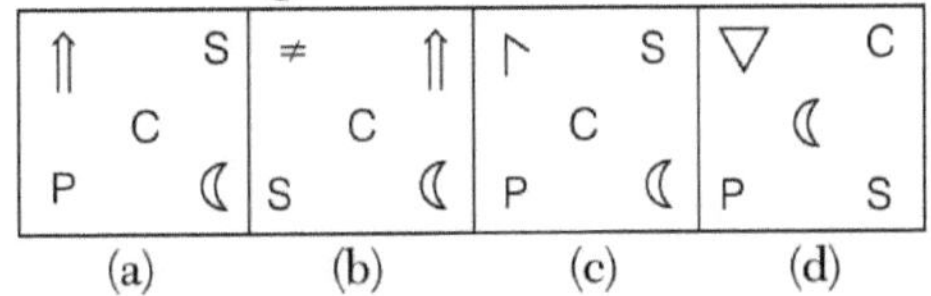

(a)   (b)   (c)   (d)

60. Problem Figures

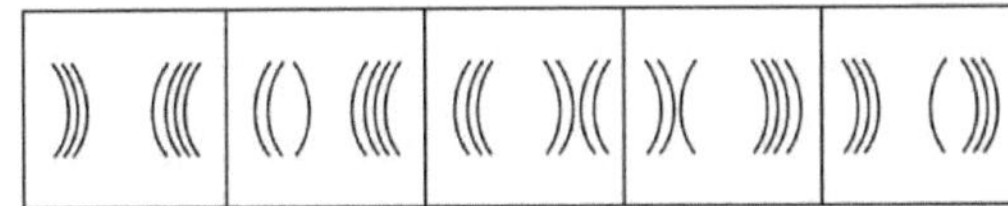

Answer Figures

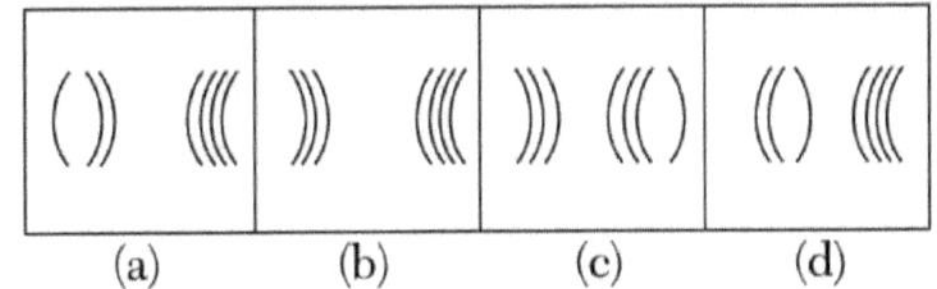

(a)   (b)   (c)   (d)

Section C : General Awareness and Current Affairs

61. Dhoni has been appointed brand ambassador of cricket in ....
(a) Bangladesh   (b) Nepal
(c) Iran   (d) China

62. The Camp David Declaration is associated with ....
(a) G-8 Summit   (b) G-20 Summit
(c) NATO Summit   (d) None of these

63. The Rajya Sabha is a
(a) permanent body
(b) temporary body
(c) House headed by the Prime Minister
(d) House having no Speaker

64. Who is Union Minister of Tourism of India ?
(a) Renuka Chaudhary
(b) Ambika Soni
(c) Subhodh Kant Sahai
(d) Praful Patel

65. Music Maestro A.R. Rahman has been conferred with his first American honorary doctorate by the
(a) Miami University   (b) Chicago University
(c) New York University   (d) None of these

66. What was global rank of India in international tourism in 2010 ?
(a) 35   (b) 40
(c) 45   (d) 50

67. Name the woman who has made history by becoming the oldest woman to scale the World's highest mountain , Mount Everest on 19th May, 2012.
(a) Sobha Ahotkar   (b) Tamae Watanabe
(c) Julia Robbinson   (d) None of these

68. The Konark temple in Orissa is dedicated to
(a) Lord Indra   (b) Lord Rama
(c) The Sun God   (d) None of these

69. The President of India is not a member of Parliament because
(a) he has to maintain his dignity of office
(b) he has to see that he remains impartial
(c) it is a constitutional requirement
(d) his position will be lowered if he becomes the member of Parliament

70. Who has been selected as the Chef-demission for the Olympics to head the Indian contingent at the London Games ?
(a) Ajit Pal Singh
(b) Gagan Narang
(c) Rajeev Shukla
(d) Surendra Singh

71. How can the Indian citizenship be terminated ?
(a) By renunciation   (b) By termination
(c) By deprivation   (d) All of these

72. Motels are
(a) the hotels on the highways
(b) the parking place for motors
(c) the hotels in the inner part of the city
(d) the hotel in the periphery of the city

73. Which is the most expensive city in the world , according to the Worldwide Cost of Living Survey - 2012 ?
(a) Mexico City   (b) Tokyo
(c) Luanda   (d) Osaka

74. Article 17 of the Constitution of India lays down for the
(a) abolition of untouchability
(b) election of the Vice-President
(c) election of the Speaker of the House of the People
(d) removal of poverty

75. Which of the following is not a fast - food chain?
(a) Mac Donald   (b) Barista
(c) Pizza Hut   (d) Dunkin Donuts

76. Which of the following property is not associated with ITc Group of Hotels?
(a) Maratha   (b) Gardenia
(c) Sonar   (d) Chunar

77. FHRAI stands for
(a) Forum of Hotels and Restaurants Association of India
(b) Federation of Hotels and Restaurants Association of India
(c) Forum of Hotels and Restaurants Association of India
(d) Federation of Hotels and Restaurants Association of India

78. Which of the following nuclear - powered submarines was inducted into the Indian Navy on 3rd April ?
(a) INS Vikrant   (b) INS Chakra
(c) INS Vikramaditya   (d) None of these

79. Where is the world's highest Tunnel-to-Tunnel bridge located ?
(a) In India   (b) In Japan
(c) In China   (d) In USA

80. Famous Leaning Tower of Pisa is in
(a) Italy   (b) Greece
(c) Cyprus   (d) Turkey

81. TFCI stands for
(a) Tourism and Food Corporation of India
(b) Travel and Food Corporation of India
(c) Tourism Finance Corporation of India
(d) Travel Finance Corporation of India

82. Which of the following places is not associated with Jainism?
(a) Mount Abu   (b) Ranakpur
(c) Shravanbelgola   (d) Lumbini

83. Name the Indian tribe which is still living on trees ?
(a) Jenu Kuruba   (b) Khasi
(c) Paharia   (d) Oangs

84. Which among the following hotel chains is not the international chain?
(a) The Grand International
(b) Best Western Group
(c) Oberoi
(d) Le Meridien

85. Which of the following is not the hotel department?
(a) House Keeping
(b) Front Office
(c) Food Processing
(d) Food and Beverages services

86. Which one of the following has the sole authority to control the expenditure of the Union Government ?
(a) The Comptroller and Auditor General
(b) The Prime Minister
(c) The Parliament
(d) The National Development Council

87. Which of the following magazines does not belong to tourism?
(a) Lonely Planet   (b) Outlook Traveller
(c) Travel Plus   (d) The Times

88. Which of the following heritage hotels does not belong to Rajasthan?
(a) Hotel Rambhag
(b) Hotel Umaid Bhawan Palace
(c) Hotel Bhanwar Niwas
(d) Hotel Lalit Mahal

89. Amitabh Bachchan is the brand ambassador of tourism of which state ?
(a) Maharashtra   (b) Gujarat
(c) Madhya Pradesh   (d) Uttar Pradesh

90. "God's Own Country" is the tourism statement of which state?
(a) Uttarakhand   (b) Assam
(c) Kerala   (d) Jammu and Kashmir

Directions (Q. Nos. 91-106) *Read the following passages to answer to questions that follow .*

PASSAGE 1

A British survey found that 44 per cent of firms, which started to use robots met with initial failure and 22 per cent abandoned them altogether , mainly because of inadequate technological know how and skills at all plant levels .

Robotisation is by and large a viable proposition . The machines can work round the clock , raise output , protect quality and industrial competitiveness.

One robot can replace between two and five production workers , while providing cheaper labour . In the US car industry a man - hour costs around $ 23 but a robot - hour costs only $ 6.

Certain jobs , mostly simple or hazardous ones , are irretrievably lost to robotics. Thus, spotwelders , press operators , spray painters , cleaners , machine leaders , grinding and polishing machine operators are endangered species .

91. In the first paragraph, the writer says that in view of initial failure
(a) 50 per cent of the firms which started using robots abandoned them
(b) half of the 44 per cent of firms which started using robots stopped the practice
(c) 22 per cent of the total number of firms which had used robots abandoned their uses
(d) British companies stopped the use of robots

92. 'A viable proposition' is
(a) a workable idea   (b) a fanciful idea
(c) an imaginative idea   (d) an unworkable idea

93. Robots are a substitute for
(a) planners   (b) production workers
(c) motor - cars   (d) any kind of labour

94. In its context the expression 'endangered species' means that
(a) workers like spot welders are in danger
(b) robots might destroy the workers mentioned
(c) robots may replace the workers in future
(d) workers are diminishing in number and we may not get them after a few years

PASSAGE 2

The report that the Union Cabinet considered the draft of a bill to prohibit the denigration of women in photographs, advertisements and films, is welcome . There has been for some time growing criticism of the projection of women in these three media.

Advertisements in the print media , as well as in films and television, frequently rely on feminine sex appeal to attract attention to products or to suggest that these products make Casanovas of ordinary mortals.

Things are even worse in the films. Some of these unabashedly rely on sex for box office success, showing scantily attired women in provocative postures. In these, as well as in many advertisements, women clearly appear as objects of erotic stimulation.

By showing heroes misbehaving with heroines and getting away with it, films invite emulation in real life, result-in the molestation of women in public places .

95. The passage says that the bill to prohibit media exploitation of women
(a) has been made a law
(b) has been discussed in the Union Cabinet
(c) is being drafted
(d) is going to create a lot of controversy

96. Feminine sex appeal is used in advertisements to
(a) entertain the customers
(b) distract the customers' attention
(c) get the attention of prospective customers
(d) show how women at home would like the product

97. 'Unabashedly' means
(a) with great shyness
(b) openly
(c) indifferently
(d) with no sign of being ashamed

98. The last sentence of the passage underlines the
(a) healthy influence of films
(b) harmful effect of bad films
(c) fact that films have nothing to do with a society's morals
(d) need to teach morals through films

PASSAGE 3

A recent report in Newsweek says that in American colleges students of Asian origin outperform not only the minority group students but the majority whites as well . Many of these students might be of Indian origin, and their achievement is something we can be proud of. It is unlikely that these talented youngsters will come back to India, and that is the familiar brain drain problem. However, recent statements by the nation's policy makers indicate that the perception of this issue is changing. 'Brain bank' and not 'brain drain' is the more appropriate idea, they suggest, since the expertise of Indians abroad is only deposited in other places and not lost .

This may be so, but this brain bank , like most of other banks, is one that primarily serves customers in its neighbourhood. The skills of the Asian now excelling in America's colleges will mainly help the USA. No matter how significant, what Non-Resident Indians do for India and what their counterparts do for other Asian lands is only a byproduct.

But it is also necessary to ask or be reminded, why Indians study more fruitfully when abroad. The Asians whose accomplishments Newsweek records would have probably had a very different fate if they had studied in India. In America, they found elbow room, books and facilities not available and not likely to be available here. The need to prove themselves in their new country and the competition of an international standard they faced there must have cured mental and physical laziness. But other things helping them in America can be obtained here if we achieve a change in social attitudes, especially towards youth. We need to learn to value individuals and their unique qualities more than conformity and respectability. We need to learn the language of encouragement to add to our skill in flattery. We might also learn to be less liberal with blame and less tight-fisted with appreciation, especially to those showing signs of independence.

HM 2012

99. Among the many groups of students in American colleges, Asian students
(a) are often written about in magazines like Newsweek
(b) are the most successful academically
(c) have proved that they are as good as the whites
(d) have only a minority status like the blacks

100. The students of Asian origin in America include
(a) a fair number from India
(b) a small group from India
(c) persons from India who are very proud
(d) Indians who are the most hardworking of all

101. In general, the talented young Indians studying in America
(a) have a reputation for being hardworking
(b) have the opportunity to contribute to India's development
(c) can solve the brain drain problem because of recent changes in policy
(d) will not return to pursue their careers in India

102. There is talk now of the 'brain bank'. This idea
(a) is a solution to be brain drain problem
(b) is a new problem caused partly by the brain drain
(c) is a new way of looking at the role of qualified Indians living abroad
(d) is based on a plan to utilise foreign exchange remittances to stimulate research and development

PASSAGE 4

A close look at the facts relating to political interference in administration shows that it is not a one - way process . There is often a nexus between power hungry and corrupt politicians and civil servants with convenient principles . Many civil servants are only too anxious to oblige the politicians, and then cash the obligation when they need some special favour.

So the attitude of self righteousness adopted by the civil service is sometimes only a way of covering their own flaws by blaming others. Every now and then some retired civil servant comes out with his memoirs, painting a glorious picture of the heights of administrative efficiency reached during his reign. There is often the suggestion that had there not been so much political interference, things would have been even more fantastic. It is not unusual for the self - styled hero to blame not only interfering politicians but also fellow civil servants who were idiots or crooks, for his failures.

This attitude of smug self satisfaction is unfortunately, developed during the years of service. Self - preservation rather than service is encouraged by our whole system of rules and procedures .

The remedy has to be drastic and quickly effected. The over - protection now granted to civil servants must end. Today to remove an erring civil servant is just not possible. And the only thing that he highest authority in the Government , both in the State and at the Centre, can do is to transfer an official from one job to another. The rules for taking disciplinary action are so complicated that, in the end, the defaulting civil servant gets away, and gets his full emoluments even for the period of the disciplinary proceedings, thus making it a paid holiday for him.

The result is that the administration has become rule-oriented and not result-oriented. Action is possible against the official who takes some interest in his work , but no action is ever taken against a person who does not deliver the goods. If the country is to adopt a result - oriented approach, it is necessary to link job performance with job retention.

103. The facts relating to the problem of political interference indicate that
(a) honest bureaucrats are always being troubled by politicians
(b) politicians are often misled and trapped by civil servants
(c) politicians and civil servants cooperate to gain mutual advantages
(d) politician and civil servants use interference as an excuse for victimising the common man

104. The attitude of self-righteousness adopted by
the civil service, according to the writer
(a) is not welcomed and supported by politicians
(b) is dishonest and conceals the facts
(c) is very difficult to maintain because of opposition
(d) does not really help the public get fair treatment

105. Civil servants who write their memoirs after
retiring
(a) claim that they would have achieved outstanding
successes if interference had not come in the way
(b) prove that constant political interference made it
impossible for them to do anything properly
(c) complain that the credit for their achievement
goes to dishonest politicians
(d) prove that people of inferior quality in the civil
service bring about interference

106. The existing system of administration seems to
encourage civil servants
(a) to become self-styled heroes and boss over others
(b) to present a glorious picture of the administration
(c) to become self-centred and concerned mainly
about their own gain
(d) to become self-righteous and fight back against
corrupt politicians

Directions (Q. Nos. 107-111) *Choose the word which
is closest in meaning to the word given below in bold.*

107. Applaud
(a) Beg   (b) Blow   (c) Clap   (d) Fruit

108. Extend
(a) Distance   (b) Far
(c) Look after   (d) Stretch

109. Nebulous
(a) Subdued   (b) Eternal
(c) Dewy   (d) Cloudy

110. Filch
(a) Hide   (b) Swindle
(c) Drop   (d) Steal

111. Querulous
(a) Peculiar   (b) Fretful
(c) Inquistive   (d) Shivering

Directions (Q. Nos. 112-116) *Choose the word which
is most opposite in meaning to the word given below in
bold .*

112. Bare
(a) Attractive   (b) Clothed
(c) Drop   (d) Full

113. Deceit
(a) Honesty   (b) Natural
(c) Plainness   (d) Sincere

114. Forbid
(a) Agreement   (b) Allow
(c) Indeed   (d) Say later

115. Mild
(a) Command (b) Enemy (c) Evil   (d) Severe

116. Modest
(a) Annoyed   (b) Boastful
(c) Courageous   (d) Disliked

Directions (Q. Nos. 117-119) *Which of the phrases
(a), (b) and (c) given below should replace the bold
part in the given sentence to make it grammatically
correct? If the sentence is correct as it is given and no
correction is required mark (d) as your answer.*

117. He is too adamant to **be effectively** in his work.
(a) to become effectively
(b) to be effective
(c) to have been effectively
(d) No correction required

118. Because the competition is **going to become**
fierce, we may have some real struggles on the
horizon.
(a) is becoming fiercely   (b) is going to be fiercely
(c) has become fiercely   (d) No correction required

119. They lost the match because they **neglected by**
the coach's valuable advice .
(a) ignored   (b) were ignored by
(c) were neglected by   (d) No correction required

Directions (Q. Nos. 120-122) *Choose the word which
is correctly spelt.*

120. (a) Occasionally   (b) Acclematise
(c) Tempareture   (d) None of these

121. (a) Sedentery   (b) Aproached
(c) Incentive   (d) Blissfull

122. (a) Satellite   (b) Forefiet
(c) Psycology   (d) Accesible

Directions (Q. Nos. 123-126) *Choose the most
appropriate preposition to fill in the blanks .*

123. Modern science began ......the influence of
Copernicus, Kepler, Galileo and Newton.
(a) by   (b) under
(c) from   (d) upon

124. Can you pay ...... all these articles ?
(a) for   (b) of   (c) off   (d) out

125. The pilot of the aircraft accepted a gift .... the
passengers who were happy about his skill.
(a) form   (b) by   (c) to   (d) about

126. Can you please drop .... ? I want to discuss some important matter.
(a) for
(b) to
(c) on
(d) in

Directions (Q. Nos. 127-129) *In each question below, a sentence is given with three words or group of words, which are labelled as (a), (b) and (c). One of them may be grammatically or structurally wrong in the context of the sentence. If there is no wrong word or group of words, your answer will be (d), i.e. No error. (Ignore the errors of punctuation , if any)*

127. (a) The need to set-up a good library in the locality/(b) has been in the minds of people/(c) for sometimes now./(d) No error

128. (a) The interviewer asked me/(b) if I knew that/(c) Kalidas was the greater than any other poet./(d) No error.

129. (a) The invigilator asked him/(b) to me that the visits they made to the island/(c) were not very frequent./(d) No error .

Directions (Q. Nos. 130-132) *In each of the following questions, the first and the last parts of a sentence are numbered as 1 and 6. The rest of the sentence is split into four parts and labelled P, Q, R and S. These four parts are not given in their proper order. Read the sentence and find out which of the four combinations is correct.*

130. 1 : When the question again came up
P : the same question arose as to why
Q : that the terms should not be
R : at the time of President Truman
S : there should be an exception to this rule
6 : more than two.
(a) PQRS
(b) PQSR
(c) PRQS
(d) RPSQ

131. 1 : Thus , it was only after 1858 that
P : to an almost uniform set of precedents,
Q : virtually be codified into a set of rules
R : this relationship was subjected
S : conventions and usages which could
6 : and regulations.
(a) QSPR
(b) RQSP
(c) PRQS
(d) RPSQ

132. 1 : We have, therefore, to
P : and fashion our political, social and economic
Q : crushed him may be removed and he may
R : think in terms of the common man
S : structure so that the burdens that have

6 : have full opportunity for growth.
(a) PQRS
(b) QSPR
(c) PRQS
(d) RPSQ

Directions (Q. Nos. 133-136) *In each of the following questions an idiom or a phrase is given followed by four alternatives. Choose and mark the alternative that best brings out the meaning of the idiom or phrase.*

133. To cross one's mind
(a) to get confused
(b) to occur
(c) to create tension
(d) to tell a lie

134. An early bird
(a) one who catches worms
(b) a cock or hen
(c) a lucky person
(d) an early riser

135. Fret and fume
(a) shout loudly
(b) burn a large fire
(c) start a fight
(d) show angry impatience

136. To set forth
(a) to impress
(b) to express
(c) to follow
(d) to clear all doubts

Directions (Q. Nos. 137-141) *In the following questions, choose the word which best expresses the meaning of the given word .*

137. PONDER
(a) Think
(b) Evaluate
(c) Anticipate
(d) Increase

138. SHIVER
(a) Shake
(b) Rock
(c) Tremble
(d) Move

139. FEEBLE
(a) Weak
(b) Vain
(c) Arrogant
(d) Sick

140. PIOUS
(a) Pure
(b) Pretentious
(c) Clean
(d) Devout

141. CHASTE
(a) Honest
(b) Dignified
(c) Virtuous
(d) Noble

Directions (Q. Nos. 142-146) *In the following questions, choose the word which is the exact OPPOSITE of the given word.*

142. FLAGITOUS
(a) Innocent
(b) Vapid
(c) Ignorant
(d) Frivolous

143. ACQUITTED
(a) Freed
(b) Burdened
(c) Convicted
(d) Entrusted

144. FICKLE
    (a) Courageous   (b) Sincere
    (c) Steadfast   (d) Humble

145. NADIR
    (a) Modernity   (b) Zenith
    (c) Liberty   (d) Progress

146. HIRSUTE
    (a) Scaly   (b) Bald
    (c) Erudite   (d) Quiet

Directions (Q. Nos. 147-150) *Choose the appropriate meaning (s) of the following plural nouns printed in capital letters.*

147. COLOURS
    (a) Hues   (b) Flag
    (c) Skin   (d) Both (a) and (b)

148. EFFECTS
    (a) Reactions   (b) Results of an action
    (c) Belongings   (d) Both (b) and (c)

149. MANNERS
    (a) Behaviour   (b) Process
    (c) Style   (d) Both (a) and (b)

150. SPECTACLES
    (a) Audiences   (b) Crowd of people
    (c) Pictures   (d) None of these

Section E : Aptitude For Service Sector

Directions (Q. Nos. 151 to 200) *Pick the one response which best describes your behaviour or the way you behave most of the times.*

151. When you are invited to attend social gatherings, you
    (a) are reluctant to attend
    (b) are in a dilly - dally mood (i.e., to attend or not to attend)
    (c) happily accept such invitations
    (d) openly criticise such gatherings and meetings

152. You are away from your home and studying in another city. Due to an urgent piece of work , your father is not able to send you money in time . Then , you
    (a) fly into a range
    (b) try to understand his handicaps
    (c) enquire from him by making phone calls
    (d) arrange money from another source and carry on your work

153. Your view about ideals and morality is the following
    (a) ideals and morality are confined to the walls of the college / educational institute
    (b) ideals and morality are confined only to books
    (c) ideals and morality are confined only to the speeches of teachers
    (d) ideals and morality are being followed even today

154. When you start your work , then on which topic, you concentrate the most ?
    (a) The nature of and plan for the piece of work
    (b) The time period and expenses involved in the execution of the piece of work
    (c) The success of failure of the piece of work
    (d) All these aspects (a), (b) and (c)

155. If someone tries to obstruct your work time and again , you will
    (a) take these events seriously
    (b) take these events in your stride
    (c) try to stop him from obstructing / interfering in your affairs
    (d) ask him the reason for obstructing / interfering and give him a suitable reply

156. When you are not capable of taking a decision, then whose suggestion or advice you would like to take ?
    (a) Of your nearest relatives
    (b) Of your parents
    (c) Of your friends
    (d) Of all those mentioned earlier

157. You consider yourself to be an able candidate for the post of a General Manager because
    (a) your father is also a General Manager
    (b) your parents nurture the ambition that you should become a General Manager
    (c) you have completed a course in Hotel Management
    (d) your friends have forwarded this suggestion / opinion

158. Your friend has received high academic degrees. But still , he has not been able to get a job. You will
    (a) try to locate a job for him
    (b) tell him that he himself has some limitation , which needs amendment
    (c) tell him that due to wrong policies of the government , most of the people are unemployed despite having good degrees
    (d) tell him not to lose heart and keep on appearing in competitive examinations . He is likely to succeed in the long run

159. You want respect and reputation in the society. Then what would you consider the right action to be?
 (a) Develop friendly relationships with all the persons
 (b) Keep on interacting with all the respected persons
 (c) Develop strong relationship with antisocial people so that all the people give you respect and treat you as a reputed person
 (d) For sake of your personal selfish interests, work for the benefit of the masses

160. While making an action plan, many aspects or facets of the plan are overlooked on the pretext of the proverb, "shall be taken care of when the time comes." What is your opinion about this ignorance?
 (a) A pessimistic thought
 (b) An optimistic thought
 (c) The best thought
 (d) A foolish idea

161. Before doing any piece of work, its plan is to be made. In this context, your opinion is that
 (a) planning is wastage of time
 (b) planning is good use of time
 (c) planning for work is only a personal opinion
 (d) planning is an indicator of success

162. You are a rich person. Therefore, your expected behaviour towards the poor is that you will
 (a) respect poor as well
 (b) help the poor to the maximum possible extent
 (c) let poor children sit in the front rows in your class
 (d) motivate the poor to make progress

163. Now-a-days, the problem of unemployment is prevalent to a large extent among the educated people . In order to remove it, your opinion is that
 (a) education should be linked to employment
 (b) education should be increased in terms of level and spread
 (c) the age of retirement of employed individuals should be reduced
 (d) educated people should adopt the teaching profession

164. If your favourite player is found to be guilty of match - fixing , you will
 (a) like a ban to be imposed on his play
 (b) meet highly placed officials in order to save his neck
 (c) like strict punitive measures to be incorporated with respect to such blunders in the rules of the game
 (d) like him to be banned from playing for a period of five years

165. That is how you behave with other passengers in a train or bus.
 (a) You give seats to old women and men
 (b) You smile at those passengers (who are standing) from your heart but don't show this feeling
 (c) If someone does not give you a seat , you get engaged in a duel or fist fight
 (d) Talk with every person with humility and warmth

166. A friend of yours is always unhappy due to your behaviour. In order to develop warm relationship with him , you will
 (a) apologise to him for your wrong behaviour
 (b) talk to him according to the make-3up of his mind and psyche
 (c) try to enquire about your misbehaviour and bring necessary reforms in the context of the same
 (d) always behave with him in a decent manner

167. Quite often, you take interest in watching movies. Due to this habit , sometimes you put off important pieces of work. Some of your friends advise you not to watch movies. You
 (a) ignore their advice
 (b) ponder over their advice
 (c) persuade them to watch cinema along with you
 (d) try to give priority to your work in the first instance

168. Some of your friends chew paan or gutkha and throw the refuse here and there. You will
 (a) tell them to spit the refuse in the spitoon only
 (b) try to tell them that they should take care of the cleanliness aspects
 (c) clean that place, which has been made awesome by them
 (d) write on walls that spitting should not be resorted to at those walls

169. If a person thinks that crossing of the way by a cat or the act of sudden sneezing of someone is a sign of ill omen , you will
 (a) try to convince that person that this is only a blind faith
 (b) tell him not to go out
 (c) give a long lecture on the issue of blind faith
 (d) tell him about the losses that may be incurred due to blind faith

170. Your view about the success of a person is that
 (a) it is the result of his hard work and efforts
 (b) he must have carned this success through dishonest and evil deeds
 (c) he must be doing his work at the right time
 (d) he must be truthful

171. You are a team leader and two of your colleagues are having a strained relationship with each other. As a result they are not contributing well in group activities. How will you handle such a situation?
(a) You will give them complementary tasks in which both have to work together
(b) You will punish them for not contributing by keeping them out of the team
(c) You will make an explicit effort to help them shake hands
(d) How am I bothered with such petty issues? At least the task is being done by others' so it is fine !

172. If you find yourself in a situation where you are required to make a Powerpoint presentation and you are already bogged down by too much work, as the manager what would you do?
(a) Pass the buck to your subordinate, you are the boss, no one can question you
(b) Prioritise your work and try to squeeze out time for it
(c) Cancel the seminar and reschedule according to your convenience
(d) Take an alternative mode of presentation

173. As an ideal leader , how would you interact with your group?
(a) Give prompt, firm, clear instructions that other members will respect and follow
(b) Respect the employees opinions and attitudes
(c) Avoid using authority
(d) Work according to your own style and not respect the opinion of the other members

174. Suppose you are the manager and one of your subordinates is not working satisfactorily. How would you approach him?
(a) Send him an e-mail pointing out his performance
(b) Call him to your room and explain the situation
(c) Hold a meeting of all the group members and discuss what is to be done
(d) Give him an ultimatum to improve his performance or else he will get the pink slip

175. To understand how employees really feel about things, the supervisor should
(a) arrange for informal private interviews with each employee
(b) keep objective records of things that reflect their feelings like production, suggestions and complaints
(c) notice their reactions to the orders and the works given to them
(d) maintain a frank, informal, give and take relationship with them

176. An angry customer wants to meet the senior manager for grievance reporting. What will you do?
(a) Talk to him yourself
(b) Tell him it is not easy to meet the senior manager
(c) Be patient and try to cool him down
(d) Try to remove his inconveniences by consulting seniors

177. You have a language handicap. Customer has many problems.
(a) Words don't matter, feelings and do services do
(b) Look for better communicator
(c) Ask for transfer
(d) Manage to find problems and set them right

178. In public dealing jobs, one must be
(a) punctual   (b) polite and humble
(c) quick at taking decisions (d) a good listener

179. I would like to go up in life
(a) personal contacts are more important
(b) quality work makes one go up in life
(c) work and relations make one reach the high positions
(d) money power can achieve anything in life

180. Your classmate comes and tells you that your friends were talking ill of you. You
(a) go to them and talk it out
(b) ask him not to tell this to you
(c) don't bother about them
(d) say you already know about it

181. After talking to somebody for the first time, you
(a) take steps to find out how your behaviour was perceived
(b) don't take it all that seriously
(c) think about how the other person improves you
(d) pick up some hints and change the behaviour accordingly

182. It is necessary for every company to advertise its products because
(a) advertising is an effective way of boosting the sale of their products
(b) every big company advertises its products
(c) it provides employment to many models
(d) it is officially recommended by the company's financial department

183. You were invited to a party, but on the day of the party you are informed that the party has been cancelled. You will
(a) try to find out the reason for its cancellation
(b) decide that you will never go to that place ever again
(c) not discuss the matter with anyone
(d) hold the party at your place instead

184. A car running with high speed crushed a child and ran away from the place of accident with the same high speed. This all happened in front of a person who was passing by the place of accident. What should he do in such a case?
(a) He should inform the police as soon as possible
(b) He should note the number of the car
(c) He should go accompanied with the child to a clinic and make arrangement for his treatment
(d) He should try to run away from the place

185. It is the midnight when a person is passing by an utterly deserted place. Just at that place a few armed persons appear who ask him to cast off his wrist watch and gold chain. What should be do in such a moment?
(a) He should tell them that they are strangers for him and so he will not do so
(b) He should offer them his wrist watch and other valuables happily
(c) He should try to run away from scene
(d) He should instead scold them for such an immoral practice

186. Five persons have been produced as eye - witnesses to an accident but the person who has been charged with commiting the accident says that he can produce fifty persons against these five persons who will say that they have not seen him committing the accidents. The argument of the accused will not be accepted because
(a) we cannot believe on an accused
(b) a witness is needed who can prove the careless driving of the accused
(c) reality of the crime depends upon the authenticity of the witness not on the number of witnesses
(d) respondents always produce false witnesses

187. If an argument starts with someone, then I invariably
(a) listen to the viewpoint of that person carefully and then, speak what is in my mind
(b) state my view at the very outset
(c) start saying whatever comes to my mind
(d) become confused and perplexed

188. You have adorned a new shirt . Your companion passes a remark that your shirt is misfit for your personal. So , you will
(a) start scolding him in the presence of all others
(b) change the shirt immediately
(c) not change the shirt but singe from the heart of your hearts
(d) laugh away the remark , starting that it is your style

189. If I were the correspondent of a magazine, then I will write on the following subject
(a) Health
(b) Cinema and theatre
(c) Current politics
(d) None of these

190. If put under pressure, I give emphasis on giving myself more time so that I may be able to think more clearly.
(a) I get into a fix
(b) Yes
(c) No
(d) Sometimes

191. Whenever someone demands any thing from me, I
(a) return him empty-handed
(b) abuse him
(c) give something
(d) do not talk to him

192. A product launched by the company is having initial hiccups and complaints. You will
(a) try and convince the customers it is temporary
(b) warn the customers for initial hiccups
(c) convey about the working and positive aspects of the product
(d) tell your boss this product should be withdrawn to save the reputation

193. You are in a contest , which has elimination rounds. Eliminated contestants are sad and others too are becoming panicky. What do you do?
(a) You leave the contest thinking that you will lose
(b) You keep yourselves calm and contented and do not bother about the others
(c) You shout at the ones who are crying
(d) You try to calm down others

194. People who aspire to work in hotel industry should have the following personality trait (s)
(a) extremely hard - working and courteous
(b) helpful attitude
(c) knowledge of a foreign language
(d) All of the above

195. Your colleague is having problems at work
(a) you avoid discussing his/her problem but do so if he/she asks.
(b) you advice him/her but let him/her decide on his/her own
(c) you lend him/her support and help him/her in resolving the issue
(d) you try to stay out of his/her affairs

196. If you have some problem with your employee, you would
(a) complain against him to your colleagues
(b) get annoyed with the employer
(c) talk to him directly
(d) do nothing

197. Status in the society can be maintained by
(a) behaviour as desired by the society
(b) being a member of political parties
(c) avoiding political parties
(d) becoming the officer of any social organisation

198. If you want to start with something new and you have little savings and few employees. What will be your first priority?
(a) Generate cash flow
(b) Figure out what business to be in
(c) Launch products
(d) Develop customers

199. The person responsible for the management of the front office of an enterprise should possess
(a) good and congenial personality
(b) strict discipline
(c) patience
(d) leadership

200. Keeping the needs of individuals in view, it is seen that
(a) all workers want challenging jobs
(b) no worker wants to have a challenging job
(c) vast majority of workers want challenging jobs
(d) not every employee is looking for a challenging job

Answers

1. (c)	2. (d)	3. (c)	4. (d)	5. (c)	6. (d)	7. (d)	8. (d)	9. (c)	10. (a)
11. (a)	12. (c)	13. (d)	14. (c)	15. (c)	16. (d)	17. (a)	18. (d)	19. (d)	20. (d)
21. (d)	22. (b)	23. (c)	24. (d)	25. (b)	26. (b)	27. (a)	28. (a)	29. (a)	30. (d)
31. (a)	32. (d)	33. (b)	34. (d)	35. (b)	36. (c)	37. (c)	38. (d)	39. (d)	40. (a)
41. (a)	42. (c)	43. (b)	44. (a)	45. (a)	46. (a)	47. (c)	48. (b)	49. (c)	50. (a)
51. (d)	52. (d)	53. (d)	54. (c)	55. (c)	56. (a)	57. (d)	58. (a)	59. (c)	60. (b)
61. (b)	62. (a)	63. (a)	64. (c)	65. (a)	66. (b)	67. (b)	68. (c)	69. (c)	70. (a)
71. (d)	72. (a)	73. (b)	74. (a)	75. (b)	76. (d)	77. (b)	78. (b)	79. (c)	80. (a)
81. (c)	82. (d)	83. (a)	84. (c)	85. (c)	86. (c)	87. (d)	88. (d)	89. (b)	90. (c)
91. (c)	92. (a)	93. (b)	94. (d)	95. (c)	96. (c)	97. (b)	98. (b)	99. (b)	100. (a)
101. (d)	102. (c)	103. (c)	104. (b)	105. (a)	106. (c)	107. (c)	108. (d)	109. (d)	110. (d)
111. (b)	112. (b)	113. (a)	114. (b)	115. (d)	116. (b)	117. (b)	118. (d)	119. (a)	120. (a)
121. (c)	122. (a)	123. (b)	124. (a)	125.. (a)	126. (d)	127. (b)	128. (c)	129. (b)	130. (d)
131. (d)	132. (d)	133. (b)	134. (d)	135. (d)	136. (b)	137. (a)	138. (c)	139. (a)	140. (d)
141. (c)	142. (a)	143. (c)	144. (c)	145. (b)	146. (b)	147. (d)	148. (d)	149. (a)	150. (d)
151. (c)	152. (d)	153. (d)	154. (d)	155. (d)	156. (d)	157. (c)	158. (b)	159. (d)	160. (d)
161. (d)	162. (b)	163. (a)	164. (c)	165. (a)	166. (c)	167. (d)	168. (b)	169. (a)	170. (a)
171. (c)	172. (b)	173. (a)	174. (b)	175. (b)	176. (d)	177. (d)	178. (d)	179. (b)	180. (c)
181. (d)	182. (a)	183. (a)	184. (c)	185. (b)	186. (c)	187. (a)	188. (d)	189. (c)	190. (b)
191. (c)	192. (a)	193. (b)	194. (d)	195. (c)	196. (c)	197. (a)	198. (b)	199. (c)	200. (c)

Hints & Solutions

1. (*c*) Let the two numbers be x and y.

According to the question,
$$\frac{70}{100} \times x = \frac{4}{5} \times y$$
$$\Rightarrow \qquad 7x \times 5 = 4y \times 10$$
$$\Rightarrow \qquad 35x = 40y \qquad \text{...(i)}$$
and
$$x - y = 100$$
$$\Rightarrow \qquad x = 100 + y$$

On putting the value of x in Eq. (i), we get
$$35(100 + y) = 40y$$
$$\Rightarrow \qquad 3500 + 35y = 40y$$
$$\Rightarrow \qquad 3500 = 5y$$
$$\Rightarrow \qquad y = \frac{3500}{5} = 700$$
$$\therefore \qquad x = 100 + 700 = 800$$

Hence, the bigger number is 800.

2. (*d*) The speed of the car A cannot be determined because given information is not sufficient.

3. (*c*) The quantity of salt in 3 L of solution $= 10\% \times 3$
$$= \frac{10}{100} \times 3 = 0.3 \text{ L}$$

Let the quantity of water to be added be x L.

Then, according to the question,
$$(x + 3) \times 5\% = 0.3$$
$$\Rightarrow \qquad (x + 3) \times \frac{5}{100} = 0.3$$
$$\Rightarrow \qquad (x + 3) = \frac{0.3 \times 100}{5}$$
$$\Rightarrow \qquad (x + 3) = \frac{30}{5}$$
$$\Rightarrow \qquad x = 6 - 3$$
$$\therefore \qquad x = 3 \text{ L}$$

4. (*d*) Let the height of the cylinder be x cm.

Then, radius of the base $= \frac{3}{4}x$ cm.

Volume of the cylindrical tank $= 38808$ mL
$$\Rightarrow \qquad \pi r^2 h = 38808$$
$$\pi \times \left(\frac{3}{4}x\right)^2 \times x = 38808$$
$$\Rightarrow \qquad x^3 = \frac{38808 \times 16}{9 \times \pi}$$
$$\Rightarrow \qquad x^3 = \frac{38808 \times 16 \times 7}{9 \times 22}$$
$$\Rightarrow \qquad x^3 = 21952$$
$$\Rightarrow \qquad x = \sqrt[3]{21952} = 28 \text{ cm}$$

So, radius of the base $= \frac{3}{4} \times 28 = 21$ cm

$\therefore$ Diameter of the base $= 2 \times r = 2 \times 21 = 42$ cm

5. (*c*) Let the speed of the boat $= x$ km/h

Then, the speed of the stream $= \frac{x}{2}$ km/h

Now, speed of downstream $= \left(x + \frac{x}{2}\right)$ km/h

We know that, Speed $= \dfrac{\text{Distance}}{\text{Time}}$
$$\Rightarrow \qquad x + \frac{x}{2} = \frac{30}{2}$$
$$\Rightarrow \qquad x + \frac{x}{2} = 15$$
$$\Rightarrow \qquad 2x + x = 15 \times 2$$
$$\Rightarrow \qquad 3x = 30$$
$$\therefore \qquad x = 10 \text{ km/h}$$

6. (*d*) Let the age of Neeta and Samir be $5x$ and $6x$ years, respectively.

According to the question,
$$\Rightarrow \qquad \frac{\frac{1}{3} \times 5x}{\frac{1}{2} \times 6x} = \frac{5}{9}$$
$$\Rightarrow \qquad \frac{5x \times 2}{3 \times 6x} = \frac{5}{9}$$
$$\Rightarrow \qquad \frac{5}{9} = \frac{5}{9}$$

We cannot find the value of x.

$\therefore$ Age of Samir cannot be determined.

7. (*d*) Let the breadth of the rectangular field be x metres.

Then, length $= x + \dfrac{15}{100} \times x$
$$= \frac{115x}{100} \text{ m}$$

Given, Area of rectangular field $= 460$ m^2
$$\Rightarrow \qquad \text{Length} \times \text{breadth} = 460$$
$$\Rightarrow \qquad \frac{115x}{100} \times x = 460$$
$$\Rightarrow \qquad x^2 = \frac{460 \times 100}{115}$$
$$\Rightarrow \qquad x^2 = 20 \times 20$$
$$\Rightarrow \qquad x = 20 \text{ m}$$

$\therefore$ The breadth of the rectangular field $= 20$ m

8. (*d*) Given, SP of article $= ₹\ 340$

Discount $(r) = 15\%$

Let the marked price of the article be $₹\ x$.

We know that,
$$\text{SP} = \left(\frac{100 - r}{100}\right) \times \text{MP}$$

$\Rightarrow \quad \dfrac{(100-15)}{100} \times x = 340 \quad \Rightarrow \quad \dfrac{85x}{100} = 340$

$\therefore \qquad\qquad x = ₹\ 400$

Given, Gain% $= 13\dfrac{1}{3}\% = \dfrac{40}{3}\%$

Now, $\quad$ CP $= \dfrac{100}{100 + \text{Gain}\%} \times$ SP

$\qquad = \dfrac{100}{100 + \dfrac{40}{3}} \times 340$

$\qquad = \dfrac{100 \times 3}{340} \times 340 = ₹\ 300$

$\therefore \quad$ Gain $= 400 - 300 = ₹\ 100$

$\therefore \quad$ Gain% $= \dfrac{\text{Gain}}{\text{CP}} \times 100\%$

$\qquad = \dfrac{100}{300} \times 100 = 33\dfrac{1}{3}\%$

9. (c) Let the radius of the cylindrical vessel be r cm.
then, its height $= 3r$ cm

Given, Volume of the cylindrical vessel $= 25.872\ l$

$\qquad\qquad\qquad = 25872$ cm^3 $\quad [\because\ 1L = 1000\ \text{cm}^3]$

$\Rightarrow \qquad \pi(r)^2 \times (3r) = 25872$

$\Rightarrow \qquad\qquad r^3 = \dfrac{25872 \times 7}{22 \times 3} = 2744$

$\Rightarrow \qquad\qquad r = \sqrt[3]{2744} = 14$ cm

$\therefore \quad$ Area of the base $=$ Area of circle

$\qquad\qquad = \pi r^2 = \pi \times (14)^2$

$\qquad\qquad = \dfrac{22}{7} \times 14 \times 14$

$\qquad\qquad = 616$ cm^2

10. (a) Let the monthly salary of Ramesh be $₹\ x$.

Then, amount spent at household expenditure

$\qquad\qquad = \dfrac{25}{100} \times x = ₹\ \dfrac{x}{4}$

Remaining amount $= x - \dfrac{x}{4} = ₹\ \dfrac{3x}{4}$

Amount spent on children education

$\qquad\qquad = \dfrac{20}{100} \times \dfrac{3x}{4} = ₹\ \dfrac{3x}{20}$

Now, the remaining amount $= \dfrac{3x}{4} - \dfrac{3x}{20}$

$\qquad\qquad = \dfrac{15x - 3x}{20} = \dfrac{12x}{20}$

$\qquad\qquad = ₹\ \dfrac{3x}{5}$

Remaining amount is invested in 3 schemes.

$\therefore$ According to the question,

$\qquad\qquad \dfrac{1}{3} \times \dfrac{3x}{5} = 5600$

$\Rightarrow \qquad\qquad x = 5600 \times 5 = ₹\ 28000$

$\therefore$ The monthly salary of Ramesh $= ₹\ 28000$

11. (a) Let the cost price of the article be $₹\ x$.

Then, according to the question,

$\qquad\qquad 625 - x = x - 435$

$\Rightarrow \qquad\qquad 2x = 625 + 435$

$\Rightarrow \qquad\qquad x = \dfrac{1060}{2} = ₹\ 530$

12. (c) Average speed of the car $= \dfrac{\text{Total distance}}{\text{Total time}}$

$\qquad\qquad = \dfrac{(35 + 69)}{\left(\dfrac{45}{60} + \dfrac{75}{60}\right)}$

$\qquad\qquad = \dfrac{104}{\left(\dfrac{3}{4} + \dfrac{5}{4}\right)} = \dfrac{104}{2}$

$\qquad\qquad = 52$ km/h

13. (d) Let the ages of Samir and Tanuj be $8x$ yr and $15x$ yr, respectively.

According to the question,

$\qquad\qquad \dfrac{8x + 9}{15x + 9} = \dfrac{11}{18}$

$\Rightarrow \qquad 144x + 162 = 165x + 99$

$\Rightarrow \qquad\qquad 21x = 63$

$\therefore \quad x = \dfrac{63}{21} = 3$

$\therefore$ Age of Samir $= 8 \times 3 = 24$ yr

and age of Tanuj $= 15 \times 3 = 45$ yr

$\therefore$ Required difference $= 45 - 24 = 21$ yr

14. (c) Let the present ages of Vishal and Shekhar be $14x$ yr and $17x$ yr, respectively.

According to the question,

$\qquad\qquad \dfrac{14x + 6}{17x + 6} = \dfrac{17}{20}$

$\Rightarrow \qquad (14x + 6)20 = 17(17x + 6)$

$\Rightarrow \qquad 280x + 120 = 289x + 102$

$\Rightarrow \qquad\qquad 9x = 18$

$\therefore \qquad\qquad x = \dfrac{18}{9} = 2$

$\therefore$ Shekhar's present age $= 2 \times 17 = 34$ yr.

15. (c) Let the cask hold x L of wine originally.

Then, quantity of wine left in cask after 4 operations

$\qquad\qquad = x\left(1 - \dfrac{8}{x}\right)^4$ L

According to the question,

$\qquad\qquad \dfrac{x\left(1 - \dfrac{8}{x}\right)^4}{x} = \dfrac{16}{81}$

$\Rightarrow \qquad \left(1 - \dfrac{8}{x}\right)^4 = \left(\dfrac{2}{3}\right)^4$

$\Rightarrow \qquad 1 - \dfrac{8}{x} = \dfrac{2}{3}$

HM 2012

$$\Rightarrow \qquad 1 - \frac{2}{3} = \frac{8}{x}$$

$$\Rightarrow \qquad \frac{1}{3} = \frac{8}{x}$$

$$x = 8 \times 3 = 24 \text{ L}$$

∴ The cask hold 24 L originally.

31. (a) As,

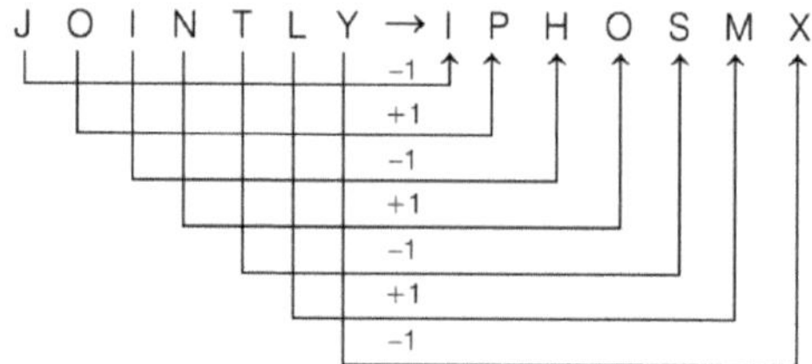

Similarly,

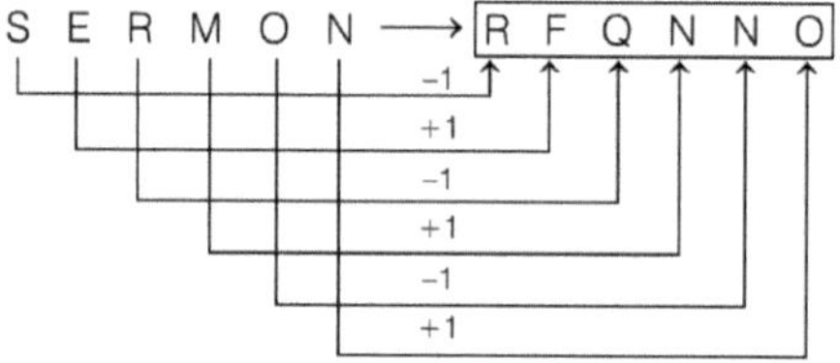

∴ SERMON is coded as RFQNNO.

32. (d) As, $143 = (12)^2 - 1$

$$168 = (13)^2 - 1$$
$$224 = (15)^2 - 1$$

But, $\quad 37 = (6)^2 + 1$

∴ 37 does not belong to that group.

33. (b) According to the question,
By using option (b), R#F★B$T

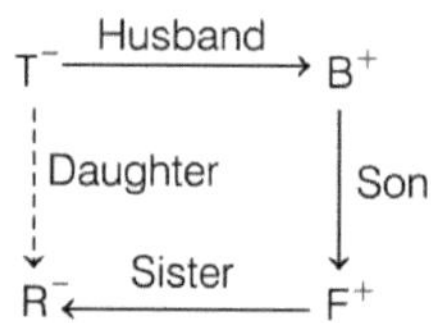

Clearly, R is the daughter of T.
Hence, option (b) is correct.

34. (d) Given, M★H@D$K
Then,

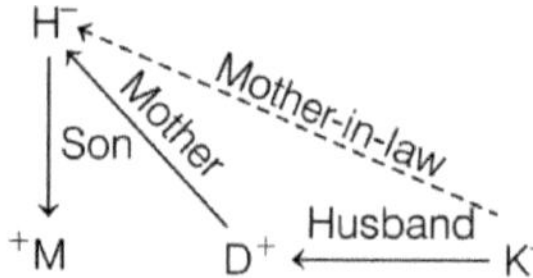

Clearly, H is mother-in-law of K.

35. (b) Given, F#J★T$R@L
Then,

Clearly, F is sister of L is definitely true.

36. (c) According to the question,

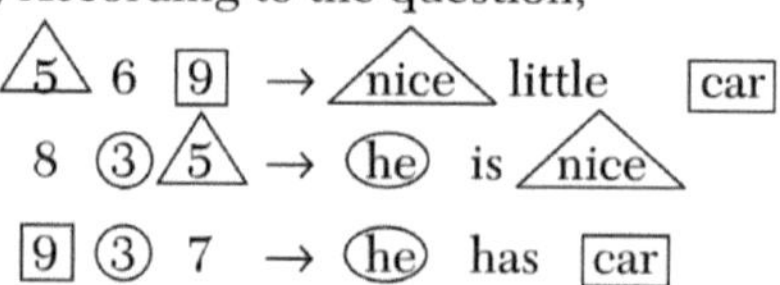

Clearly, has is coded as → 7.

37. (c) Both the conclusions are complementary pair.
So, either I or II is implicit.

38. (d) The first premise is an 1 type preposition.
Here the middle term, 'angels' forming a predicate
which is not distributed. The second premise is a
A type preposition. So, the middle term 'angels'
forming the predicate is not distributed even once in
the premises, no definite conclusion follows.

39. (d) Here, except curiosity anxiety, worry and
inhibition comes in negative sense.

∴ Curiosity is the one that does not belong to the
group.

40. (a) According to the question,

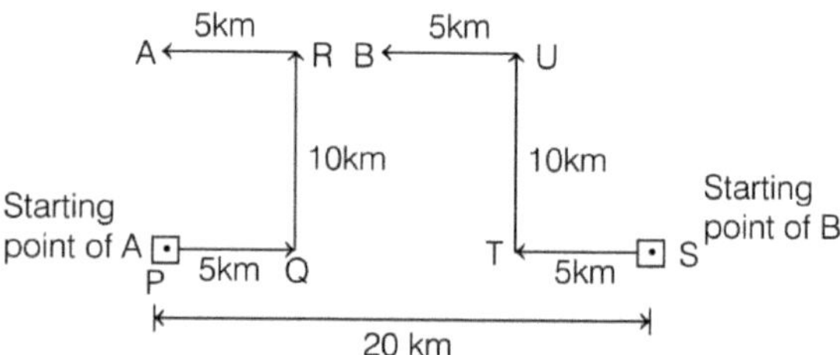

∴ Required distance between them = 5 + 5 = 10 km

41. (a) According to the question,
By using option (a), H*T%K

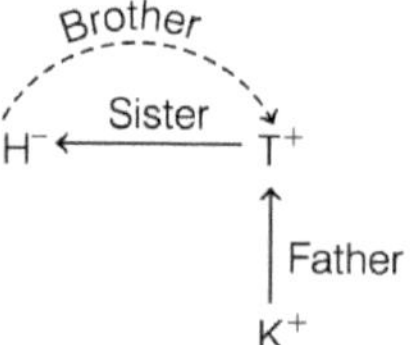

Clearly, T is the brother of H.
Hence, option (a) is correct.

42. (c) The expression H*T#F%L can be written as:

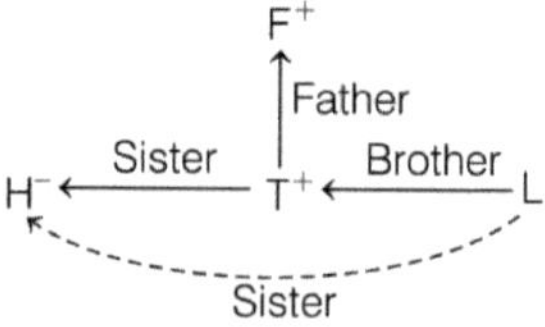

As, F is the father of L and T, and H is the sister
of T. Hence, H is also the sister of L.

43. (b) The expression M*J#R$K can be written as

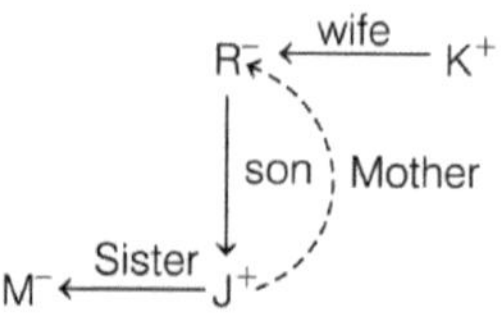

Hence, R is the mother of J.

44. (*a*) As,

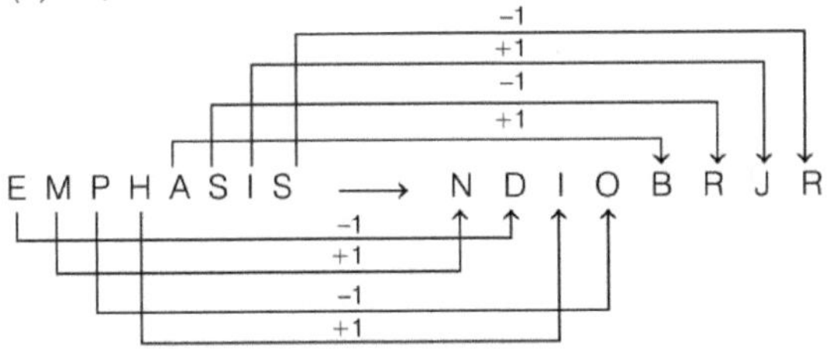

Similarly,

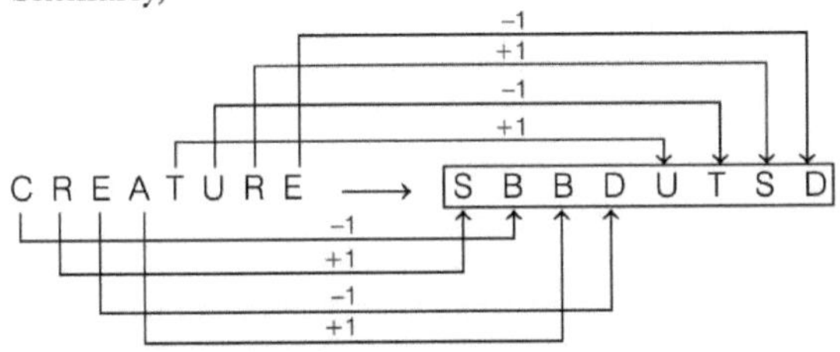

Hence, CREATURE is coded as SBBDUTSD.

45. (*a*) According to the question, the required region is one which is common to the circle A and B but lies outside the circle C. i.e. b.

46. (*a*) According to the question, the required region is one which is common to the circle A and C but lies outside the circle B i.e. d.

47. (*c*) According to the question, the required region is the one which lies inside the circle B but lies outside the circle A and the circle C. i.e. f.

48. (*b*) According to the question,

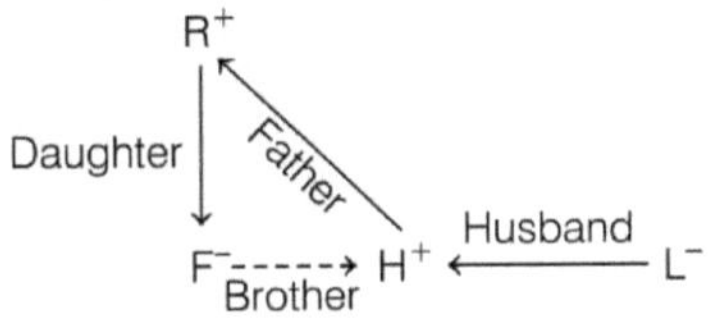

Clearly, H is brother of F.

49. (*c*) According to the question, by using option (c)

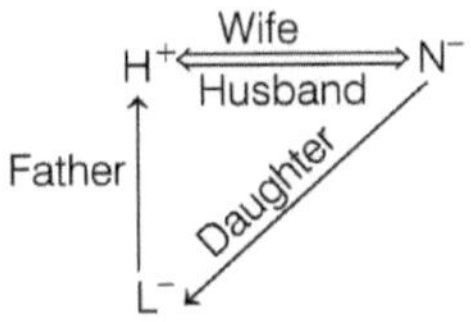

Here, H is the father of L and L is the daughter of N, then H and N are the husband wife.

So by option (c) it is clear that N is mother of L.

50. (*a*) The expression, F – R + H ÷ T can be written as

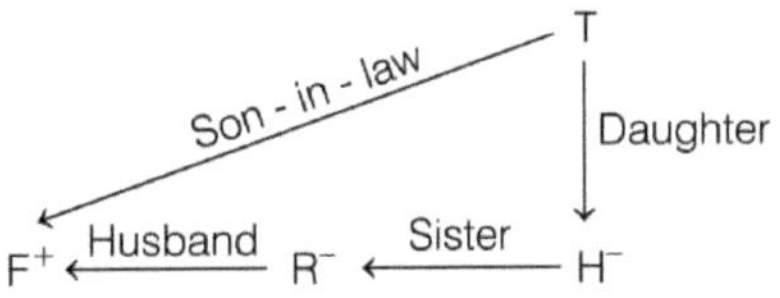

Hence, F is son-in-law of T.

51. (*d*) Without food, we feel hunger, without water we feel thirsty, without air we feel suffocation.

But pair of talent and education does not belong to that group.

52. (*d*) Pattern of the series is as follows,

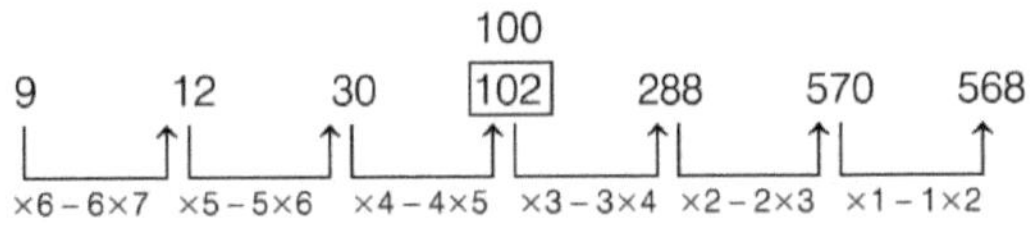

Hence, 102 is wrong number in the series.

53. (*d*) According to the question,

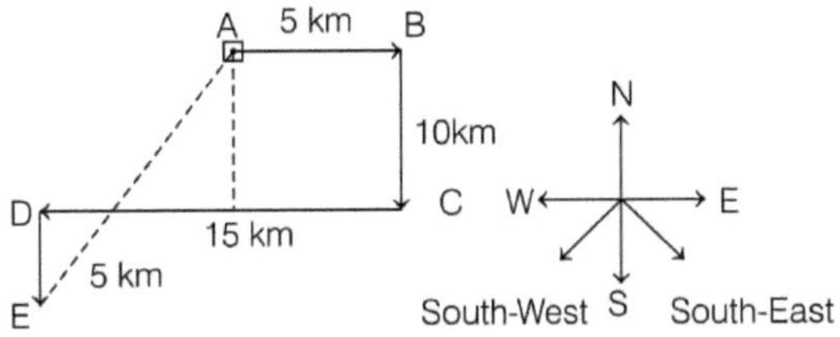

Here, E is the end point.

Hence, he is in South-West direction in relation to his starting point.

54. (*c*) A $\xrightarrow{+2}$ C $\xrightarrow{+2}$ E $\xrightarrow{+2}$ G $\xrightarrow{+2}$ I

Z $\xrightarrow{-1}$ Y $\xrightarrow{-1}$ X $\xrightarrow{-1}$ W $\xrightarrow{-1}$ V

B $\xrightarrow{+2}$ D $\xrightarrow{+2}$ F $\xrightarrow{+2}$ H $\xrightarrow{+2}$ J

∴ GWH will come in place of question mark.

55. (*c*) According to the question,

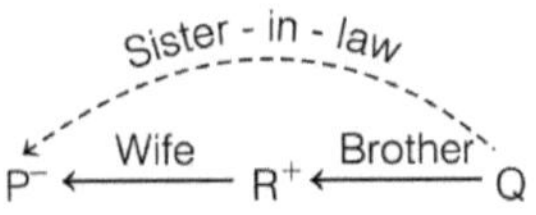

Clearly, P is the sister-in-law of Q.

56. (*a*) According to the question,

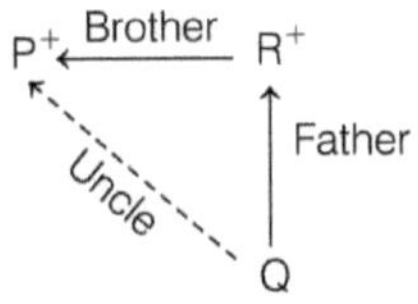

Clearly, P is the uncle of Q.

57. (*d*) According to the question,

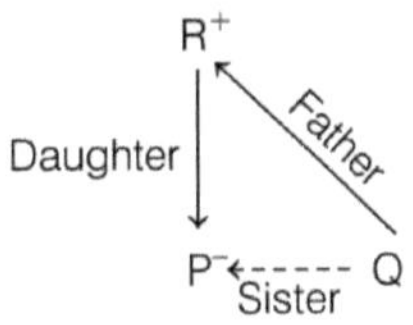

Clearly, P is the sister of Q.

58. (*a*) According to the problem figure we can see that in each subsequent figure, one new design is added to the pre-existing designs.

Also, pre-existing designs move two and half steps in anti-clockwise direction and interchange their position.

Hence, figure in option (a) will come after the problem figure to continue the sequence.

59. (*c*) According to problem figure, the movement of the designs in the figure can be shown as

1st to 2nd fig.   2nd to 3rd fig.   3rd to 4th fig.   4th to 5th fig.

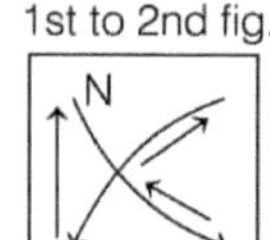 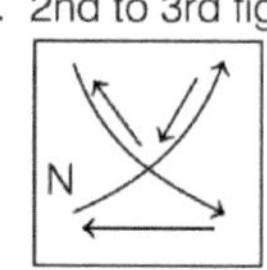 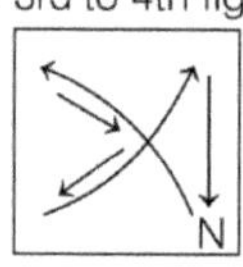 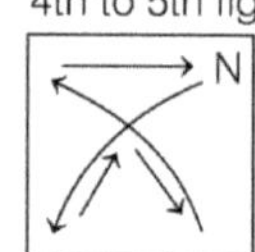

5th to 6th fig.

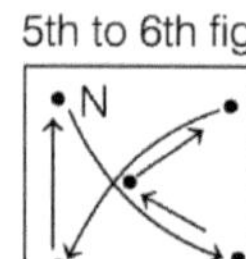

Here, N refers to new design.

Hence, option (c) is correct.

60. (*b*) According to the problem figure in each subsequent steps two, three, four, five curves are reversed respectively.

∴ The figure in option (b) will complete the given figure sequence.

107. (*c*) 'Applaud' means to show approval or praise by clapping. Hence, 'clap' is the closest in meaning to 'applaud'.

109. (*d*) 'Nebulous' means in the form of a cloud or haze. Hence, 'cloudy' is the closest in meaning to the given word 'nebulous'.

110. (*d*) 'Filch' means to pilfer or steal in a casual way. Hence, 'steal' is the closest in meaning to filch.

111. (*b*) 'Querulous' means complaining in a whining manner and 'fretful' means feeling or expressing distress or irritation. Hence, 'fretful' is the closest in meaning to querulous.

112. (*b*) 'Clothed' is the correct opposite of 'bare'. 'Bare' means not clothed or covered.

113. (*a*) 'Honesty' is the correct opposite of 'deceit'. 'Deceit' means the action of deceiving someone by misrepresenting the truth and 'honesty' means uprightness, truth and morality.

117. (*b*) The adverb 'effectively' is incorrectly used to describe the pronoun 'he'. The adjective 'effective' should be used to describe the pronoun. Hence, replace 'to be effectively' with 'to be effective' to make the sentence correct.

119. (*a*) Replace 'neglected by' with 'ignored' to make the sentence grammatically correct.

127. (*b*) Part (b) contains the error. Article 'the' should be used before 'people' to make the sentence grammatically correct.

128. (*c*) Part (c) contains the error. Article 'the' is incorrectly used in the sentence. Remove 'the' to make the sentence error free.

129. (*b*) Part (b) contains the error. Add 'tell' before 'me' to make the sentence meaningful and grammatically correct.

137. (*a*) 'Ponder' means to consider or think about something carefully. Hence, 'think' best expresses the meaning of ponder.

140. (*d*) 'Pious' means devoutly religious. Hence, 'devout' is the nearest in meaning to 'pious'.

142. (*a*) 'Innocent' is opposite in meaning to 'flagitious'. 'Flagitious' means a criminal or villainous person and 'innocent' means not guilty of any crime or offence.

143. (*c*) 'Convicted' is opposite in meaning to 'acquitted'. 'Acquitted' means to free someone from a criminal charge and 'convicted' means to declare someone to be guilty of a criminal offence.

144. (*c*) 'Steadfast' is opposite in meaning to 'fickle'. 'Fickle' means changing frequently or volatile and 'steadfast' means resolute and unwavering.

145. (*b*) 'Zenith' is opposite in meaning to 'nadir'. 'Nadir' means the lowest or most unsuccessful point in a situation and 'zenith' means high point or the time at which something is the most powerful or successful.

146. (*b*) 'Bald' is opposite in meaning to 'hirsute'. 'Hirsute' means covered in hair or shaggy.

Solved Paper 2011

Instructions

- There are Five (A–E) Sections in this Solved Paper.
- For every correct attempt, the student will be awarded **1 mark**.
- All the questions are in MCQs form and each having four options.

Marks : 200

Time : 3 hrs

Section A : Numerical Ability and Scientific Aptitude

1. Ashu spends 25% less than Nishu on Diwali fireworks. How much per cent more did Nishu spend than Ashu?

(a) 20%   (b) 25%   (c) 30%   (d) $33\frac{1}{3}\%$

2. A force of 100 dynes acts on a mass of 5 gm for 10 sec. Find the change in momentum.

(a) 10 C.G.S. units   (b) 100 C.G.S. units
(c) 1000 C.G.S. units   (d) 10000 C.G.S. units

3. What horse power engine is required to lift 1100 lbs of iron per second from a mine 20 ft deep?

(a) 40   (b) 30   (c) 20   (d) 10

4. $\sqrt{0.9} =$

(a) 0.3   (b) 0.03
(c) 0.949   (d) None of these

5. Ten years ago, the ratio of ages of A and B was $3:5$. The ratio of their present ages is $2:3$. Their respective ages in years are

(a) 16, 24   (b) 20, 30   (c) 30, 50   (d) 40, 60

6. If the price of sugar increased by 25%, by what percentage should a housewife decrease her consumption so that her expenditure on sugar remains the same?

(a) 20%   (b) 25%.
(c) 10%   (d) 30%

7. The diameter of a wheel of a cycle is 70 cm. It moves slowly along a road. How far will it go in 24 complete revolutions?

(a) 60 m   (b) 52.8 m
(c) 38.9 m   (d) 56.6 m

8. Swarna invested ₹ 2592 in buying shares of a company at ₹ 108 each. The face value of each share is ₹ 100. The company paid $12\frac{1}{2}\%$ dividend at the end of the year. Find the dividend received by Swarna at the end of the year.

(a) ₹ 300
(b) ₹ 500
(c) ₹ 400
(d) ₹ 250

9. The average of seven numbers is 24 while the average of nine numbers including these seven is 25. If the additional two numbers be in the ratio of 1 : 2, what is the smaller of these?
(a) 16 (b) 17
(c) 38 (d) None of these

10. If $\sin (A + B) = 1$ and $\cos(A - B) = 1$, find A and B.
(a) 45°, 30° (b) 60°, 30° (c) 45°, 45° (d) 60°, 60°

11. A wire of length $25\,\pi$ cm is bent so as to be along the arc of a circle of diameter 100 cm. The angle subtended by the arc at the centre of the circle is
(a) $\dfrac{\pi}{8}$ (b) $\dfrac{\pi}{4}$ (c) $\dfrac{\pi}{2}$ (d) π

12. The population of a country is 90 crores. If it increases by then 2% in first year and 10% in second year, then what will be the population after second year?
(a) 98 crores (b) 100.98 crores
(c) 102 crores (d) 105 crores

13. Find the area of the sector of a circle of radius 14 cm and angle of sector is 45°.
(a) $144\ \text{cm}^2$ (b) $77\ \text{cm}^2$
(c) $225\ \text{cm}^2$ (d) None of these

14. A and B are two sets such that $n(A) = 17$, $n(B) = 23$ and $n(A \cup B) = 38$. Then $n(A \cap B)$ is
(a) 4 (b) 8
(c) 3 (d) 2

15. Find the HCF of $(x^2 - y^2)^2$ and $(x + y)^4$.
(a) $(x - y)^2$ (b) $(x + y)^2$
(c) $(x^2 - y^2)$ (d) None of these

16. If 15% of X is the same as 20% of Y, then $X : Y$ is
(a) 3 : 4 (b) 4 : 3
(c) 17 : 16 (d) 16 : 17

17. 4.036 divided by 0.04 gives
(a) 1.009 (b) 10.9
(c) 10.09 (d) 100.9

18. $25 = ?$ of 125

The number that can replace the question mark is
(a) $\dfrac{1}{5}$ (b) 5 (c) 20 (d) 31.25

19. $\dfrac{11}{4} = \dfrac{77}{?}$
(a) $\dfrac{77}{28}$ (b) 28 (c) 44 (d) 308

20. $\sqrt[3]{\dfrac{1}{8} \times \dfrac{125}{64}} =$
(a) $\dfrac{5}{8}$ (b) $\dfrac{375}{512}$ (c) $2\dfrac{1}{2}$ (d) $15\dfrac{5}{8}$

21. ECG is a technique to record the activity of
(a) Heart (b) Lungs
(c) Brain (d) Muscles

22. Normal blood pressure of man is
(a) 80/120 mm Hg (b) 90/140 mm Hg
(c) 120/160 mm Hg (d) 85/120 mm Hg

23. The deficiency of iron in man results in
(a) Anaemia (b) Night Blindness
(c) Scurvy (d) Rickets

24. The credit of 'White Revolution' in India goes to
(a) Dr. Verghese Kurien
(b) Norman E. Borlaug
(c) Prof. Satish Dhawan
(d) Dr. Abdul Kalam

25. Mud houses are cooler in summers and warmer in winters as compared to brick houses because
(a) mud is a good conductor
(b) mud is a bad conductor
(c) mud is a poor insulator
(d) evaporation of water causes cooling in summers and sunlight coming through holes causing warming in winters

26. Montreal protocol is related with
(a) ozone depletion (b) muclear weapons
(c) lands mines (d) sea bed

27. Bits stand for
(a) Binary Digits
(b) Binary Text Interchange System
(c) Binary Interchange Transfer System
(d) Binary Inter Transfer System

28. Which of the following is correct?
(a) 1 Bit = 8 Bytes
(b) 1 Byte = 1024 Bits
(c) 1024 Bytes = 1 Giga byte
(d) I Byte = 8 Bits

29. Light from the sun reaches us in
(a) 8 minutes (b) 8 seconds
(c) 8 hours (d) 8 days

30. A vast collection of stars held together by mutual gravitational force is called a
(a) Galaxy (b) Universe
(c) Constellation (d) Nebula

Section B : Reasoning and Logical Deduction

Directions (Q. Nos. 31-34) *Refer to the word below (each letter can be used in more than one word. No letter can be repeated within a single word)*

T R I C H O G E N O U S

31. If the 1st, 5th and 8th letters of the word were taken, and then reversed and again the 1st, 5th and 8th letters taken, how many meaningful four lettered words can be formed?
   (a) Two
   (b) None
   (c) Three
   (d) Four

32. The word formed by using all of the 7th, 8th, 9th and 10th letters rhymes with
   (a) ONCE
   (b) FROG
   (c) SPAWN
   (d) MOAN

33. The word formed by using all of the 2nd, 4th, 5th, 6th and 8th letters means
   (a) Drudgery
   (b) Amusement
   (c) Bore
   (d) Task

34. On reversing the word above and taking the 4th, 6th, 8th and 10th letters and forming word using all of them, that word means
   (a) Inquire
   (b) Near
   (c) Far
   (d) Long

Directions (Q. Nos. 35-37) *In each question the numbers follow a particular logical order. Identify the number from among the given alternatives which should fill the blank space in the series.*

35. 16, 24, 34, 46, ...
   (a) 58
   (b) 60
   (c) 62
   (d) 64

36. 6, 12, 18, ...
   (a) 24
   (b) 21
   (c) 26
   (d) 28

37. 4, 12, 36, 108, ...
   (a) 304
   (b) 144
   (c) 216
   (d) 324

Directions (Q. Nos. 38-40) *For each question below, determine the relationship between the pair of capitalised words and then select the lettered pair of words which have a similar relationship as the given pair.*

38. Multiplication : Division : :
   (a) Increase : Decrease
   (b) Zero : Infinity
   (c) Calculate : Estimate
   (d) Digit : Series

39. Water: Conduit
   (a) Electricity : Magnet
   (b) Elevator : Shaft
   (c) Shell : Rifle
   (d) Noise : Cannon

40. Plaintiff : Defendant : :
   (a) Court : Law
   (b) Injured : Accused
   (c) Judge : Jury
   (d) District attorney: Lawyer

41. If day before yesterday was Thursday, then what day will be fourth after tomorrow?
   (a) Monday
   (b) Thursday
   (c) Sunday
   (d) Wednesday

42. If 'sky' is called 'sea', 'sea' is called 'water', 'water' is called 'air', 'air' is called 'cloud' and 'cloud' is called 'river', then what do we drink when thirsty?
   (a) Sky
   (b) Air
   (c) Water
   (d) Sea

43. Introducing a man, a woman said, "His wife is the only daughter of my mother." How is the woman related to that man?
   (a) Aunt
   (b) Wife
   (c) Mother-in-law
   (d) Maternal Aunt

44. Sohan walks 20 m North. Then, he turns right and walks 30 m. Then, he turns right and walks 35 m. Then, he turns left and walks 15 m. Then, he again turns left and walks 15 m. In which direction and how many metres away is he from his original position?
   (a) 15 m West
   (b) 30 m East
   (c) 30 m West
   (d) 45 m East

Directions (Q. Nos. 45 and 46) *There are two statements followed by two inferences in these questions. Select correct option following the inferences.*

45. Statements   Some teachers are followers.
      Some followers are famous.
   Inferences
      I. Some teachers are famous.
      II. Some followers are famous.
   (a) Only Inference I is true
   (b) Only Inference II is true
   (c) Either I or II is true
   (d) Both I and II are true

46. Statements   All terrorists are humans.
      All humans are bad.
   Inferences
      I. All terrorists are bad.
      II. No human can be terrorist.

(a) Only Inference I is true
(b) Only Inference II is true
(c) Neither inference is true
(d) Both I and II are true

47. If HUMIDITY is coded as UHMIIDTY, how is POLITICS coded?
(a) OPILITICS   (b) OPLIITCS
(c) OPLITISC   (d) POILTISC

Directions (Q. Nos. 48-55) *Each row consists of four figures called question figures and four options called the answer figures. The question figures make a series. You are to find which one of the answer figures would be the next one in the given series.*

48. Question Figures

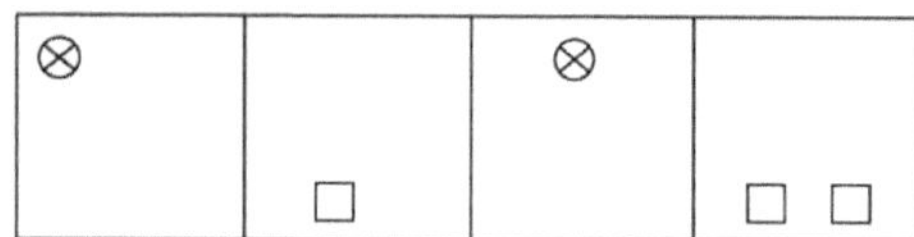

Answer Figures

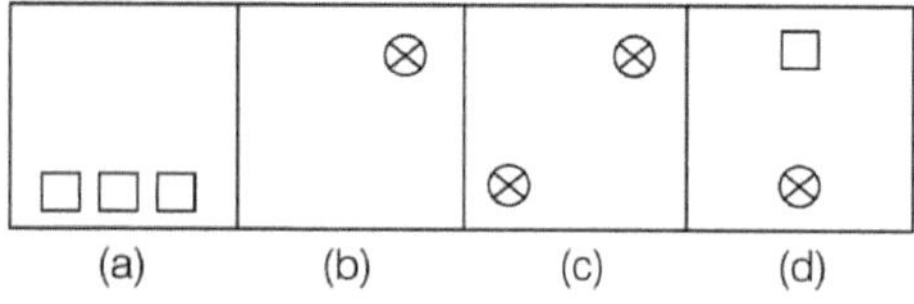

(a)   (b)   (c)   (d)

49. Question Figures

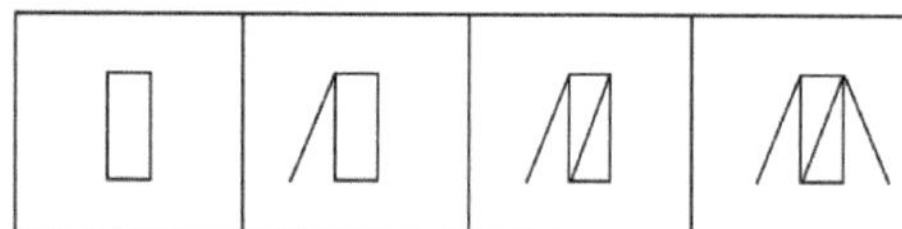

Answer Figures

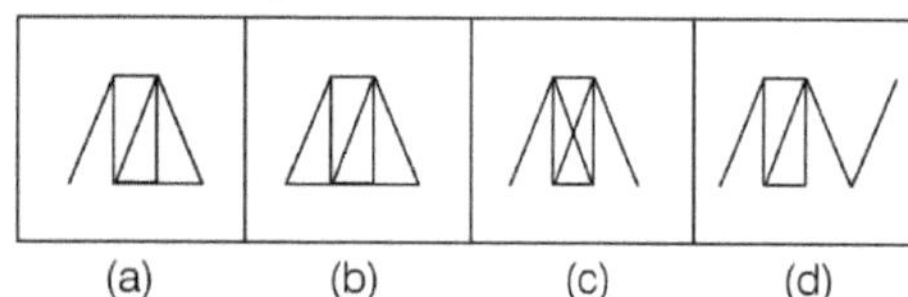

(a)   (b)   (c)   (d)

50. Question Figures

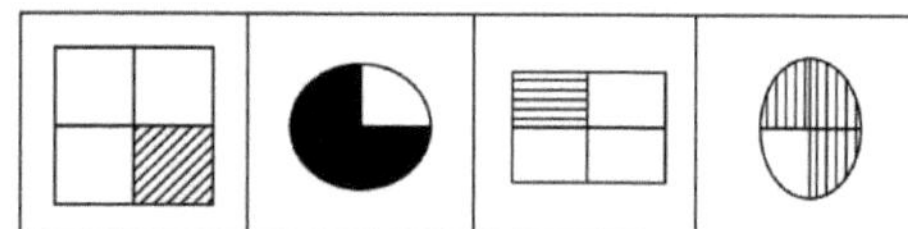

Answer Figures

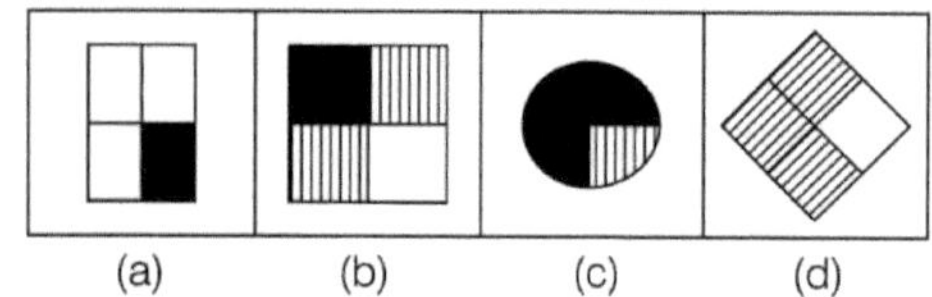

(a)   (b)   (c)   (d)

51. Question Figures

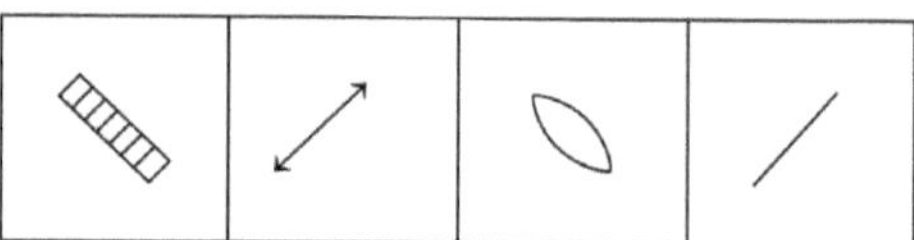

Answer Figures

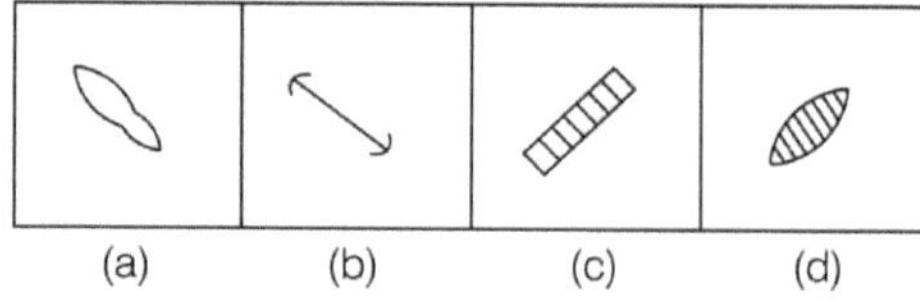

(a)   (b)   (c)   (d)

52. Question Figures

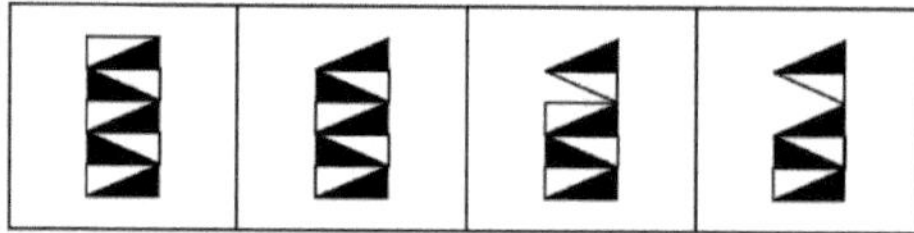

Answer Figures

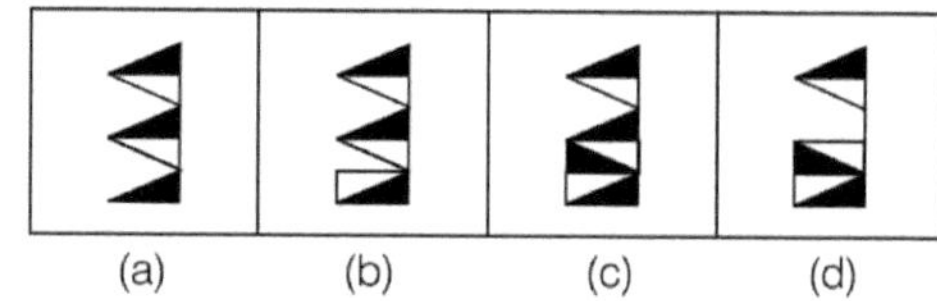

(a)   (b)   (c)   (d)

53. Question Figures

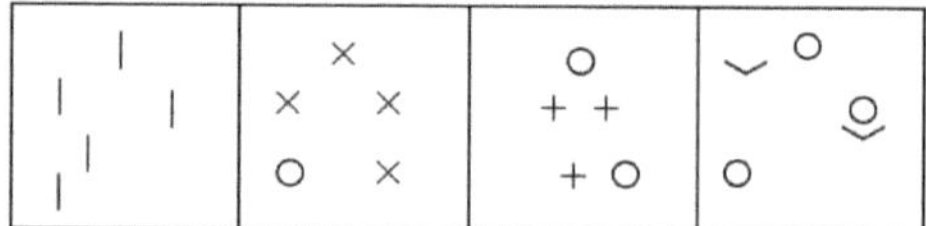

Answer Figures

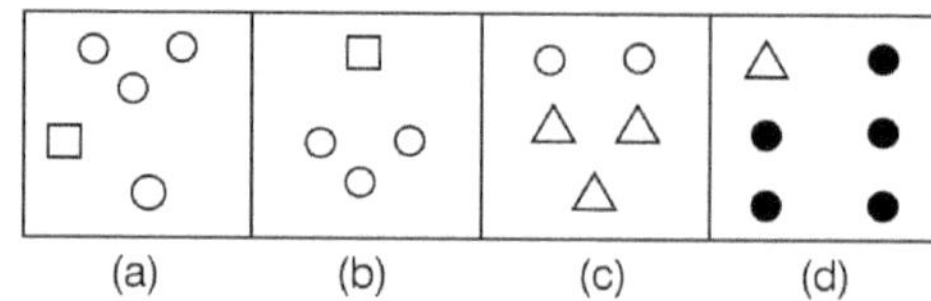

(a)   (b)   (c)   (d)

54. Question Figures

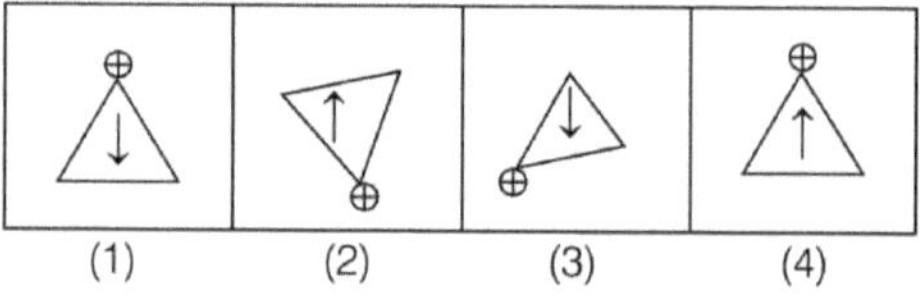

(1)   (2)   (3)   (4)

Answer Figures

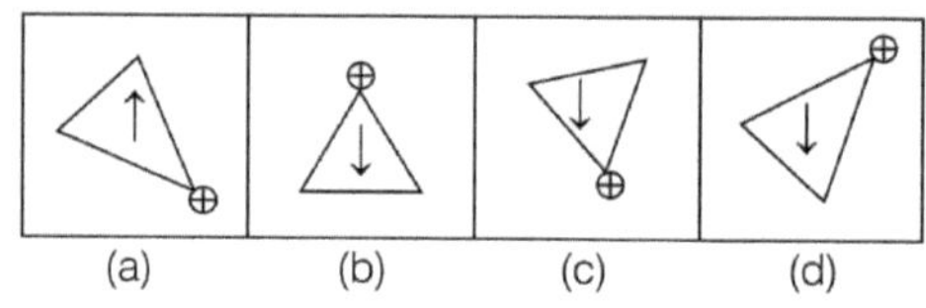

(a)   (b)   (c)   (d)

55. Question Figures

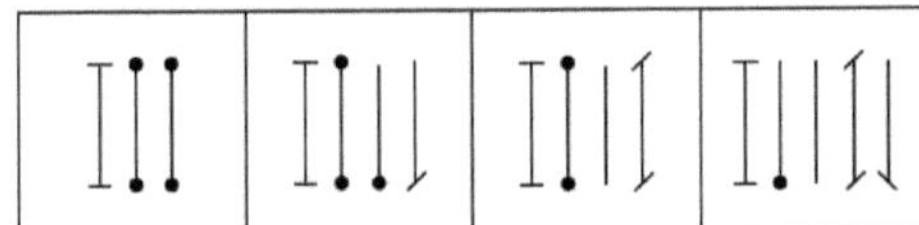

Answer Figures

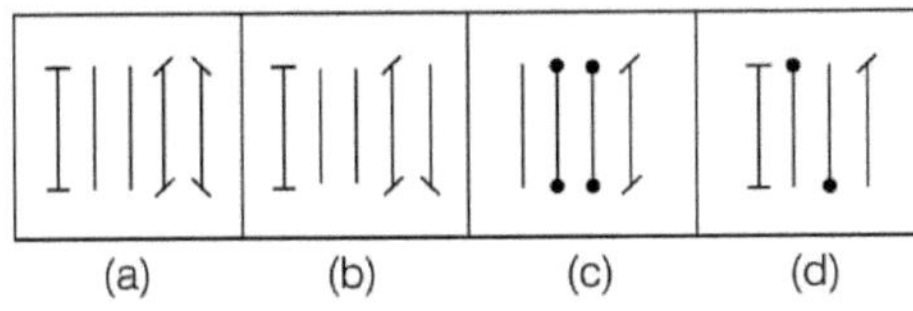

(a)   (b)   (c)   (d)

Directions (Q. Nos. 56-60) *Study the following letter number sequence and answer the questions given below.*

E 7 G B D M 4 N K H 2 A C
Z S V 3 F I J L O Q 5 P R

56. If it is possible to make a meaningful word with the first, the twelfth, the fifteenth and the twenty-first letter, which of the following letters will be the first letter of that word ? If no such word can be made, give 'X' as the answer and if more than one such words can be made, give 'M' as the answer.

(a) M   (b) T
(c) E   (d) X

57. What will come in the place of question mark (?) in the following sequence?

GDR BMP D45 ?

(a) 4NQ   (b) MNQ
(c) MKO   (d) M4Q

58. If the letters/numbers only from M to L are written in the reverse order and other letters/numbers are kept unaltered. Which letter will be third to the right of 17th letter/number from the right?

(a) C   (b) A
(c) S   (d) Z

59. If every third letter/number starting from the right replaces successive days of the week starting from Monday, which letter will replace Thursday ?

(a) A   (b) S
(c) Z   (d) F

60. If every alternate letter/number is dropped starting from E onwards, which letter/number will be second to the left of the tenth letter/number from the left ?

(a) V   (b) B
(c) A   (d) Q

Section C : General Awareness and Current Affairs

61. The country with the highest population density is
(a) China
(b) Bangladesh
(c) India
(d) Monaco

62. What do you mean by 'reserved forest'?
(a) Reserved for the local use
(b) Reserved for commercial exploitation
(c) Reserved for hunting
(d) Reserved for growing medicinal herbs

63. Atmosphere with excess of carbon dioxide as a result of pollution could result
(a) in fall in temperature
(b) in rise in temperature
(c) in no change of temperature
(d) in excess of ultra-violet rays

64. Atmospheric pressure depends on
  (i) Altitude   (ii) Temperature
(iii) Earth rotation   (iv) Moon's pull
(a) (i), (ii) and (iii)   (b) (ii) and (iii)
(c) (i) and (ii)   (d) (i), (ii), (iii) and (iv)

65. When the first metal came into being it was used for
(a) Pot making   (b) House-building
(c) Clearing jungles   (d) Making wheels

66. In the Vedic age
(a) Polygamy was unknown
(b) Child marriage became prominent
(c) Widows could remarry
(d) Hypergamy was allowed

67. The founder of the Nanda dynasty was
(a) Kalasoka   (b) Mahapadma
(c) Dhana Nanda   (d) Nagadassaka

68. How many times has Atal Bihari Vajpayee been sworn in as the Prime Minister of India?
(a) One   (b) Two
(c) Three   (d) Four

69. Dronacharya Award is given
(a) to outstanding athlete
(b) to outstanding coach
(c) for best performance in Archery
(d) for invention in Science

70. Burma (Myanmar) was separated from India in
(a) 1935 (b) 1937
(c) 1939 (d) 1941

71. Where is Dead Sea situated among continents?
(a) Europe (b) Australia
(c) Asia (d) Africa

72. Delhi became the capital of India in
(a) 1915 (b) 1911
(c) 1930 (d) 1940

73. The brand AIWA is owned by
(a) Philips (b) Sony
(c) Sanyo (d) Mitsubishi

74. Protocols is used to communicate between
(a) Similar Modules (b) Dissimilar Modules
(c) Both (a) and (b) (d) None of the above

75. Where is the European Union headquartered?
(a) London (b) Paris
(c) Brussels (d) Bonn

76. Who is the author of the book 'Is New York Burning'?
(a) John Grisham
(b) Lapierre and Collins
(c) Christopher Paolini Knopf
(d) Michael Moor

77. The prominent function of Central Statistical Organisation is
(a) to determine the money supply
(b) to collect national income estimates
(c) to collect employment details
(d) to determine prices

78. Planning and control are related in such a way that
(a) planning precedes control
(b) control precedes planning
(c) Both are concurrent
(d) Both go hand in hand with each other

79. World Tourism Day falls on
(a) 27th July (b) 27th September
(c) 16th August (d) 25th March

80. 'Ngultrum' is the currency of
(a) Denmark (b) Cyprus
(c) Bhutan (d) Myanmar

81. Who among the following is not associated with sitar?
(a) Amir
(b) Ravi Shankar
(c) Ustad Allauddin Khan
(d) Amjad Ali Khan

82. Match the following.

	Religion		Sacred Books
1.	Judaism	i.	Sutras
2.	Taoism	ii.	Torah
3.	Zoroastrianism	iii.	Hadis
4.	Buddhism	iv.	Avesta
		v.	Tao-te-Ching

Codes

	1	2	3	4		1	2	3	4
(a)	iii	iv	ii	v	(b)	ii	v	iv	i
(c)	iii	v	iv	ii	(d)	ii	iv	iii	i

83. Who was the first Indian actress to receive the Padma Shri Award?
(a) Smita Patil (b) Nargis Dutt
(c) Meena Kumari (d) None of these

84. The first Chief Justice of India was
(a) M. Patanjali (b) Mehar Chand Mahajan
(c) Hiralal J. Kania (d) B.K. Mukherjee

85. In order to win the Grand Slam in Tennis, a player must win which one of the following groups of tournaments?
(a) Australian Open, Wimbledon, French Open, US. Open
(b) Wimbledon, French Open, US. Open, Swedish Open
(c) Wimbledon, French Open, Paegas Czech Open, US. Open
(d) Davis Cup, Wimbledon, French Open, Australian Open

86. "Abhinava Bharat", a secret society of revolutionaries, was organised by
(a) Khudiram Bose (b) V.D. Savarkar
(c) Prafulla Chaki (d) Bhagat Singh

87. Endoscopy, a technique used to explore the stomach or other inner parts of the body, is based on the phenomenon of
(a) Total internal reflection (b) Interference
(c) Diffraction (d) Polarisation

88. Saina Nehwal is a famous player associated with the game of
(a) Hockey (b) Badminton
(c) Golf (d) Lawn Tennis

89. Summer Olympic of 2016 will be organised in a city in
(a) China (b) India (c) Brazil (d) Russia

90. Which of the following represents female literacy rate in India?
(As per provisional figures of Census 2011)
(a) 60% (b) 62%
(c) 65% (d) None of these

Section D : English Language

Directions (Q. Nos. 91-98) *Read the following passage carefully and answer the questions given below it. Certain words are printed in bold to help you to locate them while answering some of the questions.*

In a reversal of the norm elsewhere, in India, policymakers and economists have become optimists while bosses do the worrying. The country's Central Bank has predicted that the country's economy is likely to grow at a double digit rate during the next 20-30 years.

India has the capability with its vast labour and lauded entrepreneurial spirit. But the private sector which is supposed to do the heavy lifting that turns India from the world's tenth largest economy to its third largest by 2030 has become fed up. Business people often carp about India's problems but their irritation this time has a nervous edge.

In the first quarter of 2011, GDP grew at an annual rate of 7.8 per cent, in 2005-07 it managed 9-10 per cent. The economy may be slowing naturally as the low interest rates and public spending that got India through the global crisis are belatedly withdrawn.

At the same time the surge in inflation caused by exorbitant food prices has spread more widely, casting doubt over whether India can grow at 8-10 per cent in the medium term without overheating.

In India, as in many fast growing nations, the confidence to invest depends on the conviction that the long-term trajectory is intact and it is that which is in doubt.

Big Indian firms too sometimes seem happier to invest abroad than at home, in deals that are often hailed as symbols of the country's growing **clout** but sometimes speak to its weaknesses-purchases of natural resources that India has in abundance but struggles to get out of the ground. In fact, a further dip in investment could be self-fulfilling: if fewer roads, ports and factories are built, this will hurt both short-term growth figures and reduce the economy's long-term capacity.

There is a view that because a fair amount of growth is assured the government need not try very hard. The liberalisation reforms that began in 1991 freed markets for products and gave rise to vibrant competition, at the same time what economists call factor markets, those for basic inputs like land, power, labour etc remain unreformed and largely under state control, which creates difficulties. Clearances today can take three to four years and many employers are keen to replace workers with machines despite an abundance of labour force.

This can be attributed to labour laws which are inimical to employee creation and an education system that means finding quality manpower a major problem. In fact, the Planning Commission, concluded that even achieving 9 per cent growth will need **marked** policy action in unreformed sectors. Twenty years ago it was said that the yardstick against which India should be measured was its potential and it is clear that there remains much to do.

91. Why are employers reluctant to hire Indian labour force?

    (1) India's labour force is overqualified for the employment opportunities available.

    (2) High attrition rate among employees stemming from their entrepreneurial spirit.

    (3) Labour laws are not conducive to generating employment.

    (a) Only (3)   (b) All of these

    (c) Only (1) and (3)   (d) Only (1) and (2)

92. What is the state of India's basic input sectors at present?

    (a) These sectors attract Foreign Direct Investment (FDI) because of their vast potential.

    (b) These sectors are lagging as projects are usually awarded to foreign companies.

    (c) These sectors are stagnating and badly in need of reforms.

    (d) These sectors are well regulated as these are governed by the State.

93. Which of the following can be said about the Indian economy at present?

    (a) It can comfortably achieve double digit growth rate at present.

    (b) High food prices have led to overheating of the economy.

    (c) Citizens are affluent owing to laxity in regulation.

    (d) Private sector confidence in India's growth potential is high.

94. What impact has the GDP growth of 7.8 percent had?

    (1) Indian Industry is anxious about India's economic growth.

    (2) India has achieved status as the world's third largest economy at present.

    (3) Foreign investment in India had drastically increased.

    (a) Only (1)   (b) All of these

    (c) Only (1) and (3)   (d) Only (1) and (2)

95. Which of the following is most opposite in meaning to the word MARKED given in bold in the passage?

    (a) Decreased   (b) Ignored

    (c) Clear   (d) Imperceptible

96. What is the author's main objective in writing the passage?
   (a) Showcasing the potential of India's growth potential to entice foreign investors
   (b) Exhorting India to implement measures to live up to its potential
   (c) Recommending India's model of development to other developing countries
   (d) Berating the private sector for not bidding for infrastructure development projects

97. What measures do experts suggest be taken to ensure targeted economic growth?
   (a) Lowering of interest rates to help industries hit by recession
   (b) Prolonged financial support for basic input industries
   (c) Incentives to Indian companies to invest in infrastructure
   (d) Formulation of policies and their implementation in factor markets

98. Which of the following is most similar in meaning to the word CLOUT given in bold in the passage?
   (a) Strike   (b) Standing
   (c) Force   (d) Launch

Directions (Q. Nos. 99-105) *Read the following passage carefully and answer the questions given below it. Certain words/phrases are printed in bold to help you to locate them while answering some of the questions.*

In many countries, a combustible mixture of authoritarianism, unemployment and youth has given rise to disaffection with strongmen rulers which has in turn spilled over into uprising.

Young people in these countries are far better educated than their parents were. In 1990, the average Egyptian had 4.4 years of schooling; by 2010 the figure had risen to 7.1 years. Could it be that education, by making people less willing to put up with restrictions on freedom and more willing to question authority, **promotes** democratisation. Ideas about the links between education, income and democracy are at the heart of what social scientists have long studied. Since then plenty of economists and political scientists have looked for statistical evidence of a causal link between education and democratisation. Many have pointed to the strong correlation that exists between levels of education and measures like the pluralism of party politics and the existence of civil liberties.

The patterns are similar when income and democracy are considered. There are outliers, of course-until recently, many Arab countries managed to combine energy-based wealth and decent education with undemocratic political systems.

But some deduce from the overall picture that as China and other authoritarian states get more educated and richer, their people will agitate for greater political freedom, culminating in a shift to a more democratic form of government. This apparently reasonable intuition is shakier than it seems.

Critics of the hypothesis point out that correlation is hardly causation. The general trend over the past half-century may have been, towards rising living standards, a wider spread of basic education and more democracy, but it is entirely possible that this is being driven by another variable. Even if the correlation were not spurious. it would be difficult to know which way causation ran.

Does more education lead to greater democracy? Or are more democratic countries better at educating their citizens? A recent NBER paper compared a group of Kenyan girls in 69 primary schools whose students were randomly selected to receive a scholarship with similar students in schools which received no such financial aid. Previous studies had shown that the scholarship programme led to higher test scores and increased the likelihood that girls enrolled in secondary school.

Overall, it significantly increased the amount of education obtained. For the new study the authors tried to see how the extra schooling had affected the political and social attitudes of the women in question. Findings suggested that education may make people more interested in improving their own lives but they may not necessarily see democracy as the way to do it. Even in established democracies, more education does not always mean either more active political participation or greater faith in democracy.

Poorer and less educated people often vote in larger numbers than their more educated compatriots, who often express disdain for the **messiness of democracy** yearning for the kind of government that would deal strongly with the corrupt and build highways, railway lines and bridges at a dizzying pace of authoritarian China.

99. Which of the following is most similar in meaning to the word PROMOTES given in bold as used in the passage?
   (a) Upgrades   (b) Prefers
   (c) Recommends   (d) Advocates

100. In the context of the passage which of the following characterise(s) democracies?
   (1) Active participation of majority of educated citizens in electoral process.
   (2) Fast paced economic growth and accountability of those in power.
   (3) Better standards of living and access to higher education.
   (a) Only (2) and (3)   (b) Only (3)
   (c) Only (1) and (2)   (d) All of these

101. What according to the author has led to uprisings in authoritarian countries?
(a) Lack of access to education.
(b) Vast numbers of uneducated and unemployable youth.
(c) Frustration with the existing system of governance.
(d) Unavailability of natural energy resources like coal and oil.

102. What does the phrase "messiness of democracy" convey in the context of the passage?
(a) Democratic nations are chaotic on account of individual freedoms.
(b) Most democratic countries frequently have violent revolts among their citizens.
(c) The divide between the poor and educated is growing wider in democracies.
(d) High levels of pollution on account of frentic pace of infrastructure development.

103. Which of the following is/are true about China in the context of the passage?
(1) China's citizens are in favour of a more representative form of government.
(2) China has made huge strides in infrastructure developments.
(3) China is in the midst of a political revolution.
(a) Only (1)
(b) Only (1) and (3)
(c) Only (2)
(d) None of the above

104. What conclusion can be drawn from the statistics cited about Egypt's education system?
(a) Job prospects have been on the rise in Egypt in recent times.
(b) Authoritarian leaders have played a vital role in reforming Egypt's education system.
(c) Egypt has one of the youngest and best educated demographies in the world.
(d) There has been a rise in education levels in Egypt in recent times.

105. Which of the following most aptly describes the central theme of the passage?
(a) Democratic nations are richer and have a better track record of educating their citizens
(b) Education does not necessarily lead to greater enthusiasm for a democratic form of government
(c) Educated societies with autocratic form of government enjoy a better quality of life than democracies
(d) Citizens can fulfil their personal aspirations only under a democratic form of government

Directions (Q. Nos. 106-115) *In the following passage there are blanks, each of which has been numbered. These numbers are printed below the passage and against each, five words are suggested, one of which fits the blank appropriately. Find out the appropriate word in each case.*

Today experts all over the world are of the opinion that agriculture will affect the future of the world. The world has a serious food (**106**) and the only way to solve (**107**) is if more people take up (**108**). Moreover since the 1980s, technology and finance jobs (**109**) been the basis of America's economy. (**110**), in recent times, farmers' incomes have risen (**111**). It has also been a long time (**112**) farming was a major source of employment, but data (**113**) that unemployment in America is (**114**) in states where farming is the (**115**) occupation. As the demand for food is rising– what the world needs today is more farmers.

106. (a) trouble　　(b) problem
(c) doubt　　(d) discussion

107. (a) how　　(b) usually
(c) it　　(d) these

108. (a) farming　　(b) time
(c) matter　　(d) offer

109. (a) also　　(b) has
(c) not　　(d) have

110. (a) However　　(b) Instead
(c) Despite　　(d) Again

111. (a) much　　(b) since
(c) above　　(d) sharply

112. (a) when　　(b) since
(c) while　　(d) as

113. (a) collected　　(b) informs
(c) calculate　　(d) shows

114. (a) lowest　　(b) smaller
(c) decreased　　(d) important

115. (a) mostly　　(b) best　　(c) suitable　　(d) main

Directions (Q.Nos. 116-118) *Choose the word which is most nearly the same in meaning to the word given in bold.*

116. Yields
(a) relents　　(b) submits
(c) produces　　(d) reduces

117. Tame
(a) increase　　(b) timid
(c) study　　(d) control

118. **Still**
   (a) silent   (b) now as before
   (c) nevertheless   (d) quiet

Directions (Q.Nos. 119 and 120) *Choose the word which is most opposite in meaning of the word given in bold.*

119. **Reinforcing**
   (a) contradicting   (b) wishing
   (c) jolting   (d) forcing

120. **Slump**
   (a) output   (b) rise
   (c) slide   (d) slack

Directions (Q.Nos. 121-125) *In each question given below, a sentence with four words printed in bold is given. One of these may be either wrongly spelt or inappropriate in the context of the sentence. Find out the word, which is wrongly spelt or inappropriate, if any. The option in which the word is your answer.*

121. (a) Another **advantage**/
   (b) is that **technology**/
   (c) can be **quickly**/adapted to the client's needs
   (d) All are correct.

122. (a) It freed me to **enter**/   (b) one of the **most**/
   (c) **creatively**/   (d) **periods** of my life.

123. (a) About 4,500 **private**/
   (b) and 2000 government **hospital**
   (c) are **empanelled**/
   (d) under the **scheme**.

124. (a) More **often**/
   (b) **then**/
   (c) not we feel **concerned**/
   (d) with the development **around** us.

125. (a) **Software**/
   (b) makers in India are **facing**/
   (c) a **huge**/
   (d) **presure**

Directions (Q.Nos. 126-130) *In each of these questions, two sentences (I) and (II) are given. Each sentence has a blank in it. Four words (a), (b), (c) and (d) are suggested. Out of these only one fits at both the places in the context of each sentence. Number of that word is the answer.*

126. I. The truck stopped ....
   II. We take a ...... walk every day.
   (a) suddenly   (b) long
   (c) short   (d) distant

127. I. I got the grains .... in the machine.
   II. I do not have any .... for doubting him.
   (a) done   (b) basis
   (c) ground   (d) crushed

128. I. We were asked to design a .... of the dam.
   II. The Institute is a .... of modern thinking.
   (a) picture   (b) type
   (c) function   (d) model

129. I. Keep a ...... grip on the railing.
   II. He was .... asleep.
   (a) fast   (b) firm
   (c) deep   (d) strong

130. I. He asked me to .... over the fence.
   II. We should keep the valuables in the ....
   (a) vault   (b) cross   (c) safe   (d) tie

Directions (Q. Nos. 131-135) *Which of the phrases in the options should replace the phrase given in bold in the following sentences to make the sentences grammatically meaningful and correct ?*

131. **Most of time**, strangers have helped me in critical situations.
   (a) Many a time   (b) At time
   (c) More of time   (d) At odd period

132. The reality is **that India needs** a strong, efficient and competitive aviation sector.
   (a) what India needs
   (b) that India need
   (c) therefore India need
   (d) No correction required

133. I have known this industry **since the last two decades.**
   (a) since last two decade
   (b) ever since the last two decades
   (c) for the last two decades
   (d) from the last two decades

134. Today's children have **far most knowledge** and far less patience compared to our generation.
   (a) much most knowledge
   (b) far most knowledgeable
   (c) by far higher knowledge
   (d) far more knowledge

135. Of late, Bonsai trees have attracted the attention of **one and all**.
   (a) some and all
   (b) many and all
   (c) everyone and all
   (d) No correction required

Directions (Q.Nos. 136-145) *Read each sentence to find out whether there is any grammatical mistake/error in it. The error if any, will be in one part of sentence. Mark the number of the part with error as your answer.*

136. (a) All companies must/
(b) send its annual report to/
(c) its shareholders twenty-one days/
(d) before the Annual General Body Meeting.

137. (a) To be an effective manager/
(b) it is vital to/
(c) know the goals and vision of your organisation
(d) No error

138. (a) His aim is/
(b) provided cheap and/
(c) reliable internet facilities/
(d) to every village within five years.

139. (a) Bank notes have/
(b) many special features so/
(c) that bank staff can/
(d) easier identify fake notes.

140. (a) According to the Census Bureau.
(b) India will have/
(c) a more population/
(d) than China by 2025.

141. (a) The State Government has/
(b) issued licences to farmers/
(c) allowing them to sell/
(d) its vegetables to hotels.

142. (a) Many people decide/
(b) not to buy a car/
(c) last Diwali because of /
(d) the high price of petrol last year.

143. (a) We plan to/
(b) sell part of our/
(c) business therefore we have/
(d) to repay a loan.

144. (a) The Reserve Bank of India is/
(b) the only central bank in/
(c) Asia which have/
(d) raised interest rates in September.

145. (a) Under this scheme,/
(b) insurance companies will reimbures/
(c) any expenditure on medicines/
(d) if you submitting the original bills.

Directions (Q. Nos. 146-150) *Which of the phrases (a), (b) and (c) given below each sentence should replace the phrase printed in bold in the sentences to make it grammatically correct? If the sentence is correct as it is given and no correction is required, mark (d) as your answer.*

146. Although scared of heights, she **gather all her courage** and stood atop the 24-storey building to participate in the activities.
(a) gathered all her courage
(b) gathered all courageous
(c) gather all courageous
(d) No correction required

147. Naturally, with everything **gone so well** for them, it was time for celebration.
(a) go so well
(b) going so well
(c) gone as well
(d) No correction required

148. The ban was imposed by the state's commercial taxes department last Friday after protests by a certain community, which **had threat to burn** cinema halls screening the controversial move.
(a) had threats of burning
(b) had throated to burn
(c) had threatened to burn
(d) No correction required

149. Rakesh, an avid football player who captained his team in school and college, **will inaugurate** the match tomorrow in Pune.
(a) will be inaugurate
(b) is inauguration
(c) will inaugurating
(d) No correction required

150. At a musical night organised for them, the artistic side of the doctors **came as forward,** as they sang beautifully and made the evening truly memorable.
(a) come forward
(b) come to the fore
(c) came to the forth
(d) No correction required

Directions (Q.Nos. 151-155) *Rearrange the following six sentences (A), (B), (C), (D), (E) and (F) in the proper sequence to form a meaningful paragraph, then answer the questions given below them.*

(A) In all varieties of humour, especially the subtle ones it is therefore what the reader thinks which gives extra meaning to these verses.

(B) But such a verse may also be enjoyed at the surface level.

(C) Nonsense verse is one of the most sophisticated forms of literature.

(D) This fulfils the author's main intention in such a verse which is to give pleasure.

(E) However, the reader who understands the broad implications of the content and allusion finds greater pleasure.

(F) The reason being it requires the reader to supply a meaning beyond the surface meaning.

151. Which of the following is the **FIFTH** sentence?
(a) (D)   (b) (E)   (c) (B)   (d) (C)

152. Which of the following is the **SIXTH** (LAST) sentence?
(a) (F)   (b) (E)
(c) (D)   (d) (A)

153. Which of the following is the **FIRST** sentence?
(a) (E)   (b) (A)
(c) (F)   (d) (C)

154. Which of the following is the **SECOND** sentence?
(a) (A)   (b) (E)
(c) (F)   (d) (B)

155. Which of the following is the **THIRD** sentence?
(a) (A)   (b) (B)
(c) (F)   (d) (C)

Directions (Q. Nos. 156-160) *In each of these questions four words are given denoted by (A), (B), (C) and (D). Two of these words may be either synonyms or antonyms. Find out the correct pair in each question.*

156. (A) ECSTASY
(B) DEPRESSION
(C) INTOXICATION
(D) COMPRESSION
(a) A-B   (b) B-D   (c) B-C   (d) C-D

157. (A) TRANQUILITY
(B) LOYALTY
(C) CALAMITY
(D) UPROAR
(a) A-C   (b) B-D
(c) B-C   (d) None of these

158. (A) VILIFICATION
(B) NULLIFICATION
(C) DENIGRATION
(D) FALSIFICTION
(a) A-B   (b) B-C   (c) A-C   (d) B-D

159. (A) OPAQUE
(B) TRANSLUCENT
(C) TRANSVERSE
(D) TRANSVESTITE
(a) A-D   (b) B-D   (c) C-A   (d) B-A

160. (A) EXORBITANT
(B) EXPEDITIOUS
(C) QUICK
(D) QUEST
(a) C-D   (b) A-B   (c) A-D   (d) B-C

Directions (Q.Nos. 161-166) *In the following items, some parts of the sentence have been jumbled up. You are required to rearrange these parts which are labelled P, Q, R and S to produce the correct sentence. Choose the proper sequence and mark in your Answers Sheet accordingly.*

161. At the door
P : that he would have the door broken open
Q : the guard shouted
R : if the persons inside did not heed his call
S : at the top of his voice
The correct sequence should be
(a) S-P-R-Q (b) Q-S-P-R (c) P-R-S-Q (d) P-Q-R-S

162. P : by bandits
Q : were driving through a desert area
R : a man and his daughter
S : when they were held
The correct sequence should be
(a) S-P-R-Q   (b) R-Q-S-P
(c) S-R-P-Q   (d) P-Q-R-S
Ans. (b)

163. Our finest contemporary achievement
P : and toil
Q : in the provision of higher education
R : is our unprecedented expenditure of wealth
S : for all
The correct sequence should be
(a) P-Q-R-S   (b) R-Q-P-S
(c) R-P-Q-S   (d) P-R-Q-S

164. It seemed to him
P : like seeing one's reflection
Q : an endless quest
R : two mirrors
S : while standing between
The correct sequence should be
(a) P-R-S-Q   (b) S-P-Q-R
(c) R-S-P-Q   (d) Q-P-S-R

165. A series of shocks
P : is known as earthquake
Q : which can be recognised through seismic waves
R : that result from sudden earth movements or tremors
S : causing widespread destruction of life and property
The correct sequence should be
(a) P-Q-R-S
(b) R-P-Q-S
(c) R-S-P-Q
(d) R-Q-S P

166. P : in this world
Q : a man has
R : it is possible that the best friend
S : may turn against him
The correct sequence should be
(a) Q-P-R-S   (b) P-Q-R-S
(c) R-Q-P-S   (d) Q-R-S-P

Directions (Q.Nos. 167-170) *In the following items each passage consists of six sentences. The first sentence* (S₁) *and the sixth sentence* (S₆) *are given in the beginning. The middle four sentences in each have been removed and jumbled up. These are labelled P, Q, R and S. You are required to find out the proper sequence of the four sentences and mark accordingly on the Answer Sheet.*

167. S₁ : A city tour organised by the airport got our next vote.
S₆ : "We can only grow in height as most of our land is reclaimed from the mud brought from neighbouring countries", said Bernadette.
P : A bumboat ride through the Singapore River gave us a vantage view of the country's prized possession of skyscrapers in the central business district.
Q : The tour is very popular with transit passengers and there are many such buses doing the route.
R : We were greeted into an airconditioned volvo bus with a bottle of chilled water.
S : On the drive through the colonial heart of the city, our guide, Bernadette pointed out the Parliament House, Supreme Court and City Hall to us.
The proper sequence should be:
(a) RSQP   (b) PQSR
(c) RQSP   (d) PSQR

168. S₁ : But Bhutan is a curious mix of modern and the medieval.
S₆ : His licence plate reads simply 'BHUTAN'.
P : It was next to a speed limit sign: 8 km an hour.
Q : Even the king zips through in a navy blue Toyota Land Cruiser.
R : I noticed a rusty sign for the Kit Kat chocolate bar and realised it was the only advertisement I had seen.

S : Yet in the cities, most middle class people drive brand new Japanese cars.
The proper sequence should be
(a) SQRP
(b) RPSQ
(c) SPRQ
(d) RQSP

169. S₁ : His usually fretful features composed, Javagal Srinath announced his retirement from international cricket.
S₆ : He finished with 236 wickets in 67 Tests and 315 in 229 One-day Internationals.
P : He had spent the early years of his 13 year career sitting out nine Tests when he was at his quickest, being reminded of everything he was not.
Q : In a classic case of appreciating a good thing when it is gone, the tributes poured in for India's most successful pace bowler after Kapil Dev.
R : Not aggressive enough, not a non-vegetarian, not an all-rounder.
S : Srinath soldiered on, whether wickets were flat or causes lost, as they often were when India toured.
The proper sequence should be
(a) QPRS
(b) RSQP
(c) QSRP
(d) RSQP

170. S₁ : However, the flower industry also has its share of thorns.
S₆ : Also, there are no tax concessions from the Government.
P : Most companies have to individually invest in the transport, which is very costly.
Q : Then there are infrastructural bottlenecks– no refrigerated transport or retail chains and warehouses to store the highly perishable commodity.
R : For one, it is extremely fragmented and dominated by small players who don't have the financial muscle to expand the business
S : Ferns and Petals claims to be the only flower retailer with a multi-city presence in India.
The proper sequence should be
(a) QSRP   (b) RPQS
(c) QPRS   (d) RSQP

Section E : Aptitude For Service Sector

Directions (Q.Nos. 171-200) *Pick the one response which best describes your behaviour or the way you behave most of the times.*

171. Your colleague is not performing his duties upto the mark. You will
(a) report to the seniors
(b) try and handle his customers to maintain the company's status
(c) take advantage of it to promote yourself
(d) just do your part of the duties and enjoy your work

172. If on a tough day you are the only person available to handle the customers, you should
(a) just do your part of the work
(b) try and work to the maximum of your ability to satisfy customers
(c) take leave and go back home
(d) ask for additional help from the boss

173. A product launched by the company is having initial hiccups and complaints. You will
(a) try and convince the customers it is temporary
(b) warn the customers for initial hiccups
(c) convey about the working and positive aspects of the product
(d) tell your boss this product should be withdrawn to save the reputation

174. The front office in the organisation has a very uncomfortable physical set-up to work in. You will
(a) manage somehow with reluctance
(b) ignore everything and concentrate on your job
(c) complain to seniors about it
(d) launch a campaign to set the things right

175. Your boss has very piercing eyes and spies on your performance all the time. You will
(a) just do your work
(b) ignore the uncomfortable glances as it is his job
(c) subtly convey it to the boss
(d) tell your seniors clearly that such supervision affects your performance

176. You have opted for a course but a few weeks into it, the authorities tell you that the course has been cancelled and you need to shift to another one. You
(a) accept the new change willingly.
(b) refuse to accept the decision and take the issue up with higher authorities.
(c) reluctantly accept the new course while still trying to get the authorities to change their minds.
(d) crib about it to your friends, but accept the change.

177. You are suffering from a high fever and you have a test the next day. You
(a) work as hard as you usually would and do your best.
(b) talk to your teacher to excuse yourself from taking the test.
(c) prepare a little and take the test.
(d) forget about the test and rest instead.

178. It's your birthday and you want to spend the day with your friends, but your parents want you to spend the day at home. You
(a) spend the morning with your family and the evening with your friends.
(b) insist of spending the day with your friends.
(c) explain to your family that you would like to spend time with your friends.
(d) cancel your plans with friends and spend the day with your family.

179. You have an important exam in Mumbai. Two days before your flight, the airline calls and informs you of the cancellation of your flight. Instead, they offer you AC train tickets to your destination. You
(a) skip the exam
(b) complain about the inefficiency of the airline, but eventually take the train ticket
(c) demand tickets on another flight and threaten to sue the airline
(d) take the train ticket without complaining

180. You plan to watch a long-awaited movie with friends. Your friends decide to watch a play instead and ask you to come along. You
(a) go ahead and watch the movie alone.
(b) agree but keep reminding them that the movie would have been a better option
(c) try to convince them to go for the movie instead.
(d) agree to your friends, request and go along

181. You are in a contest, which has elimination rounds. Eliminated contestants are sad and others too are becoming panicky. What do you do?
(a) You leave the contest thinking that you will lose.
(b) You keep yourselves calm and contented and do not bother about the others.
(c) You shout at the ones who are crying.
(d) You try to calm down others.

182. Your teacher asks you a question. You
(a) blush, perspire and look blank.
(b) answer the question.
(c) tell her you don't know the answer.
(d) get a little taken aback and though you know it you can't answer it.

183. You are at the bus-stop and you see a woman wearing tight revealing clothes being eve teased. You
(a) feel sorry for her but don't want to involved.
(b) empathise with her plight, feel sorry for her and hope that someone would help her out.
(c) it's none of your business.
(d) go up to the girl and help her

184. You are a social worker. On visiting an orphanage there is one child who is not ready to let you go away.
(a) You talk to the authority and arrange for parents who can adopt him.
(b) You decide to visit him every Sunday
(c) You leave with no concern
(d) You ignore the child because you have other kids to attend

185. A wife feels neglected because of her husband's demanding job. The husband is too busy to spend enough time with her.
What, according to you, should she do?
(a) File for a divorce.
(b) Talk it out with him
(c) Indulge in self-pity and find faults.
(d) She should also develop an unconcerned attitude for him.

186. While motivating your workforce you would consider
(a) needs   (b) incentives
(c) drives   (d) All of these

187. That job is most liked by you where you can
(a) achieve administrative power
(b) have enough respect
(c) earn enough money
(d) have enough satisfaction

188. Office Manager in a hotel is the head of
(a) Lobby Manager   (b) Receptionist
(c) Guest relationship (d) All of the above

189. If you have some problem with your employee, you would
(a) complain against him to your colleagues
(b) get annoyed with the employer
(c) talk to him directly
(d) do nothing

190. In case of groupism in the organisation, you would
(a) remain indifferent
(b) encourage groupism
(c) join a group of your choice
(d) advise others to not include in groupism

191. Your immediate neighbour is quarrelsome by nature and is always fighting, even on trivial issues. You
(a) must fight back to teach him a lesson
(b) should pacify him and reason out with him
(c) should ignore him altogether
(d) must tell other neighbours about his attitude

192. Late in the night you happen to hear stränge sounds from the house of your immediate neighbour. You will
(a) ignore and opt to go off to sleep
(b) inform the police
(c) wake up your other neighbours
(d) go to your neighbour and enquire whether he needs help

193. What qualities you would look for in your life partner?
(a) Rich and very good-looking
(b) Sincere and adjusting
(c) Educated and cultured
(d) Both (b) and (c)

194. You need to book a hotel for conducting a big business meeting. You would prefer a hotel which is
(a) having good ambience
(b) reasonably priced and comfortable
(c) located in the heart of the city
(d) posh and expensive

195. People who aspire to work in hotel industry should have the following personality trait(s)
(a) extremely hard-working and courteous
(b) helpful attitude
(c) knowledge of a foreign language
(d) All of the above

196. If you find yourself in a situation where you are required to make a Powerpoint presentation and you are already bogged down by two much work, as the manager what would you do?
(a) Pass the buck to your subordinate, you are the boss, no one can question you
(b) Prioritise your work and try to squeeze out time for it
(c) Cancel the seminar and reschedule according to your convenience
(d) Take an alternative mode of presentation

197. What is your attitude like when a subordinate approaches you to discuss a work-related problem?
(a) I am the boss
(b) I am the boss but let's talk
(c) Forget I am the boss, let's talk
(d) None of the above

198. The board appoints a hard-hearted CEO on your company who is extremely uncaring, makes fun of people and criticises work for no reason. People feel scared and betrayed. No one is working and is barely able to function. As a senior HR what would you do?

(a) You allow people to vent their frustrations behind closed doors

(b) Take the role of the CEO's front and convince people that underneath all this, he wants the best for the company.

(c) Find it difficult for you to handle the situation so decide to change the job

(d) Help people cool down by listening to them without interruption and try to come to a solution.

199. You are the leader of a group and a new member joins it. How would you make the member comfortable?

(a) By making the job interesting to him by praising him when he does well

(b) Correcting him tactfully when he shows his weak points

(c) Giving him a complete set of instructions to study

(d) Explaining what the job requires, and then allowing him to develop his own methods

200. What would you normally do in a crisis situation, for instance in a situation where two of your colleagues are involved in a conflict turned bitter and one of them has resigned? This is a huge loss as he is quite a competent personnel. You would

(a) not care as long as your pay scale is not affected

(b) replace him with someone else

(c) try to rationalise with both of them and reduce the animosity between them as it will affect the harmonious working environment

(d) increase the work-load on the rest of the employees to overcome the loss

Answers

1. (d)	2. (c)	3. (a)	4. (c)	5. (d)	6. (a)	7. (b)	8. (a)	9. (d)	10. (c)
11. (c)	12. (b)	13. (b)	14. (d)	15. (b)	16. (b)	17. (d)	18. (a)	19. (b)	20. (a)
21. (a)	22. (a)	23. (a)	24. (a)	25. (d)	26. (a)	27. (a)	28. (a)	29. (a)	30. (c)
31. (b)	32. (d)	33. (d)	34. (b)	35. (b)	36. (a)	37. (d)	38. (a)	39. (b)	40. (b)
41. (b)	42. (b)	43. (b)	44. (d)	45. (b)	46. (a)	47. (b)	48. (b)	49. (c)	50. (a)
51. (b)	52. (b)	53. (a)	54. (c)	55. (a)	56. (a)	57. (b)	58. (d)	59. (b)	60. (a)
61. (d)	62. (d)	63. (b)	64. (a)	65. (a)	66. (c)	67. (b)	68. (c)	69. (b)	70. (b)
71. (c)	72. (b)	73. (b)	74. (c)	75. (c)	76. (b)	77. (b)	78. (d)	79. (b)	80. (c)
81. (d)	82. (b)	83. (b)	84. (c)	85. (a)	86. (b)	87. (a)	88. (b)	89. (c)	90. (d)
91. (a)	92. (c)	93. (a)	94. (c)	95. (d)	96. (b)	97. (b)	98. (b)	99. (d)	100. (d)
101. (c)	102. (c)	103. (a)	104. (d)	105. (d)	106. (b)	107. (c)	108. (a)	109. (d)	110. (a)
111. (d)	112. (b)	113. (d)	114. (a)	115. (d)	116. (c)	117. (d)	118. (c)	119. (a)	120. (b)
121. (d)	122. (c)	123. (b)	124. (b)	125.. (d)	126. (c)	127. (c)	128. (d)	129. (a)	130. (a)
131. (a)	132. (d)	133. (c)	134. (d)	135. (d)	136. (a)	137. (c)	138. (b)	139. (d)	140. (c)
141. (d)	142. (a)	143. (c)	144. (c)	145. (d)	146. (a)	147. (b)	148. (c)	149. (d)	150. (c)
151. (a)	152. (b)	153. (d)	154. (a)	155. (c)	156. (a)	157. (d)	158. (c)	159. (d)	160. (d)
161. (b)	162. (b)	163. (c)	164. (d)	165. (b)	166. (c)	167. (a)	168. (b)	169. (a)	170. (d)
171. (d)	172. (b)	173. (a)	174. (d)	175. (a)	176. (c)	177. (c)	178. (a)	179. (b)	180. (c)
181. (b)	182. (b)	183. (d)	184. (a)	185. (b)	186. (d)	187. (b)	188. (d)	189. (c)	190. (d)
191. (b)	192. (d)	193. (d)	194. (b)	195. (d)	196. (b)	197. (b)	198. (d)	199. (d)	200. (c)

Hints & Solutions

1. (d) As, Ashu spends 25% less than Nishu.

Here, $r = 25\%$

$\therefore$ Required percentage $= \dfrac{r}{100 - r} \times 100\%$

$$= \dfrac{25}{100 - 25} \times 100$$

$$= \dfrac{25}{75} \times 100 = \dfrac{1}{3} \times 100 = 33\dfrac{1}{3}\%$$

4. (c)

```
               0.948
        9  |   0.90
       +9  |    81
      184  |   900
       +4  |   736
     1888  | 16400
          | 15104
```

$\therefore \qquad \sqrt{0.9} = 0.948 \approx 0.949$

5. (d) Let the present ages of A and B are $2x$ yr and $3x$ yr.

$\therefore$ According to the question,

$$\dfrac{2x - 10}{3x - 10} = \dfrac{3}{5}$$

$\Rightarrow \qquad 10x - 50 = 9x - 30$

$\Rightarrow \qquad x = 20$

$\therefore$ Present ages of A and B are 40 yr and 60 yr, respectively.

6. (a) Here, $r = 25\%$

$\therefore$ Decrease in consumption $= \dfrac{r}{100 + r} \times 100\%$

$$= \dfrac{25}{100 + 25} \times 100\% = 20\%$$

7. (b) $\because$ Diameter of the wheel = 70 cm

$\therefore$ Radius, $(r) = 35$ cm

$\therefore$ Distance covered by wheel in one complete revolution $= 2\pi r$

$$= 2 \times \dfrac{22}{7} \times 35 = 220 \text{ cm}$$

$\therefore$ Distance covered in 24 revolutions $= 24 \times 220$ cm

$$= 5280 \text{ cm}$$
$$= 52.80 \text{ m}$$

8. (a) Market value of 1 share = ₹ 108

Total invested money = ₹ 2592

$\therefore$ Number of shares bought $= \dfrac{2592}{108} = 24$

Face value of 24 shares $= 100 \times 24 = ₹\ 2400$

$\therefore$ Dividend received Swarna $= \left(2400 \times \dfrac{25}{2} \times \dfrac{1}{100}\right)$

$$= ₹\ 300$$

9. (d) $\because$ Average of 7 numbers $= 24$

$\therefore$ Sum of 7 numbers $= 24 \times 7 = 168$

Average of nine numbers $= 25$

$\therefore$ Sum of nine numbers $= 25 \times 9 = 225$

$\therefore$ The sum of additional two numbers $= 225 - 168$
$$= 57$$

Let the additional two numbers be x and $2x$.

Then, $\qquad x + 2x = 57 \Rightarrow 3x = 57$

$\therefore \qquad\qquad x = \dfrac{57}{3} = 19$

Hence, the smaller number $= 19$

10. (c) $\because \qquad \sin(A + B) = 1$

$\qquad\qquad \sin(A + B) = \sin 90°$

$\Rightarrow \qquad\qquad A + B = 90°$ $\qquad$ ...(i)

$\qquad\qquad \cos(A - B) = 1$

$\qquad\qquad \cos(A - B) = \cos(0°)$

$\Rightarrow \qquad\qquad A - B = 0°$ $\qquad$ ...(ii)

From Eqs. (i) and (ii), we get
$$2A = 90°$$
$$A = 45° \text{ and } B = 45°$$

11. (c) Length of the wire $= 25\pi$ cm

Diameter $= 100$ cm $\Rightarrow$ Radius $= 50$ cm

$\therefore$ Angle subtended by arc $= \dfrac{\text{Length of arc}}{\text{Radius}}$

$$= \dfrac{25\pi}{50} = \dfrac{\pi}{2}$$

12. (b) Given, initial population $= 90$ crore

In first year, population is increased by 2%.

So, increased population after first year

$\qquad\qquad = 102\%$ of 90 crore

$$= \dfrac{102 \times 90}{100} = 91.8 \text{ crore}$$

In second year, the population is increased by 10% after the increase in first year.

So, increased population after the second year

$\qquad\qquad = 110\%$ of 91.8 crore

$$= \dfrac{110 \times 91.8}{100} = 100.98 \text{ crore}$$

13. (b) Area of the sector $= \dfrac{\theta}{360°} \times \pi r^2$

$$= \dfrac{45°}{360°} \times \pi \times (14)^2$$

$$= \dfrac{1}{8} \times \dfrac{22}{7} \times (14)^2 = 77 \text{ cm}^2$$

14. (d) Given that, $n(A) = 17 \Rightarrow n(B) = 23$

$\qquad\qquad n(A \cup B) = 38$

We know that, $n(A \cup B) = n(A) + n(B) - n(A \cap B)$

$\therefore \qquad n(A \cap B) = n(A) + n(B) - n(A \cup B)$
$$= 17 + 23 - 38 = 2$$

15. (b) $(x^2 - y^2)^2 = (x^2 - y^2)(x^2 - y^2)$

$$= (x + y)(x - y)(x + y)(x - y)$$

and $(x + y)^4 = (x + y)(x + y)(x + y)(x + y)$

$\therefore$ HCF of $(x^2 - y^2)^2$ and $(x + y)^4 = (x + y)^2$

16. (b) According to the question,

$\qquad\qquad 15\ \%$ of $X = 20\%$ of Y

$\Rightarrow \qquad \dfrac{15}{100} \times X = \dfrac{20}{100} \times Y$

$\Rightarrow \qquad\qquad 15X = 20Y$

$\Rightarrow \qquad\qquad \dfrac{X}{Y} = \dfrac{20}{15} = \dfrac{4}{3}$

$\therefore \qquad\qquad X : Y = 4 : 3$

17. (d) $\dfrac{4.036}{0.04} = \dfrac{4036}{40} = \dfrac{1009}{10} = 100.9$

18. (a) $25 = ?$ of $125 \Rightarrow 25 = ? \times 125$

$\therefore \quad ? = \dfrac{25}{125} = \dfrac{1}{5}$

19. (b) $\dfrac{11}{4} = \dfrac{77}{?}$

$\therefore \quad ? = \dfrac{77 \times 4}{11} = 7 \times 4 = 28$

20. (a) $\sqrt[3]{\dfrac{1}{8} \times \dfrac{125}{64}} = \sqrt[3]{\dfrac{(1)^3 \times (5)^3}{(2)^3 \times (4)^3}}$

$$= \dfrac{1 \times 5}{2 \times 4} = \dfrac{5}{8}$$

31. (b) Given word

1	2	3	4	5	6	7	8	9	10	11	12
Ⓣ	R	I	C	Ⓗ	O	G	Ⓔ	N	O	U	S

1st, 5th and 8th letters are T, H, E

After reversed

1	2	3	4	5	6	7	8	9	10	11	12
Ⓢ	U	O	N	Ⓔ	G	O	Ⓗ	C	I	R	T

Again 1st, 5th and 8th letters are S, E, H.

The letters are in both case, T, H, E, S (without repeating)

There is no meaningful word can be formed.

32. (d) The 7th, 8th, 9th and 10th letters are G, E, N, O.

The word formed using letters G, E, N, O is GONE

It rhymes with MOAN.

33. (d) The 2nd, 4th, 5th, 6th and 8th letters are R, C, H, O, E.

The word formed is CHORE means Task.

34. (b) Reversing the given word

1	2	3	4	5	6	7	8	9	10	11	12
S	U	O	N	E	G	O	H	C	I	R	T

The 4th, 6th, 8th and 10th letters are N, G, H, I

The meaningful word is NIGH. It means Near.

35. (*b*) Pattern of the series is as follows,

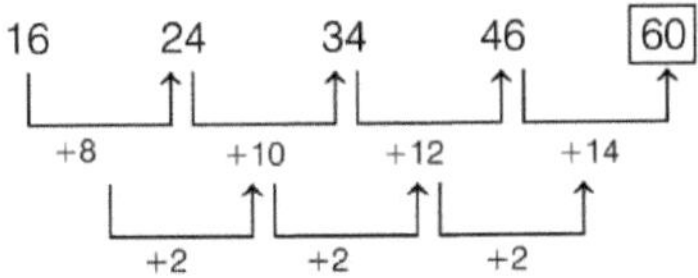

∴ 60 is the missing number.

36. (*a*) According to the question,

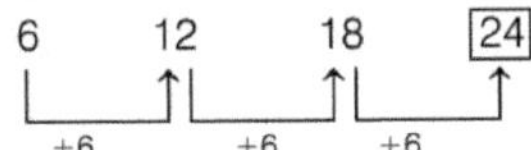

∴ 24 is the missing number.

37. (*d*) According to the question,

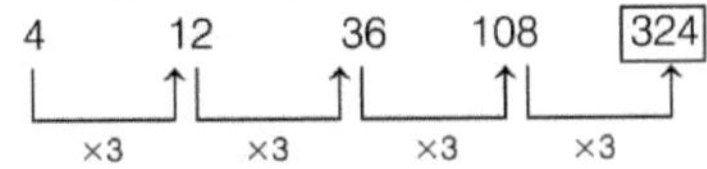

∴ 324 is the missing number.

38. (*a*) Multiplication always increases a number while Division decreases the number.

39. (*b*) An Elevator goes through and is in a Shaft just as water flows through and is in a Conduit.

40. (*b*) Plaintiff is injured while defendant is accused.
As, Plaintiff is related to injured in the same way defendant is related accused.

41. (*b*) Day before yesterday was Thursday.
∴ Yesterday was Friday.
Tomorrow will be Sunday.
∴ Fourth day after tomorrow will be Thursday.

42. (*b*) When we are thirsty we drink water.
Here, water is called air.

43. (*b*) According to the question,

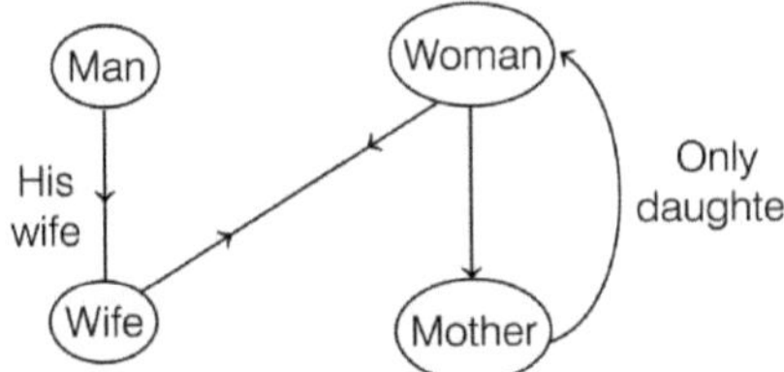

The woman is only daughter of her mother.
∴ The women is the wife of that man.

44. (*d*) According to the question,

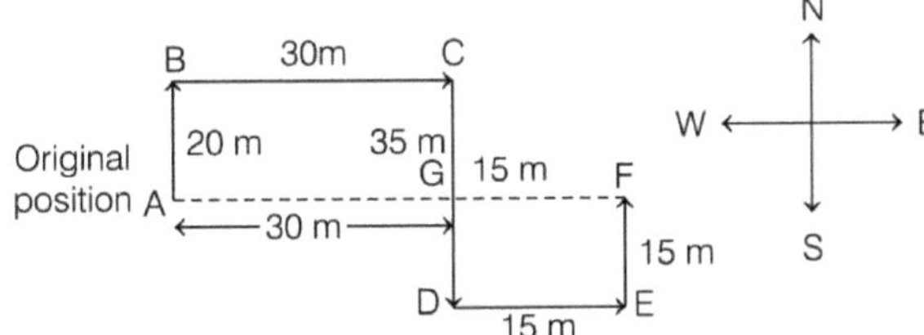

His final position is F.
∴ Required distance = AF = AG + GF
$$= 30 + 15$$
$$= 45 \text{ m}$$
The point F lies to the East of the point A.

45. (*b*) Analysis by Venn diagram,

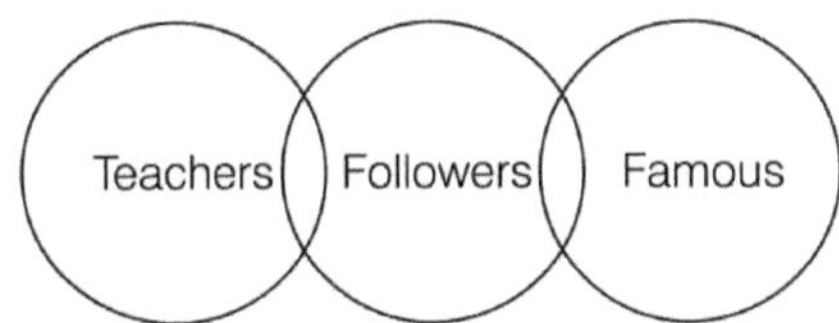

According to **Inference I :** Some teachers are famous.
It may or may not be true.
We are not sure about it.
Inference II : Some followers are famous. It is a true statement.
Hence, only Inference II is true.

46. (*a*) Analysis by Venn diagram,

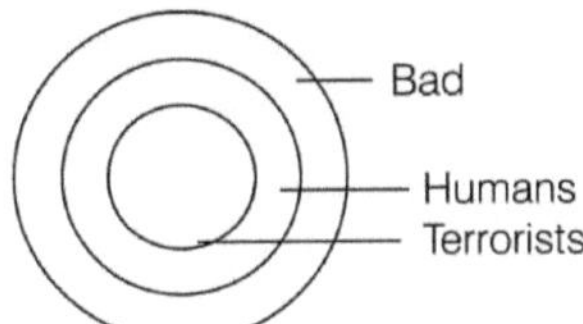

It is clear from the Venn diagram, all terrorist are bad.
But only some Humans are Terrorists.
So, Inference II is false.
Hence, only Inference I is true.

47. (*b*) As,

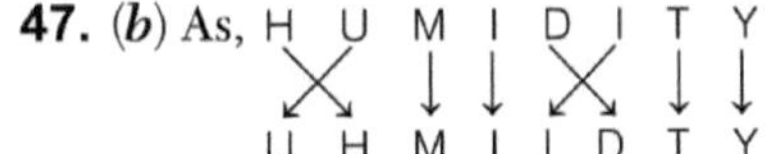

Similarly,

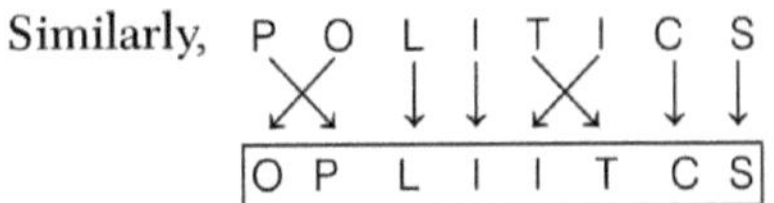

∴ POLITICS is coded as OPLIITCS.

48. (*b*) The symbol in the first figure is moving 45° in clockwise direction.
Hence, the figure in option (b) will be the next one in the given series.

49. (*c*) In each subsequent figure, one straight line is increasing.
Hence, the figure in option (c) will come next in the following series.

50. (*a*) According to the given figure sequence, the figure (a) will come next to the given figure sequence.

51. (*b*) The pattern as the next figure is a new figure and towards opposite diagonal.
Hence, option (b) figure will be the next figure of this pattern.

52. (*b*) In each subsequent figure one triangle is disappearing.
Hence, figure in option (b) will complete the given series.

53. (*a*) In each subsequent steps, the number of circle is increasing and the circle replaces the other present in the figure and the total number of symbols in each step is 5.

Hence, the figure in option (a) will complete the given series.

54. (c) The problem figure (1) is same as problem figure (4) but with inverted arrow. So, the answer figure must be same as problem figure (2) but with inverted arrow. So, option (c) must be correct choice.

55. (a) The number of dots is decreasing in each subsequent steps by 1. Also the number of the symbol dash (-) upon the straight line is increasing in each subsequent step by 1.

Hence, the figure in option (a) will complete the given figure series.

56. (a)

1	2	3	4	5	6	7	8	9
E	7	G	B	D	M	4	N	K

10	11	12	13	14	15	16	17	18	19	20
H	2	A	C	Z	S	V	3	F	I	J

21	22	23	24	25	26
L	O	Q	5	P	R

The specified letters are E, A, S, L

The word formed from the letters E, A, S, L are SALE, SEAL, LASE etc.

∴ Here more than one word is formed.

Hence, M is the required answer.

57. (b) The pattern of the given series is as,

$$G \xrightarrow{+1} B \xrightarrow{+1} E \xrightarrow{+1} \boxed{M}$$
$$D \xrightarrow{+1} M \xrightarrow{+1} 4 \xrightarrow{+1} \boxed{N}$$
$$R \xrightarrow{-1} P \xrightarrow{-1} 5 \xrightarrow{-1} \boxed{Q}$$

[from the given letter-number sequence]

∴ MNQ will come in place of question mark.

58. (d) According to the question, the arrangement of the letter-number sequence is

26	25	24	23	22	21	20	19	18
E	7	G	B	D	L	J	I	F

17	1′	2′	3′	
3	16	15	14	13
	V	S	Z	C

12	11	10	9	8	7	6	5	4	3	2	1
A	2	H	K	N	4	M	O	Q	5	P	R

Z is the third to the right of 17th letter/number from the right.

59. (b)

	Monday		Sunday		Saturday		Friday		
	↑		↑		↑		↑		
E	7	G	B	D	M	4	N	K	H	2	A	C

Z	S	V	3	F	I	J	L	O	Q	5	P	R
	↓		↓		↓		↓		
	Thursday		Wednesday		Tuesday		Monday		

'S' is the letter which will replace Thursday.

60. (a) The required arrangement will be

1	2	3	4	5	6	7	2′	1′	
7	B	M	N	H	A	Z	8	9	10
							V	F	J	O 5 R

'V' is the letter which will be second to the left of the tenth letter from the left.

95. (d) 'Marked' means clearly noticeable. Hence, 'imperceptible' meaning unnoticeable is opposite in meaning to marked.

116. (c) 'Yields' means produces or provide (a natural, agricultural or industrial product). Hence, 'produces' is the nearest in meaning to 'yields'.

117. (d) 'Tame' means to make someone or something less powerful and easier to control. Hence, 'control' is the nearest in meaning to the given word.

118. (c) 'Still' means all the same or nevertheless. Hence, 'nevertheless' is the nearest in meaning to still.

119. (a) 'Contradicting' is the correct opposite of 'reinforcing'. 'Reinforcing' means to strengthen or to support (an existing feeling, idea or habit) and 'contradicting' means disagree, or state the opposite of what someone has said.

120. (b) 'Rise' is opposite in meaning to 'slump'. 'Slump' means to undergo a sudden, severe or prolonged fall in price, value or amount and 'rise' means to soar up high or get up from lying, sitting or kneeling.

122. (c) 'Creative' is the adjective that should be used with the noun 'periods'. Hence, replace the adverb 'creatively' with 'creative' to make the sentence grammatically correct.

123. (b) Replace 'hospital' with 'hospitals' to make the sentence grammatically correct, as it should be in plural form.

124. (b) 'More often than not' is the correct phrase. Hence, replace 'then' with 'than' to make the sentence grammatically correct.

125. (d) The correct spelling of the bold word is 'pressure'.

134. (d) The sentence is making a comparison; hence, comparative degree of adjective should be used. Replace 'far most knowledge' with 'far more knowledge' to make the sentence grammatically correct.

136. (a) Part (a) contains the error. The singular form of the noun 'company' will be used in the sentence as Part (b) has the pronoun 'its'. Hence, replace 'all companies' with 'every company' to make the sentence grammatically correct.

137. (c) Part (c) contains the error. The plural form of 'vision' should be used in the sentence. Replace 'vision' with 'visions' to make the sentence grammatically correct.

138. (b) Part (b) contains the error. The verb 'provided' is used incorrectly in the sentence. Replace 'provided' with 'to provide' to make the sentence grammatically correct.

139. (*d*) Part (d) contains the error. Replace 'easier' with 'easily' to make the sentence grammatically correct.

140. (*c*) Part (c) contains the error. The order of the words in this part is incorrect. Replace 'a more population' with 'a population more' to make the sentence grammatically correct.

141. (*d*) Part (d) contains the error. The pronoun 'its' is used incorrectly because the corresponding noun 'farmers' is in plural form. Hence, replace 'its' with 'their' to make the sentence grammatically correct.

142. (*a*) Part (a) contains the error. The sentence mentions an incident from the past; hence, past tense of the verb 'decide' should be used. Replace 'decide' with 'decided' to make the sentence grammatically correct.

143. (*c*) Part (c) contains the error. Replace 'therefore' with the conjunction 'because' to make the sentence grammatically correct.

144. (*c*) Part (c) contains the error. The subject in the sentence is in singular form, i.e. Reserve Bank of India hence, according to the subject-verb agreement, it will take a singular verb. Replace 'have' with 'has' to make the sentence grammatically correct.

145. (*d*) Part (d) contains the error. Replace 'submitting' with 'submit' to make the sentence grammatically correct.

146. (*a*) The given sentence is in past tense; hence, replace 'gather all her courage' with 'gathered all her courage' to make the sentence grammatically correct.

147. (*b*) Replace 'gone so well' with 'going so well' to make the sentence grammatically correct.

148. (*c*) The given sentence is in past tense; hence, the past form of the verb 'threaten' should be used. Replace 'had threat to burn' with 'had threatened to burn' to make the sentence grammatically correct.

149. (*d*) No correction required in the given sentence.

150. (*c*) Replace 'came as forward' with 'came to the forth' to make the sentence grammatically correct.

156. (*a*) 'Ecstasy' and 'depression' are antonyms. 'Ecstasy' means an overwhelming feeling of happiness and 'depression' means feelings of severe despondency and dejection.

157. (*d*) 'Tranquility' and 'uproar' are antonyms. 'Tranquility' means calm and peace and 'uproar' means a loud and impassioned noise or disturbance. None of the options are correct.

158. (*c*) 'Vilification' and 'denigration' are synonyms. 'Vilification means abusively disparaging speech or writing and 'denigration' means the action of unfairly criticising someone or something.

159. (*d*) 'Opaque' and 'translucent' are antonyms. 'Translucent' refers to an object that allows light but not detailed shapes to pass through or semi-transparent and 'opaque' refers to an object that can't be seen through.

160. (*d*) 'Expeditious' and 'quick' are synonyms. 'Expeditious' means done with speed and efficiency and 'quick' means moving fast.

National Council for Hotel Management and Catering Technology

Solved Paper 2010

Instructions

- There are Five (A-E) Sections in this Solved Paper.
- For every correct attempt, the student will be awarded **1 mark**.
- All the questions are in MCQs form and each having four options.

Marks : 200
Time : 3 hrs

Section A : Numerical Ability and Scientific Aptitude

1. Pitch depends upon
(a) quality of sound
(b) frequency of sound
(c) intensity of sound
(d) chord of sound

2. Which of the following is heavy water?
(a) H_2O
(b) $(H_2O)_n$
(c) D_2O
(d) T_2O

3. Nitrogen is produced commercially from air by
(a) liquification and fractional distillation of air
(b) thermal decomposition of ammonium dichromate
(c) reaction of ammonia with CuO
(d) reaction between NH_4Cl and $NaNO_2$

4. Reduction is
(a) loss of electrons or gain in +ve valency
(b) loss of electrons or loss of +ve valency
(c) loss of electrons or loss of −ve valency
(d) gain of electrons or loss of +ve valency.

5. The compound of oxygen formed with non-metals are
(a) ionic
(b) covalent
(c) hydrophobic
(d) electrovalent

6. A postman walks towards North a distance of 120 m after delivering a letter. He then goes towards West for a distance of 50 m for delivering another letter. The shortest distance between the two places is
(a) 70 m
(b) 120 m
(c) 130 m
(d) 170 m

7. A certain sum of money is distributed between two friends in the ratio 5 : 11. If one of them got ₹ 1350 more than the other, the total sum was
(a) ₹ 3200
(b) ₹ 2200
(c) ₹ 3600
(d) ₹ 3000

8. On simplification, $\dfrac{1}{0.04}$ is equal to
(a) $2\dfrac{1}{2}$
(b) 25
(c) $\dfrac{2}{5}$
(d) $\dfrac{1}{40}$

9. If $x\%$ of y is the same as $\dfrac{4}{5}$ of 80, the value of xy is
(a) 320
(b) 400
(c) 640
(d) None of these

10. The HCF of two numbers is 11 and their LCM is 7700. If one of these numbers is 275, then the other is
(a) 279   (b) 283   (c) 308   (d) 318

11. If 60 C of charge flows through an electric circuit in 10s, the magnitude of current through the circuit will be
(a) 6V   (b) 6J
(c) 6W   (d) 6A

12. The direction of flow of heat depends upon
(a) quantity of heat in a body
(b) temperature difference
(c) Both (a) and (b)
(d) None of the above

13. During high jump, an athlete of mass of 40 kg jumps a height of 2.5 m. What is his potential energy at the highest point? (Assume $g = 10ms^{-2}$)
(a) 1000 J   (b) 160 J
(c) 100 J   (d) 10 J

14. For every 1°C rise of temperature, velocity of sound increases by
(a) 0.41m/s   (b) 0.51m/s
(c) 0.61m/s   (d) 0.71 m/s

15. On immersing a part of a rod obliquely in water, it appears bent. What does it exemplify?
(a) Reflection of light   (b) Refraction of light
(c) Diffraction of light   (d) Dipersion of light

16. What price should a shopkeeper mark on an article, costing him ₹ 153, to gain 20% after allowing a discount of 15%?
(a) ₹ 162   (b) ₹ 184
(c) ₹ 216   (d) ₹ 224

17. What sum will amount to ₹ 6600 in 4 yr at 8% per annum simple interest?
(a) ₹ 6000   (b) ₹ 5000   (c) ₹ 4000   (d) ₹ 6200

18. The average age of a class is 15.8 yr. The average age of the boys in the class is 16.4 yr while that of the girls is 15.4 yr. What is the ratio of boys to girls in the class?
(a) 1 : 2   (b) 3 : 4
(c) 3 : 5   (d) None of these

19. If $\frac{1}{8}$ of a pencil is black, $\frac{1}{2}$ of the remaining is yellow and the remaining $3\frac{1}{2}$ cm is blue, then the total length of the pencil is
(a) 6 cm   (b) 7 cm
(c) 8 cm   (d) 11 cm

20. If 30 kg of tea worth ₹ 540 is mixed with 15 kg of tea worth ₹ 225 and the mixture is sold at ₹ 20 per kg, the profit per cent is
(a) $11\frac{17}{11}\%$ (b) $17\frac{11}{17}\%$
(c) $11\frac{2}{3}\%$ (d) $15\frac{1}{5}\%$

21. The bond dissociation energy of H—H bond is relatively
(a) low   (b) high
(c) medium   (d) varies

22. Fertilizers of NPK type are known as
(a) single fertilizer   (b) mixed fertilizer
(c) complete fertilizer   (d) None of these

23. Mixture of aluminates and silicates of calcium is known as
(a) glass   (b) cement
(c) marble   (d) diamond

24. Artificial vegetative propagation is done by
(a) cutting   (b) grafting
(c) budding   (d) All of these

25. A true sexual reproduction is one which involves
(a) meiosis
(b) fertilisation
(c) Both (a) and (b)
(d) None of the above

26. In flowering plants meiosis occurs at the time of
(a) germination of seeds
(b) formation of buds
(c) formation of Pollen grain
(d) formation of Primodia

27. The ear drum is also known as
(a) pinna   (b) tympanum
(c) malleus   (d) incus

28. Which of the following vitamins are water soluble?
(a) Vitamin A and D
(b) Vitamin C and K
(c) Vitamin B and C
(d) Vitamin A, D, E and K

29. Which part of cell disappears during mitosis?
(a) Plastids
(b) Nucleous
(c) Plasma membrane
(d) None of the above

30. Amount of which is maximum in the blood?
(a) fructose   (b) sucrose
(c) glucose   (d) lactose

Section B : Reasoning and Logical Deduction

Directions (Q.Nos. 31-35) *Complete the series by replacing question mark (?).*

31. 1, 6, 13, 22, 33, ?
(a) 44   (b) 45   (c) 46   (d) 47

32. 3, 6, 18, 72, ?
(a) 144   (b) 216   (c) 288   (d) 360

33. 20, 19, 17, ?, 10, 5
(a) 12   (b) 13
(c) 14   (d) 15

34. AB, DEF, HIJK, ?, STUVWX
(a) MNOPQ   (b) LMNOP
(c) LMNO   (d) QRSTU

35. AZ, BY, CX, ?
(a) EF   (b) GH
(c) IJ   (d) DW

36. If day before yesterday was Thursday, then what day will be fourth after tomorrow?
(a) Monday   (b) Thursday
(c) Sunday   (d) Wednesday

37. If 'sky' is called 'sea', 'sea' is called 'water', 'water' is called 'air', 'air' is called 'cloud' and 'cloud' is called 'river', then what do we drink when thirsty?
(a) Sky   (b) Air   (c) Water   (d) Sea

38. In a code STATION is denoted by URCRKMP, then BRING is denoted in the same code by
(a) CSKLH   (b) DSGLH
(c) KSKPH   (d) None of these

39. In a certain code 'ni tim si' means 'how are you', 'ble ni si' means 'where are you', then which of the following word is used for 'where'?
(a) ni   (b) tim
(c) si   (d) None of these

40. If CLOCK is coded as 34235 and TIME as 8679, what will be the code for MOLEK?
(a) 62495   (b) 62945
(c) 72495   (d) 72945

41. If PAIN is coded as UFNS, then what will be the code for REST in that code language?
(a) QFRS   (b) WJXY
(c) PCQV   (d) ANPL

42. Pointing to a photograph, a man said, "I have no brother or sister but that man's father is my father's son". Whose photograph was it?
(a) His own   (b) His son's
(c) His father's   (d) His nephew's

43. Introducing a man, a woman said, "His wife is the only daughter of my mother". How is the woman related to that man?
(a) Aunt   (b) Wife
(c) Mother-in-law   (d) Maternal Aunt

44. Sohan walks 20 m North. Then, he turns right and walks 30 m. Then, he turns right and walks 35 m. Then, he turns left and walks 15 m. Then, he again turns left and walks 15 m. In which direction and how many metres away is he from his original position?
(a) 15 m West   (b) 30 m East
(c) 30 m West   (d) 45 m East

45. Mohit walked 25 m towards South. Then, he turned to his left and walked 20 m. He then, turned to his left and walked 25 m. He turned to his right and walked 15 m. At what distance is he from the starting point, and in which direction?
(a) 35 m East   (b) 35 m North
(c) 40 m East   (d) 60 m East

Directions (Q.Nos. 46-50) *Study the following information and answer the questions given below it.*
A blacksmith has five iron articles A, B, C, D and E; each having a different weight.
   (i) A weigh twice as much as B.
  (ii) B weigh four and a half times as much as C.
 (iii) C weigh half as much as D.
 (iv) D weigh half as much as E.

46. Which of the following represents the descending order of weights of the articles?
(a) ABEDC   (b) BDEAC
(c) ECDAB   (d) CADBE

47. E is lighter in weight than which of the other two articles?
(a) A, B   (b) D, C
(c) A, C   (d) D, B

48. Which of the following article is the heaviest in weight?
(a) A   (b) B
(c) C   (d) D

49. Which of the following is the lightest in weight?
(a) A   (b) B
(c) C   (d) D

50. E is heavier than which of the following two articles?
(a) D, B   (b) D, C   (c) A, C   (d) A, B

Directions (Q.Nos. 51-53) *In each of the following questions, there are two words on the left side of (: :) which have same relationship. The same relationship should obtain between the third word and one of the four options given. Choose the correct option.*

51. Ocean : Water :: Glacier : ?
(a) Refrigerator
(b) Ice
(c) Mountain
(d) Cave

52. Clock : Time :: Thermometer : ?
(a) Heat
(b) Radiation
(c) Energy
(d) Temperature

53. Court : Justice :: School : ?
(a) Teacher
(b) Student
(c) Ignorance
(d) Education

Directions (Q.Nos. 54-56) *In each of the following questions, four alternatives are given out of which three are same in a certain way. Choose the odd one.*

54. (a) Rose
(b) Lotus
(c) Marigold
(d) Lily

55. (a) Mango
(b) Apple
(c) Brinjal
(d) Grapes

56. (a) Tiger
(b) Lion
(c) Fox
(d) Leopard

Directions (Q. Nos. 57-60) *In each of the following questions, there are three items. These three items may or may not be related with one another. Each group of items may fit into one of the diagrams (a), (b), (c) and (d). You have to decide in which of the following diagrams a group of items may fit. The number of that diagram is the answer.*

(a) 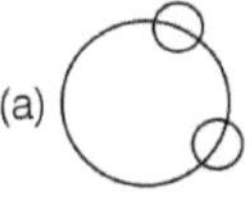 (b) 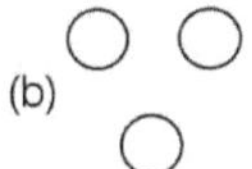 (c) 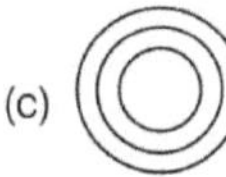 (d) 

57. Nose, Hand, Body

58. Mustard, Barley, Potato

59. Brick, House, Bridge

60. Petals, Bouquet, Flowers

Section C : General Awareness and Current Affairs

61. Which among the following National Highway routes is the longest?
(a) Agra-Mumbai
(b) Chennai-Thane
(c) Kolkata-Hajira
(d) Pune-Machilipatnam

62. The chemical name of Baking soda is
(a) Sodium carbonate
(b) Sodium bicarbonate
(c) Sodium chloride
(d) Sedium hydroxide

63. Which of the following forest types are economically most exploited?
(a) Equatorial rain forests
(b) Deciduous mixed forest
(c) Tropical hard wood forests
(d) Coniferous forests

64. Ram Prasad Bismil was associated with
(a) Kakori Conspiracy Case
(b) Alipore Bomb Case
(c) Meerut Conspiracy Case
(d) Kanpur Conspiracy Case

65. The time period of a geostationary satellite is
(a) 24 h
(b) 6 h
(c) 365 days
(d) None of these

66. Raining in Mumbai is
(a) mostly in summer
(b) mostly in winter
(c) throughout the year evenly
(d) very rare

67. Who is the first Indian batsman to score a triple century in Test Cricket?
(a) VV S Laxman
(b) Rahul Dravid
(c) Sachin Tendulkar
(d) None of these

68. The first oil well in India was dug at
(a) Bombay High
(b) Moran
(c) Digboi
(d) Naharkatiya

69. Which of the following names is wrongly mentioned among those who were hanged during the time of National Movement?
(a) Sardar Bhagat Singh
(b) Sukh Dev
(c) Ashfak-ulla Khan
(d) Chandra Shekhar Azad

70. Blue mountains are
(a) the Vindyas
(b) the Nilgiri hills
(c) the Himalayas
(d) the Aravali ranges

71. Agra city was founded by the ruler named
(a) Bahlol Lodhi
(b) Babur
(c) Sikandar Lodhi
(d) Akbar

72. Hot water is used in hot water bottles for fermentation because
(a) water can be handled easily.
(b) water can be heated quickly.
(c) water loses heat quickly due to its low specific heat.
(d) water does not lose heat quickly due to its high specific heat.

73. In childhood, Jahangir was called by the name
(a) Farid
(b) Khurram
(c) Khusrau
(d) Salim

74. The 'Grand Trunk Road' connects
(a) Kolkata and Mumbai
(b) Delhi and Chennai
(c) Kolkata and Amritsar
(d) Tirupati and Ludhiana

75. Who was the first non-European to win the Nobel Prize for Literature?
(a) Mahatma Gandhi
(b) Jawaharlal Nehru
(c) Rabindranath Tagore
(d) Sarojini Naidu

76. The World Bank's headquarters is in
(a) Geneva
(b) New York
(c) Paris
(d) Washington DC

77. 'Gandhiji's first fast in India was in connection with
(a) Champaran Satyagraha
(b) Chauri Chaura incident
(c) Communal Riots in Eastern India
(d) The strike of mill workers at Ahmedabad

78. When did the Indian National Congress adopt a resolution for complete independence of the country?
(a) 1905
(b) 1921
(c) 1929
(d) 1942

79. Secularism means
(a) suppression of all religions.
(b) freedom of worship to minorities.
(c) separation of religion from State.
(d) a system of political and social philosophy that does not favour any particular religious faith.

80. How many times has Atal Bihari Vajpayee been sworn in as the Prime Minister of India?
(a) One
(b) Two
(c) Three
(d) Four

81. Dronacharya Award is given
(a) to outstanding athlete
(b) to outstanding coach
(c) for best performance in archery
(d) for invention in science

82. Burma was separated from India in
(a) 1935
(b) 1937
(c) 1939
(d) 1941

83. Where is Dead Sea situated among continents?
(a) Europe
(b) Australia
(c) Asia
(d) Africa

84. Delhi became the capital of India in
(a) 1910
(b) 1911
(c) 1916
(d) 1923

85. The brand AIWA is owned by
(a) Philips
(b) Sony
(c) Sanyo
(d) Mitsubishi

86. A rise in 'SENSEX' means
(a) a rise in the prices of shares of all Companies registered with Bombay Stock exchange.
(b) a rise in the prices of shares of all companies registered with National Stock Exchange.
(c) an overall rise in the prices of shares of a group of companies registered with Bombay Stock Exchange .
(d) a rise in the prices of shares of all companies belonging to a group of companies registered with Bombay Stock Exchange

87. Which State of India is known as 'land of paradise'?
(a) Uttar Pradesh
(b) Jammu and Kashmir
(c) Haryana
(d) Assam

88. Which one of the following States enjoys ideal conditions for the development of petrochemical industries?
(a) Gujarat
(b) Maharashtra
(c) Tamil Nadu
(d) Uttar Pradesh

89. River Ganga does not pass through the State of
(a) Uttar Pradesh
(b) Bihar
(c) Haryana
(d) West Bengal

90. If you move towards a mirror at the speed of 10 cm/s, then your image will approach you at the speed of
(a) 5 cm/s
(b) 10 cm/s
(c) 20 cm/s
(d) Data inadequate

Section D : English Language

Directions (Q. Nos. 91-100) *Read the following passages to answer the questions given below.*

PASSAGE 1

Everything that men do or think concerns either the satisfaction of the needs they feel or the need to escape from pain. This must be kept in mind when we seek to understand spiritual or intellectual movements and the way in which they develop, for feeling and longing are the motive forces of all human striving and productivity however nobly these latter may display themselves to us.

What, then, are the feelings and the needs which have brought mankind to religious thoughts and to faith in the widest sense? A moment's consideration shows that the most varied emotions stand at the cradle of religious thoughts and experience.

In primitive people it is, first of all, fear that awakens religious ideas-fear of hunger, of wild animals, of illness and of death. Since the understanding of causal connections is usually limited on this level of existence, the human soul forges a being, more or less like itself, on whose will and activities depend the experiences which it fears. One hopes to win the favour of this being by deeds and sacrifices, which according to the tradition of the race are supposed to appease the being or to make him well disposed to man. I call this the religion of fear. This religion is considerably stabilised, though not caused, by the formation of priestly caste which claims to mediate between the people and the being they fear and so attains a position of power. Often a leader or despot will combine the function of the priesthood with its own temporal rule for the sake of greater security, or an alliance may exist between the interests of the political power and the priestly caste.

91. How did religion become firmly established?
(a) Through the constant fear of death.
(b) Through the perpetuation of faith in God.
(c) Through the establishment of religious practices.
(d) Through the growth of a priestly class.

92. How did priests come to acquire political power?
(a) By joining hand with the despotic rulers.
(b) By protecting the believers against despotic rulers.
(c) By generating fear of the unknown in the minds of rulers.
(d) By giving religious blessing to political movements.

93. 'Human soul forges a being' means
(a) that ghosts and witches are a creation of human mind
(b) that the concepts of God is a creation of human mind.
(c) Both (a) and (b)
(d) Neither (a) nor (b)

94. What motivates man's action for thinking?
(a) To satisfy his needs or to escape pain.
(b) His desire for progress or to rule.
(c) His spiritual urge.
(d) To carry out the dictates of his religious faith.

95. What feeling promoted primitive man to create religion?
(a) Love
(b) Anger
(c) Fear
(d) Spiritual revelation

PASSAGE 2

Not many people know that when the space race first began in right earnest in 1950s, the US could actually have launched a satellite before the Russian sent Sputnik I aloft. A US Army rocket which roared up from Cape Canaveral on 20th October, 1957 could have achieved orbital speed easily, but for government orders that insisted on having an empty dummy for the rocket's last stage, robbing America of a historic first. Infact, it eventually took Werner von Braun's team just 80 days to ready a satellite, once President Eisenhower's belated nod came through. So, in a way history seems to have repeated itself on Monday on the arid stretches of the Black Rock Desert in Nevada, when the rocket powered British car, the Thrust SSC, speed its way into the record books, breaking the speed of sound Mach 1 and in the process, beating its US competitor the Spirit of America.

The latter was odds-on favourite to break the sonic silence, having earlier nudged Mach 0.90 during test runs, before its aerodynamic designers called off further trials to allow more time for structural improvements. But, of course, this in no way detracts from the magnificent effort of the British team that worked round-the-clock to make what cavillers had often described as a fool's landfall-the magic figure of Mach 1, which has always been the holy girl of landspeedsters.

96. The space race first began
(a) after 1950s
(b) in 1950s
(c) before 1950s
(d) None of the above

97. The name of the first rocket launched by USSR
(a) Spirit of the USSR
(b) Mir
(c) Sputnik I
(d) None of the above

98. The first rocket sent by the USA was dummy because
(a) they were making a trial.
(b) of the government's order.
(c) the technology was not well-developed.
(d) None of the above

99. 'Eisenhower's belated nod' in the passage means
(a) Eisenhower's belated permission
(b) Eisenhower's belated interference
(c) Eisenhower's delaying technique
(d) None of the above

100. Choose a suitable title for the passage out of the options given below.
   (a) Space Loses Virginity
   (b) Achievements of the USA
   (c) Beginning Rocket Launching
   (d) Emergence of Space Era

Directions (Q. Nos. 101-110) *Choose the most appropriate option to fill the blank.*

101. In the hands of a reckless driver a car becomes a .... weapon.
   (a) lethal   (b) fatal
   (c) mortal   (d) killer

102. The numbers of orders went up............ we increased our price by 15%.
   (a) because   (b) although
   (c) when   (d) if

103. She had....... mind which kept her alert and well-informed even in old age.
   (a) an examining   (b) a demanding
   (c) an enquiring   (d) a querying

104. Their product............. more imaginatively this season.
   (a) is being marketed   (b) is marketing
   (c) is been marketed   (d) is marketed

105. They still think that women are inferior....... men.
   (a) to   (b) than
   (c) from   (d) with

106. The doctor prescribed tablets to help.............. the pain.
   (a) lighten   (b) calm
   (c) relieve   (d) rid

107. How many copies .... with the order?
   (a) did we sent
   (b) have we sended
   (c) sent we
   (d) did we send

108. The school authorities .... the child's unruly behaviour on his parents' lack of discipline.
   (a) attribute   (b) accuse
   (c) blame   (d) ascribe

109. A special committee was set up to .... on the problem of football hooliganism.
   (a) investigate   (b) inform
   (c) research   (d) report

110. If you .... in arriving late, I shall have to report to the Manager.
   (a) persist   (b) persevere
   (c) perplex   (d) perse

Directions (Q. Nos. 111-120) *Choose the word that is opposite in meaning to the word given in capital letters.*

111. IMMUTABLE
   (a) Erudite   (b) Object
   (c) Changeable   (d) Fantastic

112. COGNIZANT
   (a) Afraid   (b) Ignorant
   (c) Capable   (d) Aware

113. PROPITIATE
   (a) Anger   (b) Approach
   (c) Predict   (d) Applaud

114. REDUNDANT
   (a) Dilatory   (b) Apocryphal
   (c) Astute   (d) Insufficient

115. ABSOLVE
   (a) Bless   (b) Blame
   (c) Melt   (d) Repent

116. BENIGN
   (a) Delect   (b) Dogmatic
   (c) Dolorous   (d) Malignant

117. CALUMNIOUS
   (a) disastrous   (b) conspiratorial
   (c) querulous   (d) complementing

118. EXTIRPATE
   (a) Propagate   (b) Inseminate
   (c) Ingratiate   (d) Emasculate

119. AFFLUENT
   (a) Immigrant   (b) Conjunctive
   (c) Insufficient   (d) Filial

120. BENIGN
   (a) Captious   (b) Relevant
   (c) Robot   (d) Malevolent

Directions (Q. Nos. 121-130) *Choose the word is similar in meaning to the word given in capital letters.*

121. CELERITY
   (a) Grace   (b) Fame
   (c) Slipperiness   (d) Speed

122. SLACKEN
   (a) To grow weary   (b) To dampen
   (c) To become less active   (d) To quench

123. BARGE
   (a) To thrust forward   (b) To brag
   (c) To swell   (d) To oppose

124. DIRE
   (a) Severe   (b) Wicked
   (c) Dreadful   (d) Hopeless

125. BUTT
- (a) Bluntness
- (b) Stupidity
- (c) Target
- (d) Support

126. COMPOSURE
- (a) Assumed attitude
- (b) Liberty or musical
- (c) Restlessness
- (d) Work tranquility

127. CHAFF
- (a) Banter
- (b) Grist
- (c) Abrasion
- (d) Compost

128. LEST
- (a) Unless
- (b) But
- (c) For fear of
- (d) That

129. DEVOID
- (a) Evasive   (b) Hopeless   (c) Lacking   (d) Stupid

130. BALD
- (a) Broad   (b) Rash   (c) Unadorned   (d) Insulting

Directions (Q. Nos. 131-140) *In each of the following questions, first and last statement of a paragraph are given and marked as S_1 and S_6 respectively. The middle statements are jumbled up. Find the correct order of sentences.*

131. S_1 : Silence is unnatural to man.
- P : Even his conversation is in great measure a desperate attempt to prevent a dreadful silence.
- Q : In the interval he does all he can to make a noise in the world.
- R : There are few things of which he stands in more fear than of the absence of noise.
- S : He begins life with a cry and ends it in stillness.
- S_6 : He knows that ninety nine per cent of human conversation means no more than the buzzing of an ally, but he longs to join in the buzz and to prove that he is a man and not a wax work figure.

The proper sequence should be
- (a) SQRP   (b) PQRS   (c) QPRS   (d) PRQS

132. S_1 : Metals are today being replaced by polymers in many applications.
- P : Above all, they are cheaper and easier to process, making them a viable alternative to metals.
- Q : Polymers are essentially long chains of hydrocarbon molecules.
- R : Today polymers as strong as metals have been developed.
- S : These have replaced the traditional chromium-plated metallic bumpers in cars.
- S_6 : Many Indian Institutes of Science and Technology run special programmes on polymer Science.

The proper sequence should be
- (a) QRSP   (b) RSQP
- (c) RQSP   (d) QRPS

133. S_1 : Schweitzer goes into his little house for lunch.
- P : It is partly by this musical break in the day's work that Schweitzer keeps himself intellectually alive.
- Q : For about an hour the grand music of Back rolls away into the virgin forest.
- R : It is all too easy in the jungle for a man's mind to become stale.
- S : The meal over, he goes to his piano.
- S_6 : At two o'clock he resumes work in the surgery and continues till 6 pm.

The proper sequence should be
- (a) PSRQ   (b) SQPR
- (c) RSQP   (d) QPRS

134. S_1 : The study of speech disorders due to brain injury suggests that patients can think without having adequate control over their language.
- P : But they succeed in playing games of chess.
- Q : Some patients, for example, fail to find the names of objects presented to them.
- R : They can even use the concepts needed for chess playing, though they are unable to express many of the concepts in ordinary language.
- S : They even find it difficult to interpret long written notices.
- S_6 : How they manage to do this we do not know.

The proper sequence should be
- (a) PSQR   (b) RPSQ   (c) QSPR   (d) SRPQ

135. S_1 : A submarine is made to sink or rise by the adjustment of its specific gravity.
- P : Conversely, when water is pumped out of the submarine's ballast tanks, the specific gravity of the submarine is decreased.
- Q : Thus, when water is pumped into the submarine's ballast tanks, the specific gravity of the submarine is increased.
- R : When the specific gravity of the submarine is less than that of the water it is immersed in, it rises.
- S : When the specific gravity of the submarine is greater than that of the water it is immersed in, it sinks.

S_6 : In short, the depth of a submarine is controlled by the inflow or outflow of water ballast.

The proper sequence should be
(a) PRSQ   (b) PQSR
(c) SQRP   (d) QSPR

136. S_1 : Many people believe that it is cruel to make use of animals for laboratory studies.

P : They point out that animals too have nervous systems like us and can feel pain.

Q : These people, who have formed the Antivivisection Society, have been pleading for a more humane treatment of animals by scientists.

R : Monkeys, rabbits, mice and other mammals are used in large numbers by scientists and many of them are made to suffer diseases artificially produced in them.

S : We can avoid such cruelty to animals if we use alternative methods such as tissue culture, gas chromatography and chemical techniques.

S_6 : It is in view of these facts that the Government of India has banned the export of monkeys to America.

The proper sequence should be
(a) QPRS   (b) PRQS   (c) QRSP   (d) PSQR

137. S_1 : He could not rise.

P : All at once at a distance, he heard an elephant trumpet.

Q : He tried again with all his might, but to no use.

R : The next moment he was on his feet.

S : He stepped into the river.

S_6 : It was colder than usual.

The proper sequence should be
(a) QPRS   (b) PQSR   (c) QPSR   (d) PRQS

138. S_1 : I stood staring into the pit.

P : Across on the other side of the pit, huge and strange, lay a great flying machine.

Q : The huge engines so great and wonderful in their power, so unearthly in their shapes, rose out of the shadows.

R : They must have been experimenting with this when decay and death stopped them.

S : A crowd of dogs fought over the bodies that lay in the depth of the pit, far below me.

S_6 : At the sound of birds overhead, I looked up at the huge fighting machine that would fight no more.

The proper sequence should be
(a) QSPR   (b) QRSP   (c) PQSR   (d) SPQR

139. S_1 : Human ways of life have steadily changed.

P : From that time to this, civilisation has always been changing.

Q : About ten thousand years ago, man lived entirely by hunting.

R : Ancient Egypt-Greece-the Roman empire-the Dark Ages and the Middle Ages the Renaissance-the age of modern science and of modern nations-one has succeeded the other; and history has never stood still.

S : A settled civilised life began only when agriculture was discovered.

S_6 : During the last few years change has been even more rapid than usual.

The proper sequence should be
(a) QSRP   (b) QSPR
(c) RSQP   (d) SPRQ

140. S_1 : It is true that we cannot bring about social equality by law and that therefore there are still inequalities in Indian society.

P : In the United States of America, for instance, Negroes have equal rights under the Constitution but unfortunately these rights are not always given to them freely by the white majority.

Q : It is time for people to change their way of thinking.

R : This is a problem common to many countries.

S : It is only when we realise that social equality means not only that men are equal before the law, but also equal in the eyes of God that we can begin to have a completely casteless society.

S_6 : The secular state as found in India, recognises the importance of religion to the individual by giving him freedom to practise it and tell others about it, within the limits of the Constitution.

The proper sequence should be
(a) RQPS   (b) RPQS
(c) SRQP   (d) SPQR

Directions (Q. Nos. 141-150) *Choose the option that can substitute the given words.*

141. A person who is competent to pass critical judgement upon anything .
(a) Expert   (b) Epicurean
(c) Connoisseur   (d) Parricide

142. Lasting for a very short time
(a) Nascent   (b) Perpetual
(c) Embryonic   (d) Transient

143. A flirting woman
    (a) Virago   (b) Shrew   (c) Martinet (d) Coquette

144. Accidental solving of a crime
    (a) Investigation   (b) Detection
    (c) Sixth-sense   (d) Serendipity

145. Feeling a guilt
    (a) Reparation   (b) Remorse
    (c) Recuperation   (d) Refulgence

146. One who habitually talks in sleep
    (a) Somnambulist   (b) Insomnist
    (c) Somniloquist   (d) Blabberer

147. One who hates the institution of marriage
    (a) Misogynist   (b) Misanthrope
    (c) Philanthropy   (d) Misogamist

148. A person who believes he is always ill
    (a) Maverick   (b) Metaphysics
    (c) Neophyte   (d) Hypochondriac

149. Poetry that is silly
    (a) Observe   (b) Doggerel
    (c) Dirge   (d) Limerick

150. Something which is fit to be eaten.
    (a) Fodder   (b) Menu
    (c) Edible   (d) Gastronome

Directions (Q. Nos. 151-160) *Choose the option which contains a pair of words related to each other in the same way as the pair given in capital letters.*

151. LOVE: AFFECTION
    (a) Happiness : Joy   (b) Amity : Harmony
    (c) Enemy : Hatred   (d) Sorrow : Misery

152. SECRET : CLANDESTINE
    (a) Overt: Furtive   (b) Covert : Stealthy
    (c) Open : Closed   (d) News : Rumour

153. PEEL : PEAL
    (a) Coat : Rind   (b) Laugh : Bell
    (c) Rain : Reign   (d) Brain : Cranium

154. LOYALTY : TRAITOR
    (a) Truthfulness : Liar   (b) Hope : Optimist
    (c) Diligence : Worker   (d) Understanding : Sage

155. BACTERIA : ILLNESS
    (a) Medicine : Germs   (b) Calcium : Bones
    (c) Knife : Laceration   (d) Fire : Explosion

156. PREHISTORIC : MEDIEVAL
    (a) Akbar : British
    (b) Present : Future
    (c) Shakespeare : Tennyson
    (d) Colossus : Elephant

157. ROOM : HOUSE
    (a) Chair : Room   (b) Cabin : Ship
    (c) Wheel : Car   (d) Cockpit : Plane

158. BRICK : BUILDING
    (a) Word : Dictionary   (b) Alphabet : Letter
    (c) Platoon : Soldier   (d) Idiom : Language

159. DOUBT : FAITH
    (a) Atheist : Religious
    (b) Sceptic : Pious
    (c) Iconoclast : Idol
    (d) Apostate : State

160. PREMISE : CONCLUSION
    (a) Assumption : Inference
    (b) Hypothesis : Theory
    (c) Knowledge : Ideas
    (d) Brand : Marketing

Directions (Q. Nos. 161-170) *Against each of these questions, a sentence is broken into four parts marked (a), (b), (c) and (d). Choose the part that is not correct.*

161. (a) Passing by the damaged house
    (b) a brick was dislodged
    (c) and fell on
    (d) my shoulder.

162. (a) General is one
    (b) of the ten army officers
    (c) who held
    (d) his own flag.

163. (a) He thinks that
    (b) he will succeed
    (c) but he never has
    (d) and he never will succeed.

164. (a) Having failed
    (b) in the examination
    (c) no further attempt was made.
    (d) No error

165. (a) His all daughters   (b) are ugly
    (c) so they   (d) cannot be married.

166. (a) We are three   (b) but you have ordered
    (c) only for   (d) two drinks.

167. (a) I am hardly pressed   (b) for time
    (c) I cannot   (d) accompany you.

168. (a) My father   (b) is leaving for Poona
    (c) by the   (d) 8.30 O'clock train.

169. (a) Until you   (b) remain restless
    (c) you cannot   (d) concentrate.

170. (a) The teacher   (b) emphasised on
    (c) the point   (d) again and again.

Section E : Aptitude For Service Sector

171. Providing service to people would imply
(a) good insight
(b) planning
(c) public dealing
(d) dutifulness

172. Your colleague is having problems at work
(a) you avoid discussing his/her problem but do so if he/her asks.
(b) you advice him/her but let him/her decide on his/her own
(c) you lend him/her support and help him/her in resolving the issue
(d) you try to stay out of his/her affairs

173. Your subordinate accidentally sills soup on you in a party, you
(a) laugh it off
(b) say its 'OK' but sulk nevertheless
(c) snub him
(d) spoil his dress too

174. To take a leave you would
(a) tell the employer the genuine reason.
(b) never tell him the genuine reason.
(c) tell such a reason which seems to be justified.
(d) tell him such a reason which leaves him with no choice.

175. In an interview you are asked to describe yourself. You
(a) immediately say 'yes'
(b) immediately say 'no'
(c) ask for time to think
(d) say 'I' don't know'

176. One who has been assigned the work of managing the front office of an organisation should be
(a) disciplined
(b) a good leader
(c) full of patience
(d) owner of pleasing personality

177. You have been given a new assignment to
(a) complete it with totally new ideas.
(b) consult your colleagues for new ideas.
(c) mix old ideas with your new ideas.
(d) will think that being innovative involves risks.

178. You have a new boss. You
(a) welcome him warmly.
(b) go and flatter him as he will help you out in future.
(c) have problems adjusting as you are still loyal to your old boss.
(d) will be indifferent.

179. For an employee, the most essential thing is
(a) to discharge his duty honestly and diligently.
(b) to please the employer.
(c) to please the customer.
(d) to do his duty according to his convenience.

180. The profession of your choices is that one which provides you with sufficient
(a) opportunity to visit many places
(b) peace of mind
(c) power and authority
(d) money and fame

181. While motivating your workforce you would consider
(a) needs
(b) incentives
(c) drives
(d) All of these

182. That job is most liked by you where you can
(a) achieve administrative power
(b) have enough respect
(c) earn enough money
(d) have enough satisfaction

183. Office Manager in a hotel is the head of
(a) Lobby Manager
(b) Receptionist
(c) Guest Relationship
(d) All of these

184. If you have some problem with your employee, you would
(a) complain against him to your colleagues.
(b) get annoyed with the employer.
(c) talk to him directly
(d) do nothing

185. In case of groupism in the organisation, you would
(a) remain indifferent.
(b) encourage groupism.
(c) join a group of your choice.
(d) advise others to not include in groupism.

186. You visit the various organisations or societies because
(a) you consider it inevitable of socialisation and mental development.
(b) you consider it necessary in increase business
(c) you consider it useless
(d) you consider it essential part of your experience of work.

187. Status in the society can be maintained by
(a) behaviour as desired by the society.
(b) being a member of political parties.
(c) avoiding political parties.
(d) becoming the officer of any social organisation.

188. What would you do if you get late in the morning due to bus timings ?
(a) Let it be as it is
(b) Take the constant of management
(c) Do not do anything
(d) Make some alternative arrangement

189. Which is the best quality in man?
  (a) Ability to please others (b) Ability to work hard
  (c) Sincerity   (d) Cordiality

190. Friendship to you is
  (a) burden
  (b) a private and confidential relationship
  (c) an emotional bondage
  (d) free and frank understanding between two or
      more people

191. To be a team leader one must possess
  (a) trust
  (b) supervision
  (c) suport
  (d) decision-making ability

192. A new year's party is to be arranged in your
  college. You
  (a) try to organise it one your own.
  (b) take the help of your colleagues.
  (c) volunteer but let someone else take the lead
  (d) let them organise it themselves.

193. If you want to start with something new and you
  have little savings and few employees, what will
  be your first priority?
  (a) Generate cash flow
  (b) Figure out what business to be in
  (c) Launch products
  (d) Develop customers

194. Should the employees of an organisation be
  transferred?
  (a) No, never
  (b) Yes, annually
  (c) Only when there is urgent need
  (d) Yes, time to time

195. You
  (a) do not like to follow same routine daily.
  (b) like to escape from your daily assignment
      occasionally.
  (c) like to follow your daily routine meticulously.
  (d) feel bored and monotonous if you have to follow
      the same routine daily.

196. Service sector administration should be
  (a) restless   (b) dynamic
  (c) efficient   (d) profitable

197. Public dealings require
  (a) quick decisions
  (b) good listening
  (c) politeness
  (d) punctuality

198. In case of getting a lucrative job without social
  repect you would
  (a) continue with it.
  (b) convince your acquaintances that job is very
      good.
  (c) continue with it without telling the nature of your
      job to others.
  (d) leave it.

199. The person responsible for the management of
  the front office of an enterprise should possess
  (a) good and congenial personality
  (b) strict discipline
  (c) patience
  (d) leadership

200. A successful service is provided when the
  provider of the service is
  (a) efficient   (b) sincere
  (c) dedicated   (d) All of these

Answers

1. (b)	2. (c)	3. (a)	4. (d)	5. (b)	6. (c)	7. (c)	8. (b)	9. (d)	10. (c)
11. (d)	12. (b)	13. (a)	14. (c)	15. (b)	16. (c)	17. (b)	18. (d)	19. (c)	20. (b)
21. (b)	22. (c)	23. (b)	24. (d)	25. (c)	26. (c)	27. (b)	28. (c)	29. (b)	30. (c)
31. (c)	32. (d)	33. (c)	34. (a)	35. (d)	36. (b)	37. (b)	38. (d)	39. (d)	40. (c)
41. (b)	42. (b)	43. (b)	44. (d)	45. (a)	46. (a)	47. (a)	48. (a)	49. (c)	50. (b)
51. (b)	52. (d)	53. (d)	54. (b)	55. (c)	56. (c)	57. (d)	58. (b)	59. (a)	60. (c)
61. (c)	62. (b)	63. (c)	64. (a)	65. (a)	66. (a)	67. (d)	68. (c)	69. (d)	70. (b)
71. (c)	72. (d)	73. (d)	74. (c)	75. (c)	76. (d)	77. (d)	78. (c)	79. (d)	80. (c)
81. (b)	82. (b)	83. (c)	84. (b)	85. (b)	86. (c)	87. (b)	88. (a)	89. (c)	90. (c)
91. (d)	92. (a)	93. (b)	94. (a)	95. (c)	96. (b)	97. (c)	98. (b)	99. (a)	100. (d)
101. (a)	102. (b)	103. (c)	104. (a)	105. (a)	106. (c)	107. (d)	108. (c)	109. (d)	110. (a)
111. (c)	112. (b)	113. (a)	114. (d)	115. (b)	116. (d)	117. (d)	118. (a)	119. (c)	120. (d)
121. (d)	122. (c)	123. (a)	124. (c)	125.. (c)	126. (d)	127. (a)	128. (c)	129. (c)	130. (c)
131. (a)	132. (a)	133. (c)	134. (c)	135. (d)	136. (a)	137. (a)	138. (d)	139. (b)	140. (b)
141. (c)	142. (d)	143. (d)	144. (d)	145. (b)	146. (c)	147. (d)	148. (d)	149. (b)	150. (c)
151. (d)	152. (b)	153. (c)	154. (a)	155. (d)	156. (b)	157. (d)	158. (a)	159. (b)	160. (a)
161. (b)	162. (a)	163. (d)	164. (d)	165. (a)	166. (c)	167. (a)	168. (d)	169. (a)	170. (b)
171. (c)	172. (c)	173. (b)	174. (a)	175. (a)	176. (c)	177. (b)	178. (a)	179. (a)	180. (b)
181. (d)	182. (b)	183. (d)	184. (c)	185. (d)	186. (a)	187. (a)	188. (d)	189. (c)	190. (d)
191. (d)	192. (b)	193. (b)	194. (c)	195. (a)	196. (b)	197. (b)	198. (d)	199. (c)	200. (d)

Hints & Solutions

6. (c) According to the question,

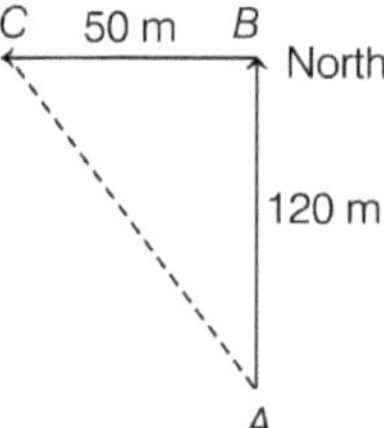

∴ The shortest distance

$$AC = \sqrt{(AB)^2 + (BC)^2}$$
$$= \sqrt{(50)^2 + (120)^2}$$
$$= \sqrt{2500 + 14400}$$
$$= \sqrt{16900} = 130 \text{ m}$$

7. (c) Let the two friends get ₹ $5x$ and ₹ $11x$ money.

∴ According to the question,

$$11x - 5x = 1350$$
$$\Rightarrow \quad 6x = 1350$$
$$\therefore \quad x = \frac{1350}{6} = 225$$

∴ Total sum $= 5x + 11x = 16x$
$$= 16 \times 225$$
$$= ₹ \ 3600$$

8. (b) $\dfrac{1}{0.04} = \dfrac{100}{4} = 25$

9. (d) According to the question,

$$\frac{x}{100} \times y = \frac{4}{5} \times 80$$
$$\Rightarrow \quad \frac{xy}{100} = 64$$
$$\therefore \quad xy = 6400$$

10. (c) We know that,

HCF × LCM = Product of two numbers
$$\Rightarrow 11 \times 7700 = 275 \times \text{other number}$$
$$\therefore \text{Other number} = \frac{11 \times 7700}{275} = 308$$

11. (d) Given $q = 60$ C

$$t = 10 \text{ s}$$

The magnitude of current in the circuit

$$i = \frac{q}{t} = \frac{60}{10} = 6 \text{ A}$$

13. (a) Potential energy of the athlele

$$U = mgh$$
$$= 40 \times 10 \times 2.5$$
$$= 1000 \text{ Joule}$$

14. (c) The velocity v_t of sound in air at a temperature $t\,°C$ given by
$$v_t = v_0 + 0.61t$$
Given, $\quad t = 1°C$
$\therefore \qquad v_1 = v_0 + 0.61$
It is clear that for 1°C increase in temperature velocity increases by 0.61 m/s.

16. (c) Given that,
Cost Price = ₹ 153
Gain = 20%
According to the formula,
$$\text{Selling price} = \left(\frac{100 + \text{gain}\%}{100}\right) \times CP$$
$$\Rightarrow \text{Selling price} = \left(\frac{100 + 20}{100}\right) \times 153$$
$$= \frac{120}{100} \times 153$$
and discount = 15%
We know that, $MP = \left(\dfrac{100}{100 - r}\right) \times SP$
$$\therefore \quad \text{Marked price} = 183.6 \times \left(\frac{100}{100 - 15}\right)$$
$$= 183.6 \times \frac{100}{85}$$
$$= ₹\ 216$$

17. (b) Let the sum be ₹ P.
We know that, $\text{Amount} = \dfrac{P \times R \times T}{100} + P$
$$\Rightarrow \qquad 6600 = \frac{P \times 8 \times 4}{100} + P$$
$$\Rightarrow \qquad 6600 = 0.32\,P + P$$
$$\Rightarrow \qquad 6600 = 1.32\,P$$
$$\Rightarrow \qquad P = \frac{6600}{1.32}$$
$$\therefore \qquad P = ₹\ 5000$$

18. (d) Let the number of boys be x and the number of girls be y.
As average age of the class = 15.8 yr
$\therefore \quad$ Total age of the class = $15.8(x + y)$ yr
As average age of the boys = 16.4 yr
$\therefore \quad$ Total age of the boys = $(16.4 \times x)$ yr
As, average age of the girls = 15.4 yr
$\therefore \quad$ Total age of the girls = $(15.4 \times y)$ yr
$$\therefore \qquad 16.4x + 15.4y = 15.8(x + y)$$
$$\Rightarrow \qquad 16.4x + 15.4y = 15.8x + 15.8y$$
$$\Rightarrow \qquad (16.4x - 15.8x) = (15.8y - 15.4y)$$
$$\Rightarrow \qquad 0.6x = 0.4y$$
$$\therefore \qquad \frac{x}{y} = \frac{0.4}{0.6} = \frac{2}{3}$$
$\therefore$ Ratio of boys to girls in the class = 2 : 3

19. (c) Let the total length of the pencil is x cm.
$\dfrac{1}{8}$ of the pencil is black.
$\therefore$ Black portion = $\dfrac{x}{8}$
Yellow portion = $\dfrac{1}{2}\left(x - \dfrac{x}{8}\right) = \dfrac{1}{2}\left(\dfrac{7x}{8}\right) = \dfrac{7x}{16}$
According to the question,
$$x = \frac{x}{8} + \frac{7x}{16} + 3\frac{1}{2}$$
$$\Rightarrow \qquad x = \frac{x}{8} + \frac{7x}{16} + \frac{7}{2}$$
$$\Rightarrow \qquad x - \left(\frac{x}{8} + \frac{7x}{16}\right) = \frac{7}{2}$$
$$\Rightarrow \qquad \frac{7x}{16} = \frac{7}{2}$$
$$\therefore \qquad x = 8$$
$\therefore$ Total length of the pencil is 8 cm.

20. (b) According to the question,
Total quantity of tea = 30 kg + 15 kg = 45 kg
Total cost price of the tea = $540 + 225$ = ₹ 765
$\therefore$ Total selling price of the tea = 20×45 = ₹ 900
$\therefore$ Profit = Selling Price − Cost Price
$$= 900 - 765 = ₹135$$
$$\therefore \text{Profit } \% = \frac{\text{Profit}}{CP} \times 100$$
$$= \frac{135}{765} \times 100$$
$$= \frac{300}{17} = 17\frac{11}{17}\%$$

31. (c) Pattern of the series is as follows,

1	6	13	22	33	46
+5	+7	+9	+11	+13	

$\therefore$ 46 comes in place of question mark.

32. (d) Pattern of the series is as follows,

3	6	18	72	360
×2	×3	×4	×5	

$\therefore$ 360 comes in place of question mark.

33. (c) Pattern of the series is as follows,

20	19	17	14	10	5
−1	−2	−3	−4	−5	

$\therefore$ 14 comes in place of question mark.

34. (a) Pattern of the series is as follows,

A B	D E F	H I J K	MNOPQ	STUVWX
+2	+2	+2	+2	

$\therefore$ MNOPQ comes in place of question mark.

35. (*d*) Pattern of the series is as follows,

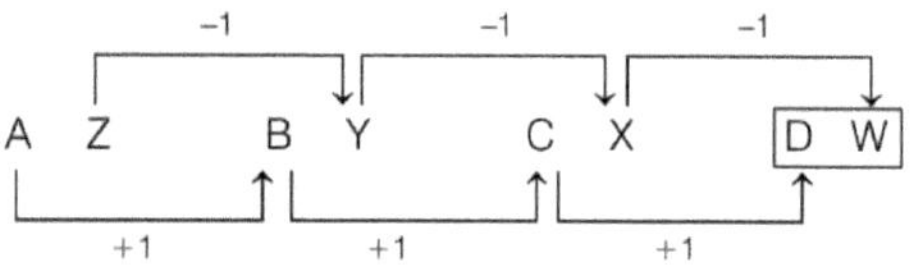

∴ DW comes in place of question mark.

36. (*b*) Given, day before yesterday was Thursday.
Then, Yesterday was Friday.
Today is Saturday.
∴ Tomorrow will be Sunday.
∴ Fourth day after tomorrow will be
$$= \text{Sunday} + 4 \text{ day} = \text{Thursday}$$

37. (*b*) We drink water when we are thirsty
but here, 'water' is coded as 'air'.
∴ So, we drink 'air' when thirsty.

38. (*d*) As,

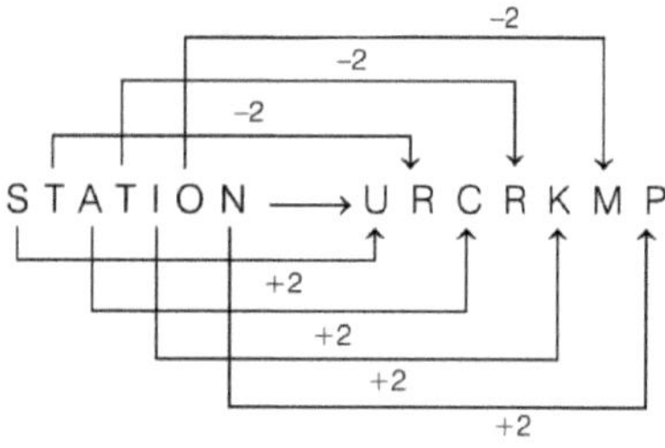

Similarly,

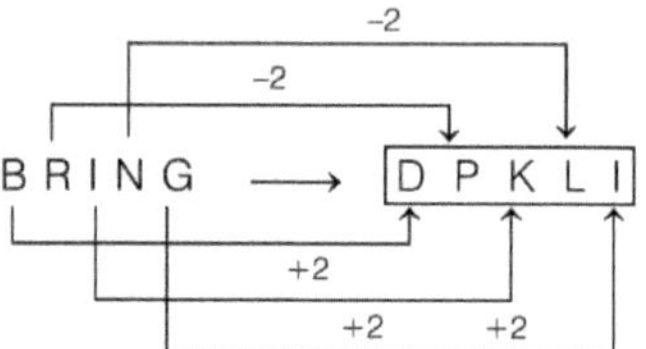

Hence, option (d) is correct.

39. (*d*) According to the question,
ni tim si ⟶ how are you
ble ni si ⟶ where are you
Here, code for are ⟶ ni/si
and code for you ⟶ni/si
Clearly, code for where ⟶ ble
Hence, option (d) is correct.

40. (*c*) As, C L O C K and T I M E

3 4 2 3 5   8 6 7 9

∴ M O L E K

7 2 4 9 5

Hence, option (c) is correct.

41. (*b*) As,

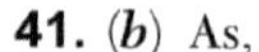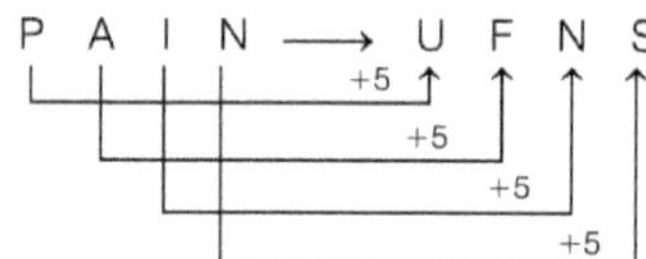

Similarly,

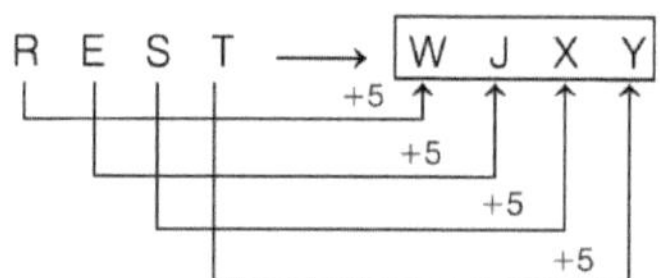

Hence, option (b) is correct.

42. (*b*) According to the question, the man has no brother
and no sister. His father's son is he himself. So, the
man who is talking is the father of the man in the
photograph. Thus the man in the photograph is his
son.

43. (*b*) According to the question,
The woman is the only daughter of her mother.
∴ The woman is the wife of that man.

44. (*d*) According to the question,

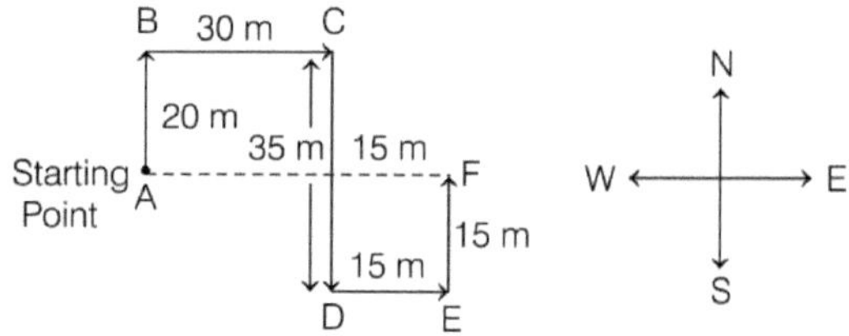

∴ Sohan is in East direction and
$(30+15) = 45$ m away from his original position.

45. (*a*) According to the questions,

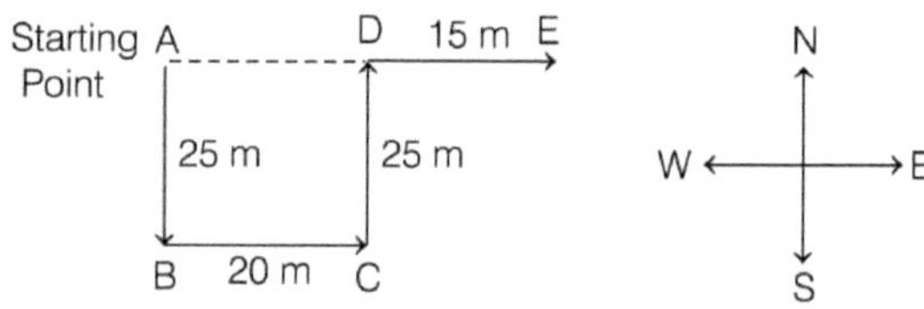

∴ Required distance = AE = AD + DE
$$= 20 + 15 \quad [\because \text{AD} = \text{BC} = 20 \text{ m}]$$
$$= 35 \text{ m}$$

and Mohit is in East direction from his original
position.

Sol. (Q. Nos. 46-50) *According to the question,*
Let the weight of *C* be *x*.
then weight of $D = 2x$
weight of $E = 4x$
weight of $B = 4.5x$
weight of $A = 9x$

46. (*a*) The correct descending order is as follows,

A > B > E > D > C

Hence, option (A) is correct.

47. (*a*) E is lighter in weight than A and B.

48. (*a*) As, weight of A is most.

∴ A is the heaviest article.

49. (*c*) As, A > B > E > D > C

Hence, C is the lightest article.

50. (*b*) As, A > B > E > D > C

Clearly, E is heavier in weight than D and C.

51. (*b*) As Ocean consists of Water.

Similarly, Glacier consists of Ice.

52. (*d*) As, Clock measures Time. Similarly, Thermometer measures Temperature.

53. (*d*) As, we get Justice in the Court. Similarly, we get Education in the School.

54. (*b*) All other except Lotus grow on land while Lotus grow in water.

55. (*c*) All others except Brinjal is the name of fruits while Brinjal is a vegetable name.

56. (*c*) All others except Fox belongs to cat family.

57. (*d*) Nose and hand are the different part of Body.

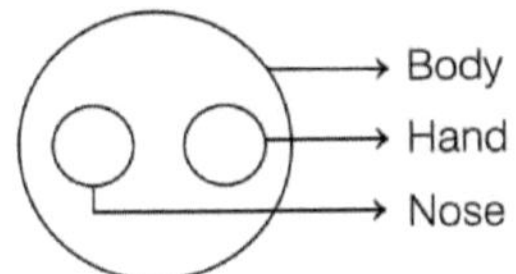

Hence, option (d) is correct.

58. (*b*) As, Mustard is categorised under oil; Barley is categorised under cereal and Potato is categorised under vegetable.

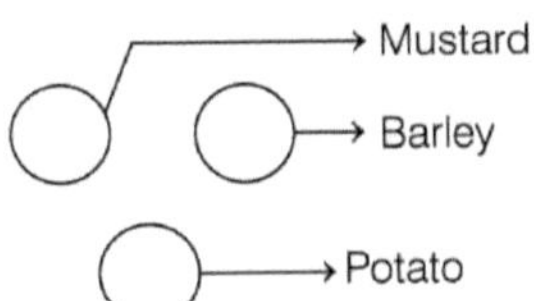

Hence, option (b) is correct.

59. (*a*) As, Brick is used in construction of both House and Bridge.

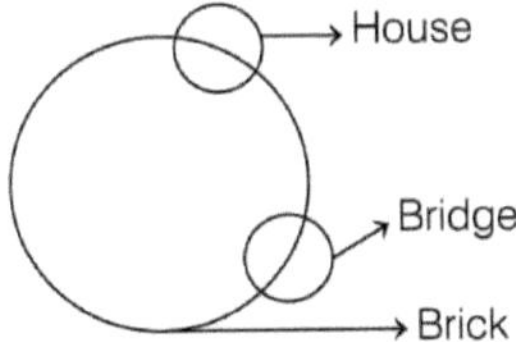

Hence, option (a) is correct.

60. (*c*) As, Flowers come under Bouquet and Petals comes under Flowers.

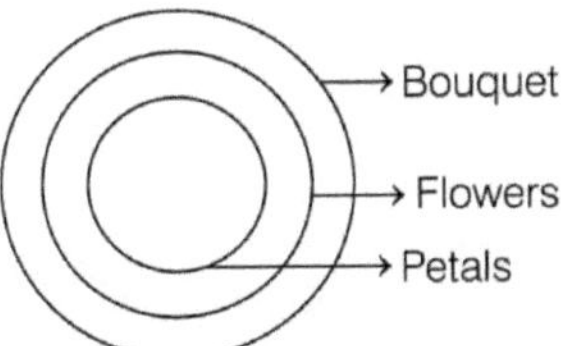

Hence, option (c) is correct.

111. (*c*) 'Changeable' is opposite in meaning to 'immutable'. 'Immutable' means unable to be changed.

112. (*b*) 'Ignorant' is opposite in meaning to 'cognizant'. 'Cognizant' means having knowledge or awareness while 'ignorant' means lacking knowledge or awareness in general.

113. (*a*) 'Anger' is opposite in meaning to 'propitiate'. 'Propitiate' means to please or placate someone while 'anger' means to annoy or provoke someone.

114. (*d*) 'Insufficient' is opposite in meaning to 'redundant'. 'Redundant' means more than what is usual or necessary or excess while 'insufficient' means not enough.

115. (*b*) 'Blame' is opposite in meaning to 'absolve'. 'Absolve' means to free someone from guilt, obligation or punishment.

116. (*d*) 'Malignant' is opposite in meaning to 'benign'. 'Benign' means kind and gentle while 'malignant' means evil or hostile in nature.

117. (*d*) 'Complementing' is opposite in meaning to 'calumnious'. 'Calumnious' means false and damaging to someone's reputation while 'complementing' means to praise someone.

118. (*a*) 'Propagate' is opposite in meaning to 'extirpate.' 'Extirpate' means to eradicate or destroy completely while 'propagate' means grow, spread and cultivate.

119. (*c*) 'Insufficient' is opposite in meaning to 'affluent'. 'Affluent' means abundance or enough of something while 'insufficient' means not enough.

120. (*d*) 'Malevolent' is opposite in meaning to 'benign'. 'Benign' means kind and gentle while 'malevolent' means evil-minded or hostile.

121. (*d*) 'Celerity' means swiftness of movement. Hence, 'speed' is similar in meaning to celerity.

122. (*c*) 'Slacken' means to become slow or inactive. Hence, to become less active' is the correct answer.

123. (*a*) 'Barge' means to hurry somewhere or through a plack in a heedless and forceful way. So, 'to thrust forward' is its correct synonym as it also means to move or advance forcibly.

124. (*c*) Both 'dire' and 'dreadful' mean extremely serious. Hence, 'dreadful' is similar in meaning to dire.

125. (*c*) 'Butt' means the person or thing at which criticism or ridicule is directed. Hence, 'target' is similar in meaning to 'butt'.

126. (*d*) 'Composure' means the state or feeling of being calm and in control of oneself. Hence, 'work tranquility' is its correct synonym.

127. (*a*) 'Chaff' means light hearted joking or teasing. Hence, 'banter' is similar in meaning to 'chaff'.

128. (*c*) 'Lest' means fearful of the possibility of something undesirable happening. Hence, 'for fear of' is the correct answer.

129. (*c*) 'Devoid' means entirely free from something. Hence, 'lacking' is similar in meaning to 'devoid'.

130. (*c*) 'Bald' means lacking adornment of amplification. Hence, 'unadorned' is similar in meaning to 'bald'.

154. (*a*) A 'traitor' is a person who betrays someone or something; hence, 'loyalty' is not their trait. Similarly, 'truthfulness' is not a trait of a 'liar'.

155. (*d*) 'Bacteria' causes 'illness' and similary, 'fire' causes 'explosion.'

156. (*b*) 'Medieval' comes after 'prehistoric' and 'similarly', 'future' comes after 'present'.

157. (*d*) 'Room' is in a 'house' and 'cockpit' is in a 'plane'.

158. (*a*) A 'building' is made of 'bricks' and a 'dictionary' is made of 'words'.

160. (*a*) "Premise' means 'assumption' and 'conclusion' means 'inference'.

161. (*b*) Option (b) is incorrect. 'Was' is used incorrectly in the given sentence. Remove 'was' to make the sentence grammatically correct.

162. (*a*) Option (a) is incorrect. In the given sentence, a particular 'General' is being talked about; hence, 'the' should be used before 'General' to make the sentence grammatically correct.

163. (*d*) Option (d) is incorrect. Remove 'succeed' to make the sentence grammatically correct as it is unnecessary.

165. (*a*) Option (a) is incorrect. The correct order of the words in option (a) is 'All his daughters'.

166. (*c*) Option (c) is incorrect. 'For' is used incorrectly in the sentence. Remove 'for' to make the sentence error free.

167. (*a*) Option (a) is incorrect. 'Hard-pressed' means burdened with urgent business. Replace 'hardly' with 'hard' to make the sentence grammatically correct.

168. (*d*) Option (d) is incorrect. The contraction 'o' clock' is only used for the exact hour. Hence, replace '8 : 30 O' clock' with '8 O' clock' to make the sentence error free.

169. (*a*) Option (a) is incorrect. A double negative cannot be used in a sentence. Hence, replace 'until' with 'so long as'.

170. (*b*) Option (b) is incorrect. Remove 'on' to make the sentence grammatically correct.

Hotel Management

National Council for Hotel Management and Catering Technology

Solved Paper 2009

Instructions

- There are Five (A-E) Sections in this Solved Paper.
- For every correct attempt, the student will be awarded **1 mark**.
- All the questions are in MCQs form and each having four options.

Marks : 200

Time : 3 hrs

Section A : Numerical Ability and Scientific Aptitude

1. The difference between a number and its three-fifth is 50. What is the number?
(a) 75
(b) 100
(c) 125
(d) None of these

2. 3.5 can be expressed in terms of percentage as
(a) 0.35%
(b) 3.5%
(c) 35%
(d) 350%

3. The square root of $(272^2 - 128^2)$ is
(a) 144
(b) 200
(c) 240
(d) 256

4. Muan obtained 76, 65, 82, 67 and 85 marks (out of 100) in English, Mathematics, Physics, Chemistry and Biology respectively. What are his average marks?
(a) 65
(b) 69
(c) 72
(d) None of these

5. By how much does $\dfrac{48}{7}$ exceed $\dfrac{6}{48}$?
(a) $6\dfrac{41}{56}$
(b) $6\dfrac{3}{4}$
(c) $7\dfrac{3}{4}$
(d) $7\dfrac{5}{6}$

6. If a and b are both odd numbers, which of the following is an even number?
(a) $a + b$
(b) $a + b + 1$
(c) ab
(d) $ab + 2$

7. The HCF of 1.75, 5.6 and 7 is
(a) 0.07
(b) 0.7
(c) 3.5
(d) 0.35

8. $337.62 + 8.591 + 34.4 = ?$
(a) 370.611
(b) 380.511
(c) 380.611
(d) 426.97

9. When a body moves uniformly along a circular path, its velocity
(a) changes
(b) is perpendicular
(c) remains unaltered
(d) None of these

10. The gravitational force with which the Earth attracts the Moon
(a) is greater than the force with which the Moon attracts the Earth
(b) is equal to the force with which the Moon attracts the Earth
(c) is less than the force with which the Moon attracts the Earth
(d) None of the above

11. Water animals can live in the severest winter because
(a) water does not freeze at the top
(b) water does not freeze at the bottom
(c) ice provides heat to animals
(d) animals can live in ice

12. In SI system the unit of energy is
(a) joule　　(b) volt
(c) calorie　　(d) erg

13. If two capillary tubes of different diameters are dipped in water, the rise of water is
(a) greater in the tube of smaller radius
(b) greater in the tube of larger radius
(c) independent of the radii and is the same in both the tubes
(d) zero in both the tubes

14. An ionic bond is formed when one of the atoms
(a) has low ionisation energy
(b) has low ionisation energy and the other has high electron affinity
(c) has high ionisation energy and the other has low electron affinity
(d) has high electron affinity

15. Alcohol is more volatile than water because
(a) it is an organic liquid
(b) its freezing point is lower than that of water
(c) its vapour pressure is 2.5 times greater than that of water
(d) its boiling point is lower than that of water

16. Light rays of different colours move in air with
(a) same velocity
(b) different velocity
(c) velocity of sound
(d) velocity of air

17. An azeotrope is one that
(a) can be separated by distillation below critical solution temperature
(b) can be separated by distillation above critical solution temperature
(c) can be separated by distillation at critical solution temperature
(d) cannot be separated by distillation

18. Colloids can be purified by
(a) precipitation　　(b) flocculation
(c) diffusion　　(d) filtration

19. How many moles of water are present in 180 gm of water?
(a) 10　　(b) 5
(c) 90　　(d) 21

20. In the concentration cells, the electrical energy is due to
(a) transfer of a substance from one solution to another solution
(b) temperature
(c) reduction of fuel
(d) chemical action

21. Which of the following acids reduce Fehling's solution?
(a) Succinic acid　　(b) Acetic acid
(c) Formic acid　　(d) Propanoic acid

22. The highest temperature at which vapour pressure of a liquid can be measured is
(a) the boiling point of the liquid
(b) critical solution temperature
(c) ionization temperature
(d) inversion temperature

23. Humus is an example of
(a) soil structure　　(b) organic colloides
(c) crystalloids　　(d) None of these

24. The smallest bone of our body is found in our
(a) Ear　　(b) Nose　　(c) Eye　　(d) Toe

25. Water plants usually have
(a) a well-developed root system
(b) a well-developed vascular system
(c) a well-developed stomatal system
(d) a reduced vascular system

26. Plankton Nekton and Benthon are not the components of which one of the following ecosystems?
(a) Marine water　　(b) Fresh water
(c) Grassland　　(d) Pond

27. Oxygen is transported to every cell of the body through
(a) RBC　　(b) WBC
(c) RBC and hormones　　(d) Both (a) and (b)

28. Rh-factor is named after
(a) monkey　　(b) chimpanzee
(c) man　　(d) None of these

29. The function of spleen in mammals is
(a) to control blood pressure
(b) to assist the liver
(c) as a haemopoietic tissue
(d) as an excretory organ

30. The protein deficiency disease is known as
(a) eczema　　(b) mycoses
(c) scurvy　　(d) kwashiorkor

Section B : Reasoning and Logical Deduction

31. Ashish is heavier than Govind, Mohit is lighter than Jack. Pawan is heavier than Jack but lighter than Govind. Who among them is the heaviest?
(a) Govind   (b) Jack   (c) Pawan   (d) Ashish

32. Going 50 m to the South of her house, Radhika turns left and goes another 20 m. Then, turning to the North, she goes 30 m and then starts walking to her house. In which direction is she walking now?
(a) North-West   (b) North
(c) South-East   (d) East

33. Nitin was counting down from 32. Sumit was counting upwards starting from 1 and he was calling out only the odd numbers. What common number will they call out at the same time if they were calling out at the same speed?
(a) 19   (b) 21
(c) 22   (d) None of these

34. Reena is twice as old as Sunita. Three years ago, she was three times as old as Sunita. How old is Reena now?
(a) 6 yr   (b) 7 yr
(c) 8 yr   (d) None of these

35. There are five different houses, A to E, in a row. A is to the right of B and E is to the left of C and right of A. B is to the right of D. Which of the houses is in the middle?
(a) A   (b) B
(c) D   (d) E

36. Raman ranks sixteenth from the top and forty-ninth from the bottom in a class. How many students are there in the class?
(a) 64   (b) 65
(c) 66   (d) Cannot be determined

Directions (Q.Nos. 37-42) *Complete the series by replacing (?).*

37. T, R, P, N, L, ?
(a) G   (b) J   (c) K   (d) I

38. H, I, K, N, ?
(a) O   (b) Q   (c) R   (d) S

39. 1, 6, 13, 22, 33, ?
(a) 44   (b) 45
(c) 46   (d) 47

40. 2, 5, 9, ?, 20, 27
(a) 14   (b) 16
(c) 18   (d) 24

41. 2, 5, 9, 14, 20, ?
(a) 27   (b) 16
(c) 18   (d) 24

42. 2B, 4C, 8E, 14H, ?
(a) 22I   (b) 20L   (c) 22L   (d) 16K

43. P, Q, R, S and T are seated around a circular table and facing centre. R is to the right of P and is second to the left of S. T is not between P and S. Who is second to the left of R?
(a) Q   (b) S
(c) T   (d) None of these

44. Rakesh is taller than Nitin but not as tall as Bhagat. Lokesh is shorter than Rakesh but taller than Gaurav. Who among them is the shortest?
(a) Rakesh
(b) Nitin
(c) Gaurav
(d) Cannot be determined

45. In a family, each daughter has the same number of brothers as she has sisters and each son has twice as many sisters as he has brothers. How many sons are there in the family?
(a) 2   (b) 3
(c) 4   (d) 5

46. One year ago, a mother was 4 times older than her son. After 6 yr, her age becomes more than double her son's age by 5 yr. The present ratio of their ages will be
(a) 13 : 12   (b) 11 : 3
(c) 3 : 1   (d) 25 : 7

47. Our mother is 3 times as old as my brother and I am 1/3rd times older than my brother. If 4 yr ago I was as old as my brother is today, what is the age of my mother?
(a) 40 yr   (b) 36 yr
(c) 44 yr   (d) 42 yr

48. Rahul is twice as old as Shiv but twice younger than Ramesh. Bhuwan is half the age of Shiv but twice the age of Naveen. Which two persons form the pair of oldest and youngest?
(a) Ramesh and Shiv
(b) Ramesh and Naveen
(c) Rahul and Ramesh
(d) None of the above

49. If FACE is coded as GBDF, then BADE will be coded as
(a) CBEF   (b) CEBF   (c) CFBE   (d) CBFE

HM 2009

50. If CHAIR is coded as FKDLU, then RAID is coded as
(a) ULGD   (b) ULKG   (c) ULDG   (d) UDLG

51. If BAD is coded as 7, HIS as 9, LOW will be coded as
(a) 50   (b) 8   (c) 23   (d) 5

52. Ravi is the brother of Amit's son's son. What is Amit's relation to Ravi?
(a) Cousin   (b) Father
(c) Grandfather   (d) Son

53. Mayank said, "My mother is the sister of Rajat's brother." What is Rajat's relation with Mayank?
(a) Cousin   (b) Maternal uncle
(c) Uncle   (d) Brother-in-law

54. If Ashokan's mother was Prakash's mother's daughter, how was Ashokan related to Prakash?
(a) Maternal uncle   (b) Aunt
(c) Sister   (d) None of these

55. If the second day of a month is a Friday, which of the following would be the last day of the next month which has 31 days?
(a) Sunday   (b) Monday
(c) Wednesday   (d) Data inadequate

56. If the seventh day of a month is three days earlier than Friday, what day will it be on the nineteenth day of the month?
(a) Sunday   (b) Monday
(c) Wednesday   (d) Friday

57. The position of how many letters in the word BRAKES remains unchanged when they are arranged in alphabetical order?
(a) One
(b) Two
(c) Three
(d) None of the above

Directions (Q.Nos. 58-60) *In each of the following questions, there are four choices. Three of them are alike and one is different. Find the odd one out.*

58. (a) Thunder
(b) Clouds
(c) Rain
(d) Rice

59. (a) Tiger   (b) Leopard
(c) Fox   (d) Wildcat

60. (a) Violet   (b) White
(c) Blue   (d) Yellow

Section C : General Awareness and Current Affairs

61. The Magsaysay Award is given for proficiency in which of the following?
(a) Literature   (b) Mountaineering
(c) Science   (d) Social Science

62. The Asian Games are organised after every
(a) 3 years   (b) 4 years   (c) 5 years   (d) 6 years

63. Sense of time is due to
(a) rotation of the Earth
(b) revolution of the Earth
(c) rotation of the Moon
(d) Both (a) and (b)

64. The velocity of winds is related to
(a) the amount of moisture they carry
(b) the nearness to the sea
(c) pressure gradient in the direction of their flow
(d) the direction in which they blow

65. Greenwich Mean Time (GMT) is the standard time of which of the following countries?
(a) India   (b) Japan   (c) UK   (d) France

66. The term 'Black Box' is more commonly used in relation to which of the following?
(a) It is a box in which high grade uranium is kept to prevent radiation
(b) It is a time capsule in which records of important events are kept to be opened at a later date
(c) It is a flight recorder in an aeroplane
(d) None of the above

67. Which of the following is not present in the blood?
(a) RBCs   (b) WBCs   (c) Placenta   (d) Plasma

68. Tides are caused by the gravitational pull of the :
(a) Earth on the Moon
(b) Earth on the Sun
(c) Sun and the Moon on the Earth
(d) Moon on the Earth

69. If a boy sitting in a train, moving at a constant velocity, throws a ball straight up into the air,
(a) the ball will fall in front of him
(b) the ball will fall behind him
(c) the ball will fall into his hand
(d) the ball will not return downwards

70. Which of the following have not undergone much of a change during the process of evolution over millions of years?
1. Crocodile   2. Cockroach   3. Horse
(a) 1 and 2   (b) 2 and 3
(c) 1 and 3   (d) All of these

71. When an object is placed between two mirrors placed parallel to each other, how many images will be formed?

(a) 2   (b) 4   (c) 6   (d) Infinite

72. The best method for improving the nutrient composition of a diet is by

(a) combining various foods
(b) use of sprouted cereals and pulses
(c) use of boiled foods
(d) use of processed foods

73. 'Let a hundred flowers bloom and let a thousand schools of thought contend' was said by

(a) Lenin
(b) Karl Marx
(c) Tolstoy
(d) Mao Tse-tung

74. Black Pagoda is in

(a) Egypt
(b) Madurai
(c) Konark
(d) None of these

75. 'Green house effect' means

(a) pollution in houses in tropical region
(b) trapping of solar energy due to atmospheric carbon dioxide
(c) prevention from ultraviolet radiations by the ozone layer
(d) None of the above

76. Arjuna Award is given for

(a) bravery on battlefield
(b) outstanding performance in sports
(c) exceptional service in emergency
(d) exceptional service to slum dwellers

77. First railway line in India was laid in

(a) 1835   (b) 1853   (c) 1917   (d) 1923

78. Khyber Pass is in

(a) India
(b) Nepal
(c) Pakistan
(d) Bangladesh

79. The Indian national calendar is based on

(a) Christian era
(b) Saka era
(c) Vikram era
(d) Hijri era

80. Who wrote the line : 'A thing of beauty is a joy for ever'?

(a) P.B. Shelley
(b) William Wordsworth
(c) John Keats
(d) Robert Browning

81. Zojila Pass connects

(a) Kashmir and Tibet
(b) Nepal and Tibet
(c) Leh and Kargil
(d) Leh and Srinagar

82. Clothes keep us warm in winter because they

(a) supply heat
(b) do not radiate heat
(c) prevent air from entering
(d) prevent the heat of the body from escaping

83. When a person enters a dark room from bright light, he cannot see anything clearly for some time. Slowly, he starts seeing things. This is because the

(a) length of lens increases
(b) iris expands
(c) iris contracts
(d) distance between the lens and retina increases

84. McMahon line demarcates the boundary between

(a) India and Pakistan
(b) India and China
(c) India and Nepal
(d) India and Bangladesh

85. Which country has the largest rail network in the world?

(a) India
(b) UK
(c) China
(d) USA

86. Who is the first Indian sportsperson to win an individual Gold medal in the Olympic Games?

(a) Leander Paes
(b) Vijender Kumar
(c) Abhinav Bindra
(d) Vikram Rathore

87. Which of the following countries is the largest producer of jute in the world?

(a) Bangladesh
(b) India
(c) Myanmar
(d) Sri Lanka

88. Who is the Governor of the Reserve Bank of India?

(a) Y.V. Reddy
(b) Shaktikanta Das
(c) Montek Singh
(d) None of the above

89. The President of Sri Lanka is

(a) Sirimavo Bhandaranaike
(b) Arjuna Ranatunga
(c) Gotabaya Rajapakse
(d) None of the above

90. Olympic Games 2012 will be held in

(a) London
(b) Paris
(c) Washington
(d) Tokyo

Section D : English Language

Directions (Q. Nos. 91-99) *Read the following passages to answer the questions given below.*

PASSAGE 1

The greatest enemy of mankind, as people have discovered, is not science, but war. Science merely reflects the prevailing social forces. It is found that, when there is peace, science is constructive; when there is war, science is perverted to destructive ends. The weapons which science gives us do not necessarily cause war, they make war increasingly terrible.

Till now, it has brought us to the doorstep of doom. Our main problem, therefore, is not to curb science, but to stop war-to substitute law for force, and international government for anarchy in the relations of one nation with another.

That is a job in which everybody must participate, including the scientists. But the bombing of Hiroshima suddenly woke us up to the fact that we have very little time. The hour is late and our work has scarcely begun.

Now we are face to face with an urgent question "Can education and tolerance, understanding and creative intelligence run fast enough to keep us abreast with our own mounting capacity to destroy?" That is the question which we shall have to answer one way or the other in this generation. Science must help us in arriving to the answer, but the main decision lies within ourselves.

91. Which of the following is opposite in meaning to the word 'anarchy' in the middle of the passage?
(a) Law and order
(b) Political dominance
(c) Economic prosperity
(d) Communal harmony

92. Which of the following would be the most suitable title for the passage?
(a) Science and social forces
(b) Science and the horrors of war
(c) Science and world peace
(d) Science and the new generation

93. According to the writer, the real enemy of mankind is not science but war, because
(a) science merely invents the weapons with which war is fought
(b) science during wars becomes destructive
(c) the weapons that science invents necessarily lead to war
(d) the weapons invented by science do not cause war, though these make it more destructive

94. According to the writer, the main problem we are faced with is to
(a) stop science from reflecting social forces
(b) stop scientific activities everywhere
(c) abolish war
(d) prevent scientists from participating in destructive activities

95. The expression 'bring to the doorstep of doom' means
(a) carry close to death and destruction
(b) lead to the threshold of a new destiny
(c) indulge in a ruinous activity
(d) introduces to an unpredictable

PASSAGE 2

True, it is the function of the army to maintain law and order in abnormal times. But in normal times there is another force that compels citizens to obey the laws and to act with due regard to the rights of others. The force also protects the lives and the properties of law abiding men.

Laws are made to secure the personal safety of its subjects and to prevent murder and crimes of violence. They are made to secure the property of the citizens against theft and damage, to protect the rights of communities and castes to carry out their customs and ceremonies, so long as they do not conflict with the rights of others.

Now the good citizen, of his own free will obey these laws and he takes care that everything he does is done with due regard to the rights and well-being of others. But the bad citizen is only restrained from breaking these laws by fear of the consequence of his actions. And the necessary steps to compel the bad citizen to act as a good citizen are taken by this force.

The supreme control of law and order in a State is in the hands of a Minister who is responsible to the State Assembly and acts through the Inspector General of Police.

96. Which of the following statements is implied in the passage?
(a) Peaceful citizens seldom violate the law, but bad citizens have to be restrained by the police.
(b) Criminals, who flout the law, are seldom brought to book.
(c) The police hardly succeed in converting bad citizens into good citizens.
(d) The police check the citizens, whether they are good or bad, from violating the law.

97. The expression "customs and ceremonies" means
  (a) fairs and festivals
  (b) habits and traditions
  (c) usual practices and religious rites
  (d) superstitions and formalities

98. According to the writer, which one of the following is not the responsibility of the police?
  (a) To protect the privileges of all citizens
  (b) To check violent activities of citizens
  (c) To ensure peace among citizens by safeguarding individual rights
  (d) To maintain peace during extraordinary circumstances

99. "They are made to secure the property of citizens against theft and damage" means that the law
  (a) helps in recovering the stolen property of the citizens
  (b) assists the citizens whose property has been stolen or destroyed
  (c) initiates process against offenders of law
  (d) safeguards people's possessions against being stolen or lost

Directions (Q. Nos. 100-110) *Choose the most appropriate option to fill in the blank.*

100. The .... transformation of the former Soviet Union or Russia as it was popularly known, remains one of biggest stories of the decade.
  (a) smooth   (b) singular
  (c) tumultuous   (d) prophetic

101. Paper money is merely a representation of wealth; therefore unlike gold or any other precious metal, it has no...value.
  (a) financial (b) fiscal   (c) inveterate (d) intrinsic

102. We must .... the tickets for the movie in advance.
  (a) draw   (b) buy   (c) remove   (d) take

103. The stenographer is very efficient. He is .... to his firm.
  (a) a credit   (b) a blessing (c) an asset (d) a boon

104. The police .... the mob.
  (a) scattered   (b) disbanded
  (c) drove   (d) dispersed

105. I cannot .... to know much about it.
  (a) imagine   (b) conceive
  (c) pretend   (d) contemplate

106. Satish was .... with a natural talent for music.
  (a) given   (b) found
  (c) endowed   (d) entrusted

107. If you drink too much, it will .... your judgement.
  (a) impede   (b) impair
  (c) impose   (d) impel

108. I did .... I could which wasn't much.
  (a) that   (b) what
  (c) how much   (d) which

109. Put your signature .... blue ink,
  (a) in   (b) through   (c) by   (d) with

110. Varun was accused of murdering his wife and though he was never......., he never recovered from the shame and the scandal.
  (a) charged   (b) booked
  (c) indicted   (d) acquitted

Directions (Q. Nos. 111-120) *Choose the word that is opposite in meaning to the word given in capital letters.*

111. CIVILISED
  (a) Palpable   (b) Civic
  (c) Incongruent   (d) Barbarian

112. WEALTHY
  (a) Wicked   (b) Famous   (c) Ill   (d) Poor

113. TRANSPARENT
  (a) Translucent   (b) Vague
  (c) Blind   (d) Opaque

114. URBAN
  (a) Rustic   (b) Rural
  (c) Civil   (d) Domestic

115. ANXIOUS
  (a) Crafty   (b) Metier
  (c) Carefree   (d) Slapdash

116. AUTHENTIC
  (a) Fictitious   (b) Duplicate
  (c) Fallacious   (d) Fake

117. PROGRESSIVE
  (a) Outmoded   (b) Brave
  (c) Revolutionary   (d) Retrograde

118. MONOTONY
  (a) Peacefulness   (b) Variety
  (c) Excitement   (d) Same

119. METICULOUS
  (a) Clumsy   (b) Irregular
  (c) Careless   (d) Irresponsible

120. FEASIBILITY
  (a) Unsuitability   (b) Impracticability
  (c) Impropriety   (d) Cheapness

Directions (Q. Nos. 121-130) *Choose the word that is similar in meaning to the word given in capital letters.*

121. INEDIBLE
(a) Unfit for human consumption
(b) Polluted
(c) Vitiated
(d) Eatable

122. DOCILE
(a) Vague　　(b) Gentle　　(c) Stupid　　(d) Stubborn

123. VIVID
(a) Brilliant　　(b) Fresh
(c) Explanatory　　(d) Picturesque

124. COMPULSORY
(a) Regular　　(b) Important
(c) Dutiful　　(d) Obligatory

125. EXEMPLARY
(a) Admirable　　(b) Clear
(c) Elementary　　(d) Ideal

126. AROMATIC
(a) Crippled　　(b) Fragrant
(c) Sentimental　　(d) Stinking

127. RIGID
(a) Sticky　　(b) Voluminous
(c) Hard　　(d) Bent

128. REFUND
(a) Deduct　　(b) Receive
(c) Distribute　　(d) Reimburse

129. CARELESS
(a) Spotless　　(b) Faceless
(c) Negligent　　(d) Vigilant

130. ELOQUENT
(a) Elusive　　(b) Articulate
(c) Frigid　　(d) Expressive

Directions (Q. Nos. 131-140) *In each of these questions, a sentence is broken into four parts marked (a), (b), (c) and (d). Choose the part that is not correct.*

131. (a) With each academic year
(b) the number of applicants
(c) are increasing
(d) in all colleges.

132. (a) The speaker highlighted
(b) the contribution of women
(c) for bringing about
(d) social changes

133. (a) India's outlook
(b) on the world
(c) is composing of
(d) these various elements.

134. (a) This exploitation
(b) of the
(c) helpless tribals
(d) need to be condemned.

135. (a) In our country women
(b) have opportunities to rise
(c) to the top in every walk of life.
(d) No error

136. (a) We met him immediately after
(b) the session in which he
(c) had been given
(d) a nice speech.

137. (a) Peoples above seventy-five
(b) years of age
(c) are not allowed to travel
(d) by air

138. (a) To make him succeed
(b) the correct thing to do
(c) is to punish him
(d) until he does not try.

139. (a) The invigilator asked him
(b) that why he had
(c) not brought
(d) his call letter.

140. (a) Now I understand　　(b) why Vishnu did not
(c) told me the reason　　(d) why he was late.

Directions (Q. Nos. 141-150) *Choose the option that can substitute the given words.*

141. One who knows many languages
(a) Linguist　　(b) Polyglot
(c) Stylist　　(d) Debator

142. A speech made to oneself
(a) Dialogue　　(b) Speech
(c) Soliloquy　　(d) Intercourse

143. Government in which all religions are honoured
(a) Fanatic　　(b) Secular
(c) Catholic　　(d) Progressive

144. A place for keeping bees
(a) Aviary　　(b) Apiary
(c) Cage　　(d) Nest

145. A place where money is coined
(a) Mint　　(b) Press　　(c) Treasury　　(d) Bank

146. A professional rider in horse races
(a) Rider　　(b) Horse courser
(c) Jockey　　(d) Coach

147. One who collects and studies postage stamps
(a) Philatelist　　(b) Stamp collector
(c) Vendor　　(d) Lexicographer

148. Place where birds are kept is called
(a) Zoo   (b) Apiary   (c) Armoury   (d) Aviary

149. An instrument for measuring the force of the wind
(a) Manometer   (b) Micrometer
(c) Telescope   (d) Anemometer

150. A decision on which all are agreed
(a) Anonymous   (b) Unanimous
(c) Obsolete   (d) Confession

Directions (Q. Nos. 151-160) *Choose the word which is correctly spelt.*

151. (a) Mustach   (b) Moustach
(c) Mustace   (d) Moustache

152. (a) Sedantry   (b) Sedentery
(c) Sedentary   (d) Sedantary

153. (a) Aproched   (b) Aproached
(c) Approched   (d) Approached

154. (a) Passanger   (b) Pessenger
(c) Pesanger   (d) Passenger

155. (a) Incentive   (b) Insentive
(c) Inscentive   (d) Inncentive

156. (a) Blisfull   (b) Blissful
(c) Blisful   (d) Blissfull

157. (a) Sattellite   (b) Satellite
(c) Sattelite   (d) Satelite

158. (a) Forefiet   (b) Forefeit
(c) Forfeit   (d) Forfiet

159. (a) Psychology   (b) Sycology
(c) Psykology   (d) Sychology.

160. (a) Accesible   (b) Accesibel
(c) Accessible   (d) Acessible

Directions (Q. Nos. 161-170) *A sentence is broken into four parts P, Q, R and S. Arrange these parts to make a logical sentence.*

161. P. four degrees below normal
Q. icy winds lashed Srinagar
R. with minimum temperature registering
S. which was already in the grip of a gruelling cold wave
(a) QSRP   (b) SRPQ
(c) RPQS   (d) PQSR

162. P. accidents are still bound to happen
Q. occasionally
R. though

S. despite everyone's best efforts
(a) SPRQ   (b) RSPQ   (c) SRPQ   (d) PQRS

163. P. through the long, hot summer
Q. if you plan to train hard
R. continually
S. you will need to acclimatise yourself
(a) QPRS   (b) SRPQ
(c) QRSP   (d) PQRS

164. P. expresses itself in many diverse art forms
Q. ancient in origin
R. the essence of the spirit of Bulgaria
S. of great creativity
(a) PQRS   (b) RQPS   (c) QPSR   (d) PSRQ

165. P. supported by soft term loans
Q. to supply imported equipment worth ₹ 8 crore
R. the Hungarian Government has offered
S. with a very low rate of interest
(a) SRQP   (b) PSRQ   (c) RQPS   (d) QPSR

166. P. and the postage
Q. I enclose a postal order
R. the price of the books
S. which will cover
(a) QPSR   (b) QSPR   (c) QSRP   (d) RPSQ

167. P. of any kind
Q. but
R. that it is without morality
S. the claim is not that science is actively anti-moral
(a) PSQR   (b) RPSQ   (c) RQSP   (d) SQRP

168. P. or even a game of tennis
Q. a typical Prakash Padukone day starts off
R. on some days
S. with an early morning
(a) QSPR   (b) SQRP
(c) RPSQ   (d) RSQP

169. P. did not know
Q. he was nervous and
R. when he heard the hue and cry at midnight
S. what to do
(a) PQRS   (b) QSPR
(c) RQPS   (d) SQPR

170. P. which one is closest in meaning
Q. read the four sentences in your text book
R. to the statement you have heard
S. when you hear a statement
(a) SRPQ   (b) SQPR   (c) SPQR   (d) QPSR

Section E : Aptitude For Service Sector

171. Your friends ask you to miss an important class to see a movie. You would
  (a) most willingly go with them
  (b) advise them not to go
  (c) think twice before deciding
  (d) politely decline to go

172. You are quite keen to buy a new model of a mobile phone with the latest features, but you know that your parents may find it too expensive. You
  (a) force your parents to buy it for you
  (b) would decide to be happy with your old phone
  (c) decide to wait for some more time
  (d) would continue complaining about it

173. You have placed an order for a few dishes of your choice in a good restaurant and the waiter brings food which you had not ordered, You
  (a) accept the food which the waiter has brought
  (b) ask the waiter to bring the correct order
  (c) create a scene to get noticed
  (d) complain to the senior staff

174. If you lose your temper over some issue, you
  (a) should count to 10 and cool down and try to reason out
  (b) should shout and scream to give vent to your anger
  (c) should just keep quiet and avoid the situation
  (d) should distract your attention from the issue of conflict

175. You tend get friendly with people who are
  (a) trendy
  (b) talkative and gossipy
  (c) simple and straightforward
  (d) markedly extroverts

176. You are working on a project along with six classmates. While dealing with them you tend to be
  (a) dominating
  (b) easy-going and remaining neutral
  (c) adjusting with others
  (d) co-operative on your terms

177. In case a subordinate is not able to accomplish a task assigned to him, you
  (a) must criticise him openly to set an example
  (b) should call him separately and guide him
  (c) compare his weakness with others in a meeting
  (d) give him another chance to perform better

178. It is seen that most effective teams have persons with diverse backgrounds and having people
  (a) fewer than 10 in number
  (b) more than 15 in number
  (c) more than 20 in number
  (d) more than 30 in number

179. A person reveals more about himself through
  (a) his body language
  (b) his verbal expression
  (c) his conduct
  (d) the way he dresses up

180. What is known to be a bigger hindrance for becoming a successful person?
  (a) Being disorganised
  (b) Having a tall ego
  (c) Being short-tempered
  (d) Taking things casually

181. To put up an excellent performance in your job, you
  (a) should have a professional attitude
  (b) should be hard-working and responsible
  (c) should be attached to your job emotionally
  (d) All of the above

182. At your workplace, what kind of relationship should you have with your colleagues?
  (a) Very close friendship
  (b) Relationship which is both friendly and informal
  (c) Formal relationship.
  (d) No relationship but exchange of only greetings

183. While purchasing a product, which of the following aspect(s) is/are considered to be most significant?
  (a) Value for money and brand
  (b) Best features
  (c) Reasonably priced
  (d) All of the above

184. Keeping the needs of individuals in view, it is seen that
  (a) all workers want challenging jobs
  (b) no worker wants to have a challenging job
  (c) vast majority of workers want challenging jobs
  (d) not every employee is looking for a challenging job

185. What type of changes can indicate stress in an individual?
  (a) Psychological changes
  (b) Behavioural changes
  (c) Biological changes
  (d) All of the above

186. If a guest loses his expensive mobile phone in the hotel premises, he should:
(a) report the matter to the police
(b) inform hotel security staff
(c) create a scene so that everyone knows about it
(d) forget about it

187. If you happen to face a serious problem at your workplace, what should you do?
(a) Pass the buck to someone and come out clear
(b) Face the problem fearlessly and look for the best option
(c) Look for help from colleagues
(d) Don't accept the blame directly and remain passive

188. In life it pays to be
(a) easy-going and casual
(b) adventurous and fun-loving
(c) caring and responsible
(d) Both (b) and (c)

189. To remain healthy and fit, one has to
(a) exercise regularly
(b) eat balanced meals
(c) avoid junk food
(d) All of the above

190. You wish to take your family out to see a movie. You would opt for:
(a) a patriotic movie, which has been a hit
(b) a famous horror movie
(c) an adult movie which is a thriller
(d) a popular family drama

191. Your immediate neighbour is quarrelsome by nature and is always fighting, even on trivial issues. You :
(a) must fight back to teach him a lesson
(b) should pacify him and reason out with him
(c) should ignore him altogether
(d) must tell other neighbours about his attitude

192. Late in the night you happen to hear strange sounds from the house of your immediate neighbour. You will
(a) ignore and opt to go off to sleep
(b) inform the police
(c) wake up your other neighbours
(d) go to your neighbour and enquire whether he need help

193. What qualities you would look for in your life partner?
(a) Rich and very good-looking
(b) Sincere and adjusting
(c) Educated and cultured
(d) Both (b) and (c)

194. You need to book a hotel for conducting a big business meeting. You would prefer a hotel which is
(a) having good ambience
(b) reasonably priced and comfortable
(c) located in the heart of the city
(d) posh and expensive

195. People who aspire to work in hotel industry should have the following personality trait(s)
(a) extremely hard-working and courteous
(b) helpful attitude
(c) knowledge of a foreign language
(d) All of the above

196. You have not been able to get admission on merit for a professional course. In such a situation you
(a) will compromise and join another course which is offered to you
(b) will decide to work harder and drop a year
(c) will pay heavy donation to get such admission
(d) will try and manipulate things to get admission

197. You tend to avoid people who are
(a) selfish
(b) cunning
(c) helpful
(d) friendly

198. You are driving to your workplace and on the way you suddenly witness an accident in which two persons are badly injured. You will
(a) avoid the scene as you are getting late for work
(b) stop and help the injured
(c) stop and motivate others to help out the injured
(d) ring up the police and proceed further

199. You wish to buy some clothes for yourself. You will choose clothes which are
(a) expensive and branded
(b) reasonably priced and durable
(c) designer-wear and trendy
(d) very reasonably priced but of low quality

200. Your grandmother suddenly feels unwell while you and your family are ready to proceed to attend a wedding of a close relation. What will you do?
(a) Leave her at home in the care of a servant
(b) Stay back yourself to look after her
(c) Ask your younger sister to stay back look after her
(d) Decide to leave her alone and attend the wedding

Answers

1. *(c)*	2. *(d)*	3. *(c)*	4. *(d)*	5. *(a)*	6. *(a)*	7. *(a)*	8. *(c)*	9. *(a)*	10. *(a)*
11. *(b)*	12. *(a)*	13. *(a)*	14. *(b)*	15. *(c)*	16. *(b)*	17. *(c)*	18. *(c)*	19. *(a)*	20. *(d)*
21. *(c)*	22. *(b)*	23. *(d)*	24. *(a)*	25. *(b)*	26. *(c)*	27. *(d)*	28. *(a)*	29. *(c)*	30. *(d)*
31. *(d)*	32. *(a)*	33. *(d)*	34. *(d)*	35. *(a)*	36. *(a)*	37. *(b)*	38. *(c)*	39. *(c)*	40. *(a)*
41. *(a)*	42. *(c)*	43. *(a)*	44. *(d)*	45. *(b)*	46. *(d)*	47. *(b)*	48. *(b)*	49. *(a)*	50. *(d)*
51. *(d)*	52. *(c)*	53. *(b)*	54. *(a)*	55. *(d)*	56. *(a)*	57. *(b)*	58. *(d)*	59. *(c)*	60. *(b)*
61. *(d)*	62. *(b)*	63. *(a)*	64. *(c)*	65. *(c)*	66. *(c)*	67. *(c)*	68. *(d)*	69. *(c)*	70. *(a)*
71. *(d)*	72. *(a)*	73. *(d)*	74. *(c)*	75. *(b)*	76. *(b)*	77. *(b)*	78. *(c)*	79. *(b)*	80. *(c)*
81. *(d)*	82. *(d)*	83. *(c)*	84. *(b)*	85. *(d)*	86. *(c)*	87. *(b)*	88. *(b)*	89. *(c)*	90. *(a)*
91. *(a)*	92. *(c)*	93. *(b)*	94. *(c)*	95. *(a)*	96. *(a)*	97. *(c)*	98. *(d)*	99. *(c)*	100. *(c)*
101. *(d)*	102. *(b)*	103. *(c)*	104. *(d)*	105. *(c)*	106. *(c)*	107. *(b)*	108. *(b)*	109. *(a)*	110. *(c)*
111. *(d)*	112. *(d)*	113. *(d)*	114. *(b)*	115. *(c)*	116. *(d)*	117. *(a)*	118. *(b)*	119. *(c)*	120. *(b)*
121. *(a)*	122. *(b)*	123. *(a)*	124. *(d)*	125.. *(d)*	126. *(b)*	127. *(c)*	128. *(d)*	129. *(c)*	130. *(d)*
131. *(c)*	132. *(c)*	133. *(c)*	134. *(d)*	135. *(d)*	136. *(c)*	137. *(a)*	138. *(d)*	139. *(b)*	140. *(c)*
141. *(b)*	142. *(c)*	143. *(b)*	144. *(b)*	145. *(a)*	146. *(c)*	147. *(a)*	148. *(d)*	149. *(d)*	150. *(b)*
151. *(d)*	152. *(c)*	153. *(d)*	154. *(d)*	155. *(a)*	156. *(b)*	157. *(b)*	158. *(c)*	159. *(a)*	160. *(c)*
161. *(a)*	162. *(a)*	163. *(c)*	164. *(b)*	165. *(c)*	166. *(c)*	167. *(d)*	168. *(a)*	169. *(c)*	170. *(b)*
171. *(d)*	172. *(c)*	173. *(b)*	174. *(a)*	175. *(d)*	176. *(c)*	177. *(b)*	178. *(a)*	179. *(c)*	180. *(d)*
181. *(a)*	182. *(b)*	183. *(d)*	184. *(c)*	185. *(d)*	186. *(b)*	187. *(b)*	188. *(c)*	189. *(d)*	190. *(d)*
191. *(b)*	192. *(d)*	193. *(d)*	194. *(b)*	195. *(d)*	196. *(b)*	197. *(a)*	198. *(b)*	199. *(b)*	200. *(b)*

Hints & Solutions

1. (*c*) Let the number be *x*.

According to the question,

$$x - \frac{3}{5} \text{ of } x = 50$$

$$\Rightarrow \quad x - \frac{3x}{5} = 50$$

$$\Rightarrow \quad \frac{2x}{5} = 50$$

$$\Rightarrow \quad x = \frac{50 \times 5}{2}$$

$$\therefore \quad x = 125$$

2. (*d*) $3.5 = \frac{35}{10} \times 100$

$$= \frac{3500}{10} = 350\%$$

3. (*c*) $(272^2 - 128^2) = (272 + 128)(272 - 128)$

$$[\because a^2 - b^2 = (a+b)(a-b)]$$

$$= 400 \times 144$$

$\therefore$ Square root of

$$(272^2 - 128^2) = \sqrt{(272^2 - 128^2)} = \sqrt{400 \times 144}$$

$$= 20 \times 12 = 240$$

4. (*d*) According to the question,

Average marks obtained by Muan

$$= \frac{76 + 65 + 82 + 67 + 85}{5}$$

$$= \frac{375}{5} = 75$$

5. (*a*) The required difference

$$= \frac{48}{7} - \frac{6}{48} = \frac{48}{7} - \frac{1}{8}$$

$$= \frac{384 - 7}{56} = \frac{377}{56} = 6\frac{41}{56}$$

6. (*a*) We know that sum of two odd numbers is always an even number.

If *a* and *b* are odd numbers, then $(a + b)$ is an even number.

Hence, option (*a*) is correct.

7. (*a*) The numbers 1.75, 5.6 and 7 can be written as

$$\frac{175}{100}, \frac{56}{10}, \frac{7}{1}.$$

Now, HCF of $\frac{175}{100}, \frac{56}{10}, \frac{7}{1} = \frac{\text{HCF of 175, 56, 7}}{\text{LCM of 100, 10, 1}}$

$$= \frac{7}{100} = 0.07$$

8. (*c*) $337.62 + 8.591 + 34.4 = ?$

$$\Rightarrow \quad ? = 337.620 + 8.591 + 34.400$$

$$\therefore \quad ? = 380.611$$

31. (*d*) According to the question,

Weight of Ashish > Weight of Govind

Weight of Govind > Weight of Pawan

Weight of Pawan > Weight of Jack

Weight of Jack > Weight of Mohit

$\therefore$ Ashish > Govind > Pawan > Jack > Mohit

Hence, Ashish is heaviest among all.

32. (*a*) According to the question,

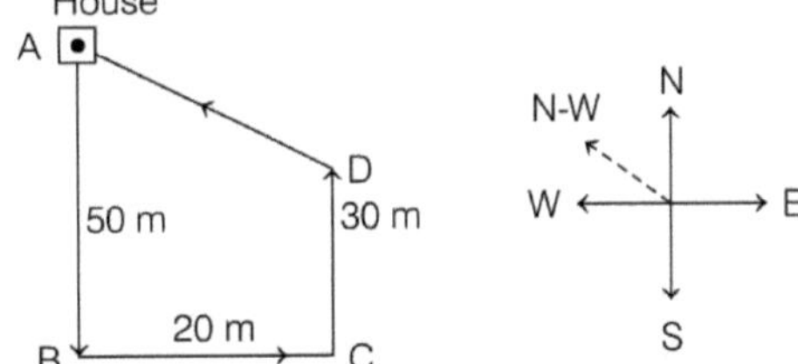

Clearly, Radhika is walking in the North-West direction.

33. (*d*) Sumit was counting only 16 digits but Nitin was counting 32 numbers. As the speed of Sumit and Nitin is same. Sumit's number will finish faster than Nitin's. Hence, they will never call out the same number.

34. (*d*) Let the age of Sunita be *x* years.

Then age of Reena = 2*x* yr

According to the question,

$$2x - 3 = 3(x - 3)$$

$$\Rightarrow \quad 2x - 3 = 3x - 9$$

$$\Rightarrow \quad x = 6$$

$\therefore$ Age of Reena $= 6 \times 2 = 12$ yr

35. (*a*) According to the question,

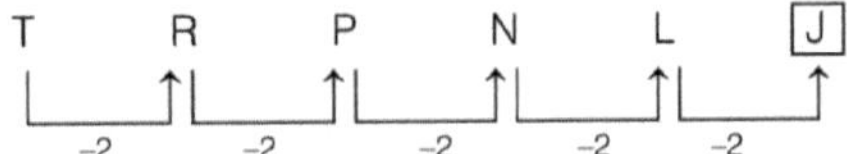

Clearly, House A is in the middle.

36. (*a*) We know that, total number of students

= (Rank from the top + Rank from the bottom − 1)

$= (16 + 49) - 1 = 65 - 1 = 64$

37. (*b*) Pattern of the series is as follows,

$\therefore$ J comes in place of '?'.

38. (*c*) Pattern of the series is as follows,

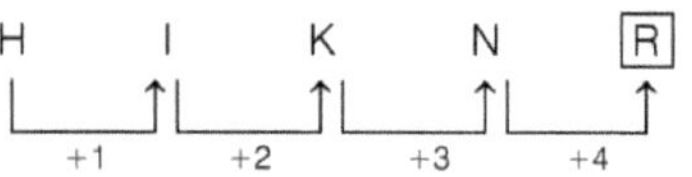

∴ R comes in place of '?'.

39. (*c*) Pattern of the series is as follows,

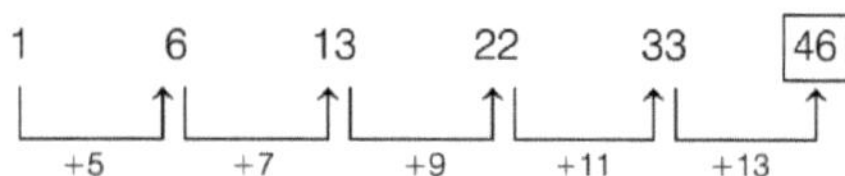

∴ 46 comes in place of ?.

40. (*a*) Pattern of the series is as follows,

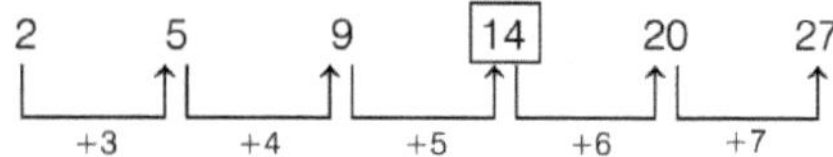

∴ 14 comes in place of ?.

41. (*a*) Pattern of the series is as follows,

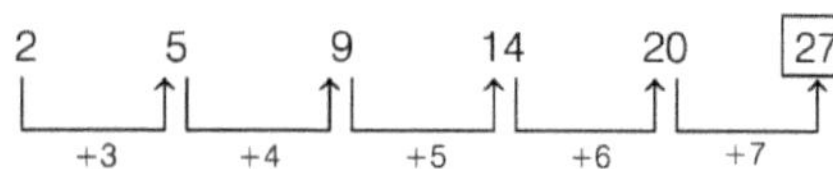

∴ 27 comes in place of '?'

42. (*c*) Pattern of the series is as follows,

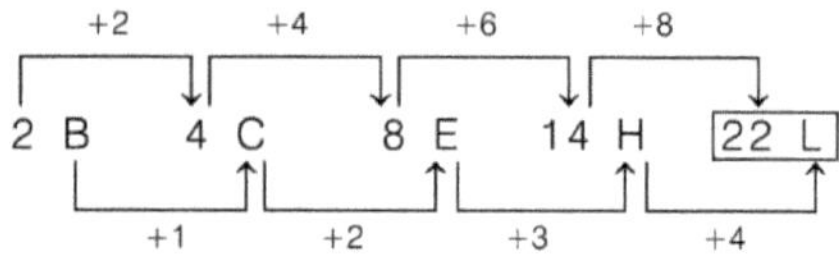

∴ 22 L comes in place of ?.

43. (*a*) According to the question,

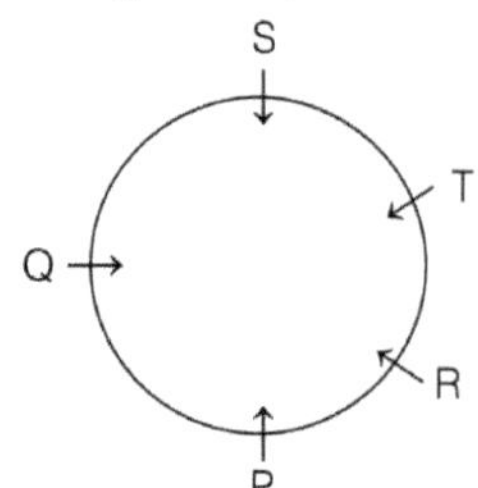

Clearly, Q is second to the left of R.

44. (*d*) According to the question,

Bhagat > Rakesh > Nitin and Rakesh > Lokesh > Gaurav.

From the given information, we cannot determine who is shortest.

45. (*b*) Let x and y represent the number of daughter and son respectively.

According to the question,

$$x - 1 = y$$
$$\Rightarrow \qquad x = y + 1 \qquad \qquad \text{...(i)}$$

and $\qquad 2(y - 1) = x$

$\Rightarrow \qquad 2(y - 1) = y + 1 \qquad\qquad$ [by Eq. (i)]

$\Rightarrow \qquad 2y - 2 = y + 1$

$\Rightarrow \qquad 2y - y = 2 + 1$

$\Rightarrow \qquad\qquad y = 3$

∴ Total number of sons in the family is 3.

46. (*d*) Let one year ago,

Mother's age = $4x$ years and son's age = x years

According to the question,

$$(4x + 7) - 2(x + 7) = 5$$
$$\Rightarrow \qquad 4x + 7 - 2x - 14 = 5$$
$$\Rightarrow \qquad\qquad 2x - 7 = 5$$
$$\Rightarrow \qquad\qquad 2x = 12$$
$$\Rightarrow \qquad\qquad x = 6$$

∴ Present age of mother $= 4x + 1$

$$= 4 \times 6 + 1 = 25 \text{ yr}$$

Present age of son $= x + 1 = 6 + 1 = 7$ yr

∴ Required ratio $= \dfrac{25}{7} = 25 : 7$

47. (*b*) Let the age of my brother = x years

Then, age of our mother = $3x$ yr

and my age $= x + \dfrac{x}{3} = \dfrac{4x}{3}$ years

According to the question,

$$x = \dfrac{4x}{3} - 4$$
$$\Rightarrow \qquad \dfrac{4x}{3} - x = 4$$
$$\Rightarrow \qquad \dfrac{4x - 3x}{3} = 4$$
$$\Rightarrow \qquad \dfrac{x}{3} = 4 \quad \Rightarrow \quad x = 12$$

∴ Present age of my mother $= 3 \times 12 = 36$ yr.

48. (*b*) According to the question,

Ramesh > Rahul > Shiv > Bhuwan > Naveen

∴ Ramesh and Naveen forms the pair of oldest and youngest.

49. (*a*) As, 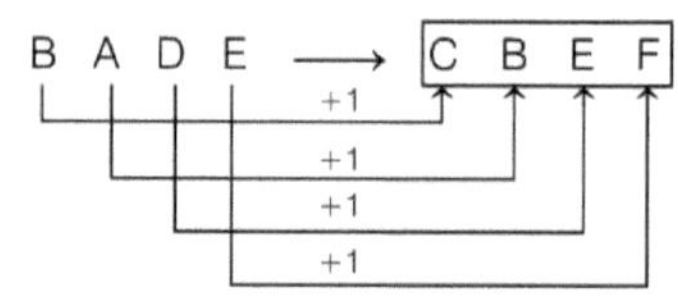

Similarly,

∴ BADE is coded as CBEF.

50. (*d*) As,

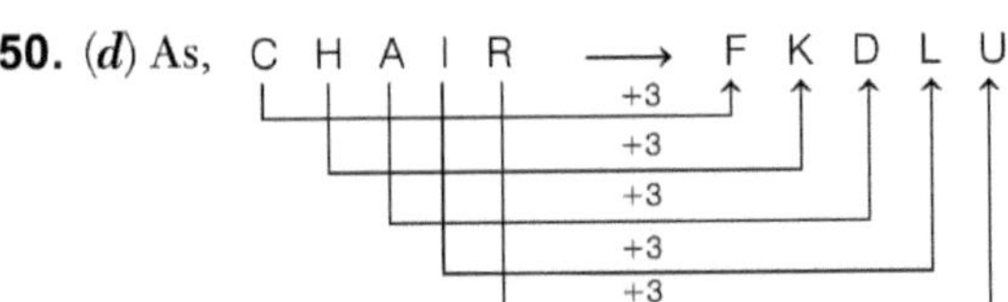

Similarly,

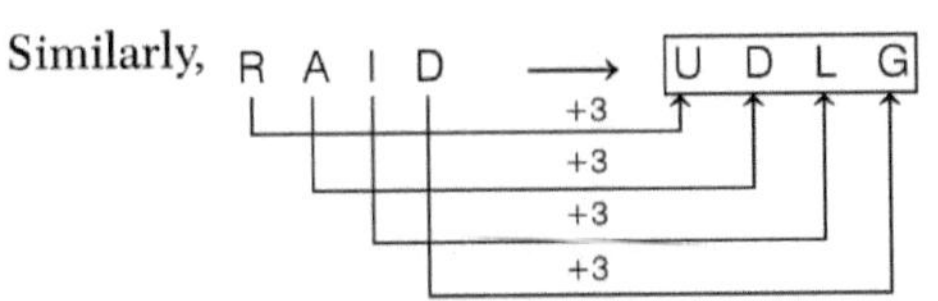

∴ RAID is coded as UDLG.

51. (*d*) As,

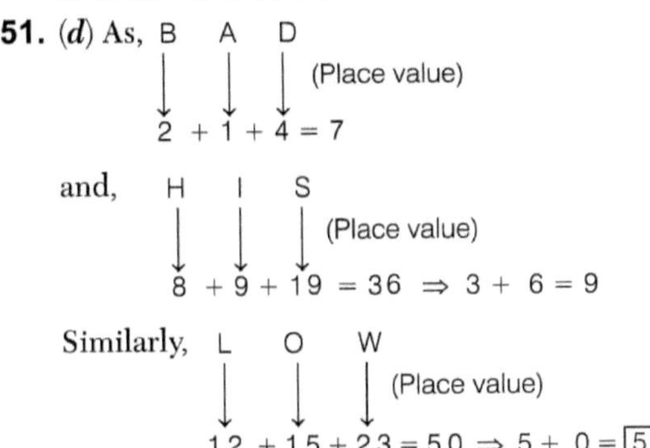

Here, the sum of place value of the letters converted into a single digit.

52. (*c*) As, Ravi is the brother of Amit's son's son. So, Amit is grandfather of Ravi.

53. (*b*) As, Mayank's mother is the sister of Rajat's brother. It means Mayank's mother is the sister of Rajat. So, Rajat is maternal uncle of Mayank.

54. (*a*) As, Ashokan's mother was Prakash's mother's daughter.

It means Ashokan's mother is the sister of Prakash.

Hence, Prakash is the maternal uncle of Ashokan.

55. (*d*) We cannot find the last day of next month. As total number of days of current month is not given.

Hence, data is inadequate here.

56. (*a*) Three days earlier than Friday is Tuesday.

∴ Seventh day of the month is Tuesday.

19th day $= ((7 \times 2) + 5)$ th day is 5th day after Tuesday.

∴ As fifth day after Tuesday is Sunday.

∴ The required day on 19th day of the month

$$= \text{Sunday}$$

57. (*b*) According to the question,

```
          B  R  A | K | E | S |
After arrangement  A  B  E | K | R | S |
```

Thus, the position of two letters remains unchanged.

58. (*d*) All others, except rice belongs to rain.

59. (*c*) All others, except fox belongs to cat family.

60. (*b*) All others, except white belongs to colours of Rainbow.

91. (*a*) 'Anarchy' means a state of disorder due to absence of authority ; or lawlessness. Hence 'law and order' is its correct antonym.

111. (*d*) 'Barbarian' is opposite in meaning to 'civilised'. 'Civilised' means polite and well-mannered while 'barbarian' means uncultured or brutish.

113. (*d*) 'Opaque' is opposite in meaning to 'transparent'. 'Transparent' means a see-through object while 'opaque' means an object that can't be seen through.

115. (*c*) 'Carefree' is opposite in meaning to 'anxious'. 'Anxious' means feeling worried or uneasy about something.

116. (*d*) 'Fake' is opposite in meaning to 'authentic'. 'Authentic' means genuine or not a copy.

117. (*a*) 'Outmoded' is opposite in meaning to 'progressive'. 'Progressive' means favouring change or innovation or modern while 'outmoded' means old-fashioned or out of date.

118. (*b*) 'Variety' is opposite in meaning to 'monotony'. 'Monotony' means lacking interest and repetitive while 'variety' means the state of being diverse.

119. (*c*) 'Careless' is opposite in meaning to 'meticulous'. 'Meticulous' means very careful and precise.

120. (*b*) 'Impracticability' is opposite in meaning to 'feasibility'. 'Feasibility' means the state of being easily or conveniently done while 'impracticability' means incapable of being performed or accomplished.

122. (*b*) 'Docile' means ready to accept instruction or complaint. Hence, 'gentle' is similar in meaning to 'docile'.

123. (*a*) 'Vivid' means intensely deep or bright. Hence, 'brilliant' is similar in meaning to vivid.

124. (*d*) 'Obligatory' means required by a legal, moral or other rule; or mandatory. Hence, it is the correct synonym of 'compulsory'.

125. (*d*) Both 'exemplary' and 'ideal' mean a desirable model or perfect. Hence, 'ideal' is similar in meaning to 'exemplary.'

126. (*b*) Both 'aromatic' and 'fragrant' mean having a pleasant or distinctive smell. Hence, 'fragrant' is similar in meaning to aromatic.

128. (*d*) 'Refund' means a repayment of a sum of money and 'reimburse' means to repay. Hence, 'reimburse' is similar in meaning to refund.

129. (*c*) 'Negligent' means failing to take proper care of something. Hence, it is similar in meaning to 'careless'.

130. (*d*) 'Eloquent' means fluent or persuasive in speaking or writing and 'expressive' means effectively conveying thought or feeling. Hence, 'expressive' is similar in meaning to 'eloquent'.

131. (*c*) Option (c) is incorrect. As the subject corresponding to the verb 'are' is 'number', i.e., singular, hence, the verb should also be used in singular form. Replace 'are' with 'is' to make the sentence grammatically correct.

132. (*c*) Option (c) is incorrect. Preposition 'for' is incorrectly used. Replace 'for' with 'in' to make the sentence grammatically correct.

133. (*c*) Option (c) is incorrect. The continuous form of the verb is used incorrectly. Replace 'composing' with 'composed' to make the sentence grammatically correct.

134. (*d*) Option (d) is incorrect. Replace 'need' with 'needs' to make the sentence grammatically correct.

135. (*d*) The given sentence is error free and grammatically correct.

136. (*c*) Option (c) is incorrect. Replace 'had been given' with 'had given' to make the sentence grammatically correct.

137. (*a*) Option (a) is incorrect. The noun 'people' remains as it is in its plural form; hence, 'peoples' is incorrect. Replace 'peoples' with 'people' to make the sentence grammatically correct.

138. (*d*) Option (d) is incorrect. Replace 'does not try' with 'tries' to make the sentence grammatically correct.

139. (*b*) Option (b) is incorrect. Replace 'that why he had' with 'why had he' to make the sentence grammatically correct.

140. (*c*) Option (c) is incorrect. The past form of verb is not used with 'did'. Replace 'told' with 'tell' to make the sentence grammatically correct.

Hotel Management

National Council for Hotel Management and Catering Technology

Solved Paper 2008

Instructions

- There are Five (A-E) Sections in this Solved Paper.
- For every correct attempt, the student will be awarded **1 mark**.
- All the questions are in MCQs form and each having four options.

Marks : 200

Time : 3 hrs

Section A : Numerical Ability and Scientific Aptitude

1. Division of 3.54 by 2.7 is same as division of ? by 27.
(a) 354
(b) 35.4
(c) 0.354
(d) None of these

2. A train runs from New Delhi to Ghaziabad, in 1 h and 20 min. If the train is running at the speed of 18 km/h, then the distance between New Delhi and Ghaziabad is
(a) 27 km
(b) 20 km
(c) 24 km
(d) 30 km

3. Between two different rational numbers, there lie(s)
(a) no fraction
(b) only one fraction
(c) infinite number of fractions
(d) only a finite number of fractions

4. Which of the following fractions is the largest ?
(a) $\dfrac{5}{6}$
(b) $\dfrac{6}{7}$
(c) $\dfrac{7}{8}$
(d) $\dfrac{8}{9}$

5. Successive discounts of 10% and 15% are equivalent to a discount of
(a) 12.5%
(b) 25%
(c) 17%
(d) 23.5%

6. Mr. Abhishek borrowed ₹ 600 and returned ₹ 856.50 at the end of 9 yr and 6 months. Thus he paid interest at the rate of
(a) 7%
(b) 6%
(c) 5%
(d) 4.5%

7. A man rowed a distance of 1 km downstream in 6 min and rowed back the same distance in half an hour. Then the speed of the man in still water is
(a) 10 km/h
(b) 6 km/h
(c) 4 km/h
(d) 2 km/h

8. Ashu spends 25% less than Nishu on Diwali fireworks. How much per cent more did Nishu spend than Ashu?
(a) 20%
(b) 25%
(c) 30%
(d) $33\dfrac{1}{3}\%$

9. A force of 100 dynes acts on a mass of 5 gm for 10 sec. Find the change in momentum.
(a) 10 C.G.S. units
(b) 100 C.G.S. units
(c) 1000 C.G.S. units
(d) 10000 C.G.S. units

10. What horse power engine is required to lift 1100 lbs of iron per second from a mine 20 ft. deep?

(a) 40   (b) 30   (c) 20   (d) 10

11. $\sqrt{0.9} =$

(a) 0.3   (b) 0.03
(c) 0.949   (d) None of these

12. Which of the rational numbers lies between $\dfrac{2}{5}$ and $\dfrac{3}{4}$?

(a) $\dfrac{3}{10}$ (b) $\dfrac{4}{5}$ (c) $\dfrac{1}{2}$ (d) $\dfrac{3}{8}$

13. If $x\sqrt{y} = \sqrt{80}$, then $y =$

(a) 5   (b) 4   (c) 10   (d) 8

14. If ₹ 400 becomes ₹ 480 in 4 yr, then the rate of simple interest per annum is

(a) 5%   (b) $8\dfrac{1}{3}\%$ (c) $12\dfrac{1}{2}\%$ (d) 15%

15. Ashu and Nishu start from home at 9 am and 11 : 30 am, respectively to meet some of their friends. If Ashu moves at a speed of 4 km per hour and Nishu at the speed of 9 km per hour, then at what time will Nishu overtake Ashu?

(a) 1 : 30 pm
(b) 2 : 30 pm
(c) 2 : 45 pm
(d) Insufficient data to predict

16. If 2 men and 3 women can finish a work in 5 h; 3 men and 2 women in 4 h, then 2 men and 1 woman can finish it in

(a) more than 5 h but less than 6 h
(b) more than 6 h but less than 7 h
(c) more than 4 h, but less than 5 h
(d) None of the above

17. Which of the following number is divisible by 11?

(a) 72594833   (b) 98673905
(c) 1642710455   (d) 365479811

18. If the sum of three consecutive integers is 15, then their product is

(a) 54   (b) 60   (c) 120   (d) 150

19. The cost of a book is 75% plus 75% of its total price. What is the price of the book?

(a) ₹ 1.50   (b) ₹ 3.50
(c) ₹ 3.75   (d) None of these

20. How many prime numbers are there between 1 and 10?

(a) 5   (b) 4
(c) 8   (d) 3

21. A galactometer measures

(a) volume of gases
(b) density of liquids
(c) length .4 curved lines
(d) absolute purity of milk

22. Which of the following is a chemical change?

(a) Solvent extraction of oil from mustard seeds
(b) Distillation of water
(c) Electrolysis of water
(d) Freezing of water

23. Which one of the following is not a constituent of a chlorophyll molecule?

(a) Magnesium   (b) Carbon
(c) Hydrogen   (d) Calcium

24. Rice is a fruit known as

(a) Follicle   (b) Pome
(c) Caryopsis   (d) Drupe

25. Electrolysis of water is a

(a) physical change   (b) chemical change
(c) radioactive change   (d) None of these

26. Wheel is an example of which kind of lever?

(a) First
(b) Second
(c) Third
(d) None of the above

27. A certain given number is divisible by 6 and 8 both. Then which of the following numbers does not necessarily divide the given number?

(a) 3   (b) 12
(c) 24   (d) 48

28. The unit of brightness is called the

(a) Foot-candle   (b) Phot
(c) Lux   (d) Lambert

29. Of the following media, the speed of sound will be greatest in

(a) metal bar   (b) water
(c) air   (d) vacuum

30. One gram weight is equal to

(a) 9.81 dynes
(b) 981 dynes
(c) 98.1 dynes
(d) 0.981 dynes

Section B : Reasoning and Logical Deduction

Directions (Q. Nos. 31-35) *Find the odd one out.*

31. Iron, Sodium, Mercury, Potassium, Gold

(a) Iron   (b) Mercury   (c) Sodium   (d) Gold

32. February, April, December, July, January.

(a) April   (b) July

(c) January   (d) February

33. Mango, Guava, Grapes, Potato, Pineapple.

(a) Guava   (b) Pineapple

(c) Potato   (d) Grapes

34. 64, 36, 9, 49, 125, 81

(a) 81   (b) 125

(c) 9   (d) 36

35. London, Washington, Riyadh, New Delhi, Allahabad

(a) Washington   (b) Riyadh

(c) New Delhi   (d) Allahabad

Directions (Q. Nos. 36 and 37) *The words in the first set have a certain relationship. Choose the word from the choices that has the same relationship with the word in the second set.*

36. Book : Paper :: ? : Thread

(a) Cotton   (b) Stitch

(c) Weaving   (d) Cloth

37. Market : Demand :: Farming : ?

(a) Farmer   (b) Loans

(c) Foodgrains   (d) Monsoon

38. If HOBBY is coded as IOBY, LOBBY is coded as MOBY, then BOBBY is coded as

(a) BOBY   (b) COBY

(c) DOBY   (d) OOBY

39. In a certain code QUIET is written as TXLHW. How is FLOAT written in that code?

(a) TORDW   (b) HNQCV

(c) INRCW   (d) IORDW

40. In a certain code BANANA is written as ANANAB. How is MELON written in that code?

(a) KENDM   (b) NFMPO

(c) NPOKS   (d) NOLEM

Directions (Q. Nos. 41-43) *For each question below, determine the relationship between the pair of capitalised words and then select the lettered pair of words which have a similar relationship as the given pair.*

41. Multiplication : Division : :

(a) Increase : Decrease

(b) Zero : Infinity

(c) Calculate : Estimate

(d) Digit : Series

42. Water : Conduit : :

(a) Electricity : Magnet   (b) Elevator : Shaft

(c) Shell : Rifle   (d) Noise : Cannon

43. Plaintiff : Defendant : :

(a) Court : Law

(b) Injured : Accused

(c) Judge : Jury

(d) District Attorney : Lawyer

Directions (Q. Nos. 44-53) *Find the missing term in each of the series.*

44. C, E, H, L, Q, (?)

(a) R   (b) W   (c) U   (d) X

45. ADG, GJM, (?)

(a) NOT   (b) MOQ

(c) MPS   (d) WTO

46. PAT, PEN, PIN, POT, (?)

(a) PIG   (b) PET

(c) PUT   (d) POT

47. 22, 15, 8, 1, (?), −13

(a) 8   (b) −8

(c) −6   (d) 0

48. 7, 9, 13, 21, (?)

(a) 31   (b) 35

(c) 32   (d) 37

49. 0, 7, 26, 63, 124, (?)

(a) 256   (b) 240

(c) 215   (d) 246

50. 2, 3, 5, 9, 17, (?)

(a) 26   (b) 15   (c) 33   (d) 18

51. 3, 11, 35, 107, (?)

(a) 111   (b) 323   (c) 413   (d) 513

52. J, F, M, A, M, (?)

(a) M   (b) J   (c) D   (d) S

53. BEH, DGJ, (?), EJO, GLQ, INS

(a) FLR   (b) FIS   (c) FKO   (d) FIL

Directions (Q. Nos. 54-60) *Which one of the four answer figures should come after the question figures if the sequence were to be completed ?*

54. Question Figures

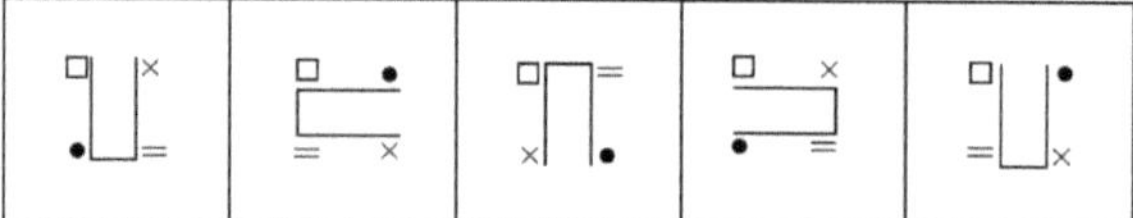

Answer Figures

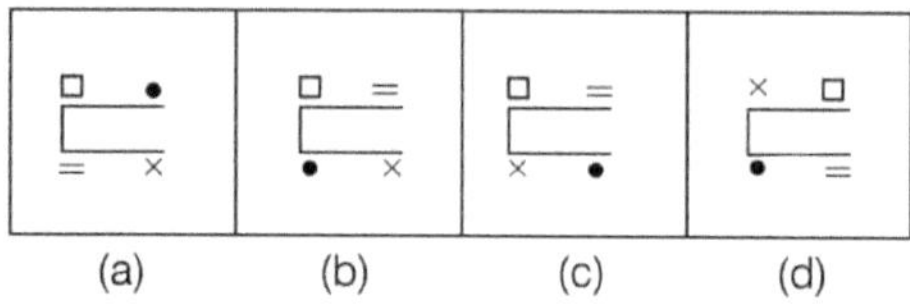

(a)   (b)   (c)   (d)

55. Question Figures

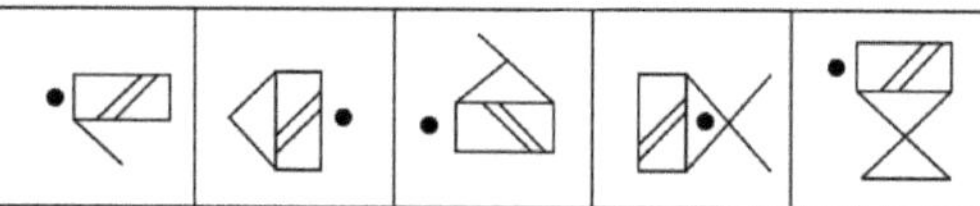

Answer Figures

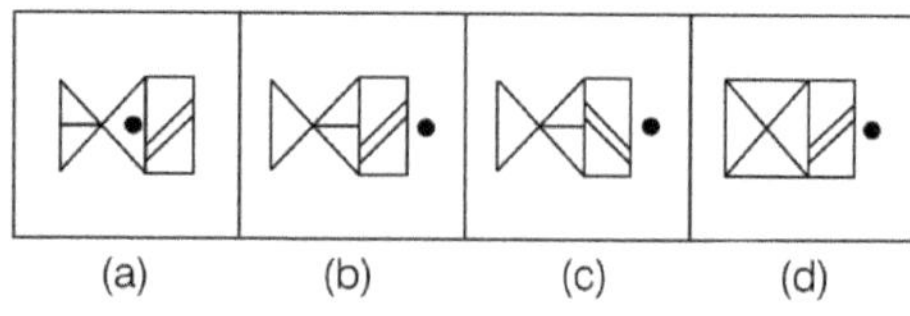

(a)   (b)   (c)   (d)

56. Question Figures

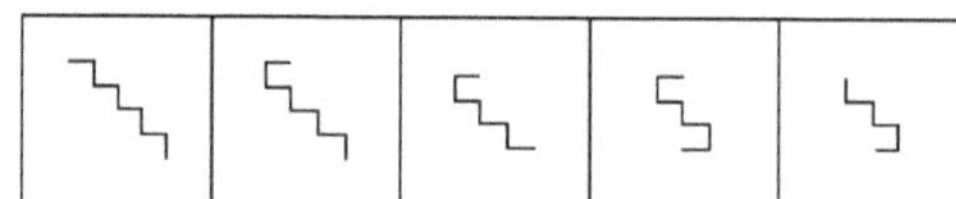

Answer Figures

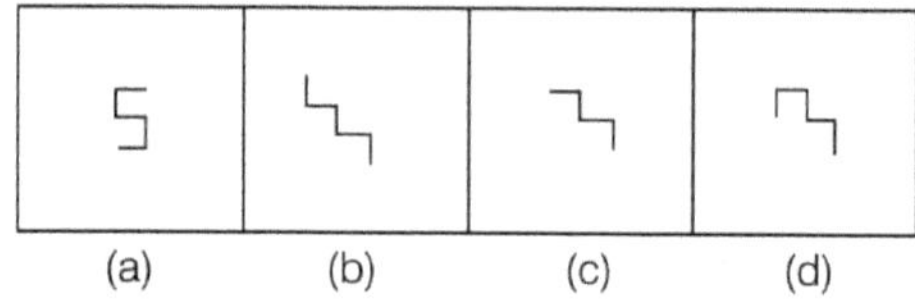

(a)   (b)   (c)   (d)

57. Question Figures

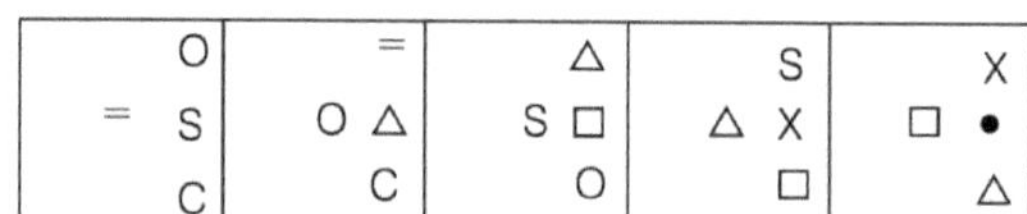

Answer Figures

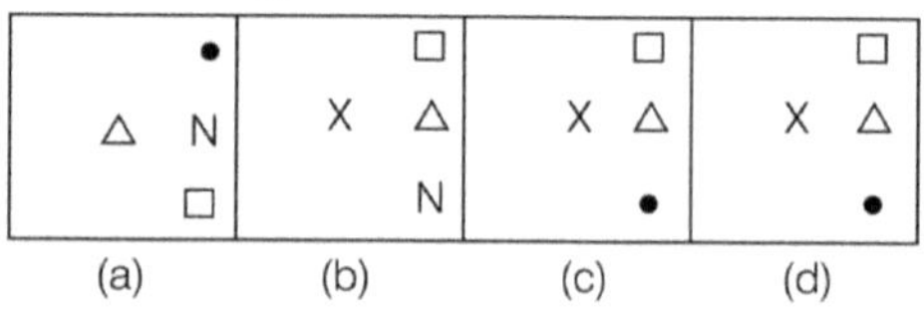

(a)   (b)   (c)   (d)

58. Question Figures

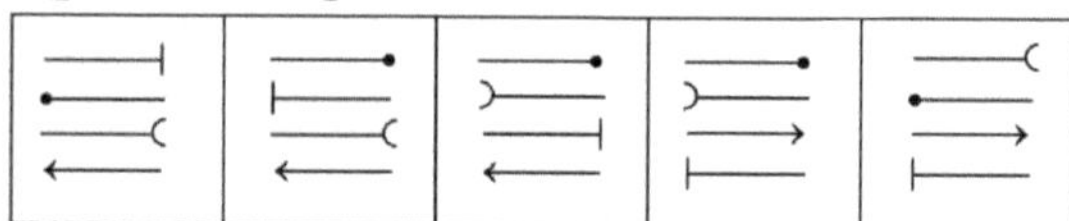

Answer Figures

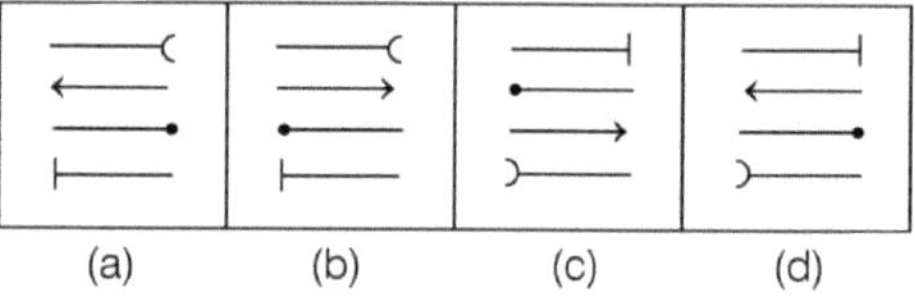

(a)   (b)   (c)   (d)

59. Question Figures

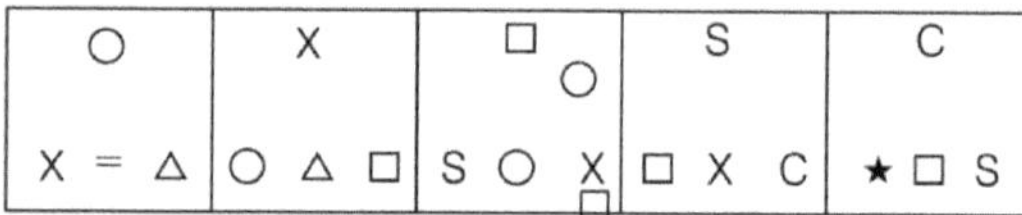

Answer Figures

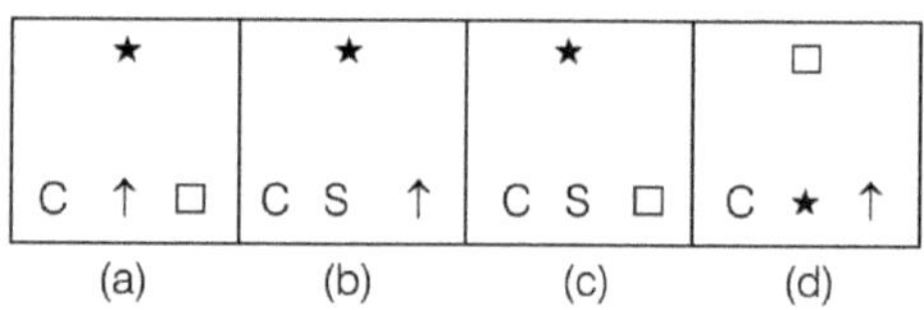

(a)   (b)   (c)   (d)

60. Question Figures

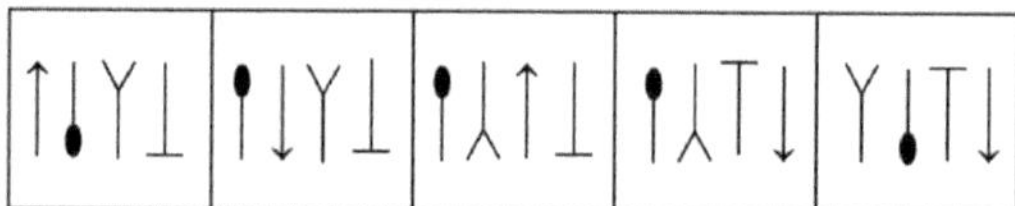

Answer Figures

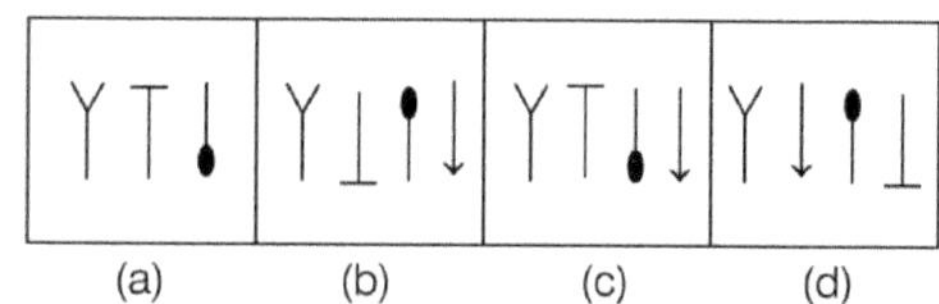

(a)   (b)   (c)   (d)

Section C : General Awareness and Current Affairs

61. In order to win the Grand Slam in Tennis, a player must win which one of the following groups of tournaments?
(a) Australian Open, Wimbledon, French Open, U.S. Open.
(b) Wimbledon, French Open, U.S. Open, Swedish Open
(c) Wimbledon, French Open, Paegas Czech Open, U.S. Open
(d) Davis Cup, Wimbledon, French Open, Australian Open

62. 'Abhinava Bharat', a secret society of revolutionaries, was organised by
(a) Khudiram Bose
(b) V.D. Savarkar
(c) Prafulla Chaki
(d) Bhagat Singh

63. Endoscopy, a technique used to explore the stomach or other inner parts of the body, is based on the phenomenon of
(a) Total internal reflection
(b) Interference
(c) Diffraction
(d) Polarisation

64. As per 1991 Census, which one of the following groups of Union Territories had the highest literacy rate?
(a) Chandigarh and Dadra & Nagar Haveli
(b) Delhi and Andaman & Nicobar Islands
(c) Andaman & Nicobar Islands and Pondicherry
(d) Pondicherry and Delhi

65. Who among the following has been appointed the National Security Advisor by the UPA Government?
(a) Brajesh Mishra   (b) J.N. Dixit
(c) Soli J. Sorabjee   (d) T.K.A.Nair

66. Who among the following is the Chief Minister of Andhra Pradesh?
(a) S.M. Krishna
(b) Chandrababu Naidu
(c) Dharam Singh
(d) Y.S. Rajasekhara Reddy

67. Which one of the following lakes forms an international boundary between Tanzania and Uganda?
(a) Chad   (b) Malawi
(c) Victoria   (d) Zambezi

68. A solemn ceremony to mark the 60th Anniversary of D—Day landings of the Allied troops during the Second World War, was held in
(a) Pearl Harbour   (b) Normandy
(c) New York   (d) Lisbon

69. Which of the following cricketers holds the world record of maximum number of sixes in Tests?
(a) Chris Cairns (New Zealand)
(b) Viv Richards (West Indies)
(c) Sachin Tendulkar (India)
(d) Wasim Akram (Pakistan)

70. Who among the following won the Miss 'Universe 2007' crown?
(a) Jennifer Hawkins   (b) Shandi Finnessey
(c) Riyo Mori   (d) None of these

71. The first feature film (talkie) produced in India was
(a) Hatimtai   (b) Alam Ara
(c) Pundalik   (d) Raja Harishchandra

72. Who is the Chairman of the Twelfth Finance Commission?
(a) Rangarajan   (b) N.N. Vohra
(c) Bimal Jalan   (d) Vijay Kelkar

73. India has signed an agreement to procure Advanced Jet Trainer (Hawk) from which of the following countries?
(a) USA   (b) UK   (c) France   (d) Russia

74. Which of the following companies became India's first listed IT firm to have crossed $1 billion turnover?
(a) Satyam   (b) HCL
(c) Wipro   (d) Enfosys Technologies

75. Who among the following persons bought the sword of Tipu Sultan in London and brought it back to India?
(a) Ratan Tata
(b) Mukesh Ambani
(c) Vijay Mallya
(d) Kumarmangalam Birla

76. USA has granted the status of major Non—NATO ally to which of the following countries recently?
(a) Pakistan   (b) India
(c) Afghanistan   (d) Myanmar

77. Who is the new Prime Minister of Sri Lanka?
(a) Chandrika Kumaratunga
(b) Ranil Wickremesinghe
(c) Mahindra Rajapakse
(d) None of the above

78. Who among the following women has become the highest individual scorer in an innings in Tests?
(a) Mithali Raj
(b) Kiran Baloch
(c) Dina Eduljee
(d) None of these

79. Who among the following has become the first Indian to score a triple century in Tests?
(a) Rahul Dravid
(b) Sachin Tendulkar
(c) V.V.S. Laxman
(d) Virender Sehwag

80. Hamas is a militant organisation fighting against which of the following countries?
(a) Sudan   (b) Israel   (c) Brazil   (d) Syria

81. Who among the following won the Femina Miss India Universe 2004 title?
(a) Lakshmi Pandit
(b) Sayali Bhagat
(c) Tanushree Dutta
(d) Jyoti Brahmin

82. The 9th South Asian Federation Games were held recently in which of the following cities?
(a) Islamabad
(b) Hyderabad
(c) Kathmandu
(d) Colombo

83. Which of the following parts of the poppy plant is used for the extraction of opium?
(a) Capsules
(b) Flowers
(c) Leaves
(d) Roots

84. A black hole is a body in space which does not allow any radiation to come out. This property is due to its
(a) very small size
(b) very large size
(c) very high density
(d) very low density

85. The 'Chilka Lake region' lies in between the deltas of
(a) Ganga and Mahanadi
(b) Godavari and Krishna
(c) Mahanadi and Godavari
(d) Krishna and Kaveri

86. The 44th Amendment of the Indian Constitution withdrew the Fundamental Right
(a) To freedom of religion
(b) To constitutional remedies
(c) To property
(d) Against exploitation

87. During the Indian freedom struggle. The Deccan Educational Society was founded by
(a) B.G. Tilak
(b) Dadabhai-Naoroji
(c) G.K. Gokhale
(d) M.G. Ranade

88. Persons below the poverty line in India are classified as such based on whether :
(a) They are entitled to a minimum prescribed food basket
(b) They get work for a prescribed minimum number of days in a year
(c) They belong to agricultural labourer, household and the Scheduled Castes/tribes social group
(d) Their daily wages fall below the prescribed minimum wages

89. The Legislative Council of a State in India can be abolished or created by
(a) The President of India in consultation with the Council of Ministers of the State concerned
(b) The Legislative Assembly of the State concerned
(c) The Parliament at a joint sitting of both the Houses
(d) The Parliament, provided the State Legislative Assembly passes a resolution to that effect

90. At which stage in its life cycle does the silkworm yield the fibre of commerce?
(a) Egg   (b) Larva   *(c) Pupa*   *(d) Imago*

Section D : English Language

Directions (Q. Nos. 91-95) *Read each sentence to find out whether there is any error in it. The error if any, is in one part of the sentence. The alphabet of that part (a), (b), (c) or (d) is your answer.*

91. <u>Do you know</u> <u>where I have</u> <u>kept my</u>
     (a)   (b)   (c)
<u>scissor</u> ?
  (d)

92. <u>Indian politics</u> <u>is similar as</u> <u>the blind</u>
     (a)   (b)   (c)
<u>leading the blind.</u>
  (d)

93. <u>I distributed</u> <u>the sweets</u> <u>between the students</u>
     (a)   (b)   (c)
<u>of my class.</u>
  (d)

94. <u>The children were</u> <u>playing with a ball</u>
     (a)   (b)
<u>and run around,</u> <u>when the accident occurred.</u>
   (c)   (d)

HM 2008

95. <u>Rita and myself</u> <u>are</u> <u>great friends</u>
      (a)   (b)   (c)

<u>since childhood.</u>
     (d)

Directions (Q. Nos. 96-109) *Fill in the blanks.*

96. Do you have enough money to pay .... these articles?
(a) of   (b) out
(c) off   (d) for

97. It is important to have an ....
development in children.
(a) all over   (b) all area
(c) all round   (d) all around

98. When selecting a perfume, buy something that really .... you.
(a) charms   (b) appeals to
(c) favours   (d) integrates with

99. He was so .... by the end of the day that the smell of food made him restless.
(a) thirsty   (b) famished (c) sleepy   (d) upset

100. Few would have suspected that this .... man had the qualities of heroism.
(a) strong   (b) soft
(c) frail   (d) weak

101. The man looked in all directions, ...
(a) anxiously   (b) apathetically
(c) indifferently   (d) efficiently

102. There was a .... of light on the street which .... the eyes of the driver.
(a) glare, dazzled   (b) ray, dazzled
(c) shine, shone in   (d) stream, sparkled

103. Millions of .... in this country are .... and without cultural roots.
(a) people, poor
(b) people, rich,
(c) persons, uneducated
(d) immigrants, homeless

104. The Prince of Wales was greeted by .... streets and .... shutters.
(a) silent, downed   (b) quiet, steel
(c) empty, downed   (d) open, closed

105. He looked forward to his first travel by air with a strange mixture of both .... and ....
(a) joy, happiness
(b) exhilaration, despondency
(c) worry, fear
(d) exhilaration, fear

106. She made .... coffee and a toast .... an electric heater.
(a) some, over   (b) some, on
(c) a, on   (d) a, at

107. It is .... when cultured and intelligent people behave like children .... of their lollipops.
(a) disheartening, acquisitive
(b) appalling, deprived
(c) upsetting, snatching
(d) encouraging, gobbling

108. The main objective of the discussion was to find a .... and not to ....   him.
(a) answer, irritate
(b) solution, irritate
(c) solution, praise
(d) way, absolve

109. A large triangular .... was cut .... from the cake.
(a) part, off   (b) piece, of
(c) wedge, off   (d) chunk, of

Directions (Q. Nos. 110-116) *Select the most appropriate option from the alternatives to replace the bold italicised word(s) to correct the sentence.*

110. I will leave when he ***will come.***
(a) will not come   (b) does not come
(c) comes   (d) No error

111. If they ***were knowing*** about the difficult climb, they would not have decided to come to this hill station.
(a) did know   (b) knew
(c) had known   (d) No error

112. If you were the principal of the college what steps ***would you have taken*** to deal with indiscipline?
(a) will you take   (b) would you take
(c) will you be taking (d) No error

113. He did not have ***some hope*** when he contested in the election.
(a) any hope   (b) few hope
(c) hopeless   (d) hopeful

114. It was just then that an unusual sound ***resounded*** through the almost sound-proof door of the room.
(a) blasted
(b) went
(c) perpetrate
(d) penetrated

115. If you want to achieve success, you need to make a *conscious effort*.
   (a) conscious efforts
   (b) tremendous efforts
   (c) effort made with consciousness
   (d) No error

116. I am not going to let you *pass on* this time. You need to take responsibility.
   (a) pass the responsibility　(b) take off
   (c) pass the buck　(d) No error

Directions (Q. Nos. 117-119) *Pick out the most effective words from the given words to fill in the blanks to make the sentences meaningfully correct.*

117. A relationship is an invisible ……… that brings people together.
   (a) cuff　(b) link　(c) rope　(d) thread

118. The mentally ill person was suffering from ……… and delusions.
   (a) hallucinations　(b) illusions
   (c) allusions　(d) conclusions

119. The most painful aspect of elections is the ……… campaigns.
   (a) expensive　(b) extensive
   (c) huge　(d) slanderous

Directions (Q. Nos. 120-123) *Choose the word which is nearly the same in meaning to the word given below in capital.*

120. SCOUNDREL
   (a) poor　(b) hunter　(c) rogue　(d) vessel
   ↪ 'Scoundrel' means a dishonest person or a rogue.

121. APPURTENANCE
   (a) opportunity　(b) an accessory
   (c) legal document　(d) equipment

122. SCOURGE
   (a) infliction　(b) clean　(c) misfortune　(d) polish

123. PATRONAGE
   (a) superior　(b) snobbish
   (c) guardian　(d) benefaction

Directions (Q. Nos. 124-128) *Which of the words/phrases, a, b, c, or d, should replace the words/phrases given in **bold italics** in each of the following sentences?*

124. He *was retired* a year ago.
   (a) is retired　(b) retired
   (c) had retired　(d) No error

125. Rohan was *entrusted* with a special talent for painting.
   (a) endowed　(b) found
   (c) given　(d) No error

126. *Every people* knows that saving money is important.
   (a) All people　(b) Everyone
   (c) Every person　(d) No error

127. Each of us loves *our* home.
   (a) their　(b) there
   (c) his　(d) No error

128. *Briefly speaking*, I do not like your way of working.
   (a) In summary　(b) Speaking in brief
   (c) In short　(d) No error

Directions (Q. Nos. 129-134) *In each question you are given certain sentences which have been jumbled and labelled P, Q, R and S. Find the proper sequence that will construct the original sentence. Choose the correct sequence.*

129. We have received, <u>went to London</u>
　　　　　　　　　　　　P
<u>no message from</u> <u>since he</u> <u>our friend</u>
　　Q　　　　　R　　　S
   (a) QSRP　(b) SQRP
   (c) PQSR　(d) RSQP

130. India has always <u>to uphold</u>
　　　　　　　　　　P
<u>extended -co-operation</u> <u>peace and freedom</u>
　　　Q　　　　　　R
<u>the cause of</u>
　　S
   (a) RQPS　(b) SQPR
   (c) PQRS　(d) QPSR

131. He is <u>but also a</u> <u>not only a</u> <u>good person</u>
　　　　P　　　　Q　　　R
<u>good cricketer</u>
　　S
   (a) PQRS　(b) QSRP
   (c) QSPR　(d) QRPS

132. Canvas being <u>manufacturing</u> <u>a durable cloth</u>
　　　　　　　　P　　　　Q
<u>shoes and tents</u> <u>is used for</u>
　　R　　　　S
   (a) PQRS　(b) QSPR
   (c) RQSP　(d) QSRP

133. Machines <u>should be simple</u>

             P

<u>may be complicated</u> <u>to operate them</u>

    Q   R

<u>but the device</u>

      S

(a) QSRP   (b) QPSR

(c) QSPR   (d) PQSR

134. It is <u>a car</u> <u>to drive</u> <u>without good brakes</u>

       P   Q   R

<u>dangerous</u>

    S

(a) SQPR   (b) QSPR

(c) PRSQ   (d) PQRS

Directions (Q. Nos. 135-139) *Read each sentence to find out if there is any grammatical error in it. If there is any error, it will be only in one part of the sentence. The alphabet of that part is your answer (Disregard punctuation errors, if any).*

135. <u>He does not</u> <u>carry any grudges</u>

     (a)   (b)

<u>against his friend for</u>

     (c)

<u>not taking him into confidence.</u>

        (d)

136. <u>She does not</u> <u>get along with</u>

     (a)   (b)

<u>her sister-in-laws.</u> <u>No error</u>

    (c)   (d)

137. <u>Please give me</u> <u>the binocular.</u> <u>I want to look</u>

     (a)   (b)   (c)

<u>at the hills.</u>

    (d)

138. <u>Myself and Rajkumar</u> <u>have been friends</u>

       (a)   (b)

<u>since childhood.</u> <u>No error.</u>

    (c)   (d)

139. <u>The syllabuses</u> <u>of all schools</u> <u>have been</u>

     (a)   (b)   (c)

<u>finalised.</u>

    (d)

Directions (Q. Nos. 140-145) *In each of the following questions, select from amongst the four alternatives, the word nearest in meaning to the word given below in capital.*

140. POIGNANT

(a) poetic   (b) solemn

(c) serious   (d) touching

141. HYPERBOLE

(a) round   (b) publicity

(c) exaggeration   (d) pure

142. MAUDLIN

(a) sentimental   (b) medicinal

(c) modern   (d) rough handling

143. AVARICE

(a) every   (b) greed

(c) postpone   (d) anger

144. NEBULOUS

(a) clear   (b) bulb

(c) light   (d) unclear

145. ABYSMAL

(a) bottomless   (b) terrible

(c) depressing   (d) total

Directions (Q. Nos. 146-155) *In the following passage, there are blank spaces numbered 146 to 155. Against each of these numbers below the passage, a choice of four words (a), (b), (c) and (d) is suggested to replace the blank spaces in the passage. Choose the best word from the alternatives (a), (b), (c) and (d).* Buddhism was **146** to Japan from India **147** China and Korea around the middle of the sixth century. After gaining **148** patronage, Buddhism was **149** by the authorities throughout the country. In the **150** ninth century, Buddhism in Japan entered a new **151** in which it catered mainly to the court nobility. In the Kamakura period (1192-1338), an **152** of great political unrest and social confusion, there emerged many new sects of Buddhism offering **153** of salvation to warriors and peasants **154**. Buddhism not only flourished as a religion but also did much to **155** the country's arts and learning.

146. (a) bring in   (b) brought in

     (c) introduced   (d) shown

147. (a) via   (b) from

     (c) through   (d) into

148. (a) imperial   (b) kingly

     (c) royalty   (d) emperor

149. (a) distributed   (b) enforced

     (c) thrust   (d) propagated

150. (a) beginning   (b) later

     (c) early   (d) end

151. (a) age   (b) era
    (c) year   (d) time

152. (a) event   (b) occasion
    (c) time   (d) age

153. (a) feeling   (b) hope
    (c) thought   (d) ray

154. (a) separately   (b) equally
    (c) alike   (d) differently

155. (a) enrich   (b) deteriorate
    (c) spoil   (d) retard

Directions (Q. Nos. 156 and 157) *In each of the following questions, select from amongst the four alternatives, the word nearest in meaning to the word given below in capital.*

156. RELEGATE
    (a) relax   (b) assign
    (c) yield   (d) enter

157. PENURY
    (a) destitution   (b) injury
    (c) needy   (d) distress

Directions (Q. Nos. 158-165) *In each of the following questions, select from amongst the four alternatives, the word most opposite in meaning to the word given below in capital.*

158. AMEND
    (a) rectify   (b) revise
    (c) maintain   (d) change

159. GIGANTIC
    (a) huge   (b) minute
    (c) mammoth   (d) large

160. GENERATE
    (a) concoct   (b) destroy
    (c) compose   (d) break

161. VERBOSE
    (a) garrulous   (b) succinct
    (c) dramatic   (d) jocular

162. PROFANE
    (a) blasphemy   (b) quiet
    (c) sinful   (d) pious

163. LACKADAISICAL
    (a) careful   (b) apathetic
    (c) concerned   (d) dreamy

164. LAMENT
    (a) weep   (b) happy
    (c) rejoice   (d) joyful

165. FOMENT
    (a) increase   (b) ferment
    (c) agitate   (d) comfort

Directions (Q. Nos. 166-170) *Read the following passage carefully and answer the questions given below.*

All of us have, at least once in our life, fantasised about being immortal. But, for James Bedford it was no fantasy. He was so obsessed with the idea that he left instructions that, after he died, his body should be frozen and preserved until science allowed it to be revived, and the disease that caused death and the ageing process reversed. Extreme behaviour? Yes, but one that is gaining in popularity.

In 1967, there were three who were frozen for posterity. In the next decade at least 100 people opted to go in for suspended inanimation. They are not cranks. They believed science would perform the marvel of resuscitation, themselves being great scientists as software programmers, physicians and so on. Welcome to the world of cryonics.

Cryonics is the practice of freezing the body of a person who has just died in order to preserve it for possible resuscitation in the future as and when a cure, for the disease that caused death, has been found. It is a sub-set of cryogenics, which is a study and use of low-temperature phenomena, referring to everything from refrigerators to rocket fuels and superconducting electromagnets.

Sure, it's a far out science, but it's not a pseudoscience. It has some heavyweight supporters like Marrin Minsky, the father of robotics and artificial intelligence and Eric Drexler, the author of the best-seller 'Engines of Creation'.

There are three institutions in US that offer the facility of suspension and these are Cryonics Institute, Trans Time and Alcor Foundation. The first two insist the entire body be preserved, while the third insists it is enough to preserve the head only. The idea is with the head preserved, the body can be regenerated. Neurosuspensions are more popular with Alcor receiving 2 heads for every one body.

How it works is simple. The blood in the body is drained out and replaced with a glycerin based cryoprotectant to prevent any ice damage to tissue, a.k.a. frostbite. The body is then placed in a cylindrical container of cryostat containing liquid nitrogen at a temperature of minus 160° C.

Whenever the technology permits, these dead people will be thawed out, and in a sense, resurrected. But thawing a frozen body invariably damages the cell membranes. The emergence of nanotechnology has given hopes and that down 30 years, damaged cells could be repaired by nanomachines or 'robodocs' that swim through your blood system.

Cryonics is not about freezing dead people at all, but rather people who had been labelled that way a little prematurely. Before Cardiopulmonary Resuscitation (CPR) was invented, a person whose heart-beat had stopped was considered dead, but with CPR, he could be revived. So, stoppage of heart-beat can no longer be considered as evidence of death.

Now, death is defined as "the destruction of the structures in the brain that encode memory and personality so that it is no longer possible in principle to restore them to an appropriate functional state". Thus, the brain forms the core of cryonics research. As of today, all parts of the body can be regenerated except the brain, whose cells cannot replicate by themselves. So, there won't be real death! There will be immortality.

But will the society afford luxuries like newly thawed people? Waking up in the future may cause severe identity crisis in the newly resurrected. Robert. C.W. Ettinger who first proposed the idea of freezing bodies in his volume, 'The Prospect of Immortality' has a few questions : Can a 'corpse' inherit ? Can the 'ice-widow' remarry ? Is it euthanasia to freeze a relation or is it murder not to?

166. What are the 'robodocs' capable of doing?
- (a) Creating new hope
- (b) Brain regeneration
- (c) Repairing cell damage
- (d) Preserving bodies

167. The new definition of death is
- (a) Destruction of the memory structure
- (b) Stoppage of heart-beat
- (c) Departure of the soul
- (d) None of the above

168. What would be the biggest problem of the resurrected persons?
- (a) Inheriting property
- (b) Identity crisis
- (c) Remarriage
- (d) Controversy between euthanasia and murder

169. What is the 'extreme behaviour' referred to in this passage?
- (a) Thinking of being immortal
- (b) Working to keep death at bay
- (c) Playing God
- (d) Being obsessed with immortality

170. What is Cryonics?
- (a) Freezing the dead body for possible resuscitation later
- (b) A kind of computer program
- (c) A study of low temperature phenomenon
- (d) None of the above

Section E : Aptitude For Service Sector

Directions *As you read the following questions carefully, please answer all the questions as best as you can without skipping any one. To each question there are four choice you can choose from, either (a), (b), (a) or (d). Make sure that you answer each question honestly and try to choose the first answer that comes to your mind without changing it because the first choice is always the true one.*

171. Your landlord exceptionally asks for rent before the due date and you have the money. You
- (a) move out since it is unacceptable for a landlord to ask for rent in advance
- (b) give half now and the other half on the due date.
- (c) give the money on the due date, as planned.
- (d) give the money right away.

172. You plan a trip with a friend and two days before the departure, he tells you that he has invited another friend along, someone you are not very comfortable with. You
- (a) hint about your feelings to your friend and hope he takes the hint and un-invites the other.
- (b) tell him straight to his face that you are uncomfortable with the person and won't go.
- (c) accept the change as an opportunity to get to know the other person better.
- (d) you travel along and do not express your discomfort.

173. On a busy day, you're walking in the street and a person who barely speaks your language approaches you and asks you for directions to the nearest metro station. You
- (a) respond by saying "I don't know the way".
- (b) accompany him to his destination.
- (c) show him the way using only gestures and hope he finds his way.
- (d) try to explain the directions but seeing he's not grasping it, you eventually walk away.

174. Your presentation has been postponed every week for the past month. This week your classmates yet again want to postpone it. You
- (a) declare the presentation over, and walk out of the class.
- (b) comply with their wishes and postpone your representation.
- (c) compromise, saying you will do part of the presentation today and the rest later.

(d) explain that you've been waiting for a long time and that you will be presenting today.

175. When faced with the issue of food in a foreign country, you would
(a) try finding a restaurant that serves food from your homeland.
(b) be eager to try a new cuisine
(c) be apprehensive about the new food but agree to give it a try.
(d) refuse to eat anything you haven't had before

176. You have an argument and you know you're in the right. How do you deal with it?
(a) Apologise and go to any lengths to make things better.
(b) State what the other has done wrong and wait for an apology.
(c) Try to foster a dialogue so that both can talk about how they feel.
(d) Give the silent treatment.

177. You are working in an organisation. Your friend-colleague wants to take half the day off but has to find a replacement. He asks you to work extra time to fill in for him with a promise to do the same for your later. You are tired and would rather go home. You
(a) help him out because you may need the favour returned later.
(b) make up an excuse and tell him you can't work extra time today, but would gladly oblige at some other time.
(c) absolutely refuse. You neither ask for nor do favours for anybody.
(d) gladly fill in for him. His cause may be more important than your need for rest.

178. You and your friend must assemble an exercise machine together. You're the hands-on kind of a person and he's the read-the-manual type. How do you resolve this?
(a) Let him read the manual and when he has grasped the instructions, build the machine together.
(b) Let him figure out the manual while you try to assemble the machine.
(c) Tell him to throw out the manual and start working.
(d) Try his approach by reading the manual with him and then work together.

179. Your friend unexpectedly lands up at your house asking to stay for a week due to renovations at his/her house. You

(a) make up an excuse and say you won't be able to accommodate him/her.
(b) agree to let him/her stay for a week without any conditions.
(c) agree to provide accommodation for a week in exchange for him/her helping around the house.
(d) agree to take him/her in but only for a few days.

180. You're meeting an old friend after a long time. You both have busy schedules. The time and place of meeting is decided
(a) according to his convenience for time and place.
(b) according to his convenience for time and place.
(c) by modifying both your schedules to create a common time and space for meeting.
(d) according to your convenience for time and place.

181. You are the manager of a group project. While making decisions you would
(a) stick to the decisions that have brought successful results in the past.
(b) try out new ideas which don't deviate too much from conventional ones.
(c) include new ideas provided they fit with past successful solutions.
(d) encourage brain-storming sessions and try out new solutions in order to get better and bigger gains.

182. Your nephew/niece asks you for a story. You
(a) make up a story of your own.
(b) recall and narrate a childhood story you once heard.
(c) read from a book.
(d) make up the story with your nephew/ niece; each contributing every alternate line.

183. You are the organiser at your college annual program. At the 11th hour you are informed that due to some unforeseen problems the show will have to be delayed. You have to explain this to your audience. You
(a) improvise, interact and play with the audience to keep them entertained (e.g. crowd games).
(b) request the Principal to explain since he is the one in charge.
(c) explain the situation making light of it using humour.
(d) explain truthfully what happened choosing the right words so that they will patiently wait.

184. You are a part of a group that has to conduct a survey on young adults. You will most likely be
(a) establishing a strategy for approaching subjects.
(b) presenting the results in front of the class
(c) doing the statistical analysis.
(d) constructing the items for the survey.

185. You have to babysit your nephew. You
    (a) let him play by himself and make sure he is safe.
    (b) take out crayons and paper and draw together.
    (c) think of a movie which he would like watch it and watch it together.
    (d) make up a game to entertain him.

186. You have a fest going on in your college. At the last minute, you realise that the stall you were planning has already been put up by someone else. You
    (a) put up the stall as planned.
    (b) come up with a totally new concept for your stall.
    (c) alter the concept for your stall to make it a bit different.
    (d) arrange it so that your stall is more attractive (e.g. put balloons and banners)

187. You are employed at a publishing house. Your job would most likely be
    (a) operating the printing press
    (b) proofreading for grammatical errors
    (c) editing and critiquing
    (d) writing the books

188. You are organising a meal for a special occasion. What's your plan?
    (a) Whip up a dish of your own and pay extra attention to presentation and decoration
    (b) Order food
    (c) Whip up a dish of your own
    (d) Try a new recipe and follow the instructions diligently

189. You just moved into a new apartment. You
    (a) give it a good coat of paint and rearrange the furniture in an aesthetically pleasing way.
    (b) Fix things that don't work.
    (c) leave it as it is.
    (d) go all out on an interior-decorating extravaganza and try to make it unique.

190. What, best describes your spiritual orientation?
    (a) I follow a religion but ponder and question its tenets.
    (b) I mix and match from different religions according to what suits me.
    (c) I read religious scriptures and adhere to my religion as it is taught.
    (d) I have found my own unique path to spirituality.

191. You have opted for a course but a few weeks into it, the authorities tell you that the course has been cancelled and you need to shift to another one. You
    (a) accept the new change willingly.
    (b) refuse to accept the decision and take the issue up with higher authorities.
    (c) reluctantly accept the new course while still trying to get the authorities to change their minds.
    (d) crib about it to your friends, but accept the change.

192. You are suffering from a high fever and you have a test the next day. You
    (a) work as hard as you usually would and do your best.
    (b) talk to your teacher to excuse yourself from taking the test.
    (c) prepare a little and take the test.
    (d) forget about the test and rest instead.

193. It's your birthday and you want to spend the day with your friends, but your parents want you to spend the day at home. You
    (a) spend the morning with your family and the evening with, your friends.
    (b) insist of spending the day with your friends.
    (c) explain to your family that you would like to spend time with your friends.
    (d) cancel your plans with friends and spend the day with your family.

194. You have an important exam in Mumbai. Two days before your flight, the airline calls and informs you of the cancellation of your flight. Instead, they offer you AC train tickets to your destination. You
    (a) skip the exam.
    (b) complain about the inefficiency of the airline, but eventually take the train ticket.
    (c) Demand tickets on another flight and threaten to sue the airline.
    (d) take the train ticket without complaining.

195. You plan to watch a long-awaited movie with friends. Your friends decide to watch a play instead and ask you to come along. You
    (a) go ahead and watch the movie alone.
    (b) agree but keep reminding them that the movie would have been a better option.
    (c) try to convince them to go for the movie instead.
    (d) agree to your friends, request and go along.

196. You are in an argument and your opponent counters your point of view. You
    (a) vehemently reject his/her views and insist on your point.
    (b) accept your opponent's view without trying to change it.
    (c) try to convince the opponent that both points are equally important.
    (d) try to prove to the opponent how important your point is

197. You are the leader of a group project. Your approach to solving problems would be

    (a) listen to each member of the group and decide according to majority vote.
    (b) listen to a few selected members of group and then you decide the solution.
    (c) listen to each member of the group and then you decide the solution.
    (d) decide depending, upon what you believe is the solution.

198. Your friend has asked you to look after her nephew while she goes out for a few hours. Just before her expected return she calls up and asks if you could wait a little longer. You
    (a) take the child with you to the next place you have to go.
    (b) ask her to try to return earlier.
    (c) refuse and ask her to return immediately
    (d) wait until she returns.

199. You are travelling by train and you have the lower berth. A fellow passenger asks you to exchange his upper berth with yours. You
    (a) make excuses so you don't have to change your berth.
    (b) make a bit of a fuss but eventually give it up.
    (c) agree willingly. It's no big deal.
    (d) refuse flatly. You have paid for that berth and you are not willing to give it up for anyone.

200. You have bought a new sweater but when you get home you .see that they have packed the wrong one. You go back to the store, but they do not have it in your size any more. You
    (a) make a fuss there and then.
    (b) ask for your money back.
    (c) ask for a credit letter and go back when the sweater arrives again.
    (d) exchange and get a different sweater that is available in your size.

Answers

1. (b)	2. (c)	3. (c)	4. (d)	5. (d)	6. (d)	7. (b)	8. (d)	9. (c)	10. (a)
11. (c)	12. (c)	13. (a)	14. (a)	15. (a)	16. (b)	17. (b)	18. (c)	19. (d)	20. (b)
21. (d)	22. (c)	23. (d)	24. (c)	25. (b)	26. (d)	27. (d)	28. (d)	29. (a)	30. (b)
31. (b)	32. (d)	33. (c)	34. (b)	35. (d)	36. (d)	37. (d)	38. (b)	39. (d)	40. (d)
41. (a)	42. (b)	43. (b)	44. (b)	45. (c)	46. (c)	47. (c)	48. (d)	49. (c)	50. (c)
51. (b)	52. (b)	53. (d)	54. (c)	55. (c)	56. (a)	57. (d)	58. (a)	59. (b)	60. (b)
61. (a)	62. (b)	63. (a)	64. (d)	65. (b)	66. (d)	67. (a)	68. (b)	69. (a)	70. (c)
71. (b)	72. (a)	73. (b)	74. (d)	75. (c)	76. (a)	77. (d)	78. (b)	79. (d)	80. (b)
81. (c)	82. (a)	83. (a)	84. (c)	85. (a)	86. (c)	87. (a)	88. (d)	89. (d)	90. (b)
91. (d)	92. (b)	93. (c)	94. (c)	95. (a)	96. (d)	97. (c)	98. (b)	99. (b)	100. (c)
101. (a)	102. (a)	103. (d)	104. (c)	105. (d)	106. (b)	107. (b)	108. (b)	109. (c)	110. (c)
111. (c)	112. (d)	113. (a)	114. (a)	115. (d)	116. (c)	117. (b)	118. (a)	119. (a)	120. (c)
121. (b)	122. (a)	123. (d)	124. (b)	125.. (a)	126. (b)	127. (d)	128. (c)	129. (a)	130. (d)
131. (c)	132. (b)	133. (a)	134. (a)	135. (b)	136. (c)	137. (b)	138. (a)	139. (b)	140. (d)
141. (c)	142. (a)	143. (b)	144. (d)	145. (b)	146. (b)	147. (a)	148. (a)	149. (b)	150. (c)
151. (b)	152. (d)	153. (b)	154. (c)	155. (a)	156. (b)	157. (a)	158. (c)	159. (b)	160. (b)
161. (b)	162. (d)	163. (a)	164. (c)	165. (d)	166. (c)	167. (a)	168. (b)	169. (d)	170. (a)
171. (d)	172. (c)	173. (b)	174. (d)	175. (c)	176. (c)	177. (a)	178. (d)	179. (b)	180. (c)
181. (d)	182. (b)	183. (a)	184. (a)	185. (a)	186. (d)	187. (c)	188. (a)	189. (a)	190. (c)
191. (c)	192. (c)	193. (a)	194. (b)	195. (c)	196. (c)	197. (a)	198. (d)	199. (c)	200. (d)

Hints & Solutions

1. (b) According to the question,

$$\frac{3.54}{2.7} = \frac{?}{27}$$

$$\Rightarrow \quad ? = 3.54 \times \frac{27}{2.7} = 35.4$$

2. (c) The required distance between New Delhi and Ghaziabad = Speed × time

$$= 18 \times \left(1 + \frac{20}{60}\right)$$

$$= 18 \times \frac{4}{3} = 24 \text{ km}$$

3. (c) Between any two different rational numbers, there lies infinite number of fractions.

Hence, option (c) is correct.

4. (d) From option (a), $\frac{5}{6} = 0.833\ldots$

From option (b), $\frac{6}{7} = 0.857\ldots$

From option (c), $\frac{7}{8} = 0.875$

From option (d), $\frac{8}{9} = 0.8888\ldots$

Clearly, $\frac{8}{9}$ is the largest fraction among the given options.

5. (d) Single discount equivalent to two successive discounts $r_1\%$ and $r_2\%$

$$= \left(r_1 + r_2 - \frac{r_1 \times r_2}{100}\right)\%$$

$$= \left(10 + 15 - \frac{10 \times 15}{100}\right)\%$$

$$= (25 - 1.5)\% = 23.5\%$$

6. (d) Let rate = $R\%$ per annum

Given, $P = ₹\,600$

Time = 9 yr 6 months = $\dfrac{19}{2}$ yr

Sum after $\dfrac{19}{2}$ yr = ₹ 856.50

$\therefore$ SI = ₹ 856.50 − ₹ 600 = ₹ 256.50

We know that, SI = $\dfrac{P \times R \times T}{100}$

$$\Rightarrow \quad 256.50 = \frac{600 \times R \times 19}{2 \times 100}$$

$$\Rightarrow \quad R = \frac{25650 \times 2}{600 \times 19} = 4.5\%$$

7. (b) According to the question,

$$\text{Downstream speed} = \frac{1}{6/60} = \frac{1}{1/10} = 10 \text{ km/h}$$

$$\text{Upstream speed} = \frac{1}{30/60} = \frac{1}{1/2} = 2 \text{ km/h}$$

$\therefore$ Speed of the man in still water

$$= \frac{\text{downstream speed} + \text{upstream speed}}{2}$$

$$= \frac{1}{2}(10 + 2)$$

$$= \frac{1}{2}(12) = 6 \text{ km/h}$$

8. (d) Let Ashu spends on Diwali fireworks = ₹ A and Nishu spends on Diwali fireworks = ₹ N

According to the question,

$$A = N \times \left(\frac{100 - 25}{100}\right)$$

$$\Rightarrow \quad A = N \times \frac{75}{100} \Rightarrow A = \frac{3N}{4}$$

$$\Rightarrow \quad 4A = 3N \Rightarrow \frac{N}{A} = \frac{4}{3}$$

$\therefore$ Required percentage = $\dfrac{4 - 3}{3} \times 100$

$$= \frac{1}{3} \times 100 = 33\frac{1}{3}\%$$

11. (c) $\sqrt{0.9} = \sqrt{\dfrac{9}{10}} = \sqrt{\dfrac{90}{100}} = \dfrac{\sqrt{90}}{10}$

Square root of 90,

```
            9.486
      ┌─────────────────
    9 │ 90.000000
      │ −81 ↓
 ─────┼─────────────────
  184 │  9 00
      │ − 736 ↓
 ─────┼─────────────────
 1888 │   16400
      │ − 15104 ↓
 ─────┼─────────────────
18966 │    129600
      │  − 113796
      │     15804
```

$\therefore \sqrt{0.9} = \dfrac{9.486}{10} = 0.9486 = 0.949$

12. (c) As, $\dfrac{2}{5} = 0.4$

and $\dfrac{3}{4} = 0.75$

From option (a), $\dfrac{3}{10} = 0.3$

From option (b), $\dfrac{4}{5} = 0.8$

From option (c), $\dfrac{1}{2} = 0.5$

From option (d), $\dfrac{3}{8} = 0.375$

Clearly, $\dfrac{1}{2}$ lies between $\dfrac{2}{5}$ and $\dfrac{3}{4}$.

13. (*a*) Given,

$x\sqrt{y} = \sqrt{80} \Rightarrow x\sqrt{y} = \sqrt{16 \times 5}$

$\Rightarrow \qquad x\sqrt{y} = \sqrt{4^2 \times 5}$

$\Rightarrow \qquad x\sqrt{y} = 4\sqrt{5}$

$\therefore \qquad\qquad y = 5$

14. (*a*) Given, $T = 4$ yr

$P = ₹\ 400$ and sum after 4 yr $= ₹\ 480$

$\therefore\ \ SI = 480 - 400 = ₹\ 80$

Now, $\quad SI = \dfrac{P \times R \times T}{100}$

$\Rightarrow \qquad 80 = \dfrac{400 \times R \times 4}{100}$

$\Rightarrow \qquad R = \dfrac{80 \times 100}{400 \times 4} = 5\%$

15. (*a*) Given, speed of Ashu $= 4$ km/h

and speed of Nishu $= 9$ km/h

Time duration between 9:00 am and 11:30 am

$\qquad = 2:30\ h = 2\ h + 30\ min$

$\qquad = 2\ h + \dfrac{30}{60}\ h = \left(2 + \dfrac{1}{2}\right) h = \dfrac{5}{2}\ h$

$\therefore$ Distance travelled by Ashu $=$ speed $\times$ time

$\qquad = 4 \times \dfrac{5}{2} = 10$ km

Relative velocity of Ashu and Nishu $= (9 - 4)$ km/h

$\qquad\qquad = 5$ km/h

Time taken by Nishu to overtake Ashu

$\qquad = \dfrac{10}{5} = 2\ h$

The time at which Nishu will overtake Ashu

$\qquad = 11:30\ am\ + 2\ h = 1:30\ pm$

16. (*b*) Let 1 h work of man and a woman is $\dfrac{1}{x}$ and $\dfrac{1}{y}$ respectively.

According to the question,

$\qquad \dfrac{2}{x} + \dfrac{3}{y} = \dfrac{1}{5} \qquad\qquad \dots$ (i)

and $\qquad \dfrac{3}{x} + \dfrac{2}{y} = \dfrac{1}{4} \qquad\qquad \dots$ (ii)

On solving Eqs. (i) and (ii), we get

$\qquad\qquad y = 50$

On putting the value of y in Eq. (i), we get

$x = \dfrac{100}{7}$

$\therefore$ (2 men + 1 woman)'s 1 h work

$\qquad = 2 \times \left(\dfrac{7}{100}\right) + \dfrac{1}{50}$

$\qquad = \dfrac{8}{50} = \dfrac{4}{25}$

Hence, (2 men + 1 woman) will complete the work

$\qquad = \dfrac{25}{4}\ h = 6\dfrac{1}{4}\ h$

i.e. more than 6 h but less than 7 h.

17. (*b*) Divisibility by 11 : If the difference between the sum of the digits at odd places and the sum of the digits at even places of the number is either 0 or multiple of 11, it is divisible by 11.

Checking option (b),

9 8 6 7 3 9 0 5

Sum of odd digits $= 9 + 6 + 3 + 0 = 18$

Sum of even digits $= 8 + 7 + 9 + 5 = 29$

Required difference $= 29 - 18 = 11$

$\therefore$ 98673905 is divisible by 11.

18. (*c*) Let the three consecutive integers are $x, (x + 1)$ and $(x + 2)$.

According to the question,

$\qquad x + (x + 1) + (x + 2) = 15$

$\Rightarrow \qquad\qquad 3x + 3 = 15$

$\Rightarrow \qquad\qquad 3x = 12$

$\therefore \qquad\qquad x = 4$

$\therefore$ The numbers are 4, 5, 6.

$\therefore$ Required product $= 4 \times 5 \times 6 = 120$

19. (*d*) Let the cost price of the book be $₹\ x$.

According to the question,

$\qquad \dfrac{75}{100} + \dfrac{75}{100} \times x = x \Rightarrow 75 + 75x = 100x$

$\Rightarrow \qquad\qquad 75 = 25x$

$\therefore \qquad\qquad x = 3$

Hence, cost price of the book $= ₹\ 3$

20. (*b*) The prime numbers between 1 and 10 are 2, 3, 5, 7.

$\therefore$ 4 prime numbers are between 1 and 10.

31. (*b*) All others except mercury are solid.

32. (*d*) All others except February has fixed number of days.

33. (*c*) All others except potato belongs to fruits category.

34. (*b*) All others except 125 are perfect squares.

35. (*d*) All others except Allahabad are capitals of countries.

36. (*d*) As, book is made up of paper. Similarly, cloth is made up of threads.

37. (*d*) As, market depends on demand. Similarly, farming depends on monsoon.

38. (*b*) As, 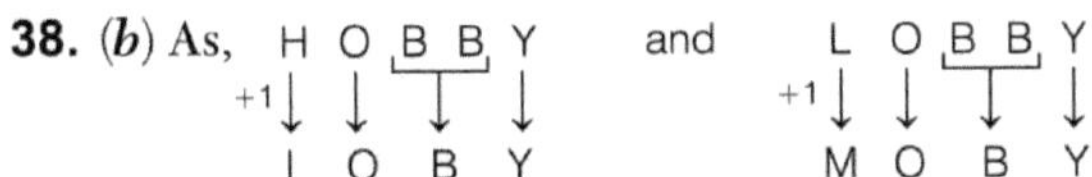

Similarly, 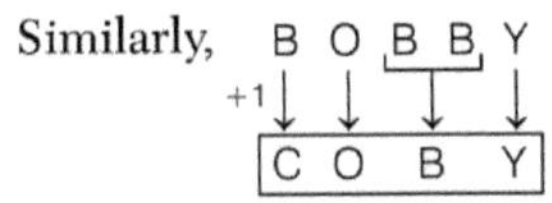

∴ BOBBY is coded as COBY.

39. (*d*) As, 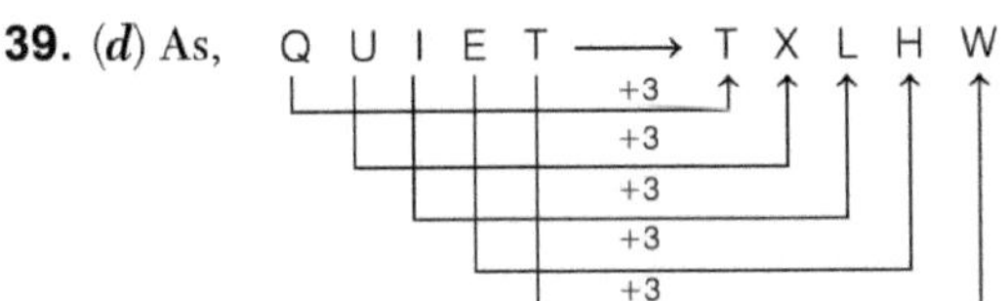

Similarly, 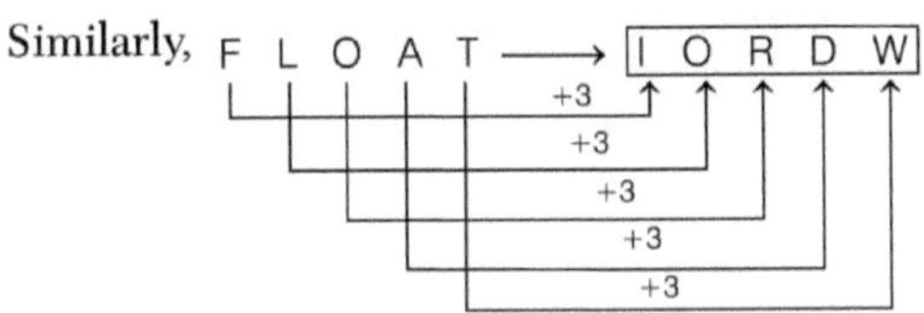

Hence, FLOAT is coded as IORDW.

40. (*d*) As, 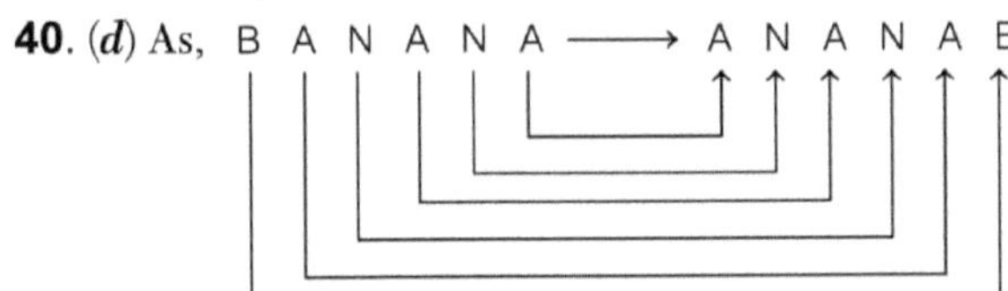

Similarly, 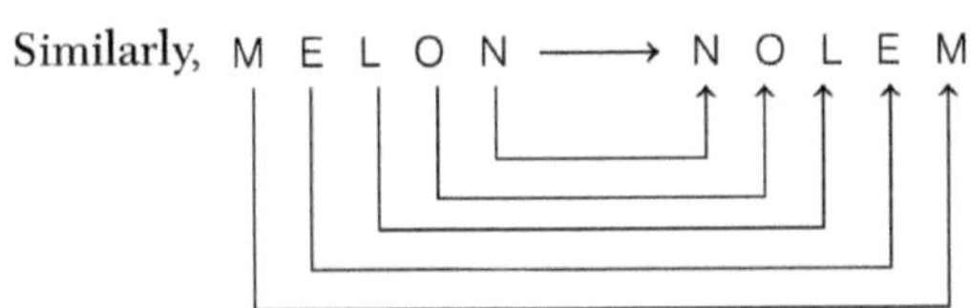

Hence, MELON is coded as NOLEM.

41. (*a*) As, multiplication is related to increase. Similarly, division is related to decrease.

42. (*b*) As, Conduit is a channel for conveying water. Similarly, Elevator is enclosed by shaft.

43. (*b*) As, plaintiff is related to the defendant. Similarly, injured is related to the accused.

44. (*b*) Pattern of the series is as follows, 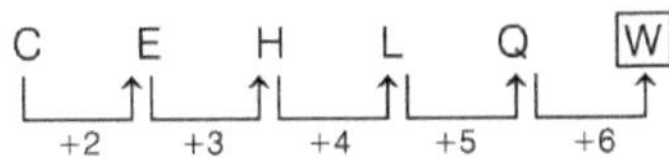

∴W comes in place of '?'.

45. (*c*) Pattern of the series is as follow,

As, 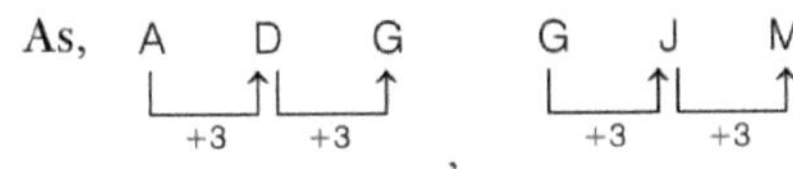

Similarly,

∴ Hence, MPS comes in place of '?'.

46. (*c*) Here, A, E, I, O, U vowels are in orders. As, P<u>A</u>T, P<u>E</u>N, P<u>I</u>N, P<u>O</u>T, PUT ∴PUT comes in place of '?' among the given options.

47. (*c*) Pattern of the series is as follow, 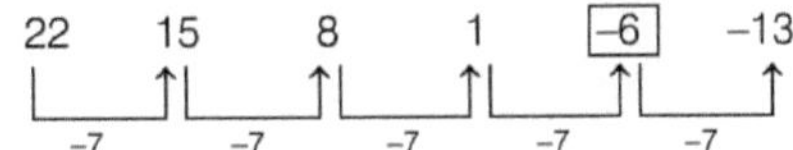

∴ − 6 will come in place of '?'.

48. (*d*) Pattern of the series is as follow, 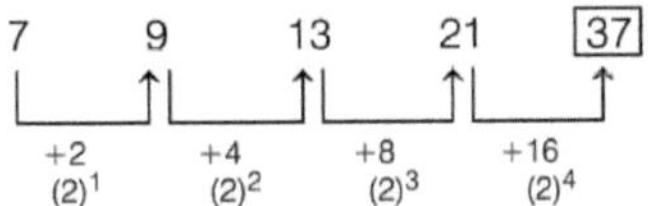

∴ 37 will come in place of '?'.

49. (*c*) Pattern of the series is as follow,

$1^3 - 1 = 0$;

$2^3 - 1 = 7$;

$3^3 - 1 = 26$;

$4^3 - 1 = 63$;

$5^3 - 1 = 124$;

$6^3 - 1 = 216 - 1 = \boxed{215}$

∴ 215 will come in place of '?'.

50. (*c*) Pattern of the series is as follow, 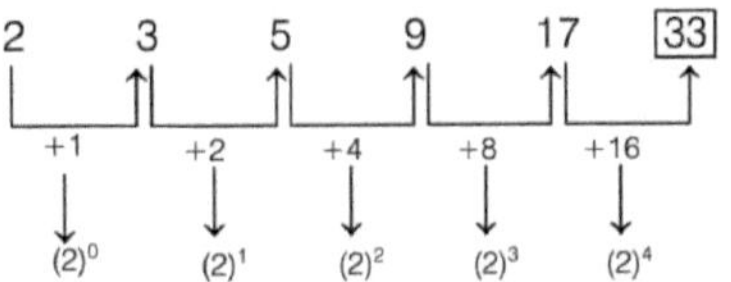

∴ 33 will come in place of '?'.

51. (*b*) Pattern of the series is as follow, 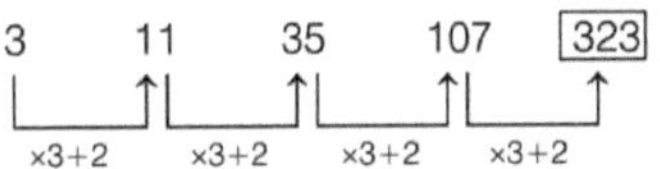

∴ 323 will come in place of '?'.

52. (*b*) Here,

J → January; F → February; M → March; A → April, M → May; J → June ∴The missing term is J.

53. (*d*) Pattern of the series is as follow, 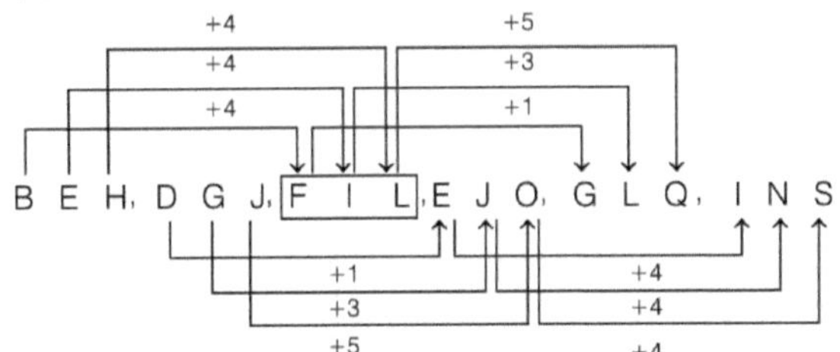

∴FIL will come in place of '?'.

54. (*c*) In each subsequent step, the figure is moving in clockwise direction at 90° and in small shapes square is moving back in one step, then changes its position with other side design in other step. So, on following this pattern option figure (c) will complete the series.

55. (*c*) In each step there is a addition of one line and the dot is exchanging its position from left to right in each step.

So, the figure in option (c) will complete the given sequence.

56. (*a*) A line first get reversed and get decreased in each of two steps. Therefore, the figure in option (a) will complete the given figure sequence.

57. (*d*) According to this pattern, option (d) will complete the given sequence.

58. (*a*) In first to fourth figures, the symbol '——⊣' come down by one position and its end get reversed in each step and the symbol ——⊣ change its position with other symbol then other symbol ends also reversed. Now, fourth figure to fifth the figure the symbol '——.'. come down by one position and its end get reversed and the symbol ——•. change its position with other symbol, then other symbol end also reversed. So, on following this pattern option figure (a) will complete the series.

59. (*b*) In the second step, × and ○ symbols have interchanged their position, and Δ shifted to middle. In the fourth step, S and □. symbols get interchanged and × shifted to middle. In the same pattern, figure (b) completes the given figure sequence.

60. (*b*) According to given pattern,

In each subsequent figure, 1st and 2nd, 2nd and 3rd, 3rd and 4th symbols interchange their position alternatively with end reversed and in fifth figure again first and second symbol interchange their position with end reversed.

∴ Figure in option (b) will complete the given sequence.

91. (*d*) Option (d) contains the error. 'Scissor' is incorrect. Hence, replace 'scissor' with 'scissors' to make the sentence correct.

92. (*b*) Option (b) contains the error. 'As .... as' is the correct format, hence, add 'as' before 'similar' to make the sentence grammatically correct.

93. (*c*) Option (c) contains the error. 'Between' is used when referring to two people. When referring to more than two people, one should use 'among'. Hence, replace 'between' with 'among' to make the sentence correct.

94. (*c*) Option (c) contains the error. The verb used in the sentence is past continuous. Hence, replace 'run' with 'running' to make the sentence correct.

95. (*a*) Option (a) contains the error. Replace 'myself' with 'I' to make the sentence error free.

114. (*a*) 'Blasted' is the correct word to be used instead of 'resounded'. Hence, replace 'resounded' with 'blasted' to make the sentence correct.

116. (*c*) 'Pass the buck' means to shift one's responsibility to someone else. Hence, replace 'pass on' with 'pass the buck' to make the sentence correct.

120. (*c*) 'Scoundrel' means a dishonest person or a rogue.

121. (*b*) 'Appurtenance' means an accessory or other item associated with a particular activity.

122. (*a*) 'Scourge' means to cause great suffering to someone 'infliction' means the action of inflicting unpleasant or painful things on someone. Hence, they both mean the same.

123. (*d*) 'Patronage' means the support given by a patron and 'benefaction' means a donation or gift. Hence, they are similar in meaning.

125. (*a*) 'Entrusted' means to trust someone with something important and 'endowed' means to provide someone with a quality or ability. Hence, replace 'entrusted' with 'endowed' to make the sentence correct.

126. (*b*) 'Every people' is incorrectly used in the sentence. Hence, replace 'every people' with 'everyone' to make the sentence grammatically correct.

135. (*b*) Option (b) contains the error. Replace 'grudges' with 'grudge' to make the sentence grammatically correct.

136. (*c*) Option (c) contains the error. The correct plural form of 'sister-in-law' is 'sisters-in-law'. Hence, replace 'sister-in-laws' with 'sisters-in-law' to make the sentence correct.

137. (*b*) Option (b) contains the error. Replace the article 'the' with 'a' to make the sentence grammatically correct.

138. (*a*) Option (a) contains the error. Replace 'myself and Rajkumar' with 'Rajkumar and I' to make the sentence grammatically correct.

139. (*b*) Option (b) contains the error. The noun 'schools' does not require the usage of article 'the'. Hence, remove 'the' to make the sentence correct.

140. (*d*) 'Poignant' means evoking a keen sense of sadness or regret. Hence, 'touching' is the nearest in meaning to poignant.

141. (*c*) 'Hyperbole' means exaggerated statements or claims not meant to be taken literally. Hence, 'exaggeration' is the nearest in meaning to hyperbole.

142. (*a*) 'Maudlin' means self-pityingly or tearfully sentimental. Hence, 'sentimental' is the nearest in meaning to maudlin.

143. (*b*) 'Avarice' means extreme greed for wealth or material gain. Hence, 'greed' is the nearest in meaning to avarice.

144. (*d*) 'Nebulous' means vague or ill-defined. Hence, 'unclear' is the nearest in meaning to nebulous.

145. (*b*) 'Abysmal' means extremely bad or appalling. Hence, 'terrible' is the nearest in meaning to abysmal.

156. (*b*) 'Relegate' means to assign an inferior rank or position to someone. Hence, 'assign' is the nearest in meaning to relegate.

157. (*a*) 'Penury' means the state of being very poor and 'destitution' means the same. Hence, 'destitution' is the nearest in meaning to penury.

158. (*c*) 'Amend' means to change something to correct it. Hence, 'maintain' is the correct opposite of amend.

161. (*b*) 'Succinct' is the opposite of 'verbose'. 'Verbose' means expresses in more words than need and 'succinct' means briefly and clearly expressed.

162. (*d*) 'Pious' is the opposite of 'profane'. 'Profane' means not relating to anything that is sacred or religious and 'pious' means devoutly religious.

163. (*a*) 'Careful' is the opposite of 'lackadaisical'. 'Lackadaisical' means lacking enthusiasm or carelessly lazy.

165. (*d*) 'Comfort' is the opposite of 'foment'. 'Foment' means to instigate or stir up an undesirable or violent course of action. Hence, 'comfort' is the correct opposite of foment.

Solved Paper 2007

Instructions

- There are Five (A–E) Sections in this Solved Paper.
- For every correct attempt, the student will be awarded **1 mark**.
- All the questions are in MCQs form and each having four options.

Marks : 200
Time : 3 hrs

Section A : Numerical Ability and Scientific Aptitude

1. A sum of money put out at compound interest amounts to ₹ 800 in 3 yr and to ₹ 840 in 4 yr. The rate of interest is
(a) 6%
(b) 5%
(c) 4%
(d) None of these

2. In an election between two candidates A and B, A got 55% of the total valid votes. 20% of the votes were invalid. If the total number of votes were 7500, find the number of valid votes polled in favour of the candidate B.
(a) 2700
(b) 2800
(c) 2300
(d) 2500

3. A student divided a number by 2 when he was required to multiply it by 2. The answer he got was 2. The correct answer should have been
(a) 12
(b) 8
(c) 6
(d) 4

4. The sum of a number and its reciprocal is $\dfrac{125}{22}$.
The number is
(a) $\dfrac{1}{4}$
(b) $\dfrac{2}{11}$
(c) $\dfrac{3}{11}$
(d) None of these

5. Which one of the following would a hydro balloon find easiest to lift?
(a) One kg of steel
(b) One kg of water
(c) One kg of lightly packed feathers
(d) All the same

6. A can do a piece of work in 40 days. He worked at it for 5 days and B finished it in 21 days. In how many days can A and B together finish the work?
(a) 12 days
(b) 16 days
(c) 15 days
(d) 14 days

7. A student walks from his house at a speed of 4 km/h and reaches his school 5 min late. If his speed had been 5 km/h, he would have reached 10 min earlier. The distance of the school from his house is
(a) 4 km
(b) 4.5 km
(c) 5 km
(d) 5.5 km

8. By selling 33 m of cloth, P gained the selling price of 11 m cloth. The percentage gain is
(a) 10%
(b) 20%
(c) 25%
(d) 50%

9. A train, 700 m long is running at the speed of 72 km/h. It is crosses a tunnel in 1 min, then the length of the tunnel is
(a) 700 m
(b) 600 m
(c) 550 m
(d) 500 m

10. A school has 20 teachers. One of them retires at the age of 60 yr and a new teacher replaces him. This change reduces the average age of the staff by 2 yr. The age of the new teacher is
(a) 28 yr
(b) 25 yr
(c) 20 yr
(d) 18 yr

11. If 11% of a number is 66, then number is
(a) 600
(b) 500
(c) 690
(d) 230

12. The price of milk increased by 25%. After that a housewife reduced her consumption of milk so that her expanses remain the same. The reduction percentage is
(a) 25%
(b) 75%
(c) 20%
(d) 80%

13. If the diameter of a circle reduced by 50%, then the area of the circle reduced by
(a) 25%
(b) 50%
(c) 75%
(d) None of these

14. $\dfrac{6}{50} = \dfrac{\sqrt{?}}{200}$
(a) 8
(b) 576
(c) 49
(d) 24

15. $\dfrac{617}{24.68} + X = 90$. Then, X is
(a) 65
(b) 68
(c) 70
(d) None of these

16. If $\dfrac{1}{x} + \dfrac{1}{y} = \dfrac{1}{2z}$, then z is equal to
(a) $\dfrac{(x+y)}{xy}$
(b) $\dfrac{(x+y)}{2xy}$
(c) $\dfrac{xy}{(x+y)}$
(d) $\dfrac{xy}{2(x+y)}$

17. Ten years ago, the ratio of ages of A and B was $3 : 5$. The ratio of their present ages is $2 : 3$. Their respective ages in years are
(a) 16, 24
(b) 20, 30
(c) 30, 50
(d) 40, 60

18. If the price of sugar increased by 25%, by what percentage should a housewife decrease her consumption so that her expenditure on sugar remains the same?
(a) 20%
(b) 25%
(c) 10%
(d) 30%

19. The diameter of a wheel of a cycle is 70 cm. It moves slowly along a road. How far will it go in 24 complete revolutions?
(a) 60 m
(b) 52.8 m
(c) 38.9 m
(d) 56.6 m

20. Swarna invested ₹ 2592 in buying shares of a company at ₹ 108 each. The face value of each share is ₹ 100. The company paid $12\dfrac{1}{2}\%$ dividend at the end of the year. Find the dividend received by Swarna at the end of the year.
(a) ₹ 300
(b) ₹ 500
(c) ₹ 400
(d) ₹ 250

21. How many electrons are present in the nucleus of Uranium ?
(a) 92
(b) 238
(c) 176
(d) Zero

22. Which one of the following metals is extracted by smelting ?
(a) Sodium
(b) Calcium
(c) Copper
(d) Aluminium

23. The outermost electronic configuration of the most electronegative element is
(a) 2, 8, 6
(b) 2, 6
(c) 2, 7
(d) 2, 5

24. The basis on which Mendeleev constructed his table is
(a) Atomic number
(b) Atomic mass
(c) Atomic volume
(d) Atomic size

25. Carbon dioxide is not a/an
(a) reducing agent
(b) acidic oxide
(c) oxidising agent
(d) extinguishing agent

26. Bernoulli's equation is important in the field of
(a) Electrical circuits
(b) Flow of liquids
(c) Magnetism
(d) Thermal conduction

27. Two bodies M and $m\,(M > m)$ are allowed to fall from the same height. If the air resistance for each be the same, then
(a) M will reach the ground earlier
(b) m will reach the ground earlier
(c) both will reach the ground simultaneously
(d) either of them may reach first depending upon their shape

28. Bones are pneumatic in
(a) Reptiles
(b) Amphibians
(c) Aves
(d) Mammals

29. The national animal of India is
(a) Lion
(b) Tiger
(c) Peacock
(d) Cow

30. When light travels from air into a glass slab, there is no change in its
(a) speed
(b) wavelength
(c) frequency
(d) amplitude

Section B : Reasoning and Logical Deduction

Directions (Q. Nos. 31 and 32) *Find the odd one out.*

31. (a) pond   (b) shore
(c) river   (d) sea

32. 87, 54, 28, 13, 5, 2, 2
(a) 28   (b) 54   (c) 123   (d) 2

33. If CLOTHES is EXHAUST and THRICE is AUMPES, then SHIRT is
(a) BLUSH   (b) STAUL
(c) THULE   (d) TUPMA

34. In a certain language 'CERTAIN' is coded as 'XVIGZRM'. How is 'MUNDANE' coded in that language ?
(a) NFMWZMV   (b) VMZWMFN
(c) NFMWZMX   (d) NFMXZMV

35. If CLEAR = RAELC, what is BEAUTY ?
(a) AUTEYB   (b) YTUAEB
(c) YUTBAE   (d) BTYUEA

36. If DOLLAR stands for EQOKYO and POUNDS stands for QQXMBP, the code for MARK will be
(a) NCUO   (b) NCUJ
(c) NCQI   (d) NCPH

Directions (Q. Nos. 37-40) *In each question below are given some statements followed by two conclusions numbered I and II. You have to take the given statements to be true even if they seem to be at variance with commonly known facts and then decide which of the given conclusions logically follows from the given statements, disregarding commonly known facts.*

Give answer
(a) If only Conclusion I follows
(b) If only Conclusion II follows
(c) If neither I nor II follows
(d) If both I and II follow

37. **Statement** Crime is a function of a criminal's biological make-up and his family relations.
Conclusions
  I. The incidence of crime is higher in identical twins that in fraternal twins.
  II. Families in which parents lack in warmth and affection fail to build children a moral conscience.

38. **Statements** 1. All keys are locks.
           2. All locks are screws.

Conclusions I. All screws are keys.
         II. Some locks are keys.

39. **Statements** 1. All pilots are brave men.
           2. All astronauts are pilots.
Conclusions I. All astronauts are brave men.
         II. Some pilots are astronauts.

40. **Statements** 1. All tigers are ships.
           2. Some ships are cupboards.
Conclusions I. Some tigers are cupboards.
         II. Some cupboards are tigers.

Directions (Q. Nos. 41 and 42) *A series of numbers which contains a wrong number in the series.*

41. 3, 6, 9, 22.5, 67.5, 236.25, 945
(a) 6   (b) 9
(c) 25.5   (d) 236.25

42. 3, 5, 8, 13, 24, 39, 72
(a) 8   (b) 13
(c) 24   (d) 39

Directions (Q. Nos. 43-47) *Find the missing term in each of the series.*

43. ACE, GIK, ?, SUW, YAC
(a) MOQ   (b) MNP
(c) MOP   (d) MPQ

44. 5760, 960, ?, 48, 16, 8
(a) 240   (b) 192
(c) 160   (d) 120

45. 78, 69, 76, 67, 74, ?, ?
(a) 65, 72   (b) 65, 67
(c) 67, 72   (d) 67, 74

46. 6, 7, 9, 13, 21, ?
(a) 25   (b) 29
(c) 37   (d) 32

47. 10, 70, ?, 5040, 50400
(a) 240
(b) 560
(c) 680
(d) None of the above

48. A man pointing to a photograph says, "The lady in the photograph is my nephew's maternal grandmother and her son is my sister's brother." How is the lady in the photograph related to his sister who has no other sister ?
(a) Mother   (b) Mother-in-law
(c) Cousin   (d) None of these

Direction (Q. No. 49) *Consider each of the statements to be true and then decide from the given conclusions which ones logically follow from the given statements.*

49. Statements   1. All glasses are roads.
               2. No road is a stick.
               3. Some sticks are pens.

   Conclusions I. Some glasses are sticks.
              II. Some pens are sticks.
             III. Some roads are sticks.
             IV. No glass is a stick.

(a) II and IV follows
(b) I or IV and II follow
(c) Either I or II and IV follow
(d) None of the above

50. In a certain code 'PENCIL' is written as RCTAMJ. Then, in that code 'BROKEN' is written as
(a) SPFLIM   (b) SVFLIN
(c) FPSMIL   (d) None of these

51. In a certain code a number 13479 is written as AQFJL and 5268 is written as DMPN. How is 396824 written in that code ?
(a) QLPNMJ   (b) QLPNMF
(c) QLPMNF   (d) QLPNDF

52. If ZUBIN is coded as ATCHO, MEHTA will be coded as
(a) NDIUB   (b) NDISB   (c) NDGSB   (d) NDHSI

Directions (Q. Nos. 53-60) *Each question consists of problem figures and answer figures. The problem figures make a series. You have to find which one of the answer figures would be the next one in the given series.*

53. Problem Figures

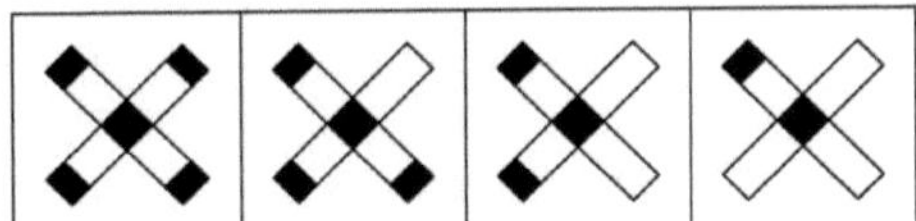

Answer Figures

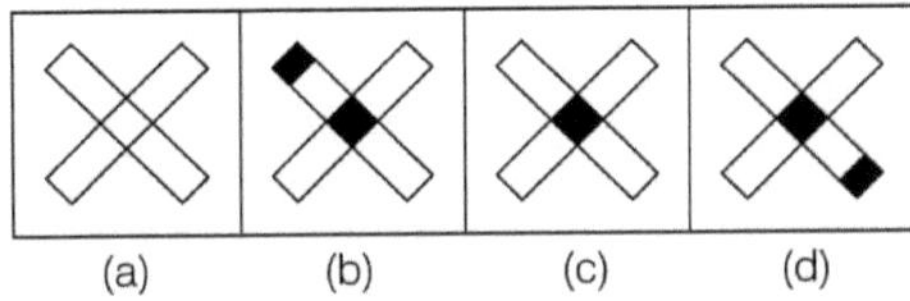

(a)   (b)   (c)   (d)

54. Problem Figures

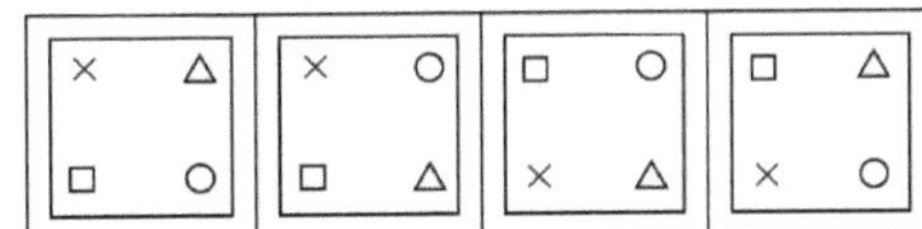

Answer Figures

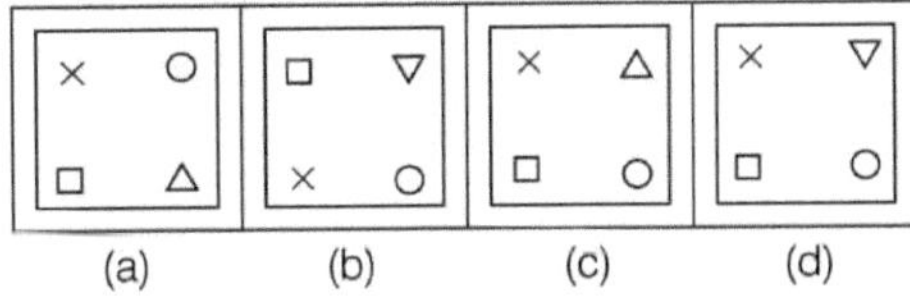

(a)   (b)   (c)   (d)

55. Problem Figures

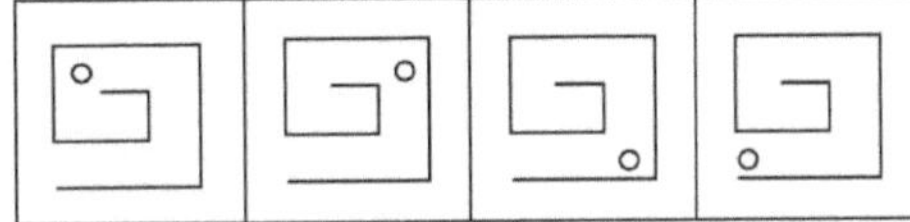

Answer Figures

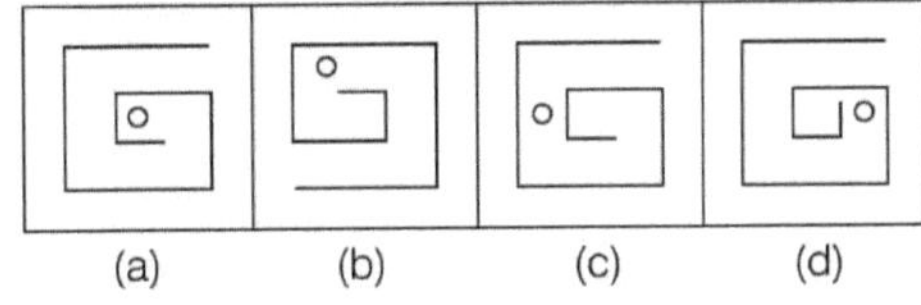

(a)   (b)   (c)   (d)

56. Problem Figures

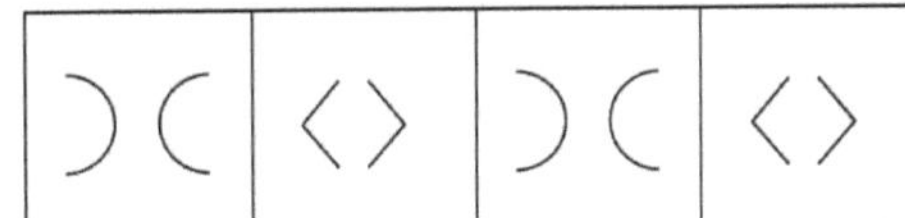

Answer Figures

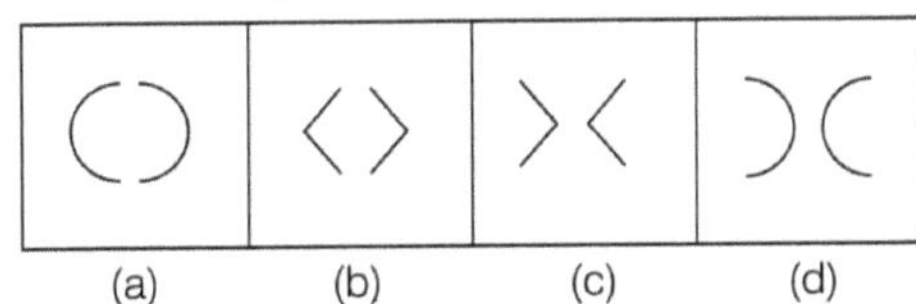

(a)   (b)   (c)   (d)

57. Problem Figures

Answer Figures

(a)   (b)   (c)   (d)

58. Problem Figures

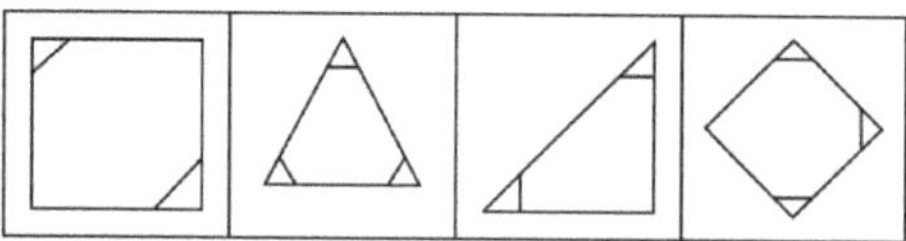

Answer Figures

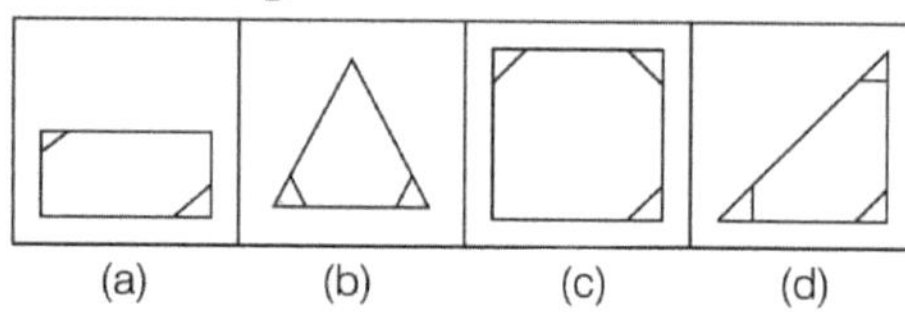

(a)   (b)   (c)   (d)

59. Problem Figures

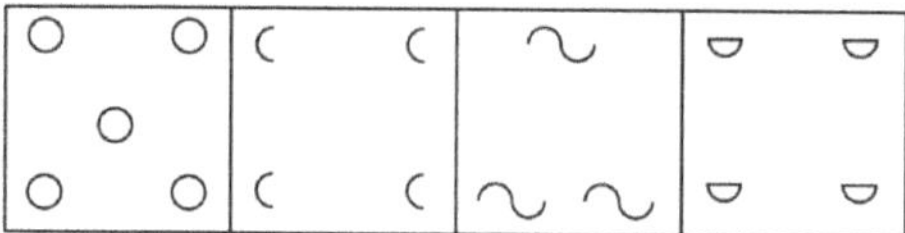

Answer Figures

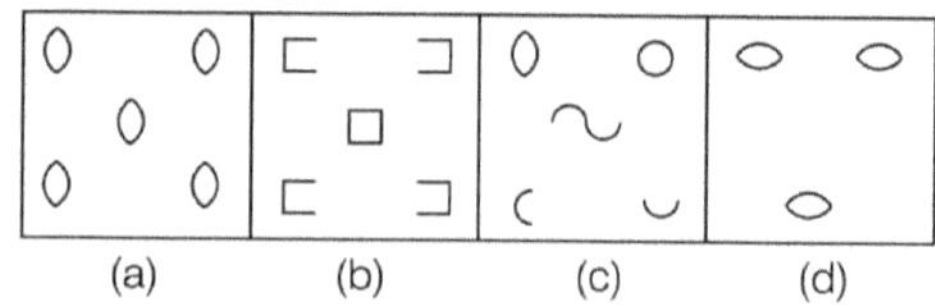

(a)   (b)   (c)   (d)

60. Problem Figures

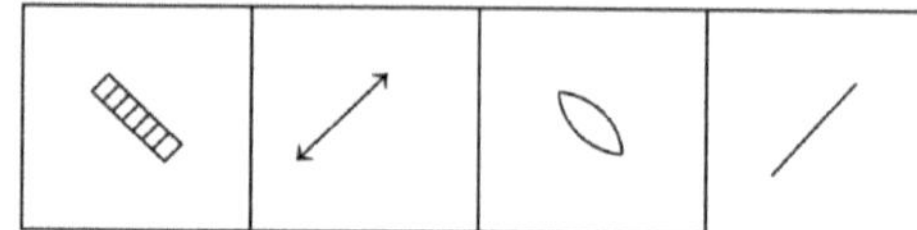

Answer Figures

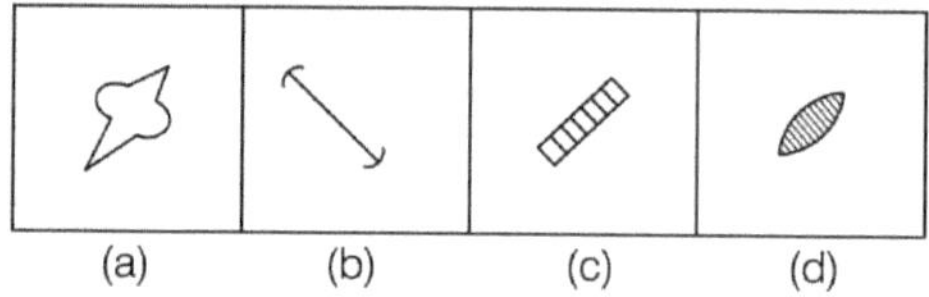

(a)   (b)   (c)   (d)

Section C : General Knowledge

HM 2007

61. Which of the following is correctly matched?

	Organisation		Headquarters
A.	International Monetary Fund	1.	Manila
B.	Asian Development Bank	2.	Lyons (France)
C.	INTERPOL	3.	Brussels
D.	NATO	4.	Washington DC

Codes

	A	B	C	D			A	B	C	D
(a)	4	1	2	3		(b)	1	2	3	4
(c)	2	3	4	1		(d)	3	4	1	2

62. Which among the following is a martial dance?
(a) Kathakali
(b) Bamboo dance in Meghalaya
(c) Chhau of Mayurbhanj
(d) Bhangra of Punjab

63. 8th March is observed as
(a) International Day for Elderly People
(b) International Children's Day
(c) International Women's Day
(d) International Human Rights Day

64. Sardar Vallabhbhai Patel was equated with
(a) Mazzini   (b) Cavour
(c) Garibaldi   (d) Bismarck

65. Mica is found in which one of the following pairs of rocks ?
(a) Slate - Sandstone   (b) Schist - Gneiss
(c) Limestone - Sandstone   (d) Shale-Limestone

66. The Tenth plan aims to reduce the poverty ratio by 2007 to
(a) 10%   (b) 30%   (c) 20%   (d) 5%

67. Which of the following Hollywood art directors, who won 11 Oscar awards, designed the Oscar statuette in 1926 ?
(a) Peter Jackson   (b) Cedric Libbons
(c) Sean Penn   (d) Tim Robbins

68. During the Non-Cooperation Movement, which award did Gandhiji return ?
(a) Right Honourable   (b) Rai Bahadur
(c) Hind Kesari   (d) Kaiser-e-Hind

69. Capital : Output Ratio of a commodity measures
(a) its per unit cost of production.
(b) the amount of capital invested per unit of output.
(c) the ratio of capital depreciation to quantity of output.
(d) the ratio of working capital employed to quantity of output.

70. Bhagirathi, a collection of poems in Sanskrit by renowned scholar Govind Chandra Pande, has been chosen for the prestigious .... for 2003.
(a) Shalaka Samman   (b) Vyas Samman
(c) Kalidas Samman   (d) Saraswati Samman

71. Which of the following is the Punjabi code for the illegal immigrants who go abroad in group on a visitor's visa or a 'sticker visa' (take visa) and then simply vanish ?
(a) Shikar   (b) Kabootar
(c) Tota   (d) Human Cargo

72. Universal receivers can receive blood from
(a) Only Group AB
(b) Only Group O
(c) Groups O, A, B, AB
(d) Groups A, AB

73. Name the first ever equity fund exclusively for power which is expected to be shortly launched as a venture capital fund.
(a) Power India Bond
(b) Power India Fund
(c) Power Finance Fund
(d) India Power Fund

74. Which one of the following is not a tool of legislative control over administration in India?
(a) Dissolution of House
(b) Resolutions
(c) Questions
(d) No confidence motion

75. Which female astronaut spent her maximum time in space?
(a) Lisa Norwak
(b) Kalpana Chawla
(c) Sunita Williams
(d) None of these

76. 13th Asian Archery Championship was held in
(a) Myanmar
(b) Singapore
(c) Taiwan
(d) Sri Lanka

77. Name the state which has been rocked by the fake stamp paper scam.
(a) Andhra Pradesh
(b) Tamil Nadu
(c) Kerala
(d) Maharashtra

78. Name the company having the punchline 'Customer power wins again'.
(a) Apollo Tyres
(b) MRF Tyres
(c) Radlab Tyres
(d) JK Tyres

79. Name the country in which MTNL (Mahanagar Telephone Nigam Limited) has won licences for operating cellular mobile, WLL and International Long Distance (ILD) services.
(a) Kenya
(b) Nepal
(c) Afghanistan
(d) Mauritius

80. Which one of the following lenses should be used to correct the defect of astigmatism ?
(a) Cylindrical lens
(b) Concave lens
(c) Convex lens
(d) Bifocal lens

81. In which of the following states is India's largest producer of poultry products, Venkateshwara Hatcheries group, situated ?
(a) Tamil Nadu
(b) Kerala
(c) Andhra Pradesh
(d) Karnataka

82. Name the company which has signed a production sharing contract with the Government for exploratory rights to two new land blocks in Tripura and the Cauvery Basin.
(a) ONGC
(b) OIL
(c) IOC
(d) GAIL

83. The causative agent of Tuberculosis is
(a) Mycobacterium
(b) Aspergillus
(c) Rhabdovirus
(d) HIV

84. What is 'Teletext' ?
(a) Flashing of telephone conversation on TV screen.
(b) Printing the text of the message on the telex machine.
(c) Connecting the local telephones with outstation telephones without STD codes.
(d) Flashing of the text of news and information on the TV screen.

85. A test tube baby means
(a) a baby grown in a test tube
(b) embryo fertilized in uterus and developed in test tube
(c) embryo fertilized and developed in uterus
(d) fertilization in vitro and then transplantation in the uterus

86. Pakistan has offered India Most-Favoured Nation (MFN) status in
(a) Railways
(b) Foods
(c) Civil Aviation
(d) Tea

87. Which of the following Indian firms has signed an agreement to acquire Australia-based Expert Information Services Pvt. Ltd. (Expert)?
(a) Sify
(b) Infosys
(c) TCS
(d) Wipro

88. The least populated state in India is
(a) Goa
(b) Sikkim
(c) Manipur
(d) Arunachal Pradesh

89. Which of the following projects has been launched by the Ministry of Science and Technology to protect India's traditional knowledge ?
(a) Traditional Knowledge Bank
(b) Pride in Past
(c) Glorious India
(d) Traditional Knowledge Digital Library

90. Why is 18th December, observed as Minorities Rights Day ?
(a) On this date in 1947 our Constituent Assembly adopted the Articles 25 and 29 regarding the protection of minorities.
(b) On this date in 1992 the United Nations adopted a declaration regarding the protection of rights of minorities.
(c) On this date in 1892, Abdul Kalam Azad was born.
(d) On this date in 1950 India gave the assurance in the UN General Assembly that it would protect the existence of the national or ethnic, cultural, religious and linguistic identity of minorities and encourage conditions for the promotion of their identity.

Section D : English Language

Directions (Q. Nos. 91-94) *Choose the word which is nearly the same in meaning to the word given below in capitals.*

91. ADMONISH
  - (a) Punish
  - (b) Curse
  - (c) Dismiss
  - (d) Reprimand

92. WRETCHED
  - (a) Poor (b) Foolish (c) Insane (d) Strained

93. ARCHAIC
  - (a) Earlier
  - (b) Outdated
  - (c) Complex
  - (d) Ancient

94. NIMBLE
  - (a) Unrhythmic
  - (b) Lively
  - (c) Quickening
  - (d) Clear

Directions (Q. Nos. 95-100) *In each question, you are given certain sentences which have been jumbled and labelled P, Q, R and S. Find the proper sequence that will construct the original sentence. Choose the correct sequence.*

95. I take it that most people who talk glibly of science think of science merely as a kind of handmaiden to make their work easier
  of course, it does make their work easier
  P
  and so it is   all science does
  Q   R
  it adds to the wealth of the nation and better conditions
  S
  but surely, science is something more than that.
  - (a) RSPQ (b) QPSR (c) PSRQ (d) QRPS

96. Many people enter the stock markets using strategies that stack the odds against their success
  predictions by economists usually vary widely
  P
  stock market pundits speak one language and technical analysts speak another
  Q
  one of the reasons this happens is because stock market is a confusing and complex phenomenon
  R
  stock market -advisory letters offer differing opinions on the prospects of individual companies.
  S

Moreover, if you listen to other investors you will hear yet different opinions.
  - (a) PSQR (b) PQRS (c) RQPS (d) RQSP

97. Equally pressing begin reconstructing
  P
  is the need to emergency footing
  Q   R
  the country of an
  S
  - (a) SRQP (b) QPSR (c) SPQR (d) QRSP

98. Georgian loyalists and rebel forces after a week of fighting
  P
  agreed to a ceasefire today
  Q   R
  in which 51 people were killed.
  S
  - (a) PQRS
  - (b) QRSP
  - (c) QPSR
  - (d) QRPS

99. Most of our farmers do not get a fair return
  P
  on the sale of their farm-products
  Q
  on their investment in back-breaking labour
  R
  and high costs of seeds and fertilizers
  S
  - (a) PQRS (b) PQSR (c) PRQS (d) PRSQ

100. He said that those who
  would miss a very interesting game
  P
  to be played between two foreign teams
  Q   R
  would not accompany him
  S
  - (a) SQRP
  - (b) SRPQ
  - (c) SPQR
  - (d) QRPS

Directions (Q. Nos. 101-106) *In each of the following questions select from amongst the four alternatives, the word most opposite in meaning to the word given below in capital.*

101. DISPARAGE
  - (a) Please
  - (b) Praise
  - (c) Belittle
  - (d) Denigrate

102. COARSE
    (a) Beautiful   (b) Attractive
    (c) Fine   (d) Smart

103. JUBILANT
    (a) Disturbed   (b) Scared
    (c) Gloomy   (d) Quiet

104. ABHOR
    (a) Admire   (b) Respect
    (c) Applaud   (d) Appreciate

105. RETROGRADE
    (a) Progressive   (b) Stubborn
    (c) Punitive   (d) Aggressive

106. HIRSUTE
    (a) Scaly   (b) Bald
    (c) Erudite   (d) Quiet

Directions (Q. Nos. 107-114) *Fill in the blanks.*

107. Your .... will .... all the benefits you derived from your hard work.
    (a) patience, delete
    (b) possessiveness, enhance
    (c) carelessness, nullify
    (d) apathy, increase

108. Nine members have .... about the decision, but the tenth one views it ....
    (a) solution, critically
    (b) consensus, similarly
    (c) disagreement, collectively
    (d) agreement, differently

109. In case you have .... his feelings, you must .... to him.
    (a) hurt, apologise   (b) evoked, surrender
    (c) touched, talk   (d) offended, appeal

110. The recent .... in oil-prices has given an unexpected additional .... to the cost-spiral.
    (a) slump, drawback   (b) cut, blow
    (c) rise, twist   (d) development, cut

111. Transforming .... bureaucracies into dynamic, customer-driven organisations is .... under any circumstances.
    (a) ideal, essential   (b) lazy, undesirable
    (c) inefficient, challenging   (d) civilised, ineffective

112. As he was the century's .... man of science, his .... was universally mourned.
    (a) wealthiest, experiment   (b) greatest, death
    (c) happiest, accepted   (d) oldest, invention

113. The issues could be .... amicably only because of his .... handling of the situation.
    (a) dropped, haphazard
    (b) raised, careful
    (c) discussed, enthusiastic
    (d) resolved, tactful

114. There are .... examples to prove that the PM .... warmly with the masses.
    (a) various, meeting   (b) several, behaves
    (c) illustrious, charms   (d) many, interact

Directions (Q. Nos. 115-121) *Select the appropriate phrase from the-alternatives to replace the underlined words to correct the sentence.*

115. India's outlook on the world <u>is composing of</u> these various elements.
    (a) is composed of
    (b) is composed by
    (c) is composing with
    (d) has been composing at

116. He could not give a/an <u>good explanation for</u> his extraordinary behaviour.
    (a) account for   (b) be satisfied with
    (c) provide evidence   (d) count on

117. He told us the story <u>in a nutshell</u>.
    (a) in the nutshell
    (b) putting it in a nut
    (c) in nutshell
    (d) No correction required

118. His suggestions were <u>so trivial and hence</u> , nobody took any cognizance of them.
    (a) so trivial that and have
    (b) very trivial and hence to
    (c) too trivial to and hence
    (d) very trivial and hence

119. His brother <u>is working</u> in this factory since 1970.
    (a) was working   (b) worked
    (c) has been working   (d) No correction required

120. I could achieve success through <u>conscious efforts</u>.
    (a) efforts made with critical awareness
    (b) tremendous efforts
    (c) efforts done after gaining consciousness
    (d) efforts done after being awakened

121. <u>If the room had been brighter</u>, I would have been able to read for a while before bed time.
    (a) If the room was brighter
    (b) If rooms are brighter
    (c) Had the room brighter
    (d) No correction required

Directions (Q. Nos. 122-131) *In the following passage, there are blank spaces numbered 122 to 131. Against each of these numbers below the passage, a choice of four words (a), (b), (c) and (d) is suggested to replace the blank spaces in the passage. First read the passage and try to understand what it is about. Then choose the best word from the alternatives (a), (b), (c) and (d).*

Something has happened in the last twenty years that surely must (**122**) anything that has happened before. Some historians are already saying that thrust (**123**) space represents a vital turning point in history. Moon flights are considered (**124**) less than steps in human evolution(**125**) to the time when life on earth emerged from the sea and established itself on land. Of course, not everyone (**126**) enraptured by space. Critics have often said that space flight has been an (**127**) use of resources that should have (**128**) to feeding, clothing and housing people. There is, however, no proof that if we had (**129**) been working on space, we would have done anything of great human value. In fact, research and exploration have (**130**) spin-offs, quite apart from the fact that they demonstrate that (**131**) is alive and insatiably curious.

HM 2007

122. (a) terminate   (b) transcend
    (c) precede   (d) recede

123. (a) on   (b) upon
    (c) in   (d) into

124. (a) nothing   (b) certainly
    (c) sufficiently   (d) probably

125. (a) exceeding   (b) contrasting
    (c) comparable   (d) matching

126. (a) was   (b) has been
    (c) had been   (d) being

127. (a) economical   (b) extravagant
    (c) appropriate   (d) benevolent

128. (a) devoted   (b) allotted
    (c) reserved   (d) gone

129. (a) not   (b) occasionally
    (c) seldom   (d) possibly

130. (a) renowned   (b) renounced
    (c) remarkable   (d) relevant

131. (a) one   (b) man
    (c) human   (d) individual

Directions (Q. Nos. 132-136) *Read the following passage carefully and answer the questions given below.*

The strength of Indian Democracy lies in its tradition, in the fusion of the ideas of democracy and national independence which was the characteristic of the Indian Nationalist Movement long before Independence. Although the British retained supreme authority in India until 1947, the provincial elections of 1937 provided real exercise in democratic practice before National Independence. During the Pacific war, India was not overrun or seriously invaded by the Japanese and after the war was over, the transfer of power to a Government of the Indian Congress Party was a peaceful one as far as Britain was concerned. By 1947, 'Indianisation' had already gone far in the Indian Civil Service and Army, so that the new government could start with effective instruments of central control.

After Independence, however, India was faced with two vast problems; the first, that of economic growth from a very low level of production, and the second was that of ethnic diversity and the aspirations of sub nationalities. The Congress leadership was more aware of the former problem than of the second.

As a new political elite which had rebelled' not only against the British Raj but also against India's old social order, they were conscious of the need to initiate economic development and undertake social reforms, but as nationalists who had led a struggle against the alien rule on behalf of all parts of India, they took the cohesion of the Indian nation too much for granted and underestimated the centrifugal forces of ethnic division, which were bound to be accentuated rather than diminished as the popular masses were more and more drawn into politics.

The Congress party, was originally opposed to the idea of recognising any division of India on a linguistic basis and preferred to retain the old provinces of British India which often cut across linguistic boundaries. However, this was later conceded as the basis for a federal 'Indian Union'. The rights granted to the States created new problems for the Central Government.

The idea of making Hindi the national language of a united India was thwarted by the recalcitrance of the speakers of other important Indian languages, and the autonomy of the States rendered central economic planning extremely difficult. Land reforms remained under the control of the States and many large-scale economic projects required a degree of cooperation between the Central Government and one or more of the States which, it was found, was impossible to achieve.

Coordination of policies was difficult even when the Congress party was in power both in the States and at the Centre. When a Congress Government in Delhi was confronted with Non-Congress parties in office in the States, it became much harder.

132. Which of the following problems was India faced with after Independence?
   (a) Military attack from a country across the border.
   (b) Lack of coordination between the Central and State Governments.
   (c) Improper coordination of various Government policies.
   (d) Increasing the production from a very low level.

133. Which of the following issues was not appropriately realised by the Central Government?
   (a) Ethnic diversity of the people.
   (b) A national language for the country.
   (c) Implementation of the formulated policies.
   (d) Centre-State relations.

134. Why was central economic planning found to be difficult?
   (a) Multiplicity of States and Union Territories.
   (b) Lack of coordination in different government departments.
   (c) Autonomy given to the States in certain matters.
   (d) Lack of will in implementing land reforms.

135. Why was the linguistic reorganisation of the States accepted?
   (a) The States were not cooperating with the Central Government.
   (b) Non-Congress Governments in the States ordered such a reorganisation of the States.
   (c) No common national language emerged.
   (d) Strong pressure from the States was exerted on the Central Government to create such States.

136. Which according to the passage, can be cited as an exercise in democratic practice in India before Independence?
   (a) The handing over of power by the British to India.
   (b) The Indianisation of the Indian Civil Service.
   (c) A neutral role played by the Army.
   (d) None of the above

Directions (Q. Nos. 137-142) *Fill in the blanks.*

137. Can you pay ……… all these articles?
   (a) for   (b) of   (c) off   (d) out

138. The workers agitated for a fair ……… for their work.
   (a) reward   (b) price   (c) salary   (d) wage

139. I could ……… see the sight since it was dark.
   (a) clearly   (b) barely   (c) obviously (d) aptly

140. Satish was …… with a natural talent for music.
   (a) given   (b) found
   (c) endowed   (d) entrusted

141. I have been awake ……… four o'clock.
   (a) for   (b) since   (c) till   (d) until

142. His life consists of ……… of drinking punctuated by periods of drunken sleep.
   (a) barrels   (b) bouts
   (c) bowls   (d) pints

Directions (Q. Nos. 143-147) *Which of the words/phrases, (a), (b), (c) or (d) should replace the words/ phrases given in bold italics in each of the following sentences?*

143. You can mix it ***with some sugar*** and eat it.
   (a) in some sugar
   (b) into some sugar
   (c) any sugar
   (d) No correction required

144. He stopped ***to work*** an hour ago.
   (a) to working
   (b) to have worked
   (c) working
   (d) No correction required

145. The tea-estate administration is ***in such mess there*** is no leader to set the things right.
   (a) in such a mess here
   (b) in a such mess that here
   (c) in such a mess that there
   (d) with such a mess that there

146. The problems of translation ***are still remain***.
   (a) are remain
   (b) will remained
   (c) will still remain
   (d) No correction required

147. The drama had many scenes which were so humorous that it was ***hardly possible to keep*** a straight face.
   (a) hardly possible for keeping
   (b) hardly impossible keeping
   (c) hardly impossible to keep
   (d) No correction required

Directions (Q. Nos. 148-152) *Read each sentence to find out if there is any grammatical error in it. If there is any error, it will be only in one part of the sentence. The alphabet of that part is your answer (Disregard punctuation errors, if any).*

148. The gentleman/ together with his/
          (a)   (b)
   wife and children/ were drowned.
          (c)   (d)

149. I complemented/ him for/
　　　(a)　　　　　　　(b)
his brilliant successes in the / examination.
　　　　　　(c)　　　　　　　　(d)

150. Naren cannot/ decide, as to which/
　　　　(a)　　　　　(b)
course he should do/ after obtaining his Degree.
　　　　(c)　　　　　　(d)

151. There will be/ increased emphasis on/
　　　　(a)　　　　　　(b)
heavy industry in planning./ no error
　　　　(c)　　　　　　(d)

152. He tried as he could/ Naveen did not/
　　　　(a)　　　　　　(b)
succeed in getting/ his car to start up.
　　　　(c)　　　　　　(d)

Directions (Q. Nos. 153-160) *In each of the following questions, select from amongst the four alternatives, the word nearest in meaning to the word given below in capital.*

153. RECOMPENSE

(a) Reward　(b) Help　(c) Praise　(d) Thank

154. QUALM

(a) Crisis　　　　　(b) Scruple
(c) Altercation　　(d) Attribute

155. LICENTIOUS

(a) Libertine　　　(b) Loafer Type
(c) Criminal　　　(d) Freelance

156. PIOUS

(a) Pure　　　　　(b) Pretentious
(c) Clean　　　　(d) Devout

157. CREDENTIALS

(a) Principles
(b) Dependability
(c) Capacity to return loans
(d) trustworthiness

158. AUDACIOUS

(a) Manifest　　　(b) Obvious
(c) Venture　　　(d) Daring

159. STRIDENCY

(a) Stress
(b) Consistency
(c) Flippant
(d) Harshness

160. HARBINGER

(a) Messenger　　(b) Steward
(c) Forerunner　　(d) Pilot

Directions (Q. Nos. 161 and 162) *In each of the following questions select from amongst the four alternatives, the word most opposite in meaning to the word given below in capital.*

161. HYPOCRITICAL

(a) Gentle　　　　(b) Sincere
(c) Amiable　　　(d) Dependable

162. FUTILITY

(a) Value　　　　(b) Usefulness
(c) Importance　　(d) Urgency

Directions (Q. Nos. 163-165) *Pick out the most effective words from the given options to fill in the blanks to make the sentences meaningfully correct.*

163. How do you expect us to stay in such a ……… building even if it can be hired on a nominal rent?

(a) scruffy　　　　(b) disparate
(c) fragmented　　(d) robust

164. It ……… during summer months.

(a) rain　　　　　(b) rains
(c) has rain　　　(d) is raining

165. He lives in the world of ………

(a) allusions　　　(b) illusions
(c) conclusions　　(d) delusions

Directions (Q. Nos. 166-170) *Read each sentence to find out whether there is any error in it. The error, if any, is in one part of the sentence. The alphabet of that part (a), (b), (c) or (d) is your answer.*

166. You must had (a)/a kind and gentle heart (b)/ if you want (c)/ to be a successful doctor (d).

167. The children were (a)/playing with a ball (b)/ and run around when the accident occurred (c)/ No error (d).

168. Bangladesh has come (a)/ into existence (b)/ thirty years ago (c)/ No error (d).

169. An anti-extortion cell is opened/ by the district police headquarter (b)/ six months ago (c)/ as a precautionary measure(d).

170. I thought that (a)/ we were meeting to talk turkey (b)/ but you have brought (c)/ your wife with you (d).

Section E : Aptitude For Service Sector

Directions *As you read the following questions carefully, please answer all the questions as best as you can without skipping any one. To each question there are four choices you can answer each question honestly and try to choose the first answer that comes to your mind without changing it because the first choice is always the true one.*

171. Even while studying alone you have to speak loudly to learn to counteract your distractions. Your flight is delayed for two hours and you are among strangers. You would
(a) chat only when others start
(b) buy a magazine and keep yourself busy
(c) start chatting with the person sitting next to you
(d) sit idle and hope time passes fast

172. You're the most recent recruit in a company, since you are new, you don't know many of the other employees. Though they are trying to make you feel comfortable from their side, what initiative would you take to interact with them?
(a) Smile at everyone and say hello
(b) Go right up to anyone who seems approachable and start talking animatedly
(c) Take part in discussions that deal with work only
(d) Be formal and wait for them to address you

173. As a treat you've taken your younger cousins out on a field trip to a new amusement park. You suddenly realize that one child is missing. You
(a) tell the remaining children in the group to stay together in one place while you go alone to look for a park official to report the missing child
(b) take the group to a quiet corner of the park and are unsure of how to proceed
(c) gather the rest of the children and take them along with you to the park officials who will then help you set about looking for the missing child while ensuring the safety of the rest of the group
(d) start calling out the missing child's name in a frantic manner

174. During an examination, the person sitting in front of you asks for your help. Before you can respond, the teacher comes up to your desk and deducts marks for being caught cheating. You
(a) are anxious throughout the paper but you continue writing
(b) continue with the exam and once it is over go up to the teacher to explain the situation as it happened in a level headed manner
(c) immediately start protesting and insist that you have not been cheating
(d) are unable to continue writing you paper and keepo n worrying about the unfair deduction of marks

175. If you have an exam coming up next week and at the same time it's your deadline to submit a project and a presentation, you would
(a) take one thing at a time and plan out a time table and work accordingly
(b) become anxious and impulsively do the tasks just for the sake of getting over with them
(c) try to do all the tasks at the same time
(d) start panicking and keep crying without being able to work effectively at any task

176. You are about to leave to meet one of your friends who has been admitted to the hospital in a serious condition. In a hurry you lock the door but forget the keys inside the house. You would
(a) mark a lot of noise, pace rapidly near your apartment expecting someone would help
(b) make a call to arrange for a duplicate key to be left with your neighbour and hurry to meet your friend in the hospital
(c) ask your neighbour to work out the keys problem for you and end up arriving late at the hospital
(d) be totally confused about the whole situation without being able to decide whether you should rush to meet your friend or tackle the keys situation

177. You work in an organisation and your boss accuses you of certain things you didn't do in front of everyone, which puts you in an embarrassing situation. You would
(a) gather the courage and discuss the matter with your boss publicly
(b) be too embarrassed to discuss it with anybody and give in your resignation letter
(c) not react in public but have a private discussion with your boss
(d) deny the accusation and move on

178. You come to know that you are suffering from tuberculosis. You would
(a) accept the diagnosis, begin with the treatment and try to live in a better way than you had previously done
(b) keep thinking about the disease and just keep waiting for it to end
(c) visit many other medical specialists to see if a wrong diagnosis has been made and then again see many doctors for treatment
(d) become totally depressed and contemplate ending your life

179. Are you happy with your social relationships?
   (a) Not at all   (b) Little
   (c) Somewhat   (d) Totally

180. You have to submit an assignment the following day. Just as you start working on it, a friend informs you that he has an extra ticket for a movie that you've wanted to see. You
   (a) plan to go for the movie and decide that you will complete your assignment, even if you have to stay up all night
   (b) decline your friends' offer and continue doing your work'
   (c) leave your work and go for the movie without giving a thought as to how you would finish your assignment
   (d) are indecisive

181. If you're faced with a problem in life, you typically
   (a) ride it out; everyone has problems, it's the getting them sorted out that matters
   (b) feel panicky because you don't know how to handle it; you feel unmotivated and do nothing
   (c) move into top gear to get it sorted; you feel guilty if you have any problem, no matter how small
   (d) you feel depressed and feel that misfortune has struck you again

182. You enter a party and see a lot of attractive boys/girls. You are there to meet your old friend. You
   (a) go directly to your friend
   (b) give him little time and then run towards other people
   (c) forget about him and get busy with other attractive people
   (d) are confused about whom to approach

183. You are asked to organise a very important event for your college. Unfortunately, in the middle of it, a personal problem-crops up. You
   (a) forget about the event and try solving the personal matter
   (b) manage both efficiently
   (c) concentrate only on organising the event, leaving the personal problem for the time being
   (d) get so burdened with both tasks that you end up giving up both the tasks

184. You are writing a well-memorised paragraph but are feeling very sleepy. You
   (a) manage to write it accurately
   (b) take regular pauses in between but complete writing
   (c) decide to sleep off and do the work later
   (d) make many errors

185. While driving
   (a) your eyes are on road and you drive nicely without doing anything else
   (b) sometimes get involved in accidents even though you paid your full attention, but still were a bit careless
   (c) you mostly end up getting involved in accidents as you are talking on your mobile or are engrossed in a song on stereo
   (d) you can do multi-tasking and still don't get involved in any accidents

186. Your teacher assigns a project to your group and nobody is ready to work on it since the winter vacations will begin in a few days and everybody is feeling restless and excited. You could
   (a) feel the same way and hope the teacher will postpone the due date
   (b) start work on the assignment yourself and hope the others will join in later
   (c) take the initiative and motivate others, in addition to beginning work on the project
   (d) shout at them for being disruptive and switch to another group

187. For the past few weeks people from the neighbouring colony have been dumping their garbage in your locality. You are extremely upset about this and decide to
   (a) call up the President of the other colony once to present you complaint
   (b) complain about the offending garbage in an informal manner whenever you meet your neighbours
   (c) hold a colony meeting, create a petition and on behalf of your colony meet and discuss the matter with the president of the other colony
   (d) remain quiet since you feel someone will ultimately solve the problem

188. After tremendous hard work your football team has reached the finals. In the final match, you and your team are performing flawlessly and there is a good chance your team may walk away with the trophy. At a crucial moment in the match, however. One of your most accomplished players suffers an injury which causes him to leave the field. Another very talented teammate is shown the red card which means he has to sit out. There is immense pressure to win and without some of your finest players, the pressure has doubled. You
   (a) get distracted by the pressure to win but concentrate on playing to the best of your abilities
   (b) continue to focus on the game and try and maintain your performance at an optimum level

(c) have already decided that winning is impossible but try and keep pace with the game

(d) spend more energy on fuming over the injustice of losing such excellent players than at the game at hand

189. One of your cousins repeatedly criticises you in front of your family members. He does it again at a family get-together and you feel extremely insulted. You

(a) talk to him openly about the way you've always felt and ask him not to do it any more

(b) go to the other members of your family rather than directly approaching him

(c) ignore the situation but continue to feel angry and hurt by his words

(d) attempt to talk to him about it but whenever you try, you end up discussing something completely unrelated

190. You meet a distant friend after many years. How would you react '?

(a) Just smile at her and head for your workplace

(b) Go up to her and start a conversation

(c) Wait for her to take the initiative

(d) Ignore her and move ahead

191. You are talking on the phone and someone from the back is listening to loud music and your favourite song is being played. You

(a) tell your friend to hold the line and listen to the song properly

(b) are able to comprehend your friend's words and are listening to the song also

(c) try to listen to the song simultaneously while talking to your friend but you cannot follow either

(d) decide to concentrate on your friend's voice

192. You got delayed leaving your workplace. It is quite late in the night and on your way home, the car breaks down. You call home and they tell you they'll be there in half an hour to pick you up. The road is deserted. Your wait extends to an hour and a half and you realise that your cell phone has switched off because the battery needs recharging. You

(a) continue to sit in the car with the windows rolled up, all the doors locked and switch on the radio and sing along, preparing for an even longer wait. while remaining alert throughout

(b) feel frightened since you can't get in touch with anybody but reason out that you will be picked up by your family soon enough

(c) experience extreme panic as the waiting period increases

(d) decide to leave your car because you can't, take the tension any more

193. You are alone with your grandmother when she suddenly collapses. You

(a) start feeling extremely panicky

(b) ask your neighbours to step in

(c) call up your parents and ask them to come over as soon as possible and wait nervously for their arrival

(d) call the family doctor immediately and go and sit beside her to keep watch in the meantime

194. You are travelling with a friend in a new city when you realise that you're lost. You

(a) blame your friend for a while but then figure out how to get back to a known area

(b) call up your parents

(c) take out/buy a map and ask for directions

(d) feel the best thing to do is visit the shops

195. You had a fight with your colleague at the office. You would

(a) ignore the whole situation old start chatting with others

(b) blame her and move ahead

(c) sit with her, talk over it and try to clear the issue

(d) vow to yourself not to talk to her again

196. Suppose your mother has given you a huge amount to deposit in the bank and you are robbed on the way. You would

(a) keep waiting on the road not knowing what to do

(b) report the incident to the police immediately and explain the entire thing to your mother

(c) call up your mother and ask her what to do

(d) start panicking and crying and decide to make excuses rather than telling the truth

197. You were saving up money to buy your favourite pair of jeans. But in the market, you realise that there is huge sale on clothes. You

(a) end up buying a pair of jeans as decided earlier

(b) get so confused that you don't buy anything

(c) forget about buying jeans and instead buy other things, which you don't really need; you buy them just because you are getting them really cheap in the sale

(d) decide to buy a pair of jeans cheap enough so that you can also buy T-shirts at sale

198. You are a part of a football team and you have to face a penalty shoot-out. The winning of the team depends on you. You

(a) get distracted because of the pressure around you

(b) feel it does not matter whether you make a goal or not. There will be other opportunities in future

(c) concentrate all your energies/attention on scoring a goal

(d) leave everything on chance

199. You have an important presentation due next month. How do you go about it ?
   (a) Complete your presentation within 1 week and keep practicing it again and again
   (b) Wait for the last few days to get started with the presentation
   (c) Plan your work in such a way that you will be able finish the presentation just on time
   (d) You leave things on time; as the pressure will build up you will start working on your own

200. While answering a question, you
   (a) beat around the bush to make the answer lengthy
   (b) try to stick to the question but get distracted as you think that other things are important even though they are not asked for
   (c) try to see how other people are going about writing the answer by asking their strategy
   (d) stick to the requirements of the question while answering

Answers

1. (b)	2. (a)	3. (b)	4. (b)	5. (c)	6. (c)	7. (c)	8. (d)	9. (d)	10. (c)
11. (a)	12. (c)	13. (c)	14. (b)	15. (a)	16. (d)	17. (d)	18. (a)	19. (b)	20. (a)
21. (a)	22. (c)	23. (c)	24. (b)	25. (a)	26. (b)	27. (c)	28. (c)	29. (b)	30. (c)
31. (b)	32. (b)	33. (d)	34. (a)	35. (b)	36. (c)	37. (b)	38. (b)	39. (d)	40. (c)
41. (a)	42. (c)	43. (a)	44. (b)	45. (a)	46. (c)	47. (b)	48. (a)	49. (a)	50. (d)
51. (b)	52. (b)	53. (b)	54. (c)	55. (b)	56. (c)	57. (d)	58. (a)	59. (a)	60. (b)
61. (a)	62. (b)	63. (c)	64. (d)	65. (a)	66. (c)	67. (d)	68. (d)	69. (d)	70. (d)
71. (b)	72. (c)	73. (d)	74. (c)	75. (c)	76. (c)	77. (d)	78. (b)	79. (d)	80. (a)
81. (c)	82. (a)	83. (a)	84. (d)	85. (d)	86. (b)	87. (b)	88. (b)	89. (d)	90. (b)
91. (d)	92. (a)	93. (b)	94. (c)	95. (d)	96. (c)	97. (b)	98. (d)	99. (d)	100. (c)
101. (b)	102. (c)	103. (c)	104. (d)	105. (a)	106. (b)	107. (c)	108. (d)	109. (a)	110. (c)
111. (c)	112. (b)	113. (d)	114. (b)	115. (a)	116. (a)	117. (d)	118. (d)	119. (c)	120. (b)
121. (d)	122. (b)	123. (b)	124. (a)	125.. (c)	126. (b)	127. (b)	128. (d)	129. (a)	130. (c)
131. (b)	132. (b)	133. (a)	134. (c)	135. (d)	136. (b)	137. (a)	138. (d)	139. (b)	140. (c)
141. (b)	142. (d)	143. (d)	144. (c)	145. (c)	146. (c)	147. (d)	148. (d)	149. (c)	150. (c)
151. (b)	152. (a)	153. (a)	154. (b)	155. (a)	156. (d)	157. (d)	158. (d)	159. (d)	160. (a)
161. (b)	162. (c)	163. (a)	164. (b)	165. (b)	166. (a)	167. (c)	168. (a)	169. (a)	170. (c)
171. (c)	172. (a)	173. (c)	174. (b)	175. (a)	176. (b)	177. (c)	178. (a)	179. (d)	180. (b)
181. (a)	182. (a)	183. (b)	184. (b)	185. (a)	186. (b)	187. (c)	188. (b)	189. (a)	190. (b)
191. (d)	192. (a)	193. (d)	194. (c)	195. (c)	196. (b)	197. (d)	198. (c)	199. (a)	200. (d)

Hints & Solutions

1. (*b*) Given, Amount of 3 yr $(A_1) = ₹\ 800$,

Amount of 4 yr $(A_2) = ₹\ 840$, $n_1 = 3$, $n_2 = 4$

Let the rate of interest be $R\%$ per annum.

$$\because \qquad A = P\left(1 + \frac{R}{100}\right)^n$$

According to the question,

$$800 = P\left(1 + \frac{R}{100}\right)^3 \qquad \text{...(i)}$$

and $\quad 840 = P\left(1 + \frac{R}{100}\right)^4 \qquad \text{...(ii)}$

Dividing Eq. (ii) by Eq. (i), we get

$$\frac{840}{800} = \frac{P\left(1 + \dfrac{R}{100}\right)^4}{P\left(1 + \dfrac{R}{100}\right)^3}$$

$$\Rightarrow \qquad \frac{840}{800} = \left(1 + \frac{R}{100}\right)$$

$$\Rightarrow \qquad 1 + \frac{40}{800} = 1 + \frac{R}{100}$$

$$\Rightarrow \qquad \frac{1}{20} = \frac{R}{100}$$

$$\Rightarrow \qquad R = \frac{100}{20} = 5\%$$

Hence, rate $= 5\%$

2. (*a*) $\because$ Total vote $= 7500$

$\because$ Invalid votes $= 20\%$

$\therefore$ Valid votes $= 80\%$

$\therefore$ Number of valid votes $= \dfrac{80}{100} \times 7500 = 6000$

$\because$ A got 55% of the total valid votes.

$\therefore$ Number of valid votes in favour of the

candidate $B = \dfrac{45}{100} \times 6000 = 2700$

3. (*b*) Let the number be x.

Then, according to the question,

$$\frac{x}{2} = 2 \quad \Rightarrow x = 4$$

$\therefore$ Required number $= 4 \times 2 = 8$

4. (*b*) Let the number be x.

According to the question,

$$x + \frac{1}{x} = \frac{125}{22}$$

$$\Rightarrow \qquad \frac{x^2 + 1}{x} = \frac{125}{22}$$

$$\Rightarrow \qquad 22x^2 + 22 = 125x$$

$$\Rightarrow \qquad 22x^2 - 125x + 22 = 0$$

$$\Rightarrow \qquad 22x^2 - 121x - 4x + 22 = 0$$

$$\Rightarrow 11x(2x - 11) - 2(2x - 11) = 0$$

$$\Rightarrow \qquad (2x - 11)(11x - 2) = 0$$

$$\therefore \qquad x = \frac{11}{2} \text{ or } \frac{2}{11}$$

6. (*c*) A can do a piece of work in 40 days.

$\therefore 1$ day's work of $A = \dfrac{1}{40}$

$\therefore 5$ day's work of $A = \dfrac{5}{40} = \dfrac{1}{8}$

$\therefore$ Remaining work $= 1 - \dfrac{1}{8} = \dfrac{7}{8}$

$\therefore B$ alone can complete $\dfrac{7}{8}$ work in 21 days.

$\therefore B$ alone can complete whole work in $\dfrac{21 \times 8}{7}$

$$= 24 \text{ days}$$

$\therefore\ 1$ day's work of $B = \dfrac{1}{24}$

$\therefore 1$ day's work of A and $B = \dfrac{1}{40} + \dfrac{1}{24}$

$$= \frac{3 + 5}{120} = \frac{8}{120} = \frac{1}{15}$$

$\therefore\ A$ and B together can finish the work in 15 days.

7. (*c*) Let the distance between the student's house and school be x km.

According to the question,

$$\frac{x}{4} - \frac{5}{60} = \frac{x}{5} + \frac{10}{60}$$

$$\Rightarrow \qquad \frac{x}{4} - \frac{x}{5} = \frac{15}{60}$$

$$\Rightarrow \qquad \frac{5x - 4x}{20} = \frac{15}{60}$$

$$\Rightarrow \qquad \frac{x}{20} = \frac{1}{4}$$

$$\therefore \qquad x = 5 \text{ km}$$

$\therefore$ The distance of the school from his house $= 5$ km

8. (*d*) Let SP of 1 m cloth $= ₹\ 1$

$\therefore\ $ SP of 33 m cloth $= ₹\ 33$

Gain $=$ SP of 11 m cloth $= ₹\ (11 \times 1) = ₹\ 11$

CP $=$ SP $-$ Gain

$$= 33 - 11 = 22$$

$\therefore$ Gain percentage $= \dfrac{\text{Gain}}{\text{CP}} \times 100 = \dfrac{11}{22} \times 100 = 50\%$

9. (*d*) Length of the train $= 700$ m

Speed of the train $= 72$ km/h

$$= 72 \times \frac{5}{18} = 20 \text{ m/s}$$

Time taken to pass the tunnel $= 1$ min

$\qquad\qquad\qquad\qquad\quad = 60$ sec

Let the length of tunnel be x m.

$\therefore$ According to the question,

$$20 = \frac{700 + x}{60} \qquad \left[\because \text{Time} = \frac{\text{Distance}}{\text{Speed}} \right]$$

$$\Rightarrow 1200 = 700 + x$$

$$\therefore \qquad x = 500$$

$\therefore$ Length of tunnel $= 500$ m

10. (c) Total number of teachers in the school $= 20$

$\therefore$ Total decrease in ages $= 2 \times 20$

$$= 40 \text{ yr}$$

$\therefore$ The age of new teacher $= 60 - 40 = 20$ yr

11. (a) Let the number be x.

According to the question,

$$11\% \text{ of } x = 66$$

$$\Rightarrow \qquad \frac{11}{100} \times x = 66$$

$$\therefore \qquad x = \frac{66 \times 100}{11} = 600$$

12. (c) Given, $r = 25\%$

$\because$ Reduction in consumption $= \left(\dfrac{r}{100 + r} \times 100 \right)\%$

$$= \left(\frac{25}{100 + 25} \times 100 \right)\%$$

$$= \frac{25}{125} \times 100\% = 20\%$$

13. (c) Here, $x = -50, y = -50$

$$\text{Reduction in area} = \left[x + y + \frac{xy}{100} \right]\%$$

$$= \left[-50 - 50 + \frac{(-50) \times (-50)}{100} \right]\%$$

$$= -75\%$$

$\therefore$ Area of the circle is reduced by 75%.

14. (b) $\dfrac{6}{50} = \dfrac{\sqrt{?}}{200}$

$$\Rightarrow \sqrt{?} = \frac{6 \times 200}{50} = 24$$

$$\therefore \quad ? = (24)^2 = 576$$

15. (a) $\dfrac{617}{24.68} + X = 90$

$$\Rightarrow X = 90 - \frac{617}{24.68} \Rightarrow X = 90 - 25$$

$$\therefore X = 65$$

16. (d) $\dfrac{1}{x} + \dfrac{1}{y} = \dfrac{1}{2z} \Rightarrow \dfrac{y + x}{xy} = \dfrac{1}{2z} \Rightarrow 2z = \dfrac{xy}{x + y}$

$$\therefore \qquad z = \frac{xy}{2(x + y)}$$

17. (d) Let the present ages of A and B be $2x$ and $3x$ respectively.

According to the question,

$$\frac{2x - 10}{3x - 10} = \frac{3}{5} \Rightarrow 10x - 50 = 9x - 30$$

$$\Rightarrow 10x - 9x = 50 - 30 \Rightarrow x = 20$$

$\therefore$ Present age of $A = 2 \times 20 = 40$ yr

and Present age of $B = 3 \times 20 = 60$ yr

18. (a) Here, $r = 25\%$

The required percentage reduction

$$= \left(\frac{r}{100 + r} \times 100 \right)\%$$

$$= \frac{25}{(100 + 25)} \times 100$$

$$= \frac{25}{125} \times 100 = 20\%$$

19. (b) $\because$ Diameter of a wheel $= 70$ cm

$\therefore$ Radius of the wheel, $r = 35$ cm

Distance covered by wheel in one complete revolution $= 2\pi r$

$$= 2 \times \frac{22}{7} \times 35 = 220 \text{ cm}$$

So, distance covered by the wheel in 24 revolutions

$$= 24 \times 220 \text{ cm}$$

$$= 5280 \text{ cm} = 52.8 \text{ m}$$

20. (a) $\because$ Dividend on ₹ $108 = ₹ 12\dfrac{1}{2} = ₹ \dfrac{25}{2}$

According to the question,

Dividend on ₹ 2592 is $= \dfrac{25 \times 2592}{2 \times 108} = \dfrac{64800}{216} = 300$

$\therefore$ Dividend received by Swarna at the end of the year is ₹ 300.

31. (b) All others except shore are the reserve of water.

32. (b) Pattern of the series is as follows,

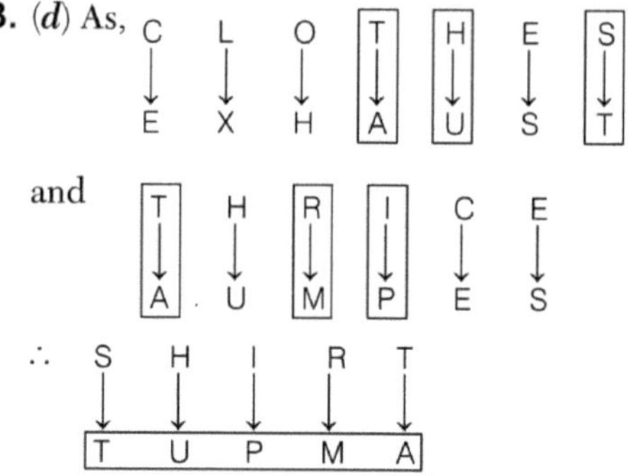

$\therefore$ 54 is the wrong number in the given pattern.

33. (d) As,

and

$\therefore$

34. (*a*) As,

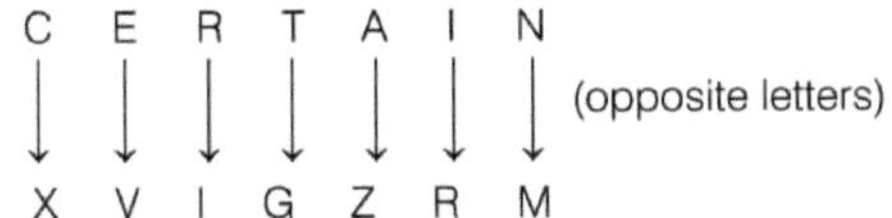

Similarly,

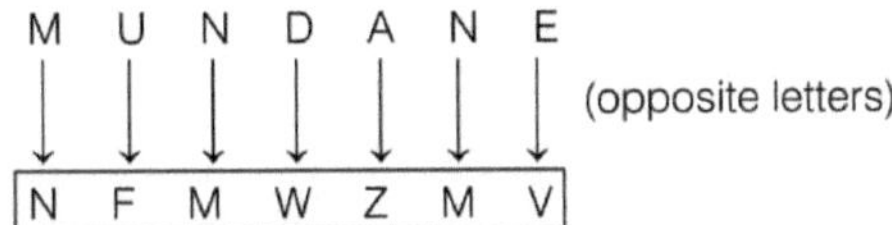

∴ MUNDANE is coded as NFMWZMV.

35. (*b*) As,   C L E A R ⟶ R A E L C

Similarly, B E A U T Y ⟶ Y T U A E B

∴ BEAUTY ⇒ YTUAEB

36. (*c*) As,

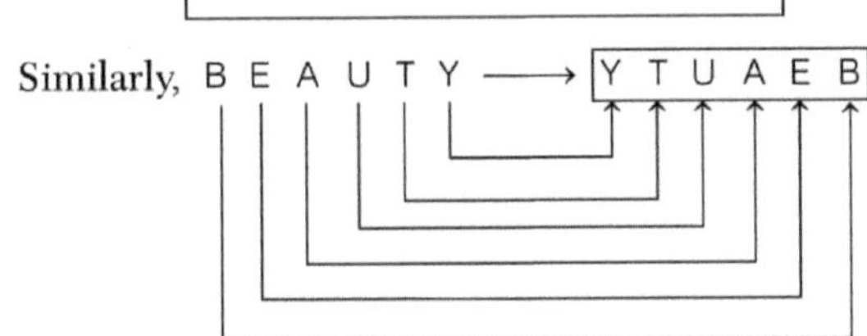

and P O U N D S ⟶ Q Q X M B P

Similarly,

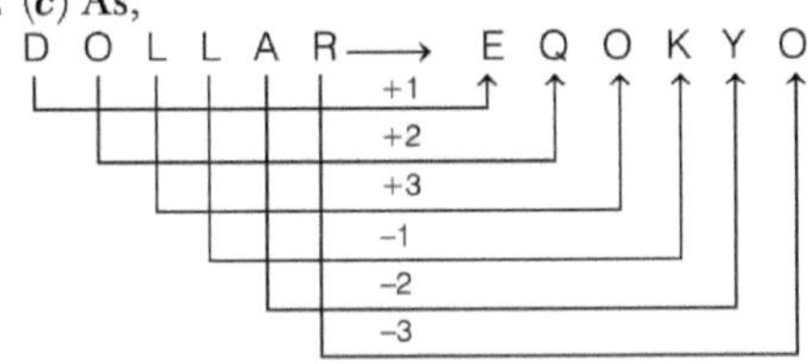

M A R K ⟶ N C Q I

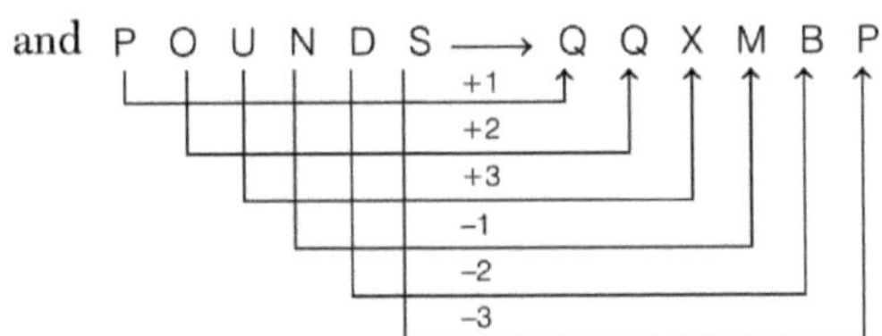

∴ MARK will be coded as NCQI.

37. (*b*) According to the Conclusion I, the incidence of crime is higher in identical twins that in fraternal twins is false conclusion. So, Conclusion I does not follow. Nothing is mentioned about identical twins in the given statement.

Hence, only Conclusion II follows.

38. (*b*) According to the statements,

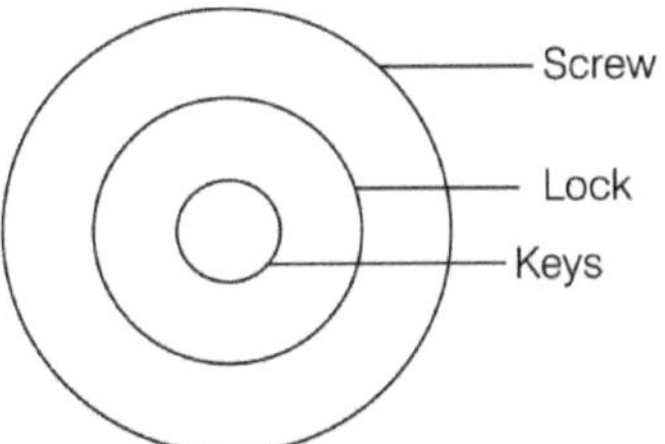

Conclusions

     I. (✗)

     II. (✓)

Hence, only Conclusion II follows.

39. (*d*) According to the question,

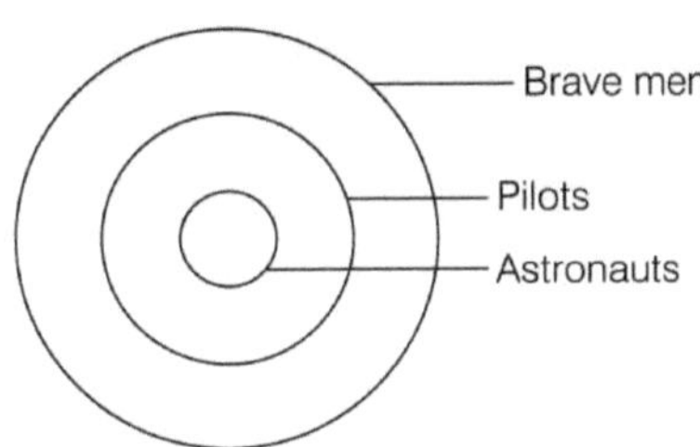

Conclusions   I. (✓)

             II. (✓)

Hence, both Conclusions follow.

40. (*c*) According to the question,

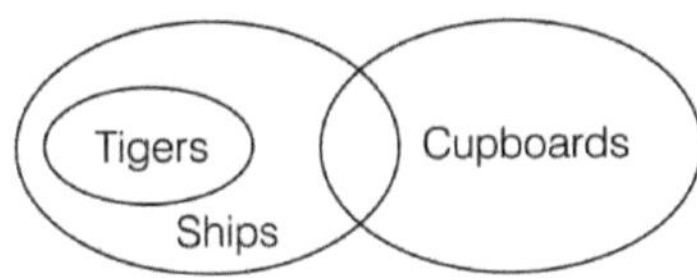

Conclusions

     I. (✗)

     II. (✗)

Hence, neither I nor II follows.

41. (*a*) Pattern of the series is as follows,

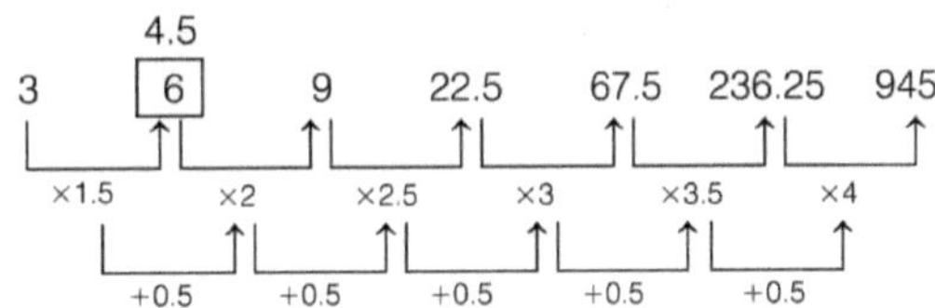

Hence, 6 is wrong number.

42. (*c*) Pattern of the series is as follows,

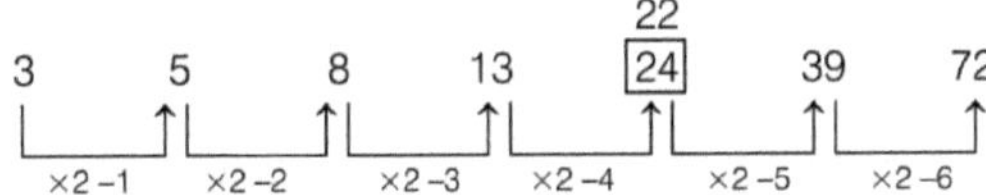

Hence, 24 is wrong number.

43. (*a*) Pattern of the series is as follows,

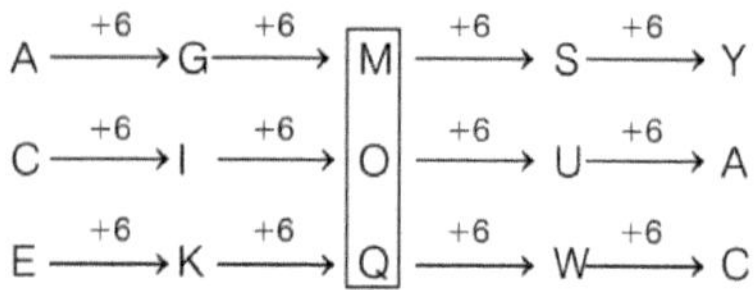

∴ MOQ will come in place of ?.

44. (*b*) Pattern of the series is as follows

$5760 \div 6 = 960$;

$960 \div 5 = \boxed{192}$;

$192 \div 4 = 48$;

$48 \div 3 = 16$;

$16 \div 2 = 8$

Hence, 192 is the missing term in the given series.

45. (*a*) Pattern of the series is as follows

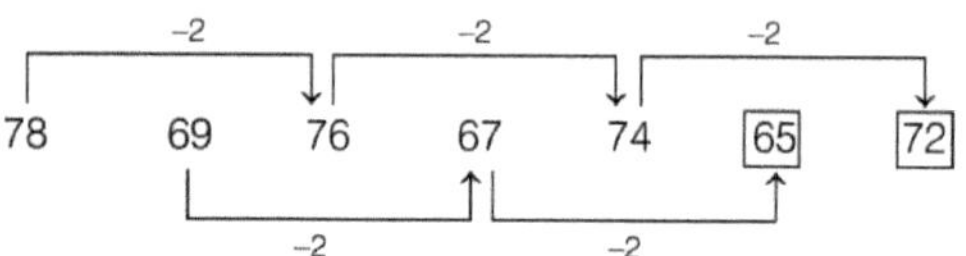

65 and 72 are the missing terms in the given sequence.

46. (*c*) Pattern of the series is as follows

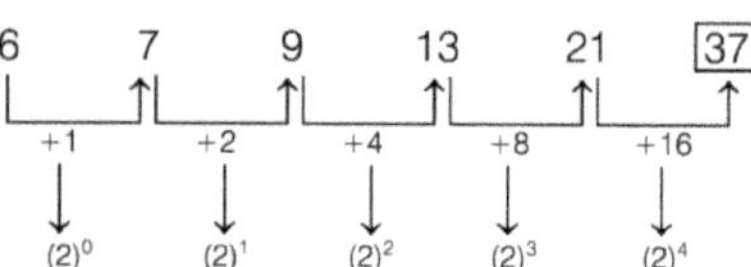

∴ 37 is the missing term.

47. (*b*) Pattern of the series is as follows

$10 \times 7 = 70$;

$70 \times 8 = \boxed{560}$;

$560 \times 9 = 5040$;

$5040 \times 10 = 50400$

∴ 560 is the missing term.

48. (*a*) According to the given statement, the maternal grandmother of the man's nephew is the mother of his only sister.

Hence, the lady is mother of the man's only sister.

49. (*a*) According to the statements,

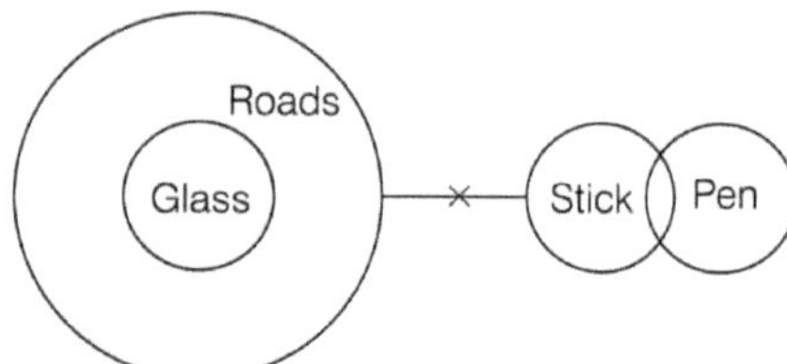

Conclusions

    I. (✗)   II. (✔)

  III. (✗)   IV. (✔)

∴ Hence, Conclusions II and IV follow.

50. (*d*) As, P E N C I L ⟶ R C T A M J

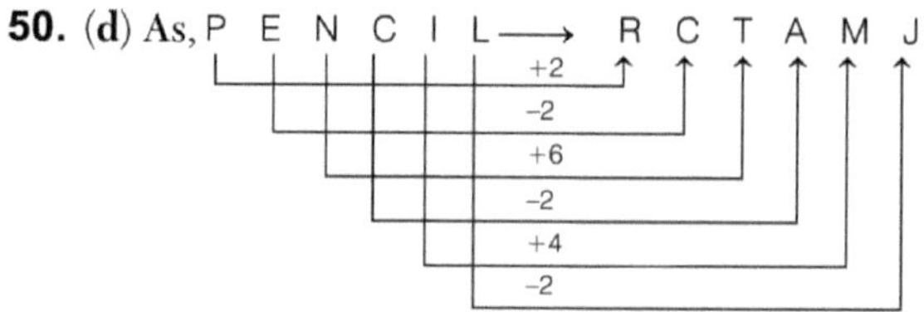

Similarly,

B R O K E N ⟶ D P U I I L

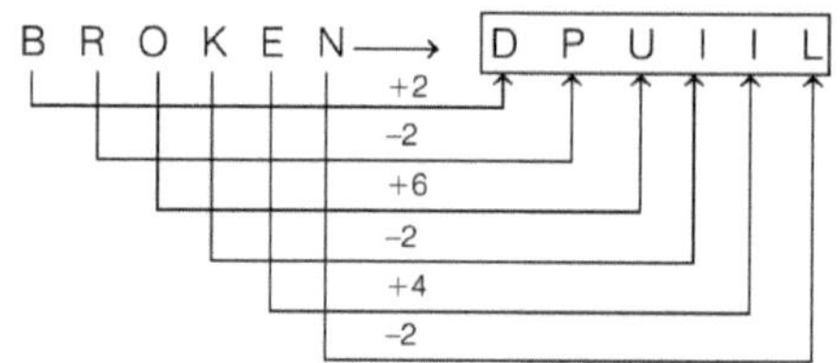

∴ BROKEN is coded as DPUIIL.

51. (*b*) As,

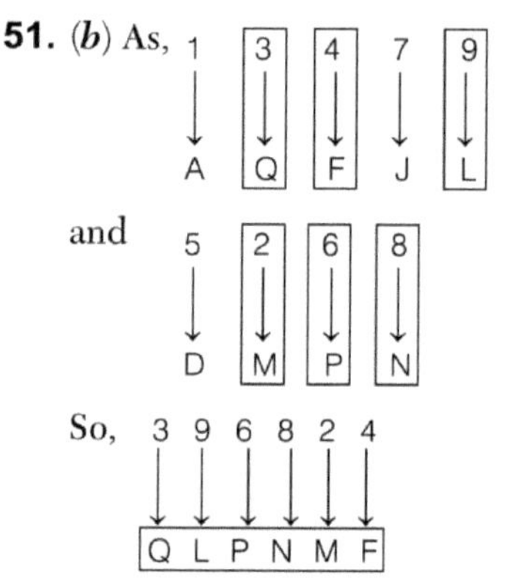

So, 3 9 6 8 2 4

QLPNMF

∴ 396824 is coded as QLPNMF.

52. (*b*) As,

Z U B I N ⟶ A T C H O

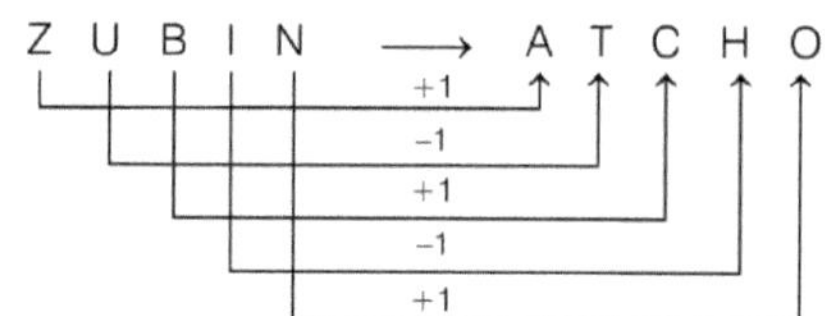

Similarly,

M E H T A ⟶ N D I S B

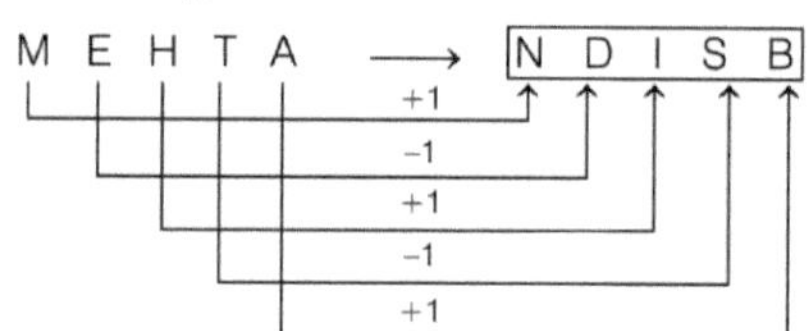

∴ MEHTA is coded as NDISB.

53. (*b*) According to the given series, two cross symbols are removed in second step while in third step, three cross symbols are added. Again in the fourth step two cross symbols are removed. Similarly three cross symbol will be added in the answer figure.

∴

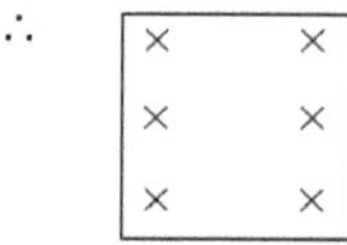

Option (b) figure will complete the given series.

54. (*c*) According to the given figures series, the symbol Δ and ○ interchange their position in second figure while × and □ remain in the same position. In the third step, ○ and Δ remain in the same position, while × and □ interchange their position.

∴ In the fifth step, same pattern will be followed as of third option.

∴ Figure in option (c) i.e. 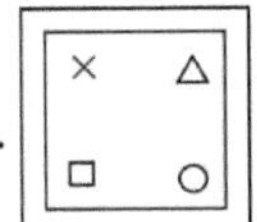 will complete the given series.

55. (*b*) In each step of figure series the symbol ○ moves clockwise. Hence, the figure in option (b) will complete the given series.

56. (*c*) According to the figure series, the rectangular spot at the end of the cross symbol is disappearing in clockwise direction in each step.

∴ The figure in option (c) complete the given series.

57. (*d*) According to the figure series, the figure in first step repeats at every odd place.

While figure in second step repeats at every even place. Hence, figure in option (d) completes the given series.

58. (*a*) In the second step the shape changes to triangle from square. In the third step, the triangle is rotated clockwise and number of angles shown is 2.

In the same pattern the figure in option (a) will complete the given sequence.

59. (*a*) In each step the symbols are of same type. In the first step the number of symbols is 5, in the second step number of symbols is 4, in the third step number of symbols is 3, in the fourth step number of symbol is 4.

∴ In the fifth step number of same type of symbol will be 5.

Hence, the figure in option (a) will complete the figure sequence.

60. (*b*) In each step the direction of figure get changed in opposite direction and figure is different in each step. Hence, the figure in option (b) will complete the given figure sequence.

91. (*d*) 'Admonish' means to warn or reprimand someone firmly. Hence, 'reprimand' is the nearest in meaning to 'admonish'.

92. (*a*) 'Wretched' refers to a person who is in a very unhappy of unfortunate state. Hence, 'poor' is the nearest in meaning to wretched.

93. (*b*) 'Archaic' means very old or old-fashioned. Hence, 'outdated' is the nearest in meaning to 'archaic'.

94. (*c*) 'Nimble' means ability to think and understand quickly. Hence, 'quickening' is the nearest in meaning to 'nimble'.

101. (*b*) 'Praise' is opposite in meaning to 'disparage'. 'Disparage' means to regard or represent someone as being of little worth and 'praise' means to admire or approve someone.

102. (*c*) 'Fine' is opposite in meaning to 'coarse'. 'Coarse' means unrefined or of inferior quality and 'fine' means of very high quality.

103. (*c*) 'Gloomy' is opposite in meaning to 'jubilant'. 'Jubilant' means feeling or expressing great happiness and 'gloomy' means causing or feeling depression.

104. (*d*) 'Appreciate' is opposite in meaning to 'abhor'. 'Abhor' means to regard with disgust and hatred and 'appreciate' means to value or respect someone.

105. (*a*) 'Progressive' is opposite in meaning to 'retrograde'. 'Retrograde' means to go back in time or position to reach an inferior condition and 'progressive' refers to a person or idea favouring change and innovation and a forward motion.

106. (*b*) 'Bald' is opposite in meaning to 'hirsute'. 'Hirsute' means covered in hair or shaggy.

115. (*a*) Here, the continuous form of verb is incorrectly used. The verb to be used in the sentence should be in past form. Hence, replace 'is composing of 'with 'is composed of' to make the sentence correct.

116. (*a*) 'Account for' means to provide a satisfactory explanations for one's actions. Hence, replace 'good explanation for' with 'account for' to make the sentence grammatically correct.

118. (*d*) Replace 'so trivial and hence' with 'very trivial and hence' to make the sentence grammatically correct.

119. (*c*) The sentence mentions an action that began in the past and is still continuing in the present, hence, present perfect continuous tense of the verb should be used. Replace 'is working' with 'has been working' to make the sentence grammatically correct.

120. (*b*) 'Tremendous' means very great in amount or impressive. Hence, replace 'conscious efforts' with 'tremendous efforts' to make the sentence grammatically correct.

121. (*d*) No correction required,

144. (*c*) The verb to be used in the given sentence should be in continuous form. Hence, replace 'to work' with 'working' to make the sentence correct.

145. (*c*) 'Such a' is the correct phrase to be used and 'that should be used as a conjunction. Hence, replace 'in such mess there' with 'in such a mess that there' to make the sentence correct.

146. (*c*) Are' is incorrectly used in the sentence. Replace 'are still remains' with 'will still remain' to make the sentence grammatically correctly.

148. (*d*) Option (d) contains the error. The verb 'were' is incorrectly used in the sentence. Remove 'were' to make the sentence correct.

149. (*c*) Option (c) contains the error. The plural form of the noun 'success' is incorrectly used. Replace 'successes' with 'success' to make the sentence correct.

150. (*c*) Option (c) contains the error. The verb 'do' is used incorrectly. Replace 'do' with 'pursue' to make the sentence grammatically correct.

151. (*b*) Option (b) contains the error. Article 'an' should be used before 'increased emphasis' in the given sentence to make the sentence grammatically correct.

152. (*a*) Option (a) contains the error. Replace 'he tried as he could' with 'he tried as hard as he could but' to make the sentence correct.

153. (*a*) 'Recompense' means to pay or reward someone for their effort or work. Hence, 'reward' is the nearest in meaning to 'recompense'.

154. (*b*) 'Qualm' means an uneasy feeling of doubt, worry or fear and 'scruple' means the same. Hence, option (b) is the correct answer.

155. (*a*) 'Licentious' means promiscuous and immoral and 'libertine' means the same. Hence, option (a) is the correct answer.

156. (*d*) 'Pious' means devoutly religious. Hence, 'devout' is the nearest in meaning to 'pious'.

157. (*d*) 'Credentials' means warranting credit or confidence. Hence, 'trustworthiness' is the nearest in meaning to 'credentials'.

158. (*d*) 'Audacious' means showing a willingness to take surprisingly bold risks. Hence, 'daring' is the nearest in meaning to 'audacious'.

159. (*d*) 'Stridency' means a state of being harsh or insistent. Hence, 'harshness' is the nearest in meaning to 'stridency'.

160. (*a*) 'Harbinger' means a person that announces or signals the approach of another. Hence, 'messenger' is the nearest in meaning to 'harbinger'.

161. (*b*) 'Sincere' is opposite in meaning to 'hypocritical'. 'Hypocritical' means behaving in a way that is more noble than the actual case and 'sincere' means genuine and truthful.

162. (*c*) 'Importance' is opposite in meaning to 'futility'. 'Futility' means pointlessness or uselessness.

166. (*a*) Option (a) contains the error. The verb to be used in the sentence should be in present form. Hence, replace 'had' with 'have' to make the sentence correct.

167. (*c*) Option (c) contains the error. The sentence is in past continuous tense. Hence, replace 'run' with 'running' to make the sentence correct.

168. (*a*) Option (a) contains the error. The correct verb form to be used in the sentence is simple past tense as it is referring to an incident in the past. Replace 'has come' with 'came' to make the sentence correct.

169. (*a*) Option (a) contains the error. The correct verb form to be used in the sentence is past perfect tense. Hence, replace, 'is opened' with 'had been opened' to make the sentence correct.

170. (*c*) Option (c) contains the error. The given sentence is in past tense. Hence, replace 'have brought' with 'brought' to make the sentence grammatically correct.

Printed by Libri Plureos GmbH in Hamburg,
Germany